Books in the Digital Age

Books in the Digital Age

The Transformation of Academic and
Higher Education Publishing in Britain
and the United States

John B. Thompson

polity

Copyright©John B. Thompson 2005

The right of John B. Thompson to be identified as Author of this Work has been asserted in accordance with the UK Copyright, Designs and Patents Act 1988.

First published in 2005 by Polity Press Ltd.

Polity Press
65 Bridge Street
Cambridge CB2 1UR, UK

Polity Press
350 Main Street
Malden, MA 02148, USA

ISBN 0 7456 3477 X
ISBN 0 7456 3478 8 (paperback)

A catalogue record for this book is available from the British Library and has been applied for from the Library of Congress.

Typeset in 10 on 12 pt Times Ten Roman
by SNP Best-set Typesetter Ltd, Hong Kong
Printed and bound in Great Britain by MPG Books Ltd, Bodmin. Cornwall

For further information on Polity, visit our website: www.polity.co.uk

Contents

Figures and tables

Figures

Tables

Preface

In the late 1990s I became interested in trying to understand the changes that were taking place in an important but hitherto largely neglected sector of the creative industries – the book publishing industry. I was struck by the fact that, while books were a pervasive feature of our social and cultural lives (and, for those of us in the academy, an essential part of what we do as teachers and researchers), we knew very little about how this industry is organized today and how it is changing. The digital revolution was fuelling (and continues to fuel) much speculation about the future of the book – and, indeed, about whether it has a future at all – but there was very little grounded knowledge of what was actually happening in an industry which was, for the most part, taken for granted.

It was against this background that I set out, in the summer of 2000, to try to gain a more systematic understanding of the book publishing industry in the English-speaking world; this book about books is the outcome of the research that preoccupied me for the following three years. I am grateful to the Economic and Social Research Council in the UK for the generous support which made this research possible. I'd also like to thank my colleagues in Cambridge for their willingness to grant me leave for two years so that I could concentrate full-time on the study. My research assistant, Alisi Mekatoa, was very resourceful in gathering data and tracking down relevant materials which have been used in various chapters, and I am grateful to her for her help. I am also grateful to Avril Symonds who transcribed a mountain of tapes with stoic perseverance and good humour; to Ann Bone who copy-edited the manuscript with extraordinary care; and to the many people at Polity – including Gill Motley, Sue Pope, Neil de Cort, Andrea Drugan, Emma Longstaff, Reitha Pattison, Breffni O'Connor and Marianne Rutter – who helped to steer this book through the publication process. Above all, my thanks go to the many individuals in the publishing industry who gave so willingly and generously of their time and who, over the course of the last few years, have shared with me their knowledge of and views on the industry of which they are part. Some of these individuals also very generously agreed to read an earlier draft of this text and commented extensively on it. In order to protect their anonymity these individuals have remained nameless, but many of the insights and ideas developed in this book belong to them. They deserve much of the credit for what follows, although I alone accept responsibility for any errors that remain.

J. B. T., Cambridge

Introduction

For more than five hundred years, books have been a key feature of modern culture and one of the foundations on which education and academic life are based. It is difficult to imagine what Western culture would be, or indeed the culture of any major civilization anywhere in the world today, without the wealth of resources that are preserved, disseminated and handed down from one generation to the next in the form of the book. But in recent years there has been much speculation about the possibility that this object we have known and valued for half a millennium may be destined to disappear. The book publishing industry today is going through a process of change which is probably as profound as anything it has experienced since Johann Gutenberg adapted the traditional screw press for the purposes of manufacturing printed texts. One of the driving forces of this change is the technological revolution ushered in by digitization. No one yet knows exactly how this revolution will play itself out in the field of book publishing. Many have wondered whether the printed book will go the way of the vinyl LP and become a collector's item, a curious relic of a bygone age, while the content that was once packaged and distributed in books will be disseminated in other ways. Will books continue to have a significant presence in a world where the computer and the television have become pervasive cultural forms, cultivating cognitive attitudes and practices that are at odds with the kind of patient attention required to read an extended text? There has been much speculation too about whether the traditional role of the publisher will survive this revolution, for why would publishers be necessary at all in a world where cultural producers could disseminate their work directly over the internet, in the way that Stephen King famously did with his novella *Riding the Bullet*? And why would consumers pay the extra premium that is likely to be charged for the content provided by publishers if they could get the content they wanted free (or much more cheaply) from other sources on the web?

In the heady days of the 1990s, speculation about the future of the book was rife. There were some commentators who claimed to discern a profound shift taking place in Western culture, one which would lead inexorably to the decline of the printed word and its eclipse by a world of electronic communication.[1] Within the publishing industry, various consultants and self-styled experts were predicting the imminent demise of the book and urging publishers to reinvent themselves for an electronic future. But as the new millennium dawned, it soon became clear that much of the speculation about the future of the book had been misguided. By the end of 2001 the much heralded ebook revolution had faltered – it was beginning to look like one of those technological revolutions that had failed, but in any case it had most definitely been postponed – and the dot.com bubble

---

[1] See, for example, Sven Birkets, *The Gutenberg Elegies: The Fate of Reading in an Electronic Age* (London: Faber & Faber, 1994).

that had pumped millions of dollars into online experiments of various kinds had burst. No one was talking seriously now about the imminent demise of the book in the face of the ebook onslaught. Publishers who had invested heavily in the 1990s in experiments in electronic publishing were counting their losses and closing down divisions. Third-party players who had hoped to ride the new wave of electronic publishing were scrambling to find alternative sources of revenue. And yet, despite the evident faltering of the ebook revolution, the book publishing industry was still going through a process of profound and turbulent change. The ebook has commanded the attention of journalists and others who like to tell dramatic stories and to speculate about the end of civilization as we know it, but the real revolution in publishing was taking place elsewhere.

So what are the key changes that are transforming the book publishing industry today? Technology undoubtedly has an important role to play, but it is only part of the story. The industry is also undergoing major changes of a social and economic kind, and we can understand the true significance of the digital revolution in publishing only by situating it within this broader context. Since the 1970s the book publishing industry has been the focus of intensive merger and acquisitions activity, and the structures of ownership and control in some sectors of the industry now bear little resemblance to the world of publishing that existed forty or fifty years ago. Today a handful of large conglomerates, many operating in an international and increasingly global arena, wield enormous power in the publishing world and harbour a growing number of formerly independent imprints under their corporate umbrellas. The idea of the gentlemanly publisher, who relied on his own cultivated judgements of quality and taste to decide which books and authors to publish and who was relatively unconstrained by such mundane matters as costs and sales, now seems like the figure of another age.

Just as some sectors of the publishing industry have changed beyond recognition, so too has the retail sector of the book trade. The independent bookstore serving a local community has not disappeared but, with the rise of the retail chains, it has found itself with its back against the wall. The dramatic expansion of the retail chains since the early 1980s has transformed the channels to market and altered the balance of power between publishers and booksellers. Today publishers depend less and less on the individual and varied decision-making processes of booksellers dispersed across the country and depend more and more on the hugely consequential decisions of centralized buyers working for the big chains. And at the same time as the bricks and mortar business of bookselling has been transformed by the rise of the retail chains, a new player, created by the digital revolution, has appeared on the scene – the online bookstore. The rise of online bookstores like Amazon has opened up new channels to market for publishers and helped to some extent to offset the decline of the independents, but it has also introduced new factors into the book trade which have disrupted traditional practices and injected further variables into a retail world in flux.

The question of how the world of book publishing is coping with this process of turbulent change is a question to which we do not yet have a clear and detailed answer. Like all sectors of modern industry, the book publishing industry produces a constant stream of reports on its own state of health[2] – this kind of 'institutional reflexivity' is,

---

[2] See, for example, the series of research reports produced by Mark Bide, Mike Shatzkin and others and sponsored by Vista Computer Services, listed in the Bibliography as Vista 1995, 1996, 1997, 1998, 1999.

one could say, a characteristic feature of modern societies.[3] Occasionally the book publishing industry has been surveyed, as one sector among others, in studies which have looked at how business organizations cope with economic and technological change.[4] Moreover, the book publishing industry is sufficiently large and important to command the attention of governments, which from time to time have commissioned their own reports on the state of the industry and its competitiveness.[5] But there have been very few recent attempts to study systematically the modern book publishing industry and to look in depth at how particular sectors of this industry, and particular firms within these sectors, have changed in recent decades. There is a large scholarly literature on the history of publishing and the history of the book, from Gutenberg through to the nineteenth and twentieth centuries,[6] and there are many works which recount the history of particular firms. But in the sphere of scholarly research, the contemporary world of book publishing has, by and large, been ignored. Why this neglect?

To some extent this is due, no doubt, to what one could describe as the 'lure of the audiovisual': for those scholars who are interested in contemporary media and cultural industries, the audiovisual sectors tend to exercise a particular fascination. Compared with the film and television industries, or with the emerging industries linked to new technologies and the internet, the world of book publishing seems rather old-fashioned – like a throw-back to the past. It hardly seems like an industry of the future. But this attitude is quite misguided. Publishing is a major industry in its own right – in Britain, for example, the turnover of the publishing industry as a whole (which includes all sectors, newspapers and magazines as well as books and journals) was £18.37 billion in 2000, of which books and journals represented about a quarter; this is significantly larger than the pharmaceuticals industry, which had a turnover of £12.03 billion.[7] Moreover, publishing underpins many spheres of contemporary culture and is a major source of content for other sectors of the media and cultural industries, including film and television. The audiovisual sector and the high-tech industries may have more glitz and glamour, but to focus on these domains at the expense of the publishing industry would be very short-sighted indeed.

While the publishing industry has received relatively little attention compared to other sectors of the media and cultural industries, it has not been completely ignored by academic researchers. Probably the best attempt to provide a detailed analysis of the modern book publishing industry is the now classic study by Coser, Kadushin and

---

[3] See Anthony Giddens, *The Consequences of Modernity* (Cambridge: Polity, 1990), pp. 36 ff.
[4] See Andrew Pettigrew and Richard Whipp, *Managing Change for Competitive Success* (Oxford: Blackwell, 1991).
[5] A recent example is the report commissioned by the Department of Trade and Industry in the UK, *Publishing in the Knowledge Economy: Competitiveness Analysis of the UK Publishing Media Sector* (London: DTI and UK Publishing Media, 2002).
[6] See, for example, Elizabeth L. Eisenstein, *The Printing Press as an Agent of Change: Communications and Cultural Transformations in Early-Modern Europe*, vols 1 and 2 (Cambridge: Cambridge University Press, 1979); Robert Darnton, *The Business of Enlightenment: A Publishing History of the Encyclopedia, 1775–1800* (Cambridge, Mass.: Harvard University Press, 1979); Roger Chartier, *The Order of Books: Readers, Authors and Libraries in Europe between the Fourteenth and Eighteenth Centuries* (Cambridge: Polity, 1993); Adrian Johns, *The Nature of the Book: Print and Knowledge in the Making* (Chicago: University of Chicago Press, 1998).
[7] *Publishing in the Knowledge Economy*, pp. 3–4.

Powell.[8] This was a study of the American book publishing industry with an emphasis on nonfiction, ranging from the New York trade (or general interest) publishers to the university presses. Coser and his associates gave particular attention to editorial decision-making and used the concept of the 'gatekeeper' to analyse the publishing process: publishers were viewed as 'gatekeepers of ideas' who, by virtue of their organizational positions, decide which books will be made available in the public domain and which will be excluded from it. This is an exemplary piece of social scientific research, rich in detail and perceptive, and it sheds a great deal of light on a world which, to the outsider, seems clothed in secrecy and governed by the most arcane practices. But however insightful, the work of Coser and his associates is no longer satisfactory for various reasons – let me highlight two.

In the first place, the notion of the gatekeeper is not really adequate as a way of characterizing the selective activities of editors and publishers. The idea of the gatekeeper suggests that there are authors queuing up to get through the gate, and the gatekeeper's job is to decide who can go through and who will be turned away. This model may have been a reasonably accurate reflection of what happened in some sectors of the publishing industry some decades ago, but it doesn't bear much resemblance to the role of an editor in most publishing firms today. Of course, there is a certain amount of this activity of selection – every publishing firm is flooded with unsolicited proposals and manuscripts from would-be authors and from agents, and many editors do spend some time wading through the pool. But in most publishing firms, the 'slush pile', as it is commonly known, is more of a distraction than a source of serious projects. Most editors – and certainly most successful editors today – are much more proactive than the notion of the gatekeeper would suggest. They actively come up with ideas for the books and authors they want to publish, and they actively go out and try to commission them. Of course, the extent to which editors are passive or proactive will vary from individual to individual and from firm to firm; it will also vary from one sector of the industry to another. But even in those sectors of the industry where the role of the editor might have looked something like that of a gatekeeper twenty or thirty years ago, such as the world of the university presses, this is less and less the case. Today editors know that their jobs depend more and more on their ability to sign up the kinds of authors and books that will do well, and to do so in the face of growing competition from other editors who would love to sign up the same authors and books. The idea that they could simply stand by the gate and decide which of the queuing projects would be allowed to pass through bears less and less resemblance to the increasingly pressurized and competitive world in which most editors work today.

A second reason why the work of Coser and his associates is of limited value is that it is now very dated. The research was carried out in the late 1970s, before the most recent wave of mergers and acquisitions which transformed the landscape of the publishing industry in the 1980s and 1990s and before the digital revolution had taken hold. In the two decades that have elapsed since their study was carried out, the industry has changed dramatically, and the key problems faced by different sectors of the industry today are simply not the same as they were in the 1970s and before. The markets for books have changed in many profound ways, the industry has become increasingly glob-

---

[8] Lewis A. Coser, Charles Kadushin and Walter W. Powell, *Books: The Culture and Commerce of Publishing* (New York: Basic Books, 1982).

alized (a factor that is of particular importance for any publisher working in the English language) and the digital revolution has transformed many aspects of the business of publishing. The study of Coser and his associates was path-breaking in its day, but it no longer provides a satisfactory account of the publishing industry at the beginning of the twenty-first century.

In more recent years, there have been a few scholars and commentators on both sides of the Atlantic who have gathered data on the book publishing industry, monitored market trends, provided useful overviews and analysed some sectors of the business.[9] But perhaps the most probing accounts of the book publishing industry in recent years are those offered by publishers themselves. André Schiffrin was the managing director of the American trade publishing house Pantheon for thirty years; he led a mass resignation from Pantheon in 1989 after falling out with the new corporate owners of Random House. (Pantheon was acquired by Random House in 1961, and Random House, which was bought by RCA in 1966, was sold to the media entrepreneur S. I. Newhouse in 1980.) Schiffrin went on to found a small independent publishing house called The New Press in 1990. In *The Business of Books* Schiffrin offers a critical, impassioned reflection on what has happened to publishing in the age of conglomerates – an age, argues Schiffrin, when the judgement of editors has been increasingly displaced by the profit-oriented priorities of accountants and shareholders and when intellectual quality and literary merit have been sacrificed on the altar of the market. 'Books today', writes Schiffrin, 'have become mere adjuncts to the world of the mass media, offering light entertainment and reassurances that all is for the best in this, the best of all possible worlds. The resulting control on the spread of ideas is stricter than anyone would have thought possible in a free society.'[10] Schiffrin sees in the work of small independent publishers and nonprofits some hope that a culture of critical debate nourished by books will not be completely extinguished, but he knows very well that the future of many of these small operations in an age of conglomerates is by no means guaranteed.

A somewhat similar broad-brushstroke account, although written from a very different perspective, is offered by Jason Epstein, for many years editorial director at Random House and one of the most distinguished editors in American trade publishing. In *Book Business* Epstein reflects on the rise of the conglomerates and the retail chains, which together, he argues, have pushed publishing in a direction that clashes with its very nature. For trade book publishing is by nature a cottage industry; it is essentially a craft, a vocation that depends on the commitment and judgement of editors and on the unpredictable tastes of the public. It is not the kind of business that lends itself to corporate synergies and high returns on investment – 'a cottage industry within an industrial conglomerate makes no sense.'[11] Hence the growing concentration within the industry is

---

[9] See, for example, Peter J. Curwen, *The UK Publishing Industry* (Oxford: Pergamon, 1981); Peter J. Curwen, *The World Book Industry* (London: Euromonitor, 1986); Albert N. Greco, *The Book Publishing Industry* (Needham Heights, Mass.: Allyn & Bacon, 1997); Irving Louis Horowitz, *Communicating Ideas: The Politics of Scholarly Publishing*, 2nd edn (New Brunswick, N.J.: Transaction, 1991); Eric de Bellaigue, *British Book Publishing as a Business since the 1960s: Selected Essays* (London: British Library, 2004).

[10] André Schiffrin, *The Business of Books: How International Conglomerates Took Over Publishing and Changed the Way We Read* (London: Verso, 2000), p. 152.

[11] Jason Epstein, *Book Business: Publishing Past, Present, and Future* (New York: W. W. Norton, 2001), p. 8.

bound to damage publishing and to disappoint the corporate chiefs. But Epstein is optimistic about the future. New technologies and the rise of the internet will, he surmises, enable publishing to become once again a cottage industry of diverse and autonomous units, able to create and disseminate content to readers on 'the global village green' of the web and to bypass the big conglomerates and superstores that have come to dominate the modern book business.

Schiffrin and Epstein are very thoughtful commentators, and their long careers in the heart of the American publishing industry have given them unique vantage points from which to view its recent history and its current troubles. But their accounts are inextricably entangled with their own personal experiences and career trajectories. These are not well-rounded and even-handed accounts of an industry in the midst of change, nor do they purport to be: they are memoirs with a critical edge. They are personal and sometimes opinionated accounts – gracefully written, rich in anecdote, tinged with a shade of nostalgia – of an industry as seen from the particular perspectives of two protagonists who have charted their own courses through the complex and turbulent world of publishing. That the protagonists have charted their courses so successfully and recounted them so eloquently is a tribute to their remarkable talents as publishers and authors, but this does not alter the fact that their accounts are, by their very nature, partial. And Epstein's vision of the kind of publishing future that will be ushered in by new technologies is, it should be said, laced with a strong dose of wishful thinking.

So how can we develop a more systematic account of the changing structure of the book publishing industry today? To begin with, it is important to see that 'the book publishing industry' is an enormously complex and varied domain. There are many different kinds of book publishing, and many different kinds of books and markets, and it would be misleading to treat them as a single whole. Commentators like Schiffrin and Epstein are writing primarily about American trade publishing, and much of what they say would apply with equal force to trade publishing in Britain, France, Germany and elsewhere. But the extent to which their accounts are relevant to other sectors of the publishing industry, such as academic or textbook publishing, is much less clear. So the generic notion of 'the book publishing industry' must be broken down. How should we do this?

One way of doing this is by introducing the concept of publishing field: the world of book publishing can be conceptualized as a set of publishing fields. We can then proceed on the assumption that each of these fields has its own characteristics and dynamics, and each has its own history that differs in some respects from the histories of other fields. The individuals who work in the publishing industry are usually embedded in one of these fields, and they may know very little about what goes on in fields other than their own. The world of publishing is like a set of games, each of which has its own rules, like chess and checkers and monopoly: you can be very good at one game but know nothing about the others, having never played them and perhaps never taken much interest in them either. So if we want to understand the world of publishing and how it is changing, we have to focus on the different publishing fields and try to reconstruct the distinctive properties and dynamics of each.

So what is a field? A field is a structured space of social positions; it is a structured space of resources and power with its own forms of competition and reward.[12] Markets

---

[12] This concept, which is borrowed from the work of the French sociologist Pierre Bourdieu, is elaborated in more detail in chapter 2.

are an important part of fields, but fields are much more than markets: they are also made up of agents and organizations and the relations between them, of networks and supply chains, of different kinds and quantities of power and resources that are distributed in certain ways, of specific practices and forms of competition, etc. Part of what I shall try to show is that each field has a distinctive dynamic – what I shall loosely call 'the logic of the field' – which is the outcome of a specific set of forces and pressures and which shapes the activities of particular agents and organizations. The logic of the field defines the conditions under which agents and organizations can participate in the field and flourish or falter within it – that is, it defines the conditions under which they can play the game. But this logic can also have unintended consequences and can throw different agents and organizations into conflict with one another, as we shall see.

There are many different publishing fields ranging from general trade publishing to a multitude of more specialized fields – the field of scholarly publishing, the field of college textbook publishing, the field of children's book publishing, the field of illustrated art book publishing, and so on. Each of these fields has its own distinctive characteristics and dynamics. Of course, these fields overlap in many ways and the boundaries between them are often blurred. The picture is further complicated by the fact that many individual publishing firms operate in several fields at the same time. Nevertheless, as I shall try to show, each field has its own peculiar properties and forms of competition. Even if a particular firm operates in several fields at once, it does not operate in these different fields in the same way. Most publishers realize that if they want to be successful in different fields, they must become experts in each: they know they cannot apply the principles of trade publishing to the field of college textbook publishing and hope to succeed. Hence the larger firms which operate in different fields tend to differentiate themselves internally and to create specialist divisions that can build up the knowledge, skills and expertise to compete effectively in particular fields. Publishing firms compete with one another only in the context of specific fields, for it is only in the context of specific fields that they run up against other firms who are seeking to acquire similar content or to sell books of a similar kind.

It is also important to distinguish publishing fields from other social fields to which they are related in various ways. For example, the field of academic or scholarly publishing cannot be understood without considering the relations between this field, on the one hand, and the field of higher education (including the world of university libraries), on the other. These fields are not the same, they have different social and institutional characteristics, but they are locked together through multiple forms of interdependency. So too with the field of college textbook publishing: this is a field that cannot be properly understood unless one takes account of its relation to the field of higher education, which provides both the principal source of content for textbook publishers (in the form of authors who are often academics employed by colleges and universities) and the principal market for the content produced by them (in the form of students who are taking courses at institutions of higher and further education). Similarly for schoolbook publishing, professional publishing, illustrated art book publishing, etc.: all of these publishing fields are linked to other social fields on which they depend and which depend to some extent on them. But these fields, while mutually interdependent, are also shaped by different interests and governed by different logics. The field of higher education, for instance, has its own structures and constraints and its own mechanisms of reward and success, and these do not coincide with those that prevail in the fields of scholarly or textbook publishing. So while the fields are closely linked through relations of mutual interdependency, they are also governed by different logics which can give rise to tension, misunderstanding and conflict.

While we can understand the world of publishing only by understanding how specific fields of publishing work and how they are related to other social fields, at the same time we can also see that there are certain broader developments that have affected the world of publishing as a whole in recent years – and, indeed, some of these developments have affected other sectors of industry as well. The particular ways in which these broader developments have been played out in the world of publishing varies from field to field. Some developments are more significant in some fields than in others, and in each field where these developments are significant, the specific ways in which they are manifested are always shaped by the distinctive properties of the field. So what are these broader developments? There are four which are particularly important and which will feature prominently in the chapters that follow.

(1) *The growing concentration of resources*   In many publishing fields, mergers and acquisitions have led to growing concentrations of power and resources in the hands of large corporations. This is a process that has proceeded in different ways and to different degrees in different fields – it is by no means a uniform process that has shaped all publishing fields in the same way and to the same extent. The process of concentration or 'conglomeratization' has been particularly marked in trade publishing, in educational publishing and in professional publishing, to mention a few; it has been much less marked in a field such as academic or scholarly publishing, partly because of the distinctive role of university presses in the scholarly publishing field. It is the growing concentration of publishing resources in the hands of large conglomerates that has particularly exercised commentators like Schiffrin and Epstein, and rightly so – it is a development of fundamental importance. But their analyses of this phenomenon are shaped largely by their own experiences and are focused primarily, if not exclusively, on the field of trade publishing. The ways in which this development has manifested itself in other fields, and the implications of this development for other sectors of the industry, are issues that Schiffrin and Epstein do not explore.

(2) *The changing structure of markets and channels to market*   Just as important as the growing concentration of resources is the changing structure of markets and of channels to market. Again, the ways in which markets have changed varies a great deal from one field of publishing to another – the developments are often quite specific to certain fields. But there are some aspects of this change that are more generic and have affected many fields. One such aspect is the changing structure of the retail trade, and in particular the rise of powerful retail chains such as Barnes & Noble and Borders in the US, and WHSmith and Waterstone's/Dillons in the UK. The rise of the retail chains has radically transformed the nature of bookselling and has altered the balance of power between publishers and booksellers; it has also exacerbated the problem of returns, which has always been a major source of uncertainty for the stock management side of publishing. Another generic aspect of the changing structure of markets has been the emergence of online retailers or 'e-tailers', like Amazon.com, barnesandnoble.com and numerous others. Online retail has opened up new channels to market that simply did not exist before, and in some fields of publishing (such as academic publishing) this has

stimulated the sales of backlist titles which are of interest to relatively small circles of specialists. But online retail has also introduced a whole series of new uncertainties into the book trade, not the least of which is the financial precariousness of the online retailers themselves.

(3) *The globalization of markets and publishing firms* The growth of publishing conglomerates, the rise of retail chains and the emergence of online retailers have all contributed to the increasing globalization of markets and publishing firms. The large conglomerates all operate on a transnational basis, and many look increasingly to foreign markets as a way of expanding their businesses. But even smaller publishing firms find themselves operating in an increasingly globalized marketplace where data about books are now readily available online to anyone anywhere in the world. This process of globalization in the sphere of publishing is deeply interwoven with the rise of English as the de facto international language, and hence the way in which this process is played out varies greatly from one country to another, from one field to another and from one firm to another. Nothing would be more misleading than to assume that globalization in the sphere of publishing – or in any sphere for that matter – is a smooth and uniform process. On the contrary, when you look carefully at what happens in practice, you find large variations in the ways that different firms and different fields are affected by, and affect in turn, developments that take place on a transnational and global scale. The kinds of opportunities and challenges faced by a medium-sized British academic publisher in an increasingly globalized marketplace are very different from the kinds of opportunities and challenges faced by, say, a small Danish firm. But even publishers working in languages other than English are finding that the conditions in which they operate are changing, partly as a result of the growing dominance of English and the increasing international circulation of ideas, authors and content.

(4) *The impact of new technologies* As I have already indicated, the digital revolution represents a major force for change in the publishing industry. At one level, the impact of new technologies in the publishing industry is no different from the impact of new technologies in other sectors of industry: digitization and computerization enable publishing firms to transform their systems for managing information and to make these systems much more efficient, comprehensive and up-to-date. They also have enormous consequences for the ways in which books are produced, from typesetting and design to printing, and for the management of stock and supplies. But the potential impact of digitization in the publishing industry goes much further than that, precisely because the very content of the publishing business is, at the end of the day, a *digitizable asset*. In this respect, the publishing business is more like other media industries, such as the music industry, than it is like those industries concerned with the production of physical objects, such as cars or refrigerators. True, the printed book is a physical object, but the digital revolution made publishers increasingly conscious of the fact that their assets comprised not just their warehouses full of books but also the *content* that was realized in those books. It was the *content*, and the control of the copyrights that governed what they could do with that content, which was in some respects their key asset, not the books themselves. Of course, the physical books were not insignificant – they were, after all, the principal means by which publishers' content was realized and exchanged in the

marketplace, and therefore the principal source of revenue. This had been so for many centuries and, for most publishers in most fields, it was still overwhelmingly the case. But it was by no means certain that physical books would remain the dominant medium of dissemination in all fields of publishing forever. The story of the impact of digitization in the world of publishing is, in part, the story of how publishers have come to realize that the content they acquire is an asset that can be manipulated and stored in digital form, and how they have experimented – sometimes successfully, sometimes disastrously – with the realization and dissemination of this content in formats other than the bound and printed book. As we shall see, this is a story in which some lessons are clear while others remain clouded in uncertainty, and we are still a long way from knowing how the plot will unravel in the end.

In exploring the ways in which these and other developments have transformed the world of publishing over the last few decades, I shall not attempt to provide a comprehensive account. Given the size and complexity of the publishing industry, a degree of superficiality would be the unavoidable consequence of any attempt to be comprehensive. I shall focus instead on two fields of publishing which are linked to one another and which stand in a close relation to the field of higher education – namely, the field of academic or scholarly publishing, on the one hand, and the field of college textbook publishing (or what I shall call 'higher education publishing'), on the other. Why these fields? There are several reasons. In the first place, these are fields that tend to be neglected by commentators on the publishing industry, since they are generally seen as less glamorous than trade publishing. It is the world of trade publishing, with its bestsellers and high-profile authors, that tends to be the focus of the attention of commentators like Schiffrin and Epstein, and it is the world of trade publishing that occasionally catches the attention of the press. It is rare for the fields of academic and college textbook publishing to be noticed, let alone analysed in depth, in the more popular commentaries on the publishing industry. Yet academic and college textbooks published represent a substantial proportion of annual book output (roughly a third of all new books published in Britain each year could be classified in this way); and educational publishing as a whole (including school and college textbooks) accounts for a substantial proportion of total book sales (combined sales of school and college textbooks account for more than a third of total book sales in the US). Moreover, academic and college textbook publishing have in many ways been at the forefront of the recent changes affecting the publishing industry, and experiments with new technologies have proceeded much further in these fields (as well as in the fields of journal publishing and reference publishing) than they have in the world of trade publishing.

But there is another reason why the fields of academic and college textbook publishing demand much more attention than they have received hitherto: these are fields upon which the whole edifice of higher education has come to some extent to depend. Academic publishing – the world of the university presses as well as commercial academic publishers – has traditionally been one of the principal means by which scholars make available the results of research and communicate with other scholars, as well as with students and other readers who are interested in serious scholarly work. Academic publishing has traditionally been one of the key mechanisms for the dissemination of scholarship, one of the key providers of high-quality content and one of the driving forces of intellectual debate in the modern world. Similarly, the whole pedagogical process within higher education has for many decades relied heavily on the availability of textbooks of various kinds which can be recommended to students and assigned as reading for courses. Where would higher education be if there were no books available for students to read? Where would it be if academics could not publish the results of their research and there were no books to discuss and debate? The two worlds of higher education, that of teaching and that of research, are dependent in many ways on the output of academic and higher education publishers, and yet those whose lives are spent within higher education know surprisingly little about this industry upon which their own activities – and to some extent their careers and livelihoods – depend.

And it is not just the academy that has come to rely in countless ways on an industry about which it knows very little: the output of academic publishers also makes a vital contribution to the broader sphere of public discussion and debate. We should not underestimate the importance of books in helping to cultivate the kind of critical and informed culture that is essential to what we could call a vibrant public sphere.[13] Books provide a readily accessible medium in which individuals can provide sustained, in-depth analyses and critical commentaries on matters of general social and political concern – analyses and commentaries which can inform and stimulate debate in other media. Of course, it is not only academic publishers who make available books of this kind: there are many trade publishers who see themselves, and justly so, as providers of serious nonfiction for the general reader. But as trade publishing has become increasingly concentrated and more oriented towards publishing authors and books which are likely to have higher and more predictable sales, the role of academic publishers in making available high-quality content in the public domain has grown. Academic publishers can take a longer-term view and can live with lower expectations in terms of sales; they don't have to be preoccupied with quick returns on investments. Hence they have more latitude, at least in principle, to publish high-quality books which may turn out to be valuable contributions to public debate, even if the real value of the contribution may become clear only later. It is significant that in the aftermath of the terrorist attacks of 11 September 2001, it was books published by university presses – such as Angus Gillespie's *Twin Towers* (published by Rutgers University Press in November 1999), Ahmed Rashid's *Taliban* (published in the US in April 2000 by Yale University Press, although originated by I. B. Tauris in Britain), and Bernard Lewis's *What Went Wrong?* (published by Oxford University Press in January 2002) – that became unexpected bestsellers, providing readers with the kind of historical background and in-depth analysis that enriched and informed public debate. At a time when developments within the publishing industry are making it more difficult for trade publishers to publish books of serious nonfiction which do not have a clear and immediate appeal, the role of academic publishers in creating a pool of high-quality content that is available if and when the need arises has become more important than ever.

The fields of academic and higher education publishing may be vital both to higher education and to the broader public sphere, but what is happening within these fields? Are they flourishing? Are they languishing? Are they on the brink of collapse? What do we know about the state of these industries upon which so much of our educational and educated culture has come to depend? What do we know about the forces and factors that are driving change in these industries? And what would happen to our edu-

---

[13] See Jürgen Habermas, *The Structural Transformation of the Public Sphere: An Inquiry into a Category of Bourgeois Society*, tr. Thomas Burger with Frederick Lawrence (Cambridge: Polity, 1989).

cational and our public culture if these industries were to founder or to change in fundamental ways? These are among the questions to which I shall seek to provide some tentative answers – or at least to provide some of the background material we shall need if we want to be able to answer these questions in a reasoned and well-informed way.

The research that forms the basis of this study was carried out over a period of three years, from 2000 to 2003. The research was restricted to the fields of academic and higher education publishing; it was also restricted to English-language publishing, and specifically to publishing in Britain and the United States. (Further details on the methodological aspects of the research can be found in the Appendix.) While this study is focused on academic and higher education publishing, the approach developed here – based on the idea of analysing the logic and development of publishing fields – could be applied with equal validity to other sectors of the publishing industry.

The study is divided into four parts. Part I deals with some general issues concerning the nature of publishing as a business – what kind of business it is, how it is organized, how the publishing supply chain works, etc. It also introduces the concept of the publishing field and examines some of the generic properties of publishing fields in more depth. Part I concludes with a chapter that explores in more detail some of the broad trends and developments that have characterized the publishing industry since 1980.

Part II is focused on the field of academic or scholarly publishing. The nature of academic publishing is defined in relation to the world of the academy which it serves and which is served by it. Against this backcloth, I then seek to uncover the key dynamics that have shaped the evolution of this field since the late 1970s and early 1980s. What are the principal factors that have driven change within this field over the last two to three decades? How have publishing organizations within the field tried to cope with these changes? And where does this leave academic publishing at the dawn of the twenty-first century?

Part III offers a similar analysis of the field of college textbook publishing – or what I prefer to describe as the field of higher education publishing. How has this field changed over the last two to three decades, and how is it changing today? What are the key factors that are driving this change? What are the implications of these developments for the nature of higher education publishing today – and, more generally, for the kinds of content that are being made available, and will be made available in the future, for the purposes of teaching and learning in the sphere of higher education?

Part IV is concerned with the impact of the digital revolution in the world of publishing. I begin by distinguishing between different levels of impact and examining some of the broader issues involved in thinking about the relations between technologies, markets and forms of content. I then examine a variety of electronic publishing initiatives that have been undertaken in the fields of academic and higher education publishing since the mid-1990s and seek to offer a preliminary assessment of them – preliminary because in many cases the experiments are still underway. In the final chapter I try to show that irrespective of the fate of these various experiments, the impact of digitization in the world of publishing has already been profound and irreversible, for it has set in motion another revolution – a quiet revolution, hidden from the gaze of most journalistic commentators – which is transforming and will continue to transform the very nature of publishing as a business and what we could call the life cycle of the book.

Part I
The Publishing Business

1
Publishing as an economic and cultural practice

The publishing firm

The book publishing business in the West has existed since the late fifteenth century, when Gutenberg's invention of the printing press gave rise to a flourishing trade in books throughout the urban centres of Europe. During the first few centuries of publishing, the distinction between printers and publishers was not clear-cut; many printers operated effectively as publisher-printers, selecting the material to print and using their own resources to print and distribute it. Many printers also relied on external financial backing to undertake particular printing jobs. In some cases they were commissioned by private financiers, publishers or booksellers to print particular texts, in other cases they were commissioned by the Church or the state to produce liturgical works or official publications. But gradually the roles of the printer and the publisher became differentiated, as publishers became increasingly concerned with the activities of selection and risk-taking, while printers operated essentially as manufacturers of printed texts. There are isolated cases where publishing and printing continue to operate today under a single administrative structure. Cambridge University Press still operates both a publishing and printing division, although this is one of the only major publishing houses in the English-speaking world which still has its own printing works. Oxford University Press had its own printing works since its origins in the seventeenth century, but the printing works were eventually closed down in the late 1980s.

For at least the last two centuries, most publishers have operated primarily as organizations concerned with acquiring symbolic content and the rights to use this content, processing the content in various ways and making available the financial capital necessary to turn it into stocks of books which can be distributed and sold in the marketplace. Publishers today are essentially *content-acquiring and risk-taking organizations oriented towards the production of a particular kind of cultural commodity.* They acquire rights in certain kinds of symbolic content and then speculatively invest capital to transform that content into physical books which they hope they can sell in sufficient quantities and at a suitable price to generate a profit. Their investment is protected by the law of copyright, the origins of which stem in part from the concern on the part of printers in early modern Europe to protect their exclusive right to print and sell books without fear of piracy. If the books sell well, the publisher may generate a healthy return on the investment; a successful title may be reprinted on numerous occasions, helping to create a backlist which provides financial stability to the firm. But the sales of a book may also fall well short of the publisher's expectations, in which case the risk is borne by the publisher, who may have to write off unsold stock.

Most publishing firms are divided into separate departments which are hierarchically structured and interconnected in terms of the workflow. A book typically begins life in the editorial department, which is responsible for acquiring new content, building and maintaining relationships with content creators, negotiating contracts with authors and others, and overseeing the intellectual development of projects. When a final manuscript has been approved by the editorial staff, it is generally handed over to a desk-editing department, which prepares the text for production. The copy-edited manuscript is then handed over to a production department, which is responsible for overseeing the production process through to the final delivery of bound and jacketed copies to the warehouse. Specific aspects of the production process, such as copy-editing, jacket design, typesetting, printing and binding, are often contracted out to freelancers or specialized firms which work for a specified fee paid by the publisher. At a certain stage in the production cycle, the marketing department begins to implement a strategy for the promotion of a specific title, which will also commonly feature in batch publicity material such as catalogues. While each department has its own specialized tasks and may have a significant degree of autonomy, the relationship between these departments tends to be hierarchically structured. The relative power of different departments, and of individuals and groups within these departments, will vary from one firm to another and from one type of publishing to another; it may also vary over time, as changing circumstances alter the relative importance of different tasks and functions within the firm.

In order to develop this analysis further, it is helpful to introduce three concepts: the *publishing cycle*, the *publishing chain* and the *publishing field*. The publishing cycle refers to the stages through which a book typically moves, from the contracting of the project to the point at which it goes out of print – it describes, in other words, the typical life cycle of the book. The publishing chain refers to the interconnection of organizations involved in the publishing, selling and distribution of books; this is a chain in which the publisher is one particular link, and where each link in the chain seeks to provide a specific range of functions or services which are valued by others. The publishing field is the structured space of positions in which different publishers, agents and other organizations are located; it is a space in which relative positions are defined by the differing kinds and quantities of capital possessed by the agents and organizations concerned. I shall examine the publishing cycle and the publishing chain in this chapter; the next chapter will be devoted to the analysis of the publishing field.

The publishing cycle

The publishing cycle defines the stages through which a book typically moves in the course of its life history. Each of these stages involves a range of specific activities which are carried out by individuals involved in the publishing process, and some stages require decisions which have a direct bearing on the financial characteristics of the project. The stages have a clear temporal and sequential structure and are typically integrated into a workflow, with certain activities necessarily following others. The financial decisions associated with these stages have varying degrees of risk and uncertainty, which are generally highest at the beginning of the sequence and which become progressively lower as the title moves along the stages of the publishing cycle.

There are four main stages of financial decision-making in the traditional publishing cycle. The first stage is usually the point at which the publisher has to decide whether to take on a project. At this stage, the book may be only an idea in the author's mind and the publisher may have no more than a brief proposal (although publishers may, in some cases, defer a decision until they have seen and assessed all or part of the manuscript). The decision to take on a project is probably the most important decision in the publishing cycle, since it commits the publisher to the investment of substantial amounts of time and capital in the development and production of a work. It is also a decision which, in many cases, carries a relatively high degree of uncertainty and risk, since those taking the decision may have very few reliable indicators of likely sales. The decision-making process may require editors to provide tentative figures on likely sales, but in the absence of actual data these figures are in many cases pretty notional. Editors may also have to decide how much to offer an author as an advance on royalties for a particular project and, in cases where publishers find themselves in a competitive situation, there is a significant risk that they may commit themselves to advances which turn out to be well in excess of the royalties actually earned by a title.

Given the relatively high degree of uncertainty that exists at the first stage of the publishing cycle, most publishers find themselves adopting in practice what could be described as the 'frog model':[1] fertilize a lot of eggs, hatch them and hope that some will survive and eventually turn from tadpoles into frogs. (This approach is also common in other sectors of the media and cultural industries, such as the music and film industries.) The frog metaphor captures well two rather sobering facts about book publishing – namely, that most books don't do very well, and very few books do very well. For most publishers, around 20 per cent of titles will account for around 80 per cent of revenue. Where the metaphor breaks down is that it misrepresents the kind of uncertainty faced by publishers when they make decisions about which projects to take on. Whether an egg makes it to the stage of a full-grown frog is largely a matter of chance, but publishers are often in a position to know that some projects and some authors *will* do very well, even if they can't be entirely sure just how many copies of a particular book they will manage to sell.

The second stage in the publishing cycle which requires important financial decisions is the point at which the initial prices and print-runs have to be set. There are sources of information and historical precedents which publishing staff can draw on in making these decisions, but there is, unavoidably, a fair degree of uncertainty at this stage. The decision concerning the price will be shaped by (a) the perception of the maximum price that the market will bear for a book of this type and size, and (b) the expectation of the likely sales at different possible prices. In general terms, publishers aim for a price that will maximize revenue over cost, where cost and revenue are dependent on price per copy, on total number of copies printed, and on total number sold. By increasing the print-run, one can lower the unit cost and thereby bring down the price per copy while achieving a reasonable margin; on the other hand, if the extra copies printed are not sold, then the potential gains will turn out to be illusory and the publisher will have to write off unsold stock.

---

[1] James Lichtenberg, 'Setting Sail on an Unknown Sea: A View from the Bridge', in Vista 1999, p. 53.

For the most part, the setting of initial prices and print-runs tends to be done in a for-mulaic fashion. The publisher categorizes a book and then uses standardized formulae to set the prices and print-runs. These formulae tend to be based on the accumulated historical experience of the firm: they are rules of thumb which seem, on the basis of past experience, to be 'about right', allowing one to produce sufficient stock to meet the sales that are likely to transpire in a given time period (varying from twelve months to several years, depending on the stock accounting practices used by the firm) while min-imizing the risks of stock write-downs. The formulae may be varied in particular cases if there are reasons to think that the sales are likely to be exceptionally good or excep-tionally bad. For example, the publisher may have reason to believe, on the basis of feedback from marketing staff and sales reps and on the basis of back orders – orders that have built up in advance of publication – that a particular title is going to do excep-tionally well, and may increase the initial print-run accordingly. On the other hand, evi-dence of this kind may also suggest that a particular title is going to flop, and the publisher may reduce the print-runs and increase the prices in order to minimize losses. While publishers can draw on various sources of information in order to make these decisions in a relatively reasoned fashion, they also tend to rely rather heavily on their 'gut instincts' about how well a particular title is likely to do.

The third stage at which key decisions have to be taken is the point at which the stock of the initial print-run has been substantially depleted and the publisher must decide whether to reprint (or to bring out a cheaper paperback edition). At this stage the risks are less than at the previous stage, since the publisher will now have a title-specific sales history to draw on. He or she will know exactly how many copies the book has sold over what period of time, and this information can be used to determine whether a reprint should be ordered and, if so, how many copies should be printed. But there are risks at this stage too. Certain kinds of books, like trade titles, may sell very strongly during the first few months after publication, when they may be getting a lot of atten-tion in the media, and sales may then suddenly drop off. It may be very difficult to predict exactly when the sales will fall off, and yet when they do the decline may be sudden and steep – 'when it's over, it really is over,' lamented one editor. An incautious reprint at the wrong moment may leave the publisher with a great deal of excess stock and may wipe out a significant proportion of the profits earned on earlier sales, as many publishers have discovered to their cost.

Another source of uncertainty stems from the nature of the publishing chain. Most publishers sell the vast majority of their stock to booksellers and wholesalers rather than directly to consumers, and, unlike most other retail sectors, booksellers and whole-salers normally buy stock on a sale-or-return basis – in effect, books are sold on con-signment. Bookstores can order stock on the understanding that if they don't sell it within a certain time period (usually twelve months), they can return it to the publisher for full credit; the only costs incurred by the bookseller are the handling and adminis-trative costs, together with the shipping costs for returning the stock. This practice was established during the Great Depression of the 1930s as a means of encouraging book-sellers to take books that they might otherwise be disinclined to stock, and it has con-tinued to the present day. It has some advantages for publishers, because it lowers the risk barrier for booksellers and thus helps to ensure that new books are stocked and displayed in bookstores. But the risks are not eliminated by this arrangement: they are simply shifted back on to the publishers, who may find themselves faced with substantial returns of unsold stock, which depresses their sales figures and can create serious stock management problems. Publishers may also find it difficult to ascertain how many copies of a particular title they have really sold, since stock supplied to bookstores may not have sold through to customers and may, in the end, be returned. Hence reprint decisions may be rendered more difficult and uncertain. A publisher may find that its stock of a particular title has been depleted and decide to reprint what appears to be a title in demand, only to find that it is subsequently inundated with returns.

The fourth stage in the publishing cycle where important financial decisions have to be taken is the point at which a publisher must decide whether to put a particular title out of print. When the rate of sale has fallen below a certain level or when the stock of a slow-selling title has been exhausted, the publisher will normally have to consider whether to put the title out of print. The cost of warehousing stock may be such that it is no longer financially sensible to keep a slow-selling title in print, and the cost of reprinting may be such that it is no longer commercially viable to reprint. In these circumstances, the publisher may decide to put the title out of print and allow the rights to revert to the author (although this is one part of the publishing cycle where digital technology has had, and is continuing to have, a significant impact, as we shall see in part IV). The degree of risk associated with this decision is minimal, since by this stage the editor has a full sales history of the title and is in a position to estimate fairly reliably what the likely future sales of the title would be if it were kept in print. The decision to put a title out of print is usually a decision about minimizing future loss rather than maximizing further gains. But once this decision is taken, the capacity of the title to generate additional revenue in the future (apart from rights income) is effectively at an end.

One important feature of the publishing cycle is that, unlike the product cycles in some other industries, it tends to be long, typically extending over several years. When a publisher signs up a book, it may be several years before the manuscript materializes, and another year or more before a final, approved version of the text is available for the publisher to begin production. For many publishers in the English-speaking world, the production process may itself take up to a year (publishers in other languages often work to tighter production schedules). It may then be another year or more before the publisher knows just how well the book is going to sell, and whether it will need to be reprinted or should be allowed to tick over until it is eventually put out of print. So it is quite common for there to be at least three or four years between the point at which a book is signed up and the point at which it becomes clear just how well it will do in the marketplace.

The length of the publishing cycle has several implications for the firm. First, it means that up-front investments in the form of advances etc. may take a long time to be recouped, during which time these investments are, in effect, unrecovered debts. This exacerbates the cash-flow problems experienced by many publishing firms, especially newer and smaller firms which have not had a chance to build up significant cash reserves. Moreover, there is a risk that a proportion of these investments may never be recovered, since some of the books signed up may never materialize (or may not materialize in a form acceptable by the publisher), and since books that are published may not sell sufficiently well to recoup the advance. A second consequence of the long cycle is that publishers generally operate under conditions in which they do not have quick and reliable feedback about the decisions they take at early stages in the cycle. At the point when an editor or editorial committee is considering whether to take on a book, there may be a great deal of discussion, speculation and even agonized deliberation about sales prospects, but by the time the book is actually published and its sales figures are clear, the earlier discussion may be largely forgotten and the book takes on a life of its own. Given the length of the publishing cycle, the feedback loop between sales performance and editorial decision-making is highly extended, and this tends to accentuate the speculative character of the decisions which characterize the early stages of the cycle.

The publishing chain

The publisher is only one of the organizations involved in the publishing chain – that is, in the network of organizations and activities involved in the publication, sale and distribution of books. This chain comprises a series of independent but interconnected organizations which are situated at specific points in the chain and which perform certain tasks or functions, for which they are remunerated in some way. These tasks or functions include the creation and development of content, the control of quality, the design of the book and the jacket, typesetting, printing, binding, warehousing, sales and marketing, distribution and so on. Many of these functions are handled by the publisher, but others are commonly performed by others – from authors to typesetters and print-ers – with whom the publisher must negotiate suitable contractual terms. Publishers are constantly reviewing the question of whether to handle certain functions themselves or to outsource them to freelancers or to specialized firms who offer their services to a variety of clients, and over the last few decades there has been a tendency in many sectors of the industry to outsource more functions. The advantage of outsourcing is that it reduces fixed overheads and increases flexibility for the publisher, but at the same time it may involve some loss of coordination and control.

The publishing chain is both a *supply chain* and a *value chain*. It is a supply chain in the sense that it provides a series of organizational links by means of which a specific product – the book – is gradually produced and transmitted via distributors and retail-ers to an end user who purchases it. Figure 1.1 offers a simple visual representation of the book supply chain. The basic steps are as follows: the author supplies the manuscript or disk to the publisher, who carries out a range of functions before delivering the final text (or the final digital file) to the printer, who prints and binds the books and deliv-ers them to the distributor, who warehouses the stock and fulfils orders from both retail-ers and wholesalers, who in turn fulfil orders from both individual consumers/readers

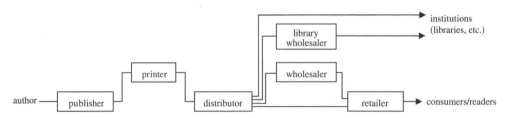

Figure 1.1   The book supply chain

and institutions (such as libraries). For most consumers/readers, the only point of contact they have with the book supply chain is when they walk into a bookstore to browse or buy a book, or when they browse the details of a book on the website of Amazon or another online retailer, or when they check out a book from a library. There are numerous intermediaries that separate the consumer/reader from the author and the publisher.

The publishing chain is also a *value chain* in the sense that each of the links purportedly adds some 'value' in the process. This notion is more complicated than it might at first seem, but the general idea is clear enough: each of the links performs a task or function which contributes something substantial to the overall task of producing the book and delivering it to the end user, and this contribution is something for which the publisher (or some other agent or organization in the chain) is willing to pay. If the task or function is not contributing anything substantial, or if the publisher (or other organization) feels that it does not add enough value to justify the expense, then the publisher may decide to cut the link out of the chain – that is, to 'disintermediate' it. Technological change may also alter the functions performed by particular links in the chain. The functions of the typesetter, for example, have been radically transformed by the advent of computerization, which has tended to eliminate the need to re-key the text, and some typesetters have sought to take on new functions, such as marking-up texts in specialized languages like XML, in order to protect their position (or to reposition themselves) in the value chain.

Figure 1.2 presents the principal tasks or functions in the publishing chain. This diagram is more elaborate than figure 1.1 because each organization in the supply chain may carry out several functions (the agents or organizations which typically perform the various tasks or functions are indicated in brackets). The starting point of the value chain is the acquisition and creation of content. Publishers seek to acquire content which is often created (at least in part) by authors, but the relation between the content creators and the content acquirers is often more complicated than a simple one-way arrow would suggest. In some cases, authors work largely independently of publishers and simply present them with a manuscript which they have conceived and produced: this model of the autonomous author is not altogether illusory, but it hardly does justice

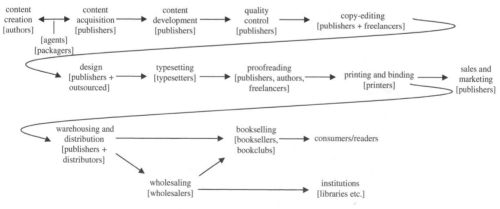

Figure 1.2 The publishing value chain

to the complex interplay between agents and organizations in the creative process. In some sectors of the publishing industry, many (or even most) book projects are conceived of by editors (or by editorial intermediaries of various kinds), and the task of the editor is then to find an author who is willing and able to write the book which the editor wants to commission. The editor may also play a very substantial role in shaping the project, either by direct interventions or by passing on the feedback of other readers or advisers. The model of the editorially driven publishing organization is not necessarily opposed to the notion of the autonomous author, and a publisher with a strongly proactive commissioning strategy may also be able and willing to accommodate a number of authors who are largely autonomous (especially if these authors are well known and well established). Different sectors of publishing, different publishing organizations and different editors tend to vary in the extent to which they are editorially driven. Some are much more single-minded in this respect, with clear commissioning objectives and elaborate systems for the development of content, while others rely much more on the cultivation of long-term relationships with particular authors who are largely left to get on with the creative process.

While authors are the main source of content creation in the publishing chain, other cultural intermediaries also play a significant role in creating content. One such intermediary is the literary agent. Agents scout for and sign up authors and then negotiate terms with publishers on behalf of their authors for specific book projects, for which they take a commission; in some cases they also come up with the idea of a book and then find an author (and perhaps a ghost writer) to write it, before they search for a publisher who is willing to sign up the project and pay an advance for it. Agents are cultural intermediaries in the publishing chain whose livelihood depends on their capacity to persuade authors that they can achieve better terms for them in negotiating with publishers than the authors could themselves, and on their capacity to persuade publishers to accept terms which are sufficiently high to generate a reasonable stream of income from the commission they charge on author's earnings. In some sectors of publishing and especially trade publishing, the role of the agent has become more important as the industry has become more concentrated, partly because, with rapid change and high staff turnover in publishing firms, the agent has in some cases replaced the editor as the principal point of contact and continuity for the author, and partly because, as the stakes have grown in the competition for bestselling authors and titles, the agent has taken on an increasingly important role as an auctioneer who solicits offers from a variety of interested publishers. For some bestselling authors, the traditional bond between author and editor has been replaced by the bond between author and agent, and the latter provides the author with the kind of continuity and point of entry into the publishing world that was once provided by an established and trusted editor.

Another cultural intermediary is the book packager. Packagers are organizations which produce and develop content for book projects, and then sell it on to the publisher. They commission writers to put together books which, the packagers believe, can be successfully marketed, and they deliver the product to a publisher who will take it over at a certain stage in the publishing cycle and publish it. Book packagers began to appear on a significant scale in Britain and the United States in the late 1960s and early 1970s. They tended to specialize in putting together books which were more complicated than the straightforward authored text, such as highly illustrated books, anthologies, reference works and other kinds of books involving contributions from multiple authors and sources. From a publisher's point of view, the attraction of the packaged book is that the time-consuming work of creating and developing content, clearing permissions, etc., has been carried out by the packager, who hands over to the publisher a more or less finished piece of content. In some cases, the book packager may also typeset, design and produce the book. The publisher can then concentrate on marketing and selling the book, without having to tie up resources in the earlier phases of the publishing chain. The disadvantage for the publisher is that the costs of acquiring and developing content in this way tend to be high, and the margins they can achieve on packaged books are likely to be much lower than the margins they can achieve on books they acquire and develop themselves.

Apart from those books that have been prepared by external packagers, publishers commonly invest a great deal of time, effort and resources in the development of content. This may involve the reading of draft material by in-house editors as well as sending material out to external readers; it may also involve picture research, copyright clearance and commissioning extra material. In complicated multi-author projects, the publisher may play a key role in commissioning and aggregating content. Publishers are also responsible for controlling the quality of the material they publish. The importance of quality control varies from one kind of publishing to another, but in some areas, such as serious nonfiction, scholarly publishing and higher education publishing, the maintaining of high standards of quality is a key component of a publisher's brand. Many of the other functions in the publishing chain, such as copy-editing, text and jacket design, typesetting, proofreading, indexing, printing and binding, warehousing and distribution, are commonly put out-of-house to freelancers or contracted out to specialized firms, although precisely which functions are contracted out will vary from one publisher to another.

Most publishers retain responsibility for sales and marketing, although some smaller publishers may buy in the services of sales reps who work for other publishers, and in some markets publishers often buy in the services of independent agents who work for a variety of publishers; in some cases publishers may also employ freelance publicists to promote specific books. Later functions in the publishing chain, such as warehousing and distribution, may be handled by the publishers themselves or outsourced, depending on the size and the policy of the organization. Some of the larger publishers handle their own warehousing and distribution, and those that do are often willing to take on other publishers as clients, charging a commission that is usually based on a percentage of sales. Many small and medium-sized publishers will outsource warehousing and distribution, since they are too small to achieve economies of scale and to maintain the level of investment in physical plant and new technologies that is required by these aspects of the business.

For the most part, publishers do not sell their books directly to consumers (although some publishers may sell a proportion in this way through mail order, publishers' websites, etc.). The publisher's main customers are not readers but rather a range of cultural intermediaries which include wholesalers and booksellers of various kinds, ranging from the small independent bookseller to the large retail chains like Barnes & Noble, Borders, WHSmith and Waterstone's. These intermediaries occupy a powerful position in the publishing chain since they are the gatekeepers who stand between the publishers and the readers, deciding how many copies of which books to stock in their bookstores, how to display them, whether to reorder when stocks are depleted and so on.

Given their powerful position, the large chains can also use their market muscle to demand improved terms and higher discounts from publishers, who may find it difficult to resist the demands for fear of alienating the key intermediaries upon whom their revenue streams depend.

Each task or function in the publishing chain exists largely by virtue of the fact that it makes some contribution, of varying degrees of significance, to the overall objective of producing and selling books. Some of these tasks (design, copy-editing, typesetting, etc.) are within the range of activities that could be done by a single publishing organization, although a publisher may decide to disaggregate the functions and contract them out in order to reduce costs and improve efficiency. Other tasks are rooted in activities which are quite distinct and which have, in historical terms, a more settled institutional differentiation. This differentiation may be characterized by harmonious relations between the agents and organizations involved, since all have something to gain from cooperation; but they can also be characterized by tension and conflict, since their interests do not always coincide. Moreover, particular positions within the chain are not necessarily fixed or permanent. Changes in working practices, economic developments and technological advances can all have a major impact on the publishing chain, as tasks that were previously commonplace or essential are bypassed or eclipsed. If a particular link in the publishing chain is no longer necessary or no longer makes a significant contribution to the value-producing process, it may find that its position is rendered increasingly marginal and it may eventually be bypassed altogether.

Given that the publishing chain is not rigid and that particular tasks or functions can be eclipsed by economic and technological change, what reason is there to believe that the role of the publisher itself might not be rendered redundant? What are the core activities or functions of the publisher? Are these activities that could be phased out by new technologies, or that could be done by others? Could publishers themselves be disintermediated from the publishing chain? The latter question has been raised often enough in recent years, but to address it properly we need to separate out the key functions of the publisher from a range of other activities that can be put out-of-house to freelancers or outsourced to specialized firms. Figure 1.3 highlights six key functions of the publisher – it is by carrying out these tasks or functions that the publisher makes a distinctive contribution to the value creation process.

The first function is content acquisition and list-building. This is in many ways the key function of the publisher: to acquire and, indeed, help to create the content that will be

Where do publishers add value?

content acquisition and list-building	financial investment and risk-taking	content development
quality control	management and coordination	sales and marketing

Figure 1.3 Functions of the publisher

turned into the books that comprise the publisher's list. The publisher acts not just as a cultural filter or gatekeeper but in many cases plays a proactive role in creating or conceiving a project – some projects simply wouldn't exist without the creative input of the publisher. Some of the best publishers are those who are able to come up with good ideas for books and to find good authors to write them, or who are able to turn what might be a rather vague idea in the mind of an author into a project that eventually becomes a good book. There is a real skill here that involves a blending together of intellectual creativity and marketing nous, and that distinguishes outstanding editors and publishers from those who are run of the mill. The second function is financial investment and risk-taking. The publisher acts as the banker who makes resources available up-front, both to pay advances to authors and to cover the costs of acquisition, development and production. And it is the publisher who takes the risks associated with publication – if the book fails to sell, it is the publisher who takes the stock write-down and who writes off any unearned advance. The third function is content development. In some cases the content provided by an author is in excellent condition and needs very little input from the publisher, but in many areas of publishing this is the exception rather than the rule. The publisher often invests a great deal of effort in content development, from actively shaping the text to providing a range of services like picture research and copyright clearance, and in so doing may add considerable value.

The fourth function is quality control: it is the responsibility of the publisher to assess the quality of the text and to ensure that it meets certain standards. These standards will of course vary from one publisher to another and a variety of assessment procedures may be used, ranging from the judgement of in-house editors to evaluations by one or more external readers who are specialists in the field. Quality control is important for the publisher because it is one of the key means by which they are able to build a distinctive profile and brand in the publishing field and thereby distinguish themselves from other publishers. The fifth function is what could be loosely described as management and coordination. This label describes a range of management activities which are an integral part of the publishing process, from the management of specific projects which may be exceptionally complex to the management of specific activities or phases in the life cycle of the book. For example, even if copy-editing is put out-of-house to freelancers, the freelancers must be given work and instructions, their terms of work must be agreed and they must be paid, and all of this requires management time and expertise (this is sometimes handled by a dedicated in-house manuscript editor or desk editor). Similarly, even though typesetting, design and printing may be outsourced to specialized firms, the whole production process from copy-edited manuscript to bound books must be managed; this is usually done in-house by a production manager or controller. Decisions must be taken about prices and print-runs, and stock must then be managed throughout the life cycle of the book. The copyright must also be managed through the sale of subsidiary rights (translations, reprints, serialization, etc.). All of these activities require a great deal of management time and expertise, and are in most cases handled by in-house managers who have responsibility for specific sectors of the production and publishing process.

The sixth and final function is sales and marketing. I have bundled these activities together although they are in fact quite distinct. Marketing comprises a range of activities concerned with informing potential customers of the availability of a book and encouraging them to order or buy it. These activities include catalogue preparation and mailing, advertising, direct mail, sending out review copies and, more recently, various kinds of telemarketing and e-marketing. Some publishers may also have a separate publicity manager and/or department whose task is to cultivate relations with the media and secure media coverage for a book – coverage which may range from reviews, extracts and interviews in the printed press to radio and television appearances, book signings and lecture tours. The task of the sales manager and the sales team is to call on the key accounts, which include the bookselling chains, the independent booksellers and the wholesalers, to inform them of forthcoming books and, where possible, to take orders for them. In the large textbook publishing firms, the sales team also commonly includes a large number of sales reps – or 'college travellers' as they are traditionally called – who call on professors at university campuses and try to secure adoptions for their textbooks.

These six key functions of the publisher define the principal respects in which publishing firms 'add value' in the publishing process. When they perform these functions well, they can make a significant difference to the quality of the book and to its success in the marketplace. The performance of these functions (and the overheads associated with them) also account for a substantial proportion of the costs incurred in the publishing process. The latter point is sometimes neglected (or not fully appreciated) by those who suggest that the electronic delivery of books would substantially reduce the costs of publishing. It is of course true that electronic delivery would eliminate the need for printing and the costs associated with printing and warehousing (including paper, binding, etc.), but these costs, while not insignificant, represent a relatively small proportion of the total costs incurred in the publishing process. We shall return to this point in a later chapter.

The economics of publishing

Book publishing is generally a low margin business. Given the overheads of publishers, the cost of manufacturing (paper, binding, jackets and covers, etc.), the number of cost-bearing links in the publishing chain, the discounts given to retailers and wholesalers and the relatively modest list price of many books, most publishers tend to generate relatively low levels of profitability. Among commercial academic publishers, it is not uncommon for overall profit margins to be in the region of 5–10 per cent. Many of the American university presses operate on a break-even basis and, in some cases, depend on grants and subsidies of various kinds from their host institutions in order to balance their accounts. In other sectors of book publishing the profit margins may be slightly higher (margins of 15–20 per cent are fairly common in textbook and professional publishing, for example), but they are rarely as high as the margins achieved in other sectors of the media and communication industries.

The financial model used by most publishing firms involves the calculation of a gross profit margin on each title published. The GPM is based on the relation between the total costs (C) per title (including pre-press costs, printing costs and royalties payable), on the one hand, and the total revenue (R) per title (number of units sold multiplied by price per unit, less discounts etc.), on the other. The GPM is calculated as revenue less costs divided by revenue; or, in simple mathematical terms, GPM = GP/R, where GP (gross profit) is revenue less costs (GP = R − C). Most publishing firms will have a target GPM which they will aim to achieve on each title published, though they will allow some variation on a title by title basis depending on the type of book it is, the competition and the prospects for long-term sales. So, for example, a firm may aim to achieve a GPM of 60 per cent on all new titles, but they may accept a lower margin of, say, 50 per cent or even 40 per cent on a title where production costs may be high and the market may be price sensitive. Another common way of setting revenue targets is to say that a title should achieve a GPM of 60 per cent or a net contribution of a certain sum; this allows for greater flexibility to take account of competitive market conditions. The publisher's task is to try to set the prices and print-runs of a title at levels that will generate a healthy margin and/or net contribution while at the same time minimizing the risks associated with over-printing (which locks up capital in stock that subsequently has to be written down) and avoiding the inefficiencies of under-printing (which may result in lost sales and may require the publisher to reprint sooner than would be desirable from the viewpoint of maximizing the margin). The GPM generated by each title over the course of its life cycle represents the contribution that the title makes to the overall GPM of the firm, from which the firm is able to cover its overheads (including staff costs) and is able, if all goes well, to generate an operating profit.

Publishers generally distinguish between pre-press costs and manufacturing costs. Pre-press costs are all the costs incurred in getting a book project to the point at which it can be delivered to a printer; they include the costs of copy-editing, typesetting, proof-reading, text and jacket design, text and picture permissions, etc. Manufacturing costs are the costs involved in manufacturing the final bound and jacketed books, including the costs of printing, paper, binding, printing covers and jackets, etc. Since pre-press costs are commonly loaded against the first print-run, the margin on the first printing of a book is usually lower than the margin that can be achieved on subsequent reprints. A book that generates a margin of, say, 52 per cent on the first print-run will often generate a margin of between 60 and 70 per cent on subsequent reprints. However, since the margin is the outcome of the relation between cost, price and units sold, reprint margins can be pushed down by low print-runs on the reprint (especially if this is combined with relatively high manufacturing costs – for instance, if the book is long or has colour illustrations). This problem is especially acute for scholarly publishers, who may find that many of their backlist titles are selling relatively slowly (at the rate of 200–300 copies per year or less). Traditionally these publishers are then faced with the decision of (a) reprinting a small quantity with a low margin, (b) increasing the print-run in order to improve the margin on the reprint, but running the risk of over-printing and hence incurring a stock write-down further down the line, or (c) putting the book out of print. As we shall see later, the development of digital printing and print on demand is beginning to provide publishers with a new set of options when faced with this difficult decision.

While the basic economics of book publishing are common to different sectors of the industry, the details vary a great deal from one type of publishing to another. Scholarly publishing traditionally uses a low volume, high price model. In scholarly publishing, it is generally assumed that demand is relatively inelastic, and hence not particularly sensitive to price: print-runs are generally low, prices are generally high, and the control of costs is one of the keys to achieving good margins. In this sphere there are certain economies of scale to be gained by achieving high throughputs and by using standardized formats for production and design, so that the amount of attention given to each

title is kept to a minimum. College textbook publishing, on the other hand, is traditionally a high volume business. A great deal of development cost may be invested in
each new title and the production costs may be high; moreover, the major college textbook publishers have relatively high overhead costs, since they commonly support large
sales forces, among other things. Hence the major college textbook publishers may be
counting on initial print-runs of 20,000 or more to justify their investment and to achieve
the kinds of margins and contributions they require. Trade publishing requires different models, since the market for trade books is more price sensitive and sales are more
unpredictable. Hence publishing for the trade is generally a much riskier proposition:
investments (in the form of advances, quality production and extensive marketing) may
be high, prices must be kept relatively low and print-runs are often difficult to determine. Sales may depend on a wide range of extraneous factors and the risks of ending
up with unsold stock are high. Successful trade books can generate handsome returns,
but many trade titles perform only moderately well in the marketplace and the margins
in trade publishing tend to be lower than in scholarly publishing, college textbook publishing and other areas such as professional and STM (scientific, technical and medical)
publishing.

One factor which has a major impact on the profitability of publishing is the discounts
offered to booksellers and wholesalers. Discounts tend to be highest in trade publishing, where publishers need booksellers to stock and display books and, in general, to
play an active role in selling them – hence discounts for trade titles are commonly
between 40 and 50 per cent. High discounts mean lower net receipts for the publisher,
and they therefore put added pressure on the publisher's margins. Scholarly monographs generally command lower discounts, typically between 25 and 30 per cent – a
'short discount', as it's commonly known. In the United States, college textbooks may
have even lower discounts, typically between 20 and 25 per cent, since it's assumed by
the textbook publishers that their reps do the selling by calling on professors, who decide
whether to adopt the book, and once a textbook has been adopted, the bookstore simply
has to stock it: students will buy the book because they've been told to buy it by their
professors. (Today many college textbook publishers in the US sell to bookstores at a
fixed price – that is, net of discount – on the understanding that the bookstore will mark
up by 20 or 25 per cent to generate their own margin.) Hence the publisher's margins
on scholarly monograph publishing and college textbook publishing will tend to be
higher than they are on trade publishing. On the other hand, bookstores, which also generally operate on very tight margins, tend to prefer trade titles since they can generate
a better margin for themselves, and they may be reluctant to stock books on which they
are receiving a discount of less than 40 per cent.

Given the direct relationship between print-runs and margins, there is a constant
temptation for publishers to increase print-runs in order to improve margins. But when
publishers print books they are locking up capital in stock which sits in a warehouse,
where it takes up space and has to be kept under conditions where it will not deteriorate or be damaged. Moreover, if they hold more stock than they are likely to sell in a
reasonable time period, they may be locking up capital in goods which are effectively
worthless (or nearly so). Hence the management of stock is a vital part of the financial
practice of publishing firms. Stock management practices vary a great deal from one
sector of the industry to another and, indeed, from one firm to another. Some firms
monitor stock very carefully and use strict rules to write down stock (for example,

writing down after a year all stock in excess of what they are likely to sell in an eighteen-month period). Other publishing firms have taken a much more relaxed view of stock management – for example, some of the American university presses have traditionally printed for a five-year period and, in some cases, have tended to turn a blind eye to excess stock (although this is a problem that has come back to haunt them in recent years). As we shall see in part IV, one of the most profound implications of recent developments in digital technologies is that it provides publishers with new ways to deal with the management of stock in those areas of publishing where turnover tends to be low, and hence provides publishers with new ways to manage the cost and the risk associated with publishing and supplying slow-selling titles.

2

The social structure of publishing fields

In the previous chapter we examined the concepts of the publishing cycle and the publishing chain. In this chapter I want to focus on the third key concept that I shall be using in this study – the publishing field. Particular firms are always embedded in structured fields which are populated by a plurality of firms, each distinguished from one another by virtue of different quantities of the different kinds of capital they possess. I shall begin by examining the different kinds of capital which constitute the principal resources of publishing firms and which determine their positions in publishing fields. I shall then explore the structural differentiation of these fields and their linguistic and spatial properties. Finally, I shall consider some aspects of the relations between publishing fields and the adjacent social fields with which they are intertwined.

The publishing field and forms of capital

I draw the concept of field from the work of Pierre Bourdieu.[1] Roughly speaking, a field is a structured space of social positions whose properties are defined primarily by the relations between these positions and by the resources attached to them. We can conceptualize the publishing field as a space of positions occupied by different publishing organizations.[2] The position of any particular publisher depends on the quantities of resources they possess. What kinds of resources do publishers possess? There are four types of resources which are particularly important for publishing firms: economic capital, human capital, symbolic capital and intellectual capital (figure 2.1). Economic

---

[1] See Pierre Bourdieu, *The Field of Cultural Production: Essays on Art and Literature*, ed. Randal Johnson (Cambridge: Polity, 1993); Pierre Bourdieu, 'Some Properties of Fields', in his *Sociology in Question*, tr. Richard Nice (London: Sage, 1993), pp. 72–7; Pierre Bourdieu, *The Rules of Art: Genesis and Structure of the Literary Field*, tr. Susan Emanuel (Cambridge: Polity, 1996). This is not the place to offer a detailed assessment of Bourdieu's work, but it should be noted that I have drawn selectively on his theory of fields and that there are aspects of his account, such as his arguments concerning the autonomy and heteronomy of literary and artistic fields, which I do not take up for various reasons. I also extend Bourdieu's approach by giving more attention than he does to the spatial and linguistic properties of fields; by examining the role of technologies in shaping the evolution of fields; by combining field theory with an analysis of the strategies and practices of firms; and by focusing on the structural transformations of fields and on the ways in which organizations respond to these changes.

[2] See Pierre Bourdieu, 'The Production of Belief: Contribution to an Economy of Symbolic Goods', in Bourdieu, *The Field of Cultural Production*, pp. 74–111; and Pierre Bourdieu, 'Une révolution conservatrice dans l'édition', *Actes de la recherche en sciences sociales*, 126–7 (Mar. 1999).

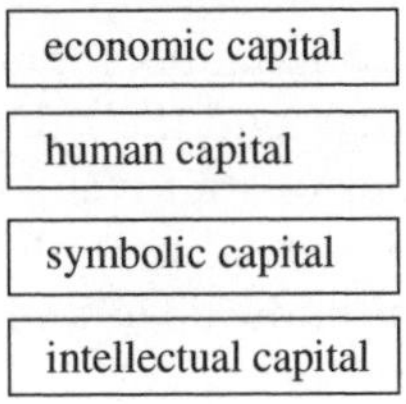

| economic capital |
| human capital |
| symbolic capital |
| intellectual capital |

Figure 2.1   Key resources of publishing firms

capital is the accumulated financial resources, including stock and plant as well as capital reserves, to which publishers have access, either directly or through their capacity to raise finance from other individuals and institutions. Human capital is the staff employed by the firm and their accumulated knowledge, skills and expertise. Symbolic capital is the accumulated prestige and status associated with the publishing house. And intellectual capital (or intellectual property) consists of the rights that a publisher owns or controls in intellectual content, rights which are attested to by their stock of contracts with authors and other bodies and which they are able to exploit through their publications and through the selling of subsidiary rights. The position of each publishing house will vary in the social space of positions, depending on the relative quantities of these four forms of capital they possess. All four types of capital are actively cultivated and accumulated by publishing organizations (albeit to varying degrees from one firm to another), since they know that their success depends on their capacity to mobilize these resources in the competitive struggle to acquire new content and achieve sales.

It is easy to see why publishers need to accumulate economic capital: as the principal risk-taker in the publishing chain, publishers must be able to draw on their financial resources (or those of financial agents and institutions to which they are linked, such as banks and shareholders) at various stages in order to finance the production and publication of books and in order to build and expand the business. Early in the publishing cycle they must be prepared to pay an advance on royalties to an author (or an author's agent) in order to acquire a book project. At subsequent stages of the publishing cycle, publishers must invest in the production of the book, paying the bills of typesetters, designers, printers, etc., and tying up resources in stock which may or may not be sold. The larger the capital reserves of the publisher, the larger the advances it is able to offer, the more able it is to cushion itself from the negative effects of unsuccessful projects and the more it can spread the risks of publishing by investing in a larger number of projects (and a larger number of more commercially promising projects) in the hope that some tadpoles will become frogs, eventually generating substantial revenue streams.

It is also easy to see why publishers need human capital: like other organizations, publishing firms are only as good as their staff. A highly trained and highly motivated workforce is a vital resource for a publishing firm and in many ways the key to its success. This is true at all levels, but particularly true at the level of editorial staff, since this is the creative core of the publishing firm. The success of the firm depends crucially on the ability to acquire, train and retain highly motivated editors who are able to come up with a strong list of new projects and develop them into commercially successful books, and who are able to form long-term relationships of trust with creative and productive authors. Editors who have the right combination of intellectual creativity, social flair and financial nous are highly valued assets, and their departure can be a major loss to the firm. The departure of a key member of staff is not only the loss of an individual who contributes to the daily workflow: it may also be the loss of someone who possesses a great deal of accumulated practical knowledge and skill, and whom it may require a great deal of time and effort to replace.

It is easy to see why publishers need economic and human capital, but what is symbolic capital and why do they need it? Symbolic capital is best understood as the accumulated prestige, recognition and respect accorded to certain individuals or institutions.[3] It is one of those intangible assets that is enormously important, indeed essential, for publishing firms. For publishers are not just employers and financial risk-takers: they are also cultural mediators and arbitrators of quality and taste. Their imprint is a 'brand', a marker of distinction in a highly competitive field. Building and maintaining a reputation for publishing high-quality books and/or prestigious authors is a way of accumulating symbolic capital, and the latter can be advantageous to publishers for several reasons. First, it enables them to attract new authors and new projects: many authors want to be published by houses which have established a high reputation in the field, such as a reputation for a strong list in scholarly publications, in trade nonfiction, in trade fiction, in poetry, in thrillers, in crime, etc. In other words, symbolic capital is a powerful acquisition tool. In the academic field, the importance of a publisher's symbolic capital is accentuated by the existence of various scholarly mechanisms, formal and informal, which endow differential degrees of symbolic reward on academics who publish with certain publishers. So, for example, an academic who publishes with a prestigious university press, such as Harvard University Press or Oxford University Press, may find that this fact weighs in his or her favour when applying for a job or being considered for promotion or tenure (the permanent establishment of their post). More formal mechanisms, like the Research Assessment Exercise in Britain, tend to consolidate and accentuate a similar system of hierarchical symbolic reward, providing further incentives for authors to sign with publishers who have accumulated substantial stocks of symbolic capital.

A second reason why symbolic capital can be advantageous to publishers is that it helps them to position and promote their books in a very competitive marketplace. Once it is published, the life of a book is shaped by the activities and responses of a range of cultural intermediaries – not only the agents and retailers who order, stock and display the book, but also by the newspapers, journals and reviewers who give attention to the book (or ignore it, as the case may be) and pass judgement on it in ways that can affect the sales of the book and the extent to which it is reviewed by others. Given the number of intermediaries involved and the many levels at which actions can be taken and judgements made which can affect the fate of a particular title, it is often extremely difficult for a publisher to predict the likely sales of a book – especially a new trade book by a relatively unknown author. Hence the surprise bestseller by a first-time author – like *Sophie's World* or the phenomenally successful Harry Potter series –

---

[3] See Pierre Bourdieu, *Language and Symbolic Power*, ed. John B. Thompson (Cambridge: Polity, 1991); John B. Thompson, *The Media and Modernity: A Social Theory of the Media* (Cambridge: Polity), p. 16.

remains an enduring feature of the publishing world. But while it may be intrinsically difficult to predict the success or failure of a particular title, the fate of a book is not an altogether indeterminate process, for it is shaped by the network of cultural intermediaries. The acts and speech-acts of a multitude of agents and organizations – including reps, booksellers, agents, rights managers and reviewers – create a web of utterances and practices which shape to some extent the life of a book. This is a network in which some publishers are well placed and others are not, and in which the accumulated symbolic capital of publishers plays a significant role. A new novel from a prestigious imprint like Faber or Bloomsbury, or a new biography from André Deutsch, Knopf or Farrar, Straus & Giroux, is more likely to get noticed and reviewed than a book by a publisher with no established reputation in the field. Publishers who are well placed in the circuits of reception will find that their books are more likely to be reviewed, and more likely to be reviewed in more places – a kind of virtuous circle of well-connected cultural intermediaries.

A third reason why accumulated symbolic capital matters to publishers is that it provides the symbolic support for the trademark of a publishing house which other individuals and organizations in the publishing chain – and even the final link in the chain, the readers – rely on to some extent. If a publisher has a high reputation as an arbitrator of quality or taste, then others will know that a book with its imprint will meet certain standards, and hence they know (or have good reason to believe) that they won't be buying a lemon. Accumulated symbolic capital serves, in this respect, to underpin relations of trust in the publishing field: a publisher with a good reputation is a brand you can trust. Most social relations and interactions in modern societies are based to some extent on relations of trust, that is, on presumptions concerning the competence, reliability and good intentions of other agents or systems of action.[4] Whenever you buy something you take a risk, but if you buy something from a dealer or a manufacturer you trust, then you are seeking to reduce the risk by basing your decision on the presumption that the dealer or manufacturer is competent, honest and reliable. This applies to publishers just as much as it applies to washing-machine manufacturers or second-hand car dealers: a publisher who has established a high reputation for quality and reliability is a publisher that agents, retailers and, ultimately, readers will be more inclined to trust. And this relation of trust will help to oil the circuits of reception of the new books which appear, since agents and retailers will be more inclined to order and stock the books, newspapers and journals may be more inclined to review them and readers more inclined to buy them.

In the case of publishing, however, the questions of reputation and trust are complicated by the fact that *authors* as well as *publishers* can accumulate symbolic capital, and while the reputations of authors and publishers can reinforce one another, they don't coincide. Authors can leave a publishing house and take their reputations with them, and the loss of a prestigious author can be a damaging blow for a publisher. Moreover, some of the organizations and individuals in the publishing chain may respond more to the reputation of the author than to the reputation of a publishing house – a new novel by Stephen King is likely to be stocked in substantial quantities by retailers and bought

---

[4] See Niklas Luhmann, 'Familiarity, Confidence, Trust: Problems and Alternatives', in Diego Gambetta (ed.), *Trust: Making and Breaking Cooperative Relations* (Oxford: Blackwell, 1988), pp. 94–107; Niklas Luhmann, *Trust and Power* (Chichester: Wiley, 1979).

by the many readers who follow Stephen King irrespective of who publishes the book. Authors who have accumulated significant quantities of symbolic capital have, in effect, established their own brand in the publishing field. This puts them in a strong position when it comes to negotiating contractual terms with publishers and tends to ensure that their new books are given prominent attention in the circuits of reception.

In the world of publishing, the importance of symbolic capital is likely to be accentuated by the sheer quantity and proliferation of books and other content. At a time when the output of new titles has tended to increase from one year to the next and when vast quantities of additional content have become available on the internet, the name or brand of a publisher is likely to become more important in the struggles for visibility that characterize the marketplace for books and as a mechanism that can help agents in the supply chain, and ultimately end users, to select material that is worthwhile from the ever expanding ocean of content that is now available. Symbolic capital, as exemplified by the publisher's brand, becomes increasingly important as a mechanism of selection and a marker of quality and distinction at a time when the sheer quantity of available content threatens to overwhelm intermediaries and end users.

We have seen why publishers need economic, human and symbolic capital, but they also possess another kind of resource which is vital to their success: intellectual capital (or intellectual property). The distinctive feature of the publishing firm is that it possesses the right to use and exploit intellectual content, to 'publish' or make available this content in forms that will generate a financial return. This right is regulated by the contracts it signs with authors or their agents and with other content-producing or content-controlling sources, such as foreign publishers. Hence a publisher's stock of contracts is potentially an extremely valuable resource, since it establishes legal entitlements to the content (or potential content) which the publisher is able to exploit. But the precise value of this resource depends on many variables. Among other things, the value of a contract for a particular book depends on (a) whether the text will actually be written and delivered in a suitable time period, (b) how profitable the book will be, that is, what kind of revenue stream less costs it is likely to generate, and (c) whether the contract entitles the publisher to subsidiary rights which are likely to yield additional revenues (such as translation rights). A contract can be a valuable resource but it can also be a liability, in the sense that it can commit the publisher to producing a book which may turn out to be a loss-maker, or it can commit the publisher to paying a substantial advance which is never recouped. A publisher's stock of contracts represents the sum total of rights it possesses over the intellectual content it seeks to acquire, develop and turn into marketable commodities, most commonly books.

All four forms of capital are vital to the success of a publishing firm, but the structure of the publishing field is shaped above all by the differential distribution of economic and symbolic capital, for it is these forms of capital that are particularly important in determining the competitive position of the firm. Publishers with substantial stocks of economic and symbolic capital will tend to find themselves in a strong position in the field, able to compete effectively against others and to see off challenges from rivals, whereas firms with very small stocks of economic and symbolic capital are in a more vulnerable position. This does not mean that firms which are less well endowed will necessarily find it difficult to survive – on the contrary, the publishing field is an enormously complex domain and there are many ways in which smaller firms can compete effectively, outmanoeuvring larger players or finding specialist niches in which they can flourish. Moreover, it is important to see that economic capital and symbolic capital do not necessarily go hand in hand: a firm with small stocks of economic capital can succeed in building up substantial stocks of symbolic capital in the domains where it is active, gaining a reputation for itself that far exceeds its strength in sheer economic terms. The accumulation of symbolic capital is dependent on processes that are very different in nature from those that lead to the accumulation of economic capital, and the possession of large quantities of one does not necessarily imply the possession of large quantities of the other.

As with other fields of activity, the publishing field is an intensely competitive domain characterized by a high degree of inter-organizational rivalry. Firms draw on their accumulated resources in an attempt to give themselves a competitive advantage over their rivals – to sign up the best authors, to publish the best-selling books, to gain the most media attention, etc.[5] The staff of particular publishing firms are constantly looking over their shoulders to see what their competitors are doing. They scrutinize one another's catalogues and study their competitors' more successful books to see whether they can pick up some clues about how they might develop their own lists. Since many of their books must be sold in a market where there are already a number of competing volumes, publishers are constantly involved in assessing the competition and trying to determine whether there are opportunities which they might be able to exploit. This kind of inter-organizational rivalry tends to produce a degree of *homogeneity* in the lists of publishing firms who publish in the same areas – for example, the textbooks published by different firms may look increasingly similar, as firms study the contents and designs of their competitors' volumes and incorporate them into their own editions. The competitive structure of the field also tends to produce a degree of *differentiation* and *specialization* among publishers, as particular firms seek to consolidate their positions and reputations in specific areas – in the way, for example, that Faber has established itself as a leading British imprint in the area of contemporary fiction and poetry, or that Butterworth dominates the area of professional law publishing in the UK.

While many fields of activity are intensely competitive, the publishing field has a competitive structure which is distinctive in some respects. In terms of their competitive position, most publishers are janus-faced organizations: they must compete both in the *market for content* and in the *market for customers*. They must compete in the market for content because most publishing organizations do not create their own content. They must acquire content by commissioning authors and others to produce content for them, and this puts them in a competitive position vis-à-vis other publishers who may wish to acquire the same or similar content. The most explicit manifestation of the competition for content is the auction of rights for the next book by a well-known author, a situation which may give rise to bidding wars between publishers in which advances are pushed to exorbitant and unrealistic levels. But the competition for content is an altogether routine feature of the publishing field, and most publishers find themselves continuously engaged in low-intensity struggles with other publishers for the signing up of titles and authors. A good deal of a publisher's commissioning activity is devoted to

[5] On the sources of competitive advantage, see especially Michael E. Porter, *Competitive Advantage* (New York: Free Press, 1985); John Kay, *Foundations of Corporate Success: How Business Strategies Add Value* (Oxford: Oxford University Press, 1993); John Kay, 'The Foundations of National Competitive Advantage', Economic and Social Research Council, London, 1994.

trying to persuade authors to sign with them rather than with some other press, and a variety of means are used to try to achieve this end. Financial inducements, such as high advances and good royalty terms, are important tools in the competition for content, but other less tangible and less quantifiable resources are also crucial – including reputation or symbolic capital, the networks upon which a publisher can draw in order to promote and market a book ('architecture' in Kay's terminology[6]) and the attractions of working with a particular editor with whom an author may have a trusting relationship (part of the human capital of the firm). Most publishers seek not only to acquire a particular manuscript but to build long-term relationships with particular authors upon whom they can rely – thanks to a kind of loyalty rewarded with good terms and special treatment – for a regular flow of content over an extended period of time.

Just as publishers have to compete for content, so too they have to compete for customers once a book has been produced. The marketplace of books is enormously crowded – and becomes ever more crowded as the number of titles published every year increases. Marketing and sales staff devote a great deal of time and effort to trying to ensure that their titles stand out from others and are not simply lost in the flood of new books which appear every season. The marketing of books can be viewed as a complex chain of information and interaction in which data about books – blurbs, jackets, endorsements, reviews, key features and other kinds of 'metadata' (ISBNs, pub dates, prices, extents, etc.) – are provided to a range of intermediaries or directly to end users, with the aim of achieving visibility for books and ensuring that they have some presence in the market. Sales and marketing staff must actively compete for the attention of intermediaries and gatekeepers in the marketing chain, from review editors and radio and TV hosts to the buyers in bookstores and chains, and their ability to gain their attention is dependent on a complex array of factors. Among the most important of these factors are the relationships which the publisher has formed with intermediaries, the networks that have been built up over time and the degree of trust that characterizes these relationships. The accumulated symbolic capital of the publisher and the author – their reputation and brand – is also a key factor.

The marketing process will always involve a series of calculations in which expenditure of time and resources is weighed against likely sales, and the precise methods used will vary from publisher to publisher and from one type of book to another. A trade book by a leading author can be sold on the basis that it is by this author and that its content is unique: the reputation of the author (his or her symbolic capital) and the uniqueness of the content are the principal selling points, and achieving visibility in the media and in the retail sector (with books prominently displayed in bookstores) may be vital. For books aimed at markets where alternative titles may be vying for market share (as with textbooks or reference books, for example), different strategies have to be used. In the case of textbook publishing, the key factor in securing sales is getting adoptions from the lecturers and professors who teach the courses for which the text may be recommended as required or supplementary reading. Hence the marketing strategy of most textbooks is geared primarily towards securing adoptions by means of giving away free copies and providing relevant back-up services (such as instructors' manuals and ancillaries of various kinds) to the pedagogical gatekeepers whose deci-

---

[6] See Kay, *Foundations of Corporate Success*, pp. 66–86.

sions can make or break the book. We shall explore the nature and significance of the adoption system in more detail in part III.

The differentiation of the publishing field

The publishing field is not a unified domain: it is differentiated into a series of fields which tend to have their own distinctive dynamics. Hence it would be more accurate to speak of 'publishing fields' in the plural, rather than 'the publishing field'. Particular firms operate in one or more of these fields, depending on the kinds of books they publish and the kinds of markets they try to reach. Competition between firms tends to be within specific fields, since these are the domains in which they are competing for authors, competing for customers and competing for the attention of intermediaries in the marketing chain. Of course, the boundaries between fields are not rigid or clear-cut – on the contrary, they are porous and blurred. Some books may cross over from one field to another, and the boundaries themselves may overlap to some extent and may shift over time. Nevertheless, the boundaries do exist and they are recognized within the publishing industry itself. Publishing firms tend to organize their activities in terms of broad distinctions between different types of publishing, since they recognize that each type of publishing has its own distinctive characteristics and requires its own skills and expertise. Particular firms which operate in two or more of these fields will often institutionalize the differences within the organizational structure of the firm – for example, by having separate departments or divisions for each publishing field.

So what are the characteristics of publishing fields, and what distinguishes one publishing field from another? A particular publishing field is a space of positions which are occupied by agents and organizations of various kinds, and these agents and organizations stand in relations of collaboration and/or competition with one another. The field is a market but it is not just a market – it is more than this. It is a complex array of networks and relationships, supply chains, forms of competition, sets of consumers, specific kinds of reward and recognition (such as prizes) and so on. The field is the structured social environment in which firms operate and exist, flourish and fail. Each publishing field has its own conditions of success, and therefore its own forms of knowledge, skill and expertise by virtue of which particular firms, and particular individuals within these firms, are able to be successful players within the field. Individuals tend to build their careers within particular fields. They learn their trade within a particular field and their ways of thinking and acting – their 'habitus', as Bourdieu would say[7] – tend to be shaped by and oriented towards the conditions of success within particular fields. It is within particular fields that individuals acquire 'a feel for the game', and it is within these fields that they earn reputations as accomplished editors or publishers. Some individuals may move between fields in the course of their careers and gain reputations as accomplished editors or publishers in more than one field, but doing this requires a deep understanding of the distinctive properties of and differences between publishing fields.

---

[7] Bourdieu uses the term 'habitus' to describe a set of durable and generative dispositions which incline agents to act in certain ways. See Pierre Bourdieu, *The Logic of Practice*, tr. Richard Nice (Cambridge: Polity, 1990), ch. 3.

What distinguishes publishing fields from one another is the *type of content* produced within them and the *kind of market* for which it is produced, together with the associated relationships, types of marketing and forms of reward and recognition that go along with this. So, for example, trade publishing constitutes a particular field. It is concerned with the production of books which are oriented towards a certain market, namely the market of general readers, and it involves a complex array of networks and relationships – including relationships with authors, agents, suppliers, printers, wholesalers, retailers, review media, etc. – by means of which particular publishing organizations are able to pursue their goals within this field and to compete with other firms. This field has its own forms of reward and recognition, including prizes that are unique to it, such as the Nobel Prize for Literature, certain of the Pulitzer prizes, the Booker Prize, the Los Angeles Times Book Prize, etc. Winning prizes is a key mechanism by means of which both authors and publishers can accumulate symbolic capital which will strengthen their position in the field (and, in the case of authors, may strengthen their position in other fields as well).

Trade publishing can be distinguished from scholarly or academic publishing, which constitutes a different field. Academic publishing is closely bound up with the world of scholarly and scientific research. It publishes books which are written by scholars and researchers and which are intended primarily for other scholars and researchers, although in some cases they may also be bought and/or read by students and other readers. The term 'monograph' is often used to refer to books of this kind – although, as we shall see, this term is notoriously ambiguous and imprecise. While monographs are intended primarily for scholars and researchers, they are often purchased by research libraries; this has consequences for the nature of the marketing chain in academic publishing, which differs significantly in this respect from trade publishing. The field of academic publishing also has its own mechanisms of reward and recognition, including an array of prizes which are often linked to particular academic disciplines (or clusters of disciplines) and administered by scholarly societies and associations.

Like academic publishing, the field of college textbook publishing is linked to the world of higher education but it constitutes a separate field. Higher education publishing is concerned primarily with the commissioning and development of textbooks and other educational materials which can be used for teaching in higher education. As we shall see, the field of higher education publishing is shaped fundamentally by the adoption system, whereby lecturers and professors act as crucial gatekeepers in the sales and marketing chain. The adoption system is one of the key features that distinguishes the field of higher education publishing from other publishing fields. It has profound implications for the way that the whole field of higher education publishing is organized, from content acquisition and development through to sales and marketing.

I have briefly sketched three publishing fields but there are many others – there is the field of reference publishing, the field of professional publishing, the field of STM publishing, the field of scientific and scholarly journal publishing, the field of school-book publishing, the field of children's books publishing, the field of illustrated art book publishing, the field of English language teaching (ELT) publishing, and so on. Moreover, each of these fields is internally differentiated, creating fields within fields which serve particular markets and meet particular needs. Publishing is a complex and highly differentiated world but it is not without order. It is structured by the existence of a plurality of fields which have their own distinctive properties and by the existence of networks and organizations of various kinds which operate in one or more of these fields.[8]

While we can distinguish between publishing fields and analyse the characteristics of each, in practice the boundaries between fields are often blurred and particular books may enjoy a life in more than one field. 'Crossover' books of this kind are relatively common; their success in more than one field may be owed, at least in part, to crossover strategies explicitly pursued by publishers in marketing their books, but sometimes the crossover phenomenon may catch publishers by surprise. An academic publisher may publish a book believing that it is primarily a scholarly work aimed at other scholars, but the book may also find its way on to reading lists at colleges and universities and be used for teaching purposes, and thus cross over into the field of higher education publishing. A scholarly book may cross over into the trade market and reach a readership beyond the world of the academy; books published as trade titles by trade houses can be picked up by academics and used as teaching texts; and so on. While publishing fields have properties that distinguish them from one another, their boundaries are porous to the flows of particular books.

It is also important to emphasize that the structure of publishing fields does not necessarily coincide with the spheres of operation of individual publishing firms. Particular firms can (and often do) operate in more than one publishing field. This can have advantages for a publisher. It can enable the firm to diversify its activities and spread its risks. It can allow it to adjust its priorities by expanding its activities in some fields and restricting them in others. It can also enable a publisher to take advantage of its networks and relationships in order to exploit potentially fruitful overlaps between adjacent fields. For example, a publisher who is strong in academic publishing may be able to commission one of its authors to write a trade book aimed at a general readership, or may commission one of its authors to write a textbook for the higher education market, and so on. Moreover, a firm with a presence in more than one field can pursue crossover strategies in marketing particular titles. But there are also dangers with this kind of multi-field activity. The firm can lose focus and find that its energies are being dissipated by trying to be successful in too many different fields. The crossover potential of many books is limited, and pursuing crossover marketing strategies may turn out to be a waste of resources. Moreover, by spreading its activities and resources across several fields, the firm may find it difficult to achieve real strength and success in any one of them. In some of the peripheral fields in which it publishes, it may simply be too small to have any real presence and to build up the kinds of networks needed to be successful. Since

---

[8] The way in which I distinguish between publishing fields does not coincide with Bourdieu's distinction between what he calls 'the field of large-scale production' and the 'field of restricted production' (see Bourdieu, *The Field of Cultural Production*, pp. 39 ff.). For Bourdieu, the field of restricted production is the field in which producers produce for other producers, whereas the field of large-scale production is the field in which producers produce for non-producers. However, this criterion is not sufficiently discriminating to account for the multiplicity of publishing fields, and the characteristics Bourdieu attributes to the field of restricted production (as an 'anti-economy' in which practices are oriented towards symbolic profit rather than economic gain and in which 'the loser wins') are not features that can be discerned unambiguously in actual publishing fields. Even in publishing fields where agents are more concerned to produce work of intellectual or cultural value than to pursue commercial goals, questions of economic value are never altogether absent and they may, at certain moments, become critical.

each field has its own distinctive properties and conditions of success, a publisher who dabbles in other fields may find that it lacks the kind of knowledge and expertise needed to succeed. It may simply be too ill-equipped, both in terms of its resource base and in terms of the knowledge and skills of its staff, to achieve positive results in adjacent fields.

One of the advantages of distinguishing between publishing fields is that it enables us to see that each form of publishing has its own conditions of success, and to see how these conditions of success change. Part of what I shall try to show is that each publishing field has its own 'logic' or dynamic that defines the conditions of success within a field and that evolves over time. The logics of publishing fields are not static because they are open to forces and pressures that stem from a variety of sources – economic pressures, technological innovations, changing social practices, etc. One of the tasks that senior managers in publishing firms set for themselves is to try to understand how economic pressures and technological innovations, among other things, are changing the nature and dynamic of the fields in which they are active – in other words, although they may not use this language, they are trying to understand how the logics of the fields are changing, and how this in turn is likely to affect their own business opportunities.

The logic of publishing fields is by its very nature a fuzzy logic. It is not the logic of the logicians but rather a practical logic – that is, a logic that can only be grasped in the practices in which and through which it is expressed.[9] It can't be summed up by a simple formula and it is not easy to pin down and specify. The logic of a particular publishing field is a set of factors and forces that determine the conditions under which individual agents and organizations can participate in the field, the conditions under which they can play the game and play it successfully. Individuals who are active in the field have some degree of practical knowledge of this logic: they know how to play the game and they have views about how the game is changing. They may not be able to sum up the logic of the field in a neat and concise fashion, but they can tell you in great detail what it was like when they first entered the field, what it is like now and how it has changed over time. The logic of the field is like the grammar of a language: individuals know how to speak correctly, and in this sense they have a practical knowledge of the rules of grammar, but they may not be able to formulate these rules in an explicit fashion. As Wittgenstein would say, their knowledge of the language is that they know how to use it, they know how to go on. Part of the task of the analyst is to listen to and reflect on the practical accounts of the agents who are active in the field, to situate them in relation to these agents' positions in the field and to seek thereby to work out the logic of the field – that is, to grasp it and formulate it in a way that is more explicit and systematic than one is likely to find in the practical accounts of the agents themselves. This is what I undertake to do in parts II and III with respect to the fields of academic publishing and higher education publishing.

The linguistic and spatial properties of publishing fields

Up until now I've been discussing publishing fields without reference to national characteristics, but one of the features of publishing fields is that they always involve certain linguistic, spatial and technological properties. Publishing fields are generally situated

[9] See Bourdieu, *The Logic of Practice*, pp. 80–97.

within certain linguistic regions – that is, language barriers tend to define the outer limits of publishing fields, since the contents of books are accessible only to those who have the linguistic capacities to read them. This does not mean, however, that publishing fields are coextensive with the boundaries of nation-states, since in some cases they may be subnational (e.g. the Catalan publishing field in Spain, or the Welsh publishing field in the UK) and in other cases they may extend well beyond the boundaries of particular nation-states – as is obviously the case with the publishing field in English, but also (although to a lesser extent) with the publishing fields in French, Spanish, Portuguese, Chinese and other languages. Individual publishing firms may operate within particular regions of a linguistically homogeneous and geographically extended publishing field – they may, in effect, operate as 'local' or 'national' publishers, concentrating their efforts on acquiring and developing content for a local or national market. But linguistic homo-geneity creates the conditions under which books can travel, thereby enabling firms to extend the range of their operations beyond particular locales or national boundaries.

In historical terms, the formation of linguistically homogeneous and geographically extended publishing fields was profoundly shaped by the legacy of colonialism. The spheres of influence and linguistic continuities created by colonial empires created homogeneous linguistic regions which extended across continents, and within which publishers could in principle distribute and market their books. So, for example, Spanish language publishers based in Spain could sell their books throughout the Spanish-speaking countries of Latin America, provided that they had systems of distribution or agents who could supply their books to booksellers or other intermediaries in cost-effective ways. Similarly, Portuguese publishers could treat Brazil as an extension of their own national market. But the flow was not only one way: with the growth of indigenous publishing firms in Latin America, Spain and Portugal also became poten-tial markets for Latin American publishers. The homogeneous linguistic regions which facilitated the expansion of publishers' activities into international markets were largely the legacy of colonialism, but the subsequent development of internationalization and globalization in the sphere of publishing (as in other spheres of the media and cultural industries) was not restricted by the traditional structures of colonial power.

Publishing firms operating in languages with significant colonial legacies were able to take advantage of the opportunities afforded by international expansion, but publishers operating in the English language benefited from a double advantage. In the first place, thanks to the British colonial expansion in the early modern period and the dominance of the British Empire in the nineteenth and early twentieth centuries, the English language was widely spoken in many parts of the world, either as a primary language or as an official language which became an integral part of state institutions in a multilingual context (as in India or Malaysia). Hence a publisher operating in English had a linguistic region which extended from the British Isles to North America, from Australia and New Zealand to India and South Africa – in effect, a linguistic region which stretched across the globe. Moreover, given the legacy of the British Empire and the rise of the United States as the major global power in the twentieth century, the English language became the *lingua franca* of international diplomacy, of business and trade, and of research and scholarship – in effect, it assumed the role in the twentieth century that Latin had once assumed in medieval Europe, although now in a global arena. Hence, even in countries where English was not the first language or an official language of state, it increasingly became the preferred second language which was taught in schools and encouraged as a means of gaining access to international arenas. As English was increasingly adopted as the preferred second language, the scope of the linguistic region of English rapidly expanded; no other language has spread around the globe as extensively and as quickly as English.[10] This expansion did not create a homogeneous linguistic region, since differing levels of education and competence created a great deal of unevenness. Nevertheless, publishers operating in English found themselves in the position of having a continuously expanding linguistic region in which English was either the primary or the preferred second language, and hence they had a continuously expanding potential market for their books.

Publishers operating in languages which did not have such an extensive colonial legacy, such as French, German, Italian or the Scandinavian languages, found themselves in a fundamentally different position. For these publishers, the opportunities for expansion into foreign markets were much more limited. French publishers could sell their books in Quebec and in some parts of Europe and Africa, and German publishers could achieve some modest expansion in countries of central Europe where the German language had established a foothold as a second language, but the sales potential for this kind of expansion was very limited. Most publishers operating in these other languages had to rely largely on their domestic markets, which, given the limited avenues for external expansion, became increasingly competitive. Their publishing fields were, to a very large extent, restricted to the boundaries of particular nation-states, and for publishers operating in nation-states with relatively small populations (such as Norway, Sweden or Denmark), the size of their markets was comparatively small.

The creation of linguistically homogeneous and geographically extended publishing fields created opportunities for publishers to expand their markets, but to do so was a costly business and not all publishers were in a position to take advantage of these opportunities. For publishers seeking to expand into international markets, there were three principal ways of doing so. One method was to collaborate with a publisher based in the foreign country or linguistic region. The originating publisher would license the foreign publisher to publish and sell the book within their country or region, and would in effect copublish the book with the foreign publisher. The two publishers would agree terms which could involve some sharing of the production costs and a suitable distribution of revenues. The originating publisher could supply bound and jacketed copies with the copublisher's imprint, or could supply camera-ready copy (or, more recently, electronic files) from which the copublisher could produce their own copies (usually in return for an offset fee to help cover the originating publisher's pre-press costs), or could simply allow the copublisher to produce their own edition from scratch. The viability of copublishing arrangements of this kind depended on an effective demarcation of the territories for the exclusive operation of each publisher. A small amount of leakage could be tolerated, but porous territorial boundaries would undermine the arrangement since it would mean that the two collaborating publishers would effectively be competing against one another for sales of the same book.

A second way for publishers to expand into foreign markets was to employ agents who would sell and distribute their books in territories where the publisher did not have

---

[10] See David Crystal, *English as a Global Language* (Cambridge: Cambridge University Press, 1997), p. 63: 'In 1950 the case for English as a world language would have been no more than plausible. Fifty years on, and the case is virtually unassailable.'

a physical presence. The main advantage of this arrangement was that the overhead costs were low, since the publisher did not have to run an office and employ staff in the foreign marketplace. But there were also disadvantages. The degree of visibility and market penetration tended to be relatively low, since the agent might represent numerous publishers simultaneously and might not be able to achieve a high profile and strong sales for the titles of any particular publisher. Moreover, the agent's commission, combined with high levels of discount and shipping costs, tended to reduce the revenue generated through export sales to a minimal level, resulting in low profit margins. Sales in foreign markets through arrangements of this kind could become financially unviable, especially if exchange rates meant that imported books were significantly overpriced in local markets.

A third way for publishers to expand into foreign markets was to develop their own operations overseas, either through indigenous growth or through mergers and acquisitions. This was a much riskier strategy which required much higher levels of investment, since the publisher had to employ staff and perhaps even open offices in foreign markets. But it was also a strategy which had the potential to generate much higher returns in the medium to long term. Publishers who expanded their own operations overseas could integrate their domestic and foreign marketing and sales operations, eliminate or reduce agents' commissions and retain more control over the financial conditions determining the profitability of their books. They could also use this expansion as a basis to develop their commissioning activities overseas, thereby creating a list which was to some extent indigenous to the foreign markets in which they wanted to expand their operations. While this kind of expansion had many attractions, it was also a very costly and risky undertaking, and one that was practicable only for the larger and more powerful publishing organizations.

While linguistic boundaries generally defined the outer limits of publishing fields, there were ways in which publishers could work across these boundaries both to acquire content and to exploit it. Translation rights were the principal vehicle: they enabled publishers to buy and sell exclusive rights for the exploitation of content in publishing fields that were defined both *linguistically* and *territorially*. The domain of exploitation was usually linguistically specific, but the territories might or might not coincide with the full extent of the linguistic region. For example, a publisher could acquire exclusive rights to publish a book in English throughout the world (in which case its territories coincided with the full extent of the linguistic region); or it could acquire exclusive rights to publish a book in English either only in the UK and the British Commonwealth (usually excluding Canada), or only in the US and Canada (in which case their territories represented a partial domain of the total linguistic region); or it could acquire exclusive rights to publish a book in English in the UK and Commonwealth and non-exclusive rights to publish it in the rest of the world with the exception of North America (in which case the total linguistic region was divided into non-competitive and competitive zones, and publishers were given exclusive rights only for the non-competitive zones).

The buying and selling of translation rights have become routine features of the activities of publishing firms, many of which have departments which are responsible for the management of rights (including translation rights). But there are also regular events in the publishing calendar which are, in effect, rights fairs – occasions when publishers, editors, rights managers and others gather together, in the same physical locale, to discuss and negotiate the buying and selling of content across the linguistic and territorial boundaries of publishing fields. The annual Frankfurt Book Fair is the most prominent of these occasions – today more than 10,000 publishers from around the world gather together for a week in October every year to talk about their new books with publishers from other fields, with a view to buying or selling content that can be exploited across linguistic and territorial boundaries. But there are many similar occasions which take place every year in other venues in Europe, Latin America and elsewhere.

Publishing fields are also shaped by technologies, since the forms in which content is stored and delivered to customers are dependent on technologies and the economics associated with them. The print-on-paper book – the traditional form in which publishers' content is transmitted to market – is a relatively heavy and bulky physical object which must be stored in warehouses and transported by road, sea or air to bookstores and customers. The costs of storage and transport, together with the costs involved in marketing and selling books, will place effective limits on the geographical scope of the field in which a particular publisher is able to operate. Even if in principle it has rights to market and sell its books throughout the world, in practice it may operate almost exclusively within a particular geographical region because the costs associated with the physical transportation and storage of books in other regions, together with the costs involved in actively marketing and selling them, would make it unprofitable for the publisher to expand its activities there. The economics of the physical book, coupled with the economics of marketing and selling, effectively shape the publishing field, so that for any particular publisher within this field the spheres of activity are skewed towards certain territories. So, for example, while the American university presses generally have world rights for the content they publish, their sales (with one or two notable exceptions) tend to be generated overwhelmingly in the United States and Canada, since the costs associated with distributing and marketing books in Europe and other regions tend to be prohibitive for organizations of this size.

Publishing and adjacent social fields

Publishing fields are not secluded and self-sufficient worlds but are commonly linked to other social fields, and in some cases they may be deeply interwoven with these other fields through complex forms of interdependency. One of the key strengths of a field approach to publishing is that it enables us – indeed, requires us – to situate publishing practices in relation to a wider array of activities with which they are interlocked. So, for example, it is essential to see that both academic publishing and higher education publishing are deeply interwoven with the world of higher education itself – or what I shall call the academic field. From the viewpoint of academic and higher education publishers, the academic field is both the principal source of authors (and hence of content) for the books they publish and the principal market for their products. From the viewpoint of teachers and scholars in the academic field, the world of academic and college textbook publishing offers a potential vehicle for publishing their work (and hence for advancing their careers as well as earning certain material and symbolic rewards) and provides the materials they need for teaching and research. The life of the academy, on the one hand, and the fields of academic and higher education publishing, on the other, are worlds that have evolved together. They need one another, they help and support one another and they are locked together in numerous and complex forms of interdependency.

In addition to providing authors and creating markets for books, the academic field also supplies publishers with multiple forms of editorial advice and input on actual or potential projects, from reading and commenting on proposals and draft manuscripts to editing series of books on specific themes or topics. Each publishing house (and indeed each editor) tends to build up a network of advisers within the academic field who comprise a kind of 'invisible college' – to use the felicitous phrase of Coser and his associates[11] – which can be called upon from time to time for ideas, suggestions and advice. Publishers typically pay a fee for this service, but the level of remuneration tends to be relatively modest in comparison to the amount of effort involved – this is, in effect, an economy of favours in which academic and higher education publishers are able to draw on forms of knowledge and expertise accumulated in the academic field. Many publishers also call upon academics to provide endorsements for new books, a practice which, they hope, will help to give visibility to the book and facilitate its reception by end users and by intermediaries in the marketing chain. But the relations of dependency are not just one way. Academics also depend on publishers to take on and support the publication of their work, even though the costs of doing so may exceed the benefits gained in purely financial terms. They also depend on publishers to ensure that their own academic field is kept alive through the constant injection of new content, whether this is in the form of scholarly monographs which are at the cutting edge of debate in the discipline or in the form of textbooks and supplementary materials which can be used in teaching.

Good editors who are truly knowledgeable about the disciplines in which they are publishing are valued not only by the publishing house: they are also valued by the academic community they are serving. They don't belong to the academic field in the same way that academics do; they are outsiders in the sense that they don't depend on it for their livelihood and career. But at the same time, good academic editors are also insiders in the sense that they actively participate in the disciplinary domains for which they publish. As one senior and respected editor in anthropology explained, 'I'm an outsider only in the sense that I don't have credentials as a fieldworker, but I'm an insider in terms of my grasp of different aspects of anthropology: people come to me and ask what's going on in anthropology.' Good editors keep abreast of debates, they go to conferences and talk to academics, and they help to shape in small ways the evolution of disciplines through the decisions they take. They are cultural intermediaries who bridge two worlds, insiders-outsiders with a foot in each camp, and their contribution to the life and well-being of a discipline may be valued as much by the academic community as their contribution to the editorial programme is valued by their bosses in the firm (and, in some cases, their contribution may be valued even more by academics than by their bosses). From time to time the academic community formally acknowledges this role by paying homage – usually in the form of a prize – to an editor's exceptional contribution to the development of a discipline.

Despite the interdependency of these worlds, they do not mesh together in a frictionless way, for the world of publishing and the world of the academy are governed by

---

[11] Coser, Kadushin and Powell, *Books*, p. 83.

different logics. The fields of academic and higher education publishing are shaped fundamentally by two concerns. On the one hand, publishing organizations in these fields are concerned with questions of quality and scholarship – indeed, for most university presses these questions are paramount. But publishing organizations are also driven by commercial concerns. The extent to which commercial considerations feature in decision-making processes varies from one field to another and from one firm to another. Commercial considerations are much more important for college textbook publishers than they are for university presses, for example. But even if commercial considerations are not uppermost in the minds of academic editors at university presses, they are not altogether absent; and as the economic conditions of scholarly publishing have become more difficult, these considerations, which had previously remained in the background of decision-making processes, have come increasingly to the fore, as we shall see.

The academic field, by contrast, is governed largely by a symbolic logic of peer recognition and acclaim. What matters in the academic field, above all, is the esteem accorded by one's peers for the work that one produces – esteem that is rendered concrete in a multitude of forms, from the acceptance of an article in a peer-reviewed journal to the reviews of a published book, from the number of times an article is cited to the winning of a prize. These and countless other *indices of scholarly esteem* become the credentials that enable individuals to advance their careers within the academic field, to secure tenure or promotion within an institution or to move to other institutions where the economic and symbolic rewards may be greater. These indices may also be incorporated into institutional mechanisms of appraisal and review, both at the level of individuals and at the level of institutions. The growing emphasis on administrative accountability within public institutions has, in some cases, resulted in the increasing formalization of these mechanisms of appraisal and review, thus giving greater salience to the indices of scholarly esteem incorporated in them. A striking example of this process is the Research Assessment Exercise in Britain, which establishes a nationwide mechanism of appraisal and review for the research output of university departments, a mechanism in which indices of scholarly esteem are explicitly embedded.

The fact that publishing fields and the academic field are governed by different concerns means that, even though these fields are woven together through relations of mutual dependency, their paths of development are likely to diverge in various ways and the priorities of individuals and institutions within them are likely to be different. This can give rise to tension and misunderstanding, or to the kind of non-coincidence of interest which leads each party to feel frustrated and disappointed by the other. We shall examine some manifestations of this tension in the chapters that follow.

3

The publishing field since 1980

While the publishing field is a differentiated domain made up of many different fields, there are nevertheless certain broad developments which have characterized the world of publishing as a whole over the last few decades. These developments cut across specific fields and shape to some extent the overall environment of publishing today, irrespective of the specific field or fields in which a particular firm may be active – although the ways in which they affect particular firms depends to some extent on the fields in which these firms are located. In this chapter I want to outline and briefly analyse the most important of these developments. I shall focus on five: the growth of title output; concentration and corporate power; the transformation of the retail sector; the globalization of markets and publishing firms; and the impact of new technologies. Let me briefly consider each.

The growth of title output

Since the middle of the twentieth century, there has been a substantial increase in the overall output of book titles. This trend has been particularly marked in Britain and the United States – two of the world's leading producers of books – but it is not unique to the English-speaking world. It is difficult to obtain reliable and strictly comparable data on title output in different countries, since the methods used for collecting data vary from one country to another. UNESCO has attempted to gather comparative data on title output over a number of years and, while the UNESCO data must be treated with caution, they provide a rough and preliminary indication of the overall growth of title output. According to UNESCO, the total number of book titles published worldwide in 1955 was around 270,000; by 1995, the total had risen to around 770,000, an increase of nearly threefold over this forty-year period.[1] The UNESCO data show that the bulk of world book output is concentrated in Europe, North America and (prior to 1989) the former Soviet Union. In 1981, Europe accounted for around 42 per cent of total world output, North America for around 16 per cent and the USSR for around 13 per cent – taken together, these three regions of the world accounted for more than 70 per cent of total world output.

---

[1] Data from UNESCO Institute of Statistics; see www.uis.unesco.org. See also Curwen, *The World Book Industry*, p. 15. The UNESCO data are incomplete in many ways, and data for particular countries (such as China) are available for some years and not for others. Moreover, the bases of data collection vary from one country to another and from one year to another; for example, in some years the data for the United States include pamphlets, federal government publications, university theses and school textbooks, while in other years these items are excluded.

Table 3.1 Position of developed countries in worldwide book production, 1965–1995

Titles ('000s)	1965	1970	1980	1995
100–110				1 UK
90–100				
80–90			1 USSR	
70–80	1 USSR	1 USA 2 USSR	2 USA	2 Germany
60–70			3 W. Germany	3 USA[1]
50–60	2 USA			4 Japan[2]
40–50		3 W. Germany	4 UK 5 Japan	5 Spain
30–40		4 UK 5 Japan	6 France	6 Korea 7 France
20–30	3 UK 4 W. Germany 5 Japan 6 France	6 France	7 Spain	
10–20	7 Spain	7 Spain		

[1] Not including pamphlets, government publications, university theses and school textbooks.
[2] 1996; first editions only; not including pamphlets.
Source: UNESCO Institute for Statistics (UIS).

Table 3.1, based on UNESCO data, shows the rank position of the leading developed countries in worldwide book production at various times between 1965 and 1995. Between 1965 and 1980, the US and the USSR vied for the top position in the world league table of new book production (although it is difficult to be sure whether the statistics are strictly comparable, since many Soviet titles were counted several times due to the multiplicity of languages in use in the old Soviet Union). By the mid-1990s the rank order had changed: the USSR had ceased to exist as a political entity and the UK had overtaken the US in the UNESCO rankings. The UNESCO data suggest that by 1995 the UK had become the leading book producer in the world, publishing 101,764 new books in 1995, followed by Germany, the United States, Japan and Spain. The UNESCO figures for ten leading book-producing countries in 1995 are given in table 3.2. (However, as we shall see below, the UNESCO figure for the United States almost certainly underestimates the actual output by a significant amount.)

The UNESCO data provide a helpful general overview of the growth and pattern of worldwide book production, but we can gain a more accurate picture of the growth of title output by looking at the statistics produced by the book publishing industries in different countries. In the United States, the principal source of data on new title output used in the publishing industry has for many years been the data gathered by the R. R. Bowker Company and published in the *American Book Publishing Record* (*ABPR*); these data are also the basis of the listings which appear in the trade journal *Publishers Weekly*. The *ABPR* is essentially a record of the titles and editions passing through

Table 3.2 Ten leading book-producing countries in 1995

Country	Titles
1 UK	101,764
2 Germany	74,174
3 US	62,039[1]
4 Japan	56,221[2]
5 Spain	48,467
6 Korea	35,864
7 France	34,766
8 Italy	34,470
9 Russia	33,623
10 Brazil	25,540

Titles are of non-periodic printed publications (books and pamphlets) published in a particular country and made available to the public. Unless otherwise indicated, statistics include both first and re-editions of books and pamphlets.
[1] Not including pamphlets, government publications, university theses and school textbooks.
[2] 1996; first editions only; not including pamphlets.
Source: UNESCO Institute for Statistics (UIS).

the Library of Congress Cataloging in Publication (CIP) programme.[2] From the early 1970s until the mid-1980s, Bowker regarded this as a reasonably accurate basis on which to produce its statistics on title output, but in the 1980s it became increasingly clear that the totals were not reflecting what was actually happening in the American book industry. The *ABPR* numbers were more accurate as a picture of the CIP's workload (which plateaued at around 50,000–60,000 titles a year) than as an account of overall industry activity. American book title production was being undercounted, particularly in relation to trade paperbacks and the output of small presses. In an attempt to produce a more accurate portrayal of industry activity, Bowker began in 1998 to compile data on new title output from its more comprehensive Books in Print database. These data are based on new ISBNs (International Standard Book Numbers – unique identifiers which are assigned to each new book and edition) issued in each calendar year in the US, and therefore include paperbacks and modified re-editions as separate titles. They also include new books produced overseas and distributed in the United States.

Table 3.3 and figure 3.1 illustrate the growth of title output in the US between 1980 and 1997 using data from the *American Book Publishing Record Annual* based on cataloguing material from the Library of Congress. Table 3.4 and figure 3.2 give the data on new title output in the US for 1997–2002 using the new method adopted by Bowker in 1998.

[2] CIP data are bibliographical records prepared by the Library of Congress for books that have not yet been published. When a book is published, the CIP data are included on the copyright page to facilitate the processing of the book by libraries and booksellers.

Table 3.3 US book title output, 1971–1997 (old method)

	New books	New editions	Total
1971	25,526	12,166	37,692
1972	26,868	11,185	38,053
1973	28,140	11,811	39,951
1974	30,575	10,271	40,846
1975	30,004	8,868	38,872
1976	32,352	9,346	41,698
1977	33,292	9,468	42,760
1978	31,802	9,414	41,216
1979	36,112	9,070	45,182
1980	34,030	8,347	42,377
1981	41,434	7,359	48,793
1982	36,230	6,712	46,935
1983	42,236	7,309	53,380
1984	40,564	6,691	51,058
1985	39,753	6,510	50,070
1986	41,925	6,992	52,637
1987	44,638	7,473	56,027
1988	44,893	7,569	55,483
1989	42,922	6,802	53,446
1990	37,049	5,726	46,743
1991	38,041	6,730	48,146
1992	38,912	6,538	49,276
1993	39,846	6,347	49,757
1994	42,454	6,751	51,863
1995	49,968	7,385	62,039
1996	55,301	8,388	68,175
1997	53,175	8,525	65,796

From 1982 on, new books and new editions comprise hardbound and trade paperbound titles only, whereas the totals include all hard- and paperbound titles; hence, from 1982 on, the totals are more than the sums of the new books and the new editions.
Source: *The Bowker Annual Library and Book Trade Almanac*, published by Information Today, Inc. (Medford, N.J.).

The earlier data tend to show that US book title output increased fairly steadily from 1971 to 1987, when the total reached 56,000; output then appears to have fallen off and remained below the 1987 total until 1995, when it increased again quite significantly, reaching a total of just over 68,000 in 1996. However, the reliability of these earlier data is called into question by the recalculation of the 1997 total using the new method adopted by Bowker in 1998. Using the old method, the 1997 total was 65,796; using the new method, the total for 1997 was 119,262 – an increase of more than 53,000 titles or 81 per cent. Calculations based on the new method indicate that total US title output hovered around 120,000 from 1997 to 2000, and then increased significantly to more than 140,000 titles in 2001 and 2002. Preliminary figures suggest that the title output for 2003 is likely to exceed 160,000, an increase of around 9 per cent on 2002. The new

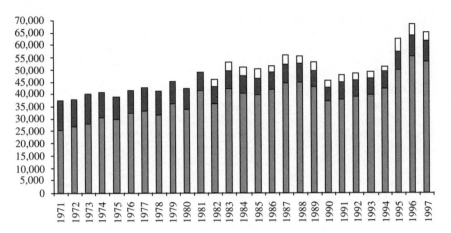

■ New editions (non-trade paperbounds not included from 1982 on)

■ New books (non-trade paperbounds not included from 1982 on)

□ Addition of non-trade paperbounds from 1982 on

Figure 3.1 US book title output, 1971–1997 (old method)
Source: The Bowker Annual Library and Book Trade Almanac, published by Information Today, Inc. (Medford, N.J.).

Table 3.4 US book title output, 1997–2002 (new method)

1997	119,262
1998	120,244
1999	119,357
2000	122,108
2001	141,703
2002	147,120

Source: The Bowker Annual Library and Book Trade Almanac, published by Information Today, Inc. (Medford, N.J.).

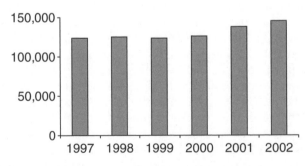

Figure 3.2 US book title output, 1997–2002 (new method)
Source: The Bowker Annual Library and Book Trade Almanac, published by Information Today, Inc. (Medford, N.J.).

Table 3.5 UK book title output, 1980–2002

	Total	Reprints and new editions
1980	48,158	10,776
1981	43,083	9,387
1982	48,304	10,360
1983	51,071	12,091
1984	51,555	11,309
1985	52,994	11,740
1986	57,845	13,671
1987	54,746	13,296
1988	56,514	13,326
1989	61,195	15,153
1990	63,980	15,928
1991	67,704	17,629
1992	78,835	19,729
1993	82,322	20,804
1994	88,718	21,236
1995	95,064	22,918
1996	101,504	23,258
1997	100,029	23,693
1998	104,634	24,688
1999	110,155	26,158
2000	116,415	–
2001	119,001	–
2002	125,390	–

Figures on reprints and new editions not provided for 2000–2.
Source: Whitaker Information Services and *The Bookseller*.

calculations place the US at the top of the list of countries ranked in terms of title output, followed closely by the UK.

In Britain, the most commonly used data on title output are those produced by Whitaker BookTrack. Publishers voluntarily submit bibliographical data to Whitaker, which publishes it on a weekly and annual basis in the trade journal *The Bookseller*. Although it relies on voluntary submission, Whitaker estimates that it has coverage of roughly 95 per cent of publishers who sell titles in Britain. Whitaker's data include new editions of earlier titles as well as new books. They also include data on the ISBNs registered by foreign publishers who distribute their books in the UK, and hence the data are not restricted to books published by British publishers. Table 3.5 and figure 3.3 show the new title output in Britain between 1980 and 2002 based on Whitaker's data. In 1950, new title output in Britain stood at around 17,000. By 1980 this figure had nearly trebled to just over 48,000. During the next fifteen years the total doubled again, reaching more than 100,000 in 1996. By 2002 total book output in the UK exceeded 125,000 – an increase of more than sevenfold since 1950. The majority of these titles were in academic, professional and STM publishing – taken together, these three categories accounted for 66,761 titles in 2002, or 53 per cent of the total.

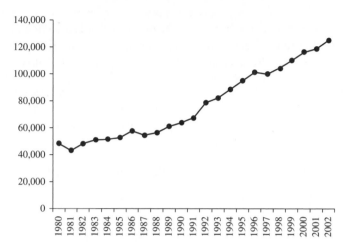

Figure 3.3   UK book title output, 1980–2002
Source: Whitaker Information Services and *The Bookseller*.

Why has output increased so significantly in the US and the UK in recent decades? Various explanations are put forward by people within the industry, although a full explanation would no doubt involve a variety of different factors. Technological changes have significantly reduced the costs associated with producing books, and hence have made it easier for small publishers to enter the field and increase their output. (There is some evidence to suggest that a substantial proportion of recent increases in title output in the US is accounted for by small and medium-sized publishers.) Moreover, in recent decades many publishers have tended to operate with what I shall describe in a later chapter as a 'higher-throughput model' of publishing – that is, they have sought to improve their financial performance by increasing the throughput of new titles, thereby building a dynamic of title growth into their business model. But the overall increase in title output may also be due in part to changing publishing strategies and to the increasing internationalization of the publishing industry. It is important to remember that the data on title output are usually based on ISBNs: these data record any edition which has its own ISBN, which may include paperback editions, new editions or re-editions of older works. A new book published simultaneously in hardback and paperback will therefore be recorded as two titles, since each edition will have its own ISBN. Hence a growing tendency to publish new books in cloth and paper simultaneously, or to bring out new editions of previously published books, would have an inflationary impact on the figures for overall title output. Moreover, since both Whitaker's data and the new system introduced by Bowker include ISBNs obtained by foreign publishers seeking to distribute their books in the UK and the US, the steep rise in titles published in these countries may reflect the increasing presence of foreign publishers in the UK and the US as much as the increased output of indigenous presses.

All of these factors probably play some role in accounting for the increased output of titles, though how much of the increase can be explained by any particular factor remains unclear. What is clear, however, is that there are many more titles published today in mature book markets like the US and the UK than was the case twenty or

thirty years ago. For external observers, this pattern of growth might seem to be symptomatic of a flourishing industry, but for many publishers it is a source of concern: they
worry about a market that is becoming saturated with the publication of more and more
new titles every year, resulting in more titles competing for the attention of review
editors, for shelf space in bookstores and for the dollars (or pounds) of consumers,
librarians and others. For publishers, the most immediate consequence of a substantial
increase in overall title output is a more crowded marketplace in which they may have
to struggle harder than ever to gain visibility for their own titles and to generate sales.

Concentration and corporate power

Another key feature of the book publishing industry in recent decades is that it has
been characterized by high levels of merger and acquisition activity, so that large corporations, many of which have interests in a variety of different media, have emerged
as dominant players in one or more publishing fields. Many of these large corporations
have also sought to expand their operations internationally and have therefore become
key players in a plurality of national markets. Today publishing fields are characterized
by very uneven distributions of financial capital as large corporations, often operating
in more than one field and more than one national market, struggle to strengthen their
positions vis-à-vis their principal competitors, in some cases through further acquisitions. Mergers and acquisitions have become an intrinsic part of the struggle for competitive advantage.

The process through which large media corporations have emerged as dominant
players in many publishing fields is a complex one with far-reaching consequences, and
here I can do no more than highlight a few salient features. The recent wave of mergers
and acquisitions in the publishing industry can be traced back at least as far as the 1960s,
when a series of major acquisitions, such as the purchase of Random House by RCA
in 1965 for $40 million, began to transform the publishing field. Some of the earlier,
high-profile acquisitions in the 1960s and 1970s involved the purchase of publishing
companies by large corporations whose principal interests were not in publishing as
such but in other industries, ranging from electronics to film and television broadcast-
ing. Some of these early acquisitions were undoubtedly driven by a belief (almost certainly overoptimistic) that the acquiring corporation would be able to forge a profitable
alliance between their own electronic resources and management expertise, on the one
hand, and the creative content of publishing firms, on the other – 'synergy' was the buzz
word at the time. As this belief turned into disappointment and the acquiring corporations realized that the profit margins in publishing were stubbornly low, some exited
from the field as quickly as they had entered it and divested themselves of their recently
acquired publishing assets.

While the acquisition of publishing firms by large corporations whose principal interests were in non-media industries may have been a passing phase, the growing role of
large media corporations in the publishing world was not. Through a series of major
mergers and acquisitions in the 1980s and 1990s, a handful of large media corporations
emerged as dominant players in the publishing field. The imprints of many previously
independent publishing houses were gathered together in one or more divisions of these
large corporations, many of which had substantial stakes in other sectors of the media,

information and entertainment industries. Media conglomerates like AOL Time Warner, Disney, Viacom/CBS, Rupert Murdoch's News Corporation, Bertelsmann, Holtzbrinck, Pearson and Thomson became increasingly powerful players in the world of book publishing, just as some were already powerful players in film, television, newspapers, magazines and other media industries.

There are three aspects of this process that are particularly noteworthy. First, the growing concentration of resources within the book publishing industry is *part of a broader process of concentration and conglomeratization which has characterized the media, information and entertainment industries as a whole*. Whereas in earlier decades, the dominant firms in any particular sector of the media industries tended to be dominant only in that sector, in recent decades the dominant firms have moved beyond particular sectors and have created diversified media conglomerates which have substantial stakes in a variety of media and related industries.[3] The large corporations which have become dominant players in the book publishing industry today are in most cases diversified media conglomerates which are also active in other media sectors. The book publishing divisions of these corporations are an important part of their overall businesses but they are by no means the only part, and in many cases they are a relatively small part in purely financial terms. AOL Time Warner, the largest of the media conglomerates formed through the merger of AOL and Time Warner in 2001, has an important stake in the book publishing industry through its ownership of Little, Brown and Company and with its own imprints such as Time Life and Warner Books, but these ventures are dwarfed by its activities in film, television, cable, music and other media sectors. Viacom/CBS, the second largest media conglomerate, created by the merger of Viacom and CBS in 2000, owns one of the largest publishers in the US (Simon & Schuster), but it also owns the largest television network in the US (CBS), one of the four largest US film studios (Paramount Pictures), the dominant video rental outlet (Blockbuster) and a variety of cable channels. For the large media conglomerates, book publishing is part of a more diversified portfolio of businesses concerned with various aspects of entertainment, information or education.

A second aspect of the process of consolidation in the book publishing industry is that it has tended to involve *a strategic restructuring of editorial activities*. In the earlier part of the twentieth century and before, publishing houses tended to be relatively heterogeneous organizations which published in a variety of different fields – fiction, nonfiction, education, higher education, professional, reference, etc. This heterogeneous character of publishing firms was often maintained and even accentuated in the early phases of conglomeratization in the 1970s and 1980s, as the conglomerates sought to expand through further acquisitions. But as the process advanced, the editorial activities of many publishing houses were gradually restructured in ways that were regarded by senior managers as more compatible with the overall strategic priorities of the corporation. For corporations whose principal activities were in the field of entertainment,

---

[3] On the rise of the media conglomerates, see Ben H. Bagdikian, *The Media Monopoly*, 5th edn (Boston: Beacon Press, 1997); Anthony Smith, *The Age of Behemoths: The Globalization of Mass Media Firms* (New York: Priority Press, 1991); Edward S. Herman and Robert W. McChesney, *The Global Media: The New Missionaries of Corporate Capitalism* (London: Cassell, 1997); Robert W. McChesney, *Rich Media, Poor Democracy: Communication Politics in Dubious Times* (New York: New Press, 1999).

it was the trade division of publishing which was valued particularly highly; other editorial activities, such as those concerned with education, were often deemed less essential and were in many cases sold off – even though the profit margins in educational publishing were generally higher than in trade publishing, and the sales more reliable.

The history of Simon & Schuster illustrates this process very well. One of the great imprints of the American publishing industry, Simon & Schuster began in a one-room office on W. 57th Street in New York in 1924, when Richard Simon and Max Schuster published their first book, a compilation of crossword puzzles that became a national bestseller. By the mid-1960s, Simon & Schuster had evolved into a major publishing company with an annual turnover of more than $40 million and seven divisions, including a trade division, several paperback divisions and a couple of divisions producing books aimed at different sectors of the educational market. In 1975 Simon & Schuster was sold to Gulf & Western, a conglomerate with interests in many different industries, including construction, natural resources, manufacturing, leisure and film (it owned Paramount Pictures among other things). In the 1980s and 1990s, Gulf & Western went through a period of intense corporate expansion, acquiring more than sixty companies between 1984 and 1994, including several major educational, professional and reference publishers such as Prentice Hall and the Macmillan Publishing Company. In 1989 Gulf & Western was restructured and became Paramount Communications, and in 1994 Paramount was in turn acquired by Viacom. In 1998, Viacom decided to streamline its publishing activities by selling its educational publishing businesses to Pearson, the UK-based media conglomerate which was consolidating its position as a leading international player in educational publishing. In 2000, Viacom purchased CBS for $37 billion in what was then the biggest media deal in history (though it was subsequently dwarfed by the $106 billion merger of AOL and Time Warner in 2001). In 2002, Simon & Schuster, now divested of its educational and professional divisions, was integrated with the Paramount motion picture and television studios as part of the Viacom Entertainment Group.

A third aspect of the process of consolidation in the book publishing industry is that it has become *increasingly international in character*. The large media corporations that play a dominant role in the book publishing industry today are also organizations that operate increasingly in an international arena. This trend is not altogether new; corporations like Pearson, Thomson and News Corporation have operated in an international arena for some while, but the trend has become more pronounced since the 1980s. There are a variety of different factors that have stimulated the media conglomerates to internationalize their activities. For the large US-based media corporations, overseas markets offer opportunities to generate additional revenue through the export of products and the sale of rights. Corporations like AOL Time Warner, Disney and Viacom generate the vast majority of their revenues from the US market, but they see the increase in sales in non-US markets as vital to their future growth. On the other hand, for media corporations based in the UK and Europe, expansion in the US market is generally regarded as essential, since the US market is by far the largest and most affluent market for media, educational and information products. When in 1998 Pearson acquired the educational businesses of Simon & Schuster, which included major imprints such as Prentice Hall, it moved into a dominant position in the US market for textbooks and educational products. For continental European conglomerates, there is an added incentive for investing in the acquisition of US and UK publishers: it provides them with a means of entering the English language market through indigenous pub-lishing operations. Since English has become the dominant global language, the acqui-sition of major publishing operations in the US and the UK provides continental European corporations with a basis for building a global publishing business in the new *lingua franca* of culture and commerce. The German media conglomerate Bertelsmann has pursued this strategy with great determination, acquiring a range of publishing houses in the US and the UK – including the purchase of Random House in 1998 for $1.4 billion – to become the largest trade book publisher both in the US, where it com-manded 17 per cent of trade and mass market sales in 2001, and in the world. In 1999, ten of the twenty largest publishing companies in the US were foreign-owned.

The mergers and acquisitions which have characterized the publishing industry – and the media industries more generally – since the 1960s have undoubtedly resulted in a growing concentration of resources in the hands of large corporations, which between them account for a steadily increasing share of the book market. In 1980, the total US book market was estimated to be worth around $7 billion; of this, the top ten publish-ers accounted for just under 46 per cent. By 1994, the US book market was worth around $19 billion, and the top ten publishers accounted for just over 62 per cent of this. By 2002, the US book market was worth around $27 billion, of which the top ten publish-ers accounted for around 70 per cent. In 2002, the top twenty publishers accounted for around 82 per cent of total sales in the US.[4]

Table 3.6 lists the twenty largest book publishers in North America in 2002 based on data gathered by Subtext, a Connecticut-based organization which monitors trends in the publishing industry. Pearson, a UK-based company, is the largest publisher both internationally and in the US, with US book sales of $3.9 billion in 2002; the Penguin Group (a subsidiary of Pearson) accounts for about a quarter of Pearson's global book sales, and Pearson Education accounts for around three-quarters of the total. Two other publishers with a strong presence in professional and educational publishing – the Canadian-based International Thomson and the Anglo-Dutch company Reed Elsevier – ranked second and third with US book sales of $3.4 billion and $2.7 billion respec-tively. The children's publisher Scholastic ranked fourth in the US, its sales boosted by the phenomenal success of the Harry Potter books. US-based McGraw-Hill ranked fifth and Random House, part of the German-based Bertelsmann group, ranked sixth, each with sales in the US of around $1.5 billion.

In examining patterns of concentration in the book publishing industry, it is impor-tant to bear several points in mind. First, particular corporations such as Pearson often include many different publishing imprints and many different activities, and the revenue generated from North American book sales may represent only part of the cor-poration's total global sales generated from all activities (Pearson reported total sales of £4.3 billion ($7 billion)[5] in 2002). Second, particular publishing firms, which are often treated as distinct entities in descriptions of the major publishers, are in some cases

---

[4] Source for 1980 and 1994: Simba Information, reproduced in Martin P. Levin, 'The Positive Role of Large Corporations in US Book Publishing', *Logos*, 7/1 (1996). Source for 2002: Subtext, *Perspective on Book Publishing: 2003–2004* (Darien, Conn.: Open Book, 2004), p. 27.
[5] The exchange rate has varied significantly in recent years, ranging from £1 = $1.40 to £1 = $1.85. In this study I have used an average exchange rate of £1 = $1.60, although the exchange rates used in some of the tables may differ from this.

Table 3.6 Twenty largest book publishers in North America, 2002 (ranked by 2002 world revenues and breaking out US revenues (books only))

Rank	Publisher	2002 world sales ($m)	2002 US sales ($m)	US sales as % of total
1	Pearson[1]	5,786	3,900*	67.4
2	International Thomson[2]	4,226*	3,400*	80.5
3	Reed Elsevier[3]	4,214*	2,700*	64.1
4	McGraw-Hill	2,804	1,496	53.3
5	Wolters Kluwer[4]	2,628*	1,300*	49.5
6	Random House	2,090	1,463	68.7
7	Scholastic	1,958	1,639	83.7
8	Houghton Mifflin[5]	1,195	1,180*	98.7
9	HarperCollins	1,162	855*	73.6
10	Reader's Digest	1,082	604*	55.8
11	John Wiley & Sons	854	524	61.4
12	Simon & Schuster	688*	660*	95.9
13	Harlequin Books[6]	415	340*	66.8
14	AOL/Time Warner[7]	410*	350*	85.4
15	Encyclopaedia Britannica	365*	280*	76.7
16	Holtzbrinck Group[8]	320*	320*	100
17	BNA	263	263	100
18	Rodale Press	235*	215*	91.5
19	WCR Media[9]	210	210	100
20	Thomas Nelson	188	188	100
	Total	31,093	21,887	70.39

* Estimates.
[1] Penguin Group, $1.3 billion; Pearson Education, $4.4 billion; exchange rate: £1 = $1.46.
[2] Estimate for 2002 includes full year sales for Harcourt's higher education division. Thomson acquired the division from Reed in July 2001.
[3] Reed acquired Harcourt General in July 2001; the 2002 estimate includes full year of Harcourt's sales. Estimate also includes book sales of Reed's professional businesses.
[4] Based on Wolters Kluwer's non-electronic sales worldwide for legal/professional, medical and educational businesses.
[5] The majority of Houghton Mifflin's sales are derived from its US businesses. Overseas sales come from the Kingfisher La Rouse properties, which Houghton Mifflin recently acquired.
[6] North American sales.
[7] Warner Books and Little, Brown. Time Warner's continuity program not included.
[8] Includes St Martin's Press, Farrar, Straus & Giroux, Henry Holt, St Martin's Press college and Scientific American publications.
[9] Formerly Ripplewood Holdings, WCR Media is comprised of a number of educational companies acquired in 1999. These include Weekly Reader, American Guidance, World Almanac and Compass Learning.
Source: Subtext, *Perspective on Book Publishing: 2003–2004* (Darien, Conn.: Open Book, 2004).

owned by larger media conglomerates with interests in a diverse array of media. So, for example, while Random House is listed as a distinct entity in table 3.6, it is owned by Bertelsmann; HarperCollins is owned by Rupert Murdoch's News Corporation; and Simon & Schuster is owned by Viacom/CBS. Third, the patterns of concentration tend to vary considerably from one field of publishing to another. This is an important point and I shall pursue it in more detail below, but first let us briefly consider the UK.

Table 3.7 Top ten consolidated publishing groups in the UK, 2002

Rank	Group	Total consumer market sales (£m)	2002 sales as % of total consumer market
1	Pearson	183.3	13.8
2	Bertelsmann	168.3	12.7
3	News Corporation	126.0	9.5
4	WHSmith	91.7	6.9
5	Hachette	77.8	5.8
6	Holtzbrinck	60.0	4.5
7	Time Warner	38.3	2.9
8	BBC	37.8	2.8
9	Bloomsbury	29.0	2.2
10	Oxford University Press	24.7	1.9
	Total	836.9	62.9

Nielsen BookScan estimates that its total consumer market (TCM) data reflected 85% of all retail and internet sales in the UK in 2002.
Source: Nielsen BookScan 2002.

A very similar process of consolidation has occurred in the UK publishing industry over the last couple of decades, and many of the key players are the same. The UK market is much smaller than the US market (the total book market in the UK in 2002 was around £3.5 billion ($5.6 billion), compared to a total US market in 2002 of around $27 billion), but the dominant role of large corporations is nevertheless clear. Table 3.7 lists the top ten consolidated groups in the UK general retail market in 2002 based on data gathered by Nielsen BookScan; it gives the total sales of each group in the general retail market and its market share. In 2002 the top six publishing groups in the general retail market in the UK were Pearson (comprising imprints such as Penguin, Viking, Michael Joseph, Hamish Hamilton and Dorling Kindersley), Bertelsmann (including Random House, Transworld, Jonathan Cape, Chatto, Vintage, Harvill, Pimlico, Century Heinemann, Hutchinson, Arrow and Ebury Press, among others), News Corporation (including HarperCollins and Fourth Estate), WHSmith (including Hodder Headline and John Murray), Hachette (including Orion, Octopus, Victor Gollancz and Weidenfeld & Nicolson) and Holtzbrinck (including Macmillan, Pan and Picador). Pearson's share of the general retail market was 13.8 per cent, Bertelsmann's was 12.7 per cent, News Corporation's was 9.5 per cent, WHSmith's was 6.9 per cent, Hachette's was 5.8 per cent and Holtzbrinck's was 4.5 per cent.[6] Together these six groups accounted for just over half (53.2 per cent) of general retail sales. After that, the market shares of the leading groups fall off quite quickly – the top ten groups, taken together, account for nearly two-thirds (62.9 per cent) of general retail sales.

[6] Hachette is set to become the second largest book publisher in the UK following its purchase of Hodder Headline from WHSmith. The £223 million acquisition, announced in August 2004, will give Hachette over 13% of the UK market. Hachette, a division of the French conglomerate Lagardère, is already the largest publisher in France.

Table 3.8 Top five educational publishers in the US, 2002 (revenue estimates in $m)

Rank	Publisher	2002 ($m)	2001 ($m)	Change (%)
1	Pearson[1]	4,410	4,166	5.9
2	McGraw-Hill[2]	2,357	2,322	1.5
3	International Thomson[3]	2,290	1,851	23.7
4	Harcourt Education[4]	1,589	926	71.5
5	Houghton Mifflin[5]	985	980	0.5
	Total	11,631	10,245	13.5

[1] Sales for Pearson Education: worldwide school, $1.842 billion (£1.151 billion); worldwide college, $1.240 billion (£775 million); professional, $1.254 million (£784 million); and FT Knowledge, $74 million (£46 million); £1 = $1.60.

[2] Sales for McGraw-Hill Education, which consists of the school education group (around 60% of sales) and the higher education, professional and international group (around 40% of sales).

[3] Sales for Thomson Learning, which consists of school and higher education publishing, library reference, and corporate training and testing. Thomson acquired Harcourt's college publishing business from Reed Elsevier in July 2001.

[4] Sales for Harcourt Education: US schools and testing, $1.354 billion (£846 million) and international, $235 million (£147 million). Harcourt Education was acquired by Reed Elsevier in July 2001. Sales for 2001 reflect six months only of Harcourt sales (July to December 2001). £1 = $1.60.

[5] Combined school and college publishing sales reported in SEC filing, 30 May 2003. Houghton Mifflin was sold by Vivendi Universal in 2002 to a consortium of private investment firms led by Thomas H. Lee Partners and Bain Capital.

Source: Subtext, *Perspective on Book Publishing: 2003–2004* (Darien, Conn.: Open Book, 2004).

While the process of consolidation in the book publishing industry has resulted overall in a growing concentration of resources and market share in the hands of a relatively small number of large corporations, in practice the way in which this process has unfolded has varied considerably from one field of publishing to another. Some publishing fields have experienced much higher levels of concentration than others and, while some corporations are active in more than one field, each field tends to have its own dynamic of mergers and acquisitions and its own dominant players. One striking feature of table 3.6 is that the five largest book publishers in North America in 2002 were publishers who are active in educational and professional publishing – Pearson, International Thomson, Reed Elsevier, McGraw-Hill, and Wolters Kluwer. The fields of educational and professional publishing have experienced particularly high levels of consolidation over the last few decades, driven in part by the high costs of investment in technology and by the levels of investment required to secure large adoptions in the schoolbook and college textbook markets. In the field of educational publishing, there are three large international corporations which have been the dominant players in the process of consolidation which has restructured the field over the last two decades: Pearson, McGraw-Hill and International Thomson, all of which had sales well in excess of $2 billion from their educational divisions in 2002. Table 3.8 lists the top five educational publishers in the US in 2002 (comprising all aspects of educational publishing, from school to higher education). With sales of $4.4 billion in 2002, Pearson is the largest overall educational publisher, with substantial stakes in the school, college and professional markets and major international operations. McGraw-Hill ranks second, with total educational sales of $2.35 billion, and International Thomson ranks third with sales of $2.29 billion. These three corporations – Pearson, McGraw-Hill and International Thomson – are also the key players in the field of higher education publishing, as we shall see in chapter 8.

The field of general trade publishing has also undergone a process of consolidation in recent decades, although here some of the players are different, partly because trade publishers have been seen as attractive acquisitions by media conglomerates which have substantial stakes in the world of entertainment. Hence media conglomerates such as Bertelsmann, Viacom/CBS, AOL Time Warner and Murdoch's News Corporation have played key roles in the process of consolidation in the field of trade publishing. In 2002–3, six of the top seven trade houses in the US were owned by conglomerates, and together they accounted for over 50 per cent of all sales generated in the adult, children and mass market sectors – see table 3.9. Random House, owned by Bertelsmann, is by far the largest trade publisher in the US, with trade sales in the US of $1.46 billion in 2002 and global sales of around $2 billion. The Penguin Group (owned by Pearson) and HarperCollins (owned by News Corporation) vie for second place, with trade sales in the US of just over $800 million and global sales of around $1.1–1.3 billion. Simon & Schuster (owned by Viacom/CBS), Warner and Little, Brown (owned by AOL Time Warner), John Wiley & Sons, and St Martin's, Holt and Farrar, Straus & Giroux (owned by Holtzbrinck) derive most of their book sales from the US, where they are the fourth, fifth, sixth and seventh largest trade publishers respectively. Together, these seven groups have around 54.9 per cent of the total US trade market. The top ten trade publishers, taken together, account for just over 61 per cent of the total US trade market.

In effect, the process of consolidation in the book publishing industry has contributed to the increasing differentiation of the world of publishing into relatively distinct fields, with trade publishing becoming increasingly dominated by a small set of media conglomerates which have substantial stakes in the world of entertainment, with educational publishing becoming increasingly dominated by a small set of international corporations which are geared more to the world of education, and so on. This differentiation is not clear-cut and there are major players, such as Pearson, who have dominant positions in more than one field. There are also some fields, such as professional and educational publishing, which overlap to a significant extent and where some of the major players are the same. Nevertheless, even where there is overlap, the rank order of the dominant players tends to vary from one publishing field to another – and indeed, the rank order within any particular field can change from one year to the next as the leading players seek to strengthen their positions within those fields, both nationally and internationally, through further acquisitions when the opportunities arise.

There are some publishing fields where the process of consolidation has proceeded more slowly and less decisively, although these fields have experienced the consequences of consolidation in other, more indirect ways. The field of academic (or scholarly) publishing is a good example. This is partly because academic publishing is less profitable than other types of publishing, and is therefore of little interest to the large commercial firms, and partly because a substantial part of academic publishing has been carried out by the university presses, whose position as not-for-profit organizations linked to universities has protected them to a large extent from the logic of mergers and acquisitions characteristic of the commercial sector. But the process of consolidation in the publishing industry has had an impact on academic publishing in other ways. The rise of powerful corporate players in the fields of STM publishing and journal publishing has squeezed

Table 3.9 Seven largest US trade publishers, 2002–2003

Rank	Publisher	Parent company	World trade/mass market revenues ($m)	Estimated US trade/mass market revenues ($m)	% of total US trade/mass market
1	Random House[1]	Bertelsmann	2,090	1,463*	17.0
2	Penguin Putnam	Pearson	1,349	810	9.4
3	HarperCollins[2]	News Corporation	1,162	835	9.6
4	Simon & Schuster[3]	Viacom	688	660	7.6
5	Warner/Little, Brown[4]	AOL Time Warner	410	350	4.0
6	John Wiley & Sons[5]	John Wiley	369	322*	3.7
7	St Martin's/Holt/FSG[6]	Holtzbrinck	320	320	3.7
	Total		Global: 6,388	US: 4,760	% US: 54.9

Trade publishing here includes adult hardcover, adult paperback, children's hardcover and paperback, and mass market paperback.
Figures are for all sales, domestic and overseas. Numbers for financial years ending 31 Dec. 2002 and in the first half of 2003.
The final column is calculated on the basis of total US trade sales, as compiled by the Association of American Publishers, of $6,929.8 million and total US mass market sales of $1,726.8 million, giving a grand total of $8,656.6 million. Combined US sales of top seven trade/mass market publishers: $4,760 million, representing 54.9% of the total domestic market.
* Actual numbers; all other numbers in this column are estimated.
[1] Revenue for financial year ended 31 Dec. 2002.
[2] Financial year ended 30 June 2003. Includes Zondervan Publishers, with sales estimated at $70 million for 2002.
[3] Estimated, financial year ended 31 Dec. 2002.
[4] Estimated, year ended 31 Dec. 2002.
[5] Professional/trade segment for financial year ended 30 April 2003.
[6] Estimated, year ended 31 Dec. 2002.
Source: Subtext, *Perspective on Book Publishing: 2003–2004* (Darien, Conn.: Open Book, 2004).

the budgets of university libraries with dire consequences for academic publishers, as we shall see. Moreover, those academic publishers who, in response to the difficulties they face in their own field, have sought to increase their presence in the fields of trade publishing and higher education publishing have found themselves having to cope with competitive dynamics that are shaped by corporate players much more powerful than themselves. So even if the field of academic publishing has not experienced the process of consolidation to the same extent as other fields, this process has had a profound impact on academic publishing and has shaped the overall environment within which all publishers, including academic publishers, operate today.

The fact that resources in the publishing industry have become increasingly concentrated in the hands of large media conglomerates does not mean that small publishers have been squeezed out of existence – on the contrary, there are a surprising number of small publishers in markets which are increasingly dominated by the large conglomerates. According to the Department of Commerce, the number of publishers in the US with fewer than twenty employees grew from almost 1,400 in 1977 to almost 1,900 in 1987, and grew again to 2,174 in 1997. The Department of Commerce's Economic Census for 1997 lists a total of 2,541 publishing companies in the US, of which 85 per cent have fewer than twenty employees and nearly 60 per cent have fewer than five. Of course, the output of small companies represents a relatively small proportion of the total output of the industry (in 1997, establishments with fewer than twenty employees accounted for less than 5 per cent of the total value of shipments in the US, and many of these establishments may be publishing a small number of titles each year), but there are no signs that the number of small publishing companies is declining over time.[7] And it is not difficult to see why this might be so. Publishing is a highly diverse and differentiated domain, and in many fields (such as trade publishing) the costs of entry are relatively low. Technological changes, and especially those associated with digitization and computerization, have made it even cheaper and easier for small publishers to enter the field. As many traditional publishing companies have been bought up by large corporations, their editorial strategies have changed in various ways, and this process has created new opportunities for enterprising individuals and small publishing operations which are willing to take risks with new authors and projects and which are able to cater for small, niche markets. Hence the growing concentration of resources in the hands of large conglomerates does not necessarily spell the demise of small publishers. On the contrary, the two may go hand in hand, as small publishers are able to cater for more specialized tastes and needs that the large corporations, by virtue of the financial logic that tends to prevail within them, are unable to meet.

The rise of the media conglomerates is undoubtedly one of the most significant developments that have characterized the book publishing industry in recent decades. By acquiring many formerly independent publishing companies and integrating them into the structures of large corporations, the media conglomerates have transformed the world of book publishing. Many of the great publishing houses that rose to fame in the first half of the twentieth century have, since the 1960s and 1970s, become operational divisions of large corporations. Today more than ever before, a large proportion of the books that are produced and sold in particular publishing fields are produced and sold by a handful of large corporations, many of which have interests in a variety of media

[7] See www.census.gov/prod/ec97/97m5111c.pdf.

sectors. The consequences of this development are varied and complex. They vary from one corporation to another, since corporations differ in the ways that they manage their subsidiary companies, and they vary from one publishing field to another, since publishing fields differ in the extent to which large corporations play a dominant role within them. In part II we shall examine a field – that of academic (or scholarly) publishing – in which large corporations play a minor role, although they do have a profound (if more indirect) impact on the field as a whole. In part III we shall examine an adjacent field – higher education publishing – in which a small handful of large corporations have become dominant players, not only in the lucrative US market but also, and increasingly, in the international arena.

The transformation of the retail sector

It is not only the structure of publishing firms which has changed quite profoundly in recent decades: the retail sector has also undergone a veritable revolution. The transformation of the retail sector has radically altered the conditions in which publishers operate, for the various organizations that comprise the retail sector – the bookstores, wholesalers, online retail outlets, etc. – are the intermediaries that provide publishers with their channels to market. They provide the crucial links in the supply chain between publishers and the customers who ultimately buy books. They are also publishers' shop windows and they take responsibility for stocking, displaying and selling the books that publishers produce. Given the importance of the retail sector for publishers, it is likely that fundamental changes within this sector will have an impact on the activities of publishers themselves, although the precise nature of this impact may be complex and difficult to trace through.

The most important changes that have characterized the retail sector since 1980 are (1) the rise of the retail chain superstores, (2) the decline of the independents, and (3) the advent of online retailers. These changes are particularly marked in the US and Britain, but they are by no means unique to these countries – similar developments can be seen elsewhere. Let me comment briefly on each.

(1) *The rise of the retail chain superstores*   The rise of the superstores is associated most commonly with Borders and Barnes & Noble in the US and with Waterstone's in Britain, but the origins of the book superstore date back to the 1960s. In 1966 the Dayton Hudson Corporation – a company formed by the merger of two department stores in the American Midwest – opened the first B. Dalton bookstore in a suburban shopping mall in Dayton, Ohio.[8] In 1969 Dayton Hudson bought the Pickwick Bookshop in Hollywood, together with other Pickwick outlets, and in 1972 the two operations were merged to form B. Dalton Booksellers. By 1980 there were more than 450 B. Dalton stores located in shopping malls across the United States. At roughly the same time, Waldenbooks – another bookstore chain that emerged from a network of rental libraries established on the East Coast by Lawrence Hoyt in the 1930s – expanded by also opening bookstores in malls across the United States. By 1981 Waldenbooks had 750

---

[8] See Thomas Whiteside, *The Blockbuster Complex: Conglomerates, Show Business, and Book Publishing* (Middletown, Conn.: Wesleyan University Press, 1980), pp. 44 ff.

Table 3.10   The expansion of Borders and Barnes & Noble, 1993–1994

	Sales ($m)		Number of stores	
	1993	1994	1993	1994
Borders				
Borders superstores	225	425	44	85
Waldenbooks	1,146	1,086	1,159	1,102
Total	1,371	1,511		
Barnes & Noble				
Barnes & Noble superstores	600*	958	200*	268
B. Dalton	737*	665	750*	698
Total	1,337	1,623		

* Estimate.
Source: Stephen Horvath, 'The Rise of the Book Chain Superstore', *Logos*, 7/1 (1996).

sites and claimed to be the first bookseller to operate bookstores in all fifty states. In 1984 Waldenbooks was acquired by the retail giant Kmart.

The mall-based chains of the 1960s and 1970s were the origins of the modern retail chain superstores, but the book retail business was transformed in the 1980s and 1990s by the extraordinary growth of Borders and Barnes & Noble. Tom and Lewis Borders opened a small bookstore in Ann Arbor, Michigan, a major university town, and ran it successfully for many years. In 1985 they opened a second bookstore in Detroit to see whether they could replicate their success in a less academic setting. The success of the Detroit store encouraged them to expand into other locations in the Midwest and Northeast. Borders' expansion also encouraged Len Riggio of Barnes & Noble to expand his bookselling operation, which was based in New York. In 1987 Barnes & Noble acquired B. Dalton and in 1989 they acquired Scribner's Bookstores and Bookstop/Bookstar, a regional chain in the south and west of the United States. In 1992 Borders was acquired by Kmart, which merged Borders with Waldenbooks to form the Borders Group, which went public in 1995. By this stage, the Borders Group and the Barnes & Noble group had emerged as the dominant book retail chains in the United States and their sales were five to ten times those of the other national chains, such as Crown and Books-A-Million. Both Borders and Barnes & Noble expanded rapidly, as table 3.10 illustrates, and an intense competition grew up between them.[9]

In the year from 1993 to 1994, Borders nearly doubled the number of superstores from 44 to 85, and Barnes & Noble increased the number of superstores from around 200 to 268. Riggio took the view that the fastest national roll-out would establish the brand and serve the company well in the long run, while Borders adopted a more cautious approach. At the same time, both Borders and Barnes & Noble were closing some of the traditional mall-based stores in their Walden and B. Dalton chains – Borders closed 57 Walden stores between 1993 and 1994, and Barnes & Noble closed around 52 B. Dalton stores. The old mall sites were gradually giving way to the rise of the superstores.

[9] See Stephen Horvath, 'The Rise of the Book Chain Superstore', *Logos*, 7/1 (1996), p. 41.

As pioneered by Borders and Barnes & Noble, the rise of the book superstores has transformed the nature of bookselling. It has brought intensified competition based on location, size, price, range and depth of inventory, customer service, extended opening hours and amenities. Each chain has a mix of flagship superstores in prime city locations, suburban sites and stores in smaller towns. Barnes & Noble is prominent in Manhattan, while Borders is more visible in downtown Chicago and in the cities of the Midwest. Throughout the 1990s, both chains sought to saturate the major metropolitan areas by rushing to open large stores in prime city locations. They competed with one another and with the other chains and independents by giving deep discounts (30–40 per cent) on bestsellers, modest discounts on other hardcovers (10–20 per cent), and by the range and depth of their stock. Purchasing, stock allocation and inventory control were centralized; this gave the chains a great deal of leverage in their discussions with suppliers and enabled them to realize substantial economies of scale. The chains emphasized customer service and attractive, eye-catching displays. They were open for up to a hundred hours a week, seven days a week. The superstores were designed as appealing places to browse – clean, spacious, carpeted, well-lit stores with sofas and coffee shops – and in many cases they stocked merchandise other than books, such as magazines, music CDs, computer games and videos.

By 2002, Barnes & Noble was operating 886 bookstores across the United States, which included 628 under the Barnes & Noble, Bookstop and Bookstar trade names and 258 under the B. Dalton, Doubleday and Scribner's names; its total sales were around $3.9 billion. The company also diversified into the video games and computer software retail business, acquiring a 63 per cent stake in GameStop and operating 1,231 video game and entertainment software stores under various trade names, including GameStop, Babbage's and Software Etc. The Borders Group, with total sales of around $3.5 billion, was operating around 1,185 bookstores in the US, including 410 superstores under the Borders trade name and around 775 mall-based Waldenbooks stores. Borders had also expanded internationally, operating 33 Borders stores outside the US (mainly in the UK and the Pacific Rim) and 37 Books Etc. stores in the UK (Borders acquired Books Etc. in 1997 for around £40 million). The combined revenues of Barnes & Noble and Borders were around $7.4 billion in 2002, which represented about 28 per cent of total book sales in the US and about 57 per cent of the estimated $13 billion US bookselling market. The third largest bookstore chain in the US is Books-A-Million, but with sales of $442 million in 2002 it was dwarfed by the two superstore chains.

Although on a much smaller scale, the phenomenon of the retail chain superstore had entered the UK market long before Borders opened its first store in the UK. In the early 1980s there were various long-established bookstore chains in the UK market, from the general high street bookseller and stationer WHSmith to more specialized bookstore chains such as Blackwell's, Hammicks and Websters, Pentos and Sherratt & Hughes. But the bookselling environment began to change significantly in the 1980s, thanks largely to the rapid rise of Waterstone's. Tim Waterstone was sacked from WHSmith in 1982 and went on to raise £100,000 in venture capital to set up Waterstone's Booksellers, opening his first store in the Old Brompton Road in London. Waterstone's quickly expanded the number of branches, opening large stores in central, high street locations and designing them in ways that were attractive to customers and conducive to browsing. From its beginnings in 1982, Waterstone's grew into a major retail chain that rivalled both Blackwell's and Pentos (which owned the Dillons

Table 3.11   Number of branches of specialist bookstore chains in the UK, 1984–1989

	1984	1985	1986	1987	1988	1989	Average size (sq. ft)
Blackwell's	44	44	48	55	54	56[1]	2,500
Hammicks	7	15	15	20	26	30	2,300
Hatchards	5	9	21[2]	26	29	27	3,500
Pentos[3]	23	27	34	47	56	59	4,400
Sherratt & Hughes	31	34	38	44	48	54	3,500
Waterstone's	5	7	13	22	35	34	6,000

[1] Includes satellites counted for the first time.
[2] Includes Claude Gill.
[3] Includes Athena bookshops.
Source: The Bookseller.

Table 3.12   Sales by bookstore chains in the UK, 1983/84 to 1988/89 (£m)

	1983/84	1984/85	1985/86	1986/87	1987/88	1988/89
Blackwell's	30	33	37	40	42	45
Hammicks	4	5	7	10	12	15
Hatchards	4	8	15	18	22	28
Pentos[1]	16	21	24	30	46	58
Sherratt & Hughes	14	15	18	20	25	33
Waterstone's	3	6	9	15	29	40

[1] Includes Athena bookshops.
Source: The Bookseller.

bookstores among other things) in terms of number of branches and sales (see tables 3.11 and 3.12).

The 1990s were a period of consolidation in the UK book retail sector. Between 1989 and 1993, WHSmith acquired all of Waterstone's shares and the business was integrated with 48 Sherratt & Hughes stores, which were converted into the Waterstone's brand. As an autonomous business within the WHSmith Group, Waterstone's expanded rapidly and became the leading specialist bookseller in the UK. In 1998 Waterstone's merged with the Dillons chain. Established in 1936, Dillons was acquired by the Pentos Group in 1981, but Pentos was declared bankrupt in 1995 and the Dillons stores were sold to HMV. The HMV Media Group was set up in 1998, under the chairmanship of Tim Waterstone, in order to acquire the two bookselling chains. It paid £300 million for 115 Waterstone's stores and £500 million for EMI's two chains, comprising 78 Dillons stores and 271 HMV music stores. For a year the two rival bookselling brands were maintained, but in 1999 the Dillons name was dropped and the stores were rebranded as Waterstone's. In 2002 the HMV Group operated 197 Waterstone's stores, mostly in the UK and Ireland, as well as 328 HMV stores selling music, videos and games. WHSmith also expanded its holdings in the 1990s, using the proceeds from its sale of Waterstone's to acquire the 232 stores of the Scottish-based John Menzies chain in 1998, bringing the total number of branches in WHSmith's high street and travel chains to 741. And Borders continued to increase its holdings in the UK, both through the opening of its own superstores and through the acquisition of Books Etc.

It is primarily Waterstone's and Borders that have been responsible for the rise of the book superstore in the UK. Tim Waterstone's conception of book retailing was always close to the idea of the superstore, which was partly why he was able to expand so rapidly in the 1980s and early 1990s, and the merger of Waterstone's and Dillons within the HMV Group gave Waterstone's the financial strength to increase its super-store programme. The idea of the superstore was also the cornerstone of Borders' strat-egy in entering the UK market in the 1990s. As Waterstone's and Borders began to open more superstores, it became increasingly clear that they were going to be competing head-to-head in many of the major metropolitan centres, just as Barnes & Noble and Borders were competing with one another in the US.

(2) *The decline of the independents* The other side of the rise of the retail chain superstores has been the precipitous decline of the independent booksellers. Once again, this decline predates the rise of the superstores. In 1958, one-store independent booksellers were selling 72 per cent of trade books in the US; by 1980 their share had fallen to less than 40 per cent of trade sales.[10] But there can be no doubt that the decline of the independents was further hastened by the rise of the retail chain superstores. As the chains were rushing to open new superstores in the metropolitan centres across America in the 1990s, more and more independents were closing down, forced out of business by the two-pronged pressure of rising overheads (and especially the rising costs of real estate) and declining revenues. In the early 1990s there were around 5,400 inde-pendent bookstores in the US; by the end of the decade, the number had fallen to around 3,200, a decline of some 40 per cent.[11] In 1993, the chains accounted for around 23 per cent of retail sales in the US; by the end of the decade, this had risen to over 50 per cent. During the same period, four out of every ten independent bookstores failed and their market share fell from 24 per cent to around 16 per cent.

Concerns about the decline of the independents have frequently been expressed in the UK as well, and many felt that the demise of the Net Book Agreement in the mid-1990s would only hasten their demise. The Net Book Agreement (NBA) was a retail price maintenance mechanism that was introduced by publishers as a voluntary agree-ment in 1900 to protect specialist booksellers from the effects of discounting by general traders. In the mid-1990s, a number of retailers, including Pentos (owner of Dillons), began to experiment with non-net titles, and in 1995 Random House and HarperCollins struck a deal with WHSmith and announced they would withdraw from the NBA. Other publishers soon followed suit and the NBA collapsed. In March 1997 the Restrictive Practices Court decided that the NBA was no longer in the public interest and declared it illegal. Many of the fears about the impact of the collapse of the NBA proved to be unfounded,[12] but the growth of the superstore chains has undoubtedly made life more difficult for many independents and for the smaller chains. The small chains have been

---

[10] Whiteside, *The Blockbuster Complex*, p. 41.
[11] Schiffrin, *The Business of Books*, p. 125.
[12] See Francis Fishwick and Sharon FitzSimons, *Report into the Effects of the Abandonment of the Net Book Agreement* (London: Book Trust, 1998).

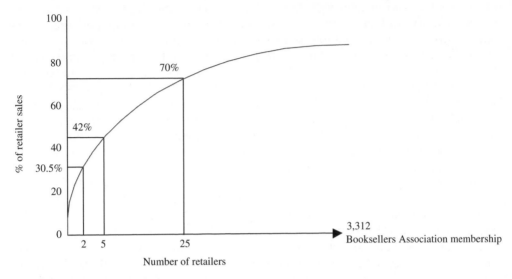

Figure 3.4 Concentration in the UK book retail sector
Source: The UK Book Industry: Unlocking the Supply Chain's Hidden Prize (London: Booksellers Association/KPMG, 1998).

particularly vulnerable, and in the course of the 1990s several small local and regional chains were absorbed by medium-sized chains that were seeking to strengthen their positions in the face of competition from the big retailers. Blackwell Retail absorbed several smaller chains – Austicks (4 shops), Thornes (6 shops) and Heffers (10 shops). James Thin, the Edinburgh-based chain, bought Volume One (18 shops) in 1994, and Ottakar's bought Bell's Bookshops and Bookworms in 1998.

Despite the consolidation among the small and medium-sized retail chains, the gap between the big retailers and the medium-sized chains in the UK remains large. At the end of the 1990s, HMV Media Group accounted for around 16 per cent of the UK retail book market, and WHSmith accounted for 14.5 per cent; Blackwell Retail was in third position but accounted for only 2.5 per cent of the market (this was before the purchase of Heffers). The pattern of concentration in the UK retail sector is illustrated by figure 3.4.[13] The top two retailing groups, HMV and WHSmith, accounted for 30.5 per cent of sales in 1998; the top five groups accounted for 42 per cent; and the top twenty-five retailers accounted for 70 per cent. The remaining 30 per cent of sales came from over 3,000 smaller accounts.[14]

The decline of the independents in the US appears to have levelled off in recent years and those that survived the rise of the superstore chains appear to have a certain resilience. Many independents fought back by offering discounts (or increasing the range of their discounted titles), improving their service to customers and hosting events

[13] See *The UK Book Industry: Unlocking the Supply Chain's Hidden Prize* (London: Booksellers Association/KPMG, 1998); *Book Retailing in Britain* (London: Bookseller Publications, 1999), p. 74.
[14] *Book Retailing in Britain*, pp. 71–4.

of various kinds to deepen their links with local communities. In some cases, independents sought to find a niche which would enable them to differentiate themselves more clearly from the superstores. Some moved increasingly into selling used books and remaindered stock, since these kinds of business generated higher margins and enabled them to offset to some extent the lower margins on discounted titles. The struggle against the chains was also fought on the legal front. In 1998, the American Booksellers Association (ABA) filed a suit against Borders and Barnes & Noble, alleging that the two chains had secured special (and hence illegal) deals on discounts and cooperative reimbursement. The case went to trial in 2001 but Borders and Barnes & Noble settled after six days with a cash payment of $4.7 million. Neither Borders nor Barnes & Noble accepted liability for any of the illegal practices alleged in the suit.

There can be no doubt that the rise of the retail chain superstores, and the attendant decline of the independents, has transformed the landscape of bookselling over the last two decades, but the impact of these changes on book publishers has been more complex and ambiguous than has sometimes been suggested. It is undoubtedly the case that the rise of the retail chain superstores has accentuated the importance attributed to commercial bestsellers and bestselling authors and has shifted the focus of the trade increasingly towards high-profile frontlist titles at the expense of mid-list and backlist books (a point emphasized by Epstein among others[15]); it has also given certain advantages to the larger publishers and media conglomerates, which are able to make available substantial amounts of co-op money in order to buy prominent display space in shop windows or on the tables and racks at the front of the store. However, it was not only the larger publishers which benefited from the rise of the retail chain superstores in the 1990s. As the chains expanded by opening more and more stores, they ordered books from many publishers to fill the growing aisles of bookshelves. Smaller publishers, including the university presses, benefited from this dramatic increase in retail shelf space. For many publishers (including the university presses), sales soared in the 1990s as the expansion of the chains sucked more and more books into the bookstores. However, this sales growth was to some extent an illusion, since many of the books that were being ordered to fill the shelves of the superstores were not being sold on to customers and would eventually be returned to the publishers.

The main consequence of the growth of the retail chains has been a shift in the balance of power between publishers and retailers, as publishers become increasingly dependent on a small number of mega-chains which play an increasingly important role in determining the channels to market. Selling new books into the major chains has become an increasingly important task for publishers who hope to achieve sales in the general retail market. Moreover, given that the major chains (especially in the US) rely to a large extent on centralized buying, the key decisions affecting the availability of books in the stores of the major chains are taken by a relatively small number of individuals. A decision by the buyer at a major chain to stock a particular title in significant quantities at all or most of the chain's bookstores can transform the prospects for a book and give it much greater visibility nationwide than it otherwise would have had. But equally, a decision to stock a particular title cautiously can significantly limit its visibility and sales. As the market share of the national chains grows and the number of independent bookstores declines, the centralized buyers become increasingly important

---

[15] See Epstein, *Book Business*, pp. 104 ff., 156 ff.; Whiteside, *The Blockbuster Complex*, pp. 45–8.

gatekeepers in controlling the channels to market and determining the visibility and sales of books.

The increasing power of the chains is also reflected in the problem of returns, which has become a growing source of tension between publishers and retailers. A central buyer can transform the prospects of a book by deciding to stock it nationwide, but if the stock doesn't sell through it is likely to be returned in substantial numbers, leaving the publisher with large quantities of unsold stock. Moreover, given the share of the market commanded by the chains, a high-level decision to reduce the depth of the stockholding and to return slow-moving stock can result in massive returns. During the expansion of the superstore chains in the 1990s, this was not a major problem, as the chains were eager to have books to fill the shelves and they prided themselves on the depth of their collections. But as the programmes of expansion began to slow down at the end of the decade and the cost of the real estate began to hit home, the chains began to reassess their policies and practices on the depth of their stockholdings and on slow-moving stock. A shakeout was bound to occur and in 2000–1 returns began to soar. The university presses experienced this with particular force, since many of their titles were slow-moving stock that had been to some extent 'protected' (as one buyer confided), in the sense that a book was allowed to sit on the shelf for at least a year before a decision was taken on returns (and in the case of some university press paper-backs, it was allowed to sit there indefinitely). But by 2000–1 the circumstances had changed and the university presses, among others, experienced the consequences of policy changes in the big chains, as we shall see.

(3)   *The advent of online retailers*   Another factor that influenced the changing poli-cies of the chains in the late 1990s was that by this time another player had appeared on the scene and was beginning to take a significant share of the market: the online retailer. The key player here is Amazon, but numerous other 'e-tailers' have emerged since the mid-1990s. The brainchild of Jeff Bezos, a Princeton computer science graduate, Amazon.com opened for business from a suburban garage in Seattle in July 1995; by the end of 1998 it had become the third largest bookseller in the US, with annual sales of $610 million.[16] Amazon's sales grew at a phenomenal rate throughout the late 1990s, as is shown in table 3.13, but so too did its losses: by 1998, Amazon was reporting losses of $124.5 million, which was more than 20 per cent of its turnover. By 2000, Amazon's cumulative losses were a staggering $1.2 billion. Achieving profitability became an increasingly urgent corporate goal. At the end of 2002 Amazon reported its first annual operating profit of $64 million – a modest 1.6 per cent of overall

Table 3.13   Financial performance of Amazon.com, 1995–1998

	1995	1996	1997	1998
Turnover (US$m)	0.5	15.75	147.79	610.0
Net profit (loss) (US$m)	(0.3)	(6.25)	(31.0)	(124.5)
Loss as a % of sales	60.0	39.7	21.0	20.4

[16] Robert Spector, *Amazon.com: Get Big Fast* (London: Random House, 2000), p. 216.

sales – although it was still reporting a net annual loss of $149 million. In 2003 Amazon's operating profit rose to $270 million, which was around 5 per cent of overall sales of $5.2 billion, and the company reported its first net annual profit of $35 million.

In the late 1990s, Amazon internationalized and diversified its business activities. A significant proportion of Amazon's client base had always been overseas, but in 1998 Amazon moved directly into the European market by acquiring the British online bookseller Bookpages and the German online bookseller Telebuch and using them to launch Amazon.co.uk and Amazon.de. Other international branches were subsequently opened in Japan, France and Canada. Amazon also began to diversify beyond its core business of books, in part by acquiring other online retailers and adding them to what was rapidly becoming a vast online shopping centre. In 1998 it added music CDs and videos, in early 1999 it moved into toys and electronics, and in September 1999 it launched zShops, an online shopping zone offering a wide range of goods from clothes and household appliances to pet supplies.

Spurred on by the phenomenal growth of Amazon in the 1990s, others began to enter the online bookselling market. Barnes & Noble had watched the rise of Amazon with growing concern, and in March 1997 it opened its own online bookstore, b&n.com. In 1998 Bertelsmann, which had already been planning to launch its own internet business, BooksOnline, acquired a 50 per cent stake in b&n.com for $200 million and rolled its proposed US operation into it. By 1999, b&n.com was posting sales of $202 million, making it the fifth largest bookselling establishment in the US. Although b&n.com is separate from Barnes & Noble and has a different corporate structure, the two companies work together closely and collaborate on the purchasing and managing of inventory, among other things. This gives b&n.com a certain competitive advantage vis-à-vis Amazon, its main rival, since it enables b&n.com to draw on a more extensive range of in-house inventory. (B&n.com currently claims to offer more than 30 million titles on its site, including out-of-print, rare and used books, and it probably carries around 850,000 titles in stock. Amazon claims to offer around 25 million titles but it probably carries fewer than 200,000 in stock – although the precise stock-holding figure is a closely guarded secret.) The Borders group also launched its own online operation in 1997, but Borders.com trailed far behind Amazon and b&n.com, achieving sales of only $27 million in 2000. In 2001 Borders announced that it was handing its loss-making online operation over to Amazon, which became responsible for running the operation, fulfilling orders and providing customer service.

The great advantage of the online retailers is that they are able to offer a huge range of titles – many times more than the bricks-and-mortar bookstore. When Amazon.com started business, they claimed to offer over a million titles – 'Earth's Biggest Bookstore' was the tagline – compared with about 175,000 titles in the largest terrestrial bookstore in the US. But, of course, the comparison was not entirely fair, since Amazon's listings were derived from the database of *Books in Print* and the books were not actually held as inventory. Amazon relied heavily on the major wholesalers, Ingrams and Baker & Taylor, to supply the inventory: when Amazon received an order from a customer, it ordered the book from one of the wholesalers, unpacked it when it arrived in its Seattle distribution centre, repacked it and mailed it to the customer. This model had the huge advantage of being inventory-free, but the disadvantage was that it was relatively slow since books had to be ordered and mailed twice. So in 1996 Amazon began to expand its warehouse capacity and to build regional distribution centres so that it could fulfil orders more quickly and reduce the costs involved in double-handling the books. But the more Amazon moved in the direction of warehousing its own inventory, the more capital it tied up in physical stock and in real estate, and the more it began to look like a traditional retailer and to experience the financial pressures and problems associated with conventional bricks-and-mortar operations.

The online retailers competed with one another and with terrestrial bookstores not only in terms of the range of titles offered and those held in stock, but also by deep discounting. Amazon was preoccupied with 'the customer experience', and its research had led it to conclude that the three things that mattered most to book-buying customers were selection, convenience and price. By offering over a million titles it could excel on selection; by being open 24/7 and aiming to ship books directly to the customer as quickly as possible, it could score high on convenience; and by discounting a substantial proportion of its titles it could compete against the superstores on price. Amazon offered a discount of 10 per cent on 300,000 titles, a discount of 30 per cent on the top twenty hardback and top twenty paperback titles, and a discount of 40 per cent on a select number of titles. When b&n.com went live in 1997, it offered discounts on 400,000 titles, including discounts of up to 50 per cent on some bestsellers. To some extent, the online retailers could offer deep discounts of this kind because their overheads were lower than those of bricks-and-mortar bookstores, but they continued to offer substantial discounts despite the fact that they were running losses year on year because they regarded this as crucial to their ability to compete with the superstores. Both Amazon and b&n.com also introduced free shipping on orders over a certain amount to ensure that the total price of purchases remained low.

For publishers, the meteoric rise of Amazon and other online retailers was a very welcome addition to the existing channels to market. At a time when terrestrial retailing was being consolidated increasingly in the hands of the large retail chains and many independents were falling by the wayside, the emergence of online retailing represented a major reconfiguration of the bookselling business. It proved to be particularly good for selling older backlist titles and books of a more specialized kind which were seldom stocked by the bricks-and-mortar bookstores. The university presses and many smaller publishers found that Amazon would quickly become one of their most important accounts. But just as online retailing would prove to be good for selling older backlist titles, so too it would prove to be an ideal medium for selling used books, since the prices of new and used books could be easily compared online. As Amazon and b&n.com began to list used books on their sites and a variety of more specialized used book vendors began to appear online, the used book business, which had long been a thorn in the side of college textbook publishers, would experience rapid growth and would become a source of increasing concern to publishers in other sectors of the industry, including the mainsteam trade houses.

By 2002, online bookselling accounted for about 8 per cent of the adult trade market in the US and it appears to have stabilized at around that level.[17] Amazon.com was the clear leader in online bookselling, with sales in its books/music/video division of $1.87 billion in 2002 and a net income of $211 million. B&n.com remains Amazon's main online competitor in the US, with sales in 2002 of $423 million and a net loss of $74

---

[17] Subtext, *Perspective on Book Publishing*, p. 70.

million. In the UK, online bookselling has increased rapidly since 1999, though there is some evidence that this is now flattening out at around 5 per cent of the retail market.[18] The market share of online retailers has not grown as quickly as some of the early forecasters predicted and they have yet to demonstrate stable long-term profitability (although Amazon's financial performance in 2002 and 2003 represented a significant turnaround). But the dramatic rise of online bookselling in the late 1990s has demonstrated beyond any doubt that the internet is an attractive medium for consumers to use in searching for and purchasing books. It has introduced a significant new ingredient into the book retailing mix and has provided publishers with an important new channel to market, one which has had a particularly beneficial effect on backlist sales and on the sales of more specialized books.

The globalization of markets and publishing firms

The emergence of online retailing has accentuated another set of developments that were already underway by the early 1990s – namely, the globalization of the markets for books and the growing tendency for publishers to operate on an international scale. I noted in the previous chapter that publishing fields tended to develop within certain linguistically homogeneous regions, and that the formation of linguistically homogeneous and geographically extended publishing fields was profoundly shaped by the legacy of colonialism. The dominance of the British Empire in the nineteenth and early twentieth centuries and the rise of the United States as the major global power in the twentieth century have helped to ensure the global pre-eminence of the English language, and hence have helped to extend the boundaries of the publishing field in English so that it became increasingly global in scope. However, for much of the twentieth century, the field of English-language publishing was divided into territorially discrete markets, so that books could be sold by publishers and other parties within exclusive domains of operation. The international trade in books was based on a system of territorial rights that carved the world up into different regions and granted publishers exclusive rights to distribute and sell works within each territory.

In the aftermath of the Second World War, this system of territorial rights was given a settled institutional form in the British Commonwealth Market Agreement. In 1947 British publishers agreed among themselves that when they sold US rights to an American publisher, they would retain the exclusive right to distribute and sell the book throughout the British Commonwealth. Similarly, when they acquired rights from an American publisher, they would do so for the whole of the Commonwealth and not just for the UK. This agreement protected the export market of British publishers by preventing US editions from seeping into it. However, the agreement faced various legal and political challenges from the 1960s on, as a number of countries sought to distance themselves from blanket arrangements of this kind. By the late 1960s India had unofficially become an open market, and booksellers in Australia, New Zealand and elsewhere expressed growing unease about being tied to British rather than American editions, especially when the American editions were cheaper (as, from the 1970s on, they often were). The agreement was dealt a final blow in 1976 when the US Depart-

[18] Joel Rickett, 'Internet Sales Flatten Out', *The Bookseller*, 11 May 2001.

ment of Justice indicated that it believed it to be illegal under anti-trust law; faced with the potentially high costs of defending the agreement, UK publishers agreed to revoke it. The collapse of the agreement brought an end to the protection of exclusive British rights in the Commonwealth: it was now possible for US editions to enter Australia and other Commonwealth territories that were formerly the exclusive domain of British publishers. The carving up of the world into exclusive spheres of operation was becoming increasingly difficult to sustain. British and American publishers could continue to acquire exclusive rights for the publication, distribution and sale of particular titles in their own markets, but they could no longer take it for granted that the rest of the English-speaking world could be carved up between them into exclusive spheres of operation, nor could they presume any longer that publishers from across the Atlantic would restrict their activities to their traditional territorial domains.

The challenges to the system of territorial rights were also economic and technological. As publishing firms expanded through mergers, acquisitions and organic growth in the latter half of the twentieth century, many became increasingly international in both composition and orientation. Many British and European-based publishing firms sought to expand their presence in the US, which was the largest and most mature market for English-language books, and some of the larger US-based publishers also sought to increase their sales in overseas markets. The more that publishing organizations sought to expand their sphere of operations internationally, and especially to cross the US–UK territorial divide, the more eager they would be to secure and retain world rights for the content they published. This would enable them to exploit the content in different markets and even, for the largest corporations, in different languages. It would also enable them to build a global brand by publishing their valued authors and books throughout the world. Of course, they would in some cases face resistance from authors and their agents (or, in the case of translations, from foreign publishers and rights managers), since authors and agents often have a financial interest in segmenting the English-language market and selling rights to two or more publishers. But the international expansion of publishing firms, and the rise of multinational media conglomerates into which many publishing firms have been integrated, have inclined many publishing firms to press for global rights deals and have tended to erode the traditional system of territorial rights.

The other significant source of pressure on the system of territorial rights has been the rise of the internet. The system of territorial rights is based on the idea that publishers can be assigned exclusive spheres of operation within clearly defined boundaries. The boundaries were never impermeable; there has always been some degree of 'leakage', as intermediaries of various kinds move books (often illicitly) from one territory to another and as buyers (individuals as well as institutions) search for the cheapest editions. But with the rise of the internet and the emergence of online retailers like Amazon, territorial boundaries have become more porous than ever before. An individual anywhere in the world can now go to a site like Amazon.com and check the availability and the price of virtually any book in print. If the book is available in more than one edition, the prices of the different editions can be compared with relative ease – indeed, they are often listed on the same site.

Hence, thanks to the rise of online booksellers, publishers now find themselves operating in a world of *globalized metadata* where their prices can be inspected and compared by consumers and others irrespective of where they happen to be located. This in turn has had two tangible consequences for the practices of publishing firms. First, for publishers who operate in different territorial regions, the creation of globalized metadata has tended to undermine the traditional practice of pricing to market (i.e. tailoring prices to particular markets) which was common in the book trade, and has induced some publishers to adopt a system of world pricing (standard prices translated into different currencies throughout the world). The extent to which publishers have moved to world pricing tends to vary from one field of publishing to another – it is more common today in scholarly monograph publishing, for example, than it is in the field of higher education publishing, where significant price discrepancies remain (we shall return to this later). But the existence of globalized metadata and the relative ease with which buyers (both individual and institutional) can check prices have undoubtedly made it more difficult to maintain substantial price differentials in different markets.

Second, the creation of globalized metadata has also placed further pressure on the system of territorial rights. In practice, an individual in the UK can order a US edition of a book from Amazon.com even though a British publisher may have exclusive rights to distribute and sell the book in the UK market (and vice versa). The individual is unlikely to know anything about the territorial rights and is unlikely to care; what matters to the individual is that he or she is able to get the book easily, quickly and at the cheapest price. Existing copyright law does not provide a clear way of dealing with this situation. UK copyright law prevents UK booksellers from selling imported copies which infringe territorial rights, whether these copies are sold over the counter or over the internet, but an individual visiting another country can buy a copy of a local edition there and bring it back to the UK for private use. Similarly, an internet bookseller operating outside the UK could claim that its sales to individual customers were made outside the UK. When an individual in London buys a copy of a book from Amazon.com, is the transaction taking place in London or in Seattle? When an individual in New York buys a copy of a book from Amazon.co.uk, is the transaction taking place in New York or in Slough? Jeff Bezos has no qualms: an American buying a book on Amazon.co.uk is, in his view, 'no different than if you go to London on a vacation and pick up a book and take it home in your suitcase'.[19] The views of Bezos and others have yet to be tested in the courts and, in the meantime, the online retailers continue to fulfil orders regardless of where the orders come from. Moreover, while an online bookseller based in the UK may technically be in breach of copyright law if it sells an edition which should not be available in the UK, in practice it is very easy for information on such editions to find its way into the metadata systems. The more automated the metadata systems become, the easier it is for information to flow between the systems and the harder it is to prevent metadata from cropping up in a system where, from a purely legal point of view, it shouldn't be. The appearance of the metadata on a US edition in the system of a UK-based online retail organization (or vice versa) may have nothing to do with illicit intent but may simply be the outcome of automated bibliographical feeds which are not being properly monitored. Globalized metadata do not always convey accurate information on territorial rights and, given that the people running these systems have many other pressing things to do, no one is bothering to check.

---

[19] Jeff Bezos, quoted in Spector, *Amazon.com*, pp. 189–90.

While the emergence of online retailers and the creation of globalized metadata have undoubtedly placed pressure on the traditional system of territorial rights, they have by no means destroyed the system. There were some commentators in the 1990s who predicted that the rise of the internet would be the death-knell of territorial rights, but their predictions were premature and probably overstated. There are parties (especially authors, agents and rights managers) who have strong interests in segmenting markets and selling territorial rights for specific titles, and these interests will continue to shape publishing practices for some time to come. Moreover, despite the growth of online booksellers, sales through online retail organizations remain a relatively small proportion of overall book sales, and hence many publishers are still willing to acquire territorially delimited rights for certain kinds of books – especially those which are likely to have significant trade potential in their exclusive markets. The postage costs involved in sending books overseas are relatively high and may cancel out any gains that could be made from marginally lower prices. At least in trade publishing, the system of territorial rights is likely to continue for the foreseeable future, even if territorial boundaries have been rendered much more porous by the rise of the internet.

The impact of new technologies

The rise of the internet is only one aspect of the digital revolution, a technological transformation which has had, and continues to have, a profound impact on the publishing industry. Since the early 1980s, the publishing industry has been in a state of continuous debate about the impact of new technologies on its working practices, management systems and supply chains. Every sector of the industry has been affected in some way by digitization and computerization, from the introduction of electronic point of sale (EPOS) facilities and the use of electronic ordering services in bookstores, which have revolutionized stock control and supply chain management, to the computerization of typesetting and text design, which have brought down costs dramatically and transformed the process of book production. The rise of online retailers like Amazon, and the much publicized debates about ebooks, are only the more visible manifestations of a revolution which has affected the publishing industry at every level of the value chain.

In part IV we shall examine in detail the impact of the digital revolution in the fields of academic and higher education publishing. But before we do this, we must focus our attention more sharply on the fields of academic and higher education publishing and see if we can determine their distinctive characteristics and dynamics.

Part II
The Field of Academic Publishing

4

Academic publishing under pressure

At the beginning of the twenty-first century, academic publishing is going through difficult times. Many of the university presses are experiencing the most difficult conditions they have known for several decades, and the commercial publishers who are still active in this field are struggling to find ways to continue publishing scholarly work. To say that academic publishing today is in crisis may be overstating the case, but there can be no doubt that it is under serious pressure. Why? What are the sources of the pressure that is bearing down on academic publishers today? How has academic publishing changed over the last few decades, and why has this made life so difficult for the university presses and others who are active in this field? What are the implications of these changes for the future of academic publishing and for the intellectual disciplines which are served by it?

In this and the following chapters I shall try to answer at least some of these questions. I shall try to show that we can understand the difficulties faced by academic publishers today only by reconstructing the nature and evolution of the field of which they are part, for their current difficulties are the outcome of a process of change which has characterized the field as a whole. I shall begin by examining the nature of the field of academic publishing and situating this field in relation to what I shall call 'the research process'. I shall then look back over the last couple of decades and analyse the principal forces and pressures that have shaped the evolution of the field. Against the backcloth of this analysis, the subsequent chapters will examine the ways in which academic publishers have tried to cope with the changes.

The field of academic publishing

Academic publishing and the research process

The field of academic or scholarly publishing[1] is defined by the distinctive relation between publishing organizations, on the one hand, and the institutions and activities of scholarly and scientific research, on the other. Academic publishing is an integral part of a broader research process, the key components of which are highlighted by figure 4.1. Individual researchers as well as research groups or teams engage in what we could

[1] I shall generally use the term 'academic publishing' rather than 'scholarly publishing' to refer to this field, although I use these terms interchangeably. The term 'academic publishing' is sometimes used more loosely to refer to any kind of publishing that has an academic content, ranging from scholarly monographs to textbooks, but this is not a usage I shall follow here.

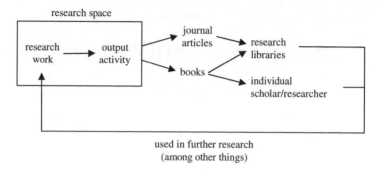

Figure 4.1 The research process

generically describe as research work. The exact nature of this research work varies a great deal from one research field to another – the work of a research group in the sciences is very different from the work of a historian, a philosopher or a literary critic, for example. But all research takes place in a context which is shaped in part by previous research and reflection, and it is an accepted part of scientific and scholarly practice that researchers should take account of the results of previous research as expressed in outputs of various kinds. Researchers and scholars are themselves generally subjected to certain pressures to produce outputs from their own research. These pressures range from contractual obligations to grant-giving bodies to the pressures associated with tenure and career advancement. In Britain an additional and very powerful set of output pressures has been created by the Research Assessment Exercise – we shall have more to say about this later.

Taken together, research work and output activity comprise what we could describe as the 'research space'. The research space is generally situated within an institutional setting – a college or university, a state-funded research organization, a think-tank, a non-governmental organization (NGO), or, in the case of some research fields such as pharmaceuticals, biotechnology and IT, a private corporation. For most individuals employed by colleges or universities, this research space is constantly being squeezed by demands stemming from other sources – demands from their faculties for teaching and administrative outputs and demands from students for time and attention, as well as demands stemming from other organizational and personal commitments. Juggling these various demands and trying to prevent the research space from being shrunk or even closed down are a continuous struggle for most academics.

It is important to see that the production of research outputs fulfils two distinct but equally important functions – *dissemination* and *certification*. The function of dissemination involves more than simply making the results of research available: it also involves making them available in ways and in contexts that will be noticed and taken into account by others. Hence publication in a journal that is widely distributed, or in a book that is extensively and effectively marketed, is quite different from making the results available in a format that will be noticed only by a few specialists. The function of certification (or 'consecration', to use Bourdieu's term) is equally important: the organization that makes the results available also bestows a degree of legitimacy or symbolic value on the output, and thereby gives the output a standing which it would not have if it were simply made available by the researcher as an unpublished paper. To some extent, the legitimacy bestowed by the publishing organization is a reflection of the mechanisms of selection and approval used by it, and especially the mechanism of peer review. Subjecting the output to a rigorous process of selection tends to ensure that the content meets certain quality thresholds (although quality may not be the only factor which enters into the selection process, as we shall see). But the legitimacy bestowed by the journal or publishing organization is also a reflection of the accumulated prestige or symbolic capital of the journal or organization itself, which is transferred to the material published under its name. For scholars and researchers who wish to publish their work, the legitimacy bestowed by the journal or publishing organization becomes a form of symbolic capital – a credit or credential – which they can use for their own purposes. They can add it to their CV and use it for the advancement of their own career, whether they are applying for research grants, seeking promotion or pursuing some other career-enhancing goal. Indeed, the kind of recognition they gain for their work, both in terms of the legitimacy bestowed by the journal or publisher and in terms of other forms of peer recognition such as reviews and prizes, is for many scholars and researchers the most important benefit of publication, far outweighing any direct financial return. The imprimatur of the journal or publisher has benefits for end users too, for it operates as a filter to guide their own research and scholarly activities. It saves them time and effort, since they know that the material published by this journal or organization has passed through a selection process which provides some guarantees about its quality and authenticity. The publication of research is never just a matter of disseminating results: it is an intrinsic part of a cultural economy of research, a complex system of symbolic and economic rewards which shapes the life chances of the individuals who wish to pursue their careers in the world of the academy and of scientific and scholarly research.

While most scholars and researchers experience pressures (and in many cases, intensifying pressures) to produce research outputs, the specific forms in which these outputs are produced varies a great deal from one research field to another. In the natural sciences and in certain social sciences (such as economics), the publication of articles in peer-reviewed journals is the accepted and valued form of research output. The articles are often jointly authored, reflecting the collaborative nature of much research work in these disciplines. The *output sanctions* in these disciplines ensure that the article in a peer-reviewed journal is the form in which researchers are *expected* to make their results available and are *recognized* and *rewarded* for doing so (in the form of symbolic credits which they can accumulate on their CV and use to advance their careers). And the higher the status of the journal within the discipline or research field, the greater the credit which accrues to the researcher who publishes in it. In the humanities, in some of the so-called 'softer' social sciences like sociology, anthropology and politics and in interdisciplinary fields like gender studies, regional studies and media and cultural studies, research outputs tend to assume more varied forms. Articles in peer-reviewed journals are important in these disciplines too, but scholars and researchers in these disciplines also commonly publish the results of their research in the form of books which range from high-level scholarly monographs and collections of articles on specialized topics to books written for a broader readership. The output sanctions in the humanities and social sciences are less uniformly focused on the peer-reviewed journal: this is an important and highly valued output form but it is not the only form, and books also have an important and valued role to play.

The forms of research output are not static, and in recent decades there have been significant shifts in the nature of these forms and the relative symbolic credit associated with them. The peer-reviewed journal has become increasingly important in many disciplines and fields of research beyond the natural sciences. Moreover, since the early 1990s, many journals have been made available in electronic as well as print formats. Most journals continue to be distributed in both formats, partly because the main customers for scientific and scholarly periodicals – the research libraries – prefer to have both formats and have yet to be convinced that electronic-only access would provide a secure and long-term solution to the archiving problem. While publication of articles in peer-reviewed journals is important (and increasingly so) in the humanities and social sciences, the output sanctions in many of these disciplines continue to value books as a medium of research output and in some circumstances place a high premium on books – for example, with regard to tenure decisions at American universities, an issue to which we shall return. However, as we shall see in this and the following chapters, the organizations that help to make these outputs available are also changing in fundamental ways, and these changes are creating new tensions (and exacerbating old ones) in the relationship between the world of scholarship and research, on the one hand, and the world of scholarly publishing, on the other. The so-called 'crisis of the monograph' is rooted in a disjunction – which is growing more and more pronounced – between the output sanctions of the disciplines and the market demand for scholarly monographs.

So what are the organizations that help to make research outputs available? A variety of organizations are relevant here, but there are two key sets of organizations which are particularly important – the scientific and scholarly journal business, and the scholarly or academic book business. I shall be focusing here on the latter. A comprehensive analysis of the cultural economy of research would also have to take account of the changing nature of the scholarly journal business and of the changing relations between books and journals (for, as we shall see, the fate of these two publishing fields is closely intertwined). But the field of scientific and scholarly journal publishing is a complex one in its own right, with its own characteristics and dynamics and its own players (some of whom, but by no means all, overlap with the key players in academic book publishing), and while I shall have something to say about journal publishing in this and subsequent chapters, a detailed analysis of the evolution of this field would be beyond the scope of this study.

One of the principal outputs of the scholarly or academic book business is the scholarly monograph – the monograph is the principal form of content circulation in the field of academic book publishing. But what exactly is a monograph? Can it be defined? Most people working in the business of academic publishing acknowledge that this is a very slippery notion. One publisher's monograph is – with a different title and a four-colour jacket – another publisher's academic-trade title. So can we give an effective definition of a monograph? In strict etymological terms, a monograph is 'a separate treatise on a single object or class of objects'.[2] However, this definition does not pin down clearly enough the way that the notion of the scholarly monograph is used in the world of publishing. To do this, we must take account of the way the book is written and the principal audience for whom it is intended. Bearing this in mind, we could define a scholarly monograph as *a work of scholarship on a particular topic or theme which is written by*

---

[2] *The Shorter Oxford English Dictionary*, vol. 2 (Oxford: Oxford University Press, 1973), p. 1349.

a scholar (or scholars) and intended for use primarily by other scholars. The scholarly monograph is a focused work of scholarship pitched at a relatively high level of intellectual sophistication. It takes a good deal for granted on the part of the reader; it assumes that the reader is knowledgeable about the subject matter and has a professional interest in it. It is not a book written for the general reader with no background in the field. Of course, it is not always easy to draw a clear line between a scholarly monograph understood in this way, on the one hand, and a trade or 'academic-trade' title, on the other, and those involved in the scholarly publishing business are constantly crossing and blurring this boundary in various ways, as we shall see.

The scholarly monograph supply chain

The supply chain in the field of academic publishing has its own structures and characteristics which distinguish it from the supply chains that exist in other fields of publishing. Academic publishers are the principal suppliers and risk-takers in the scholarly monograph supply chain, and research libraries together with scholars and researchers are the principal market. Figure 4.2 provides a schematic representation of this supply chain. The publisher acquires content from scholars or researchers who are writing either on their own as the sole author of a text or in collaboration with others. Once the publisher has gone through the process of developing the content and producing the book (see figures 1.1 and 1.2 in chapter 1) and has received stock in its warehouse, it supplies copies to booksellers and wholesalers. The library wholesalers (or 'jobbers') play a particularly important role in the scholarly monograph supply chain. Research libraries are a key market for scholarly monographs, but for the most part libraries purchase books from booksellers and library jobbers rather than directly from the publishers. Most research libraries have what are called 'approval plans' with a wholesaler like Baker & Taylor, Yankee Book Peddler (now owned by Baker & Taylor) or Blackwell's Book Services. The approval plan operates in effect like a standing order. The library completes a detailed profile of the books that it would like to receive depending on the kind of collection it wishes to build, and the wholesaler then sends to the library all new books which match the profile. The library is generally given the option of accepting the book or returning it within a certain time period. The wholesaler might also perform other functions for the library – for example, it can catalogue the book so that it is shelf-ready when it arrives. For the library, the use of an approval plan saves a great deal of time and effort. There is no need for the acquisitions staff in the library

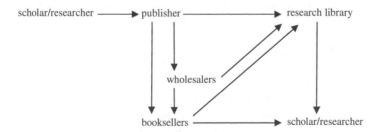

Figure 4.2   The scholarly monograph supply chain

to spend time trawling through the catalogues of the main scholarly publishers and deciding which books to order on a title-by-title basis. The acquisitions staff can concentrate their efforts on building specialist collections where the library has real strengths and can spend time searching for the books and 'grey literature' which are more difficult to obtain, leaving the more routine acquisitions activity to the library jobbers.

The research libraries are the main customers for scholarly monographs, which may then be used, borrowed, consulted and/or read by scholars, researchers, students and others. Some individuals will also buy monographs for their own personal use, but the extent to which this occurs depends on the subject area, the price and whether the book is available only in a cloth edition or in paperback as well. The traditional practice of academic publishers in the English-speaking world was to publish scholarly monographs in hardback only in the first instance, with a view to achieving sales to research libraries and to some individuals who have a specialist interest in the topic. If the book was well received by the academic community, the publisher might decide to bring out a new paperback edition at a lower price about eighteen months after the original cloth edition, in the hope of achieving more individual sales and perhaps some course adoptions. In recent years, however, many publishers have experimented with alternatives to this traditional practice in an attempt to cope with declining sales of hardback editions (with mixed results, as we shall see).

The extent to which individuals are willing to buy relatively expensive hardback books tends to vary from one discipline to another. There are some subjects, such as classics, where there is a culture of book buying among individual scholars, who are inclined to build their own personal collections. Hence scholarly monographs published in this field tend to achieve significant sales to individual scholars even when they are published in hardback only and at relatively high prices. On the other hand, there are subjects like literary criticism, some fields of history, anthropology and interdisciplinary fields like gender studies and cultural studies where the market among individual scholars for books published in hardback only and at relatively high prices is much weaker. Hence it is in these fields above all that publishers have tended to experiment with alternatives to the traditional practice of scholarly monograph publication.

The structure of the field

The field of academic publishing in the English-speaking world is occupied by a multitude of publishing organizations which differ from one another in many ways. We can begin to analyse the structure of this field by distinguishing four axes or criteria which are of particular significance for the ways in which these organizations operate and for the ways in which other individuals and organizations relate to them. The four axes are (1) ownership status, (2) economic capital, (3) symbolic capital, and (4) geographical reach. I shall discuss each of these dimensions, but before I do so I want to add one caveat. The structure of a publishing field is not static – on the contrary, it is constantly changing as particular organizations change, some growing and expanding while others decline, and as new players enter the field and others exit from it. In this section I shall offer a very brief sketch of the field of academic publishing in English today – a rough snapshot, as it were, taken at a particular point in time. Later in this chapter and in subsequent chapters, I shall then look back over the last few decades and examine some of the changes that have taken place in this field, as well as the impact these changes have had on the activities and practices of the organizations within it.

I shall begin with ownership status because this criterion plays a particularly important role in the field of academic publishing in the English-speaking world, where we must distinguish between the university presses and commercial publishing firms. University presses are not unique to the English-speaking world, but there are many more university presses operating in English than there are in other linguistic regions of the world. As part of their constitutional remit, university presses are committed to publishing scholarly works. For the most part these presses are registered as charities or not-for-profits, and hence are not liable (in all or nearly all of their territories of operation) to pay corporation tax. In some cases these presses are constituted as departments within their host universities; in other cases they are established as administrative units within the universities and report to a particular officer (some American university presses report to the president of the university, while others report to the head librarian). All university presses have one or more committees – such as the Board of Syndics at Cambridge and the Board of Delegates at Oxford – in which members of the host university oversee the activities, both editorial and financial, of the press.

Apart from the university presses, there is a range of commercial firms which are active in the field of academic publishing. Unlike the university presses, commercial firms operating in the field of academic publishing do not have any special remit to publish scholarly works, nor do they have any special tax status. Their activities in the field of academic publishing are subject to the commercial constraints of the organization and the financial objectives set by its management (or by the management of the controlling corporation). In most cases these commercial firms are active in fields other than academic publishing – most commonly, the fields of higher education publishing, journal publishing, reference publishing and, in some cases, trade publishing and professional publishing. Their commitment to the field of academic publishing is contingent and historical rather than constitutional (as it is with the university presses), and if the conditions of academic publishing deteriorate, it cannot be taken for granted that the commercial firms will maintain the same level of activity within the field as they have done in the past.

In both the university press sector and the commercial sector, firms vary greatly in terms of the accumulated reserves of economic and symbolic capital and in terms of their geographical reach. While all university presses share certain broad structural features in common, this sector is enormously varied and the differences between organizations within it are considerable. The two major British-based university presses, Oxford University Press (OUP) and Cambridge University Press (CUP), are in a league of their own. Let me highlight four ways in which they differ from the American university presses. In the first place, Oxford and Cambridge are much larger than any other university press. OUP is roughly thirteen times the size of the largest of the American university presses, and CUP is more than four times the size of its nearest American rival. OUP's turnover in the year ended 31 March 2001 was £366 million ($585 million), generating a net surplus of £44 million ($70 million), and CUP's turnover in the year ended 31 December 2000 was £121 million (($194 million), with a trading surplus of £4.5 million ($7.2 million). By contrast, the largest of the American university presses had a turnover of less than $40 million (£25 million) in the same period. There are around a hundred American univer-

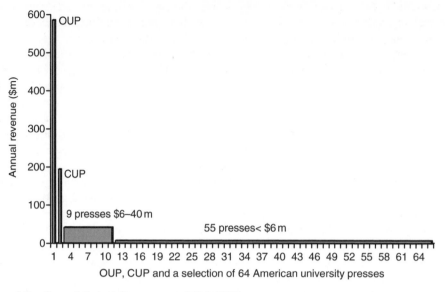

Figure 4.3 Size of university presses, 2000–2001

sity presses (in 2001 there were 121 scholarly presses affiliated to the Association of American University Presses (AAUP), but these include a number of foundations and scholarly society publishers as well as several overseas university presses). A small handful of the American university presses have annual sales of between $20 million and $40 million, but the vast majority of the American university presses had turnovers of less than $20 million in 2001 (and in most cases, much less than this). If we were to look at OUP and CUP alongside a selection of sixty-four of the American university presses and categorize them according to annual turnover, we would find that OUP is far ahead of all others, CUP is second and is also well ahead of the American university presses, nine of the American university presses fall into a band of between $6 million and $40 million, and the remaining fifty-five presses fall into a band of less than $6 million. Figure 4.3 provides a rough illustration of these differences in size.

Apart from the differences in size, the university presses also vary greatly in terms of their financial arrangements. Many of the American university presses have traditionally received financial assistance from their host institutions in various forms, ranging from annual operating grants to cover deficits to rent-free accommodation, free employee benefits and interest-free overdraft facilities. A few of the larger of the American university presses – notably Harvard and Princeton – have also had special endowments they could draw on to support their scholarly publishing activities. However, not all American university presses receive direct financial assistance from their host institutions.[3] Some are expected to break even, and in recent decades many

[3] Of the sixty-four university presses who responded to an AAUP inquiry in 2001, forty-two (or two-thirds) received annual operating grants, but half of these were small presses with sales of under $3 million. Of the nine presses with sales over $6 million, only one received an annual operating grant (although many of these received other, more indirect forms of assistance, such as free legal and audit services).

of the university presses have experienced growing pressure to reduce their dependence on their host institutions (a point to which we shall return). The position of OUP
and CUP is quite different. In recent years, both OUP and CUP have generated sufficient surpluses to transfer funds to their host institutions, although the amounts transferred by OUP have been considerably more than those transferred by CUP: in 2001
OUP transferred £11.7 million ($18.7 million) to the university, and in the five years
from 1998 to 2003, OUP transferred a total of £202 million ($323 million); in 2000 CUP
transferred £2.2 million ($3.5 million) to its host institution.

A third major difference is that OUP and CUP are much more diversified than any
of the other university presses and they operate in many more publishing fields. Both
OUP and CUP have substantial programmes in the field of academic publishing and
they publish large numbers of scholarly monographs across the whole range of academic
disciplines, but they also have strong programmes in other fields including journals,
reference publishing, trade publishing, professional publishing, college textbook publishing, schoolbook publishing and English Language Teaching publishing. The ELT
programmes at both OUP and CUP have been particularly successful and have served
in many ways as the engines of growth for both organizations in the period since 1980.
The academic publishing programmes at OUP and CUP are undoubtedly a core activity of these presses and they define to a large extent their profile as publishers, but in
terms of turnover they represent less than 40 per cent of the overall revenue (and, in
the case of OUP, less than 30 per cent).

The fourth major difference is that OUP and CUP have much greater geographical
reach than the other university presses. While both are based in the UK, they have a
major presence in the US and offices in a variety of countries throughout the world
including Canada, Australia, South Africa, India, Singapore, Spain and Brazil. Sales in
the UK represent a relatively small proportion of their overall sales (less than a quarter)
and, while the US is a major market for both OUP and CUP, both presses also generate strong sales in Europe and other parts of the world. By contrast, the American university presses operate overwhelmingly in the North American market. Several have
offices in the UK and many have distribution arrangements with UK-based organizations, but in nearly all cases the revenue generated from sales outside of North America
represents a small proportion of their total sales – generally in the region of 10–15 per
cent. (MIT Press is an exception and a higher proportion of its revenue – about 30 per
cent – is generated from sales outside the US, partly because of the nature of its list.)

The explanation of these differences in geographical reach is partly historical, partly
economic. Both OUP and CUP began expanding their activities outside the UK in the
late nineteenth and early twentieth centuries. Taking advantage of the trading networks
created by the British Empire, they made distribution arrangements in various overseas
territories to build on what was then a thriving business in bibles and schoolbooks
among other things. OUP opened a branch in New York in 1896; CUP set up a special
agency arrangement in the US with Macmillan in 1890, turning this into an independent branch of the press in 1948. By the 1960s, the US-based operations of both OUP
and CUP had taken on their own editorial staff who were actively engaged in commissioning books in the US. OUP and CUP also expanded their activities in Africa, Asia,
Spain and elsewhere in order to take advantage of a growing market in schoolbooks
(here the presses benefited from the operations of the Examination Boards controlled
by the University of Oxford and the University of Cambridge). These networks subse-

quently provided strong bases from which, from the early 1980s on, they could develop and expand their programmes in ELT. By contrast, the American university presses were always conceived of, and tended to conceive of themselves (with a few exceptions), much more as pure academic publishers whose primary purpose was to publish scholarly works. They had neither the diversified publishing base nor the resources to expand significantly in overseas markets.

While OUP and CUP differ in many important ways from other university presses, they also differ from one another in several significant respects. OUP is much larger than CUP – roughly three times the size in terms of turnover – and in recent years it has tended to produce much more substantial surpluses. OUP and CUP are also organized differently and have been structured by rather different managerial philosophies. CUP has a much more centralized administrative structure than OUP. For example, in the case of CUP all new book projects are submitted to the Board of Syndics in Cambridge, where the final decisions are taken, and this practice applies irrespective of whether the projects are generated by editors based in Cambridge, New York, Australia or elsewhere. In the case of OUP, by contrast, the local branches have a large degree of autonomy to make their own decisions about which new book projects to take on, and they simply submit a list of the projects to the Board of Delegates in Oxford. Whereas the senior management at CUP has tended to see the press as a single, integrated global organization with the centre located in Cambridge, the senior management at OUP has taken a more decentralized approach, giving the various branches and divisions more leeway and autonomy to develop their own initiatives and publishing programmes. OUP has also tended to adopt a more commercial approach, allowing its trade divisions to grow on both sides of the Atlantic, investing in schools publishing throughout the world and expanding its ELT programme more aggressively and more successfully than CUP. As a result, OUP has become a more diversified publishing organization with a stronger presence in different publishing fields, a fact that has enabled it to cope more effectively than CUP with the difficult economic conditions of recent years. So while OUP and CUP are quite different from the American university presses, they also differ from one another in ways that have become increasingly marked with time.

Just as one can differentiate between the university presses in terms of economic resources and geographical reach, so too one can draw some broad distinctions in terms of symbolic capital. This is by nature more complex and controversial. One cannot quantify symbolic capital in the same way that one can quantify economic capital, and judgements of symbolic value are always open to question; but equally one cannot deny that the university presses rank differently in the eyes of the academics and others who are potential authors and consumers, and differently in the eyes of the various agents who are part of the publishing field. The two largest university presses, Oxford and Cambridge, are undoubtedly among the most prestigious: these are organizations which possess large quantities of symbolic as well as economic capital. But the quantity of symbolic capital possessed by an academic publisher is not determined simply by the size or turnover of the press, for symbolic capital is generated and accumulated by processes that are not just economic in character. In the field of academic publishing, the most important source of symbolic capital is the perceived quality of the list in particular subject areas, as attested to by the perceived quality of the authors and the books. In this respect, symbolic capital is a resource that flows back and forth between the academic field and the field of academic publishing: a publisher can augment its symbolic capital by publishing authors who have gained a high reputation in the academic field and, at the same time, an author can increase his or her standing in the academic field by publishing with a press that has accumulated large quantities of symbolic capital. University presses also draw some symbolic capital from the prestige attached to their host institutions, although this is not the most important source. The university presses of Oxford, Cambridge, Harvard and Princeton – to name a few – undoubtedly benefit from the fact that their host institutions are widely regarded as outstanding universities, but the symbolic capital derived from this association would be squandered if the quality of the list were widely perceived to be poor.

The field of academic publishing is hierarchically structured in terms of the distribution of symbolic capital among university presses. Some presses, such as those just mentioned, have substantial stores of symbolic capital which they are able to use as a valuable resource in the struggle to sign outstanding authors and acquire new content. Others, such as the smaller presses located at less prestigious universities, are less well endowed with symbolic capital and will find themselves disadvantaged in the competitive marketplace for new content. As one university press director observed,

> the cachet of the university name is a very big factor in the pecking order, in the hierarchy of publishing. This doesn't mean that every elite university has a top-notch press, but it does mean Harvard, Princeton, Yale, Chicago carry a certain cachet which the University of Mississippi or the University of North Carolina never will. So that flows into acquisitions activities, all sorts of things. And depending on where you sit, that's an obstacle to be overcome or to be celebrated.

The presses at the less prestigious universities may find themselves at a double disadvantage: their stocks of both economic and symbolic capital may be a good deal less plentiful than those of their more well-endowed competitors. Editors at these presses are therefore obliged to adopt different strategies to acquire content and build a list. For example, they can form strong relationships with local authors based at their institution (or neighbouring institutions) and offer the kind of personal attention that an editor at a more prestigious but distant press may find difficult to match. Or they can build lists in specific fields where they can hope to gain a high reputation among specialists, even if they cannot reasonably expect to match the kind of generalized recognition accorded to the most prestigious presses.

The university presses are key players in the field of academic publishing but they are not the only players. The field also comprises a variety of commercial firms which are similarly differentiated in terms of their ownership structure, economic capital, symbolic capital and geographical reach. Some of these commercial firms, such as Blackwell and Sage, are private, largely family-owned businesses. Others are companies quoted on the stock market – Taylor & Francis, for example, went public in 1998 and bought Routledge (among other imprints) with the cash generated through flotation. Other commercial academic publishers are wholly or partly owned subsidiaries of larger corporations – for example, Penguin and Longman are among the numerous wholly owned subsidiaries of Pearson; Edward Arnold is a subsidiary of Hodder Headline, which was itself acquired by the retailer WHSmith in 1999; and the Macmillan Group, which includes the academic imprint now known as Palgrave Macmillan, is owned by the German-based publishing conglomerate Georg von Holtzbrinck, which acquired a

70 per cent stake in the company in 1995 and now controls the whole company. As in other fields of publishing, the commercial sector of academic publishing has been characterized by many mergers and acquisitions in recent decades. The ownership of many commercial houses has changed hands (in some cases, such as Routledge, more than once) and many formerly independent presses have become imprints within larger corporations.

Partly as a result of these mergers and acquisitions, there is a great deal of unevenness in the distribution of economic capital in the commercial sector of academic publishing. Some commercial publishers active in the field of academic publishing are parts of large conglomerates which have gross turnovers of several billion dollars, but gross figures of this kind tell one very little about the economic power of these organizations in the field of academic publishing, since the academic programmes of the subsidiaries represent a tiny fraction of these totals. It would make more sense to separate out the subsidiaries with academic programmes and treat them as separate players in the field. At the other extreme, there are a variety of small publishing organizations in academic publishing – some of them niche publishers specializing in particular disciplines or sub-disciplines – with annual sales under $5 million. Between the large corporations and the small niche publishers, there are a number of medium-sized publishers with varying ownership status, such as Blackwell, Palgrave Macmillan, Taylor & Francis and Sage, with annual sales ranging from $300 million down to $30 million. Most of these commercial firms are diversified in their publishing activities and are active in fields other than academic book publishing – many have strong journal programmes and are active in textbook publishing, reference publishing and professional publishing, among other things. As with the larger university presses, most of the revenue generated by many of these commercial firms stems from activities other than academic book publishing.

Commercial academic publishers also vary in terms of their geographical reach and in terms of their accumulated reserves of symbolic capital. Some UK-based commercial firms, like Blackwell and Taylor & Francis (and Routledge before it was acquired by Taylor & Francis), have invested heavily in developing a presence in the US, establishing offices there and hiring US-based commissioning editors. Other UK-based firms have tended to rely on a combination of copublishing and dedicated distribution arrangements with partners in the US as a means of reaching the US market. Some US-based commercial academic publishers, such as Sage, have established a strong presence in the UK, while others have remained largely focused on the North American market. Some of the commercial firms have built strong brands as scholarly publishers and have developed a high reputation for their publishing programmes in particular subject areas (e.g. Blackwell in philosophy, economics and linguistics, Palgrave Macmillan in politics and history, Routledge in literature and media and cultural studies, etc.). Unlike the university presses, the commercial academic publishers cannot draw on the symbolic capital of their host institutions, and hence they must rely, for the purposes of accumulating symbolic capital, on the quality of the list they have built up over time. And once again, while some commercial presses which have substantial quantities of economic capital may also be well endowed with symbolic capital, there is no necessary correlation between the two: small presses can succeed in establishing high reputations in particular fields.

Up until now I have been sketching the structure of the field of academic publishing in the English-speaking world as it exists today. This sketch is, of course, very rough and incomplete. There are around a hundred university presses in the English-speaking world and many commercial firms of various kinds which are active in the field of academic publishing – I have mentioned only a handful. But my concern at this stage is not to provide a comprehensive survey of the field nor to discuss particular firms in detail; rather, it is to outline the structure of the field and to define the key dimensions which determine how particular publishing organizations are positioned within it. Having outlined this structure, I now want to look back over the last few decades and examine how the field has changed. What are the most significant developments that have taken place in the field of academic publishing in recent years and how have these affected the ways that publishing firms operate? Is there any particular development that stands out as of fundamental importance for shaping what we could describe as the logic of the field?

The decline of the scholarly monograph

As it happens, there is one key development in the field of academic publishing over the last few decades that stands out above all others: the decline of the scholarly monograph. Ask any senior manager or director in the field of academic publishing what changes have affected them most in the last decade or two and, with very few exceptions, the decline in the sales of scholarly monographs will be high in their list. It is difficult to get reliable and genuinely comparable figures of actual sales which would back up this general observation, but it is reasonable to assume that the views of senior managers who have been involved in academic publishing throughout the 1970s, 1980s and 1990s are well grounded in a deep knowledge of the experiences of particular firms. Viewed from the perspective of the present, the 1970s seem like halcyon days to many who have lived through the difficult times that followed. In the 1970s academic publishers would commonly print between 2,000 and 3,000 hardback copies of a scholarly monograph. Of course, they may not have sold all of these copies (and in many cases they did not); print-runs were undoubtedly shaped by inflated sales expectations which were not being adjusted downwards quickly enough to take account of declining sales, thus leaving publishers with a growing problem of excess stock. Nevertheless, the market for scholarly monographs was sufficiently robust in the 1970s to make academic publishing a relatively straightforward matter. The principal task of many academic publishers at that time was one of selection: to decide which of the scholarly projects presented to them was of sufficiently high quality to merit publication. If ever there was a time when the editorial practices of academic publishers bore some resemblance to the gatekeeper model, then this was it. Once the decision to publish had been taken, it was generally assumed that the financial aspects could be worked out, in the knowledge that the print-runs could be set high enough to make most monographs financially viable. As one senior manager of a British-based academic publisher who was an editor in the 1970s recalls, 'publishing monographs then was easy compared to what it is now. It was really easy and one could print 2,500 expecting to sell them all.'

By the mid-1980s it was clear to many in the world of academic publishing that the market for scholarly monographs was changing, although at the time it was difficult to tell how fundamental the changes were and what their long-term consequences would be. The experience of most academic publishers on both sides of the Atlantic was that, in most subject areas, the unit sales of scholarly monographs published in hardback only were declining. The evidence was beginning to appear in the sales figures, though publishing organizations (and especially university presses) have a tendency to bury their heads in the sand when it comes to sales figures that don't live up to initial (and usually overoptimistic) expectations. As one senior manager recalled,

> It was very common to print 3,000 copies of a hardback monograph but they weren't being sold. I remember some absurd conversations with a colleague who didn't want to accept this fact, and I would thrust printouts in his face and he would say, 'it's sold more than you think.' So there were some pressures to overcome there. But significant numbers weren't being sold and I've got the records of some of those still.

The decline in the sales of scholarly monographs generated a great deal of internal discussion and forced many academic publishers to re-examine their practices; it also precipitated some fundamental transformations in terms of the strategies, orientations and organizational cultures of academic publishing firms. It fuelled debates about the so-called 'crisis of the monograph' which have continued in one form or another to the present day.

Although different academic publishers will report different experiences in terms of the decline in the unit sales of monographs published in hardback only, the overall picture at the beginning of the twenty-first century is very different from the 1970s. Today many academic publishers say that total sales of hardback-only monographs are often as low as 400–500 copies worldwide. They will often print more than this – it is still relatively common for academic publishers to set the initial print-run of a hardback monograph between 600 and 1,000, depending on the book and the subject area. But they know that in many cases they will find themselves with unsold stock in the warehouse, even if they can't be sure which books will sell out their print-run and which will not.

The decline in the sales of scholarly monographs has undoubtedly been one of the most significant trends with which academic publishers have had to deal over the last two decades – more than any other single factor, it has transformed the economic conditions of scholarly publishing. The unit sales of scholarly monographs have fallen to a quarter or less of what they were in the 1970s, and what was once a relatively straightforward and profitable type of publishing has become much more difficult in financial terms. Academic publishers have had to change and adapt in various ways – we shall examine these changes in the following chapters. But before we pursue these issues any further, it is important to stress that the pattern of decline is in fact more varied and complex than I have indicated so far. There is not a single, uniform pattern here but rather a complex array of patterns that vary from publisher to publisher and from one subject area to another.

The differentiated pattern of monograph sales

In order to explore these complexities further, let us consider in more detail the actual experience of two university presses. The first press – let us call it UP1 – has a large and varied list of scholarly publications. Each year it publishes a substantial number of new monographs in hardback only across the full range of academic subjects, from the humanities and social sciences to the natural sciences. Like other academic publishers, UP1 used to print between 2,000 and 3,000 hardback copies of each new monograph – this was its standard print-run for this kind of book in the 1970s. It may have been somewhat excessive; the sales of each title were not monitored carefully and stock management was rather lax, and there were undoubtedly cases where it had printed many more copies than it was able to sell. But broadly speaking, the sales of hardback monographs were sufficiently strong that the question of how many copies of an individual title it was likely to sell was not an issue of great concern.

Throughout the 1980s and 1990s, managers and editorial directors at UP1 became increasingly aware that they were over-printing their new monographs, and that actual sales were not living up to the expectations built into the print-run figures. It became increasingly clear that they were storing up serious stock management problems, as attested to by rising stock/sales ratios: for a substantial proportion of their scholarly monographs, they were holding far more stock than they were ever likely to sell. They adjusted the print-runs of new monographs downwards, but the adjustments always lagged behind the actual decline in sales. The lowering of print-runs meant that they had to control their costs and increase their prices in order to achieve adequate margins on their new monographs. But there was growing concern within the press about whether they would be able to meet even the reduced sales targets, and hence about whether they would be able to find any combination of price, print-run and cost that would enable them to publish monographs in a financially viable way.

In the late 1990s UP1 undertook a detailed review of the press's experience of monograph publishing. Among other things the press wanted to see how its new monographs were actually performing, and to see whether there were any significant variations across broad subject areas. It looked at the actual sales of hardback-only monographs to the end of July 1998 for all titles published in 1997. In UP1's experience, the typical sales pattern for monographs of this kind was that around 80 per cent of sales were achieved in the first year, 15 per cent in the second year and the remaining 5 per cent were spread fairly evenly over the next five years. The results, broken down into humanities and social sciences monographs and natural sciences monographs, are summarized in table 4.1.

UP1 found that nearly half – 47 per cent – of their monographs in the humanities and social sciences had sold fewer than 500 copies in this period, and the vast majority – 85 per cent – had sold fewer than 750 copies. The figures for monographs in the sciences were very similar – 49 per cent sold fewer than 500 copies in this period, and 78 per cent sold fewer than 750 – so the problems were not unique to the humanities and social sciences. Given the typical sales pattern for monographs of this kind, it is likely that

Table 4.1 Monograph sales for UP1

	First-year sales of hardback-only monographs published by UP1 in 1997	
	Fewer than 500	Fewer than 750
Humanities and social sciences	47%	85%
Natural sciences	49%	78%

Table 4.2 Monograph sales for UP2

	Three-year sales of hardback-only monographs published by UP2		
	1980		1997
Book A	1,385	Book F	2,086
Book B	1,149	Book G	1,995
Book C	709	Book H	1,342
Book D	1,638	Book I	1,621
Book E	1,572	Book J	1,319
Mean	*1,290*		*1,672*

nearly half of UP1's monograph output during this period would never sell more than around 500 copies (and many would sell fewer), and around three-quarters of its monograph output would never sell more than 750 copies.

Let us now compare UP1's experience with that of another university press – UP2. Whereas UP1 has a large academic list that spreads across many different disciplines, UP2 has a more focused list and publishes in a much smaller range of subject areas. Within these areas, they continue to publish a significant number of new titles each year as hardback-only monographs. Unlike many other academic publishers, senior management at UP2 were not particularly concerned about the decline in monograph sales. Their impression was that the sales of their hardback-only monographs had held up fairly well over the years, and they didn't sense any need to carry out a fundamental review of their policy on monograph publishing. To test this impression, we took a small selection of monographs published in 1980 and compared their sales over a three-year period with the sales of a small selection published in 1997. The titles were chosen in a way that would broadly represent the different subject areas in which UP2 was active. Table 4.2 shows the sales. The titles published in 1980 sold on average 1,290 copies over a three-year period, and the titles published in 1997 sold on average 1,672 copies over a three-year period. Of course, one must be careful about generalizing from such a small selection of titles, since it is difficult to be sure that the titles are truly representative of the list as a whole and since one strong or weak performance can have a significant impact on the mean. Nevertheless, these figures do lend some support to the view held by senior managers at UP2. For this particular publisher, there does not appear to have been a significant decline in the sales of hardback-only monographs across this seventeen-year period. The sales figures for the two sets of titles are roughly comparable – indeed, on the basis of this selection of titles, unit sales appear to have improved.

How can we explain the different experiences of UP1 and UP2? The most plausible explanation lies in the differing character of the lists. Like many university presses, UP1 publishes across the whole range of disciplines, reflecting the range of disciplines taught at its host university. It has a strong presence in the humanities (monographs in literature and history accounted for 30 per cent of the monographs it published in 1997). By contrast, UP2 publishes in a small number of disciplines or subdisciplines, and it has focused on subjects which are relatively robust in terms of the market for scholarly books. UP2 has built up a strong reputation in each of these subject areas and is known by booksellers, librarians, reviewers and academics as a leading publisher in this domain. Hence any new book published by UP2 will be received with interest by intermediaries in the publishing chain; it is more likely to be stocked by booksellers and wholesalers, and more likely to be bought by libraries and individuals with a specialist interest in the subject, than books published by other university presses.

While the experience of UP2 is certainly interesting, it does appear to be exceptional in the world of university presses. For the vast majority of university presses, the experience of UP1 is likely to reflect their own experiences more closely than that of UP2, and many had come to realize by the late 1990s that the life sales of a significant proportion of their hardback-only monographs were likely to be no more than several hundred copies. Most commercial publishers who remained active in the field of academic publishing experienced a similar pattern of decline. It also became increasingly clear to academic publishers that some disciplines or subdisciplines provided more robust markets for hardback-only monographs than others, and that there were some disciplines or subdisciplines where it was becoming increasingly difficult to publish monographs in a financially viable way. The more robust markets were to be found in disciplines such as economics, linguistics, mathematics, computer science and some areas of philosophy and classics; these were disciplines where library sales held up relatively well, where sales into international markets were relatively strong and where there were communities of individuals who were able and willing to buy expensive, high-level scholarly books. There were other disciplines or subdisciplines, such as literary criticism, some fields of history (including British history and European history), some of the 'softer' social sciences (like sociology and anthropology), some interdisciplinary fields (like gender studies and cultural studies) and some area studies (including African studies, Middle East studies and Latin American studies) where publishers were finding that the sales of hardback-only monographs were falling to alarmingly low levels.

We shall examine how publishers responded to these developments in the following chapters, but there is one general issue that should be highlighted at this stage: given the differentiated pattern of monograph sales, some disciplines or subdisciplines were becoming less and less attractive to publishers as areas for scholarly monograph publishing. If they were to going to continue publishing in those disciplines, then either they had to change their publishing strategy (for example, publish simultaneously in paperback and hardback rather than in hardback only, in the hope of reaching a market that was proving increasingly refractory to hardback-only monographs) or they had to publish different kinds of books (e.g. more textbooks aimed at students, rather than high-level works of scholarship). Each of these strategies had its own risks and costs, as we shall see. But many publishers were also led to reconsider their publishing priorities. Was it worth their while to continue publishing scholarly monographs in subject areas where the sales seemed to be falling to unmanageably low levels? If they had a series of scholarly monographs in an area where sales were consistently poor, should they close down the series? How could they afford to continue publishing scholarly work in areas where the demand for monographs seemed to be falling to levels that were too low to enable them to meet even their most conservative projections?

Questions of this kind posed (and continue to pose) serious difficulties for academic publishers and especially for university presses, who find themselves caught on the horns of a dilemma. On the one hand, as academic publishers who see themselves as having a certain responsibility to serve the scholarly communities from which they draw their authors and to whom they sell their books, many publishers feel an obligation to publish high-quality scholarly work in a variety of disciplines – and in the case of university presses, they may feel some pressure to continue publishing in those disciplines which have a strong and vocal constituency within their own universities. On the other hand, the changing market conditions of scholarly publishing make it increasingly difficult to publish scholarly work in certain areas in a financially viable way, thus forcing publishers to consider whether they should withdraw from those areas (or gradually wind down their activities within them) or whether they should continue to remain active in those areas but do so at a loss. For many commercial academic publishers, the way out of this dilemma was not too difficult to see: at the end of the day, commercial logic would tend to override any obligation they might feel to the scholarly community. But for many university presses, the dilemma was experienced in a more acute form and the solutions were less easy to find, partly because many university presses felt some obligation to publish in many (or even all) of the areas where their host universities had active programmes of teaching and research, and partly because many university presses were vulnerable to pressures from vocal individuals and constituencies within their host institutions. We shall return to the question of how the university presses have struggled to cope with this dilemma and whether these conflicting pressures can ultimately be resolved without some more fundamental shift in the expectations that are placed on university presses by their host institutions and others.

Up to now I've been trying to identify and document a crucial development in the field of academic publishing, but I haven't yet tried to explain why this development has occurred. Why have the sales of scholarly monographs declined so dramatically for most academic publishers since the 1970s? In order to explain this decline, we have to return to the scholarly monograph supply chain and look at what has happened to one of the key intermediaries further down the chain – namely, the research libraries, which form a crucial part of the market for scholarly monographs.

The changing structure of the library market

The most important factor in explaining the decline in the sales of scholarly monographs is to be found in the financial pressures faced by the research libraries at the major universities. The growth of academic publishing in the 1950s and 1960s was fuelled by the expansion of universities in the United States, Britain and elsewhere (see below, pp. 180ff). The massive expansion of higher education was accompanied by increased investment in university libraries – both in the building of new libraries and in the provision of increased resources for existing libraries. As budgets for new acquisitions grew, the demand for books, periodicals and content in other forms (such as microfilm) increased, and academic publishers in the English-speaking world found themselves riding a wave of increasing demand for scholarly content. But from the early 1970s on, the growth in demand began to fall off, as the economic boom of the 1960s gave way to more turbulent economic conditions and as government priorities began to change. During the economic recession of the 1980s, many universities dependent on public funding found that their budgets were being squeezed, and university administrators looked for ways to cut costs. Library budgets – and especially budgets for new acquisitions – were vulnerable.

Since the early 1980s, two additional factors have played an increasingly important role in squeezing the budgets for new book acquisitions by university libraries: the growing proportion of acquisitions budgets which is spent on periodicals, and the growing expenditure by libraries on IT services and on the acquisition of content in electronic formats. Let us briefly examine each.

The periodicals squeeze

The fact that university libraries spend a growing proportion of their acquisitions budgets on periodicals is the outcome of the increased volume and the increased cost of journal content. Today there are around 12,000 scientific journals with an international reach, and over the last decade the number of new journals published each year has increased by between 200 and 300 each year. Many of these new journals are highly specialized periodicals which reflect the increasing specialization of scientific and scholarly research. Moreover, throughout the 1980s and 1990s, the prices of journals were increased year on year well above the rate of inflation. The increases were particularly dramatic in what is broadly described as the STM (scientific, technical and medical) field, but the cost of journal subscriptions has increased significantly in the social sciences and humanities as well. The steep rise in the cost of journals has been well documented in the literature and here I shall simply highlight a few relevant features of this trend.

In 1997 journals were thirty times more expensive than they were in 1970 – an average annual increase of more than 13 per cent.[4] The pressure on library budgets created by increasing journal prices is exacerbated by several additional considerations. In the first place, once a library has begun to build up the back issues of a particular journal, it is often difficult to cancel the subscription and many librarians do so only with some reluctance. For many librarians, building collections is part of what good research libraries do, and cancelling a subscription to a journal means that the collection of back issues will be incomplete. Moreover, librarians often face a good deal of pressure from faculty members to maintain subscriptions to particular journals, especially to those journals which are regarded as important forums for the publication of scholarly and scientific research. Well-established journals are often regarded as 'must-have' content by academics and researchers in the field: they must have access to them if they are to be able to keep up with the latest research. This is particularly true of the natural sciences and of those areas in the social sciences, like economics and psychology, which rely most heavily on journal publication as the principal form of research output. Hence, despite a significant increase in prices, the librarians' hands may be tied. Many librarians regularly review their journal subscriptions and try to cancel some subscriptions to offset the steep increase in journal prices, but in the context of a research university, there are many cases where cancellation is simply not an option. Librarians are caught between the needs of faculty members to have access to journal content, on the one hand, and the increasing prices of journal publishers, on the other, and at the end of the day they may have little option but to pay the increasing fees.

[4] John Cox, 'The Great Journals Crisis: A Complex Present, but a Collegial Future', *Logos*, 9/1 (1998), p. 31.

The pressure on librarians' budgets has also been exacerbated by consolidation in the field of journal publishing. Especially in the area of STM journal publishing, a small number of publishers have emerged as the key players, controlling a large proportion of the most important titles. This has put them in a position of considerable strength when it comes to determining price increases and negotiating with libraries and library consortia. With the move to electronic delivery of journal content, the traditional subscription model has been supplemented by site licences whereby institutions pay for access to a bundle of journals published by a particular publisher. Publishers who control a large number of key journals are in a strong position to bundle their journals and to negotiate prices for electronic site licences. Bundling enables subscribing institutions to gain access to more of a publisher's journals, but it also reduces the ability of librarians to control the content of their collections and obliges them to pay the entire subscription for a specified time period. They cannot unsubscribe to certain journals and free up resources to use for other purposes (contracts place strict limits on the number of journals that can be cancelled in any given year). The costs of electronic access are often linked to the continued supply of printed copies of journals, which further increases the overall costs to libraries.

The Anglo-Dutch conglomerate Reed Elsevier is often cited as a prime example of how consolidation in the field of journal publishing goes hand in hand with substantial price increases. Over the last couple of decades Elsevier has emerged as the world's leading scientific journals publisher. Prior to its acquisition of Harcourt in 2001, Elsevier published over 1,200 research journals and was the largest single journals publisher, both in terms of number of titles and their value; with the acquisition of Harcourt, it added another 500 STM journals to its stable. (The proposed acquisition was referred to the Competition Commission in the UK to consider whether it would be against the public interest, but it was allowed to go through.) At the same time, Elsevier has earned a reputation in the library community for being particularly aggressive about increasing its journal prices. More recently, with the development of its ambitious ScienceDirect project, which has effectively transposed its journals publishing programme into an online environment, Elsevier has developed new pricing models which enable subscribing institutions to gain access to the full range of its journals. This has given Elsevier a great deal of power in negotiating with institutions, since the advantages of subscribing to ScienceDirect are considerable (given the enormous range of journals included and the must-have character of some of them) and the costs of exclusion are high.

While Elsevier is often singled out as being particularly aggressive in terms of its pricing policy, it is by no means unique, as table 4.3 shows. This table uses 1994/95 prices as an index to show how Elsevier's prices moved relative to the industry between 1994 and 2001. It suggests that Elsevier increased prices well above the industry average between 1995 and 1997, but since then it has increased prices slightly below the industry average, so that it was only just above the average annual increase for the period.[5]

While Elsevier's price increases are broadly in line with the industry averages, there remains a significant gulf between the prices of journals published by commercial publishers and the prices of non-profit journals – that is, journals published by professional

[5] See Competition Commission, *Reed Elsevier plc and Harcourt General, Inc: A Report on the Proposed Merger* (London: Competition Commission, 2001), p. 75, based on a US library journal survey and data provided by Elsevier.

Table 4.3 Elsevier journal price increases compared to industry average (index 1994/95 = 100; based on $ prices)

	Elsevier		Industry average	
		Increase on previous year		Increase on previous year
1994	100		100	
1995	111	11	111	11
1996	139	28	128	17
1997	161	22	143	15
1998	173	12	156	13
1999	182	9	170	14
2000	196	14	185	15
2001	209	13	201	16
Average annual increase		15.8		14.4

Source: Competition Commission, *Reed Elsevier plc and Harcourt General, Inc.: A Report on the Proposed Merger* (London: Competition Commission, 2001).

societies and university presses. A recent study of economics journals found that the average price per page of the ten most cited commercial journals was about six times as high as the average price per page of the ten most cited non-profit journals, and the gulf is growing – in 1985 the difference was three times.[6] However, since a growing proportion of journals in many scholarly fields are published by commercial publishers, the pricing policies of the commercial firms have played an increasingly important role in determining the subscription costs of research libraries. In 1960 there were around thirty English-language economics journals and nearly all of them were published by non-profit organizations; by 2000 there were almost 300 economics journals in English and more than two-thirds of them were published by commercial firms. In real terms, the average subscription price to libraries of the top ten non-profit economics journals increased by about 80 per cent between 1985 and 2001; the average real subscription price of the top ten commercial economics journals increased by 379 per cent during the same period.[7]

The steep increase in the prices of scientific and scholarly journals has been the topic of much debate in recent years and has become a matter of serious concern within the scholarly community. There are many in higher education who have been sharply critical of the current system of scholarly communication: university staff are paid, often by the public purse, to undertake research and make the results available, and the intel-

[6] Theodore C. Bergstrom, 'Free Labor for Costly Journals?' University of California at Santa Barbara, 2000. This picture is rendered more complicated by the fact that some journals are owned (and in some cases published) by learned societies, which may affect subscription prices. Some learned societies and non-profit journals also apply page charges to authors to enable them to keep down subscription costs.
[7] Ibid., pp. 6–7.

lectual content is then being handed over to journals publishers who are charging university libraries substantial sums to buy the content back, generating a handsome profit in the process. Publishers respond to criticisms of their pricing policies by emphasizing that they add considerable value in the publication process, that the size of many journals has increased in recent years and that the costs associated with the development and constant upgrading of electronic delivery systems are high. But dissatisfaction among academics and librarians has stimulated the development of alternative forums for the dissemination of scholarly output. These include the development of electronic pre-print open-access servers which allow authors to archive their articles before they are published. The best known of these is the Los Alamos Physics Archive, which was set up in 1991 and now contains more than a million papers in physics; similar archives have been established in computer science, biomedical science and other subjects.[8] More recently, a group of scientific researchers formed the Public Library of Science and, with the help of a $9 million grant from the Gordon and Betty Moore Foundation, launched the first issue of its first open-access journal, *PloS Biology*, in October 2003.[9] Librarians have also formed coalitions aimed at fostering alternatives to the high-priced journals of the major commercial publishers. The most prominent of these coalitions is SPARC, the Scholarly Publishing and Academic Resources Coalition, a US-based alliance of libraries which seeks to create partnerships with publishers who wish to develop high-quality but modestly priced periodicals.[10]

The pressure mounted on the major journals publishers by library consortia and other groups has helped to highlight some of the economic issues involved in scientific journal publishing, but whether it will have a significant long-term impact on the structure of the field remains unclear.[11] The rate of price increases may have slowed down in recent years, but viewed over the longer term, the steep rise in journals prices has required research libraries to use a growing proportion of their acquisitions budgets to meet the cost of journal subscriptions and site licences. In individual institutions librarians were able to take some measures that would help to offset the increases, such as cancelling subscriptions to infrequently used journals or to journals which were duplicated by other libraries or faculties within the university. But for the most part, these measures simply slowed down the rate of increase; they did not arrest or reverse it.

The cost of IT

From the mid-1980s on, librarians found themselves faced with another type of expenditure which would demand a growing proportion of their budgets: expenditure on information technology and on electronic products and services of various kinds. Some of this expenditure was non-recurrent infrastructural cost (such as the provision of new or updated computer equipment) and some was expenditure on technical staff and

---

[8] See http://arxiv.org.
[9] See www.plos.org.
[10] See www.arl.org/sparc.
[11] For a more detailed discussion of recent economic trends and possible future scenarios in scientific journal publishing, see *Economic Analysis of Scientific Research Publishing* (London: Wellcome Trust, 2003), available at www.wellcome.ac.uk/en/1/awtpubrepeas.html.

training, but as more and more information and content was made available in electronic formats (initially CD-ROM but increasingly online), many librarians used a growing proportion of their budgets to acquire electronic products and services. These included citation indexes, bibliographical resources and a rapidly expanding range of databases of various kinds, such as ISI/Thomson's Web of Science, Reed Elsevier's LexisNexis, Bell & Howell/Chadwyck-Healey's ProQuest, etc. Once librarians had begun to subscribe to these electronic resources, they found it difficult to pull back – 'they're quite addictive,' explained one librarian. 'You cut LexisNexis and everybody will scream.' So there has been a trend for a growing proportion of the acquisitions budgets of university libraries to be spent on journals and electronic resources of various kinds. And what have been squeezed in this process are the resources available to libraries for the acquisition of new books and other printed materials.

Downward pressure on monograph acquisitions

This trend can be seen very clearly in the data gathered by ARL (Association of Research Libraries) in the US and by Sconul (Society of College, National and University Libraries) in the UK. Figure 4.4 summarizes the expenditure trends in the 122

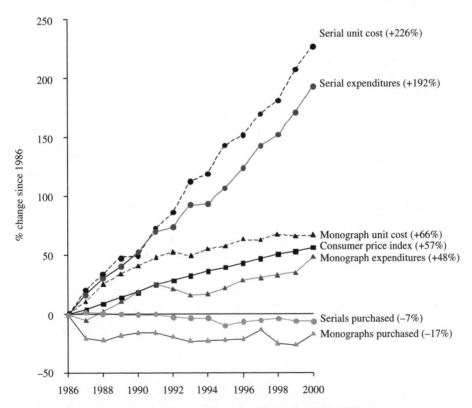

Figure 4.4 Monograph and serial costs in ARL libraries, 1986–2000
Source: ARL Statistics 1999–2000 (Washington DC: Association of Research Libraries, 2001).

Table 4.4 Breakdown of expenditure on information provision in UK higher education libraries, 1991/92 to 1999/00 (%)

	91/92	92/93	93/94	94/95	95/96	96/97	97/98	98/99	99/00
Books	40.2	40.2	39.6	38.5	36.6	34.7	35.0	34.0	32.6
Serials	48.6	48.0	48.4	50.0	51.1	46.5	45.3	46.8	48.4
Electronic	2.3	2.6	2.7	2.7	2.9	9.5	10.7	11.1	11.5
Binding	4.7	4.6	4.2	3.8	4.0	4.0	3.7	3.3	4.0
Interlibrary loans	4.2	4.6	5.1	4.9	5.4	5.3	5.3	4.7	3.5
	100.0	100.0	100.0	100.0	100.0	100.0	100.0	100.0	100.0

Source: Claire Creaser, *Sconul Library Statistics: Trend Analysis to 1999–2000* (Loughborough: Library and Information Statistics Unit, Loughborough University, 2001).

research libraries affiliated to ARL between 1986 and 2000.[12] It shows that expenditure on serials increased by 192 per cent over this period, despite the fact that, due to cancellations, the libraries bought 7 per cent fewer serial titles. The increase in the serial unit cost[13] during this period was 226 per cent, which was around four times more than the increase in the consumer price index (CPI), which rose by 57 per cent during the same period. Expenditure on monographs increased by 48 per cent over this period, which was less than the increase in the monograph unit cost, which rose by 66 per cent; the increase in the monograph unit cost (66 per cent) was only just above the rise in the CPI (57 per cent). As libraries shifted expenditures from monographs to serials to meet some of the demands of increasing serial prices, the number of monographs purchased declined from a median figure of 32,679 in 1986 to 24,294 in 1998–9, a decline of more than 25 per cent. The number of monographs purchased rose to 27,059 in 2000, but this figure still represents a decline of 17 per cent over a fourteen-year period.[14]

The Sconul statistics display a similar pattern. Table 4.4 gives the breakdown of expenditure on information provision among UK higher education libraries between 1991 and 2000;[15] the proportions are represented visually in figure 4.5.[16] In 1991/92 expenditure on serials accounted for 48.6 per cent of total information provision expenditure; this proportion rose to 51.1 per cent by 1995/96, then dipped between 1996/97 and 1998/99, returning to 48.4 per cent in 1999/00. (The dip between 1995/96 and 1998/99 is explained by the fact that definitions were changed so that the provision of electronic documents was included as 'electronic' expenditure rather than as 'books' or 'serials'; hence the proportion spent on electronic materials increased sharply from 2.9 per cent in 1995/96

[12] See *ARL Statistics 1999–2000*, compiled and ed. Martha Kyrillidou and Mark Young (Washington, DC: Association of Research Libraries, 2001), p. 14, available at www.arl.org/stats/arlstat.
[13] In this context, 'serial unit cost' and 'monograph unit cost' means the cost of purchase, i.e. the price. It should not be confused with what publishers normally understand by 'unit cost', which is the cost of production.
[14] *ARL Statistics*, p. 10.
[15] Based on personal correspondence, 15 Nov. 2001.
[16] From Claire Creaser, *Sconul Library Statistics: Trend Analysis to 1999–2000* (Loughborough: Library and Information Statistics Unit, Loughborough University, 2001), p. 25. I have restricted the analysis here to the 1990s, since it is difficult to get comparable figures from the 1980s.

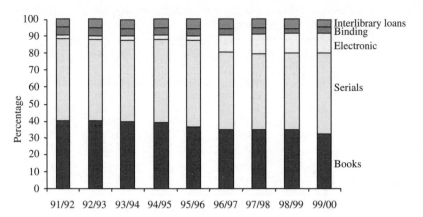

Figure 4.5 Breakdown of expenditure on information provision in UK higher education libraries, 1991/92 to 1999/00
Source: Claire Creaser, *Sconul Library Statistics: Trend Analysis to 1999–2000* (Loughborough: Library and Information Statistics Unit, Loughborough University, 2001).

to 9.5 per cent in 1996/97, and continued to increase steadily after that. In 1999/00 electronic serials were put back into serials, and data were collected separately for electronic, print and combined subscriptions, though it is difficult to be sure whether these definitions are adhered to closely.)[17] Taken together, expenditure on serials and electronic products rose from 50.9 per cent in 1991/92 to 59.9 per cent in 1999/00. By contrast, the proportion of total expenditure accounted for by book purchases over this nine-year period declined at a steady rate, falling from 40.2 per cent in 1991/92 to 32.6 per cent in 1999/00.

If we look at actual expenditure for new acquisitions in UK universities and higher education colleges, we can see that expenditure on books has increased in recent years but has increased at a much lower rate than expenditure on periodicals and electronic materials. Table 4.5 and figure 4.6 summarize the acquisitions spending in all universities and higher education colleges in the UK for the period 1994–2000.[18] As these figures show, expenditure on periodicals in UK universities and higher education colleges increased by 28 per cent over this six-year period and expenditure on electronic materials increased sixfold (although these figures are also affected by the change in classification criteria noted in the previous paragraph). Expenditure on books also increased during this period but by a much smaller extent: 9.5 per cent overall. During the same period the average price of new UK academic and professional titles increased from £35.35 to £44.18, an increase of 25 per cent. So while overall expenditure on books in UK institutions of higher education was increasing over this period, the increase was well below the rate at which the price of new titles was increasing. Hence the number of new titles acquired every year by libraries has tended to decline over time. In 1991/92 Sconul libraries acquired on average 27,294 new books and pamphlets to add to their

[17] Personal correspondence, 15 Nov. 2001.
[18] From Peter Sowden, *University Library Spending on Books, Journals and Electronic Resources*, 2002 Update (London: Publishers Association, 2002), pp. 5–6.

Table 4.5 Acquisitions spending in all UK universities and higher education colleges, 1994/95 to 1999/00 (£000s, actual spending)

	1994/95	1995/96	1996/97	1997/98	1998/99	1999/00
Books	44,270	44,453	44,013	46,751	47,447	48,471
+/– previous year		0.4%	–1.0%	6.2%	1.5%	2.2%
Periodicals	54,140	58,684	56,452	57,763	63,022	69,313
+/– previous year		8.4%	–3.8%	2.3%	9.1%	10.0%
Electronic	2,781	3,164	10,567	12,435	15,110	16,631
+/– previous year		13.8%	234.0%	17.7%	21.5%	10.1%
Total	101,191	106,301	111,032	116,949	125,579	134,415
+/– previous year		5.0%	4.5%	5.3%	7.4%	7.0%

Source: Peter Sowden, *University Library Spending on Books, Journals and Electronic Resources,* 2002 Update (London: Publishers Association, 2002).

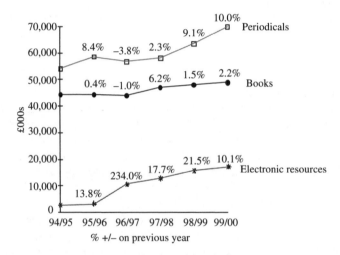

Figure 4.6 Acquisitions spending in all UK universities and higher education colleges, 1994/95 to 1999/00
Source: Peter Sowden, *University Library Spending on Books, Journals and Electronic Resources,* 2002 Update (London: Publishers Association, 2002).

stock;[19] by 1999/00 this figure had fallen to 22,545,[20] a decline of 17 per cent over this eight-year period.

The problems created by the squeeze on library budgets have been exacerbated by the fact that the output of new academic and professional titles has increased significantly in recent years. In the UK, for example, the number of new academic and professional titles published annually more than doubled in the 1990s, rising from 20,609 in 1991 to 42,424 in 2000 (this includes new editions). Hence there are many more titles competing for a library spend which is increasing at a very modest rate overall (and in the case of some institutions, actually declining over time – in the case of the Univer-

[19] *Sconul Annual Statistics 1991–1992* (London: Sconul, 1993), p. 4b.
[20] *Sconul Annual Library Statistics 1999–2000* (London: Sconul, 2001), p. 9.

sity of Reading, for example, library expenditure on book acquisitions fell from £368,000 in 1994–5 to £241,000 in 1999–2000, a decline of 34.5 per cent[21]). In these circumstances, academic publishers are likely to find that they are selling fewer numbers of their scholarly monographs into university libraries and that the revenue generated per title from sales to libraries is declining with time.

The general trends outlined by these statistics are broadly confirmed by the experience of librarians. In interviews, librarians at universities in the US and the UK tend to confirm that the budgets for new book acquisitions have been squeezed over the years by the steep rise in serial prices and the increasing levels of expenditure on IT and electronic products. Of course, the experience of librarians varies from one institution to another. In some of the larger, well-endowed institutions, librarians have been able to protect their book acquisition budgets from substantial erosion, but in many of the smaller institutions and in libraries where the collections are strongly oriented towards the natural sciences, many librarians have experienced strong downward pressure on book acquisition budgets. Commenting on the experience of librarians in the US, a librarian at one of the major research libraries put it like this:

> Thus far the actual acquisition of books has been fairly constant for many of the large research libraries – in the sheer number of books we buy, we're buying as many or more than we did before. But this has to be qualified on two levels: one, the category of library, and two, the subject. Science libraries have increasingly moved away from book acquisition – for science libraries, books have become a very small part of what they do. The other qualification one has to add is that smaller libraries are making significant cuts to what they're acquiring and how they're acquiring materials, in their commitment to certain fields and their willingness to build collections in certain fields. They need to be very selective in terms of the areas they can really support in their research collections.

By being more selective in terms of the subject areas they support, librarians at the smaller and less well-endowed institutions can continue to build their collections while at the same time reducing their book acquisitions overall.

The erosion of library budgets for new book acquisitions has undoubtedly had a significant impact on the sales of scholarly books, since university libraries are a principal market for books of this kind. When an academic publisher brings out a scholarly book in hardback only at a relatively high price, it is generally expecting to sell a significant proportion of the print-run to libraries; it may also get some sales to individuals who have a specialist interest in the topic, but the principal market is institutional. Hence a long-term erosion in real terms of library budgets for new book acquisitions will have serious consequences for the sales of scholarly books. More than anything else, this is the factor that has shaped the field of academic publishing over the last two decades. But it is not the only factor. At the same time as the erosion of library budgets was cutting into the sales of scholarly monographs, many of the American university presses were coming under pressure from another source: their host institutions.

---

[21] For a full breakdown by institution, see Sowden, *University Library Spending*, table 3.2a.

Institutional pressures on university presses

To understand why this happened, we have to look back briefly at the history of the American university presses. The oldest of these presses, such as Johns Hopkins, Chicago, Cornell, California and Columbia, date back to the late nineteenth century; another nine, including Princeton, Harvard and Yale, emerged in the first two decades of the twentieth century.[22] By 1967 there were sixty university presses affiliated to universities in the US and Canada. For the most part, the American university presses were set up with the aim of advancing and disseminating knowledge by publishing high-quality scholarly work; they were generally seen as an integral part of the function of the university. It was commonly assumed that the university presses would require subsidies and support of various kinds from their host institutions and from benefactors, since a good deal of what they published was the kind of scholarly work that would not be taken on by commercial presses. Presses were also able to apply for grants for specific projects from a variety of grant-giving bodies and charitable foundations, such as the National Endowment for the Humanities (NEH) and the Andrew Mellon Foundation.

In the 1970s and 1980s, this situation began to change, and some university presses found themselves faced with growing pressure from their host institutions to reduce their financial dependency. This was linked to broader changes within the sphere of higher education and in the levels of funding – both public and private – available to universities. As many universities found their budgets being squeezed, they began to scrutinize their activities with a renewed sense of purpose, and the subsidies provided to university presses were viewed by some in university administrations as inessential expenditures. In the course of the 1980s, a chill wind of financial accountability swept through the world of the university presses. In some cases (though by no means all), subsidies were pared down or withdrawn, and some presses were told by university administrators that they should aim to break even. At the same time, some of the pro-grammes that had been available to subsidize specific book projects were closed down, thus making it much more difficult to secure support for scholarly projects which were worthy in intellectual terms but commercially unviable.

The impact of this new climate of financial accountability on the activities of university presses varied greatly from one institution to another. Some presses were in a much stronger position than others – in a few cases because they had independent endowments which helped to insulate them from institutional pressures, in some cases because they had built strong coalitions of support within their host institutions which served them well in less auspicious times, in other cases because they had been forced to put their houses in order at an earlier stage, and hence they were in a relatively robust financial state when the pressures of the 1980s and 1990s came to bear. Other presses were more vulnerable and found themselves having to restructure their activities and implement significant cost-saving measures. The presses at state universities were generally more exposed than the presses at the large, well-endowed private universities, since the resources available to state universities were dependent on state budgets and hence uni-

---

[22] See Gene R. Hawes, *To Advance Knowledge: A Handbook on American University Press Publishing* (New York: American University Press Services, 1967), ch. 2.

versity budgets tended to be squeezed when state budgets came under pressure. Questions were asked in some universities about whether it was necessary to have a press at all, and in one case (Iowa State University Press) the press was sold off to a commercial publisher (Blackwell Science).

The new climate of financial accountability exposed the perilous position of some of the American university presses and highlighted their dependence on financial support from their host institutions, but it did not necessarily result in an overall reduction in the level of support they received. There are many different ways in which the university presses receive assistance; some are relatively easy to identify (such as annual subsidies to cover operating costs, salaries and benefits), while others are more difficult to quantify (such as rent-free or subsidized accommodation, interest-free overdraft facilities and one-off allowances to absorb losses or stock write-downs). Exactly how the issue of subsidies is handled varies from one press to another, and many continue to receive some form of assistance from their host institutions even if the nature and scale of assistance is now subjected to more intensive scrutiny. Some university presses report reductions in subsidies from one year to the next, some report a continuation of subsidies at levels comparable to earlier years and some report real increases in support – there is no single, uniform pattern here. But what has unquestionably happened is that the university presses have been subjected to more intensive financial scrutiny than was commonly the case in the past. They have been forced to re-examine their practices, and in some cases they have had their practices re-examined for them by external consultants. Many presses continue to receive subsidies of various kinds but this now takes place in a context of intensive and continuous financial scrutiny.

The new climate of financial accountability has not only subjected the university presses to more intensive forms of scrutiny: it has also highlighted a deep uncertainty within universities about the nature and purpose of a university press. On the one hand, many universities want to have a press which publishes scholarly work of the highest quality, and thus both reflects and contributes to the standing of the university as a centre of research and excellence (that is, contributes to its symbolic capital). On the other hand, there are some senior administrators within universities who, in the new climate of financial accountability, expect their presses to operate as commercially viable organizations, breaking even financially or making little demand on university resources. But given the deterioration in the market for scholarly books, the expectation that university presses should contribute to the symbolic capital of the university while making little or no demand on its economic capital was unrealistic. Something had to give. Either the presses had to persuade their host institutions to continue to support them (albeit at reduced levels) or they had to find other ways of generating cash (for example, by shifting the emphasis of their publishing programmes towards more lucrative fields of publishing). And in many cases they had to do both (as well as other things).

In contrast to the American university presses, OUP and CUP were insulated to a large extent from the kinds of institutional pressures experienced by their American colleagues in the 1980s and 1990s. Although a new climate of financial accountability also swept through British higher education in the 1980s, the university presses of Oxford and Cambridge were much larger, more diversified and more international than the American university presses, and hence were in a much less vulnerable position. CUP had been forced into a major restructuring by a financial crisis in the late 1960s and early 1970s and, under the stewardship of Geoffrey Cass, it enjoyed a long period of financial growth throughout the 1970s and 1980s. From the early 1980s on, both OUP and CUP developed very successful ELT publishing programmes which generated resources that could be used to support scholarly publishing and costly one-off projects. Throughout the 1980s and 1990s, the university presses of Oxford and Cambridge were in a cash-positive position and were not making financial demands on their host institutions. This does not mean that OUP and CUP were immune from the need to adapt in the face of the changing economic conditions of academic publishing – they too had to find ways of coping with these changes. But thanks to their distinctive histories and their large, diversified and international character, OUP and CUP were in a much stronger position, and they were not subjected to the same kinds of pressures from their host institutions as the American university presses experienced in the 1980s and 1990s.

5
Academic publishing in transition (1): changing organizational cultures

How have academic publishers responded to and tried to cope with the developments outlined in the previous chapter? How has academic publishing been transformed by the pressures – both economic and institutional – that have impinged on publishing firms? As publishers became aware of the fact that the sales of scholarly monographs were declining and unsold stock was accumulating in their warehouses at an increasingly alarming rate, they took measures of various kinds to try to limit the damage. They also began to think about broader strategic issues and, in some cases, took bold steps to try to reposition the firm and redefine its publishing activities. Individual publishing firms responded to these developments and pressures in different ways – there was no single, uniform response. But if one examines the responses of a variety of publishing firms, one can identify certain common themes, a distinctive set of responses that recurs from one firm to another and that tends to form a common currency of discussion and debate within and among the presses that occupy the field.

In this and the following chapter, I want to examine this distinctive set of responses. In doing so, I don't want to suggest that all academic publishers have adopted the same coping strategies and grappled with the issues in the same way, as if there was only one possible move in the game – that is manifestly not the case. How individual firms respond to changing circumstances is always going to be shaped by a complex range of factors, some historical, some institutional and some personal. Even the university presses, which share many things in common, have responded in differing ways depending on the specific circumstances in which they found themselves, the resources at their disposal, the historical legacies of the presses, the personal dispositions of the directors and other senior managers and the attitudes adopted by administrators in their host institutions. The picture is complicated still further when one takes account of the changing practices of commercial academic publishers, who, being generally less constrained by constitutional obligations but more exposed to market realities, have often followed other paths (or have followed similar paths but in more radical ways). I do not wish to oversimplify the very complex array of changes that have characterized the field of academic publishing over the last few decades. But by focusing on certain key themes, we can begin to develop some frameworks of interpretation which will help us to understand the historical trajectories of individual publishing firms and which will enable us to explore some of the tensions and trends that characterize the field of academic publishing as a whole. In the following discussion I shall examine the following seven themes:

- reduction of costs;
- increase of prices;
- changing publishing strategies;
- greater selectivity in title acquisition and list-building;
- growth of marketing concerns;
- changing organizational cultures;
- diversification and field migration.

In this chapter I shall examine the first six themes. The next chapter will be devoted to the theme of diversification and field migration.

Reduction of costs

The most direct and immediate way of dealing with the falling demand for scholarly monographs was to reduce costs and increase prices. By taking these steps, publishers could maintain their margins on monographs (or limit the extent to which they declined) while lowering their print-runs – provided that, and this is an important qualification, they actually managed to sell the copies they printed. Publishers were able to reduce the costs associated with scholarly monograph publishing in various ways, the most important of which were the following: (1) reducing typesetting costs, (2) lowering royalties, (3) streamlining production processes, and (4) bringing down overheads by outsourcing and other methods. Let me deal briefly with each.

(1)   The reduction in typesetting costs was a consequence of a series of technological changes associated with digitization and computerization in the publishing industry, changes that began to take effect in the early to mid 1980s. I shall examine these changes in more detail in part IV; here I want simply to highlight the significance of these changes for the costs involved in typesetting. Prior to the mid-1980s, the common practice among publishers was to copy-edit the typescript submitted by an author and then send the copy-edited script to a typesetter to be manually keyed in and typeset. The typesetter would generate page proofs which would be checked and corrected by the publisher and/or author, and the corrections would then be rekeyed by the typesetter and 'pasted in' to the made-up pages. All of this was very time-consuming and costly. However, as traditional typesetting equipment was replaced by computer-based composition and as personal computers became more widespread among authors and academics, the costs of typesetting began to fall. By the late 1980s, some publishers were beginning to receive texts from authors on electronic disks rather than simply as typescripts. Although initially most publishers continued to copy-edit on typescript rather than onscreen, it was no longer necessary for the typesetter to key in the entire text; the typesetter now had the more limited task of incorporating the copy-editor's amendments and following the instructions concerning layout and design to make up the book pages using various software packages such as Quark or PageMaker. The changing role of the typesetter also stimulated the emergence of new competitors, many located in India and the Far East, which placed downward pressure on costs. The subsequent development of the internet made it even easier for publishers in the UK and elsewhere to use typesetters overseas, since electronic files could be sent back and forth quickly and cheaply. The

cumulative effect of these changes has been a dramatic decline in the cost of typeset-ting. One academic publisher put it like this: 'We were spending vast sums of money on Rolls-Royce production standards. The typesetting cost of a monograph, I remember to this day, was £14 a page in 1978. Twenty years later it's a fraction of that. So we've made major economies in typesetting, helped by new technology.'

The decline in typesetting costs undoubtedly helped publishers to reduce the overall costs of production, and helped academic publishers in particular to reduce their costs at a time when many were finding it necessary to cut the print-runs of their scholarly monographs. If some publishers were paying around £14 a page in 1978,[1] in 2003 they were typically paying around £2.80 ($4.50) a page – that's a fifth of what it cost twenty-five years ago, and that's without taking account of inflation. (If one were to take account of inflation, the figure would be more like one-twentieth.) Of course, typesetting costs are only one component in the array of costs involved in book production, and a sig-nificant reduction in typesetting costs would not by itself transform the business of scholarly publishing. But there can be no doubt that it helped to ease the pressure on margins at a time when the trends in the marketplace were making life a good deal more difficult for academic publishers.

(2)   Many academic publishers also sought to ease the pressure on margins by negoti-ating lower royalties with authors. Most of the authors of scholarly monographs were either academics or researchers whose careers were within the academic field; for them, publishing scholarly monographs was primarily a means of making available the results of their research and advancing their careers, since securing tenure or promotion often depended on publication. As the financial pressures on scholarly publishing increased, some publishers took the view that authors should be offered lower royalties on schol-arly monographs, and in many cases they found that authors were quite willing to be flexible on this point. What mattered most to many academics was that their work was published, preferably by a prestigious press. To many academics it also mattered that their book was published attractively – the quality of the product was more important than strict financial remuneration. Hence publishers who sought to negotiate lower royalties for scholarly monographs often found that authors were amenable. As one publisher recalled,

> I looked at author's royalties and I was amazed to see that scholars who had been paid salaries by the universities to do research and write books were getting royalties of 10 per cent of the published price on books which had very modest sales. And this was completely non-commercial behaviour in my view. It was equivalent to 15 per cent of the sales. Well, you only had to reduce that by 5 percentage points to have a bottom line and, of course, when you actually talked to authors about it, they saw the sense of it. And you had to be careful to pay competitively. You had to make sure that other publishers weren't making themselves much more attractive than you were. But fortunately most people began to realize this at about the same time and so there was a general lowering of royalties paid to authors on scholarly books.

[1] This figure may be on the high side. This publisher was using a typesetter who was part of its own organization and who was probably charging above-market rates. Other publishers were spending less on typesetting in the late 1970s, but even so they were spending much more per page twenty to thirty years ago than they are today.

Given the pressure on the margins of scholarly monographs caused by declining sales and falling print-runs, a small modification to royalties could make a significant difference to the publisher. Changing a royalty from 10 per cent of list price to 7.5 per cent of list would make a difference of around 4 per cent to the gross margin. If, in addition, the basis of calculation for royalties was changed from list price to net receipts, then the difference would be even greater – around 6–7 per cent, depending on the level of discount offered to booksellers and wholesalers. In the course of the 1980s and 1990s, it became increasingly common for academic publishers to offer lower royalties for scholarly monographs (or to offer a sliding scale of royalties with the first step pitched at a lower level); it also became increasingly common for publishers to move to net receipts as a basis for royalty calculation. Of course, this was not a uniform trend across the publishing industry as a whole, and in fields where there was intense competition for key authors (such as trade publishing), publishers were commonly faced with escalating royalties and advances, especially when agents were involved. (This affected many academic publishers too, as we shall see in the following chapter.) But in the field of academic publishing, a downward movement in royalty levels provided many publishers with some much-needed room to manoeuvre in trying to cope with the falling demand for scholarly monographs.

(3)   Academic publishers also sought to reduce costs by streamlining their production processes. Academic publishing is a field where the values associated with high-quality book production are deeply rooted. Many academic publishers have long prided themselves on the quality of the books they produce. They invest a great deal of time and effort in the design of each book, and use high-quality materials in the production process – 'Rolls-Royce production standards', to use the phrase quoted earlier. Production values of this kind are particularly evident among the university presses, but some commercial academic publishers have also placed a great deal of emphasis on high-quality book production. However, with the growing pressures on scholarly monograph publishing, many academic publishers began to look for ways to streamline production processes so that some of the costs involved in monograph production could be squeezed out of the system. The aim was to lower costs while at the same time ensuring that the overall quality of the final product remained high. One way of doing this was to introduce standardized templates: monographs were 'batched' and cover designs were simplified and standardized. Cost savings could be made by reducing the amount of individualized attention devoted to each book. In some cases, lower quality materials (such as cheaper paper) and simplified techniques (such as glued rather than stitched bindings) were also used. Undoubtedly this involved some loss of quality, and this was a source of concern in some organizations. There were some – especially some production staff who were accustomed to traditional methods of working – who felt that the new practices were sacrificing quality on the altar of commerce. But there were others who took a more pragmatic view, arguing that traditional standards of production may have been appropriate in the past but that, in the changing circumstances of scholarly publishing, one had to be prepared to modify the standards. 'I have to admit there has been some decline in standards,' said one senior academic publisher. 'You no longer get a wonderful buckram binding and thick creamy paper that you used to have, but neither does anybody else. The market has moved on and people's expectations change. It's just like you no longer get lovely seats in railway trains. It is one of the sad factors of mass production.'

While many academic publishers looked for ways to make modest reductions in cost by streamlining production processes without compromising overall quality, there were a few commercial publishers who took more radical steps. They sought to make scholarly monograph publishing profitable despite the declining print-runs by increasing prices and keeping development and production costs as low as possible. In some cases authors were expected to deliver manuscripts as camera-ready copy (CRC), so that copy-editing and typesetting could be bypassed altogether and the publisher could shoot film from the final text submitted by the author. However, more radical approaches of this kind elicited much criticism from and dissatisfaction among authors, librarians and readers. The production quality of these books was simply too low, especially in view of the prices that were being charged, and there were many who felt that these presses were publishing material (including a good number of doctoral dissertations) that did not deserve to be published in book form. Sales were generally very modest and the symbolic capital that an author derived from publishing with a monograph publisher of this kind was relatively low. This radical strategy did not succeed and many of the presses that adopted it in the 1980s and 1990s have either abandoned it or disappeared as viable publishing operations.

(4)   Another way that publishers sought to cut costs was by bringing down their over-heads. Outsourcing became increasingly common, as publishers made more use of free-lancers who could work from their own premises and use their own equipment. This provided publishers with greater flexibility while at the same time reducing their over-heads and salary commitments. Copy-editing was one area which lent itself to out-sourcing, since copy-editing was an activity that could easily be done from home. Traditionally, many of the American university presses employed manuscript editors who worked in-house, copy-editing manuscripts and in some cases investing a great deal of time and effort in checking references, compiling bibliographies, etc. This ensured high levels of accuracy and a good deal of consistency from one book to the next, but it was a costly practice. Many of the university presses moved to outsourcing at least a proportion of their throughput, using a set of freelancers who were managed by an in-house editor and trained in the house style. Some publishers also isolated other functions, such as cover design, which could be outsourced to freelance individuals or firms in order to reduce overhead costs.

The restructuring of production processes was in many cases a continuous process of change, shaped both by the economic need to reduce costs and by the technological revolution that was taking place at more or less the same time. In many organizations this restructuring process went relatively smoothly, as employees accepted and adapted to the new realities. But there were some organizations where staff found it difficult to adapt to the new roles and expectations. In some of the university presses, for example, where high-quality production was cherished by some members of staff, the attempt to restructure and streamline production processes was met by resistance in some quarters, and disagreements concerning this issue created a tense atmosphere which in some cases lasted for years. The director of one American university press, who had begun his publishing career many years ago as a manuscript editor, recalled how difficult and stressful this process had been:

> It was not easy. There were resignations from the manuscript editing department. When I first came here as a manuscript editor everything was edited in-house, just about. Now we

edit nothing. This was very difficult because the staff were people who were very fine desk editors who found their jobs changed to managing freelancers. I had a managing editor who was wonderful but who finally retired early out of frustration with all these changes and because I had in the meanwhile hired a crackerjack production manager after demoting the person who'd been here for thirty years and who had turned that into a completely dysfunctional department. The new production manager had transformed that department in about one and a half years and then said the then managing editor is the anchor that's dragging this all down. There was terrible tension between the then managing editor and the new-kid-on-the-block production editor. It was tough but it's now transformed. We are not in never-never land, it is not that there aren't sometimes tensions. But we are no longer working at cross-purposes to each other and the result is that schedules make sense and people talk to each other. It's much better.

Increase of prices

The other immediate way of easing the pressure on margins in a context of falling demand was to increase the prices of scholarly monographs. Some of the most radical thinking about the prices of scholarly monographs was initiated in the early 1970s by Geoffrey Cass as director of Cambridge University Press. Cass had joined Cambridge in December 1971, taking over as managing director in January 1972, in a context where the press was running up large overdrafts and facing a serious financial crisis.[2] Cass realized that the press was holding a great deal of stock that had been printed years ago, and was still selling these books at prices that had been set when they were originally printed. Since the late 1960s and early 1970s was a time of relatively high inflation, he concluded that these backlist titles were being sold at prices that were too low. He argued that the prices of backlist titles should be determined, not by their original production costs, but by what it would cost to replace them. He thus undertook a thorough repricing of CUP's backlist, completing it just before the government put a freeze on price increases in an attempt to slow down the rate of inflation. Cass's repricing policy was a radical innovation at the time, although it has since become commonplace among academic publishers. The policy helped to transform the fortunes of Cambridge University Press, which soon overcame the crisis of the late 1960s and began an extended period of growth.

Cass's early innovations were concerned primarily with the repricing of the backlist, but as the downward pressure on monograph sales led many publishers to reduce print-runs on new titles, many were also led to increase the prices of new monographs in an attempt to maintain margins. Figure 4.4 (see p. 103) shows that the average monograph unit price in the US rose by 50 per cent between 1986 and 1992, although the rate of increase declined after that (the unit price rose by another 16 per cent between 1992 and 2000). The increase between 1986 and 1992 was roughly twice the rate of increase of the consumer price index, although the overall increase in the average monograph unit price between 1986 and 2000 was only just ahead of the increase in the CPI.

While the average prices of monographs increased in the 1980s and 1990s by more than the rise in the CPI, the increases were not uniform across the field of academic

---

[2] See Michael Black, *Cambridge University Press, 1584–1984* (Cambridge: Cambridge University Press, 1984), pp. 236–64.

publishing. The average net selling price of American university press books remained remarkably stable over the decade of the 1990s, rising from an average price of $16.55 ($22.41 for cloth, $9.77 for paper) in 1991 to $16.77 ($22.12 for cloth, $11.04 for paper) in 2000. (The stability of the net selling prices of university press books may be partly explained by higher discounts.) There is some evidence to suggest that the commercial academic presses have been more aggressive about increasing prices for their scholarly books than the American university presses.[3] It is also the case that UK-based academic publishers – OUP and CUP as well as the commercial presses – have generally been more willing to increase prices than US presses, especially American university presses. In 2002, for example, it was common for a UK-based academic publisher to price a hardback-only monograph in the humanities and social sciences in the region of £50–60 ($80–95) or more, whereas many American university presses would generally aim to keep the price below $50 (£31) and would often price it below $40 (£25).

Why have the American university presses been so cautious about raising prices? There are several reasons. Partly it is because they believe, rightly or wrongly, that the market for scholarly monographs is elastic and that they will sell more copies to individuals if the price is kept at an affordable level. Partly it is because the presses tend to take their price bearings from other university presses (and, in some cases, from the New York trade houses); university press managers regularly scrutinize the catalogues of other university presses, and no press wants to be seen to adopt a more aggressive pricing policy than their competitors. And partly it is because, in the case of at least some American university presses, making scholarship available at affordable prices is seen as part of the mission of the university press. But this is beginning to change. The pressures on margins in the context of falling print-runs is forcing the American university presses – even those which have traditionally prided themselves on their relatively modest prices – to increase the prices of the more specialized monographs. As one director remarked,

> One of the other things we have resisted here is going to Cambridge and Oxford prices, although I see us inching up there. We have $55 books now and when I got here and wanted to price books at $35, they were aghast. That was the argument here – you don't price these books for the market, you price to create the image that we are giving these away to poor people. That is something I have had to combat. So I think we are now saying, if there is no elasticity of demand here we are going to price them at $75. With some you can't do that. Social sciences you can do that. Lit crit, if you price a book at $75 you wouldn't sell any. So we are damned if we do and damned if we don't. What do we do with this book that really needs to be $45 if we are going to be close to break-even?

Changing publishing strategies

The reduction of costs and increase of prices undoubtedly helped academic publishers to relieve the pressure on margins, but neither of these strategies would enable them to arrest or reverse the pattern of declining sales. It was partly in order to address the latter

[3] Albert N. Greco, Walter F. O'Connor, Sharon P. Smith and Robert M. Wharton, *The Price of University Press Books, 1989–2000* (New York: Association of American University Presses, 2003).

problem that many academic publishers began to experiment with different publishing strategies. The most common practice in this regard was to move from the publication of scholarly books as hardback-only monographs to the simultaneous publication of hardback and paperback editions. This practice became increasingly common among academic publishers in the 1980s and 1990s, but it has remained controversial in the academic publishing community. Most academic publishers today would take the view that the optimal publishing strategy for scholarly work depends not only on the content of the work itself but also on the discipline in which it falls. Most publishers would agree that if they are going to publish scholarly work in subject areas such as anthropology, cultural studies and gender studies, they have to be prepared to publish much (if not all) of this work in paperback immediately in order to achieve a viable level of sales, but many publishers would argue that the traditional method of publishing scholarly books remains preferable in other disciplines.

The traditional method was to publish a scholarly book in a hardback or cloth-only edition in the first instance, with a view to achieving sales in the library market and among individuals with a specialist interest in the topic. Prior to 1960, most university presses tended to publish in cloth only; some presses occasionally released paperback editions of successful hardbacks, or sold paperback rights to commercial houses. The development of paperback lines in university presses began in a systematic way in the 1960s, when a number of presses – including Harvard, Cornell, California, Chicago and Yale – started to release their own paperback editions of books previously published in cloth. If the book did well and sold all or most of its hardback print-run, the publisher would consider whether to bring out a new-in-paperback edition (or 'NIP'); books were rarely published simultaneously in cloth and paperback editions. The main advantages of this strategy were twofold: first, the publisher could sell hardback copies into the library market without running the risk of hardback sales being cannibalized by the availability of a cheaper paperback edition; and second, the publisher could test the market and get some sense of a book's reception before deciding whether to bring out a NIP. But as the sale of hardback copies began to decline from the 1970s on, many academic publishers experimented increasingly with the strategy of publishing scholarly books simultaneously in cloth and paperback. The hope was that libraries would continue to buy the hardback edition and that, at the same time, publishers would be able to secure additional revenue from sales of the paperback edition to academics, students and other interested individuals. Increasingly publishers also hoped that in at least some cases they would be able to secure course adoptions for books which were released immediately in paperback and which could be used as supplementary texts for teaching purposes.

The shift towards simultaneous cloth and paperback publication is apparent from the data presented in table 5.1 and figure 5.1, which show the overall proportion of new books published in different formats by American university presses between 1986 and 2000.[4] The data show that in 1986, just under 60 per cent of new books published by university presses were published in cloth only. By 1998 this had fallen to 37.5 per cent, though it rose to 40 per cent in 2000. On the other hand, in 1986 only 17.5 per cent of

[4] Data presented at the AAUP annual meeting in Toronto, 2001, from: *Annual University Press Statistics*.

Table 5.1 Formats of new titles published by American university presses, 1986–2000 (%)

	1986	1989	1992	1995	1998	1999	2000
Cloth only	59.6	54.5	49.4	43.2	37.5	37.8	40.0
Paper only	22.8	21.2	26.6	28.4	28.8	29.3	27.1
Simultaneous	17.5	24.2	22.8	27.2	32.5	32.9	31.8
Other	0.0	0.0	1.3	1.2	1.3	0.0	1.2
	100.0	100.0	100.0	100.0	100.0	100.0	100.0

Source: Annual University Press Statistics (New York: Association of American University Presses).

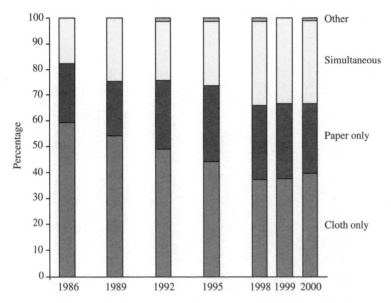

Figure 5.1 Formats of new titles published by American university presses, 1986–2000
Source: Annual University Press Statistics (New York: Association of American University Presses).

new university press books were published in simultaneous cloth and paper editions. By 1999 this had risen to just under 33 per cent, falling slightly to 31.8 per cent in 2000. Paper-only editions increased from 22.8 per cent in 1986 to 29.3 per cent in 1999, falling back to 27.1 per cent in 2000.

From other data we know that the actual number of cloth-only editions published by the university presses did not decline during this period – on average they published the same number in 2000 as they did in 1986. But the actual numbers of simultaneous and paper-only publications increased significantly during this period – hence the steep decline in the proportion of new books represented by cloth-only editions. The data also show that the increase was particularly marked among presses with annual sales

Table 5.2 Average number of new titles published annually by the large American university presses, by format, 1986–2000

	1986	1989	1992	1995	1998	1999	2000
Cloth only	106	111	95	98	101	100	115
Paper only	26	38	55	57	65	71	60
Simultaneous	13	27	42	48	48	49	49
Other	0	1	1	1	1	0	2
Total	145	177	193	204	215	220	226

Source: Annual University Press Statistics (New York: Association of American University Presses).

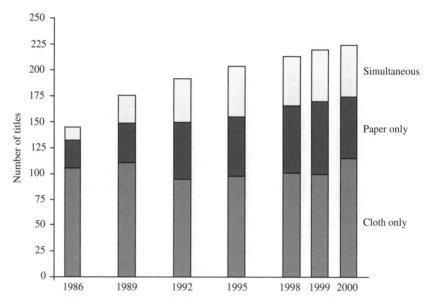

Figure 5.2 Average number of new titles published annually by the large American university presses, by format, 1986–2000
Source: Annual University Press Statistics (New York: Association of American University Presses).

between $3 million and $6 million, and among presses with annual sales above $6 million – in both categories, the number of simultaneous publications more than trebled during this period. The actual numbers of new publications in different formats for the larger American university presses (sales over $6 million) are displayed in table 5.2 and figure 5.2.[5]

Given these changing publishing strategies together with the decline of the library market, it is not surprising that the proportions of the revenue generated by cloth and paper editions have changed significantly in the university presses over time, as can be

[5] Ibid.

Table 5.3 Breakdown between total cloth sales and total paperback sales of American university presses (%)

	1968	1982	1991	1992	1993	1994	1995	1996	1997	1998	1999	2000
Units												
Cloth		37	34	33	32	32	30	31	30	30	30	32
Paper		63	66	67	68	68	70	69	70	70	70	68
Dollars												
Cloth	75	66	56	56	54	52	50	50	48	48	48	49
Paper	25	34	44	44	46	48	50	50	52	52	52	51

Source: *Annual University Press Statistics* (New York: Association of American University Presses).

seen from table 5.3.[6] Back in 1968, around 75 per cent of the sales of the American university presses was accounted for by cloth editions, and only 25 per cent by paper. By 1982, the proportion of sales accounted for by cloth editions had fallen from 75 per cent to 66 per cent, while the proportion accounted for by paper editions had increased from 25 per cent to 33 per cent. By 1995, the proportions were equal – 50 per cent cloth, 50 per cent paper. By 1997, the sales of paper editions were accounting for a larger proportion of the total revenue than the sales of cloth – 52 per cent paper, 48 per cent cloth.

The tendency among university presses (and academic publishers more generally) to release a growing proportion of their new books as simultaneous editions was an understandable response to the decline of hardback-only sales, but there were risks and costs associated with this strategy. The strategy worked best when there was a clearly defined course-adoption market for a book: in these cases, the book would be recommended by lecturers and professors, and the availability of the paperback edition would generate sales among students. Editors at university presses can cite numerous cases of books which were published simultaneously in cloth and paper and which took off in paperback, getting good course adoptions and selling thousands of copies year after year. But publishers also found that many of the academic books they published simultaneously did not actually secure significant coursebook adoptions, despite expectations (in some cases based on confident predictions by external readers) that they would do so. Books based on revised dissertations were particularly prone to underperform as simultaneous publications, although disappointing sales were not unique to revised dissertations. Most academic publishers can provide many examples of books published simultaneously which sold no more than a few hundred copies in paper and even fewer in cloth. Given that the revenue generated by each paperback sale is significantly less than the revenue generated by the sale of a cloth edition and that the margin on paperbacks is generally lower, it was necessary to sell many more copies of a book when it was released in paperback than when it was published only in hardback in order to cover costs, let alone generate a surplus. But the paperback sales of many of the titles released as dual editions simply did not live up to the expectations of editors and authors.

In addition to disappointing paperback sales, there was another risk associated with simultaneous publication – namely, that some libraries would shift their new acquisi-

[6] Ibid.

Table 5.4 Differentials in average list prices of cloth and paper editions

	Comparison of nine university presses, May 2000–April 2001			
	Average list $ cloth	Average list $ paper	Factor	Paper/Cloth?
Press 1	$46.77	$21.62	2.16	Paper
Press 2	$67.93	$23.44	2.90	Paper
Press 3	$39.29	$21.46	1.83	Paper
Press 4	$60.53	$20.08	3.01	Paper
Press 5	$60.57	$20.75	2.92	Paper
Press 6	$38.43	$19.80	1.94	Paper
Press 7	$33.97	$27.10	1.25	Cloth
Press 8	$32.13	$20.10	1.61	Cloth
Press 9	$29.05	$ 9.95	2.92	Paper

Source: Dana Courtney, 'The Paper–Cloth Conundrum', *Against the Grain*, 14/2 (Apr. 2002).

tions from hardback to paperback, eroding still further the sales of hardback editions. Throughout the 1980s and 1990s, librarians were searching for ways to ease the growing pressures on their acquisitions budgets, as we have seen. When academic publishers began to make an increasing proportion of their new books available in dual editions, many librarians saw the purchase of paperback editions rather than cloth editions as a way of reducing the costs of new book acquisitions. Library wholesalers like Yankee Book Peddler began to offer what they called 'paper-preferred approval plans' to librarians from the early 1990s on: these plans enabled librarians to refine their approval plans in order to stipulate that, when a new title was released in a paper as well as a cloth edition, the wholesaler should supply the paper edition. In deciding whether to buy a cloth or paper edition, librarians' decisions are generally based on two considerations: the price differential between the cloth and paper editions, and the durability of the binding. There are some librarians who will always buy the cloth edition on grounds of durability, but there are others – especially those who face tighter constraints on their budgets – who will choose to buy the paper edition if the price of the cloth edition exceeds the price of the paper edition by a factor of 1.8 or more. Table 5.4 compares the average list price of cloth and paper editions of nine American university presses in the period May 2000 to April 2001, based on data gathered by Yankee Book Peddler. The final column indicates which edition many librarians would choose given the differential between the prices of the cloth and paper editions.[7]

Librarians who buy paper editions vary in the way they use them. Some will put them on the shelves as paper editions, and will strengthen or replace the binding if and when it begins to deteriorate. Others may simply dispose of the book if and when it begins to fall apart, especially if the demand for it has fallen off. Some librarians may arrange for the wholesaler to rebind the book before it is sent to them under their approval plan.

[7] Data supplied by Dana Courtney, Yankee Book Peddler, AAUP annual meeting in Toronto, 2001; subsequently published in Dana Courtney, 'The Paper–Cloth Conundrum', *Against the Grain*, 14/2 (Apr. 2002), pp. 28–33.

Since some wholesalers charge between $7 and $8 on average to rebind a book, it is often much cheaper for a librarian to buy the paper edition and have it rebound than it is to buy the original hardback edition. Dana Courtney at Yankee Book Peddler – one of the leading library wholesalers in the US – felt confident that the trend towards paper-preferred approval plans would continue: 'Simultaneous paper editions are a huge money-saver for libraries and my prediction is that more and more will opt for paper-preferred approval plans and choose paper over cloth for their firm orders. If publishers continue to price their cloth editions at two and three times their paper editions, I think it's guaranteed.'

So, ironically, by shifting to a strategy of simultaneous cloth/paper editions as a way of trying to compensate for the decline of hardback sales, publishers contributed unwittingly to the very problem they were hoping to alleviate. They discovered that when they published new books in both cloth and paper, the sales of the cloth edition commonly fell to even lower levels – by 2000, some academic publishers had found that the sales of the cloth edition had fallen to as low as 200 copies worldwide. The falling hardback sales meant that the financial viability of a new book published in dual editions depended increasingly on the sales of the paper edition, but in many cases the paper sales were simply too modest to make up the lost ground.

The dangers of the simultaneous strategy have led many academic publishers in recent years to reconsider the wisdom of releasing scholarly works immediately in paperback, and many publishers have moved back towards the view that scholarly books should be published initially in hardback only unless there is a good reason not to. If there are reasons to believe that a new book has the potential to be adopted as a course text, then it would clearly be sensible to publish the book immediately in paperback – if it were released in cloth only, the potential adoptions might well be lost. But the climate within many academic publishing firms today is no longer to assume that simultaneous publication would be the best way to proceed. The onus is increasingly on editorial and marketing staff to justify the decision to release a book immediately in paperback. As one editorial director of an American university press remarked:

> We're really at a reality checkpoint. Whereas in the past we were looking for reasons to do a book in paperback, I think we've now reversed that and our default mode is increasingly becoming hardback. We're looking for reasons to publish in cloth. If you've got a season full of paperbacks, just trying to meet your sales goals becomes almost impossible. If we're doing a paperback edition, try to justify it then: are there courses out there? Give us hard figures. What are the courses? Who teaches the courses? That's sometimes difficult to determine and we have to make judgment calls but increasingly we're trying to be more hard-nosed in decisions on what the market for the paperback is. Our cloth runs are now down to about 250 copies, with sales often below 200 on simultaneous runs. So one has to ask, is it worth it?

Editors like this tend to adopt a mixed strategy, publishing a proportion of their new books in cloth only (and, as we've seen, this proportion has increased slightly in recent years, thus reversing the dominant trend of the 1980s and 1990s) and a proportion in simultaneous cloth and paper editions. They might also publish some new books in hardback initially while at the same time planning a delayed paperback release, printing f&gs (i.e. sheets which are printed, folded and gathered) and extra covers and binding up the paperback at a later date. The advantages of f&gs are that the publisher saves costs on printing, since the printer doesn't have to make new plates for a subsequent paperback, and the publisher also has the option of binding up more f&gs as hardbacks if the cloth edition sells better than expected. The danger is that the sales of the hardback edition may be disappointing and the publisher may be landed with a large quantity of f&gs that cannot be sold in either cloth or paper editions. An editor might also choose to release a certain number of new books in paperback only, in cases where there is little prospect of significant library sales; but the paperback-only option is more likely to apply in those sectors of the list which are not strictly academic.

While the pendulum has to some extent swung back in recent years towards hardback-only publication, there are some academic disciplines or interdisciplinary subjects where it seems particularly difficult to achieve sales in hardback and where many publishers therefore feel obliged, if they are going to publish in these subjects at all, to publish new books immediately in paperback. These are subjects like anthropology, some areas of sociology (i.e. the so-called 'softer' social sciences) and many of the interdisciplinary subjects like media and cultural studies, gender studies, ethnic studies and environmental studies. Why these subjects should be less amenable to a hardback-only publishing strategy is not entirely clear; it may be that the library market is generally less robust for books in these subjects, and individual scholars working in these areas are less willing to pay the price of a hardback. In any case, those academic publishers who are active in these subjects tend to take the view that there is a strong market preference in these subject areas for paperbacks, and while they do sometimes publish new books in these areas in hardback only, the default position for new publications tends to be dual cloth–paper editions.

Another important factor which sometimes influences decisions concerning publishing strategy is the preference of authors. Many academics have a strong preference to see their books published immediately in paperback and they have become increasingly inclined to treat this as an issue to be discussed and negotiated with publishers. It is not uncommon for an author to ask for an assurance from a publisher that his or her book will be published immediately in paperback, and there are many instances where a publisher will feel obliged to give this assurance in order to increase the chance of signing up a book, especially if several presses are after the book and/or the author. Even in cases where no such assurance has been given, an author may place pressure on an editor to publish his or her book immediately in paperback, and an editor may feel obliged to do so in order to remain on good terms with the author, in the hope that he or she might be inclined to stay with the press and write more books for it in the future. In a highly competitive marketplace for content, the question of how best to publish a book cannot be entirely divorced from the question of how to attract and keep the creators of content.

So while the experience of the last two decades has made many academic publishers more cautious about publishing new scholarly books in simultaneous editions, there are a variety of factors which are likely to ensure that simultaneous publication will remain a common practice, especially in certain subject areas. In recent years the pendulum has begun to swing back towards hardback-only publications but it is unlikely to return to anything like the level of the past. Most academic publishers will adopt a mixed strategy today, assessing on a title-by-title, author-by-author and subject-by-subject basis how best to publish a new book. Editors will be encouraged (and have been encouraged in recent years, as we shall see below) to talk with sales and marketing staff about the best way to publish a particular book in order to maximize its potential (or minimize the risk). It is also likely that decisions concerning the publishing strategy for scholarly books will be affected in significant ways by new technological developments such as digital printing and print on demand, an issue to which we shall return.

Greater selectivity in title acquisition and list-building

The declining sales of scholarly monographs have also led academic publishers to scrutinize more carefully the kinds of books they are publishing. In the 1970s and 1980s, many academic publishers tended to operate with what we could describe as a 'higher-throughput model' of monograph publishing – that is, it was assumed that you could improve the bottom line by increasing the throughput of new titles while holding your costs constant (or even reducing them). This kind of approach was viewed by some academic publishers as a way of improving the productivity of the organization, since, by streamlining systems and redeploying staff, one could increase the throughput of titles without increasing the number of employees (and perhaps even reducing the number overall). The higher-throughput model worked well so long as the sales of new monographs held up, but the declining sales of the 1980s and 1990s placed growing pressure on this approach. The ability to improve the bottom line by increasing the throughput of new titles was gradually undermined by the decreasing revenue per title; publishers found themselves running faster and faster to generate the same amount of revenue (or even less), putting more and more books into the system in a somewhat desperate attempt to meet the annual sales targets. As one sales manager who has worked in academic publishing for many years observed:

> Presses that had previously grown by producing monographs found themselves in an uncontrollable situation. The best analogy I can think of is like a mouse on a treadmill where they were running faster and faster and faster just to stand still. Because what was happening is the next year they produced 10 per cent more titles, going up from, say, 150 monographs to 165. But instead of the revenue growing by 10 per cent as it had done previously, the sales, the units sold to the libraries, were dropping by 10 per cent. So they were having to produce more and more titles to produce an income that was at best flat or still declining.

The only way to escape from this situation in the medium to long term was for publishers to change the kind of books they produced. Hence many academic publishers began to move away from the higher-throughput model and to adopt a policy of *increased selectivity*, with a view to being more discriminating in terms of the monographs that were published and changing the 'mix' of the list in favour of books that would have stronger sales and a longer life as an active backlist title. The objective was to give more attention to fewer books, and to seek to acquire titles that would make a more substantial overall contribution to the financial performance of the press. The policy of increased selectivity involved several distinct components, the most important of which were the following: (1) increased selectivity in monograph acquisition, (2) changing the mix of the list, (3) focusing on some subject areas at the expense of others, and (4) developing a more proactive commissioning strategy. Let us briefly examine each.

(1)   It is a common belief among academic publishers that one of the reasons why some scholarly monographs do not sell well is that the quality is simply not high enough. Partly because they implicitly accepted the higher-throughput model, academic publishers got into the habit of taking on and publishing books which were very good but not truly outstanding, and now they are paying the price. Doctoral dissertations – revised and unrevised theses – are commonly singled out as the main culprit, but they are not the only problem. Academic series of specialist monographs in certain fields – such as particular periods of history or of literature, or particular area studies – have also become a source of difficulty for many publishers. In the 1970s and 1980s, setting up monograph series with academics as series editors was a relatively easy and cost-effective way to increase the throughput of new titles. But as the sales of monographs began to decline, many of these series began to look increasingly like liabilities. All too often they formed clusters of highly specialized books (many of which are based on doctoral dissertations) that consistently underperformed in sales terms.

In response to these developments, a number of academic publishers have tried to introduce greater selectivity into the acquisition of new monographs. They have sought to raise the quality threshold – to eliminate (or at least to thin out) the category of the 'merely worthy' and to seek to publish only those monographs that are truly outstanding. In some cases they have also closed down a number of monograph series which were underperforming in sales terms, and sought to give more attention to the management of those series they wished to maintain, in order to improve the quality and performance of the list. One senior figure in the university press world put it like this:

> I think the greater financial discipline has actually led to greater selectivity and a higher quality in what is published. It certainly has become more difficult to publish monographs, and publishers will say it's because they won't sell. That's true because they sell less than they did. But when you look at a lot of the monographs that aren't being published as a result, I think it is mostly those theses which were pouring forth from the presses in the sixties and early seventies. I don't think it's the important work. Not that we are turning away stuff we should be publishing – if anything, we are slightly overpublishing. And I don't mind sharing with you the fact that we have agreed this year that we don't want to increase our output of monographs. We want to publish fewer books which are what we would call 'worthy but dull'.

In an effort to exercise greater selectivity, some academic publishers have raised the threshold in terms of what monographs they are prepared to take on. They are more willing to turn down projects that they would have taken on in the past, on the grounds that, while they may be perfectly worthy contributions to the academic literature, they do not appear to be truly outstanding. As the director of a large university press remarked, 'We have turned away a lot of books which I think we would have published two or three years ago – books that could be regarded as worthy, competent, wouldn't blemish our imprint in any way at all, but were not outstanding in their field and actually wouldn't have made any financial contribution either.'

Greater selectivity in terms of title acquisition may be an entirely sensible strategy, but there are two problems with this kind of response. The first is that it assumes a correlation between the quality of a monograph and its likely sales which may not be fully justified. There are some senior figures in academic publishing who strongly believe that such a correlation exists – as one manager remarked, 'the better the book, the more commercially viable it intrinsically will be; even if it sells in small quantities, it will sell at a high price. That's the key thing about academic publishing which a lot of people have never grasped.' But not all academic publishers share this view; not all are so sure that there is a direct and reliable correlation between quality and commercial viability. 'We used to tout this line that there is always a market for excellence,' said one senior academic publisher, 'but I can tell you it's crap, it's not true and the world does not recognize the value that we're putting into these books.' And indeed, most academic publishers can come up with numerous examples of high-quality monographs that sold poorly. In so far as there is some doubt about the relation between quality and sales, it's not clear that raising the quality threshold will succeed in reducing the number of poor-selling monographs, since monographs that are judged to be outstanding in the peer review process may still turn out to sell in small numbers. The sales of monographs may be determined more by factors such as the disciplinary subject area and the breadth or narrowness of the treatment than by the quality of the monograph per se. Raising the quality threshold may be a sensible and laudable step for academic publishers to take, but this step by itself may not have a significant impact on the sales performance of the list.

The second problem with the strategy of increased selectivity is that it is often difficult to implement in practice. Partly this is because judgements of quality are by nature controversial and there is often room for disagreement, especially in the humanities and social sciences. One reader may say that a manuscript is the best thing he or she has read on the subject for a decade, while another may be unimpressed. Hence 'quality' is not the kind of criterion that can be applied in precisely calibrated degrees. It may be the intention of senior management to take on only the truly outstanding monographs and to turn down the merely worthy, but drawing the line between the truly outstanding and the merely worthy is often difficult to do in practice. It is also difficult to implement this strategy partly because, in the day-to-day flow of editorial activity, there is an institutional inertia that is hard to change. Editors are constantly sifting through a large number of potential monograph projects and are already exercising a high degree of selectivity in deciding which projects to take forward and which to turn down. They may feel that they are already doing everything they can to identify those monographs that are truly exceptional in terms of quality, and they may find it difficult in practice to be more exacting. So exhortations from senior management to raise the quality threshold may not be sufficient to reduce the number of monographs taken on. It may be necessary to introduce other measures, such as formal or informal quotas which put a ceiling on the number of monographs signed by an editor or by the press as a whole during a given period, in order to achieve an actual reduction.

Another reason why it is often difficult to implement the policy of increased selectivity is that, faced with the immediate and pressing need to make your sales forecast, the temptation to go for higher throughput is not easy to resist. While many senior managers would agree with the view that it would be better in principle to publish fewer books but ones which generated higher revenue and had stronger backlist potential, in practice it may be difficult to give up the immediate injection of frontlist revenue provided by the release of new books, even if they are scholarly monographs. Restructuring the revenue basis of an academic publishing firm is a long-term process; it takes time to commission different kinds of books, time to write and develop them and time to turn them into revenue-generating titles. Hence if a publisher cuts back on monographs while it is still waiting for the higher revenue-generating titles to come through, it is likely to experience a temporary downturn in overall revenue. So if a senior manager is faced with pressure to ensure that the results don't fall short of the sales forecast for the year, as many are, then reducing the throughput of new titles doesn't necessarily look like the most sensible short-term strategy, even if it makes good sense in a longer-term perspective.

(2)   The second component of the policy of increased selectivity involves changing the mix of the list. An academic publisher who is active in a particular subject area often publishes different kinds of books in that area, including scholarly monographs, textbooks, reference works, anthologies and books which have some trade potential ('academic-trade' titles). The mix gives a certain 'architecture' to the list that is attractive to academic publishers for a number of reasons. In the first place, it spreads the risks in financial terms, since textbooks, reference works, etc., may perform better than monographs and make a more substantial financial contribution. Second, it strengthens the foothold of the publisher in a particular subject area and provides benefits and synergies that come from having a certain critical mass in a field – for example, it provides some economies of scale in terms of marketing. Third, it strengthens the hand of the publisher in the competitive struggle for new content, since the publisher can demonstrate a wide-ranging commitment to a subject area and can make a plausible case that it is able effectively to market different kinds of books within it. Fourth, it also increases the job satisfaction of editors and other staff, since it enables them to work on different kinds of projects and to share some of the excitement that comes from working on books that could sell – and in some cases actually do sell – exceptionally well.

When applied to the architecture of the list, the policy of increased selectivity generally amounts to a structured shift of emphasis: staff are urged to spend less time and fewer resources on the acquisition, development and marketing of monographs and to devote more attention to acquiring, developing and marketing other kinds of books. Exactly how publishers try to achieve this shift of emphasis – and how far they try to shift it – varies from one organization to another and depends on a variety of factors, including the size of the organization, its constitutional status and the managerial and organizational cultures that prevail within it. In some cases, senior managers have merely indicated a preference for editors to commission some books other than monographs, while in other cases they have introduced specific targets or quotas for different types of books. In some cases managers have tried to change the mix of the list by redirecting the commissioning activities of existing editors without changing the organizational structure; in other cases they have set up new departments (e.g. for textbooks) and brought in new staff in order to increase commissioning activity in certain areas, thus redirecting resources in ways that were aimed at producing a structured shift of emphasis in the publishing programme. In some cases managers have viewed the shift of emphasis as a way of complementing and supporting the continued publication of scholarly monographs; in other cases they have sought to restructure their publishing programmes in more radical ways, reducing or even winding down their monograph programme and replacing it with a dedicated focus on different kinds of publishing.

The structured shift of emphasis with regard to the architecture of the list is an issue of enormous significance. It has fundamental implications not only for the nature and future of academic publishing but also for the academic communities which are served by it. I shall therefore return to this shift in the following chapter and examine its nature and consequences in greater detail.

(3)   A third aspect of the policy of increased selectivity has to do with the willingness and ability of publishers to focus on some subject areas at the expense of others. Traditionally it was common practice for academic publishers – both university presses and commercial firms – to publish across a wide range of academic disciplines. In the case of many university presses, this disciplinary catholicism was a reflection of the fact that the press was generally regarded as the publishing wing of the university itself, and hence had a responsibility to cater for all the scholarly communities represented within the university of which it was part. However, in an environment characterized by declining monograph sales and increasing competitiveness among firms, there are certain disadvantages in pursuing a policy of disciplinary catholicism. Given that the resources of most academic publishers are quite limited, an organization that tries to publish across too many subject areas runs the risk of spreading itself too thinly. It may end up building a list that has a presence in many subject areas but excels in none, and it may find itself publishing in areas where it will never be able to compete effectively with the major players in the field. The efforts and energy of editorial staff may be dispersed across too many subject areas, and this may limit their ability to develop the kinds of networks and relationships that would underpin real success in any of them. Moreover, it will have to spread its marketing resources across titles aimed at different constituencies; it may find it difficult to achieve the scale it needs in order to bring its new titles to market in a cost-effective way. In short, it may find that the costs of doing business in some subject areas are exceeding the benefits gained, especially when the kinds of books it is publishing in these subject areas are largely scholarly monographs with declining sales.

Academic publishers have responded to this dilemma in differing ways. Many commercial academic publishers have sought to consolidate their lists in certain subject areas where they have an established strength; they have actively invested in areas which they believe to offer the potential for growth and for profitable publishing, while winding down or axing their investment in areas which are not yielding the kinds of results they would like to see. Since, ultimately, commercial publishers do not have to answer to any constituencies other than their shareholders, they are relatively free to change the disciplinary focus of the list in accordance with their assessment of its actual and likely financial performance. In the case of the university presses, however, it is much more difficult to restrict and change the disciplinary focus of the list, and any attempt to do so runs the risk of alienating certain academic constituencies within their host universities. Many of the university presses have nonetheless sought, in differing ways and with differing degrees of success, to move away from the kind of disciplinary catholicism that was a common feature of university presses in the past, and have tried to concentrate their efforts and resources in certain subject areas.

The move towards disciplinary specialization among the university presses was pioneered by one or two directors in the 1970s and early 1980s – most notably by Frank Urbanowski at MIT Press. When Urbanowski arrived at MIT in 1976, the press was running a serious deficit and had a great deal of stock in the warehouse which, with the decline of the library market, would never be sold – a situation that was not uncommon among university presses at the time. And like most university presses, MIT Press was publishing in many different subject areas, from linguistics and architecture to political science, urban studies and fiction. As part of the development plan for the press, Urbanowski proposed to refocus the list on a small number of subject areas – 'we selected half a dozen areas and said, "This is going to be our core publishing program. We're not going to publish anywhere else."' The areas chosen were linguistics, philosophy, computer science and artificial intelligence, economics, architecture, and cognitive science. All their acquisition, development and marketing efforts were refocused on these six subject areas.

The decision to focus the list on certain disciplinary areas undoubtedly paid dividends for MIT Press, which went on to become one of the largest of the American university presses. There was a price to be paid for this disciplinary specialization – the press could no longer hope to achieve a significant presence in many academic fields, including many of the fields in which its host university, the Massachusetts Institute of Technology, was a leading institution of teaching and research, and there were some academics at MIT who were very unhappy to see lists in their subjects discontinued. But there were considerable benefits in terms of concerted list-building and marketing in a shrewdly chosen range of subject areas. These areas included subjects – like linguistics, economics and architecture – where most other university presses tended to be weak or to have no presence at all, and hence MIT Press could build a reputation as a leading publisher in the field. They also included subjects – such as computer science and cognitive science – that were emerging and expanding fields and where demand for cutting-edge content would grow. Moreover, they were subjects where the host institution tended to be strong, and hence the press had a pool of potential authors at its doorstep. They were also subjects where monograph sales would remain relatively buoyant and where scholarly work would travel well in the international marketplace.

MIT Press was an early mover in the shift towards greater disciplinary specialization among the university presses and today it is regarded by some as a model to be emulated. But the move towards disciplinary specialization has been a very complex and uneven process in the world of the university presses; by no means all of them have gone in this direction and it remains a hotly contested issue. Many university presses continue to practise a much higher degree of disciplinary catholicism than MIT Press, but the increasingly difficult economic conditions of recent years have forced the senior management at many presses to review the scope of their editorial activities. Some have tried to give greater disciplinary focus to their list-building activities, and to wind down their commissioning in areas which are marginal to their core concerns and/or where the financial performance of their list has been particularly disappointing. In some cases this has involved pulling out of whole subject areas and refocusing editorial energies on a selected and limited set of disciplines, along the lines of MIT press. In other cases it has involved more subtle shifts of emphasis – for example, many American university presses which are active in history have sought to wind down their lists in European history and Latin American history, where sales have declined sharply in recent years, and to give more emphasis to American history or even to specific areas of American history, such as Civil War history or the history of the American South. Many presses have tried to bring about these shifts of emphasis in relatively gentle ways. Editors can be encouraged to redirect their energies, to focus on new areas or subareas while cutting down the numbers of books they do in other areas, which, while not being axed completely, are left to 'wither on the vine'. Publishers who try to proceed in a more abrupt and explicit fashion may find themselves paying a high price in terms of public relations, both within the host university and in the broader academic and public domain – as OUP, among others, discovered to its cost.[8]

While methods and tactics vary from one university press to another, depending on the size and circumstances of the press and on the nature of its relationship to its host institution, there are many senior managers in the university press world who feel that in the increasingly difficult conditions of academic publishing, the disciplinary catholicism of the past is no longer a viable option. They believe that they must proactively shape their list-building activities and concentrate their resources so that they can compete effectively in those subject areas where they stand a chance of becoming a serious player. But at the same time some directors, especially at the larger university presses, find that their ability to shape the list proactively is constrained by the traditional expectations of a university press that are held by many academics and administrators in their host institutions. One senior manager at a large university press expressed this tension very well:

> I suppose the challenge for us is that we are an extremely overdiversified sort of business in terms of the number of disciplines in which we publish and that's because we are expected to represent the range of the university's intellectual interests. I don't actually think that is a sustainable model in the long run in the sort of competitive environment that we are in. We are spreading ourselves too thinly and we are paying the price for that. Academic publishing is like most forms of activity, it's about expertise, and being a good history publisher is actually different from being a good physics publisher. Your market is different, your editorial practice is different, there are common things like warehousing and book production that are similar, but the editorial and marketing side is very different according to the discipline that you are operating in. If you are operating in about forty disciplines or more, you are going to be less effective than if you are operating in ten. But that is not something the delegates of the university are comfortable with. So there is a tension here because I'm giving one form of advice and they're giving another. One just has to accept that that's one of the issues.

(4)   A fourth aspect of the policy of increased selectivity involves the adoption and cultivation of a more proactive commissioning strategy. All publishers receive a large number of unsolicited proposals and inquiries from authors and potential authors; the more well known a publisher is in a particular field, the larger the number of unsolicited proposals it receives. Academic publishers are frequently swamped with unsolicited proposals for books based on Ph.D. theses, conference papers and research projects. In practice these unsolicited proposals are commonly allowed to accumulate for a period of time. Occasionally someone sifts through the slush pile and selects a handful of proposals, manuscripts and letters of inquiry that seem worth pursuing. This can be a time-consuming process, although experienced editors are usually able to form a judgement very quickly as to whether a project is worth the investment of further time and effort.

For academic publishers whose output includes a significant number of scholarly monographs, unsolicited proposals can be an important source of new books. As a press

---

[8] In 1999 OUP decided to close down its contemporary poetry list and its UK music books list, a decision which elicited a good deal of hostile criticism within the university and in the national press; it was even discussed in the House of Lords, where the Lord Bishop of Oxford asked if the government 'will be making representations to save the Oxford Poet's list'.

gains a reputation and a profile in a particular academic subject area, scholars who are doing research in that area will be increasingly inclined to send their book proposals to it, in the hope that the press will recognize the merits of the project and want to add the book to its list. In the case of university presses, the flow of unsolicited material is increased further by the fact that university presses are traditionally seen by many academics in the host institution as a natural home for their research publications, and hence a natural port of call when they are beginning to think about how to publish the outcome of their research. Even if an editor is very experienced and can separate fairly quickly the projects that are worth pursuing from those that are not, the task of following up the unsolicited proposals that seem worthwhile can become an administrative treadmill. Corresponding with authors, sending proposals or manuscripts out to external readers, considering readers' reports and liaising with authors about possible changes, preparing proposals for editorial boards and so on – all of this can take a great deal of time. When added together with the other administrative tasks that an editor has to carry out, there may be little time left over to take independent initiatives or to develop and pursue commissioning plans. Just coping with the relentless day-to-day throughput of proposals and manuscripts at various stages of development can easily become all-absorbing. An organization can become locked into a kind of administrative inertia in which editorial staff are fully preoccupied in coping with the throughput of projects and in which there is little or no space for editorial initiatives that would result in the publication of different kinds of books.

As part of an attempt to take a more proactive role in shaping the nature of their lists and the kinds of books they are publishing, many academic publishers have tried to move away from this model of the acquisitions editor as a relatively passive filter and processor of incoming material, and move towards a rather different model of the editor as a proactive commissioner of new projects. Of course, these two models of the editorial role are not mutually exclusive, and in practice many individual editors combine elements of both. But to create the space and the motivational structures for proactive commissioning often requires managerial intervention and the cultivation of an entrepreneurial culture which is not necessarily present in academic publishing houses. This kind of entrepreneurial culture is more commonly found in the commercial sector, and hence the model of the editor as a proactive commissioner has long been a feature of commercial academic publishers. The model has also featured for many years in the more commercially oriented university presses, which have long encouraged editors to take a more entrepreneurial approach to content acquisition. But as the sales of scholarly monographs declined and the financial pressures on university presses intensified, more and more university presses began to re-examine their commissioning practices and to consider whether and how they could create the space and the incentives to enable – and, in some cases, to require – their editors to adopt a more proactive approach. One editorial director at a university press put it like this:

> The guy I worked for when I arrived here in the late seventies was purely reactive. I was his assistant and I watched the way he worked. He would get proposals in his inbox and he'd read them and he'd decide whether to review them. He never travelled. He couldn't even drive. He was the shyest person on the face of the earth. He would stammer and stutter and never look you in the eye. He would just react to what came across his desk or what somebody phoned in and told him to do. That was possible then. That was a very possible way of acquiring books twenty years ago – no problem. We had several editors like that.

But today, she explained, it's no longer like that. The editors have to be much more proactive. They travel to campuses and call on professors; they go to conferences and listen to papers and try to nab the people who seem good; they think up book ideas and try to find authors to write them. 'Most of us do that – I mean, it's a battle and you have to fight.'

The methods used by academic publishers to achieve this reorientation of editorial activity varied from publisher to publisher. In some cases, editors were asked to draw up their commissioning plans for the coming year and these were discussed with the managing director (or editorial director); progress against the plan was then assessed in a review at the end of the year, during which the plans for the following year were also discussed. In other cases, senior managers drew up specific commissioning targets for each editor on an annual basis; the targets would be agreed at the beginning of a year and each editor's performance would be assessed against the targets during an end-of-year review. The targets could be defined in various ways – in terms of the total numbers of new books of different types that he or she would be expected to sign up during a given year, or in terms of the total amount of revenue likely to be generated during a specifiable period (such as the first year or two of sales) by the books signed up during the year, or in terms of some combination of books, revenue and margins. Each academic publisher which introduced commissioning targets for its editors tended to do so in its own way, adopting a framework that seemed to suit the local culture of the organization and adapting the framework as and when it seemed appropriate to do so. Target-setting had the advantage of formalizing the expectations associated with a more proactive model of commissioning and provided clear benchmarks for assessing an individual's performance against expectations. But it also involved the introduction of measures of productivity which, in the context of a university press, were viewed with anxiety, scepticism or even hostility by some editors.

While some form of target-setting for editors has become increasingly common among academic publishers, there are some senior managers within the university presses who continue to feel that the introduction of formal measures of editorial productivity is not necessarily the most effective way to improve the overall quality and quantity of the press's output. They don't regard explicit quotas as essential and they feel that they may even have counterproductive consequences – for example, by encouraging editors to sign up particular projects in order to meet their targets rather than because they are really strong books. One editorial director at an American university press who has resisted the idea of introducing quotas explained his reasons in the following way:

> There's a bit of pressure in that direction and I've resisted it. I don't want to give people hard targets. I would still say be open and let's have some pots going on every burner. In the same way we don't say to an editor, 'you're expected to acquire fifteen books this year.' We've never said that, partly because it can lead to a kind of desperation in acquisition. Nine months of the year have gone and you've only brought in nine books, and you go look in your drawer and say, 'hey, you guys just got really lucky.' We have drawers full of manuscripts. We have no problems with numbers. We don't want any eighty books in the catalogue. We want eighty books that we've acquired for a reason. When an editor's pitching a book to me, that's what I'm listening for. Do they really believe in the book and when it comes out are they going to be glad? It's not true of every book we've published but that's what I listen for.

Growth of marketing concerns

As academic publishers searched for ways to improve and redirect their commissioning activities and to achieve better financial performances from the books they published, the roles of sales and marketing staff began to change in certain ways. In traditional academic publishing, sales and marketing staff tended to be situated at the final stage of a process that was to a large extent linear: editors commissioned new books, the production staff produced them and sales and marketing staff announced them to potential customers and to various intermediaries in the marketing chain. In this traditional linear model, the commissioning editors were in the position of real power and authority: they were responsible for bringing in new content, and it was the judgements of editors (resting in many cases on the judgements of external readers) that was crucial in deciding whether to take on a project. The key questions in deciding whether to take on a project were questions of quality: How good is the material? How good is the author? How important is the topic? In many academic publishing organizations, sales and marketing staff were not even consulted at this stage, since it was assumed that high-quality scholarly books would sell in sufficient quantities to make them financially viable. And in the days when there was a robust library market for scholarly monographs, this assumption was not altogether unfounded.

But as the library market eroded and the sales of scholarly monographs declined, editors were encouraged (and, in many cases, required) to think more carefully about the sales potential of the new projects they were proposing and the input of sales and marketing staff began to assume a more significant role. In many presses, new procedures were introduced that required editors to estimate likely sales for the new books they were proposing. Editors were encouraged or even required to get the views of sales and/or marketing staff on the sales potential for new projects and on the best way to publish them. The traditional hierarchical and largely one-way relation between editorial staff, on the one hand, and sales and marketing staff, on the other, was gradually replaced by a more interactive model in which sales and marketing staff were given a more prominent role in editorial processes and editors were actively encouraged to solicit their views at various stages of the commissioning process. In short, the traditional linear model (figure 5.3) was gradually replaced by a circular model (figure 5.4).

Exactly how sales and marketing staff were incorporated into earlier decision-making processes, and exactly what role they were expected to play, varied from one press to another. In many cases, senior managers decided that the sales and/or marketing manager should attend editorial meetings and should scrutinize the sales projections for the new books that were being proposed by commissioning editors. Sales and marketing managers were also encouraged to express their views about how best to publish and 'package' the book – should it be published as a scholarly monograph or did it have the potential to be developed and marketed as a trade book, for example? Should the title be changed? Should it be published in hardback only in the first instance, or in hardback and paperback simultaneously? What would be the best price, given the market for which it was being published? In other words, sales and marketing staff were invited to act as a kind of reality check on sales projections, offering their opinions on the sales figures outlined by editors, and they were encouraged to express their views on publishing strategy, that is, on how best to maximize the sales potential of a new project.

Figure 5.3   Traditional linear model

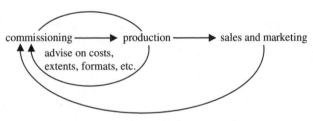

- pre-selection screening device
- advise on how to publish
- some role in deciding which new projects to take on

Figure 5.4   Circular model

The decision to give sales and marketing staff a greater role in editorial processes was often taken by the director or managing director of a press, as part of a broader attempt to create a more market-conscious attitude within the editorial group. In the past, editors at university presses did not completely disregard market considerations, but these considerations were very much secondary to the question of intellectual quality: if the book was judged to be outstanding by the readers, if it fitted the list and the editor wanted to publish it, then the press would generally take it on, believing (and hoping) that the library market would be sufficiently robust to absorb a sufficient number of copies. But at most university presses, that way of thinking is now gone. As one editor put it:

> Twenty years ago we could take the market for granted. We didn't even have the need to focus on certain areas. We really did anything the editor liked and where there was the supporting documentation from the experts. It was very luxurious; it was very much a gentleman's profession. But now we are being asked to function as a business. We are being asked as editors to look at markets, to define those, to justify them in a way that we haven't had to do before. It wasn't that we didn't care about the markets entirely, but it would be after the fact. It was an editorial decision – if it was an excellent book, we published it. Now the market is part of the decision early on. So when we sit at our weekly editors' meeting, there are many marketing people sitting there. They don't make any decision but they give a lot of feedback and ask a lot of questions.

While sales and marketing staff were drawn increasingly into editorial deliberations, they were not always given a significant role in deciding whether a new project should be taken on. In some cases they were encouraged to express their views about the commercial viability of a new project, but in other cases their role was limited to that of advising editorial staff about how best to publish a book they had already decided to do. There was a potential source of tension here; roles were changing and the new responsibilities that were being given to (or being assumed by) sales and marketing staff were not always clearly defined. Senior management perceived the need to take more account of the views of sales and marketing staff, but in many cases editors were reluctant to cede the power they traditionally wielded to decide which books were worth publishing and which were not. This potential source of tension sometimes manifested itself in open disagreement between editorial and marketing staff. 'I can comment but I don't approve,' explained the director of marketing and sales at one of the larger American university presses. 'I pick my battles. If there is something that is a disaster, then I really will say that. But I can't do that too often. It becomes emotional. I wish it was a more business-like decision and that marketing and production and everyone had an equal voice, but that just is not the case.'

While open disagreement in editorial meetings is not uncommon, for the most part the differences of opinion between editorial and marketing staff are dealt with by informal discussions between individuals before a project reaches a formal decision-making process. As part of the incorporation of sales and marketing staff into editorial processes, editors were actively encouraged to talk with them at an early stage about potential projects, and to get their feedback before they invested time and effort in developing a formal proposal, getting reviews, and so on. This would help an editor to decide whether it would be worth their while to invest the time and effort, since it would give them an early indication of how the project would be received if it was developed into a formal proposal. In other words, the opinions of sales and marketing staff increasingly assumed the role of *pre-selection screening devices* that were used by editorial staff to decide whether a potential project was worth pursuing and, more generally, to decide how best to focus their commissioning activities.

Although I have dealt here with the growing involvement of sales and marketing staff in the editorial process, there was also a parallel development in the relationship between editorial and production staff. With the growing pressure on margins, editors were increasingly encouraged (and, in some cases, required) to get the views of production staff on the likely costs associated with particular projects. In some cases, new systems were introduced to ensure that editors obtained estimated unit costs from production as part of the formal proposal submitted to an editorial board – that is, before the board decided whether to take on a project. This would help the board to see whether the proposed combination of costs, prices and expected sales would enable a book to be published in a financially viable way, that is, in a way that would make a positive financial contribution. It might also help editors to see how they could improve the financial contribution of a project – for example, by reducing the number of illustrations or cutting the length of the manuscript. Heavily illustrated books are costly to produce and, in the case of some scholarly monographs, the likely sales may be insufficient to justify the costs. This is an issue that more and more academic publishers have found themselves having to confront and, in some cases, they have turned down projects on these grounds, even though the quality in intellectual terms may be high. The issue of length has similarly become an increasingly important issue for many academic publishers precisely because it is one of the key variables affecting the margin on scholarly books when the overall print-runs are relatively low.

The growth of marketing concerns is attested to by the increasing involvement of sales and marketing staff in editorial processes, but it is also evidenced by the increasing size and professionalization of sales and marketing departments in many academic publishing houses. As one American university press director observed,

What changed in the 1990s is that marketing really became professionalized. It's the last department of scholarly publishing to really become professionalized. We are much more aware of a rapidly changing marketplace at every level – retail, wholesale, distribution – and we talk about it more than we ever did. And if you looked at the growth by departments of university presses, I would bet you that the biggest growth across the board in presses of any size would be in the marketing department. And that's in the last decade, maybe a long decade if you want to make it fifteen years.

Partly this professionalization and expansion of sales and marketing departments reflects the changing nature of the lists – the more emphasis that is placed on publishing books for the trade market, for example, the more these books have to be supported with sales and marketing staff, including staff with particular skills in publicity. It also reflects the changing nature of the retail trade and the need to devote more time and expertise to understanding and cultivating relationships with the key players, including the increasingly powerful retail chains, wholesalers and online booksellers. But the expansion of sales and marketing departments in many academic publishing houses is also indicative of a change of attitude that has gradually taken hold in the field of academic publishing over the last couple of decades as senior managers came increasingly to realize that they could no longer take it for granted that the market would continue to absorb scholarly books, and that they had to place much more emphasis on getting everyone within the organization, including editors, to think more systematically about sales and marketing issues. 'We talk a great deal more about the market, publicity, distribution and sales opportunities,' commented one university press director, 'and I think editors are much smarter and much better educated about all of that because they have more colleagues in marketing and those colleagues are more professional.'

Changing organizational cultures

Thanks in part to the changes examined in this chapter, academic publishing firms have been in the throes of a profound transformation for more than a decade, and the impact of this transformation is still being played out in the day-to-day running of these organizations. The traditional culture of academic publishing, which was concerned above all with building a list of high-quality scholarly books in a broad range of subject areas, has increasingly given way to a more market-conscious culture. Questions of quality have certainly not been brushed aside – the suggestion that quality has been sacrificed on the altar of the market would be an oversimplification of the dynamic of this field.[9] But questions of quality have been supplemented in myriad ways by considerations of the sales potential and financial viability of new book projects. The culture of academic publishing houses has become permeated with a much greater awareness of the importance of the market as managers have struggled to come to terms with the consequences of declining sales. Editors have been obliged to become more market-conscious in their own day-to-day practices. They have incorporated a sense of the importance of the market in their day-to-day judgements about which projects are worth pursuing and which are not, in the way they advise authors about how to develop their work and in

[9] See Schiffrin, *The Business of Books*, p. 140.

the decisions they take about how best to invest their own time and effort. In other words, an awareness of the importance of the market has increasingly become part of their habitus, of their practical schemes of judgement and evaluation and of their way of understanding the nature of their role and task as editors.

Of course, not all editors have adapted so well to this transformation in the organizational culture of academic publishing firms. Some editors who were trained in the more traditional methods of scholarly publishing have found it difficult to accept this new, more market-conscious approach. For some, scholarly publishing was always about publishing works of real quality and intellectual worth, and questions of sales and margins were secondary concerns – these were matters for others to think about and they did not weigh heavily in their editorial judgements. In some cases, these editors have found themselves on a collision course with senior managers who felt obliged to introduce changes into the working practices of their staff. This is not just a clash of attitudes and of different ways of thinking about what is involved in academic publishing: it is a clash of different worlds and worldviews. There are some editors and other professional staff whose practices and ways of thinking were shaped by the kind of academic publishing that existed in the 1970s and early 1980s who feel that it is not just their professional judgement that is being called into question by the new, more market-oriented culture of academic publishing: it is their whole livelihood and way of being that is at stake.

One can see signs of this clash of worldviews in many different contexts – it has become one of the central lines of tension, anxiety and, in some cases, open conflict within the world of academic publishing. Most academic publishing houses have experienced, or are experiencing, this clash in some form and to some extent. But the appointment of a new director or senior management team is often an occasion when this clash of worldviews comes into sharp relief. A new director may come in with a remit to change some of the traditional practices of the organization, to introduce new accounting and management systems and perhaps to change the editorial direction with a view to improving the financial performance of the press. Editors who have been at the press for many years and who have been trained in the traditional practices of academic publishing may resent what they see as the imposition of a business culture and mentality into a world where it is ill-suited and which it doesn't really understand. One senior editor who found himself in just this situation expressed his dismay in these terms:

> I have certain colleagues here who are in the books division but are really administrators and who as far as I'm concerned don't have any relationship to what I consider to be what I'm doing because they're not book people, they're not involved with ideas, they don't know where ideas come from, they don't know what they're about, they don't know what their importance is. They're looking at markets, they're looking at the management of information, they're looking at accounts, they're looking primarily at form and procedure and not content. It's a culture of surveillance and suspicion and emphasis on procedure which makes everyone feel that there's a kind of conspiracy.

This view may be somewhat extreme but it highlights vividly a tension that is real. Book publishing – including academic book publishing – has always been about both ideas and markets, culture and commerce, but the decline of the sales of scholarly monographs over the last two to three decades has forced most academic publishing firms to grapple with the question of markets in ways that they were not accustomed to doing in the past, and this has given rise to tension, anxiety and conflict in the very heart of the firm. Many editors have accepted the need to change and have embraced the new ethos, while others have remained suspicious and have felt that, whatever the merits of the new emphasis on markets and marketability, it is not for them – 'It's fine as long as nobody says that I have to do it,' said one. 'If I have to do it then I'll just have to admit that I don't know how to do that kind of thing.' In some cases, editors who were out of tune with the new ethos were pushed aside or even sacked, while senior managers promoted or sought to recruit editors who would help to instil a more market-conscious approach.

This profound transformation in the organizational culture of academic publishing raises many important questions, but the fundamental question is this: how can an organization continue to operate as an academic publisher when the market for its principal output – the scholarly monograph – is in serious and seemingly continuous decline? This is the central question with which all the players in the field of academic publishing have been struggling in one way or another over the last two decades. The various strategies documented in this chapter have provided publishers with an array of methods to manage this decline and to try to stem the haemorrhaging caused by the erosion of the library market. But most senior managers came to realize, in the course of the 1980s and 1990s, that they could survive in the field of academic publishing only in so far as they also became something other than an academic publisher in the strict sense of the term. This is the fundamental paradox of academic publishing today: *it is possible to survive as an academic publisher only in so far as you are able and willing to move beyond the field of academic publishing per se and to publish different kinds of books for different kinds of markets.* One thoughtful editor at a university press put it like this:

> There's a tension between *responding* to a market demand, which is what Bourdieu would call a heteronomous approach, and *creating* a market demand, and the exciting type of publishing that we do here is creating a demand for a certain kind of book, a book that cuts across fields and suddenly opens up a new area of research for people and gives them something new and fresh to do. But in order to do that kind of book, we have to put the brakes on somewhat in terms of the agenda that we have been following and at least make some concessions to the market if we want to stay alive. In my view, it's not the mission of this press to do that kind of heteronomous publishing but we're going to have to do some of it in order to be able to continue to do what it is our mission to do. The upshot of this debate is that as editors in the book division we have all had to have our consciousnesses raised about the mix of books that we're doing.

It is this paradox and its implications – in terms of the kinds of books that are published by academic publishers and, indeed, in terms of what it means to be an academic publisher today – that we shall explore in the following chapter.

6

Academic publishing in transition (2): list diversification and field migration

We have seen how, in response to the declining sales of scholarly monographs, many academic publishers have tried to bring about a structured shift of emphasis in their list-building activities, and in differing ways have tried to build up their publishing programmes in areas other than traditional monograph publishing. In most cases they have not abandoned monograph publishing – on the contrary, most have continued to publish scholarly monographs and, especially in the case of the university presses, this has remained an important part of what they do. But in a context where the pressures on monograph publishing were becoming more severe every year and seemed unlikely to go away, many academic publishers looked increasingly to other fields of publishing in an attempt to strengthen their financial positions and, if possible, to create some growth. For whatever the future held for scholarly monograph publishing, it seemed increasingly clear to many that this field would offer few prospects for sustained growth in the foreseeable future.

From the viewpoint of the strategic planning of publishing firms which had an active presence in the field of academic publishing, this quest for greener pastures took on a variety of forms. In some cases it was a matter of diverting resources to other kinds of publishing in which the firm was already actively engaged, such as reference or journal publishing. In other cases, the quest for greener pastures assumed more subtle forms – for example, publishing organizations sought to alter the mix of their lists by encouraging editors to redirect their energies towards the acquisition and development of books other than scholarly monographs. This 'mixed portfolio' strategy has been favoured by the smaller publishers and by many of the American university presses which were not large enough to redeploy resources on a significant scale from one internal division to another.

In this chapter I want to analyse in a more systematic way these shifts of emphasis in the list-building activities of academic publishers. I want to look at this process not simply from the viewpoint of particular publishing firms (or particular editors within these firms), but also from the broader viewpoint of publishing fields and the changing positions of firms within these fields. If we look back over the last two or three decades, we can see that the difficulties in the sphere of academic publishing have induced many academic publishers to think strategically about the fields in which they are publishing, and in many cases have led them to try to increase their presence in other, often adjacent fields where they perceive some opportunities for growth. They begin to reposition themselves in relation to the different fields in which they have been or could be active; they begin to commission different kinds of books, and to develop the necessary support services, in order to establish or increase their presence in fields other than academic publishing in the strict sense. In some cases they even begin to redefine the kind of publisher they are, to reinvent themselves and reorient the firm towards a different kind of publishing activity – for example, they no longer think of themselves as an 'academic publisher' but rather as an 'educational publisher' concerned with commissioning, developing and marketing books for a different kind of market.

I shall use two concepts to help make sense of these developments. The first concept is what we could describe as *list diversification*. Viewed from the perspective of the publishing firm, the mixed portfolio strategy is, in effect, a form of diversification – not necessarily a diversification in terms of the *disciplines* in which the publisher is active, but a diversification in terms of the *types of books* that are published. The aim of list diversification is to shift the balance away from scholarly monographs so that the organization is less dependent on them as a source of revenue. The problem with scholarly monographs from a financial point of view is not simply that the unit sales are declining with the erosion of the library market: it is also that the revenue they generate tends to be skewed towards the first year of publication, and the sales in subsequent years tend to be relatively modest. A list which is heavily dependent on scholarly monographs will therefore tend to be frontlist-driven – hence the temptation for academic publishers with a substantial scholarly monograph programme to adopt, explicitly or implicitly, the higher-throughput model. Over the last couple of decades, many academic publishers have come to the view that they must try to get off the treadmill created by the dependence on the revenue patterns of scholarly monographs, and one way of doing this is to diversify the list so that they rely less on monographs and more on books which have different kinds of revenue profiles – especially books that generate substantially more revenue per title and have a much longer and more lucrative life as a backlist title.

Viewed from the perspective of the firm, the emphasis on different types of books can be seen as a form of diversification, but viewed from the perspective of the theory of fields, this same phenomenon takes on a different significance. For different types of books live and breathe in different fields – they are part of a broader set of relations and networks that extend far beyond the confines of particular publishing firms. So when a particular firm takes a decision to diversify its list – for example, to limit or even reduce its output of scholarly monographs and to increase its output of textbooks or trade titles – it is, in effect, altering its relation to various publishing fields. It is, either implicitly or explicitly, knowingly or unwittingly, repositioning itself vis-à-vis these fields. I shall introduce the concept of *field migration* in order to make sense of this phenomenon. Seen from the perspective of the theory of fields, the restructuring of a list is much more than an internal process of redeploying resources and encouraging editors to commission different types of books: it is the migration of the organization into adjacent publishing fields and a shifting of the extent to which they are actively involved in these fields.

Why introduce the concept of field migration when the notion of list diversification would surely do? It's important to take this broader perspective because we cannot understand the problems faced by individual organizations or the implications of their decisions if we view them only from the perspective of particular publishing firms. An academic publisher may take the decision – which is perfectly rational from the financial viewpoint of the firm – to reduce its output of scholarly monographs and increase its output of textbooks or trade titles, but in doing so it is staking its future on its ability to perform in fields other than that of academic publishing per se. What makes decisions of this kind attractive to academic publishers is that these other fields do offer real opportunities for sales and growth and, if they get it right, the difficulties caused by the declining sales of scholarly monographs can be offset, at least to some extent, by successful publishing in adjacent fields. But there are real dangers too, and organizations which are primarily academic publishers may find themselves out of their depth when it comes to publishing in fields that are structured in different ways and that have their own logics of which academic publishers may be only dimly aware. Field migration has benefits but it has risks and costs too – and not only for academic publishers but for the academic community as well.

I shall organize this chapter in a thematic way and I shall use the experience of different publishing organizations to illustrate general arguments and themes. Once again, it should be stressed that there is a great deal of variability in the ways in which individual publishing firms have behaved. The large UK-based university presses, OUP and CUP, have a scale and international scope that provide them with an altogether different basis on which to respond to the changing conditions of academic publishing than the American university presses, which are much smaller and less oriented towards international markets. Similarly, the commercial academic publishers generally have much more leeway for field migration than the university presses. Since it is part of the remit or 'mission' of university presses to publish scholarly work, there is a limit to how far they can withdraw from the field of academic publishing, even if this limit is never clearly defined. Commercial academic publishers, on the other hand, can decide to exit the field if they wish – they may pay a price for doing so in terms of a loss of symbolic capital and a deterioration of their relations with the academic community, but they are not prevented from doing so by virtue of their legal or constitutional status.

The pursuit of diversification

Many publishers who are active in the field of academic publishing have, in fact, been active in other publishing fields for a long time – there is nothing new about the idea of developing a diversified list. The university presses of Oxford and Cambridge, for example, were major publishers of the Bible and other liturgical texts as early as the sixteenth century and, although Bible publishing has long ceased to be a major source of revenue for them, they have diversified into many other fields of publishing. But the decline of the market for scholarly monographs since the early 1970s has induced many academic publishers to reassess their priorities and actively pursue strategies of list diversification. Various notions are used by academic publishers to crystallize these strategies. The notion of 'the balanced list' is perhaps the most common notion, but other metaphors are also used: 'the architecture of the list', 'the balanced portfolio', etc.

The arguments in favour of list diversification for academic publishers are basically twofold. The first is economic: the decline of the market for scholarly monographs has forced publishers who are active in the field of academic publishing to look at other kinds of publishing. Senior managers look at adjacent fields – fields in which the organization may or may not already be active – and consider whether it would make strategic sense to expand their activities there. The hope and the expectation is that by expanding their activities in these adjacent fields, they will be able to shift the balance of their publishing away from scholarly monograph publishing, with its distinctive financial model of frontlist-driven revenue and high-priced books with low (and declining) unit sales, to other kinds of publishing which are geared to different financial models – models which place greater emphasis on the backlist and the longevity of the title, and which generate much higher unit sales and overall revenue per title over time.

While the principal argument in favour of list diversification for academic publishers is unquestionably economic, there is also an argument of a more aesthetic kind concerning the 'architecture' of the list and the benefits that a more diversified list can produce – ranging from marketing synergies to the job satisfaction of editors. There are some senior managers who believe that good academic lists have their own architecture and that the role of an editor is to take responsibility for the list as a whole, thereby ensuring that the subject is well represented at all the levels at which it is studied and taught. One director of a major university press put it like this:

> It has been very much part of our model of editorial development – which was a very idealistic one in a way – that an editor was responsible for a subject area and in that subject area they could produce a list that had a certain kind of architecture that had its own aesthetic appeal almost. A very powerful idea actually – that you would have at the bottom your monograph series, you would then have your intermediate textbooks, your advanced textbooks and your reference books. It would be like a little city that you were building with various kinds of building. By virtue of your management of that whole publishing programme, you could achieve the right kind of balance in this list. Some editors have done that very well and in some subjects it is very fully articulated – there is a good balance between reference, textbook and monograph publishing. But it is not one that we've achieved in all subject areas and it is one that we're trying to achieve in those where we think that it is practicable.

This vision of the architecture of the list provides an argument for diversification that is independent of the economic argument – and, indeed, in the case of this particular university press, list diversification was pursued as a desirable goal in its own right, quite apart from the economic arguments in favour of it. But there can be no doubt that the deepening economic difficulties of scholarly monograph publishing have added fresh appeal to a strategy that has attractions for other reasons as well.

The adoption of a strategy of list diversification does not by itself dictate how one should implement this strategy, and the ways of implementing it vary considerably from one organization to another. If a publisher holds the view that it is part of the job of an editor to be responsible for a subject area and to commission different kinds of books within it, then it is likely to try to achieve list diversification by encouraging editors (through incentives of various kinds), or even requiring them (by a system of targets or quotas), to redirect their commissioning activities towards the acquisition and development of books other than scholarly monographs. This is likely to be the favoured strategy of most of the American university presses, which are simply too small to set up internal divisions or departments which are dedicated to commissioning and developing particular types of books: they will move towards the model of the polymath editor who takes responsibility for a whole subject area and is encouraged or obliged to commission different types of books within it, although in practice what often happens is that particular individuals find that they have a flair for certain kinds of commissioning and take more responsibility for them within the organization. A different way of implementing the strategy of list diversification is to create specialized divisions or groups dedicated to commissioning and developing certain kinds of books, whether these are textbooks, reference books or trade titles. This kind of specialization has real advantages, in that it enables the organization to create dedicated centres which can build up the skills, knowledge and expertise needed in order to become an effective player in different fields of publishing. But it can also give rise to resentment among editorial staff who feel that part of their list is being hived off. One senior academic publisher described his experience like this:

> In the early nineties we were looking around, partly because of the declining monograph scene, for something we could grow. So we set up a textbook unit within the humanities and social science department but within the academic department. We actually found that it was quite difficult for it to forge its own culture and its own way of doing things because it was still part of another department, still using the same marketing resources; the editors were different but still using the same marketing resources and the same production resources. Some of the editors were trying to do monographs as well as textbooks which is difficult because there is a completely different process. So eventually we decided we've got to have our own department. Making a change like that is a big deal because you make the academic editors unhappy because they can no longer do textbooks. They complained a lot – I tell you it was a big deal. Anyway, we've done it and sales are growing by over 10 per cent.

So while internal specialization of this kind has some clear advantages in terms of the potential effectiveness of new publishing initiatives in adjacent fields, it can give rise to internal complications within the organization and dissatisfaction among the editorial staff. It also requires a certain scale that most of the American university presses and the smaller commercial academic publishers simply do not have.

In the context of declining sales of scholarly monographs, the attractions of list diversification for academic publishers are not difficult to see, but what are the risks and dangers? The most obvious risk is a certain *amateurishness* and an inability to compete effectively in a field about which the staff may know very little. Different publishing fields work in different ways, and a publishing organization whose staff are trained primarily in the methods of academic publishing may find it very difficult to become an effective player in a different field. It may simply not know what it's doing, and may lose a lot of money on experiments and risky publishing projects that go wrong. It may also find that its limited resources are not sufficient to do what needs to be done in order to succeed in the field. It becomes a dabbler in other fields, an innocent abroad who doesn't understand the cultures in which it finds itself, and where it lacks the knowledge and resources it needs to succeed.

Another danger is that list diversification can give rise to new kinds of vulnerability. By moving into new fields, academic publishers may be able to create growth while the markets are strong and expanding, but when these markets contract the publishers may find themselves exposed in a particularly dangerous way, with one foot in a declining market for scholarly monographs and another foot in a market to which they had turned for growth but which is now contracting and therefore unable to deliver the hoped-for injections of extra revenue. What may have seemed like a sure-fire strategy for bolstering the finances of the organization and compensating for the decline of scholarly monograph sales suddenly turns into a quagmire, as the organization finds itself trying to come to terms with disappointing performances in several fields at once. This is exactly what happened to many academic publishers – and especially the American university presses – in 2001 and 2002, as we shall see.

So far I've been examining the rationales for list diversification and some of the risks associated with it, but I haven't considered the types of publishing that lend themselves to strategies of diversification by academic publishers. What types of publishing do they regard as suitable arenas for diversification? The answer to this question varies considerably from one publishing organization to another – a great deal depends on the nature of the organization and its specific history. Many of the larger organizations which are active in the field of academic publishing have also been active for many years in fields such as reference publishing, journal publishing, professional publishing and textbook publishing, and it is relatively easy for them to shift the emphasis of their publishing by diverting more resources into their activities in these other fields – by taking on new editors, seeking to expand the journals programme by acquiring more journals, etc. For those academic publishers who have journals programmes, there is a real financial incentive to expand further in this domain because the economics of journal publishing are much more attractive than those of book publishing (and especially scholarly monograph publishing). But journal publishing is a field that has a complex dynamic of its own, a dynamic that tends to favour incumbents and to favour size.[1] Hence, for academic publishers who don't already have a presence in the field of journal publishing, the opportunity to diversify by building a journals list has become increasingly unrealistic over the last couple of decades. And for those academic publishers who remain in the field of journal publishing, the costs of remaining a competitive player have increased significantly, so much so that some have begun to wonder whether they can afford to remain in the game.

There are, however, three fields which have had a particularly strong 'pull' for academic publishers over the last two to three decades: (1) textbook publishing, (2) trade publishing, and, for the American university presses, (3) regional publishing. There are other fields which have proved attractive to some academic publishers, such as reference publishing and professional publishing, but their appeal has not been quite as widespread. In the following sections I shall therefore concentrate on these three fields and try to explain why they have exerted a particularly magnetic effect on academic publishers.

---

[1] The increasing competitiveness of the field of journal publishing, combined with the high costs associated with the move to electronic environments of journal delivery and storage, have made it increasingly costly to remain in the field and increasingly difficult for new publishers to enter it. The field of journal publishing has a logic of its own which is shaped by, among other things, the uneasy relation of cooperation and benefit maximization between publishers and copyright holders (sometimes the copyright is owned by the publishers but often it is not, and the copyright holders can move to other publishers if they are not satisfied with the terms of their licensing agreement); the benefits that stem from scale (both in terms of economies of scale and in terms of negotiating power with libraries, library consortia and other intermediaries of various kinds); and the very substantial costs associated with the move to an electronic environment for journal delivery and storage. Given the logic of the field, journal publishing tends to favour the larger players who become increasingly aggressive in their acquisitive moves. Publishers who are active in journal publishing find themselves spending more and more time trying to retain the journals they publish, to acquire new journals and to fend off acquisitive moves from other publishers. They also find themselves having to invest more and more in the development of electronic systems of delivery and storage. The costs of remaining in the field have grown while the costs of entering it have become increasingly prohibitive.

The pull of the textbook market

For many academic publishers who, in the course of the 1980s and 1990s, were searching for ways to cope with the precipitous decline of scholarly monograph sales, the textbook market looked more and more attractive. There were several reasons for this. First and foremost, the economics of textbook publishing are very different from those of scholarly monograph publishing and they match more closely the kinds of revenue profiles that managers were seeking to create as a way of offsetting the decline of the monograph. Whereas monograph publishing tends to be frontlist-driven with rapid backlist decay, textbook publishing is oriented much more to the development of a backlist with ongoing sales. As one senior sales manager in an academic publishing firm in the UK put it,

> With monographs you get a one-off sale and the book is dead. Now developing a textbook is more time-consuming, you might need to spend 25 or 30 per cent more time on it. But instead of a book being dead in two years, if you get it right, it is a book that has a life, an increased sale and a life-edition of four to five years and the potential to revise very easily with minimal tweaks. It is potentially a book that could last thirty years and five editions.

Not only were the economics of textbook publishing more attractive, but the market seemed to be a good deal more robust than the market for scholarly monographs. The sale of scholarly monographs relied very heavily on a library market which, as we have seen, was being squeezed by the downward pressure on acquisition budgets, on the one hand, and the rapidly escalating costs of scientific and scholarly periodicals, on the other – the pool of available resources in the market was slowly drying up, and the resources that remained for monograph acquisitions were being spread ever more thinly. By contrast, there were large numbers of students going into institutions of higher education – from the mid-1980s, these numbers increased significantly in both Britain and the United States. Unlike the market for scholarly monographs, the market for textbooks seemed to be expanding. Moreover, given the complexity and progressive structure of higher education systems, there are many different levels at which a publisher can enter the field. While the large courses at the lower levels of the curriculum may be particularly attractive, there are also many upper-level courses where smaller publishers can find niches for more specialized texts. Since most courses are taught to new sets of students year after year, texts which are adopted for teaching purposes are likely to have recurring sales; they may become strong-selling backlist titles and – since pre-press costs have by then been recouped – they may have high margins, thus making a strong positive contribution to the bottom line. So for publishers faced with declining monograph sales and growing pressure on margins, the commissioning and development of textbooks which have adoption potential has clear financial attractions.

Another reason why textbook publishing was attractive for academic publishers is that it is an *adjacent* field, and the boundary between these fields is relatively porous. Many of the books published by academic publishers were already selling into the textbook market: they were turning up on reading lists and being recommended to students. Even if they weren't commissioned and developed explicitly *as* textbooks, they were nevertheless being used for teaching purposes and thus circulating within the textbook market. Hence most academic publishers already had a foothold in the textbook market and had some experience of it – including some experience of how books, once adopted for teaching purposes, would perform. The porous boundaries between the fields of academic publishing and higher education publishing meant that it was relatively easy for academic publishers to redirect their energies towards the textbook market. They could move into this field, or expand their presence in it, without necessarily having to create an entirely new publishing operation (although some chose to create a new operation in order to concentrate skills and expertise in a single unit, as we have seen). The move into textbook publishing was also facilitated by the fact that the author bases for academic publishing and higher education publishing overlap to a significant extent. An editor who is seeking to commission a textbook for higher education will generally be looking for an academic (or group of academics) to write the book; he or she will be talking to the same people who, with different aims in mind, would also be the authors of scholarly monographs.

Finally, textbook publishing was attractive for academic publishers because there was some degree of overlap in terms of markets. The markets do not coincide – the principal market for scholarly monographs consists of university libraries and individual scholars and researchers, as we have seen, whereas the market for textbooks consists primarily of students taking courses (together with the libraries that cater for the needs of students). The systems needed for marketing textbooks are therefore different from those needed for marketing scholarly monographs. But in both cases the principal markets are located within the world of higher education, and in both cases academics are key players in the marketing chain. In the case of scholarly monographs, academics are the principal category of intended readers whose research interests are being catered for by librarians when they build their research collections; academics sometimes recommend books to librarians, and may occasionally buy scholarly monographs for their own personal collections. In the case of textbooks, academics as lecturers and professors are the key gatekeepers to the student market. Whether students buy a textbook depends to a very large extent on whether it has been adopted as a set text by the lecturer or professor who is teaching the course on which the students are enrolled. Hence, although students are the ultimate purchasers of textbooks, the marketing effort must be directed above all at the gatekeepers who make the adoption decisions – that is, broadly speaking, at the community of academics.

While there were many factors that made the textbook market attractive to academic publishers in the 1980s and 1990s, in practice UK-based academic publishers were more inclined to move into this field than the American university presses. UK-based publishers such as Blackwell, Macmillan (subsequently Palgrave Macmillan) and Routledge (subsequently Taylor & Francis) moved concertedly and effectively into the textbook market, significantly increasing their presence in a field where they already had some role. The major UK-based university presses, OUP and CUP, also moved in this direction in their own distinctive ways. By contrast, the American university presses (with a few notable exceptions) moved much more haltingly and erratically into the textbook market. How can we explain this different strategic response?

There are two main factors that explain the difference. The first has to do with the differing structures of the fields of higher education publishing in the US and the UK. We shall examine these differences in more detail in part III, but here let me highlight one key difference: in the UK, where the system of higher education is much smaller than in the US and the adoption system is much more flexible, the textbook market has traditionally been relatively 'open' in the sense that it was relatively easy for small and medium-sized players to enter the field. Hence there were relatively few barriers to entry for those academic publishers who saw the opportunity to expand their presence in the textbook market – even very small publishers could establish a significant foothold in targeted subject areas. There are clear signs that this is beginning to change today, but the absence of barriers to entry created real opportunities for academic publishers who were searching for ways to compensate for the decline in monograph sales. In North America, by contrast, college textbook publishing has been dominated by the large textbook publishers for several decades and the industry has become increasingly concentrated in recent years. The lower levels of the curriculum have been colonized by the big commercial players, who invest large sums in commissioning, developing and marketing textbooks aimed at the core first- and second-year courses. They also develop textbooks for upper-level courses where the student numbers justify the level of investment required. For a university press operating in the American context, the prospect of competing head-to-head with these powerful commercial players is simply a non-starter. The American university presses knew very well that if they wanted to enter the textbook market, they would have to do so in ways that did not compete directly with the commercial sector; hence they tended to understand what they were doing in terms of publishing 'supplemental texts' primarily for use in upper-level courses. Those academic publishers who tried to enter the US textbook market at lower levels (including some UK-based publishers with a less direct knowledge of the US market) were generally forced, as one publisher working in the US for a UK-based firm recalled, 'to beat a hasty retreat up the curriculum'.

A second factor that tended to discourage many of the American university presses from entering the textbook market is that they did not see textbook publishing (and many still do not see it) as essential to their mission as university presses. For many editors at American university presses, the primary purpose of the university press is to publish high-quality, original works – books that are recognized as outstanding by the scholarly community and that will make a real contribution to scholarship. This is how many editors understand their craft: commissioning and publishing books of this kind is what they know how to do and what they believe they should be doing. The idea of publishing textbooks in the strong sense of 'textbook' – pedagogical texts which are explicitly designed for teaching purposes – simply does not concur with the way that many editors at university presses understand their role, nor is it something that many of them feel able and trained to do. This is changing in many of the American university presses, but the existence of this gulf between the traditional habitus of the university press editor, on the one hand, and the idea of textbook publishing, on the other, tended to slow down (or in some cases even block) the migration of American university presses into the field of textbook publishing.

There were, however, other fields of publishing that were particularly attractive to the American university presses (though less attractive to UK-based academic publishers). Trade publishing was undoubtedly the most important of these other fields, although regional publishing has also played (and continues to play) a very important role in the world of the American university presses.

The lure of the trade

There is a long tradition of developing scholarly books for a general readership and selling them through bookstores at affordable prices, either as paperbacks or as hardbacks with cover prices that are much lower than the prices of scholarly monographs. This kind of publishing was developed very successfully by Penguin/Allen Lane and others in the UK and by a variety of up-market trade publishers in the US, such as Basic Books, the Free Press and W. W. Norton. OUP and CUP have also published high-quality trade books for many years – something that OUP has done more energetically than its counterpart in Cambridge. Among the American university presses, Harvard stands out as a publisher which has successfully ploughed the ground between academic and trade publishing. In Harvard's case, the move into trade publishing stems largely from the appointment of Arthur Rosenthal as director in 1972. The founder of Basic Books, Rosenthal was a New York publisher who had a great deal of experience publishing books by scholars and scientists for a general readership. He arrived at Harvard at a time when the press was in serious financial difficulties, having suffered a deficit of more than half a million dollars in 1970–1 on sales of around $3 million, and a deficit of $350,000 in 1971–2; the cumulative deficit from 1969 to 1972 was over $1 million.[2] Rosenthal reoriented the activities of the press and gave it a new profile as an up-market trade house, publishing ten or twelve titles per season (out of a total of around fifty to sixty titles per season) which had the potential to get national review coverage and to do well in the trade. As one colleague remarked, 'he had the vision to see where he wanted to lay his bets and a few of those go a long way in creating the image.'

Harvard's success in ploughing the ground between academic and trade publishing provided a model which other university presses have sought to emulate with varying degrees of dedication and success. The key assumption of this model is that high-quality books with a scholarly content, often (but not always) written by scholars, have the capacity to sell into a general trade market if they are developed and marketed properly. Hence an academic publisher, if it chooses its books well and develops and markets them effectively, can find markets beyond the diminishing library market and, indeed, beyond the academy. Some of these books may also get adopted as coursebooks at the university level, but they are not being developed *as* textbooks. They are being developed above all as books which have the capacity to cross over into the general trade market; however, having established themselves as books which make a significant intellectual contribution, they may also be used by some professors for teaching purposes.

Now there is, in fact, a degree of ambiguity and confusion among academic publishers about what exactly a 'trade book' is, and it is important to see that this rather vague term covers a variety of different kinds of books and forms of publishing. The term 'trade publishing' is normally used to refer to the publication of books (both fiction and nonfiction) which are aimed at the general consumer, although in practice this broad domain is differentiated into a variety of more specific fields with their own distinctive characteristics. In general terms, the trade publishing supply chain involves relations between publishers, wholesalers and booksellers and consumers, as indicated by figure 6.1. The publisher does not interact directly with consumers but tries to influence their purchasing decisions through marketing, promotion and publicity. Making books 'visible' in the media and in the bookstores is a vital part of the selling process. Hence marketing budgets for trade publishing tend to be much higher than the marketing budgets for scholarly monograph publishing, and successful trade publishing usually

[2] See Max Hall, *Harvard University Press: A History* (Cambridge, Mass.: Harvard University Press, 1986), p. 186.

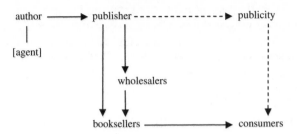

Figure 6.1 The trade publishing supply chain

requires concerted publicity campaigns aimed at securing media coverage. Getting books into the bookstores is one thing; getting the kind of publicity you need to induce individuals to buy the books, so that the sell-through is sufficient to avoid high returns, is another. Moreover, since trade publishing depends heavily on the role that booksellers play in stocking, displaying and promoting books, the discounts on trade books are much higher than the discounts for scholarly monographs – in the US, the discounts for trade books are generally between 40 and 50 per cent, compared to discounts of between 20 and 30 per cent for textbooks and scholarly monographs.

While figure 6.1 outlines the supply chain for trade publishing in the full sense of the term 'trade', there is a hybrid version of trade publishing which lies on the boundaries between academic and trade – indeed, many in the field of academic publishing describe this as 'academic-trade'. This is a kind of publishing in which works of a fairly scholarly character are developed in a way that is intended to reach beyond a narrow circle of specialists and appeal to a broader readership, although exactly how broad that readership will be varies considerably from one title to another. There are cases when books 'break out' of the academic domain and sell to a broader, non-academic readership. Many senior managers at American university presses can describe examples from their own experience of real successes of this kind – and in many cases they were successes that were not at all anticipated by the editors or sales staff at the press. But these are undoubtedly the exceptions. A great deal of what the American university presses publish as 'trade' books are, in fact 'academic-trade' books. This type of book lies in between the scholarly monograph and the true trade book. Its market is broader than that of the scholarly monograph but it doesn't sell in any significant quantities to non-academic readers. Whereas trade books, as understood by a trade publisher like Random House, are books written essentially for a general readership, academic-trade titles are books whose primary market is likely to be found in the academic world. They are books which have a broad, interdisciplinary character and which are written in an accessible way for a non-specialist but largely academic readership – 'good books written by scholars for audiences consisting mostly of other scholars', as one university press editor put it. They break out of the narrow circle of specialists and out of a particular discipline, selling to a wider range of academics and students than a typical scholarly monograph would do. On some occasions they may also break out of the academic world and sell to a broader non-academic readership, but in practice this is rare and the number of books that sell to non-academic readers is generally very small. 'We need to be honest with ourselves about what our markets are,' reflected an editorial director at one of the larger university presses. 'Our markets are academic markets and the books that succeed for us are, for the vast majority of university presses, books that are methodologically not discipline-specific.' Books of this kind can sell several thousand copies in cloth at an academic-trade price in the $25–30 range. The discounts given to wholesalers and booksellers for books of this kind are typically more than the discounts given on scholarly monographs but typically less than the discounts given on full trade titles.

In the context of the declining sales of scholarly monographs, it is easy to see why many of the American university presses looked to the model pioneered so successfully by Harvard as a possible way forward. If a press could publish a number of books each year which broke out of narrow disciplinary specializations – and perhaps even, in some cases, broke out of the academy and sold into a more general trade market – then this could help to create substantial new revenue streams to offset the declining sales of scholarly monographs. A number of books selling 3,000 or more hardback copies, even at academic-trade prices and discounts, could make a significant contribution to frontlist revenue, and the subsequent release of a paperback edition, with perhaps some course adoptions as supplemental reading, could strengthen backlist sales. Moreover, successes with trade and academic-trade titles could also help to raise the profile of the press and give it greater visibility both in the academy and in the broader public domain.

But in the late 1980s and 1990s, there were two other factors that also favoured the migration of academic publishers into trade (or academic-trade) publishing, especially in the American context. One factor was the growing concentration and conglomeratization within the world of trade publishing itself (a trend which we briefly documented in chapter 3). As many of the once-independent publishing houses in New York, London and elsewhere were bought up by the large conglomerates and either integrated into them or maintained as separate imprints under the conglomerate's financial and organizational umbrella, the sales expectations within the world of trade publishing were gradually ratcheted up. Editors were encouraged or even required to look for titles that would sell in sufficiently large quantities to meet the heightened expectations of contribution and profitability that were generally held by directors and senior managers of the large corporations. Hence the commissioning practices of mainstream trade publishers became increasingly oriented towards the acquisition of books with higher sales potential. They looked to sign authors with a proven track record and they became increasingly risk-averse. Books that they might have taken on previously in the hope that they might do well, even though the author had no track record as a successful trade author, were increasingly passed over by trade publishers who were searching for projects that bore the more obvious signs of probable success, such as the name-recognition of the author and/or a previous book which had done exceptionally well in the trade.

Partly as a result of this development, there was a growing pool of so-called 'mid-list' titles which were in search of new homes, and publishers with strong academic lists – including many of the university presses – were able to move into this space. While a mainstream trade publisher might be looking to commission books that would sell 10,000 copies or more as a trade hardback and might consider anything less to be marginal, many academic publishers would be delighted to sell 3,000 copies of a cloth edition before bringing out a paperback edition. The sales thresholds and expectations of the university presses were much lower, and therefore they were able to move into a space in the field of trade publishing that was being increasingly vacated by the big trade houses. But the university presses were not just picking up projects that were being passed over by mainstream trade publishers: they were also seeking actively to commission books which they thought they could develop for and sell into the trade (or academic-trade) market. In some cases they did this by working with academic authors and encouraging them to write for a wider audience – by broadening the scope of the book, making the text more accessible stylistically, using a more trade-oriented title, etc. In other cases they looked to acquire books from abroad, either by acquiring rights from copublishers in the UK or by acquiring translation rights on books originally published in other languages, which they thought they could sell into the US trade market.

A second development which favoured the migration of university presses into trade publishing was the rise of the retail chains. The rapid growth of the chains – especially Barnes & Noble and Borders in the US – created an increased demand for books which were needed to stock the newly opened superstores, and many academic publishers found that they could secure substantial orders from the chains for books which were perceived to have some trade potential. In sharp contrast to the declining library market for scholarly monographs, the late 1980s and 1990s were a period of more or less steadily expanding demand for scholarly books which crossed over into the general trade, particularly in the North American context. Some of the American university presses invested a great deal of effort in cultivating good working relations with the retail chains, which became an increasingly important retail outlet for them. And the more they depended on the retail chains to order and stock their books, the more they oriented themselves to acquiring and developing books which they thought would appeal to the central buyers at Barnes & Nobles and Borders. In other words, the acquisition practices of some university presses gradually migrated towards the commissioning of content that they thought would sell into the chains, from which they were deriving a substantial and growing proportion of their revenue.

The academic-trade book has come to assume a particularly prominent position in the editorial thinking of American university presses. There are some in the university press world who have come to see this type of book – pioneered so brilliantly by Harvard – as a kind of ideal to which the American university presses aspire. One university press director put it like this:

> If you ask me or any of my colleagues what is the ideal university press book to publish, I think we would all come up with the same answer. It wouldn't be a monograph, it wouldn't be a text and it wouldn't be twenty-five walks in New Jersey. It would be serious nonfiction written by a master scholar, about 300 pages with twenty illustrations at $27. It would be written for a high-level general audience. It would have some course use after its initial year. It would have book club potential because it would be at that level. These are books on major topics of general interest written to satisfy scholars but at a level that pulls in everyone else. You would have consensus on this issue. We all know what the perfect book is. The problem is that there are precious few scholars writing them and we all want them.

While many university presses were increasingly attracted by the idea of academic-trade publishing (and even, in some cases, more straightforward trade publishing), there were significant costs and risks associated with this shift – let me highlight six. In the first place, trade and academic-trade publishing generally requires much higher investment and higher risks in terms of advances than scholarly monograph publishing. The more that university presses find themselves competing for authors and book projects which are being sought after by other presses – both by other university presses and by some of the up-market trade houses like Norton or the US trade division of OUP – then the higher the advances are likely to go and the greater the risks. As they move increasingly in the direction of trade and academic-trade publishing, they find themselves searching for projects which are more trade and less academic. They are more likely to find themselves trying to sign up authors who are journalists or writers rather than scholars – or authors who, whether journalists or scholars, are 'big names' and have accumulated the kind of symbolic capital or 'author brand' that is so highly valued in the field of trade publishing. They find themselves drawn more and more into competitive situations where agents and auctions are involved and where advances begin to soar.

This is one of the points at which those university presses that have moved towards trade publishing find themselves struggling to cope with the logic of a field which is very different from that of academic publishing. And one of the ways in which it differs is that the level of advances in trade publishing has escalated dramatically in recent years. This is partly due to the increasing role of agents as intermediaries in trade publishing: agents have significantly upped the ante in terms of advances. Some agents have also seen opportunities to take on academics as clients and have altered expectations among academic authors about the kinds of advances their books might be able to command. 'What's shocking to me is how many associate professors at every university have an agent,' commented one publisher. 'Agents have become savvier about looking on college campuses for clients. They actually go out and seek them out.' As more and more academics enter into relationships with agents, the university presses find that the expectations within its traditional author base are changing. The advances for their trade-oriented books are rising both because more of these books are agented and because competition for the most desirable books and authors is increasing. These are circumstances in which all but the largest and most well endowed of the American university presses are likely to find it increasingly difficult to compete for the most attractive authors and projects, and in which those who do choose to compete are likely to run ever greater risks. There are still many opportunities for the smaller university presses to engage in academic-trade publishing if they choose their projects carefully and if they nourish academic-trade books which emerge organically from their traditional academic author base and steer clear of the most sought-after authors. But even in these cases, the competitive dynamic of trade and academic-trade publishing – even if the competition is only among a cluster of university presses – is likely to ratchet up the stakes.

Second, trade and academic-trade publishing are also riskier in terms of print-runs and the dangers of unsold stock. To publish for these markets at the kinds of prices and discounts required, a publisher has to print 2,000–3,000 copies at the very least, and in many cases it is likely to print substantially more – perhaps 5,000 or 10,000 copies or even more. It has to be prepared to take a gamble on likely sales or it simply cannot play the game. And the higher the print-run, the greater the risk that it will be left with unsold stock, perhaps even a very large quantity of unsold stock. This kind of gamble runs against the grain of many university presses, which are inclined to print much more conservatively and, in the context of the declining sales of scholarly monographs, have become accustomed to lowering their sales expectations and reducing print-runs. The inherently risk-taking character of trade publishing clashes with the more conservative mindset of the university press world. As one trade publisher who is intimately familiar with the world of the university presses put it,

> Trade publishing is all about risk, the willingness to take risks, and if you're not willing to do that, you just can't do it – that's the first rule. And that's the problem for the university presses: they say they want to be trade publishers but they're scared that it's going to cost them too much money or that a book might fail. You have to be willing to have the courage of your convictions.

Third, publishing trade and academic-trade books tends to produce a downward pressure on margins because the books have to have low prices and the bookstores and chains have to be given high discounts. They also have to be produced well, often with four-colour covers and internal illustrations. Fourth, this kind of publishing also requires higher investment in terms of marketing, since publicity and review coverage are vital to the success of books of this kind. Hence those university presses which have moved in this direction have found that they've had to increase significantly their expenditure on marketing and publicity, both in terms of their budgets for particular titles and, more broadly, in terms of their overall levels of staffing. If one is not careful, the benefits that may come from higher sales on trade and academic-trade titles can be wiped out by the higher costs involved in marketing them.

Fifth, publishing trade and academic-trade books also increases the dependence of university presses on the retail chains and increases their exposure to returns. (The move into the textbook market also increases their exposure to returns, although for different reasons, as we shall see in part III.) With the growth of the retail chains and the decline of the independents, the chains have become more and more important as retail outlets for books aimed at a general readership – the chains 'make or break the book', as one trade publisher put it. Hence, to the extent that university presses increase their output of trade and academic-trade books, they become more dependent on sales through the major retail chains. This can work very much to their advantage when times are good. Throughout the 1990s, the university presses benefited significantly from the expansion of the chains, as we noted earlier. But when the chains realized that many of these books were not selling through, they returned them in large numbers and began to revise their orders of new books downwards. The impact of these changing practices of the chains on the fortunes of the university presses has been dramatic: as a result of these and other developments, returns soared to record levels in 2001 and 2002 and helped to produce substantial deficits for many university presses. We shall return to this point in the following chapter.

A sixth danger faced by the university presses is the danger of fooling themselves – that is, the danger of thinking that a scholarly book has trade potential when, in fact, its sales beyond a relatively narrow academic market are likely to be minimal. An erroneous decision of this kind can carry heavy costs – not only in terms of excess stock, but also in terms of the extra expenditure that went into high-quality production and extra marketing and the revenue lost through low prices and high discounts. A book that might have made a reasonable financial contribution if it had been published in accordance with a monograph business model – streamlined production, modest print-runs, high prices and low discounts – may turn out to be a serious loss-maker when published as an unsuccessful academic-trade title. All too often the decision to publish a book as an academic-trade title is a victory of wishful thinking over sober commercial logic, and the publisher may also have to deal with a disappointed author whose expectations have been falsely raised.

For understandable reasons, the move into trade and academic-trade publishing has been, and remains, an attractive option for the American university presses. These are fields in which it is possible to do very well, and many editors and directors can pick out a number of books from their backlist which have done exceptionally well, selling thousands of copies in cloth and many thousands more in paperback – they are the kinds of figures that gladden the heart of publishers who have suffered for decades from the seemingly relentless decline of scholarly monograph sales. It's also fun and exciting to publish books which have a real chance of getting reviewed in the national press and of selling many more copies than the typical scholarly monograph. 'In every breathing editor there beats the heart of Maxwell Perkins,' commented one well-established university press editor. 'Everybody wants to play in the big leagues and be on the *New York Times* bestseller list.' But trade publishing, and even the hybrid form of academic-trade publishing, is a risky business, and for publishers who are not accustomed to assessing and taking risks of this kind, it's easy to lose out (and even, on occasion, to lose your shirt). Some university presses have had some extraordinary successes with trade or academic-trade titles, but serendipity plays a much greater role here than in other fields of publishing; it's hard to plan for successes of this kind and easy to end up with failures.

The attractions of the region

Another field of publishing which has proved increasingly attractive for many of the American university presses is regional publishing. The practice of regional publishing is not a new development for the American university presses – some of them have been publishing books dealing with local and regional subjects since the 1920s. The University of North Carolina Press at Chapel Hill was one of the pioneers in this regard, thanks largely to the efforts of an enterprising scholar at the university, Howard W. Odum. Odum established an Institute for Research in Social Science at Chapel Hill and he and his colleagues produced numerous studies of the American South, many of which were published by the press.[3] The University of North Carolina Press gained a reputation as a publisher which, in addition to having a strong programme of scholarly publications, had a flair for publishing innovative books on regional themes and issues, with a particular emphasis on the history, culture and natural history of the South.

Since its origins in the South, the development of regional publishing spread to other university presses in all parts of the United States and today it represents one of the few growth areas for American university presses. The move of university presses into regional publishing is a development that was made possible by certain historical and geographical features of the American publishing industry. Historically, the American publishing industry was concentrated in the large cities on the eastern seaboard, especially New York and Boston. The New York commercial houses tended to orient their activities towards the publication of books that would be read nationwide; if they pub-

[3] Hawes, *To Advance Knowledge*, pp. 22–3.

lished books with a local flavour, the local reference points tended to be taken from the large urban metropolises of the East Coast. But the university presses discovered that there was a market for serious nonfiction books about the states and regions in which they, as university presses scattered across the country, were located, and which was not being catered for by the East Coast commercial houses. They could draw on the specialist knowledge about their regions which could in many cases be found in their own universities, and they could develop books which would sell into a local and regional trade market – that is, which would sell not just to academics and libraries but to a wider readership of individuals who had an interest in the culture, politics, history and natural history of the state and the region.

What kinds of books are published by university presses in their regional publishing programmes and how does this kind of publishing fit within the remit of a university press? 'Regional publishing' is, in fact, a very elastic term; it gives a geographical focus to one's publishing activities, but a focus of this kind can be applied to different fields of publishing. So, for example, a regional programme at a university press may include scholarly works and reference works dealing with the region as well as books on the flora and fauna of the region, books on regional culture, cuisine and traditions and regional travel guides. The latter kinds of books are aimed essentially at a regional trade market: they are intended for general readers who have a particular interest in the region. So how does this kind of publishing fit with the remit of a university press? Those university presses which have regional programmes tend to see this as an integral part of the 'public outreach' role of the university, a role which is particularly important in the self-understanding of the state universities. As one university press director put it,

> I think nearly all public universities have as part of their mission a component of public outreach and public service. That's very much a part of this university's mission, and therefore an important part of ours. And it's in that context that I think about the regional publishing that we do, which is to say that I think of it as both a responsibility and an opportunity.

In other words, regional publishing is a way in which university presses can make available books which help to interpret the region for a popular audience. In some cases these books will be written by academics – for example, by a historian, a botanist or a marine biologist at the state university. But in other cases they will be written by a local author who is not an academic but who is knowledgeable about some aspect of the state or region.

So is there anything that distinguishes the kinds of regional books published by a university press from the kinds of books and travel guides that would be published by a local commercial press? When asked this question, editors at university presses tend to respond by saying that they generally expect their regional books to have some kind of educational content. They are not simply picture books or lists of restaurants, since they make some attempt to interpret the region. As one senior editor explained,

> We bring to those books something of a scholarly press approach. So let's take a guidebook. Generally if you look at our guidebooks you'll see that they have an educational component. They are not bed and breakfast guides. They are not where to eat. They are generally guides that have a cultural side to them, an historical side to them. Right now we're working for example on some books to support cultural tourism in the region. There

are guides that support cultural tourism that are really no more than brochures, that make no attempt to interpret the region, no attempt to give the person using them any experience of the region. They're simply guides to get the person to stay a day longer. We don't publish that kind of thing. Whatever we do we try to bring something of the seriousness of the kind of work we do to them.

While regional publishing has an extended history among the American university presses, the financial pressures of recent decades have encouraged many university presses to give more attention to the development of their regional publishing programmes – or, in some cases, to begin publishing regional books for the first time. Since the field of regional publishing tends by nature to be spatially fragmented and university presses tend to restrict their regional publishing programmes to their own state and region, the degree of competition between university presses tends to be less than in the academic and more trade-oriented publishing programmes. Some competition does exist, since there are several university presses within regions like the South, the Southeast, the Southwest or the West Coast, but a university press in the South will generally not be competing with a university press on the West Coast in the field of regional publishing. Hence there tends to be a culture of collaboration among university presses at the editorial level in the field of regional publishing – much more so than in the fields of academic or trade publishing, where university presses are more likely to find themselves competing with one another for the same authors and books. Editors responsible for the development of regional publishing programmes tend to talk to editors at other university presses about the books they have published or are planning to publish, about which have done well and which have not, etc. A successful regional book published by one university press becomes a model which other university presses can replicate in their own states and regions. One senior editor put it like this:

> One thing that's nice about regional trade publishing is that you can use the ideas of presses in other regions without seeming to steal them or compete. So there's more sharing in regional trade publishing, and there's a more collaborative feel. Someone calls me and wants to know sales: I have no problem sharing an experience. If someone wants to know how our book on quilts did because they're going to do Indiana quilts, I'll tell them the whole story, no problem. I think that most of us have taken up the idea that interpreting the region, publishing about the region that they happen to be located in, both in their scholarly work and in their regional trade side, is good for the press, and good publishing.

There are clear economic advantages for university presses in developing regional lists. There is relatively little competition and the books, if you get them right, can do very well. A good regional travel guide, for example, can sell 20,000 copies – a different league from the kinds of sales generally achieved in scholarly monograph publishing. They can also become good backlist titles and go through multiple editions. On rare occasions a regional title can break into the national trade market and sell hundreds of thousands of copies, transforming the finances of the press. This point was illustrated all too poignantly by the performance of the University of North Carolina Press in 2001, a year when most of the American university presses suffered exceptionally high returns and sales shortfalls. UNC Press bucked the trend, thanks largely to the tremendous success they had with two regional cookbooks – *Not Afraid of Flavor*, which sold nearly 20,000 copies, and *Mama Dip's Kitchen*, which sold over 80,000 copies. While these books were regional trade titles, they reached a nationwide audience. In the case of *Mama Dip's Kitchen*, this was due largely to the fact that the author – an African-American self-taught restaurateur named Mildred Council – appeared on a cable TV cooking programme and on the shopping channel QVC. Thanks to these TV appearances, sales took off in a way that had not been expected at all by the press ('Our first printing was 1,000 jacketed cloth and 5,000 paperback. We expected that to be a two to three year supply.') These two titles alone generated revenue of $750,000 and helped to cushion UNC Press from what was experienced by all other university presses as an extremely difficult financial year.

While the financial attractions of regional publishing are easy to see, there are potential downsides. Perhaps the greatest risk is the possibility that the reputation of the university press will be increasingly defined by its regional specificity, a characteristic that might make it more and more difficult for the press to attract the very best international scholars in particular disciplines. There are some in the university press world who also worry that the reputation of a press could be damaged – 'the danger is that you move so down-market that people don't take you seriously,' said one university press director. Certainly the question is asked from time to time whether it is really within the purview of a university press to publish cookbooks and travel guides, and there are some critics who see this as yet another sign that the university presses are veering away from their scholarly mission in the pursuit of higher selling titles ('mission drift', as it is sometimes euphemistically called). There may be specific occasions when this criticism has some force, but as a general appraisal of the role of regional publishing in the university press world, it is wide of the mark. Regional publishing has a much more fundamental connection to the mission of university presses and to the geography of American publishing than this kind of criticism suggests. And the increasing importance of regional publishing is linked in a much more profound way to the logic of the field of academic publishing, a logic which has made the issue of list diversification a matter of life and death for many of the university presses.

Given the precipitous decline of scholarly monograph sales, the American university presses have been forced into a strategy of list diversification. What might appear to the outside observer to be a loss of focus and a dilution of the scholarly mission of university presses is, in most cases, part of a self-conscious strategy to diversify the list. Exactly how this strategy is developed will vary from one university press to another, depending on their size, their history, their position in the field and their geographical reach, as well as the preferences and choices of their directors and editors. Some will lean more strongly towards trade (or academic-trade) publishing, others more strongly towards regional publishing and others will place greater emphasis on supplemental coursebooks. Others will try to achieve a balance between all of these, while still carrying on with the scholarly monograph programme. The key is the mix of books – achieving a 'balanced list' has increasingly become the goal to which the university presses aspire, a goal forced upon them by the logic of the field. 'We are very comfortable with a mix of books,' commented one university press director:

> We will do a few monographs if they are very impressive and fit our programme; we look for books of supplemental reading for courses and that's really our bread and butter; we look for general interest trade books; and we look very much for regional books, which is one of the things American university presses do so well . . . Diversification, or the mix of books, is essentially what we do.

One of the questions raised by this structural shift, however, is whether university presses – many of which are relatively small organizations whose resources are already stretched – can become effective players in so many different fields of publishing without spreading themselves too thinly. This is a question to which we shall return.

Exiting the field

While the university presses sought to diversify their lists, they nevertheless maintained their commitment to publishing scholarly work – it was, after all, part of their constitutional remit to do so. But commercial academic publishers were not tied to the field of academic publishing in the same way. If the sales of scholarly monographs were falling to unsustainable levels, commercial publishers could wind down their scholarly publishing programmes and could even, in the most extreme cases, exit the field.

Consider the example of one medium-sized UK-based commercial academic publisher with a tradition of publishing high-quality scholarly work in the humanities and social sciences – I shall refer to this publisher as AC1. In the early 1980s, few publishers could match AC1 in terms of the sheer quality of its list: in its core subject areas, such as philosophy and economics, it was regarded by many academics as the pre-eminent scholarly press. Like the university presses, AC1 commonly published its new books as hardback-only monographs in the first instance, printing 1,500 or 2,000 copies for its own markets and another 1,500 copies or so for a US copublisher. These were healthy print-runs and, with the injection of cash from a good copublication deal, it was easy to make the margins work. But as the sales of hardback monographs began to fall off on both sides of the Atlantic, the numbers became increasingly unmanageable and the organization found itself facing a growing financial crisis. The management was forced into a process of intensive self-examination about the nature of its publishing programme. In the late 1980s it embarked on various publishing experiments, from professional and reference publishing to trade and business books, many of which turned out to be costly failures. The decline of monograph sales was boxing it ever more tightly into a corner and it was searching, with a growing sense of urgency, for a way out. 'This was a time of real stress about who we were and what we were trying to do,' recalled the managing director. Eventually AC1 settled on what it came to see as the only viable way forward: to abandon scholarly monograph publishing altogether and to redefine itself as a different kind of publisher. As one senior manager recalls,

> I think in this organization it was the managing director who said, we must undergo radical change. The business that we've got at the moment isn't working and unless we do something absolutely different then we are in big trouble. So he was the Moses coming down from the top of the mountain and on one of his stone tablets was the word 'textbook'. He thought that our publishing programme needed to turn around 180 degrees. The problem was, though, it was one thing for him to say we're doing textbook publishing, it's quite another to have the organizational skills to do it. We just didn't know how to go about it, and I remember at the time describing this to people in terms of being a journalist working at *The Times* and then being told that you've got to produce a tabloid like the *Daily Mirror*. To an outsider you think OK, you're all journalists, I'm sure you can do it. But it's a completely different way of life, a completely different culture.

Unlike the university presses, AC1 was not constrained by its constitutional remit to continue publishing scholarly work. It could drop it if it believed that there was no commercial future in scholarly monograph publishing and it could redirect its publishing efforts elsewhere. And this is exactly what it did. It withdrew from scholarly monograph publishing and redefined itself as an 'educational publisher' with a dedicated focus on textbooks and teaching materials for higher education.

Why did AC1 adopt such a radical approach to the problems created by the decline of scholarly monograph sales? Why didn't it take a more piecemeal approach, streamlining its production processes, controlling its costs more carefully and diversifying its list, as most of the university presses have done? In fact, it did try these various strategies. It introduced production templates to standardize procedures and reduce costs, it reduced print-runs and raised prices and it experimented with simultaneous publication, but all of these seemed like so many half-measures that were unlikely to resolve the fundamental problem:

> I suspect that psychologically and collectively we preferred to do something that clearly had significant commercial potential rather than struggle on with a publishing model that seemed to be running into the ground. We did explore some technological experiments with, for example, authors keying into word templates which we then ran out. But a lot of those early experiments got cocked up and things went wrong and so the organization didn't really have the stomach for making monograph publishing work. Fundamentally, as a commercial organization, I don't think we felt the need to make it work in the way that, presumably, university presses did. I guess those guys said, OK, it's commercially difficult, but we've got to do it. We, actually quite courageously at the time, said, no, we don't need to do this and we are better off out of it.

But there was another reason why AC1 decided to take this radical approach. The managing director took the view that to be successful as a textbook publisher, you had to change the mindset of the whole organization, from editorial through to production and marketing. If the firm continued to publish monographs and other types of book such as trade titles, then there would be a chronic lack of clarity and focus about the fundamental aims of the organization. There would be endless arguments and disagreements about whether a particular monograph should be taken on, whether it was really a monograph or a textbook, why one monograph could be taken on and not another and so on, and all of this would distract attention from the goal of building a textbook programme. As the managing director explained,

> We needed more clarity about (a) margins have to be higher, and (b) we needed to publish a certain type of book. You may understand the subtle difference between book type A and book type B, but it's difficult to communicate this to other people and it confuses them and they say, 'well, hey, why are we publishing this monograph here, I thought we weren't publishing monographs.' And that clarity throughout the whole organization has meant fewer political battles. We don't have battles at editorial board meetings any more about what we should and shouldn't publish because everybody has been involved in this planning process.

Once the decision had been taken to stop publishing monographs and to focus on textbook publishing, the senior management wanted to try to ensure that this goal was pursued with single-minded dedication and that no one, from editors to marketing staff, got distracted by other kinds of publishing.

The decision to stop publishing scholarly monographs and to regear the organization to the task of commissioning and publishing textbooks required AC1 to adopt a long-term view. It takes a long time to retrain staff and to wait for the results of their commissioning activity to begin generating new revenue streams – as publishers sometimes say, it's like trying to turn around a supertanker. And in the meantime, the loss of revenue from monograph sales may lead to a short-term decline in overall sales. The fact that AC1 was a private company, largely family-owned, gave it the financial breathing space it needed to carry out a fundamental restructuring of the organization – had it been a publicly quoted company, this would have been much more difficult. 'The decision to stop publishing monographs was only possible when you could take a long-term view, i.e. we were a private company,' explained the managing director. 'Textbooks take longer to develop and you have to forgo the dues or US bulk sale revenue. So if you are already in financial trouble with monographs, moving to textbooks meant even more short-term pain.' Thanks to its status as a private company, AC1 was able to absorb the short-term losses involved in discontinuing its monograph publishing programme and in restructuring the organization as a textbook publisher, and the strategy eventually paid off in financial terms.

There were, however, casualties on the way. There were editors who didn't share this single-minded focus on textbook publishing – some left, others were forced out. 'What it tended to boil down to', said one senior manager, 'was the tension between author-driven and market-driven publishing.' The editors who no longer fitted in this new environment were those who had built their lists by forming personal relationships with key academics who were the leading people in the field: by publishing their work, they built the list and established a reputation as a leading publisher in that subject. But this model was now being replaced by a new, market-driven approach which would be focused on mapping out the structure of the higher education curriculum in different subjects, identifying courses where textbooks might be needed, doing some market research and competitor analysis, and then trying to find authors who were willing to write the textbook that you wanted to commission. This was not every editor's cup of tea:

> We've lost some good people because it wasn't part of the mission that they wanted to adhere to. But we've also turned lots of other people around, thinking this is really quite an exciting mission to be taking the cutting-edge of research and translating it into the cutting-edge of pedagogy, to be getting people who are mostly researchers into thinking, yeah, I want to do a textbook.

There were other costs too. AC1 also faced criticism from some sectors of the academic community who felt that the press was no longer committed to scholarship. Some academics complained loudly and vociferously that AC1 was no longer supporting the subject – the philosophers were particularly aggrieved. 'There were many impassioned arguments between editors here and various British philosophers who essentially said "it's your responsibility as a publisher to support the philosophy monograph", to which we said "well, would you rather we published monographs and went out of business or carried on in business and didn't?"' But the senior managers knew that the issues were not so straightforward. They had decided to discontinue scholarly monograph publishing on financial grounds, but in taking this decision they ran the risk of damaging their reputation as an academic publisher and alienating the academic community upon whose support they would continue to depend. Their success as a publishing firm required them to accumulate and protect their symbolic capital as well as their financial capital, and the course of action they had adopted in order to turn the company around financially was in danger of undermining their symbolic capital. And this mattered to them precisely because, as an academic publisher, they knew that the academic community was vital to them. It was the source of their authors, of their content creators; it was also the principal market for their products, since academics bought books and acted as the crucial gatekeepers in the textbook adoption system. AC1 wanted to present itself as an organization that provided a service to the academic community and was responsive to its needs. How could it do this when at the same time it was withdrawing from a form of publishing that mattered greatly to certain sectors of the academic community?

One way in which AC1 tried to address this problem was to draw a clear distinction between teaching and research, and to say to the academic community that its book publishing programme was geared to teaching while its journals programme was geared to research. Hence it was able to serve the academic community in both teaching and research, although each would be handled by a different medium. The problem with this response, however, is that there are many disciplines in the humanities and social sciences where the book continues to play an important role as a means of making available the results of research and as a medium for the development of extended analyses and arguments – not all scholarly work in the humanities and social sciences can be accommodated in the framework of the twenty-page journal article. So the criticism of AC1 from certain sectors of the academic community did not go away and eventually the senior management began to contemplate a limited degree of backtracking:

> That debate with the philosophy community still lingers on such that even now we have been thinking very hard about how to protect our academic reputation to the philosophy community and are deliberately commissioning books which we think will essentially be good for our academic image while at the same time not lose us shed-loads of money.

The economic conditions of academic publishing had driven AC1 to withdraw from monograph publishing and this improved their financial position in the medium term, but the improvement came at a cost: it strained AC1's relations with some sectors of the academic community and threatened to damage its reputation – its symbolic capital – in the eyes of the very academics upon whom it depended.

Sequestering the monograph

Not all commercial academic publishers responded to the decline of scholarly monograph sales in such a radical way as AC1. There were others who decided to remain in the field of academic publishing but sought to manage the decline of scholarly monograph sales by separating off this form of publishing and rigorously controlling the conditions so that it would be a profitable, or at least not a seriously loss-making, activity. I shall describe this strategy as 'sequestering the monograph'. This strategy was pursued by several UK-based academic publishers in the course of the 1990s, and is still pursued by them today.

Consider the example of AC2, a medium-sized commercial academic publisher based in the UK. AC2 used to publish a large number of scholarly monographs throughout the humanities and social sciences. As the sales of monographs began to decline, its initial response was to cut costs – to simplify and standardize production processes, eliminate four-colour covers, reduce royalties, etc. 'That was partly successful in that it gave a lease of life for several years while it sort of found its feet,' recalled the managing director. But AC2 paid a price in symbolic value for this initial response: 'We drove down costs too far, we became unprestigious, we lost some of the prestige we used to have.' So it adopted a different strategy: it created a separate organizational unit within the firm which was focused exclusively on publishing scholarly monographs. The task of the unit was to control all the factors – cost, price, quality – with a high degree of rigour:

> Of course, success is getting the very best authors and a whole bunch of things right, but in this very tight game, because the margins are very tight, you are looking at a lot of dials to fly this particular aeroplane and you're tweaking when you see one of the needles flicker in the wrong direction. We follow the moving total units at six months, at twelve months; we have a whole bunch of stuff, the average price per page we spend on typesetting, our average print-runs and all the rest of it. We just look at all these dials and you've just got to watch them going into the red and fine-tune as much as you possibly can.

By carefully controlling all the variables – print-runs as low as 300–400 copies for the global market, prices as high as £60–70, standardized formats for production, extent rigorously limited, etc. – this kind of scholarly monograph publishing can still be financially worthwhile for a commercial academic publisher. But margins are razor-thin and there is very little room to manoeuvre. Tight control of all the variables is the key. Production has to be standardized and one simply cannot afford to give individual attention to any book – to design a separate cover for it or to depart from the standard format in some other way. As one academic publisher described it, using a somewhat less elegant metaphor, 'It has to be a finely honed sausage factory. By putting the monograph through almost like a sausage-making machine, we are able to keep it profitable.' Having designed the machine in a way that enables costs to be driven down, a certain volume of throughput is also needed to make it worthwhile financially, since the overall contribution per title is generally modest and most sales are in the first year. The more throughput there is, the greater the revenue that will flow through to the bottom line, provided overheads can be kept constant. Volume also enables the marketing costs to be spread across a larger number of titles.

By separating out the monograph publishing programme and treating it as an organizationally distinct operation, the commercial academic publisher is able to keep tight control on all the variables that affect the financial viability of the monograph. The organizational sequestration of monograph publishing also forces one to be clear about the likely market for books of this kind. As the managing director of AC2 explained,

> It forces you to say, will a substantial number of people buy this out of their private pocket? If so, I deem it a textbook, it goes into paperback, etc. If not, then it is a library purchase. You have to price highly. Although this is a great simplification, that's the way we divide it. And I've got the organizational divide to force people not to equivocate over that divide.

On one side of this organizational divide, there's the academic division which is responsible for monograph publishing; on the other side, there's the college division that does textbooks, including high-level undergraduate and graduate level texts. Monographs are published as high-priced hardbacks in low print-runs with costs strictly controlled; textbooks, including upper-level textbooks, are published in paperback. Occasionally the academic division experiences pressure from authors to publish their books in paperback, and sometimes they have to concede. 'But by and large there is a mental self-image that this is a hardback and therefore a high-priced piece of activity, and you can't fool yourself that those extra few hundred copies are worth doing and all the rest of it.'

Like all academic publishers, AC2 has experienced the precipitous decline of scholarly monograph sales over the last couple of decades. Where it used to print 1,500–2,000 hardback copies, it is now printing between 300 and 400 for a global market. So why does it continue to publish them? If it sequesters scholarly monograph publishing in this way, carefully controls the costs and prices high, it can still make it work in financial terms. 'It's tricky and it's wafer-thin, you haven't got fat margins to play with', but it is still profitable. Moreover, given the difficulties of scholarly monograph publishing, the competition has thinned out. Monograph publishing has become deeply unattractive to the big commercial publishers, 'so they're off our backs', and some of the smaller and medium-sized academic publishers have effectively withdrawn from the field, as we have seen. This has left the university presses and some commercial academic publishers like AC2. And whereas the university presses may have an advantage in terms of their symbolic value, their prestige and their appeal to academics, the commercial presses may have other advantages. 'In terms of discipline and commercial rigour and just cleverness, we are often better than them,' contends the managing director of AC2, and this 'gives a predominantly UK-based, academic non-university press publisher room for competitive advantage'.

Does the strategy of sequestering the monograph have a future? Will commercial academic publishers like AC2 continue to publish monographs in this way, or continue to do so with the same volume of throughput? It's difficult to say. There are many, including the managing director of AC2, who expect it to get harder and harder, as library budgets continue to be squeezed. Others take a more optimistic view, suggesting that the situation is likely to stabilize at print-runs around 300–400 copies, although they acknowledge that this depends entirely on library budgets and on what happens in the journals market, with which the fate of the monograph is inextricably linked. Still others believe that the decline will eventually level off but they're not sure what the final numbers will be – 'I think it will bottom out somewhere but I am not quite sure where,' commented one senior editor. Whichever way you look at it, it's clear that the commercial academic publishers who remain in the field of scholarly monograph publishing have little room to manoeuvre. Any further significant decline in the sales of monographs would turn a marginally profitable business into a loss-making operation, and if this were to happen, their continued presence in the field could not be guaranteed.

Some consequences of field migration

What are the consequences of field migration for academic publishing? Does it herald the imminent demise of academic publishing, as publishers search for strategic exits from the field? Or does it signal a more complex structural transformation of the field, as the players within it seek to reposition themselves both within this field and in relation to other fields? The evidence to date lends support to the latter interpretation, although further significant decline in the market for scholarly monographs could lend support to a more pessimistic view. To the extent that field migration is producing a structural transformation of the field rather than destroying the field altogether, what are the main lines of this transformation? Let me draw this chapter to a close by highlighting four key aspects of this structural transformation of the field of academic publishing.

(1)   The field of academic publishing is thinning out, as the number of active players declines and those who remain active in the field seek to reduce the numbers of monographs they publish through policies of increased selectivity and list diversification. The university presses remain more committed to monograph publishing than the commercial firms, largely because university presses have a constitutional remit to publish scholarly work and see this as part of their educational mission (for which they are entitled to their status as charities or not-for-profits and exempt from corporation tax), whereas commercial firms are more inclined to make strategic decisions on the basis of strict financial criteria. Some commercial firms do nevertheless retain active programmes of monograph publishing, but these tend to be pared down and run as discrete operations. As the field of monograph publishing thins out, the pool of potential monographs seeking publishers grows and the pressures on those publishers who remain active in the field intensify. They are faced with an ever increasing number of inquiries and unsolicited manuscripts from academics and prospective academics in search of a publisher for books based on their research.

(2)   Within particular publishing organizations, scholarly monograph publishing becomes an increasingly sequestrated and delimited activity, operating within boundaries that are defined with increasing clarity and precision. Attempts are made to control the overheads on monograph publishing as carefully as possible by using standardized formats and reducing the attention given to detail and to individualized production. Print-runs are brought down and prices are put up. The ways in which these various factors are combined varies from one organization to another. The UK-based university presses and the UK-based commercial academic publishers tend to be much more assertive in terms of standardizing production to cut costs, reducing print-runs and increasing prices than the American university presses. The latter tend to give more individualized attention to monographs, to print more and to price well below the UK-based academic publishers. But even in the case of the American university presses, these practices have been changing and are likely to continue to do so. Scholarly monograph publishing remains an important part of what the university presses do on both sides of the Atlantic, but it is no longer seen as a means of driving expansion and growth as it was in the 1970s and before. The university presses and some commercial firms continue to support scholarly monograph publishing, but very few publishers see monograph publishing as an activity in which they would now wish to increase significantly their level of investment and commitment. They look increasingly to other fields, such as textbook publishing, trade publishing and regional publishing, as arenas in which increased activity could yield more positive financial returns.

(3)   In contrast to the field of academic publishing, the fields into which academic publishers migrate are becoming increasingly crowded, as more and more publishers seek to compensate for the decline in monograph sales by shifting their commissioning activities into more lucrative domains. Competition in the destination fields intensifies – not only between the academic publishers who may be relatively new entrants, but also between these new entrants and the already existing incumbents of these fields who now find themselves faced with an ever growing number of migrant firms. This competition becomes particularly intense in textbook publishing and trade publishing, which are less spatially fragmented than regional publishing and where there are already many well-entrenched and well-resourced competitors. As the fields become more crowded, the stakes are constantly ratcheted up, as more and more publishers seek to commission the same or similar content. Authors, agents and foreign publishers (in cases where rights are being sold) demand, and in some cases are able to secure, higher and higher advances, and some new entrants find themselves faced with levels of investment and risk to which they were unaccustomed in the field of academic publishing. Early successes in the new fields become harder to repeat, and new entrants must constantly search for new ways to position themselves and achieve success in increasingly crowded and competitive markets.

(4)   The relations between academic publishers, on the one hand, and academics in the academic field, on the other, become increasingly strained, as the trajectories of field migration propel publishers in directions that do not coincide with, and in some respects directly conflict with, the aims and priorities of academics. While the difficulties of monograph publishing have forced many academic publishers to try to limit or scale down their monograph publishing operations (or even, in some cases, to close them down) and to refocus their activities elsewhere, the constraints and conditions of success in the academic field place ever greater pressure on academics and prospective academics to publish scholarly work based on original research and to avoid investing time and energy in writing material which is introductory and pedagogical in character. Publishers want academics to write textbooks, but many academics, under pressure from sources internal to their own field, eschew the idea of textbook writing and want publishers to take on their scholarly work. Publishers find it increasingly difficult to persuade academics to write the kinds of books they need in order to compete effectively in the textbook and trade markets, while academics become increasingly frustrated and disappointed by what they see as the growing unwillingness of publishers to take on works of scholarship, and thereby support the academic community by helping to disseminate the results of research and provide the forms of certification that individuals need in order to advance their careers in the academic field. Thanks to the differing logics of the publishing field and the academic field, the stage is set for a play of conflicting interests, multiple misunderstandings and half-baked compromises, some scenes of which we shall examine in the following chapter.

7

Academic publishing at the crossroads

The transformation of the field

For more than two decades, the field of academic publishing has been driven by a dynamic of change that has made it more and more difficult to engage in the kind of publishing that was once central to academic presses. As we have seen, the sales of scholarly monographs have declined dramatically since the 1970s, largely due to the contraction of the library market and the need to use more and more library resources to meet the escalating costs of serials and the growing costs of electronic products and IT. Academic publishers have found themselves in a situation where more and more titles are chasing resources that are relatively static or diminishing over time. Some commercial academic publishers, unconstrained by constitutional obligations, saw the writing on the wall and exited the field. But for the university presses, exiting the field was never an option. They felt obliged to continue publishing scholarly work, both because this was a central part of their educational mission and because they were locked into a system of certification in the academic world from which they could not easily extricate themselves. The university presses found themselves in the increasingly uncomfortable position of having to continue with a form of publishing where revenues and margins were declining while at the same time trying to ensure that their overall financial position was secure.

To some extent, the major UK-based university presses, OUP and CUP, were shielded from the worst consequences of this structural transformation of the field by the fact that they were large, global and diversified organizations. Throughout the 1980s and 1990s, they were heavily involved in other publishing fields where the dynamics were very different and where there were real opportunities for growth – most notably ELT publishing, but also reference publishing, journals publishing, professional publishing and other fields. The sheer scale of OUP and CUP and the surpluses generated by their activities in other fields provided them with some room to manoeuvre. The UK-based university presses were also proactive about restructuring their academic publishing programmes in response to the declining sales of scholarly monographs – more so than many of the American university presses. Among other things, they reduced costs, streamlined production, lowered print-runs and significantly increased prices on scholarly monographs, with the aim of trying to ensure that their academic publishing programmes could be continued on a financially sound basis. They did not go as far as the UK-based commercial academic publishers who remained in the field – production quality mattered too much to the university presses and they would have abjured any talk of a 'sausage machine'. They were willing to make some concessions on quality in order to reduce costs, but they were not willing to lower quality to the extent that it might damage their reputation. There was a point where the symbolic damage caused by further reductions in quality could begin to overshadow the financial gains, and that was a point beyond which the university presses were generally unwilling to go.

The American university presses found themselves in a different position – or, to be more precise, in different positions, since the circumstances varied greatly from one press to another. They did not have the scale, the diversity and the global reach of OUP and CUP; they were more dependent on their host institutions for support, more dependent on scholarly monograph sales for their revenue and more dependent on the US market for their sales. In various ways they sought to transform their scholarly monograph publishing programmes to cope with the consequences of declining sales – though, taking their cues from one another and from the US market, they were reluctant to standardize production as thoroughly and to increase prices as sharply as the UK-based university presses and commercial firms. They sought to introduce a more market-conscious set of attitudes and practices within the organization, encouraging editors to think more proactively about the kinds of books they were commissioning and the markets for which they were publishing, and involving sales and marketing staff more directly in editorial processes. Economic considerations began to weigh more heavily in their editorial deliberations – not because economic considerations didn't matter in the past (they did), but because the relatively buoyant institutional market of earlier decades, which had supported the scholarly monograph business and afforded academic publishers the luxury of being able to take sales for granted while focusing their attention on questions of quality and intellectual worth, had fallen away from under their feet. Above all, they sought to diversify their lists, branching out into fields of publishing that were adjacent to academic publishing but that offered better opportunities to increase revenue and generate growth. Whereas OUP and CUP were already diversified publishing organizations, the American university presses increasingly sought to *become* diversified. The migration of the American university presses into trade publishing, textbook publishing and regional publishing did not begin with the decline of scholarly monograph sales in the 1980s and 1990s, but this decline undoubtedly accelerated the shift.

The transformation of the field of academic publishing has placed the American university presses in a particularly difficult situation. For various reasons they feel obliged to continue publishing scholarly monographs, but given the contraction of the library market and the attendant decline of monograph sales, given the standards of production they feel obliged to maintain and the price bands with which they feel obliged to operate, and given the level of overheads they carry, this kind of publishing has increasingly become a loss-making activity for many of the university presses. Senior managers at university presses vary in their assessments of the profitability or otherwise of their monograph publishing programmes and there are no hard and fast rules about how to carry out an assessment of this kind (much depends, for example, on exactly how overhead costs are apportioned between the different kinds of books published). But many university press directors have no doubts at all that monograph publishing has become a loss-making activity for them:

> Our monograph publishing programme, if I thought of it as a separate entity, would be a *colossal* loser financially, just colossal, astronomical. I've done the figures and we'd lose, over the lifetime of each monograph, $13,000 to $15,000. But beyond that, we would get no

reputational oomph for having done it. Very few people would say, 'Oh, I'll bring you my grand new opus because you published those ten narrow little twigs of scholarship.' We would get no reputational oomph from bookstores – bookstores would not say, 'Oh, you've published so many of these things that I'm going to order more of them.' It's even questionable whether we'd get much oomph, or psazz, or whatever the word is, from our bosses here, because those books are like trees falling in the wilderness when there's no one around to hear.

In the view of this university press director, scholarly monograph publishing has become a serious financial liability – and, on top of that, it is no longer clear whether it contributes much to the symbolic capital (the 'reputational oomph') of the press. They can and will continue to publish monographs, since they see it as part of their mission as a university press. But they can continue to do this only if they diversify the list, because it is from other kinds of books – from trade and academic-trade books, from supplemental texts and regional books – that they are able to generate the revenue streams they need in order to flourish (or indeed survive) as a publishing organization.

The paradoxical outcome of this logic of transformation is that the university presses and other academic publishers can remain in the field of academic publishing only if they are able to move beyond it. They have to be in adjacent fields already, or migrate into adjacent fields, in order to generate the kind of revenue they need in order to compensate for the declining sales of scholarly monographs. Hence they can remain academic publishers only if they are or become something else as well – if they are or become trade or academic-trade publishers, if they are or become publishers of textbooks or supplemental texts, if they are or become regional publishers, etc. The decline of scholarly monograph sales has made it very difficult, if not impossible, for a publisher to survive by being active *only* in the field of academic publishing.

Indeed, some American university presses have found themselves caught in a kind of pincer movement by the transformations of the last couple of decades. On the one hand, in the course of the 1980s and 1990s, university administrators at some host institutions expected the university presses to reduce their dependence on direct or indirect subsidies and to become more autonomous financially – 'self-supporting' was the term often used. Many universities were themselves coming under financial pressure and they began to look for ways to reduce their costs – although exactly how this was played out in terms of the university presses varied greatly from one institution to another. As one director put it,

> People began to go after the presses and expect them to be much more self-supporting than they had been in the past. So you get tugs of war within the universities which have never been resolved along the following lines: What are these presses? Are they academic units or are they so-called enterprise or business units? How these issues are addressed varies dramatically from one university to another and depending on who is in the administration. But there is no doubt that by the mid- to late 1980s, there is greater pressure on the presses to be so-called self-supporting – although what self-supporting means from university to university is as varied as the number of universities.

On the other hand, at the same time as many of the university presses were experiencing pressure from above to improve their financial performance, the market for their principal output, the scholarly monograph, was steadily declining, and hence their traditional revenue base was eroding. The conjunction of these two sources of pressure in the course of the 1980s and 1990s forced many of the university presses to review and reform their internal policies and practices. This process has undoubtedly led to many improvements in terms of their organizational structure and efficiency, but it has also propelled them with a degree of urgency on to the path of diversification, compelling them to migrate into other fields of publishing for which they are not always very well equipped and which carry substantial risks of their own.

Uncertain times

In fact, despite the decline in scholarly monograph sales, the period of the 1980s and 1990s was a relatively buoyant period for many publishers who were active in the field of academic publishing, including the American university presses. Many publishers experienced a 'long decade' of growth from the early 1980s to 2000, with growth particularly marked in the late 1980s and early 1990s. No doubt there were many factors underlying this trend, and the relevance of each factor will vary from one organization to another. For many publishers, this growth undoubtedly reflects some success in achieving a diversified publishing programme. This was a time when many of the UK-based commercial academic publishers, as well as some of the UK-based university presses, moved energetically into the field of textbook publishing, and some of their success during this period is no doubt linked to this shift in the focus of their activities. It was also a time when many of the American university presses moved into other fields of publishing, including trade and academic-trade publishing. A few of the larger of the American university presses facilitated this shift into trade publishing by importing general books on art, art history and other subjects from UK publishers and cultural institutions (such as art museums and the BBC) which they could sell as trade titles in the US, and in some cases they did so with considerable success. But this was a risk-laden activity, and while it helped to generate impressive levels of growth for some of the American university presses in the late 1980s and 1990s, it also exposed them to dangers that would become fully apparent in 2001.

Another factor which underpinned the growth of academic publishers in the long decade of the late 1980s and 1990s was the expansion of the retail chains and the rise of the internet booksellers. The expansion of the retail chains was particularly significant in North America, where the rapid growth of Barnes & Nobles and Borders in the late 1980s and throughout the 1990s created a significant demand for books to stock the new superstores that were being opened in urban centres across the country. The expansion of the retail chains sucked books out of the warehouses of university presses and other academic publishers, stimulating a growth in sales throughout the long decade. But part of this growth in sales was an illusion, because a significant proportion of these books were not selling through. They were simply being moved from one warehouse to another, and they were lining the shelves of the superstores like wallpaper. As one publisher observed, 'they'd bought all those books to fill up the floorspace almost, it felt like they were buying books as furniture, and then two years later when they saw that most of those books weren't working and they had so much money tied up in inventory, the books started to come back in droves.'

Trade publishers were particularly exposed to the high level of returns from the chains – one publisher said that returns in their trade division had reached 40 per cent of sales

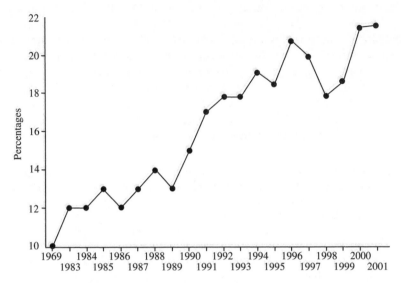

Figure 7.1 Returns as a percentage of gross sales for American university presses, 1969–2001
Source: Annual University Press Statistics (New York: Association of American University Presses).

in 2001 and 2002, compared to returns of around 26 per cent in the mid-1990s. But the university presses were also exposed to higher levels of returns throughout the 1990s, especially in so far as they were moving increasingly into trade and textbook publishing. This is illustrated by figure 7.1, which shows the returns experienced by American university presses as a percentage of gross sales from 1969 to 2001. In 1969, returns for the university presses were 10 per cent of sales, and were still only 13 per cent of sales in 1989. But they rose steeply in the 1990s, reaching nearly 22 per cent in 2000 and 2001. The situation deteriorated still further in 2001–2, especially for the larger university presses with strong trade and academic-trade lists. One university press director said that their returns had reached 34 per cent in 2001–2, whereas in previous years they had stood at around 24 per cent. While gross sales of the press were up in 2001–2, the steep rise in returns meant that its net sales were down on the previous year for the second year in succession.

High levels of returns are a problem not only in the trade market: the levels of returns are also high in the American textbook market. One university press reported that its returns from college stores were running as high as 55 per cent in 2001–2. For many who work in the university press sector, the discovery that the American textbook market is characterized by high levels of returns has come as something of a surprise. An in-depth knowledge of how this market works – the structure of the used book market, the ordering and stocking practices of the college bookstores, etc. – is not widely shared among editors and other staff in the university presses. There are some editors and directors in the university presses who began their careers in college textbook publishing before moving into the university press sector and who therefore understand textbook publishing very well, but they are the exception rather than the rule. For most editors and others in the university presses, college textbook publishing is another world.

The problems caused by high levels of returns are not simply that they significantly reduce net sales and introduce higher levels of uncertainty into the publishing process: they also increase administrative and handling costs. Returns have to be processed, which means that they have to be unpacked, inspected and returned to the appropriate bins in the warehouse or destroyed if they are damaged. Staff become tied up in processes of checking and negotiation which can become messy, costly and time-consuming. One university press director gave a vivid illustration of the problem:

> Among the returns that we've just opened were galley proofs that we had shipped out that they were returning for full credit. We opened up some of these books, they were high-lighted and underlined and marked 'used'. So they were returning their used books to us for full credit. You don't know how much of that is in the system. I'm hoping that it's not much but you can't be sure. So you have to get someone to go through the returns and they discover things. Then, of course, their response is 'oops, sorry, we made a mistake'. But, you know, how many mistakes like that are they making with that publisher? It is just a tremen-dously inefficient system.

Most publishers now meet regularly with the retail chains to discuss the growing problem of returns and what can be done about it. Some have even considered ship-ping less stock than the chains order, especially of the more trade-oriented titles, so that the chains have fewer books to return. What is not clear at this stage is whether the high levels of returns in 2001 and 2002 were a temporary aberration, precipitated by a one-off adjustment in the stock-holding capacity of the chains and the wholesalers and a shift in their stock-ordering practices as the long decade of superstore expansion came to an end (exacerbated by the economic downturn and the shock of 11 September), or whether this is the beginning of a new phase in which publishers will have to learn how to cope with significantly higher levels of returns as a routine feature of their business.

What is clear is that 2001–2 was a rude awakening for many of the American uni-versity presses. Many had become accustomed to steady growth during the long decade of the late 1980s and 1990s, but in 2001–2 they experienced a sudden change of fortunes that caught many by surprise. The year on year growth of the 1980s and 1990s was sud-denly replaced by substantial shortfalls, and in the financial year ending in June 2001 many of the American university presses were significantly down on their previous year's sales. Many saw their deficits grow to alarming levels – one of the larger presses reported a deficit of nearly $5 million on sales of around $18 million. This downturn is highlighted by figure 7.2, which shows the average compound growth rate of the American university presses for various periods between 1983 and 2001. Sales growth for 1998–2001 was 1 per cent – the lowest since 1983 and a dramatic decline from the four-year growth of 34 per cent in 1986–9.

For many of the American university presses, the deteriorating economic conditions of 2001–2 raised serious questions about the strategies they had adopted since the early 1980s to manage the decline of the scholarly monograph. What had seemed to be a suc-cessful strategy that was capable of delivering growth year on year – a strategy involv-ing above all the diversification of the list and the migration into trade/academic-trade publishing, supplemental texts and regional publishing – suddenly began to look more

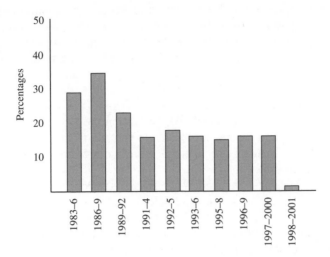

Figure 7.2 Compound growth rates of the American university presses
Source: Annual University Press Statistics (New York: Association of American University Presses).

precarious. The more the university presses moved into trade and textbook publishing, the more exposed they were to the increasing levels of returns that had characterized the industry since the mid-1990s. Some of the larger university presses that had sought, in the course of the 1990s, to counterbalance the declining sales of monographs by acquiring a set of trade titles every season that would generate high frontlist revenue (such as the University of California Press) suddenly found themselves faced in 2001–2 with unprecedented levels of returns, wiping out any gains they may have made in gross sales. Many of the university presses had tried to cope with the declining sales of monographs and the simultaneous demand from university administrators to improve their financial positions by diversifying their lists and moving into what appeared to be greener pastures. In 2001–2 they discovered that these pastures are full of quicksand.

The difficulties of 2001–2 have precipitated much soul-searching in the world of the American university presses. Recent annual meetings of the Association of American University Presses have been preoccupied with the difficult economic conditions and how to cope with them. ('Hard Times: A Glimpse of the Future or a Bump in the Road?' was the title of the plenary session in 2002; 'We're All In This Together' was the plenary session in 2003.) Some university presses (or their host institutions) have initiated wide-ranging reviews, in some cases carried out by external management consultants, and in many presses the changes that were already underway have been accelerated. As it happened, the downturn occurred at a time when the directors of some of the larger university presses were due to retire, and the appointment of new directors at these institutions will undoubtedly have some impact on the courses they adopt in the coming years.

The difficult economic conditions of 2001 and 2002 have also affected the UK-based academic publishers, although less dramatically than the American university presses. Most UK-based academic publishers with a significant presence in the US market experienced high returns in 2001, just as the American university presses had done, and this depressed their North American sales. Many have also experienced further downward pressure on monograph sales and, with state budgets under pressure and stock market earnings down, the resources available to libraries in both the state universities and the private colleges are likely to contract still further in the near future. While the scale, the global reach and the diversified character of OUP and CUP give them some degree of protection from the decline of scholarly monograph sales and from the vicissitudes in the US market, they are by no means insulated from these developments, as the experience of CUP illustrates all too well.[1] Both OUP and CUP maintain large academic publishing programmes and are heavily dependent on the US market for sales of their scholarly monographs, and hence significant downturns in the US market, or further contractions in library budgets, are likely to have a direct impact on these aspects of their publishing operations.

For the UK-based commercial academic publishers, success today depends largely on their ability to publish textbooks for the higher education market, both in the UK and in the US. They have long ceased to think of themselves primarily as scholarly monograph publishers, and those that continue to publish scholarly monographs do so only under rigorously controlled conditions – by separating off the monograph operation and running it according to a carefully calibrated formula of streamlined low-cost production, low print-runs and high prices. The danger with this system is that, with such a finely balanced operation, any significant alteration in the publishing environment can turn a marginally profitable operation into a loss-making one. Hence, if the book acquisitions budgets of the American research libraries are squeezed further by declining state budgets and declining stock market revenues, the monograph operations of the commercial academic publishers could feel the pinch. The margins are very tight on these operations and you need to sell all 300 or 400 copies in order to make it profitable – 'until you sell that last 10 per cent of the units, you are not breaking into profit.' These publishers have very little room to manoeuvre on their monograph operations and further contractions in the library market could easily tip these operations into the red.

Conflicting logics

I have been analysing the logic of transformation of the field of academic publishing in relation to the activities of publishing firms, but it is also vital to see that this transformation is interwoven in complex ways with the world of the academy itself. As I emphasized in chapter 4, academic publishing is part of a broader research process which is

[1] Like many of the American university presses, CUP experienced a sharp downturn in its economic performance in 2001 and 2002. CUP's sales in the year ended 31 December 2001 were £132 million ($211 million), with a net trading loss of £5.8 million ($9.3 million), compared to a net surplus of £4.5 million ($7.2 million) in the previous year. In the year ended 31 December 2002, CUP's sales were £129 million ($206 million), with a net trading loss of £2.5 million ($4 million). By contrast, OUP has performed relatively well despite the harsh economic climate. In the year ended 31 March 2002, OUP's sales were £375 million ($600 million), with a net surplus of £46 million ($74 million); in the year ended 31 March 2003, OUP's net sales rose to £392 million ($627 million), with a net surplus of £58 million ($93 million). As a much larger, more diversified and more commercially oriented organization, OUP was in a much stronger position to weather the difficult economic conditions of recent years.

located primarily within institutions of higher education, and the production of scholarly work fulfils two functions in the research space – dissemination and certification. Scholarly outputs, whether journal articles or scholarly books, are the principal means of disseminating and communicating ideas and the results of research among scholars and researchers in the subject. But scholarly outputs are also means of certification in the academic world. Anyone who wishes to pursue an academic career, or to advance their career in the academic world, knows that they have to publish the kind of work that is recognized and rewarded in that world. This is not an option, it is a necessity. Credentials are essential for career progression in the academic world, and academic publishers (along with journal publishers) are among the key institutions of academic certification.

But the fact that academic publishers are key purveyors of academic credentials has only exacerbated the problems they face, since it has produced a gulf between the supply of scholarly content and the demand for scholarly books that has grown ever wider with time. As the universities produce more and more Ph.D. students who are seeking to pursue academic careers, there are more and more prospective authors who are hoping to find an academic press to publish a version of their thesis. As the competition for academic jobs and promotion to senior posts intensifies, the pressure on academics and prospective academics to publish scholarly work grows, and academic publishers find themselves faced with an ever growing avalanche of scholarly book projects. And yet the expansion in the supply of scholarly content, driven by the logic of the academic field and linked to the hopes and expectations of individual academics and prospective academics whose careers depend on their ability to publish, has occurred at the same time as the market for scholarly books has collapsed. Academic publishers find themselves caught in the middle of these conflicting logics and struggling to reconcile them. Academic publishing has become one of the terrains on which the logics of two different worlds – the world of publishing and the world of the academy – come together and clash, leading on occasion to tension, misunderstanding and mutual recriminations.

In the American context, this clash of logics is expressed with growing disquiet in the controversies over the role of the university presses in the tenure system. In many American colleges and universities, young academics are commonly appointed in the first instance to junior tenure-track positions. After an initial period of two or three years, they are subjected to a review process to decide whether they should be upgraded to a tenured post. A crucial part of this review process is the publication record of the individual, and in the humanities and social sciences the publication of at least one book (often based on a Ph.D. thesis) is regarded as essential in many institutions and departments. In this respect, the decisions of academic publishers, and especially of the university presses, have come to play a pivotal role in the tenure and promotion processes of the universities themselves. Academic publishers in general, and the university presses in particular, have become key players in the provision and legitimation of the credentials of prospective academics. The more prestigious the publisher – that is, the more symbolic capital it possesses in the eyes of academics – the more clout it has as a credential legitimator: in the tenure and promotion processes of the universities, it matters a great deal that a candidate has a book published by Harvard or Princeton or Yale, and the imprimatur of these and other prestigious university presses carries a lot more weight than the name of a small and less prestigious press.

This arrangement suits the universities because it provides a seemingly external yardstick to measure the performance and productivity of the candidate. Lindsay Waters, executive editor at Harvard University Press and a forceful critic of this arrangement, expressed the point with elegant simplicity: 'The benefit of the system is that it allows universities to outsource tenure decisions to university presses.'[2] The fact that the decisions of academic publishers might be taken on grounds other than those that should matter most in decisions concerning the tenure or promotion of an academic may be of little significance to the tenure or promotion committees, for what matters to them is the fact of publication and the symbolic value of the press or imprint, not the grounds on which a manuscript may or may not have been accepted for publication.

The role of academic publishers in oiling the wheels of the tenure system also suited the publishers so long as there was a buoyant market for scholarly monographs: it provided them with a steady flow of new material which they could turn into monographs and sell into a library market that was relatively flush with cash. It was a cosy arrangement that suited all parties. But two developments undermined this. One was the erosion of the library market, which, as we've seen, led to a substantial decline in the sales of scholarly monographs in most subject areas. The other development was the increasing difficulty of securing tenure and the raising of the expectations of tenure and promotion committees concerning the publication records of candidates. As universities came under financial pressure, they made increasing use of adjunct professors, and tenure-track jobs became scarcer. There were fewer opportunities to secure tenure and the hurdles were raised: in the best colleges and universities, it became increasingly common to expect candidates to have published not just one monograph but two before they would be seriously considered for tenure. The tightening of the market for academic posts has inflated the demand for credentials.

As a result of these two developments, the cosy arrangement of earlier decades collapsed and academic publishers found themselves moving in directions that were diametrically opposed to the expectations of many academics, prospective academics and university administrators. The continued functioning of the tenure system required academics and prospective academics to publish more scholarly monographs than ever before, but the pressures within the field of academic publishing meant that most academic publishers (including most university presses) were seeking to publish fewer monographs and were trying to persuade academics to write different kinds of books. And the kinds of books they wanted academics to write were not necessarily the kinds of books that would fulfil the function of legitimating their credentials for tenure and promotion. The pressure to publish for the purposes of securing tenure encourages young academics to publish quickly, and to publish books that will be recognized by other academics as worthy or even significant contributions to the field. The publication of books that are recognized and praised by other academics is a form of currency that young and/or prospective academics must acquire in order to gain permanent entry to the academic field. But academic publishers (including the university presses) are less and less interested in publishing books which are high-level contributions to a specialized field of scholarship; they are looking, instead, for books which have a broader

---

[2] Lindsay Waters, 'Rescue Tenure from the Tyranny of the Monograph', *Chronicle of Higher Education*, 20 Apr. 2001, p. B9. See also his *Enemies of Promise: Publishing, Perishing, and the Eclipse of Scholarship* (Chicago: Prickly Paradigm Press, 2004), esp. pp. 18–30.

appeal, which tackle broader topics and spill over disciplinary boundaries, perhaps even spill over into a general trade market. They are looking for books which take time to write, which are the results of years of reflection and are not rushed out to satisfy the demands of tenure committees. They are also looking for books which are written for students and will be adopted for teaching purposes, either as textbooks or as supplemental texts. But while these are the kinds of books that academic publishers are seeking with increasing determination to publish, they are not the kinds of books that would necessarily be most valued by tenure committees, nor are they the kinds of books that young academics seeking tenure would be most likely (and most able) to produce.

Both textbooks and trade (or academic-trade) books require an approach to the writing and development of content which is at odds with the rush to publish encouraged (indeed required) by the tenure process. Good textbooks, for example, are often written by academics who have considerable experience as teachers and an authoritative overview of the subject; they require careful development, with numerous reviews by external readers who teach the subject and extensive revision by the author in the light of this feedback. Rushing this process is likely to result in a textbook which has not been properly developed to meet the needs of professors, lecturers and students. Similarly, for an academic to write a book that will succeed as a trade (or academic-trade) title often takes time – both time to write it, revise it and present it in a style that will be accessible and interesting to a non-specialist readership and, perhaps more importantly, time for the ideas and the arguments to mature. It is not easy for young academics who are still struggling to gain the recognition of their peers and to secure a position in the academic field, and who in addition are often faced with heavy demands on their time in terms of teaching and administrative commitments, to write the kinds of books that will succeed in either the trade or the textbook market.

Equally importantly, these are not the kinds of books for which young academics will be most rewarded in the competitive struggle that matters most to them at this point in their careers. For what matters most to them is to secure tenure and promotion in the academic field, and what tenure committees are looking for above all, in assessing the publication record of young academics, is whether they are producing scholarly work which makes an original and perhaps even significant contribution to the field. As fields of scholarship develop, in many cases they become increasingly fragmented, and academics (or prospective academics) find themselves making contributions to scholarly fields that are ever more narrowly defined – what some publishers describe as 'the twigging effect', as the branches of scholarship begin to split more and more into twigs. The dynamics of scholarly fields tend to encourage the production of scholarship which is ever-more specialized in character and to reward scholars for publishing works which are judged by other scholars to be original contributions to the field. 'If you want to get tenure you identify the narrow, and that's the book that, except for your dissertation committee, nobody else really cares about and we're supposed to publish,' complained one university press director. Given the dynamics of the field of academic publishing over the last couple of decades, these are the very works that the university presses and other academic publishers are increasingly reluctant to take on.

The cumulative consequence of these developments is that the field of academic publishing and the field of the academy are being propelled in opposite directions. The requirements of the tenure system are placing growing pressure on academic publishers (and especially on the university presses) to publish scholarly monographs, since these are credentials that are increasingly necessary for the tenure process (and, with the credential inflation of recent years, necessary at increasing levels of attainment). But the decline in the market for scholarly monographs, coupled with the institutional pressures on university presses, have placed growing pressure on academic publishers to restrict or reduce their output of scholarly monographs and to devote more attention and resources to commissioning and developing other kinds of books, such as textbooks and trade (or academic-trade) titles. Academics and administrators in the university system want and expect academic publishers to continue to fulfil the role of credential legitimators (and, indeed, they are counting on this more than ever before), but at the same time academic publishers, faced with two decades of declining monograph sales, feel increasingly obliged to devote more of their energy and resources to publishing other kinds of books.

This structural tension affects all academic publishers, but it impinges with particular force on the American university presses. This is partly because the American university presses have been interwoven with the tenure system for a long time and the expectations associated with their role are deeply entrenched; it is also because the presses are closely linked to the universities, receive various kinds of support from them, often have academics from their host institutions sitting on their boards and are regarded by many academics as having some responsibility (however vaguely defined) to serve the academic community. There are occasions when editors or directors at university presses find themselves having to deal directly with tenure-related issues. In the vast majority of cases, these are simply inquiries about the review process, often from prospective authors who are facing tenure decisions and are anxious to know about the fate of their manuscript. But occasionally a university press will find itself faced with pressure of a more insidious kind, as one press director recalled:

> The most common way in which it expresses itself is you get authors who are submitting manuscripts in which you have expressed an interest and you ask to see the thing and send it out for review and then you are told that the tenure clock is ticking and they need a decision by such and such a time and, oh, by the way, because of this they've submitted the thing to three or four other presses. Some editors are very good at just ignoring all this. I think more junior editors tend to get themselves into situations where they are manipulated by a situation like that. The second way in which it expresses itself, which is more egregious, is when the clock of the press, which is either reviewing or in fact editing and producing the manuscript/book, doesn't coincide with the clock of the tenure committee and the editor or director begins to get sometimes very unpleasant calls from either the tenure committee chair or the Dean who wants to know this, that and the other. When I hear that this is happening I generally call up these people and tell them that it is not their matter. We are not in the business of supplying the certification that they need in order to make their decision.

The problem is that, from the viewpoint of many tenure committees, the university presses *are* in the business of supplying the certification they need – or at least part of the certification they need – to make their decisions. The occasions when university presses find themselves faced with direct pressure from members of tenure committees to speed up their decision-making processes are no doubt rare, but the structural tension is deeply embedded in the tenure system. The university presses have become part of a process of certification on which decisions concerning tenure in the academic world have come to depend, and this is a role from which they cannot easily extricate themselves.

The problems generated by the tenure system are exacerbated by the fact that not all universities have university presses, and not all university presses have the same status as credential legitimators. For a young academic to have a monograph published by Harvard or Princeton or another high-status university press will generally matter more in the tenure stakes than if the same book were published by a small and less prestigious press. Hence the tasks of credential legitimation tend to be differentially distributed among publishers, and those presses that have the most symbolic capital in the eyes of academics tend to carry the heaviest burden of expectation in terms of their contribution to the tenure system. Indeed, the tasks of credential legitimation are differentially distributed not just among publishers but among universities, since there are many colleges and universities which do not support university presses but which rely on those university presses that do exist to legitimate the credentials of their academic staff. It is hardly surprising that staff at the most prestigious university presses might feel some resentment at finding themselves charged with a disproportionate responsibility for performing a role that they had no wish to assume in the first place. 'That's an unfair allocation of resources,' commented the director of one such press, 'because a lot of these people we publish come from places where there are no presses, and the places are not contributing but they're gaining. They're gaining the use of our name in their recruitment brochures. They haven't published with their own colleges because they're too cheap to have a press.'

What can be done about this situation? Many academic publishers would like universities to disconnect the tenure system from the publication of scholarly monographs – 'rescue tenure from the tyranny of the monograph', to use Lindsay Waters's words. From the publisher's point of view, this would have the bonus of freeing university presses from the obligation to provide tenure committees with certifications of academic excellence. In Waters's view, the reliance of tenure committees on the publication decisions of university presses is an abdication of responsibility on the part of the academic community: the members of the tenure committees do not have to read a candidate's work for themselves and make up their own minds about its quality and significance but can rely instead on the seemingly external assessment processes of the university presses. Waters is undoubtedly right to urge the academic community to re-examine its practices in this regard. At the very least, tenure committees in the humanities and social sciences should reflect on the changing conditions of academic publishing and take account of the fact that the publication decisions of university presses are shaped by a range of considerations which have very little to do with the sheer quality of a scholar's work. There are some signs that this message is beginning to be heard in some sectors of the academic community – in 2002, for example, Stephen Greenblatt, as president of the Modern Language Association of America, circulated a letter to members of the MLA outlining some of the problems faced by the university presses and urging them to bear this in mind when reviewing the tenure of junior faculty. 'These faculty members find themselves in a maddening double bind,' explained Greenblatt. 'They face a challenge – under inflexible time constraints and with very high stakes – that many of them may be unable to meet successfully, no matter how strong or serious their scholarly achievement, because academic presses simply cannot afford to publish their books.' Greenblatt urged academics to try to persuade their departments and universities to change their expectations for tenure reviews – 'The book has only fairly recently emerged as the sine qua non and even now is not uniformly the requirement in all academic fields.'[3]

It is too early to say whether interventions of this kind are likely to have a significant impact. The MLA has recently carried out its own inquiry into the future of scholarly publishing and has similarly urged that tenure committees review their criteria of assessment: 'By ceasing to regard book publication as the gold standard for tenure and promotion, universities and colleges would be able to place more emphasis on the quality of publications rather than on their external format.'[4] But ingrained practices are hard to change, and in a context of fewer tenure-track jobs and increasing competition for those that do exist, it may be difficult to break the cycle of credential inflation that has placed growing pressure on the university presses. Greenblatt's intervention and the MLA report display a growing acknowledgement from within the academic community of the deep problems faced by the university presses, an acknowledgement that is long overdue. There may be the beginnings here of a change of attitude, perhaps even the beginnings of a more constructive dialogue between the various constituencies upon which the future of scholarly publishing depends – the librarians and university administrators as well as the academics and university presses. But one should not underestimate the difficulty of bringing about any significant change in the tenure system and the support provided for scholarly publishing, especially when the competition for tenure is likely to become more intense and when the resources available to both libraries and presses are likely to come under increasing pressure.

The debates in the United States over the role of the university presses in the tenure system exemplify very well the tensions created by the conflicting logics of the academic world and the field of academic publishing. A similar tension exists in the UK, in so far as scholarly monographs continue to play an important role in decisions concerning academic appointments and promotions in British universities, especially in the humanities and the softer social sciences. However, British universities do not have the same kind of tenure-track system as American universities, and hence the tenure decision has not become a focal point of tension in the UK in the way that it has in the US. In the British context, it is the Research Assessment Exercise – the RAE – which has become the key focal point where the conflicting logics of the academic world and the world of publishing are expressed. But since this conflict bears as much on the field of textbook publishing as it does on the field of academic publishing, I shall postpone the discussion of the RAE until chapter 10.

Academic publishing in the face of an uncertain future

We have examined in some detail the transformation of the field of academic publishing over the last few decades, but it is also important to see that this transformation is part and parcel of a broader structural change in the field of higher education itself. In

---

[3] The full letter can be found at www.mla.org/rep_scholarly_pub.
[4] *The Future of Scholarly Publishing* (New York: Modern Language Association, 2002), p. 179. Available at www.mla.org/resources/documents/issues_scholarly_pub.

the United States, the history of higher education since the Second World War can be roughly divided into two periods.[5] The first period, from 1945 to around 1975, was a period of growth and expansion – this was the Golden Age of American higher education. The number of American undergraduates increased by almost 500 per cent and the number of graduate students increased by nearly 900 per cent. In the 1960s alone, enrolments more than doubled, the number of doctorates awarded annually tripled and more members of faculty were hired than had been hired in the entire 325-year history of American higher education up to that point.[6] This growth was fuelled by three developments: the baby boom, the relatively high domestic economic growth rate of the postwar period and the Cold War. During the Second World War, the federal government instituted the practice of contracting out its scientific research to the universities, and during the Cold War the federal government began to subsidize higher education directly, partly in response to fears about a technological lag behind the Soviet Union. The 1958 National Defense Education Act identified two fields, science and foreign languages, that were particularly deserving of public investment.

The Golden Age came to an end around 1975 and American higher education entered a new phase. The college age population levelled off, the sustained economic growth of the postwar period turned into recession and the political climate of the 1960s, which had viewed the support of higher education as a bulwark against communism, began to change. Partly in order to maintain enrolments, the admissions policies of colleges and universities began to adapt, leading to greater diversification in terms of the student body and a broad shift away from the traditional liberal arts degree. In 1970, English majors in American colleges and universities accounted for 7.6 per cent of all BAs; by 1997, they represented 4.2 per cent. In absolute numbers, English majors declined from 64,342 in 1970 to 49,345 in 1997. By contrast, subjects such as business, education and healthcare grew significantly. Today 20 per cent of all BAs are awarded in business – it is by far the biggest undergraduate major in American higher education, followed by education (10 per cent) and the health professions (7 per cent). (We shall discuss these trends in more detail in chapter 9.)

The changing structure of American higher education has shaped the evolution of the field of academic publishing, simply because the American system of higher education is the most important single market for the output of academic publishers in the English language, whether they are American university presses or UK-based university presses and commercial firms. With the benefit of hindsight, one can see that the Golden Age created an inflated market for the output of academic publishers: the expansion of the system of higher education, together with the pumping of federal funds into higher education, fuelled the demand for books and other content to fill the libraries of an expanding system. In effect, university presses and other academic publishers were being subsidized indirectly by a federal government which saw the expansion of higher education as part of its Cold War strategy. The university presses were also playing their part in the expansion of the system by taking on the role of credential legitimators for the faculties that were rapidly increasing their staff. One university press director described this as the emergence of the 'Big Deal':

[5] See Louis Menand, 'College: The End of the Golden Age', *New York Review of Books*, 18 Oct. 2001.
[6] Ibid., p. 2.

The emergence of the Big Deal took place at a time when there was money to support what was essentially a closed circle in which presses expanded to produce this product, libraries bought this product and had the money to buy it in a way that basically covered the presses' costs. It was also a period in which, because of the explosion of the number of people in graduate school, the notion that a book was needed in order to get tenure, which was already well institutionalized at the major research universities, began very quickly to spread to the second-rank universities, the liberal arts colleges and on down beyond that. This dovetailed beautifully with what the graduate schools were turning out, because there was a change in the whole way that graduate students were being trained by the late 1960s – you were really being trained to write a book. The whole culture fed and sustained this set of assumptions, which there was sufficient money for a while to support.

The waning of the Golden Age was also the beginning of the long-term decline of the market for scholarly monographs, a decline that has been exacerbated since the early 1980s by the rapidly escalating costs of scientific and scholarly journals. The American university presses were particularly vulnerable to the impact of this long-term structural change for several reasons. First, they were much less diversified and much less global than OUP, CUP and the large UK-based academic publishers, and hence they were much more dependent on a US scholarly monograph market that was in decline. Second, with one or two notable exceptions, the American university presses did not have substantial journals programmes, and hence they were not able to benefit as much as other academic publishers from the escalation of journal subscription prices (and, in any case, the university presses have generally not increased their journal prices at anything like the rate of the commercial publishers, as we saw in chapter 4). Third, again with a couple of notable exceptions, the American university presses have traditionally been strongly oriented towards the humanities and the softer social sciences. Their publishing programmes have therefore tended to be focused on those subjects which are part of the traditional liberal arts curriculum, whereas the real growth of the American higher education system in recent decades has been elsewhere. And fourth, while the resources that flowed into the system during the Golden Age have declined or been diverted elsewhere, the expectation that the American university presses should continue to play the role of credential legitimators for the universities has remained intact and has if anything been raised to higher levels, since the increased competition for tenured posts, especially in the humanities and social sciences, has inflated the demand for credentials.

We have seen how the university presses have struggled to cope with the changing circumstances in which they have found themselves, changes that are rooted in deep structural transformations that go back to the 1960s and before. They sought, with varying degrees of determination and effectiveness, to transform their own internal structures and practices in all aspects of the organization, from editorial to production, sales and marketing. They sought, again with varying degrees of success, to turn themselves into organizations that were more business-like and market-conscious, as it became increasingly clear that the market for scholarly monographs could no longer be taken for granted as it had been by many in the 1970s and before. Many of the university presses also sought to diversify their lists, to move away from their traditional reliance on scholarly monographs and to migrate into fields of publishing where they thought they could generate higher sales.

Thanks to these and other changes (including important changes in the retail sector), the fortunes of many of the American university presses improved during the late 1980s and 1990s, but the fundamental structural problems inherent in the field of academic publishing remained intact. Throughout the late 1980s and 1990s, the university presses were, in effect, managing decline in the field of academic publishing by redirecting their energies into more fertile fields – a strategy that worked so long as the other fields remained fertile. To some extent, the university presses found, in the rise of the retail chains and the online bookstores, a temporary reprieve from the long-term decline of the library market. But when the inflated market created by the expansion of the retail chains began to contract, resulting in unprecedented levels of returns, the precariousness of this strategy became all too apparent. This is not to say that list diversification was (or is) misguided – on the contrary, it was undoubtedly a sensible move, even if it did expose university presses to much higher levels of risk than they were accustomed to taking, especially when they tried to move into trade publishing. But it is to say that the problems faced by the university presses are unlikely to be solved by a strategy of list diversification alone.

So what are the university presses to do? Many of the American university presses face a very uncertain future. Undoubtedly the larger university presses – and especially those, like Harvard and Princeton, which can draw on substantial endowments – will be secure, but it is by no means clear that all of the smaller presses will survive if the economic conditions continue to deteriorate. At a time when many colleges and universities are facing growing pressure on their finances, some may be forced to take tough decisions about which activities they regard as essential and worthy of continued support and which they regard as dispensable, and it cannot be taken for granted that a subsidized university press will always fall on the fortunate side of the line.[7] So what can university presses do to increase their chances of weathering difficult times? The university presses have come up with many answers themselves, and the more successful presses have already gone a long way to implementing them. So without wishing to suggest that these points are particularly novel, I would highlight the following four measures: (1) further changes in publishing strategies; (2) greater selectivity in list-building; (3) more emphasis on textbook publishing; and (4) more effort devoted to public relations.

(1) *Publishing strategies*   The American university presses tend to publish scholarly monographs in ways that were shaped by different market conditions. They have taken significant steps to reduce costs, but they tend to maintain very high standards of production and to devote a great deal of attention to each book they publish. They have also been reluctant to increase prices and have tended to remain within certain price bands for both their hardback and paperback editions. As I noted earlier, this is partly because they see it as part of their mission to make scholarship available at affordable prices, and partly because they take their pricing reference points from one another and

---

[7] In early 2004, two universities announced their intention to close their presses, the University of Idaho and Northeastern University. In both cases, the reason given was that the press was a drain on the university's resources. The decisions have generated a good deal of controversy and discussions are underway to see whether there might be some alternative solution which would enable publishing operations to continue in some form.

from the New York trade houses: no university press is inclined to increase its prices beyond certain price points unless it sees others doing the same, and the result is that no one does it. But the consequence of these largely self-imposed constraints is that many of the university presses make a significant loss on most of the monographs they publish, once overhead costs are factored in. Judged in relation to the revenue generated in current market conditions, the American university presses are overproducing and underpricing their scholarly monographs. They are able to do this provided that their host institutions are willing to subsidize the press and/or provided that they are able to generate surpluses in their other publishing activities, which they can use to create an internal subsidy for their monograph programme. But as the university presses come under increasing pressure to reduce their dependence on their host institutions and as their ability to generate surpluses from other publishing activities is jeopardized by weakened markets and high returns, they may have little alternative but to reform more radically their monograph publishing practices. This would include introducing further measures to reduce costs, such as streamlining production processes and introducing more stringent controls on the length and complexity of manuscripts. It would include the willingness to continue to reduce print-runs to reflect actual sales of scholarly books, so that the presses' warehouses are not filling up with unsold and unsaleable stock. And above all it would involve a willingness to push the prices of both cloth and paperback editions significantly higher, so that they are charging prices that are geared more accurately to recovering the costs they are actually incurring in their monograph publishing programmes.

(2) *List-building*   A second measure that would strengthen the position of the university presses would be to be even more selective in terms of their list-building activities. The higher-throughput model of monograph publishing may have seemed like an attractive strategy in the 1970s and early 1980s, but the decline in unit sales has turned this model into a treadmill. The only way to get off this treadmill is for university presses to be more selective about the monographs they take on and to be more proactive about building their lists in ways that will create a more robust revenue base in which a higher proportion of revenue is generated from the backlist. Greater selectivity implies a willingness to restrict or even reduce the numbers of monographs the university presses publish: the growth in monograph output has been driven not by an overall growth in demand for scholarly monographs but by a combination of other factors (including the growth in the supply of manuscripts, the demand for certification from the academic community and the short-term need of the university presses to meet their sales forecasts). Publishing fewer monographs and concentrating only on works of outstanding scholarship might result in some temporary shortfalls in frontlist revenue but, if it is accompanied by an effective shift of editorial strategy to other kinds of commissioning, it would strengthen the position of the university presses in the longer term.

Greater selectivity also implies a determination to reduce the range of subjects in which the university presses publish and a willingness to consider building their lists in areas that have traditionally been neglected by them. One of the most burdensome legacies of the university presses is their disciplinary catholicism and their traditional emphasis on the humanities and the softer social sciences, to the neglect of those disciplines – including the natural sciences, the harder social sciences and emerging fields like information technology and computer science – that lie outside the traditional liberal arts curriculum. The problem with disciplinary catholicism is not simply that it gives rise to a publishing programme that lacks focus: it is also costly because it gives rise to marketing costs in subject areas where the press lacks sufficient critical mass to justify them. Many of the university presses would do well to follow the example set by MIT Press in the late 1970s when it chose to restrict its commissioning activities to a selected range of disciplines. The more that the press can focus its list-building activities on a limited set of subject areas where it can build up real expertise and critical mass, the more effective its publishing programme is likely to be; and the more that the press can focus on those subject areas which are likely to be more robust in terms of the sales of scholarly monographs, the more able it will be to stave off the debilitating effects of the long-term decline in the market for scholarly books. It is clear that different subject areas vary in terms of their capacity to absorb scholarly books and that some of the areas which have been the traditional focus of university press publishing – especially humanities subjects like history and literary studies – are among the areas where the sales of scholarly books have become, and are likely to remain, the weakest.

(3) *Textbook publishing* However, if my analysis of the field of academic publishing is sound, then it will not be sufficient for the university presses simply to improve the ways they publish scholarly work – by itself, scholarly monograph publishing will simply not generate sufficient revenue for the presses to survive. They will have to find other ways to make up the revenues they will need, and the more that their host institutions wind down their subsidies and expect the presses to break even, the more urgently they will need to search elsewhere for the kind of revenue they will need to support their monograph publishing programme – in other words, they will have to migrate into other fields. External subsidies from host institutions will have to be replaced by (or, in cases where they remain, augmented by) internal subsidies which can be created by moving into more profitable forms of publishing. As we've seen, many of the university presses have already undertaken some degree of field migration, but the movement of the American university presses into adjacent fields has been heavily skewed towards trade and academic-trade publishing to the relative neglect of the textbook market. To some extent, this skewing of the process of migration was shaped by the success of Harvard in reinventing itself in the 1970s as a highbrow trade publisher with an academic list, a model that was emulated by several of the larger university presses in the 1980s and admired by many others. It was also shaped by the glamour associated with trade publishing, which undoubtedly exerted some appeal on university presses, by the rise of the retail chains, which created an expanding market for trade and academic-trade titles in the late 1980s and 1990s, and by the cultural dispositions of university press editors, who were inclined to think of the trade market as the most likely source of additional revenue. But for many university presses, migrating into the trade market was not necessarily the most prudent move. It was a path strewn with dangers. University presses were drawn into the practice of giving high trade discounts to books that were academic-trade books at best. Attracted by the lure of the trade, it was easy for publishers to delude themselves about the sales potential of what was essentially an academic book, and hence to over-print it, overproduce it, underprice it and give it a discount which gave away margin and increased the risk of high returns. They were building lists that were heavily dependent on frontlist revenue and therefore highly vulnerable to downturns in the economy and to changes in the practices of the retail chains.

There are signs that some of the university presses are taking a more realistic approach to the trade potential of their books, partly in response to the devastating impact of high returns. There are also signs that the university presses are putting more concerted effort into reference publishing and into commissioning books that stand a good chance of securing course adoptions at colleges and universities. These are undoubtedly sensible measures. The university presses could strengthen their positions considerably – and this is the third measure I wish to highlight – by focusing their attention more systematically on publishing for the higher education market, and especially for the upper levels of the undergraduate curriculum and graduate courses. This would enable them to take advantage of their links with the academic community – the same academics who write scholarly monographs for them are the potential authors of textbooks. Indeed, editors at university presses are probably more closely and regularly in contact with a wide range of potential academic authors than the editors at the large textbook publishing firms, who tend to rely more on the intelligence gathered by the sales force of college reps. Publishing for the textbook and course adoption market has not been neglected by the university presses, but in many cases these books are adopted because they are judged by the academics teaching the courses to be significant contributions to the field rather than because the books were explicitly designed for teaching purposes. Both types of books have an important role to play in the curricula of higher education, and the university presses could do much more to develop an organizational culture which was more systematically oriented to the commissioning and development of content for teaching and learning in higher education (we shall return to this issue in chapter 9). This would not compromise or exclude their commitment to publishing original works of scholarship but would be complementary to it and would be entirely consistent with their overall educational mission.

(4) *Public relations*   The fourth point has to do with the relations between the university presses and their host institutions. In essence, the fundamental problem faced by the university presses is that they are expected to fulfil two very different objectives, one intellectual and the other financial. When the market conditions in the field of academic publishing were relatively buoyant, the university presses could pursue their goal of publishing high-quality scholarship without worrying greatly about the financial consequences. But over the last twenty to thirty years these market conditions have deteriorated at the same time as many of the host institutions have raised their expectations in terms of the financial performance of the presses. Hence the goal of publishing high-quality scholarship has diverged increasingly from the financial goals that have been set for the university presses by their host institutions: the presses are expected to continue to publish high-quality scholarship in conditions when publishing of this kind has become incapable of sustaining the press. In the late 1940s, the then director of Harvard University Press, Thomas Wilson, was reputed to have said that 'a university press exists to publish as many good scholarly books as possible short of bankruptcy.'[8] The problem for the university presses today is that it has become more and more difficult to publish high-quality scholarly books while remaining on the virtuous side of insolvency. How can they reconcile their scholarly mission with the need to generate sufficient revenue

[8] Quoted in Hall, *Harvard University Press*, p. 125.

to ensure their survival? This is the key question that all university presses have to face today with a greater sense of urgency than ever before.

Within the context of the university, the tension between the scholarly and financial goals is often expressed in terms of the conflicting expectations of university administrators, on the one hand, and the academics who take an interest in the press, on the other. One university press director expressed this tension very well:

> The press directors report usually to an administrator and that administrator is usually somebody who cares about financial concerns. There is also either an editorial board or an academic group at the university that cares about the press. That group is usually uninformed about publishing and completely uncaring about the financial implications of what they want. They are ignorant in both ways, but they are quite vocal and sometimes quite powerful. The press director is almost always trying to reconcile two unreconcilable goals. The director is trying to please two masters and it is almost impossible to please even one.

Hence an essential part of the work of a university press director is a kind of political work aimed at building relations with the two key constituencies within the university – the administrators who control the purse strings and the faculty who take an academic interest in the press. How exactly these relations evolve over time, what kind of power the constituencies have and how well they understand the problems of the presses, varies greatly from one university to another, and most generalizations about these issues would be misleading. But there is undoubtedly room for the university presses to do more to explain their predicament to their constituencies – both to seek to persuade university administrators and others that the presses perform a role which is worthy of some degree of support (and some degree of tolerance when the business cycle turns down), and to try to explain to faculty that their academic agendas (as well as their tenure conditions) have financial costs and consequences. For at the end of the day, decisions concerning the future of the university presses lie not in the hands of the presses themselves but in the hands of those to whom they report and those for whom their core activity – the publication of high-quality scholarly work – is carried out. When the going gets tough, the future of a press may well depend on the extent to which it has secured the support of university administrators or, in cases where that is lacking, on the extent to which faculty and others are willing to mobilize support on its behalf. 'If a press has lost the support of the local faculty,' commented one well-placed observer, 'then I think it is doomed. Then you're depending entirely on the goodwill of an administration that is under an increasing amount of pressure and I think that's probably hopeless.' Cultivating good relations with the local faculty is not just sensible from the viewpoint of running a good scholarly publishing programme: it is vital to the long-term survival of the press.

I have concentrated here on the predicament of the American university presses, but the two major UK-based university presses are exposed to similar pressures and faced with similar difficulties. Both OUP and CUP have been much more proactive than the American university presses in terms of reducing costs, cutting print-runs and raising prices for scholarly monographs, and hence their monographs tend to carry significantly higher prices than those published by the American university presses. This has helped OUP and CUP to maintain the margins on monographs in the context of declining sales and declining print-runs, but it hasn't arrested the overall pattern of decline. Hence OUP and CUP have also had to face, and will undoubtedly continue to have to face, difficult decisions about whether to remain in certain specialized academic fields where the sales of scholarly monographs are particularly poor. They too will have to grapple with the legacy of disciplinary catholicism, which perhaps weighs even more heavily on them given their scale and the intellectual diversity of their host institutions.

But the real challenges faced by OUP and CUP stem from the very conditions that distinguish them from the American university presses, namely their diversified character and their global reach. Their ability to weather the storms in the field of academic publishing depends crucially on their success in other publishing fields – especially in the field of ELT publishing, which has been the real engine of growth for both presses (and especially for OUP) since the early 1980s. Without the surpluses generated from ELT publishing, the financial performances of both OUP and CUP over the last two decades would have been much weaker. But ELT publishing is a highly competitive field with its own logic and dynamic of change, and both OUP and CUP are likely to face increasing competition from local publishers in Spain, Latin America and elsewhere who are eager to supply their domestic market with ELT materials and who are well networked with local schools and educational authorities. OUP and CUP have important competitive advantages in these markets, including their brands and the quality of their products, but they know very well that these advantages could be eroded by well-organized local competitors (as well as by intensified competition from UK-based commercial publishers who are already key players in the field). And if they were to experience a significant decline in the performance of their ELT publishing programmes (or, in the case of CUP, an inability to expand it quickly and substantially), this could place renewed pressure on other aspects of their businesses including their academic divisions, which have traditionally benefited from the surpluses generated by ELT publishing.

OUP and CUP also have to deal with a different set of expectations in their host institutions. For several years both OUP and CUP have been net financial contributors to their universities rather than the other way around, but whether they (and especially CUP) will be able to sustain this in a harsher economic climate is unclear. At a time when the universities of Oxford and Cambridge are both experiencing serious financial difficulties and running substantial annual deficits, a significant decline in the contribution of the presses to the university chests could well become a source of strain. Ultimately these issues will depend on the establishment of a more satisfactory arrangement for the funding of institutions of higher education in the UK. But in the meantime, it may well be necessary for both OUP and CUP to invest additional time and energy in the management of their relations with their host institutions.

Whereas the university presses will remain in the field of academic publishing so long as they remain going concerns since it is part of their constitutional remit to do so, the same could not be said of the commercial academic publishers. As we have seen, some of these publishers have found ways to remain active in the field by sequestering the monograph and carefully controlling the conditions of publication. But whether they will remain in the field will depend on whether these operations remain profitable for them – it is as simple as that. There are other reasons why these commercial academic publishers would like to remain in the field: it adds symbolic value to the list and it strengthens their relations with the academic community, who can see that the press is willing to serve it by publishing scholarly works. But the symbolic benefits of remaining in the field will be overshadowed by financial considerations. And if these considerations turn into serious liabilities, the commercial academic publishers are likely to follow the course taken by other commercial publishers and exit the field.

The transformation of the field of academic publishing has major implications not only for the university presses and the commercial publishers who remain active in the field, but also for the academic community itself. The academic world has come to depend on the field of academic publishing (together with that of scholarly journals) as a principal means for the dissemination of scholarly work and as a key mechanism of professional certification, and yet, ironically, most academics are woefully ignorant of what is happening in this field upon which so much of their own success now depends. 'I think that academics are very, very, very sadly misinformed,' commented one university press director. 'I'd say that after ten years of proselytizing about this, I've made zero inroads.' This director had her own theory of why academics were so ill-informed about the real conditions of academic publishing: because so much of their own self-esteem is wrapped up in their scholarly work, they tend to share only the success stories with their colleagues. 'The people who have the sad stories are not going to be as likely to share them. So because of the secretive nature of academics and the privacy that's needed when the stakes are so high, it's only the good stories that get out – and also the horror stories about publishers.' Whether or not her theory is correct, it is undoubtedly the case that most academics understand very little about the real conditions of academic publishing and how they have changed in recent decades. Many are aware that things are changing but they have little in-depth understanding of why this is so and of what the implications might be for the disciplines in which they are engaged.

And yet it is not difficult to see that the implications are potentially far-reaching. If academic publishers are systematically withdrawing from certain disciplinary fields or subfields because the sales of scholarly monographs in those fields are too poor to justify their continued presence in them, then how are young scholars in those fields going to publish their work in the future? How are new ideas going to emerge and new developments take shape? Will the vitality of intellectual disciplines be determined by the decisions taken by publishing organizations whose actions are governed by an altogether different logic? It may well be that, in many disciplines, the dissemination of scholarly work will increasingly gravitate towards the journal, as is already the case in the natural sciences and in the harder social sciences like economics. But in many of the humanities and social sciences, books continue to play a vital role in the ways that scholars communicate their work and their ideas. Books are often the focus of discussion, controversy and debate; they are key reference points for both teaching and research and a crucial means by which these disciplines evolve. So a fundamental transformation of the conditions of scholarly publishing should be a matter of concern to anyone who has an interest in the nature, vitality and future of academic disciplines.

These developments are likely to affect all disciplines in which monographs have traditionally played some role in the processes of scholarly communication and professional certification, but they will undoubtedly affect some disciplines more than others. Humanities subjects like literary studies and certain fields of history are particularly vulnerable, since these are subjects where the decline in the sales of scholarly monographs has been particularly dramatic. While these disciplines have traditionally relied on the university presses to publish and disseminate scholarly work in their fields, it would be unwise to count on this in the future. 'At the end of the day,' remarked one university press director, 'staying in existence is going to trump any warm-hearted feelings about English scholarship.' How these disciplines will cope with a situation in which the university presses become more and more reluctant to publish scholarly monographs, and how this will affect the nature of knowledge and intellectual development within these disciplines, are questions to which, at this moment, we have no clear answers.

Will these problems be solved by technology? Will the coming of electronic systems of content delivery do away with the need to publish scholarly monographs in the traditional printed format, replacing them with electronic texts that can be accessed anywhere and anytime? There are many who have dreamt of an 'electronic solution to the monograph problem' – a phrase that has often been used in the technical literature. And indeed, there can be no doubt that the digital revolution has had, and will continue to have, a profound impact on the field of academic publishing and, more generally, on the nature and forms of scholarly communication. But the issues are less clear-cut than many of the early advocates of electronic publishing tended to assume. While many of the experiments are still underway, we now know enough to draw one reasonably firm conclusion: just as the digital revolution was not the origin of the problems faced by academic publishers today, so too it is unlikely to be their salvation. (We shall examine these issues in more detail in part IV.)

In the final analysis, the future of academic publishing in general, and of the university presses in particular, is dependent on the world of the academy itself, for this is the social field to which academic publishing is inextricably tied. When there were sufficient resources available in university libraries to make scholarly monograph publishing an unambiguously profitable business, it was not necessary to ask too many questions about what purposes were served by publishing books of this kind, and the academic community could enjoy the benefits of this system of scholarly communication and professional certification without having to worry about who was picking up the tab. But as the economic conditions which underpinned this system deteriorate, the principal beneficiaries can no longer take it for granted that the services provided by academic publishers will continue as before. They must therefore ask themselves which of these services they continue to value and how they should be funded in the future. It is encouraging that there are some within the academic community who have begun to ask whether their institutions can and should continue to rely on the output of scholarly publishers to provide the credentials upon which their systems of tenure and promotion are based – many scholarly publishers would be only too pleased to be relieved of what they have come to see as an unwanted burden. But even if the link between the publication of scholarly monographs and the certification of academic credentials were attenuated (and any movement in this direction is likely to be modest for the foreseeable future), the key questions concerning the future of scholarly publishing would remain. For the principal rationale for continuing to publish scholarly monographs despite the long-term decline in sales has to do, not with the needs of tenure committees, but rather with the intellectual life of the disciplines: scholarly monographs merit publication in so far as they make important contributions to knowledge which are vital for the development of disciplines and valued by the academic community. And to the extent that scholarly monographs are valued by the academic community as a means of disseminating research and advancing knowledge in their fields, then the academic community cannot relinquish all responsibility for ensuring that the organizations saddled with the task of making scholarly monographs available are able to do so without being driven to the wall. It cannot shift all the responsibility onto the university presses and other academic publishers and expect them to cover the costs of providing a service to the academic community which has become increasingly difficult to sustain in economic terms. Expecting academic publishers to continue to publish scholarly monographs in the context of a declining market is a matter of willing the ends without the means. The scholarly monograph can survive only if there is a recognition on the part of the academic community that it remains a valuable medium for the dissemination of research and scholarship which deserves the active support of the academic community itself – through, among other things, the vigorous defence of the book acquisitions budgets of university libraries, the provision of subsidies for specific publication projects and, above all, the willingness of host institutions to support their university presses in difficult times.

Part III

The Field of Higher Education Publishing

8
Higher education publishing in the US (1): the formation of the field

At the beginning of the twenty-first century, the field of higher education publishing looks very different from the kind of field that existed thirty years ago. This is a world that has undergone enormous change in a relatively short period of time, and many of the firms who were key players thirty years ago are no longer there – or if they are still there, they are no longer in control of their own destinies. How has this field changed and why has it changed so much? Have the upheavals that have characterized the field of higher education publishing in the United States also occurred in the United Kingdom? If not, why not? Is this simply a cultural and economic lag that will be eclipsed with time, or does the field of higher education publishing in the UK differ in important ways from the US field? What are the implications of these developments for the firms which are active in the field, or for those which are seeking to increase their presence in it? And what are the implications for the field of higher education itself, for the professors, lecturers and students who depend on the products of higher education publishers for the teaching and learning that takes place in our colleges and universities?

These are some of the questions that I shall seek to address in this and the following chapters. I shall begin by analysing the field of higher education publishing in relation to the social field of higher education itself and the pedagogical activities that take place in colleges and universities – in relation, that is, to what could be called 'the pedagogical process'. I shall then focus on the nature and evolution of the field of higher education publishing in the United States since the 1970s, with a view to highlighting the structure and the logic of transformation of this field (this chapter and the next). Finally, I shall turn to the field of higher education publishing in the UK, exploring the differences between the US and the UK and the changing nature of higher education publishing in Britain today (chapters 10 and 11).

The field of higher education publishing

There are two keys to understanding the nature of higher education publishing. First, higher education publishing must be understood in relation to the pedagogical activities of higher education, for higher education publishing exists only by virtue of the fact that it meets a demand for teaching and learning materials that arises within the field of higher education itself. Second, the nature of the relation between higher education publishing, on the one hand, and the field of higher education, on the other, is defined above all by a particular structure of decision-making which has become institutionally sedimented in both higher education publishing and higher education itself – namely, the adoption system.

Higher education publishing and the pedagogical process

The field of higher education publishing is defined by the distinctive relation between publishing organizations and the teaching activities of educational institutions. Publishers develop teaching materials for every level of the curriculum, from kindergarten through to advanced graduate-level courses at the best universities. In the North American context, publishers generally distinguish between what they call the 'K-12' market (sometimes referred to as 'elhi' – elementary to high school), which runs from kindergarten through the twelfth grade and comprises elementary and secondary school, on the one hand, and the higher education market, which runs from freshman year at college through to graduate school, on the other. The professional market, which includes STM, business and computing, is often treated as a separate division, as is material produced for what is sometimes called 'lifelong' or 'lifetime' learning. My focus here is on higher education publishing – that is, the publishing of content for use as teaching material in courses at colleges and universities, from first-year undergraduate through to postgraduate levels.

Traditionally, the principal form for the provision of educational content for higher education has been the textbook. Indeed, in the North American context, publishers who were active in this field were traditionally described as 'college textbook publishers'. In more recent years, this label has tended to give way to the more generic term 'higher education publisher', partly in recognition of the growing importance of educational materials which are supplied in forms other than the traditional textbook. Many publishers in this field prefer today to describe themselves as an 'education' or 'higher education' publisher, and to describe their division as the 'education' or 'higher education' division, on the grounds that these terms are neutral with regard to the particular medium or media in which the educational content is packaged and delivered to end users. In practice, however, the printed textbook remains the principal medium for the delivery of educational content in the area of higher education and the principal mechanism of revenue generation for higher education publishers.

What is a textbook? This is a term which is as slippery and difficult to define as 'monograph'. In the broadest sense, a textbook could be defined as *a book which is written for and used by teachers and students for the purposes of teaching and learning*. But this broad definition covers a multitude of different kinds of books, from basic or 'core' textbooks which are carefully developed for first-year college students through to books of a more specialized kind which are used by professors as supplementary texts in teaching more advanced subjects and topics. The textbook market is, in fact, highly differentiated, reflecting the fact that both the system and the curriculum of higher education are themselves highly differentiated. In most academic subjects, students move from more basic courses in the first and second years to more advanced and specialized courses in the third and fourth years, and then on to courses which are still more advanced and specialized at the graduate level. As one moves to higher levels, the numbers of students tend to diminish, and hence the potential market shrinks. So publishers who are looking for the largest unit sales will tend to concentrate their efforts at the lower levels of the curriculum, where the competition between publishers tends

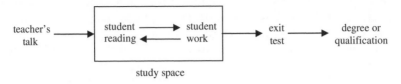

study space

Figure 8.1 The pedagogical process

to be most intense. They will also tend to focus their efforts on those sectors of the higher education system where the student numbers are largest, such as the big state universities, the state colleges and the community colleges.

In addition to the market differentiation created by the progressive structure of the curriculum and the stratification of the higher education system, the textbook market is further differentiated by the varied nature of academic disciplines and the varied pedagogical practices of academics. There are some academic disciplines, such as mathematics, physics, biology, chemistry, economics and psychology, where there are accepted bodies of knowledge that can be structured systematically and taught progressively. It is relatively easy in such cases to design textbooks that can be used at specific levels of the curriculum and that stand a good chance of being used in a substantial number of institutions of higher education. In many of the humanities and social sciences, however, it is less easy to design textbooks of this kind and to achieve adoptions across a multiplicity of institutions, partly because the bodies of knowledge in these disciplines have a more varied and contested character and partly because many academics prefer to teach by using original texts or case study material of various kinds rather than (or sometimes in addition to) textbooks. Certainly, textbooks have a role to play in subjects such as literature, history, philosophy, politics, sociology and anthropology, but the ways in which textbooks and other texts are used in teaching contexts in these subjects are not necessarily the same as the ways they are used in maths, physics or biology. (We shall explore these differences in more detail in the following chapter.)

What role do textbooks play in the pedagogical process? There is no single answer to this question – the answer varies from subject to subject, from course to course, from one institution to another and, indeed, from one professor or lecturer to another. We shall examine some of these variations in the following chapters. But for the time being we can outline a very general model of the pedagogical process which will help to situate the role of textbooks in the learning environment of higher education. Figure 8.1 illustrates, in the most basic fashion, the key components of a typical college course. In the US, the typical college course is a credit-bearing course for which there is a tuition fee of some kind. In the UK, the course may or may not involve a system of formal credits and a tuition fee, but the course will be a certifiable component of an undergraduate or postgraduate degree. A course typically involves at least four components: teacher's talk (e.g. lectures, classes, etc.); student reading (of textbooks and other materials); student work (e.g. written work, problem solving, etc.); and exit tests. Taken together, student reading and student work comprise what we could call the 'study space'. How exactly do students go about their activities in the study space? In fact, we don't know much about this. It seems likely that in most subjects, students do relatively little reading until they have first been exposed to teachers' talk in the form of lectures, classes or other forms of teacher guidance. In some subjects (like the natural sciences, engineering and maths), any reading the students do may be determined largely by the need to solve problems they encounter in the course of their assignments and practical work (e.g., if they can't solve a problem, they may go to the textbook to try to find some help). A large part of the activity that takes place in the study space is likely to be oriented towards very concrete goals – completing assignments or writing essays by specific dead-lines, preparing for classes and preparing for exams. Students' time and resources are limited and there are many things (academic and otherwise) that make demands upon them. Hence the activities of many students in the study space are likely to be oriented towards achieving the best results they can in the most efficient way – that is, with the least expenditure in terms of time, effort and cost.

Textbooks are one kind of resource that students can use in the study space, and as a resource they have certain advantages – clarity, comprehensiveness, ease of use, an abundance of pedagogical devices to facilitate understanding and, most important of all, an integral connection (in the case of an adopted textbook) with teacher's talk, student's work and exit tests. But just as we know relatively little about how students actually go about their activities in the study space, so too we know relatively little about the extent to which they actually use textbooks as distinct from other resources, how these practices vary from subject to subject and whether they are changing (for example, whether students today are relying more on alternative sources such as the internet to gather material for their work). Textbook publishers are not alone in knowing very little about what actually happens in the study space – most professors and lecturers know relatively little as well. The study space is in many ways a black box and what happens within it is shrouded in mystery.

While textbooks have certain advantages for students, they also have advantages for professors and lecturers. Textbooks provide clear and well-structured presentations of material which professors can assign to the students who are taking their courses. Well-developed textbooks will be tailored closely to the structure and content of the syllabus that a professor is likely to want to cover at a certain level of the curriculum. Hence having a single text (or several texts used together) covering the curriculum can make life a lot easier for the professor, who can rely on the textbook to convey much of the basic material to the students taking the course. It also ensures a degree of uniformity and consistency in the resources made available to and used by students – something which is particularly important when the number of students is large, as it often is on the introductory courses at the big state universities in the US. Moreover, it is common for several professors to be assigned to teach different sections of an introductory course, and using a common core textbook helps to ensure common coverage of the different sections. The use of textbooks can make life easier for professors and lectur-ers in other ways too and can ease the pressure on their time, since the textbook pub-lishers have sought increasingly to provide the professors and lecturers who adopt their books with a range of supplementary materials. To understand how and why this occurs, we have to understand the basic structure of decision-making which underpins all college textbook publishing.

The adoption system

While textbook publishing is a highly differentiated field, there is one feature of this type of publishing that tends to distinguish it from other types of publishing – namely, *the adoption system.* In the traditional model of textbook publishing, the textbook is *marketed* to professors and lecturers and *sold* to students. The professors, lecturers and teachers are the gatekeepers in the marketing chain – they have the power to decide which textbook is going to be adopted for which course. Sometimes this decision is made by individual professors, who compile the reading lists for the courses they teach; in other cases (e.g. for first-year courses at some of the big American universities), the adoption decisions are taken by departmental committees which examine a range of textbooks and choose the one that best suits their needs. Once the adoption decision has been taken, students will be told which textbook or textbooks they should buy for the course; hence their purchasing decisions are largely determined by the adoption decisions of the professors. The adoption decision is a form of *authorization* which warrants that a particular pedagogical product has been selected and approved by the figure of authority in the pedagogical situation, often to the exclusion of all other products. Hence, securing the adoption is the vital factor in ensuring the success of a textbook. The adoption decision creates a captive market. On the other hand, failure to secure adoptions can result in the complete failure of a textbook, since a textbook is unlikely to be bought by students unless it has been adopted by the professor or lecturer teaching the course.

So in the traditional textbook model, professors function as gatekeepers and publishers seek to generate sales by persuading professors to adopt their textbooks in preference to the textbooks produced by other publishers. The publisher does not have to persuade the ultimate end user to buy the book but has to persuade the gatekeeper to adopt it. So a great deal of effort and resources is invested by textbook publishers at every stage in trying to ensure that their textbook will meet the needs and expectations of professors, who in the end decide whether the book will be adopted in preference to the available alternatives. Outlines and draft chapters are sent out to professors (who are, at the same time, potential adopters) for their comments and feedback, and authors are asked to revise the text in order to ensure that it covers the material in ways that will be acceptable to a significant proportion of the professors who teach the relevant courses. The extensive review process used by the major textbook publishers is both a way of improving the quality and adoptability of the textbook and a form of 'market seeding', since the more professors involved in the reviewing process, the more extensive the network of gatekeepers who know about the book, who are mentioned and thanked in the preface and who have some stake (however minor) in a textbook for which they are a potential adopter. The use of focus groups involving both professors and students has also become increasingly common among the big American textbook publishers as a means of tailoring content to the needs and expectations of users and as a form of market seeding. And a great deal of supplementary material is produced, much of it electronic in format, in order to facilitate the adoption process.

When it comes to marketing, it is the gatekeeper – the professor or lecturer – who is the principal focus of the marketing effort. The big American textbook publishers employ a large number of sales reps or 'college travellers' who regularly visit the major university campuses and call on individual professors, presenting them with their new textbooks and the various supplements, talking them through the key features of their textbooks and their advantages relative to competing volumes, and responding to their requests and concerns in the hope of securing adoptions. The college rep system is in many ways the keystone of the traditional textbook publishing model, since the

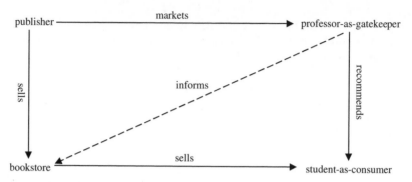

Figure 8.2 Traditional textbook model

interaction between the rep and the professor is the crucial point where the big adoptions that make or break a textbook are secured. Hence the sales reps tend to have a
higher status in college textbook publishing than they do in other sectors of publishing,
and many editors and senior managers in college textbook publishing firms began their
careers as college travellers. Traditionally, the college rep system was the training ground
for aspiring editors and managers; it was the first necessary step on the career path for
anyone who hoped to succeed in the textbook publishing business.

Once a textbook has been adopted, information is supplied to a local bookstore (or
bookstores) serving the college or university. In the US these bookstores typically have
special floors or sections dedicated to textbook sales, with shelves earmarked for specific textbooks which have been adopted by individual professors for their courses.
Bookstore staff will order stock so that it is available for the beginning of the semester
during which the relevant course will be taught. They generally use two criteria to decide
how many copies of a textbook to order: first, how many students are taking the course;
and second, how well the book sold in previous years. Students, having been told by
their professor that a particular book is a set text for the course, will then purchase the
book from the local bookstore or from some other retailer – at least this is how it works
in principle. Figure 8.2 illustrates the main elements of this traditional textbook model.

A key feature of the traditional textbook model, and of the adoption system on which
it is based, is that the person who recommends the product is not the person who buys
it. Hence the considerations that weigh uppermost in the minds of the gatekeepers in
deciding which textbook to adopt may not be the considerations that matter most to
the students who are ultimately required to buy the book – at the end of the day, it is
the student, not the gatekeeper, who pays the bill. In this respect, explained one senior
textbook publisher,

> It is very much like the pharmaceutical business. The person who needs the product and
> who is buying the product is not the decision-maker. In the pharmaceutical industry, the
> decision-maker is the doctor. In the academic community, it is the professor. Large sales
> forces give away the product. The decision-maker isn't the buyer. The patient goes to the
> pharmacy, the student goes to the bookstore. So the whole process is very analogous.

This structure is fundamental to the adoption system. It creates a form of *non-price
competition* – that is, competition between publishers on grounds other than price –

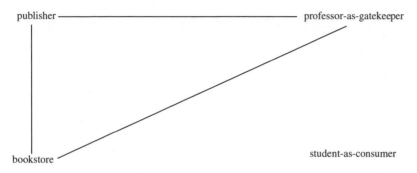

Figure 8.3   The knowledge triangle

which has had profound implications for the evolution of the textbook publishing business, as we shall see.

Another consequence of the traditional textbook model and the adoption system is that publishers tend to know quite a lot about professors and what they want, since they are the gatekeepers and their reps interact with them on a regular basis, but in general publishers don't know much about students, that is, the end users who eventually buy the textbooks. They assume that students will buy what the professor tells them to buy, just as patients will buy whatever medicine the doctor tells them to buy. We could speak here of a *knowledge triangle* (figure 8.3) that embraces the publisher, the professor-as-gatekeeper and the bookstore, but excludes the end users, the students. In developing their textbooks, both new textbooks and new editions, editors consult extensively with professors who teach the relevant courses, and they receive feedback from their sales reps who are talking to professors as they travel from campus to campus. Publishers also know quite a lot about the needs and concerns of the bookstores and the retail chains, because they are their immediate customers and they communicate with them on a regular and continuous basis. But publishers know relatively little about the needs, concerns, practices and habits of their ultimate customers – the students who either do or don't buy their books. What publishers know about students tends to be based on what professors know about them, since they don't generally interact directly with students. As one senior manager in a textbook publishing firm said, 'We know instructors and we know what instructors know about students, so we know their version. But we have no independent knowledge about the students.'

As a general rule, publishers don't try to take account of the views of students in the same kind of systematic way that they consult the gatekeepers. In recent years some of the big textbook publishers have involved students in focus group discussions, but this involvement of students tends to be shaped by the structure of the adoption system – that is, the main purpose of consulting students is not to find out what students need and want, but rather to find out what they need and want in order to influence the adoption decisions of professors. As one seasoned textbook editor put it, 'We are trying to include students more. But the way you use students is you find out what they want and then you tell the professor that you've found that out from the students. You use that to try to influence the professor.' The publisher's principal relations are with the gatekeepers (the professors) and with the intermediaries in the supply chain (the bookstores, retail chains and wholesalers), not with the end users (the students) as such.

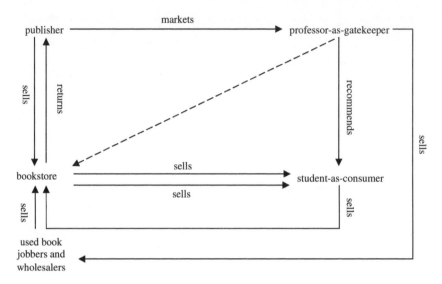

Figure 8.4 The textbook model in the context of the used book market

The traditional textbook model is a relatively simple structure which relies crucially on the role of professor-as-gatekeeper, but there are various ways in which this model becomes more complicated in practice. One way is that there are various options open to the gatekeeper – it is not simply a yes–no decision. The professor can adopt the book as a *required* text or as a *recommended* or *supplementary* text. If it is a required text then students are much more likely to buy the book. If it is merely a recommended or supplementary text, then purchase is optional and many students will refrain from buying the book. The major textbook publishers are really only interested in getting their books adopted as required texts, since this is the only reasonably reliable way of ensuring that adoptions will translate into sales. But even in the case of required texts, the adoption of a textbook by a professor does not necessarily translate into a publisher's sale to every student taking a course. Individual students may fail to buy, or may look for ways to reduce their expenditure – for example, by borrowing books from libraries, by pooling resources with one or more friends to buy one book which can be shared between them, by photocopying texts or, most significantly, by buying used or second-hand books. The rise of the used book market has become such an important feature of the textbook business in the US that we shall devote a section to it below. For the time being, we can illustrate how the rise of the used book market has complicated the traditional textbook model by figure 8.4. As in the traditional textbook model, the professor still acts as the gatekeeper, deciding which textbook will be adopted for a particular course and recommending this to the students. But thanks to the used book market, the textbooks available to students include not only the new books supplied by the publisher but also an array of used books which are supplied through the used book supply chain and sold by the same college bookstores at prices that are significantly lower than the prices of new textbooks.

The fact that the adoption of a textbook does not necessarily translate into a publisher's sale for each student taking a course is sometimes referred to in the business as 'sell-through breakdown'. The growth of the used book market is the most significant factor in creating sell-through breakdown, but there are other factors too. For example, in cases where students are taking courses simply to fulfil certain requirements but have no intention of pursuing the subject at a higher level (e.g. a student who is majoring in business but takes a course in geography to fulfil a science requirement), they may be particularly inclined to try to get through the course without buying the textbook, or may be more inclined to pool resources with one or two friends and share a copy between them. There is some evidence to suggest that the problem of sell-through breakdown is getting significantly worse – we shall return to this issue at the end of the chapter and try to understand why this might be so.

So although the adoption system creates a captive market, it is often difficult for a bookstore to predict exactly how well a textbook will sell, and difficult to determine exactly how many copies it should stock. A professor may tell the campus bookstore that there are 300 students taking a course and may ask the bookstore to order 300 books, but the bookstore may only sell 150 or 200 books and the remaining copies will be returned to the publisher. Sometimes courses will change at the last minute, or the actual number of students will turn out to be less than the professor thought. Moreover, in many cases students will have access to more than one bookstore to buy their text-books (or may order the textbook from an online retailer), so a particular bookseller cannot count on the fact that all the students taking a course will buy their textbooks from that bookstore. As a result of these and other factors, the level of returns in text-book publishing tends to be relatively high – returns of 30–33 per cent are common. College bookstores develop their own systems – sometimes quite elaborate systems – to control and try to reduce the level of returns. For example, many will keep comput-erized records of how many copies of which books they have sold for which courses in previous years and, rather than taking the enrolment figures at face value, the textbook buyers will refine their orders by taking account of their actual sales experience.

College textbook publishing has a long history in the United States and some of the firms which have been active in this field – McGraw-Hill, Prentice Hall, Harcourt Brace, Houghton Mifflin, John Wiley & Sons, W. W. Norton, etc. – date back to the nineteenth and early twentieth centuries. But over the last twenty to thirty years the industry has changed in fundamental ways, so much so that the industry today is very different from the one that existed as recently as the 1960s. There are three developments in the field of higher education publishing in the United States which are particularly important and which, taken together, have come to define the logic of the field: (1) the rise of the textbook conglomerates, (2) the package wars, and (3) the growth of the used book market. Let me briefly discuss each in turn.

The rise of the textbook conglomerates

In 1980 there were roughly twenty to twenty-five major higher education publishers operating in the United States. In the early 1980s this began to change, as a number of large corporations began to buy up publishing companies, including companies operat-ing in the field of higher education. The process of consolidation which characterized the publishing industry generally in the late twentieth century was replicated in the field of higher education publishing. The result of these mergers and acquisitions is that three

Table 8.1 Top five college publishers in the US, 2002

Rank	Publisher	2002 ($m)	2001 ($m)	% change	2002 sales as % of total US college market
1	Pearson[1]	998	918	8.7	30.5
2	Thomson[2]	864	735	17.6	26.4
3	McGraw-Hill[3]	530	495	7.3	16.2
4	Houghton Mifflin[4]	212	186	14.0	6.5
5	Wiley[5]	148	141	5.0	4.5
	Total	2,752	2,475	11.2	84.1

[1] Pearson reports US college sales of £624 million in 2002. £1 = $1.60.
[2] Subtext estimates Thomson's college publishing sales at $864 million. Thomson claims to have a 24% market share of a US college publishing market that it estimates at $3.6 billion.
[3] Subtext estimates McGraw-Hill's college sales at $530 million in 2002. Total sales for the Higher Education, Professional and International Group are estimated at just more than $1 billion in 2002.
[4] According to SEC filing, 30 May 2003. Sold by Vivendi in 2002 to Bain Capital and Thomas H. Lee investment group.
[5] Domestic college publishing sales for fiscal year ended 30 April 2003. For the January–December 2002 period, Wiley said its college sales rose 12% to about $142 million from $127 million in the previous calendar year.
Source: Subtext, *Perspective on Book Publishing: 2003–2004* (Darien, Conn.: Open Book, 2004).

large conglomerates have emerged as the dominant players in the field of US higher education publishing today: Pearson, McGraw-Hill and International Thomson. There are a number of other significant players, including Houghton Mifflin, Wiley, Norton and smaller conglomerates like the Holtzbrinck group, but Pearson, McGraw-Hill and Thomson have established themselves as the dominant players in the field.

Table 8.1 lists the top five college publishers in the US in 2002, with a comparison for 2001. Following its acquisition of the educational businesses of Simon & Schuster in 1998, Pearson became the dominant player in US college publishing, with sales reaching $998 million in 2002. Thomson's acquisition of Harcourt's college publishing business from Reed Elsevier in 2001 pushed Thomson into second place, with total college sales of $864 million in 2002. McGraw-Hill ranked third, with college sales of $530 million in 2002, and Houghton Mifflin ranked fourth with sales of just over $200 million. Wiley ranked fifth with college sales of just under $150 million in 2002. Given that the total higher education market in the US was around $3.273 billion in 2002, Pearson had just over 30 per cent of the market, Thomson had just over 26 per cent of the market and McGraw-Hill had around 16 per cent of the market. Taken together, the top three players controlled nearly three-quarters (73.1 per cent) of the higher education market in the US, and the top five players controlled more than four-fifths (84.1 per cent) of the market.

Pearson began as a small construction company in Yorkshire, in the north of England, in 1844. It grew rapidly by taking on large construction projects – it built the docks at Milford Haven, London and Southampton, it built railways across Spain, Mexico, Columbia and China, and it built reservoirs, dams and tunnels, including the Manhattan tunnel projects. By the time Pearson relocated to London in 1882, it was one of the largest contracting firms in the world. In 1920, Pearson moved into the media world, acquiring a group of provincial newspapers that formed the basis of Westminster Press.

Over the next fifty years, it increased its media portfolio, acquiring the *Financial Times* in 1957, acquiring Longman in 1968 and acquiring Penguin in 1970. In 1988, Pearson purchased the American textbook publisher Addison-Wesley, which specialized in maths and science, and merged it with Longman to create Addison-Wesley Longman. And in 1998, Pearson paid $4.6 billion for the educational businesses of Simon & Schuster, which owned one of the major US textbook publishers, Prentice Hall. The Simon & Schuster businesses were merged with Addison-Wesley Longman to create Pearson Education. Today Pearson plc is a global media corporation with substantial stakes in television, educational publishing, financial and professional publishing (including the Financial Times group) and general trade publishing (including the Penguin group). Its overall turnover in 2002 was around £4.3 billion ($7 billion). Pearson Education is the largest of the four main operating groups within Pearson, with a turnover of around $4.4 billion in 2002. Pearson is the largest book publisher in North America, and Pearson Education is the largest educational publisher. It is also the leading higher education publisher in the US and the UK and a major presence in Europe, Asia and the rest of the world. It comprises numerous imprints which are well known in higher education publishing including Prentice Hall, Allyn & Bacon and Scott Foresman, as well as Addison-Wesley and Longman.

The origins of the Thomson Corporation lay in the activities of a Canadian entrepreneur, Roy Thomson, who began his career in the media industries by starting up a local radio station and buying a local newspaper in Timmins, Ontario in the early 1930s. During the next two decades, he expanded the business by acquiring a stable of Canadian newspapers and other companies. In the early 1950s Thomson turned his attention to the UK, acquiring the *Scotsman* in 1953 and the Kemsley Group – a public company comprising a range of national and regional newspapers including the *Sunday Times* – in 1959. Thomson also diversified his activities, taking a stake in television, buying several package holiday companies and joining a consortium to explore for oil and gas in the North Sea. From the late 1970s on, the company expanded its operations in book publishing and information services, acquiring Wadsworth (a major US college textbook and professional book publisher) in 1978, acquiring Gale (a leading provider of information services for libraries, schools and businesses) in 1985, acquiring Sweet & Maxwell, Carswell and The Law Publishing Company (leading law publishers in the UK, Canada and Australia) and Associated Book Publishers (a UK-based academic publishing group) in 1987, and acquiring Lawyers Cooperative Publishing (a major US legal publisher) in 1989. As part of the sale of Harcourt to Reed Elsevier in 2001, Thomson acquired Harcourt's college publishing business and much of its corporate and professional services business for $2.06 billion. By 2002 the overall revenue of the Thomson Corporation was around $7.8 billion. The corporation is now divided into four groups – legal and regulatory (which includes the law publishers), Thomson Learning (which includes Wadsworth, Gale and other brands), Financial, and Scientific and Healthcare. With overall revenues of around $2.3 billion in 2002, Thomson Learning is a major educational publisher in the US, and its acquisition of Harcourt's college business has pushed it into second place in the league of college publishers. Thomson also has a significant presence in the UK, Europe and other parts of the world.

McGraw-Hill was formed through the merger of the McGraw Publishing Company and the Hill Publishing Company in 1909. Both companies had started life in the 1880s as publishers of technical and trade journals on railways. During the first half of the twentieth century, McGraw-Hill expanded its publications into other fields of science, engineering and transport and into business, management and the social sciences. It became a major college textbook publisher and moved increasingly into elementary and high school publishing. In 1966, McGraw-Hill acquired Standard & Poor, one of the major providers of financial services. Today McGraw-Hill is a diversified media corporation with a turnover of around $4.8 billion in 2002. Educational publishing is one of its three main divisions, the other two being financial services (Standard & Poor) and information and media services. McGraw-Hill Education vies closely with Pearson as the largest K-12 publisher in the US, and it ranks third among college publishers. The higher education division of McGraw-Hill also has a significant presence in the UK, Europe, Latin America and elsewhere, although its presence in the UK and Europe is less substantial than that of Pearson.

While the field of higher education publishing in the US is now dominated by these three conglomerates, there a number of other players which have a significant presence in the field. Dating back to the 1830s, the Boston-based firm Houghton Mifflin is one of the oldest publishing houses in the US. It publishes in a variety of fields, from fiction and nonfiction to children's books and dictionaries, and it has a strong programme in educational publishing at both the school and college levels. In recent years, Houghton Mifflin has been through two changes of ownership. In 2001 it was bought for about $2.2 billion by the French media group Vivendi Universal, one of the largest of the global media conglomerates. Thanks to its ownership of Houghton Mifflin, Vivendi ranked fourth among US college publishers in 2001, with sales of around $186 million. However, Vivendi's growing financial difficulties forced it to divest itself of some of its assets, and in 2002 Houghton Mifflin was sold for $1.66 billion to a consortium of private investment firms led by Thomas H. Lee Partners and Bain Capital and including funds from the Blackstone Group.

The German-based Holtzbrinck Group also became a player in the US college textbook market with the acquisition of Bedford/St Martin's, Freeman and Worth in the 1980s, and became a player in the UK higher education market with the purchase of a majority stake in Macmillan in the mid-1990s. Bedford/St Martin's is a major imprint in English language and literature textbooks, Freeman is a publisher of science textbooks and Worth is well known for its textbooks in psychology, business and the social sciences. Holtzbrinck also has a major presence in the trade market in the US thanks to its acquisition of Henry Holt in the 1980s and Farrar, Straus & Giroux in 1994.

The most notable of the textbook publishers that remain independent is John Wiley & Sons. Wiley is another publisher with a long history. It dates back to the beginning of the nineteenth century, when it published a number of authors who would become major American writers, such as James Fenimore Cooper; it subsequently became an important college textbook publisher with an international presence and a particularly strong list in the sciences and engineering. With sales in the college market of around $148 million in 2002, Wiley ranked among the top five US higher education publishers.

Another important textbook publisher that remains independent is W. W. Norton. Norton was established in 1923 by W. Warder Norton as the People's Institute Publishing Company, a house that was dedicated to publishing books of an academic kind that were written for a general readership. It gradually evolved into a publishing house that was serving both the general trade and the higher education market, and it now has a trade and a college division. Norton's textbook publishing is primarily in the humanities and the social sciences, and its anthologies of literature and histories of music have become standard texts in their fields.

The rise of the textbook conglomerates reflects the broader trend towards consolidation which has characterized the publishing world since the 1960s. However, there are three features of the post-1980 wave of mergers and acquisitions in the field of higher education publishing which deserve special comment. One feature is that this process has been fundamentally *international*, or *multinational*, in character. Of the three dominant corporations in the field of US higher education publishing, only one is US-based – McGraw-Hill. The other two are international corporations with their bases nominally in the UK and Canada respectively. With Pearson's acquisition of Addison-Wesley and Simon & Schuster, with Thomson's acquisition of Wadsworth (and, more recently, part of the Harcourt group), with Holtzbrinck's acquisition of Bedford/St Martin's, Freeman and Worth, and with Vivendi's acquisition of Houghton Mifflin, publishing groups based outside the US have increased their stake in the field of US higher education publishing (albeit temporarily in the case of Vivendi). At the same time, these moves have increased the international presence of US college textbook publishers, which are given greater access to international markets by being integrated into global media conglomerates. As the English language increasingly becomes the dominant language of higher education, especially in the sciences and in harder subjects like economics, business and IT, it becomes more and more vital for the leading higher education publishers to have a substantial stake in the English language market, and above all in the US.

The second important feature of the post-1980 wave of mergers and acquisitions is that it has involved what could be described as a *de-diversification* of publishing firms. Traditionally many of the large publishing firms operated in a variety of different fields – they were trade publishers as well as being college textbook publishers, professional publishers and so on. It was common among the larger houses like Random House, Harper & Row and Little, Brown to have a trade division and a textbook division, with a fair amount of information exchanged across the divisions. But as these houses were themselves bought up by larger conglomerates – Random House by Bertelsmann, Harper & Row by Rupert Murdoch's News Corporation (Harper & Row was subsequently merged with another Murdoch acquisition, Collins, to form HarperCollins) and Little, Brown by Time Inc. (as it then was) – they gradually divested themselves of their college textbook divisions, selling them in many cases to the emerging higher education conglomerates. So, for example, Random House sold its textbook division to McGraw-Hill in the 1980s, HarperCollins sold its education division to Pearson in 1996 and Times Mirror sold its higher education companies to McGraw-Hill in 1996. Under their new corporate managers, trade and textbook publishing were splitting apart. Old imprints like Random House and Harper & Row (the latter now restructured as HarperCollins), which had previously embraced both trade and textbook publishing, became focused more sharply on trade publishing, while textbook publishing became increasingly integrated into conglomerates which were focused primarily on educational and professional markets. These conglomerates cover the whole range of education, from kindergarten and primary/secondary school (K-12) through higher education, further education and corporate training. Hence textbook publishing has increasingly become part of the activities of global conglomerates which have a dedicated focus on the educational and professional markets. Houghton Mifflin, Wiley and W. W. Norton are among the few remaining textbook publishers who have so far bucked the trend.

While there were undoubtedly many forces behind this process of de-diversification, the following factors probably played some role. On the 'push' side, many of the corporations that began to buy up publishing companies in the 1980s (and before then in some cases) were organizations that had interests in other media and entertainment businesses, including newspapers, television and film. In acquiring publishing houses they hoped to achieve at least two things: first, by a certain amount of restructuring, they hoped to be able to achieve profits in excess of 15 per cent; and second, they hoped to be able to create 'synergy' between different sectors of their media and entertainment businesses – in the way, for example, that a novel could become the basis for a film. As we noted in chapter 3, the idea of creating synergies between different sectors of the business was an important factor driving the acquisitions process of the 1970s and 1980s; whether it generated real benefits for the corporations concerned is a moot point, but it undoubtedly played a role in the strategic thinking of senior corporate executives. When these executives realized that it was going to be difficult to achieve the levels of profitability that they and their shareholders expected, they began to divest themselves of some of their publishing acquisitions. They had to decide whether they were going to expand significantly the size of their college division, with its costly sales force, or get rid of it. Continuing to run a medium-sized college division in an increasingly competitive publishing field, and in a context where the publishing acquisitions were generating lower than expected levels of profitability, did not seem like a realistic option. Most of these corporations therefore decided to sell their college divisions.

From a strictly financial viewpoint, it might have made more sense for these corporations to sell off the trade division rather than the college division, since textbook publishing is generally more profitable than trade publishing. (This is primarily because of the discount structure: trade books are generally sold to bookstores and wholesalers at a discount of 45–50 per cent, whereas textbooks are generally sold at a discount of 20–25 per cent.) But if a media-oriented company is looking for synergies from its publishing acquisitions, then it is more likely to sell off the education divisions and hold on to the trade division, since trade titles are the more likely source of film and television spin-offs. In other words, for corporations in search of synergies between publishing and entertainment, college textbook lists were strategically dispensable items.

On the other hand, on the 'pull' side, the college textbook lists of traditional publishing houses were attractive acquisitions for the emerging conglomerates in the field of higher education publishing. Acquiring these established lists enabled them to grow quickly and in some cases quite dramatically, and to short-circuit the long gestation period of the normal publishing cycle. It enabled them to increase significantly their stocks of content and of revenue-generating copyrights, and thus helped them to consolidate their positions as dominant players in the field. But there were other factors at work here too. One was a growing recognition that the traditional markets occupied by these publishers were becoming increasingly saturated: acquiring an established list was an effective way of expanding market share in increasingly saturated and highly competitive markets. Moreover, if growth is going to get more difficult on the top line, then ways have to be found to make the most of the bottom line, and some cost reductions and economies of scale can be achieved by combining forces. So even if sales are not going to increase significantly, at least profits can be grown by merging lists and rationalizing internally.

Recent mergers and acquisitions in the field of higher education publishing have also been driven by the increasing levels of *investment* required to compete effectively in the field, and especially the levels of investment required in terms of IT – this is a third important feature of the post-1980 mergers and acquisitions in this field. Especially in the North American context, the ability to develop textbooks that will secure adoptions at the lower levels of the curriculum requires very substantial investment – in advances to authors who are increasingly aware of the value of their output, in the development and production of lavishly illustrated four- and five-colour books and in the development of a sophisticated array of electronic supplements and technology tools to support the print product. The large conglomerates are also able to invest much more heavily in the development of IT infrastructures and in innovative web-based learning projects, and are thus able to take a leading position in exploring the uses of new technologies in the provision of learning materials for higher and further education. As one senior executive put it:

> The trend towards consolidation is not just about improving profitability. I think it's increasingly to do with being able to invest on a larger scale, and get the return on a larger scale. So, for example, if we were to invest in technology tools that support our print products, then the bigger the base of print product that we've got, the more we can amortize the expense of doing that – or another way of putting it would be, the more we can afford to invest in doing it. So again, it is to do with investment, it is not just to do with improving profitability.

There are many reasons why the big higher education publishers find themselves obliged to invest more and more heavily in IT infrastructure and in the development of new products. The digital revolution of the 1980s and 1990s and the rise of the internet from the mid-1990s on were undoubtedly key factors – higher education publishing today has become inextricably interwoven with information technology and the provision of content in online environments. No higher education publisher today can afford to ignore these technological developments, and to stay abreast of these developments, let alone lead the way, requires substantial investment. But it is also important to see that the need to invest more and more in technology was not driven by technology itself, nor was it driven exclusively or even primarily by a concern to improve the quality of the learning materials made available to students. Rather, the growing levels of investment in new IT products of various kinds was rooted in a cycle that was part of the competitive logic of the textbook publishing field. This cycle is commonly described by those within the industry as the package wars.

The package wars

The so-called package wars began in the US in the late 1970s and early 1980s. The term is used by people in the industry to refer to the ever intensifying cycle of providing more and more elaborate 'packages' of supplementary materials or ancillaries to accompany textbooks, which were themselves becoming more and more elaborate and costly to produce. As one senior editor recalled,

> It really started in the late seventies/early eighties, especially in the business and econom-
> ics field. That was where it started I think because that was where the enrolment shift went,
> to business, economics and management courses – intro to business, intro to marketing,
> intro to accounting, all with humungous packages. I remember copublishing a marketing
> text and it had this elaborate box of supplements. It was like a file box with things stacked
> in it. The texts were published in slip cases and they often had dust jackets and were just
> trying to dazzle the public.

Some of the material in these early packages was designed for students, but most of it
was aimed at the gatekeepers – the professors. In essence, the package wars were started
by textbook publishers in order to gain competitive advantage in the struggle for adoptions. The package wars were spurred on by the technological possibilities created by
the digital revolution, but the real driving force behind them, and behind the constantly
escalating scale of investment in ever more sophisticated packages, was the desire to
win over the gatekeepers and to outmanoeuvre one's competitors in the struggle to
secure adoptions.

In the early 1970s and before, textbook authors were generally expected to write an
instructor's manual (IM) and some test items along with the textbook itself. The publisher would print a few hundred copies of the IM in black and white and give them
away to professors to facilitate the adoption process. But as competition for adoptions
intensified and new technologies increased the range of options available to publishers,
the packages became increasingly elaborate. Test files were supplied electronically in
both Mac and IBM formats, overhead transparencies were added to the packages, then
video tapes and a whole range of software – floppy disks, laser disks, CD-ROMs, etc. –
were included. With the rise of the internet, the development of dedicated or 'companion' websites became an essential component, and the companion websites themselves became ever more elaborate. 'We are actually reaching the point', commented
one senior editor, 'where the number of print elements is on the decline. The number
of electronic elements is on the increase, and in many cases the print elements are
becoming electronic elements – in some cases not even printed at all but only offered
online or on a disk.' The cost of developing and providing all of this electronic supplementation can be huge. For many textbooks today, the cost is likely to be between
$15,000 and $20,000, but in exceptional cases – for the big textbooks in areas where the
student numbers are high – the expenditure can be a good deal more. 'I'm sure there
are a number of books being signed now where they are budgeting for about a quarter
of a million dollars just for electronic supplements,' observed the same editor, adding:
'I wouldn't rule out the possibility that people are spending half a million dollars,
especially in an area like psychology.'

What is driving the ever increasing scale of investment in electronic supplements?
Why do textbook publishers invest so much money in developing and providing supplements of various kinds? This spiralling investment can be understood only by seeing
that it is intrinsically linked to the competitive logic built into the adoption system. The
textbook publishers hope that by creating more elaborate packages, they can win over
the professors who make the adoption decisions – 'Professor, we are going to do more
for you than the competition does.' The fact that adoption decisions for some of the
core introductory courses at the big universities – especially in the natural sciences –
are made by committees of professors has added another incentive for publishers to
invest in electronic supplements:

It may be that nine out of ten people on the adoption committee don't care about this but the one who cares about it cares much more than the other nine do. It's not that they object to it, they just don't care that much about it, and he, or she, comes on as being a very, very vocal proponent of media, and the others will take advantage of that and say, ok, well if she wants media, it's one of the criteria, so we can tell that publisher we don't want their product if they don't have it.

Many universities also have policies to encourage their students to use IT as part of their education, and this increases the power of those members of the adoption committees who want electronic supplements and strengthens the positions of the publishers who provide them. Given the intensity of the competition for adoptions at the level of the core introductory courses and the consequences of failing to get adoptions, publishers who wish to compete at this level simply cannot take the risk of alienating those members of the adoption committees who may feel strongly about electronic supplements, and hence cannot avoid investing substantial sums in developing and providing elaborate packages.

The committee adoption structure has also tended to drive up the scale of investment in the textbook itself – not only in terms of the quality of production, but in terms of the scope of coverage of the text. Increasingly publishers find themselves adding chapters to make textbooks more and more comprehensive, for fear that some member of an adoption committee might object to their book because it doesn't cover a topic that they regard as important. One editor recounted this story:

> What really drives the whole thing are the committee adoptions. I remember presenting a book that happened to be an introductory sociology text at a sales meeting one time and I said, 'It's like a bottle of wine. The wine bottle is the size of the course and the text is the content, and the content of most of these 23-chapter books spills all over the floor.' I said all this came about because people called us and said they wanted us to add chapters, and they wanted their books to be much longer. Now one of these chapters was a chapter on sexuality and there was somebody who wanted it, so we put it in and the others didn't mind if we had it. Somebody else wanted a chapter on medical sociology, so we added a chapter there . . . These books are made for committees.

The adoption system thus encouraged publishers to invest in the development of ever more elaborate textbooks – comprehensive in their coverage, lavishly illustrated and beautifully produced in four or five colours – and in the development of ever more elaborate packages of electronic supplements. If you wanted to compete in certain subjects at the level of the core introductory courses, then investment of this kind was not really an option: it was a condition of playing the game. 'In most cases, professors simply will not consider your book unless you have an attractive array of freebies to give them,' observed one director of a college division. While lavishly illustrated textbooks and elaborate packages had become a condition of playing the textbook game, the extent to which this was true varied from subject to subject. It was certainly true of economics, business studies, psychology, all of the natural sciences, engineering, mathematics, computer science, among others – these were 'core' textbook subjects. It was somewhat less true in the 'softer' social sciences, like sociology, anthropology and political science, and even less true in most of the humanities subjects, like history, literature, philosophy and classics. These differences are important and we shall return to them in the next chapter.

While the struggle for adoptions tended to ratchet up the scale of investment on both textbooks and the accompanying packages of supplementary materials, the only way of generating a return on this investment was through the sale of printed textbooks (often shrinkwrapped with supplements of various kinds) to students. The printed textbook remained the revenue-generating product, and most of the electronic supplementation was given away to professors with the aim of influencing their adoption decisions. Hence the printed textbook had to bear an ever increasing burden of investment, and the only way to recoup these costs was (a) to concentrate on those levels of the curriculum where the student numbers were large, and (b) to increase the prices of textbooks. The big textbook publishers did both. They focused their principal textbook publishing efforts on the first and second years of the college curriculum – the core introductory courses of the freshman year (intro to psych, intro to economics, etc.) and on the so-called 'gateway' courses of the sophomore year (child psychology, abnormal psychology, social psychology, principles of macro economics, principles of micro economics, etc.). They also increased textbook prices – today prices of between $80 and $120 are fairly standard for the big core introductory textbooks. But the increase in prices tended in turn to fuel another development which has played a fundamental role in the field of US textbook publishing: the growth of the used book market.

The growth of the used book market

The buying and selling of used books has been around for a long time. Books are durable and portable objects that lend themselves to the second-hand trade. This was true in the textbook business too – the practice of buying and selling used textbooks is not new. But in the 1970s and 1980s the used book market for college textbooks in the US began to grow into an industry of its own. In the past, the used book market for textbooks was largely a *local* and *fragmented* market; students sold books back to the bookstores on their campuses or to other students. But in the course of the 1970s and 1980s, the used book market became increasingly *national* and *organized*. The crucial developments here were the proliferation of used book jobbers, who bought up used textbooks and sold them on to wholesalers and retail outlets, and the increasing involvement of the retail sector in the used textbook business. The buying and selling of used textbooks became an increasingly routine and taken-for-granted feature of the retail side of the book business. Students bought textbooks knowing that they could sell them back to bookstores when they had finished with them, and increasingly they looked to buy a used textbook rather than a new textbook at the beginning of their course. The major college bookstores and chains – including Barnes & Noble College and Follett's – became not just retail outlets for publishers but also used book brokers in an increasingly sophisticated marketplace for second-hand textbooks.

The economics of the used textbook business are simple and straightforward. A college bookstore or retail chain will typically buy back a textbook from a student at 50 per cent of the price she bought it for, provided that (a) it is reasonably confident it can resell it (e.g. it knows that the course will continue to run next year and the faculty member will continue to adopt this text, and it knows it has fewer books in stock than it will need), and (b) the book is in a resaleable condition. The bookseller will then sell the used book at a mark-up of 50 per cent. So if the original selling price was, say, $100, the bookstore will buy it back for $50 and then resell it for $75. The student who sells back the book ends up with $50 in her pocket; the bookseller, if it manages to resell the book, will get a margin of 33 per cent, which is better than the 20 or 25 per cent margin it normally gets on the sale of new textbooks; and the student who buys the book will get it for $25 less than the cost of a new textbook. Everyone wins – except, of course, the publisher and the author, both of whom get nothing from this transaction and have lost a possible sale. Booksellers will also buy back used books using the same principles, provided that the two conditions apply.

A college bookseller can also acquire used books from used book wholesalers. One of the advantages of the big retail chains like Barnes & Noble College and Follett's is that they have created their own computerized networks for used textbooks which enable individual stores to enter their used book stock on a centralized database. Before any store orders new textbook stock, it can check the database to see whether another Barnes & Noble or Follett store has used books that it wants to offload, effectively creating a nationwide pool of used books that can be shipped around the country according to demand. So when a bookstore manager is planning his stock provision for September (the beginning of the academic year), he can try to provide most of the textbooks he thinks he will need by increasing his stock of used books before he orders any new books from the publisher.

To illustrate this point, one college bookstore manager described how he generally orders his textbooks for the fall semester. If it's a freshman course with an enrolment of, say, 1,000 students and with one textbook adopted as required reading, he assumes he will need about 850 copies of this text. If the adopted textbook has been around for a year, he knows that there will be used books; he knows that many students will be eager to sell and that the new students, if they're given the choice, will almost always choose to buy the cheaper used books. He assumes the store can buy back 350 books from its student body. The store then searches to fill the remaining need from book wholesalers, including but not only the chain of which his store is part – he will probably be able to acquire another 300 used books this way. This leaves a shortfall of 200, which he meets by ordering 200 new textbooks from the publisher. The bookstore will always sell the used books first, given student preferences, and may sell 100 of the 200 new books. The bookstore therefore ends up with 100 unsold new textbooks, which it returns to the publisher. So of the 750 books sold, only 100 (less than 15 per cent) are new textbooks supplied by the publisher. And, to make matters even worse, the publisher in this case would end up with a 50 per cent return rate on an order of 200 copies.

From the viewpoint of booksellers, this is good business. They're not concerned about whether the books they're selling are new or used, provided they are selling books and the margin is healthy. The main risk from the booksellers' viewpoint is that if they can't sell the books they buy back, they will find themselves holding stock that can't be returned to a publisher, so they have to do what they can to try to ensure that there will be a continuing demand for the textbook. If they do find themselves left with stock of used textbooks they can't resell – if, for example, a professor suddenly cancels a course or adopts a different text – they can make the unsold stock available in the nationwide pool of a chain (if they belong to a chain) or sell it on to a used book wholesaler, who will store it in a warehouse and fulfil orders from booksellers elsewhere in the country.

Students are the principal source of supply for used textbooks but they are not the only source. As the used book market began to grow, some professors began to sell some of the books that were being given to them by publishers as examination copies. Just as the sales reps of the big textbook publishers would go to the campuses and visit professors to try to persuade them to adopt their new textbooks, giving away complimentary copies of the books, so too enterprising used book jobbers began to visit the campuses as well and knock on the doors of professors, offering to buy examination copies of textbooks for which the professors had no use. 'My next-door neighbour started a used book company,' commented one senior editor. 'He had guys with wheelbarrows going down the hallways buying the desk copies from professors. All he did was used books.' There are even stories of professors actually ordering books from publishers as examination copies for the sole purpose of selling them on – 'there was a lot of that going on.' Many publishers felt that there was something unethical about all this – that it was immoral for students and professors to sell their books. They may have been right if they were thinking of cases where professors were ordering examination copies with the explicit intention of selling them, but whether professors were behaving improperly if they accepted cash from someone who offered to take away books that had been sent to them unsolicited by a publisher is much less clear. 'If you send a book to a professor who didn't ask for it and he wants to sell it, I guess he can,' reflected one editor. 'If Lever Brothers or Colgate Palmolive send me a bar of soap and I wanted to sell it at a garage sale, I suppose that would be my right.'

Whatever the ethical issues, from a strictly economic point of view the rise of the used book market was disastrous for the textbook publishers. It meant, in effect, that the attrition rate from year one to year two increased dramatically. Before the used book market really took off in the 1980s, textbook publishers generally assumed an attrition rate of 10–20 per cent – that is, if a textbook sold, say, 20,000 copies in year one, they would generally assume that it would sell about 16,000 in year two. But with the rise of the used book market, the attrition rate skyrocketed to 60–70 per cent, in some cases to 80 per cent or more. So now the textbook that sells 20,000 copies in year one will typically sell only 6,000–8,000 in year two, and by year three it will be dead in its tracks. This was disastrous for publishers because they traditionally relied on second and third year sales to recoup the substantial up-front costs involved in textbook development and production. With the dramatic increase in the rate of attrition, this backlist revenue stream dried up.

The increase in the rate of attrition varied somewhat from subject to subject and course to course. The impact was particularly strong in the big service courses in which very few students would major, and it was strong in subjects like anthropology, which were popular credit courses for students who were majoring in other subjects. 'Anthropology is horrible,' said one senior editor:

> You might sell 18,000 copies of an anthropology book in the 0 + 1 year[1] and in year two you might sell 3,000. In year three you might sell 1,500. This wasn't because people were dropping the book, this was because of used books. It was because the great majority of the students taking anthropology were not anthropology majors. They see no value in keeping the book. So they turn around and sell them as soon as the semester is over.

---

[1] Some of the big textbook publishers bring out their new textbooks in August and treat August through December as zero year, and then the first calendar year is the first year – hence they refer to this first sixteen months as the 0 + 1 year.

The textbook publishers developed their own strategies to try to counter the growth of the used book market. One strategy was to create textbook packages for students. The textbooks were packaged together with other items, such as study guides and supplements of various kinds, and the package was shrinkwrapped and given its own ISBN. The publishers' reps urged the professors to adopt the package rather than the textbook on its own, on the grounds that the package contains materials that will be helpful for students. This would, in effect, take the used book off the market, since students would be required to buy the shrinkwrapped package rather than a used textbook on its own. But booksellers, who realized that they could no longer buy back individual textbooks if students were going to be required to buy packages, responded by talking directly to the professors themselves. As one bookseller recalled,

> We went to talk to the faculty member to understand what package is being created, because the faculty member is hearing a story from the publisher's rep that this would be beneficial for the student, and what we want to do is to communicate with the faculty member and let them understand what the impact is for the student in terms of being able to sell their book, because believe me those students will go to that faculty member and be very upset with him when we have to tell them 'we can't buy this book back from you because the faculty member is requiring that package – why don't you talk to the faculty member?' So we want to explain what the implication is to the faculty member, and a lotta times they totally understand. We also have a strategy that we will break the package down in our system and we'll still buy back the individual books and we'll put them on the shelf and we'll let the student make a decision. So there's a lot of communication that goes on because of the packages.

The growth of the used book market creates new lines of conflict between publishers and booksellers, and as publishers search for strategies to counter the impact of the used book market on the sale of new textbooks, booksellers search for their own ways to counter the strategies of publishers, drawing on their own connections with the gatekeepers – the professors – in the colleges and universities they serve in an attempt to influence their decisions in ways that will elevate the interests of booksellers and students, both of whom have a stake in the used book market, over the interests of publishers, for whom the used book market is nothing but trouble.

But there was one card the publishers could play which would be difficult for the booksellers to counter: they could speed up the cycle of new editions. Twenty or thirty years ago, a textbook publisher would bring out a new edition of a successful textbook every four or five years. This would enable them to keep the book up to date and help to ensure that they did not lose market share to competing volumes. However, as the used book market took off, publishers began to speed up the cycle of new editions in order to render earlier editions obsolete. Now the typical cycle for new editions of the most successful textbooks is two or three years – every two or three years a new edition of the textbook will be brought out, revised, repackaged and re-presented to professors with the aim of persuading them to renew their adoptions and, indeed, securing new ones. The speeding up of the revision cycle was not dictated by – or at least not primarily by – the need to improve the content of the book; it was dictated above all by the need to neutralize the effects of the used book market. 'Very often there's little to change,' commented one editor, 'so you're putting out a new product that claims to be a new edition when almost nothing has changed.' In practice, the nature and extent of the revisions vary from one edition to another. In some cases the modifications may be largely cosmetic – a new cover design, some fresh illustrations in the text, some updated references, a new preface, etc. – while in other cases the revisions are more thorough and far-reaching. But since, thanks to the used book market, three-quarters of the sales of major textbooks may be in the first year and the sales will be minimal by year three, a publisher who does not work to a revision cycle of two or three years will soon find that its textbook is dead.

From the viewpoint of sales, working to a two-year revision cycle would be ideal, since 90–95 per cent of the sales of a major textbook are likely to be in the first two years. 'In any large sizeable market, the most we can hope for now is three semesters worth of real sales, one and a half years,' explained one editor. But in practice, working to a two-year revision cycle is very demanding, and many publishers will settle for a three-year revision cycle for most of their textbooks. What this means in practice is that the first year is spent selling the textbook and monitoring sales; the second year is spent gathering information on how the book is being received, what is working and what isn't, what needs to be changed for the next edition, etc., and feeding this information back to the author who is, during this year, engaged in revising the text for the new edition; and the third year is spent producing the new edition. And then the cycle begins all over again.

Textbook publishers must therefore invest a great deal of time and effort in maintaining their successful textbooks in what is virtually a state of continuous revision. Sales reps provide a constant source of grounded feedback. As they travel from campus to campus and talk to professors and instructors, they get a good sense of what the gatekeepers like and dislike about a textbook. The sales reps have their ears to the ground and they relay this information back to the sponsoring editors – indeed, the sales reps operate more and more like 'editors in the field'. The big textbook publishers also employ development editors who manage the revision process, commissioning reviews from adopters and non-adopters and providing the author with comprehensive feedback on a chapter-by-chapter basis. As chapters are revised and new text and features are written, they are sent back to reviewers to ensure that they meet with approval from potential adopters. Sometimes focus groups are used to explore the strengths and limitations of a textbook and to identify areas in need of improvement. The aim of this intensive development process is to get the author – either on his or her own or with the assistance of one or more co-authors – to revise the text in the ways that actual and potential adopters judge to be desirable, and hence to revise the text in a manner that will enable the sales force to win adoptions for the new edition of the textbook and kill off the sales of the previous edition in the used book market.

The revision process often goes smoothly, but not always. It's very demanding on authors as well as on other staff, and successful textbook authors may find that they have become prisoners to their own work. Sometimes authors refuse to go along with this process and the textbook effectively dies. As one senior editor remarked,

Sometimes it is difficult. Sometimes the authors won't do it. Sometimes the books die because the author has refused to do that. The authors insist that the way they do things is the right way and if other people don't want it, that's too bad. We insist that we've made a tremendous investment in this and we have to protect our investment by making sure that it changes in the ways that it should. Some of the human factors are the most difficult –

they are not just legal issues, they are human issues. It is convincing people to do this. This is still a fairly gentle industry in terms of the way we treat our authors and the way we treat our customers.

Employing researchers or taking on one or more co-authors may ease the pressure on authors who are too busy to keep to this tight revision schedule, or who are unable or unwilling for other reasons to be chained to the relentless revision cycle of the modern textbook. Hence it is not uncommon for successful textbooks to metamorphose in terms of their authorship, usually retaining the original author who remains the brand name while acquiring one or more co-authors who update, revise and develop the content for the new editions.

Speeding up the revision cycle to every two or three years was an effective strategy for countering the effects of the used book market – indeed, it was, at the end of the day, the only effective strategy. Earlier editions of textbooks are still used by some students but the production of a new edition greatly devalues earlier editions on the used book market, even if it does not render them entirely obsolete. However, this strategy has come at a cost. Textbook publishers must invest a great deal of their time, effort and resources in striving to maintain the value of their existing assets – their copyrights – in a market that quickly penalizes publishers who leave their content unchanged. Continuous revision of content and frequent repackaging are the only ways to prevent your assets from rapidly declining in value.

Moreover, the fact that new editions had shorter lives meant that the sales horizon of textbooks had changed profoundly. In the past, textbook publishers could offset the low initial margins they usually faced on the first print-run of a textbook by the higher margins they would be able to achieve on subsequent reprints, when the textbook had become a healthy backlist title. But if the textbook was dead by year three, it had no backlist life and the publisher could no longer count on the healthy margins earned on later reprints. Hence all the costs involved in developing and producing the textbook, the extra expense involved in frequent revisions as well as the costs involved in producing the packages for both the professors and the students, had to be recouped in a sales horizon of two to three years. There was tremendous pressure on publishers to increase the prices of textbooks (we shall return to this point below). And increasing prices stimulated still further the used book market, exacerbating the vicious circle in which textbook publishers had become ensnared.

The vicious circle of used books and frequent revisions has resulted in what one editor described as a 'tremendous wastage of resources and time on the part of the major players in the college market trying to fend off used books'. Whether the textbook publishers realistically could have done anything to avoid this outcome is difficult to say. There are some who believe that textbook publishers could have responded differently; they could have been less moralistic and could have seen the rise of the used book market as an opportunity rather than a threat. 'They didn't get into the business themselves because they felt above it,' reflected one senior editor. 'It was the biggest mistake college publishers made. It killed them in the end.' It's not clear whether publishers themselves could have become effective players in the used book market, as this editor suggests; it's difficult to see how publishers could have avoided paying authors' royalties, for instance, and this would have put them at a competitive disadvantage in the market. In any case, having remained outside the used book business, the only truly effective strategy left for the textbook publishers was to invest more and more time and resources in speeding up the revision cycle so that they could try to neutralize the effects of the used book market on the sale of new books.

Some consequences

What are the consequences of the three developments – the rise of the conglomerates, the package wars and the growth of the used book market – which together comprise what we could describe as the logic of the field of higher education publishing? How has the logic or dynamic of this field altered the behaviour of the players within it? What consequences has it had for the practices of textbook publishers and for the nature of what they produce?

Few would deny that textbooks today are produced to a much higher standard than they were twenty or thirty years ago – they are more attractive, better illustrated, more up to date, easier to understand, filled with a variety of interesting sidelines and useful pedagogical devices and accompanied by a range of helpful ancillaries. Whether students care about all this much less clear. As one seasoned editor remarked:

> Students do not care a whit about the better qualities of the modern child psych text. In market research publishers have done, when students or professors are polled, the vast majority of students say they would prefer a lower priced text without color to the high-priced text with color. Yet, professors, when examining new texts, will rarely consider a one-color text in child psychology, no matter how inexpensive it is. Publishers have tried with one-color texts that are low-priced, but they have simply failed. So there is apparently no turning back.

Students would prefer cheaper books, but given the structure of the adoption system, students' preferences are not the factor that drives the practices of the textbook publishers. Their practices are driven by sales, and sales are determined to a very large extent by the decisions of the gatekeepers who are swayed by factors other than price. By constantly upping the ante in the struggle to win adoptions, the publishers have, in the opinion of this same seasoned editor, painted themselves into a corner:

> It seems to me that publishers have indeed painted themselves into an interesting corner as an industry by raising the ante every year, adding more and more sizzle for smaller and smaller shares of a market that has not grown nearly as much as our costs. In trying to beat the competition, we have gone beyond common sense in pursuit of market dominance.

The big textbook publishers are locked into a cycle of producing ever more elaborate textbooks and packages and of continuous revision which, together with the connivance of the gatekeepers, is very much of their own making. The stakes are high, the barriers to entry at the lower levels of the curriculum are prohibitive and the competition is intense. Not all will survive, and further consolidation among the commercial textbook publishers seems likely.

I shall explore some of the consequences of these developments by focusing in this section on five issues: (1) disciplinary encroachment, (2) the end of one-off publishing,

(3) the homogenization of content and practices, (4) the decline of representation and the marginalization of low priority texts, and (5) representation fatigue. In the following section I shall pursue a sixth issue which is becoming increasingly important – the problem of sell-through breakdown.

(1) *Disciplinary encroachment* In the 1970s and before, most textbook publishers tended to focus on certain disciplines which they made their own, and tended to steer clear of other disciplines where they knew their competitors were particularly strong. It was an approach that involved a mixture of strategic self-interest (concentrating on one's strengths and not trying to do everything) and an attitude of mutual respect characteristic of the traditional gentlemanly publisher. But as the conglomerates got bigger and the competition intensified, this attitude of mutual respect went out of the window and publishers sought to expand their textbook programmes in any subject area where opportunities seemed to present themselves, irrespective of whether that subject area was one in which they had traditionally been strong. The large conglomerates became omnivorous in disciplinary terms. They encroached on the disciplinary territories of their competitors and sought to develop competing texts which, they hoped, would take away some of the market share of the textbooks which had established themselves as dominant in the field. The mixture of mutual respect and strategic self-interest which had once kept the textbook publishers at arm's length from one another in terms of their disciplinary specializations gradually gave way to a kind of free for all in which the main textbook publishers compete against one another across many (if not all) of the core textbook subjects. One managing director put it this way:

> The biggest difference from twenty-five years ago is that none of us publishers has the proper respect for the other in the sense that, roughly speaking, when I came into the business there was a dominant textbook, maybe two dominant textbooks in each field and everybody sort of said, OK, Norton's got English literature, I've got economics, I'm going to be happy with my economics, Norton can have its Anthology of English Literature and that American history book that Harcourt publishes will be the major American history textbook. But what's really changed now is that some publishers began to say, OK, we're doing really well in history but let's also try to do an economics textbook to compete with McGraw-Hill's textbook. And we've started to do the same thing too, to fill in the holes.

The result is that the big textbook publishers become locked into increasingly intensive struggles for adoptions and market share across the whole range of core textbook subjects, as each organization tries to cover more and more subject areas. Moreover, as the large conglomerates acquire more firms and incorporate more and more titles into their ever expanding lists, their publishing programmes tend to become more diversified. Thanks to acquisitions, the large conglomerates also tend to find themselves with numerous textbooks in the same subject area pitched at roughly the same level of the curriculum, which creates problems of its own – we shall return to this point below.

(2) *The end of one-off publishing* As the large conglomerates acquire more and more critical mass in certain subject areas, they gain certain competitive advantages. They can invest large sums of money in developing the package for one key textbook and then use the package (or parts of it) for a cluster of other textbooks in the same

subject area, thus spreading the costs over half a dozen or more texts. It becomes much harder for smaller publishers with only one major textbook in a certain subject area to spread their costs in this way. Hence the smaller publishers have to decide either to expand their list in a particular area and to try to compete seriously with the big players or to get out of the area altogether. 'You can no longer be a one-off publisher, which is the term used if you want to dabble in a field,' remarked one senior editor at a smaller house. 'What the conglomerates have forced us to do is to stop doing one-off publishing and to develop entire lists in an area.'

The problem is that this is costly and risky – and increasingly so as the competition gets more intense. If a publisher wants to have any presence at all in a field, it has to invest more and more in expanding its list in that area so that it has a growing set of textbooks over which it can spread the ever increasing costs of waging the adoption struggles. The costs of entering a field are high, and if it wants to enter a new field it has to make very smart business decisions. 'If you're going to start a list in biology, you better be damn sure that you've backed the right horses with that first key book and that it does beautifully, so that you can then do all these satellite books around it having developed the brand name.' A publisher can lose a great deal of money if it gets these initial decisions wrong. The intensity of the competition means that either it has to invest heavily with the aim of becoming a major player in the field or it should stay out altogether, and if it does decide to invest the risks are high. 'It's forced the issue: now you need to do systematic, across-the-board, discipline-based fully fleshed out lists, but it puts a lot of pressure on doing it right.'

(3) *The homogenization of content and practices*   As the commercial textbook publishers strive to maximize the sales potential of their core textbooks and to strengthen the market position of subsequent editions, the size of the textbooks tends to grow and the content tends to become more and more similar from one textbook to another. The development process involves consulting a large number of potential adopters, and authors are encouraged to revise the text in ways that will appeal to the broadest market segment. The aim is to develop the text so that it will match the syllabus as it is taught at a range of institutions, and to do so in a way that will maximize the adoption potential. Authors are generally discouraged from expressing strong views which could offend some potential adopters, or from developing views which could be regarded as idiosyncratic. Moreover, since adoptions for some core textbooks are made by committees at some of the larger universities, the publishers are generally inclined to make their textbooks more and more comprehensive, covering all the major topics and subfields, since it is not worth the risk of alienating a particular member of an adoption committee by leaving some topics out. And of course, the publishers themselves are constantly looking over their shoulders to see what their competitors are doing. They know which textbooks are the leaders in the field and they scrutinize their structure and content carefully, often modelling their own textbooks on the market leaders. Hence the major competing texts put out by the big textbook publishers begin to look increasingly similar, covering similar topics in a similar style and tone, produced in a broadly similar way and always accompanied by an elaborate array of supplements.

It is difficult for a publisher to deviate too much from this if it wants to compete in the core textbook market, because the more distinctive its textbook is, the more it risks losing adoptions and hence the more cautious it has to be in terms of what it can afford to provide in the way of internal illustrations, electronic supplements, etc. If it wants to be able to justify a large development budget, it has to aim for the largest segment of the market, which means comprehensive coverage and an even-handed, non-controversial approach. Asked about the implications of these trends, and especially of the growing consolidation within the industry, for the nature of the educational products, one senior editor responded like this:

> Well, I think they've homogenized them to a tremendous degree. To compete today they have to be very, very mainstream. It's like the department stores. When I was a kid you could go to Sears and buy almost anything. Now you can only buy what they think you are going to buy before you go there. So they don't offer nearly as much in the lines. They discontinue departments because there aren't enough people.

> *Does the competitiveness of the textbook business today mean that in your commissioning and development processes you have to try to satisfy as many different constituents as possible and, therefore, you have to avoid being overly controversial?*

> I think to a degree. If you are aiming at a particular part of the market, you want to have some edges to things and you want to be able to appeal a little bit outside of the center of that particular market segment. But it is extremely difficult to do that. You are asking people to give up too many things. You are asking people to give up color. You are asking people to give up electronic supplements, test files. How many things are you going to ask them to give up in the process?

As the big publishers move increasingly towards the production of more standardized, homogenized 'vanilla' textbooks, they create opportunities for smaller players to develop texts which have a more distinctive perspective and flavour. In some cases the smaller players may emphasize this distinctiveness as a way of differentiating their textbooks from the more standardized products of the big publishers. But the more distinctive the approach, the more difficult it generally is to gain a significant market share at the lower levels of the curriculum in the core textbook subjects. It is more like 'nibbling away at the edges', as one senior editor put it.

It's not just the homogenization of content that is at issue: it's also the homogenization of practices. With growing concentration in the industry, there are fewer major players and they all tend to operate in fairly similar ways. They use similar methods of commissioning, developing and marketing textbooks, they prepare similar kinds of packages and staff are trained in similar ways. Moreover, key personnel often move from one corporation to another, so many have some personal experience of the methods used by their competitors. 'The real danger', said one senior manager, 'is that we are very similar to each other. We are in-breeding. That's risky.' He elaborated:

> There are far fewer players than there used to be, which means by definition that it is more competitive because you've got five or six major players frankly doing similar things. Through acquisition and through people moving and changing, it is a fairly incestuous industry. The training process, the missions, the publishing styles, the production qualities, the supplement usage are very similar across all of those publishers. So you are in a very competitive market, a very similar market where the ability to differentiate one's self is harder than it used to be ten to fifteen years ago, which means you've got to be a lot better at what you do, as does everyone else.

(4)   *The decline of representation and the marginalization on low priority texts*   Despite the many changes that have occurred in college textbook publishing over the last twenty years, the adoption system remains intact and the major textbook publishers continue to count on the capacity of their sales reps – the college travellers – to win adoptions for their new textbooks and new editions. But the dynamic of the field has meant that, for the large textbook publishers, the efforts of the sales reps to win adoptions have become increasingly focused on the core textbooks aimed at the lower levels of the curriculum, at the expense of those textbooks which are aimed at higher level courses where the numbers are smaller. The big textbooks for the large freshman courses demand more and more of the sales reps' time and attention – winning adoptions for these texts is the real prize (and is appropriately rewarded by the bonus system). Reps may have neither the time nor the incentives to call on professors teaching upper-level courses where the numbers are smaller and where winning adoptions will never translate into sales on the same scale as adoptions at the freshman level. The result is that textbooks for upper level courses are not given the same kind of representation as the big freshman textbooks or the gateway sophomore textbooks. Indeed in many cases they are not represented at all by the college travellers but are promoted by direct mail or by what's known as 'blind comping' – that is, sending out complimentary copies to professors who appear to be teaching relevant courses, with little or no follow-up.

The problem of representation is exacerbated by the increasing consolidation within the industry. As a result of mergers and acquisitions, many textbooks that previously would have been stellar titles on smaller lists now find themselves sitting alongside numerous other titles on a large list, and they may be competing with some of these other titles for market share. An editor in psychology or economics may now find that she has eight, nine, ten or more intro psych books or principles of economics texts where formerly, in a smaller firm before the days of conglomeratization, she would have had only one. Given the pressures on staff within the large conglomerates, not all of these titles can in practice be given the same degree of attention or promoted with the same degree of effort. Prioritization will inevitably occur, and the titles with lower sales figures and smaller market shares will tend to be marginalized in favour of the titles with stronger sales histories.

The marginalization of low priority titles tends to occur at two different levels. In the first place, editors and development teams cannot treat all of the textbooks equally, and cannot give all of them the same degree of attention and investment when it comes to producing new editions. Hence the quality of some of the textbooks will tend to decline relative to the competitors, and they will gradually lose market share. As one editorial director put it,

> You have a diminution of quality editorially because you can't do as good a job. Anyone who's a quality person will say that a good textbook is crafted very carefully, and you really have to pay close attention and work with your customers and your author and a development team to craft that tool so that it works just about as perfectly as it can in the classroom, and that includes a huge support package now. So if you've got seventeen intro psych books and one psych editor – or maybe now you have two psych editors – you can't control it. You're into a Darwinian situation now: survival of the fittest.

The large corporations pour more and more resources into the most successful textbooks on their list, revising them and supporting them with huge budgets in the attempt to maintain or increase their market share, while the less successful textbooks tend to get neglected. Some will wither on the vine as their sales and market share decline. Some of the more marginal textbooks may eventually be discontinued and their authors cut loose ('I get calls all the time from authors who've been released,' said one well-connected editor at a smaller house). As the battle between the titans turns increasingly into a struggle for market share at the lower levels of the curriculum, those textbooks that are not vital stakes in this struggle will tend to become increasingly marginalized in the editorial development process and their quality and market share will gradually decline.

The marginalization of the low priority texts also occurs in the repping process. When a conglomerate acquires a whole new set of textbooks that formerly belonged to another house, the sales reps may find themselves in the awkward position of trying to win adoptions for two or more textbooks that cover the same material and are pitched at the same level – in effect, the books are competing against one another for market share. In practice the reps are bound to engage in some degree of prioritization, and to push some textbooks in certain contexts harder than others. The inevitable result is that some textbooks are going to be given less representation; they may be very fine textbooks, but they may not have the same kind of market share in the conglomerate's expanding stable of intro psych or intro economics books and hence they will not be given the same degree of attention and push in the day-to-day process of repping. There are some in the industry who see this skewing of the representation process as a serious loss for authors and as the real tragedy of conglomeratization. The managing director of one of the smaller textbook publishing firms put it like this:

> What's also happened with all the conglomeratization is that some of the big publishing groups will have at least twenty introductory economic textbooks among their various lists. I would argue that, first of all, the situation is much worse for an author because you would rather be a publisher's only introductory economics author, even if they have only forty reps, than one of twenty introductory economics authors even though you might have three hundred reps. If you are the biggest fish in that big pond you are happier, but the nineteen others would be a good deal sadder. I actually think that's the real tragedy of this conglomeratization. I think that there is a lot less variety. But there is a lot less good representation for some books that really were wonderful and strong and important. If they had been published by a smaller publisher, they'd still be getting their good, strong representation. But because they're just slightly less successful than another book at a conglomerate, they don't do as well.

In practice, the prioritization of some textbooks within the large conglomerates means that those texts with strong sales histories and significant market shares will command more and more resources and will become the focus of more editorial and marketing effort, while those texts with less impressive track records in sales terms will become increasingly marginalized even though, in terms of the intrinsic quality of the text, they may be excellent books. There are winners in this game – the resources that are poured into the most successful textbooks are unprecedented, as is the development and representation effort. But there are losers too, and many of the books that are not prioritized in this way will gradually fall by the wayside.

(5) *Representation fatigue* The changes of the last two decades and the intensified competition at the lower levels of the curriculum have also had an impact on the nature

of representation and the relation between sales reps and potential adopters. It is easy to romanticize the past and to paint an excessively rosy picture of how reps and professors interacted in earlier decades, but there are some people who have been in the business for a long time who believe that there has been a real change in this regard:

> In the old days it was much more collegial, the publishing rep was a purveyor of information – what's going on out there? What are the trends in my discipline? These kinds of conversations don't take place anymore. The traditional model is broken in the sense that the trust that used to exist between a professor and a publishing rep is gone. They know that the big commercial publishing rep is coming down the hall to stuff something down their throat and all they want is the business.

The traditional relationship between the sales rep and the professor was a rather genteel relation based a form of trust and mutual respect that was built up over time. But as the conglomerates have grown in size and the investment in the big freshman textbooks has escalated, the struggle to win the big freshman adoptions and to increase market share for the flagship textbooks has become more intense. There is a lot at stake for the corporations and for their sales reps, and the interactions with potential adopters tend to veer towards the hard sell. Some professors respond with a kind of weariness, a 'representation fatigue' – they see the rep coming down the corridor and they walk the other way. They don't want to know. 'Intro psych is the perfect example of people running the other way, closing their doors. They don't want to go through the ritual. They've got a stack this high of intro psych books and you can see their eyes glazing over.' They are happy to see you if they've already adopted your textbook but – apart from a few quite exceptional cases – they don't want to sit through another presentation of yet another introductory textbook in a field which is already overflowing with intro books.

The problems are exacerbated by the fact that professors are busier than ever and are often reluctant to spend time listening to a rep talking about a new textbook when they already have more than enough to choose from. They are also exacerbated by increasing turnover among sales reps. In circumstances where the big core textbooks begin to look more and more the same, covering similar topics and accompanied by similar packages of supplementary materials, the personal relationships formed between sales reps and professors may play an increasingly important role in adoption decisions. Having long tenure in the field and taking the time to form relationships with professors – 'shooting the breeze' as one former rep put it – can make all the difference. But if there is a high turnover among sales reps, it becomes very difficult to form long-term relationships of this kind. Some of the big textbook publishers have become increasingly conscious of the importance of this factor and have introduced incentive schemes to encourage reps to remain in the field. They've become increasingly aware that, as the big textbooks become more and more similar, more and more depends on what happens in the sales relationship. As the textbooks and packages become more indistinguishable, the selling process becomes more important. 'If I were assigning percentages to what counts in the adoption,' explained one senior executive, 'I would say that in most of these very mature markets where there are five or six really good choices, 70 per cent is the book, 20 per cent is the rest of package that goes with it and 10 per cent is the rep – except if everybody has got that 70 and that 20, then in fact the way the decision plays out, the rep is 50 per cent or more of what actually happens in the end.'

Given how much is at stake, some of the big publishers are willing to go to considerable lengths to win key adoptions. If a professor would like special materials to help teach a course, such as a customized set of slides or a modified test bank, the sales rep may try to provide it even though it is not part of the standard package for the text. Stories abound of practices which are more dubious in character, including some which amount to a kind of soft corruption ('dirty adoptions', as they are sometimes called) – such as cases where the publisher pays a dollar or two into an 'education fund' for a particular faculty for every copy sold to its students, or where the publisher makes a small alteration to the text to 'customize' it for a particular professor who is then treated as a co-author and paid a share of the royalties on every copy sold of this edition, or where the publisher agrees to pay excessively large reviewer fees to instructors on condition that they adopt the book, and so on. These practices are no doubt the exception rather than the rule, but they do highlight what is at stake today in the college textbook business. Everything depends on winning the big adoptions, and if on occasion this requires an exchange of favours between the publisher and the gatekeepers in the adoption system, this is not necessarily ruled out.

In the final analysis, however, a great deal still depends on the intrinsic quality of the textbook. There are many in the industry who will say – providing examples to back it up – that no matter how much money you throw at a new textbook and no matter how hard your sales reps push it, if the text isn't good enough it simply won't succeed. 'Everyone says the textbook is just a commodity, it's all package-driven and it's all rep-driven – in the end it's not,' observed one experienced editor. 'There are too many really good books out there for that to be the case. The best books dominate because they are the best books.' The other side of this is that, despite the fact that the freshman market is very crowded, it is still possible to launch a new textbook into this market if it has the right author and the right content, and if it is heavily backed with investment in development and production – including the full package of supplements – and with a bonus scheme for reps. Substantial investment in textbook development, four- or five-colour production, elaborate multimedia packages and a sales force of reps with suitable incentives are all necessary conditions to win the adoption battles in the crowded and intensely competitive freshman markets, but they are not sufficient conditions. They are the entry conditions, the conditions that must be fulfilled if you want to play the game, but these conditions alone don't determine success. Quality does still matter.

The problem of sell-through breakdown

We have been examining some of the consequences of conglomeratization and of the dynamic that has driven the textbook publishing industry over the last two decades, but there is one very important issue that we have not yet addressed – the problem of sell-through breakdown. Many of the textbook publishers report that during the last couple of years the problem of sell-through breakdown appears to be getting significantly worse, resulting in declining unit sales and even higher returns from the bookstores – one textbook publisher reported that its returns were running at 37 per cent in 2002. The contrast with twenty years ago is striking. One senior figure who has been in the business for many years put it like this: in 1980, if you secured an adoption for a course with 300 students, in the first year of the first edition of the textbook you could count on nearly 300 sales – in other words, the sell-through would be close to 100 per cent. Of course, the sell-through in subsequent years would decline, thanks largely to the used book market. By 2000, however, an adoption for a course with 300 students would typically generate sales of only 150 units in the first year of the first edition – the sell-through had fallen to around 50 per cent. And this is before you take account of the used book market, which only really kicks in during the second year. The sell-through problem has now become so serious that it is being openly talked about in the industry and has become a source of growing concern.[2]

What is the source of this problem? The origins of the problem can be traced back to the rise of the used book market and to the competitive dynamic that is built into the adoption system. As we saw, the rise of the used book market greatly shortened the sales horizon of textbook publishers. The backlist life of the textbook was increasingly undermined and most of the revenue for a particular edition of a textbook had to be generated in the first year of sales either by increasing unit sales during the first year or by increasing prices (or both). Moreover, textbook publishers poured more and more resources into the development and production of textbooks and of elaborate packages to keep up with their competitors and to try to outmanoeuvre them in the struggle for adoptions, and they had to absorb the escalating costs of these adoption struggles by raising the prices of the textbooks. The multimedia packages (and subsequently the companion websites) were key weapons in the struggle to win adoptions, but the packages were effectively given away to the professors – they were freebies, not revenue-generating products. The only way the publishers could generate revenue was by selling textbooks to students, and the increasing costs of textbooks and packages could be recovered only by increasing prices. Since the decision-makers were not the ultimate purchasers, the logic of the adoption system created a form of non-price competition between publishers, who simply increased their textbook prices in order to meet the costs of waging the increasingly expensive struggle to win adoptions.

So the combination of the shortened sales horizon caused by the rise of the used book market and the increasing costs of waging the adoption struggles created a strong and constant pressure to increase the prices of textbooks. Indeed textbook publishers settled into the practice of raising their prices every six months almost as a matter of routine. Even if they weren't achieving significant increases in unit sales, they could still increase their revenue year on year by steadily increasing their prices. In recent years the industry has settled into a practice of raising its prices twice a year by about 3 per cent each time. There are some who say that this is what accounts for most of the growth in the industry, which in the last few years has been about 6–8 per cent per annum. It was generally assumed that the ultimate consumers – the students – were a captive market and that they would buy whatever their professors told them to buy. So the key thing was to win over the professor, and the cost of doing so could be passed on to the student in the form of higher prices.

---

[2] It should be noted that senior figures in the industry offer differing assessments of the scale and significance of this problem. One senior executive at a major textbook publishing firm disputed the view that the problem of sell-through breakdown is getting worse. He contended that their textbooks were still selling through in their first year at more or less 100%, and that the steep decline in years two and three was due entirely to the used book market. However, this is very much a minority view. Most senior executives are concerned – and increasingly so – about what they perceive to be a growing trend in the market.

But there are signs that this cosy arrangement, which has underpinned the growth of the textbook industry over the last few decades, is beginning to come unstuck. The student was always the silent partner in the traditional textbook model. Publishers listened very carefully to the gatekeepers because they needed their adoptions in order to survive, and they interacted with booksellers because they were their immediate customers, but they didn't pay much attention to students because they assumed that students would buy what they were told to buy. It was the gatekeepers who mattered, and it was the gatekeepers upon whom they lavished ever more elaborate packages to help them teach and examine their courses. But now the silent partner in this deal is demanding to be heard in the only voice that really matters: they are refusing to buy. They regard the prices as too high and they are inventing all sorts of ways to avoid doing the one thing they were supposed to do, which was to buy the books. One senior manager put it like this:

> As an industry and in all sectors, we have reached the absolute ceiling in terms of prices. The sell-through is half of what it was. Students are actually signing up for the same courses as roommates so that they can go halves on a book, or they're just not buying the book, or the bookstores are letting them read the books in the bookstores, or they're renting them for a week before finals and then returning them to the publishers. So you have a 300-student course and maybe 120–50 copies get sold.

The same manager cited a case where a professor told a rep that he wasn't going to use a textbook any more because the prices were simply too high – 'I'm going to put together my own coursepack. I don't need a textbook and I don't need my students to spend $110 on one.' The fact that concerns about prices are now being expressed by the gatekeepers is significant. In the past, reps often asked professors whether the price of textbooks mattered, and up to the late 1990s they always said it didn't matter. They would choose what they thought was the best book; price wasn't an issue. But now price is becoming an issue.[3] Professors are talking about it and they are telling reps that it does make a difference in terms of their adoption decisions. Why? 'Because the students are screaming bloody murder at these professors. They're saying I'm just not going to buy the book, sorry.'

The high prices of textbooks have also encouraged students to shop around and look for cheaper ways of acquiring them, often going online to compare prices and search for used copies. There has been a proliferation of online bookstores – campusbooks.com, eCampus.com, textbookx.com, cheap-textbooks.com, etc. – which offer specialized services to students seeking the cheapest available textbooks, new or used. This creates growing problems for campus bookstores, who are losing sales to online retailers and finding themselves obliged to return even more copies to publishers at the end of the semester. It also creates new problems for the publishers, who find that the same textbooks which their overseas subsidiaries are selling at lower prices – often half the price or less – are being imported back into the US and undercutting their own sales, as well

---

[3] It's even become a public issue, making it onto the pages of the *New York Times* and taken up by Senator Charles Schumer of New York. See Tamar Lewin, 'When Books Break the Bank: College Students Venture beyond the Campus Store', *New York Times*, 16 Sept. 2003, section B, p. 1.

as generating more bad publicity for the publishers.[4] Given that the internet has created a system of globalized metadata where prices can be compared by consumers irrespective of where they happen to be located, it seems likely that the big textbook publishers will become increasingly cautious about allowing their key textbooks to be sold at heavily discounted prices in overseas markets. They simply cannot allow their domestic US sales to be undercut by the seepage of cheaper overseas editions back into the US market.

The problem of sell-through breakdown presses to the very heart of college textbook publishing. For, as we have seen, the whole industry is based on a particular model of decision-making which defines the relations between the publishers, the professors who make the decisions about whether to adopt a textbook and the students who ultimately buy the book, and it is this model – the adoption system – which is being called into question by the growing problem of sell-through breakdown. For now the party who has been the silent partner in the system, and whose willingness to buy the books adopted by their professors has kept the industry going and funded the package wars that have been waged in their name, is beginning to say that this game is getting too costly and they're not sure they want to play it any more. For years, students were largely excluded from the knowledge triangle, but now, with sell-through breakdown on the rise, the publishers are beginning to listen. As one college publisher observed,

> College publishers have been great about listening to their customer who was the professor, but now they're realizing that there's another customer who's entered the picture who wasn't there before – the student. And that student is making himself heard, and he's saying 'sorry, but you guys have been playing without me and I'm really the consumer and guess what, I count.' And think about it: what the student has paid for over the last twenty years is the *comfort* of the professor – the free test banks, the laser disks, the video tapes, the software, you name it, they get it, it's endless. All this stuff is free, and it all gets added on as a cost and the only way to make it up is price. The student has funded this whole free-for-all in terms of free ancillaries, and now the student is saying the chickens are coming home to roost.

The views of students were not completely ignored in the past. Some publishers have involved students in the development of textbooks, soliciting their views on content, presentation, etc. – the students get paid, they get their names in the book and so on. But the extent to which the big publishers actually took account of students' views was generally very limited. 'In the end, that's all marketing,' commented one senior editor. 'The real student point of view is price.'

What makes the problem of sell-through breakdown so worrying for the textbook publishers is that it's not entirely clear what they can do about it. The competitive dynamic of the adoption system has raised the bar of expectation in terms of the production quality of textbooks and the array of supplements that are provided to professors free of charge, and it would now be difficult to go back on these features without

---

[4] Tamar Lewin, 'Students Find $100 Textbooks Cost $50, Purchased Overseas', *New York Times*, 21 Oct. 2003, p. 1. 'We think it's frightening, and it's wrong, that the same American textbooks our stores buy here for $100 can be shipped in from some other country for $50,' Laura Nakoneczny, a spokeswoman for the National Association of College Stores, is quoted as saying. 'It represents price-gouging of the American public generally and college students in particular.'

running the risk of losing adoptions. 'We've got into one of those unfortunate vicious circles where the books are too expensive and no one knows how to make them cheaper any more', as one managing director put it. Some publishers have tried to introduce cheaper one-colour textbooks that could be priced much lower, but in the past experiments of this kind have not been very successful. Many professors seem to have become accustomed to the lavish four-colour production and the array of supplements which are intended to make their life easier, and they seem reluctant to do without them. Whether a growing sensitivity to prices on the part of some professors will create a more congenial environment for less lavish editions remains to be seen. Some publishers are now offering a range of what they call 'lower-cost alternatives' – e.g. selected textbooks which are being offered at $15 or $20 less than competing titles, or textbooks which are being offered in looseleaf at 30 per cent off – in the hope that these will appeal to some professors who are concerned about price. (The looseleaf editions have the added advantage, from the publisher's viewpoint, of undercutting the used book market, since used book vendors can't be sure the editions are complete and are therefore unlikely to want to buy them back.) Some publishers are placing renewed emphasis on customized editions of the big textbooks, in the hope that by tailoring the contents more closely to the needs of professors and students they will be able to bring down costs and increase sell-through (we shall return to the customization of textbooks in chapter 14). Some are also setting up their own online bookstores to sell textbooks directly to students in the hope that, by cutting out the bookseller's margin, they will be able to reduce the final price to students and increase overall sales.

Could publishers simply lower the prices of their textbooks without reducing the quality or slimming down the package? Are they simply charging too much for their existing textbooks and being too greedy in terms of the profit margins they are generating for themselves? The problem for the big textbook publishers is twofold: first, their overheads are high; and second, while margins may be very good on the most successful textbooks, there are many textbooks on their lists, with first-year unit sales in the region of 15,000–20,000 copies, where the margins are already under considerable pressure given the level of expenditure involved. The smaller textbook publishers have lower overheads and may therefore have more room to manoeuvre in terms of price freezes or even price cuts, but even they would find this very difficult because the competitive logic of the adoption system militates against it. As one editor at a smaller textbook publisher put it, 'it's hard to envisage lowering prices given the climate we're in where there's tremendous pressure to do more with the package and to make the books heavily and more expensively illustrated.'

Might there be price wars among the big textbook publishers? No one rules it out but few think that it's likely. The role of the adoption system in the struggle for market share is too important and would probably override the growing concerns about sell-through breakdown. As one managing director put it,

> As the big publishers become increasingly desperate for market share, I think that rather than a price war we're going to continue with non-price competition. They're going to throw more and more money at lavish video supplements to their textbooks, CD-ROM supplements, test preparation, test corrections, etc. They will probably try to find ways to make it very, very expensive for smaller publishers to be involved in the market. To some extent they may lose money doing that and willingly so, just to force people out of the market.

While sell-through breakdown is perceived as a growing problem by the big textbook publishers, their preoccupation with gaining market share may override their concern with prices, at least in the short run. Whether they will be able to put this problem aside if the sell-through continues to decline as it has in the last couple of years is not at all clear.

Some in the industry express the hope that new technologies will provide at least part of the solution to the problem of sell-through breakdown in the medium to long term. The hope is that new technologies will enable publishers to reduce the size of the big textbooks and shift most of the illustrative material onto companion websites or CD-ROMs. As one senior executive put it,

> I see a textbook of the future that is still going to be a printed book but it's not going to have all the illustrations in it. The student will have her computer on while she's reading her assignment and for some of the best illustrations will turn to her computer screen and a CD-ROM or some form of delivery that gives her the lovely four-colour illustrations. That may prove to be a much less expensive textbook. It may be less expensive to give kids a CD-ROM and a one-colour textbook and that may ease the pricing pressure in a helpful way.

This scenario is a possibility, and the growing problems of sell-through breakdown have encouraged some of the big textbook publishers to experiment with ways of delivering content electronically in the hope that, by enabling them to bring down prices, it will stimulate sales. But, as we shall see in a later chapter, the history of experiments in this domain does not provide a strong basis of evidence to suggest that these new initiatives will be strikingly successful, at least in the short term. The printed textbook remains the core revenue-generating product for higher education publishers, and the competitive logic of this intensely competitive field has tended to drive the big players to produce ever more elaborate packages and has discouraged them from scaling down the printed versions of their key textbooks in any significant way.

Not everyone in the industry would agree that the problem of sell-through breakdown is the most serious problem facing textbook publishers today, but most would agree that it *is* a major problem and many fear that it could get worse. With returns increasing, sell-through declining and students not buying in the way they used to, these are challenging times for textbook publishers, and how these developments will play themselves out in the coming years is by no means clear.

9

Higher education publishing in the US (2): the differentiation of the field

In the previous chapter I examined the evolution of the field of higher education publishing with reference primarily to the activities of the large textbook publishers. We saw how the logic of the field, and in particular the increasing scale of investment precipitated by the package wars, obliged the large textbook publishers to concentrate their efforts increasingly on the lower levels of the curriculum where they could hope to secure the kinds of adoptions that would translate into substantial sales. Hence the competition at the lower levels of the curriculum has become increasingly intense, and it has become more and more difficult for smaller publishers or new entrants to compete at this level – the barriers to entry are simply too high. But the more that the large textbook publishers were forced to move down the curriculum, the more opportunities there were for smaller publishers and migrants from other fields to find market niches at the upper levels, at the junior and senior levels of the undergraduate programme and at the graduate level. Moreover, there are some subjects, such as the humanities (history, literature, philosophy, etc.) and the 'softer' social sciences (sociology, anthropology, political science, etc.), where many professors are inclined to use materials other than standard textbooks in their classes, either as supplements to a textbook or, in some cases, as alternatives to it. So the more you move up the curriculum and the more you move into subjects like the humanities and the softer social sciences, the more complex the picture becomes in terms of the provision of the textbooks and other teaching materials which are used by professors and students in higher education.

While the previous chapter focused on the overall structure of the field of higher education publishing in the US and sought to identify the central logic or dynamic that has shaped the evolution of this field in recent decades, in this chapter I want to focus on the differentiation of the field and to bring out some of its internal complexity. I shall begin by analysing some of the main dimensions of differentiation. I shall then look at the results of an important study which examined the material actually used for teaching in history and literature at a number of universities. This will provide the backcloth against which I shall explore in more detail the changing role of the university presses in the field of higher education publishing and the rise of the coursepack business.

Differentiated markets for textbooks

The field of higher education publishing in the United States is stratified and differentiated in various ways – I have already mentioned some, but now I want to analyse these patterns in a more systematic way. There are essentially three axes of differentiation: (1) the institution, (2) the curriculum, and (3) the discipline. Let me deal briefly with each.

(1) *Institutional differentiation* The American system of higher education is enormously diverse, and both the teaching practices of professors and the needs of students vary considerably from one type of institution to another. There are many ways that one could analyse the structure of the American system of higher education – for the purposes of understanding the business of higher education publishing, it's helpful to distinguish between six different types of institution. First, there are the elite liberal arts colleges – the Ivy League (Harvard, Princeton, Yale, Columbia, Cornell, etc.) and the top tier of liberal arts colleges. Many of these are relatively small, well-endowed private institutions which draw students who are generally very able and well prepared for higher education. But not all of the top liberal arts colleges are small – Columbia has an enrolment of more than 23,000 students, for example, and at New York University (NYU) there are more than 48,000 students taking courses at six different locations in Manhattan. Second, there are many other liberal arts colleges which may not be among the elite but which are nevertheless high-quality teaching institutions. They range from well-known and highly regarded colleges like Duke and Notre Dame to a variety of smaller and lesser known colleges spread across the country. Third, there are the large state universities, like the University of California or the University of Illinois, each of which has several campuses in different locations across the state. The state universities tend to be much larger than the liberal arts colleges and to cater for a much broader spectrum of students. In terms of academic standards, the best state universities are as good as the top liberal arts colleges, although given the numbers of students involved in the state university sector, the teaching methods are likely to be different. Fourth, there are the four-year state colleges, like East Michigan State or San José State University in California. Again, compared to the liberal arts colleges, the four-year state colleges tend to be large institutions which cater for a more varied student intake. Fifth, there are the two-year community colleges which offer the Associate of Arts or the Associate of Science degree. There are many students who will start higher education at a two-year community college and then transfer to a four-year institution to complete a bachelor's degree. There are also many students at two-year community colleges and four-year state colleges who are taking courses on a part-time basis and combining study with full-time or part-time employment. Sixth, there are the technical schools, which are a breed apart. The world of the technical schools is itself stratified, with the top-brand schools like MIT and Cal Tech at one end and the lower level vocational schools at the other. In the academic year 2000/01, there were a total of 4,182 accredited institutions in the US offering degrees at the associate level and above.

Table 9.1 and figure 9.1 show the overall enrolment in degree-granting institutions – that is, in accredited colleges and universities, four-year and two-year, public and private – in the US from 1965 to 2000.[1] Enrolment increased sharply from 1965 to 1975 and then levelled off in the late 1970s and early 1980s, before growing again sharply in the second half of the 1980s. There was a slight decline in enrolment between 1992 and 1995,

---

[1] National Center for Education Statistics, table 173. The data used in this and the following paragraph are drawn from NCES; see www.nces.ed.gov.

Table 9.1   Enrolment in accredited colleges and universities in the US, 1965–2000

	Four-year institutions	Two-year institutions	Total
1965	4,747,912	1,172,952	5,920,864
1966	5,063,902	1,325,970	6,389,872
1967	5,398,986	1,512,762	6,911,748
1968	5,720,795	1,792,296	7,513,091
1969	5,937,127	2,067,533	8,004,660
1970	6,261,502	2,319,385	8,580,887
1971	6,369,355	2,579,289	8,948,644
1972	6,458,634	2,756,186	9,214,820
1973	6,590,023	3,012,100	9,602,123
1974	6,819,735	3,403,994	10,223,729
1975	7,214,740	3,970,119	11,184,859
1976	7,128,816	3,883,321	11,012,137
1977	7,242,845	4,042,942	11,285,787
1978	7,231,625	4,028,467	11,260,092
1979	7,353,233	4,216,666	11,569,899
1980	7,570,608	4,526,287	12,096,895
1981	7,655,461	4,716,211	12,371,672
1982	7,654,074	4,771,706	12,425,780
1983	7,741,195	4,723,466	12,464,661
1984	7,711,167	4,530,773	12,241,940
1985	7,715,978	4,531,077	12,247,055
1986	7,823,963	4,679,548	12,503,511
1987	7,990,420	4,776,222	12,766,642
1988	8,180,182	4,875,155	13,055,337
1989	8,387,671	5,150,889	13,538,560
1990	8,578,554	5,240,083	13,818,637
1991	8,707,053	5,651,900	14,358,953
1992	8,764,969	5,722,390	14,487,359
1993	8,738,936	5,565,867	14,304,803
1994	8,749,080	5,529,710	14,278,790
1995	8,769,252	5,492,529	14,261,781
1996	8,802,835	5,497,420	14,300,255
1997	8,874,676	5,470,740	14,345,416
1998	9,017,653	5,489,314	14,506,967
1999	9,198,525	5,592,699	14,791,224
2000	9,363,858	5,948,431	15,312,289

Source: National Center for Education Statistics, US Department of Education.

followed by large increases in the late 1990s. By 2000, total enrolment in degree-granting institutions was 15.3 million. Much of this growth was in female enrolment – between 1990 and 2000, male enrolment increased by 7 per cent while female enrolment increased by 14 per cent. The proportion of students from ethnic minorities has also increased significantly – in 1976, 15 per cent were from ethnic minorities, compared with 28 per cent in 2000. About three-quarters of the students enrolled in 2000 were in

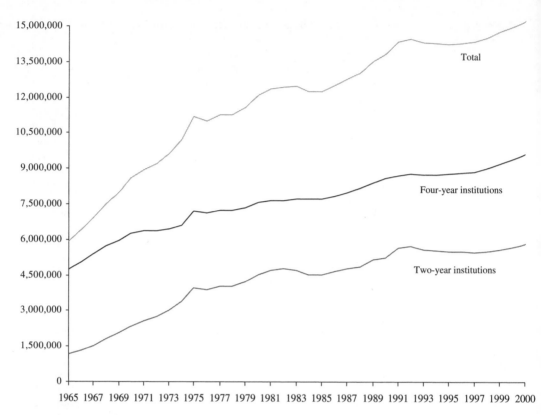

Figure 9.1 Enrolment in accredited colleges and universities in the US, 1965–2000
Source: National Center for Education Statistics, US Department of Education.

public institutions of various kinds. Most students were also attending the larger colleges and universities. Of the 4,182 accredited institutions in 2000, 10 per cent of the campuses had enrolments of 10,000 or more, and these campuses accounted for 50 per cent of total college enrolment. Table 9.2 lists the ten largest college and university campuses in fall 2000.

In terms of bachelor degrees conferred, the largest subject by far at American colleges and universities is business – about 20 per cent of all B.A.s conferred in 1999–2000 were in business. Social sciences and history (10 per cent), education (9 per cent), health and related sciences (6 per cent) and psychology (6 per cent) are also popular subjects. English language and literature represented about 4 per cent of all B.A.s conferred in 1999–2000, and liberal arts and sciences represented about 3 per cent. At the master's level, the largest subjects by a significant margin are education (27 per cent of all degrees conferred in 1999–2000) and business (25 per cent). Health and related sciences accounted for 9 per cent of all masters degrees, and public administration accounted for 6 per cent. Social sciences and history accounted for 3 per cent of masters degrees, as did psychology. English language and literature represented about 1.5 per cent of masters degrees.

The institutional differentiation of the field of higher education in the United States has important implications for the activities of higher education publishers, since the

Table 9.2 Enrolment in the ten largest college and university campuses in the US, fall 2000

Institution	State	Rank	Total enrolment
University of Texas at Austin	Texas	1	49,996
Ohio State University, Main Campus	Ohio	2	47,952
Miami-Dade Community College	Florida	3	46,834
University of Minnesota, Twin Cities	Minnesota	4	45,481
University of Florida	Florida	5	45,114
Arizona State University, Main Campus	Arizona	6	44,126
Texas A&M University	Texas	7	44,026
Michigan State University	Michigan	8	43,336
Houston Community College	Texas	9	40,929
University of Wisconsin, Madison	Wisconsin	10	40,658

Source: National Center for Education Statistics, US Department of Education.

pedagogical practices of professors and the needs of students vary from one type of institution to another. At the large state universities, the numbers of students involved in the freshman intro courses and the sophomore gateway courses are such that the only sensible and feasible way to teach these courses is to adopt a core textbook. The textbook will provide all students with a common basis for their studies, and the package of supplementary materials will reduce the amount of time and effort that must be invested by the professor. At the elite liberal arts colleges, professors may be more inclined and more able to use more challenging teaching methods, such as encouraging students to read a variety of texts and more original works rather than relying largely or exclusively on core textbooks. Given that the student numbers are generally smaller and the staff–student ratios are more favourable, a more customized approach to teaching is possible, even at the lower levels of the curriculum. At the other end of the spectrum, teaching staff at the two-year colleges are more likely to rely on textbooks for many of their courses. Staff at these colleges are more likely to be on short-term and part-time contracts (in 1999 only 35 per cent of faculty at public two-year colleges were employed full-time, compared with 73 per cent at public four-year colleges and universities). Hence teachers at two-year colleges have less time for preparation and are likely to value textbooks – together with the package of supplements – which save them time and effort and which are tailored to the needs of their students, who generally have fewer qualifications, less preparation and less time (since many are working) than students at four-year colleges and universities. Moreover, in a two-year college that relies heavily on part-time teachers ('freeway flyers', as they are called in California), an adopted textbook can give continuity and stability to the curriculum in a context where the teaching staff may be in a state of flux.

The textbook publishers themselves tend to segment the market according to type of institution and to develop their books for specific segments. Partly this is because they perceive that the needs of professors and students tend to vary from one type of institution to another, and partly it is because this enables them to make the most effective use of their sales force. As one textbook publisher whose books are developed primarily for the private liberal arts colleges and the better state universities down through the mid-range state universities remarked, 'we are unlikely to take on a textbook whose main market would be community college students because it would be a mismatch between the book's audience and our sales force.' On the other hand, some of the large textbook publishers explicitly develop a range of textbooks for the four-year state colleges and two-year community colleges, gearing the level of the text to the perceived needs of teachers and students in these institutions.

(2)   *The curriculum*   The field is differentiated not only in terms of the kinds of institutions which students attend but also in terms of the curriculum. In all colleges and universities, most subjects tend to be taught in a progressive and cumulative fashion, beginning with broader and more introductory courses in the freshman year, more focused (or 'gateway') courses in the sophomore year, followed by more specialized courses in the junior and senior years. In psychology, for example, a student will typically take a basic 'intro psych' course in the freshman year, followed by gateway courses in subjects such as social psychology, child psychology and abnormal psychology in the sophomore year, followed by more specialized courses in the junior and senior years. By the time students reach the graduate level, it is generally assumed that they understand the basic principles and concepts of the subject and that they can engage with problems, issues and theories at a more advanced level. Publishers hoping to secure adoptions for textbooks have to ensure that their texts are carefully geared to the needs and background knowledge of students at specific levels of the curriculum. Moreover, in the American higher education system students often take courses in subjects in order to gain credits and fulfil certain requirements even though they do not intend to major in that subject; in such cases they may be less likely to buy books for these courses, and more likely to sell them back when they've finished the course.

   In the previous chapter we saw how the dynamic of the field of higher education publishing has forced the big textbook publishers to concentrate their efforts on the lower levels of the curriculum, on the large freshman intro courses and the sophomore gateway courses, where the student numbers are largest and where there is more comparability in terms of pedagogical content from one institution to another. Given the levels of investment required for the core textbooks and their packages and given the costs involved in sustaining a substantial force of college travellers, it is only at the lower levels of the curriculum that one can hope to achieve the kinds of print-runs necessary to achieve a profitable return. The big textbook publishers do move higher up the curriculum and are willing to publish for junior and senior courses and even for graduate courses if the numbers of students involved are sufficient to justify the investment. But textbooks aimed at upper-level courses will generally be given less attention by the sales team, and the publisher is more likely to rely on comping rather than the face-to-face methods of the college travellers to sell these books.

(3)   *Disciplinary differentiation*   Just as teaching practices vary across institutions and types of institution, so too they differ from one academic subject or discipline to another. In subjects like economics, business, psychology, the natural sciences (physics, biology, chemistry, etc.), mathematics and engineering, it is common practice at many institutions for professors to use core textbooks at the lower levels of the curriculum and even, in some subject areas, at junior, senior and graduate levels. On the other hand, in the humanities and the 'softer' social sciences, it is common for professors to use a more

varied range of teaching materials at both lower and upper levels of the curriculum (though the extent to which they do so in practice will depend on the nature of the insti- tution as well as the personal preferences of the professor). The more varied range of teaching materials may include books of a more original kind – primary texts (in the case of English literature or philosophy, for example), trade paperbacks, a selection of articles or extracts which have been compiled in an anthology or in a coursepack, and so on. Sometimes these materials are used alongside a core textbook and sometimes they are used as an alternative to it – the approach varies from subject to subject and from professor to professor. Some history professors, for example, are loath to use what they would see as someone's predigested account of US or European history, and prefer to teach by requiring their students to read a variety of books and articles which can be discussed in class. As one textbook publisher explained,

> In history there's a lot more tendency to say, rather than adopt that big textbook I'm going to have my kids buy eight or twelve paperbacks and we're going to read our way through the first half of US history, or twentieth-century US history, or something like that. English literature is another area – there's more of a tendency there than in a lot of the other dis- ciplines at the introductory level to ask students to buy a bunch of paperbacks rather than to buy a single textbook.

The fact that some professors in history or literature prefer to teach introductory courses with materials other than textbooks does not mean, however, that textbooks do not exist in humanities subjects – on the contrary, they do exist and in some areas they are very successful. English composition is a big textbook subject with large numbers of students. In English literature, the equivalent of the textbook at the lower level of the curriculum is the big anthology which includes selections and extracts from origi- nal works – the kind of volume for which Norton has become particularly well known. Western civilization and US history are big textbook subjects, even if some professors prefer to teach in other ways. And,

> if you want to go all the way to what some would say is the soft end of the humanities, you're going to wind up at music and art, and those are very big textbook areas. The music appreciation course in the United States is one of the great textbook areas, the history of Western music course is a very big and textbook-dominated market, Janson's *History of Art* is one of the great classic textbooks, and so on. What makes the music and art books work is that you can get all that wonderful art into one place and that's terribly expensive. These textbooks to some extent just become nice big boxes into which all kinds of neat things can be collected.

So textbooks are used in subjects like history, English, art and music, but they are used more selectively and less exclusively, and often in conjunction with other books.

To some extent these differences are linked to differences in subject matter. In the natural sciences, mathematics, economics and so on, there is a core body of material that all students are expected to cover at the lower levels of the curriculum. This material can be covered by a textbook in a clear and comprehensive way, and the textbook can be structured in a way that maps on to the sequential structure of the course – 'eco- nomics 101 is economics 101 is economics 101,' as one senior executive put it. In sub- jects like history and literature, however, the structure of knowledge is less cumulative in character – it has a more open texture, and greater emphasis is often placed on different perspectives or points of view, on debates and the development of arguments, and so on. Textbooks tend to be less common in those subject areas where professors want to teach the debates and to sensitize their students to different perspectives rather than to teach some core and well-established body of knowledge, and this more open-ended pedagogical approach tends to be more prevalent in the humanities and the softer social sciences than in the natural sciences, mathematics, etc.

Those who work within the textbook industry tend to structure their own field by drawing a broad distinction between the 'hard side' and the 'soft side' – this structuring schema is deeply embedded in the field. The hard side comprises the natural sciences, mathematics, engineering, computer science and related subjects, while the soft side generally comprises the social sciences and humanities. Business, economics and psychology are in a somewhat ambiguous position: some firms treat these as hard side subjects, some regard them as the 'hard end' of the soft side and some treat business and economics as comprising a category of their own ('B & E'). The hard side–soft side distinction has a long history in the textbook industry. It was formally institutionalized by Prentice Hall many years ago when it divided its sales force into hard side and soft side, thereby acknowledging that there were systematic differences between these broad clusters of disciplines. On the hard side, most of the courses students take – especially in the early stages of the curriculum – are required. Students tend to be more motivated to buy textbooks, and more motivated to hold on to them when they are part of a career trajectory (as in engineering or pre-med, for example). Hence sell-through tends to be relatively high, the price thresholds are high and sell-back into the used book market tends to be somewhat lower than in soft side subjects. On the soft side, many courses are elective – that is, students take them to fulfil a *generic* requirement. Hence students are less likely to use the textbook later in their career, and more likely to sell it as soon as they can (or to try to get by without one).

The prices of textbooks in many soft side subjects tend to be significantly lower than they are in hard side subjects. It's not uncommon for a first-year or second-year textbook in biology or physics to cost between $100 and $120 or even more, but a first-year textbook in literature, English composition or history might cost between $30 and $50 – between a third and half the price of a first-year textbook in a hard side subject. What explains this large price differential between hard side and soft side textbooks? Are the books less elaborate in terms of their production quality and less expensive to produce? Not necessarily – some of the anthologies are very large and carry high permission fees, some of the English composition textbooks and history textbooks are printed in four colours and heavily illustrated, some come with elaborate packages and so on. In fact, it's not easy to explain the difference – when asked about this, many people who have spent their lives working in the industry will shrug their shoulders and say they have no idea what accounts for it. So how can we explain it?

There are perhaps three factors that underpin this price differential. One factor is that pricing in the textbook business tends to be parity pricing. The first thing any editor or manager does before they set the price of a textbook is to check the prices of the competing textbooks, and they try to set the price of their textbook at the same level. 'There's a book called Follett's blue book,' explained one textbook editor, 'and it basically gives you the price of every competing text, and that's the first thing an editor does to price the book: what are my competitors pricing this book at?' So prices tend to be fixed in relation to the norms which operate in specific textbook fields – the price of English composition textbooks tends to be fixed in relation to the price norms of English composition textbooks, the price of American history textbooks tends to be fixed in relation to the price norms of American history textbooks and so on – and these norms are not generalizable across textbook fields.

The second factor that underpins the price differential is that students in the humanities and softer social sciences are often expected to buy more than one book. For example, a student taking a history course may be expected to buy four or five trade paperback books in addition to, or perhaps instead of, a core textbook on Western civilization or American history. There is an understanding within the industry that the prices of books aimed at the lower levels of the curriculum in some soft side subjects have to be lower in order to allow for the fact that students may be required to buy more than one book. This contrasts with subjects like economics and psychology where professors tend to use big textbooks at the introductory level and to require students to buy only these textbooks. The result is that it's very difficult for a publisher to get anywhere with a book that is intended to be supplementary reading for students taking intro economics or intro psych. 'I can't tell you how often we see proposals from authors who would like to write a really interesting book that might be used as a paperback alongside an introductory textbook in economics or psychology,' explained one textbook publisher:

> We can't publish those things, we just can't make them work, because teachers are aware that their students have just plonked down $80 or $100 for the textbook and they are on the whole unwilling to ask them to plonk down another $10 or $15 in order to buy a paperback to accompany it. And if there are really interesting trends, we textbook publishers are going to start incorporating some of those themes. So I think it's increasingly a challenge even to get extra reading onto a list with a big fat textbook.

The third factor that underpins the price differential is that soft side professors tend to be more price conscious, and they take more account of the prices of textbooks when they make their adoption decisions. So while in general it is accurate to say that the adoption system tends to generate a form of non-price competition between textbook publishers, this generalization has to be qualified when it comes to certain soft side subjects like English and history, where price tends to play a more significant role in adoption decisions. One managing director put it like this:

> English teachers and history teachers are much better at asking us what the price of our textbook is and making that part of their textbook decision. Because they like to buy lots of books is my theory, and so they know what it is to go into a bookstore and to think about, at the end of buying four books or six books or eight books, how much money am I paying at the cash register.

By contrast, in subjects like economics, there has traditionally been very little incentive to keep prices down:

> It's always interested me that economists, who believe in competitive marketplaces, just assume that the prices of all textbooks must be the same. We used to try to price our books 15 per cent cheaper than the competition and use that as a sales point and the professors

thought there was something wrong with our book. Why are we selling the book so cheaply? There must be something wrong with it. And so there came to be very little incentive for us to mark down the prices on these books.

The fact that price tends to play a more significant role in adoption decisions in soft side subjects like English and history produces a downward pressure on the prices of textbooks in these subjects which – at least up till now – has not existed in hard side subjects like economics, psychology, engineering and the natural sciences.

Partly as a result of the price differential, hard side textbook publishing tends to be more profitable than soft side publishing. You can get big adoptions in subjects like English and history, but you can't charge as much for the textbooks and hence these tend to be relatively low-profit fields compared to hard side subjects like economics, physics, chemistry and maths.

The BYTES study

The fact that teaching practices vary across the disciplines means that, while the big textbook publishers tend to dominate the market for content provision at the lower levels of the curriculum in hard side subjects, the sources of the content used for teaching in soft side subjects tend to be more diverse. This was brought out very clearly by an interesting recent study called 'BYTES' – 'Books You Teach Every Semester'.[2] The study, which was funded by the Andrew W. Mellon Foundation, set out to examine which books were being put on the reserve reading lists in libraries during two academic terms in 2000 for history and English literature at nine colleges that were part of the NorthEast Research Libraries consortium (NERL). Reserve reading lists are made up of selections of books and articles which professors teaching particular courses have assigned to their students and have asked the library to hold in a reserve section, so that they can be used by students in the library and, in some cases, borrowed on a short-loan basis; putting this material on a reserve list helps to ensure that it will be available to all students taking the course. The colleges involved in the BYTES study were Columbia, Cornell, Dartmouth, Harvard, NYU, Syracuse, University of Connecticut, University of Massachusetts (Amherst) and Yale. The main purpose of the study was to see how much overlap there was in the readings that were being assigned at different colleges, and to consider the implications of this for the ways that libraries manage their resources. There was an electronic agenda here too. For if it emerged that there was a core set of texts that were regularly used for teaching purposes across different institutions, this could have implications for the ways in which libraries think about their digital strategy: making high use texts available in electronic formats could turn out to be a more effective way of meeting the pedagogical needs of students and professors.

In total they examined 972 courses (60 per cent history, 40 per cent English). They found that nearly 13,000 books published by 375 different publishers were put on

[2] Ann Okerson, 'Wanted: A Model for E-Reserves', *Library Journal*, 126/14 (Sept. 2001), pp. 56–9. For the full report, see www.library.yale.edu/~okerson/BYTESFinal070401.PDF. The data in the article differ slightly from the data in the full report; here I've used the data from the published article.

reserve for these courses in these nine schools during 2000. But the top 51 publishers (that is, less than 15 per cent of the total) accounted for two-thirds (65.5 per cent) of the total number of books. Who were these publishers? Which publishers dominated the list? Somewhat surprisingly, they weren't the big textbook publishers – they were the university presses. Of the top ten publishers with most titles on the reserve lists, eight were university presses (see table 9.3). Oxford University Press was first with 743 titles, Cambridge was second with 428 titles, Harvard was third with 333 titles. The only publishers who were not university presses in the top ten were Penguin (ranked fourth) and Norton (ranked tenth). Of the 41 publishers with 50 or more titles in the collections, university presses accounted for 3,574 titles (58 per cent of the total) and non-university presses accounted for 2,569 titles (42 per cent). Overall, books published by British and American university presses accounted for two-thirds of the assigned readings.

Of course, one must be careful about the conclusions one draws from this study. It was a limited piece of research that focused on the reserve reading lists in two humanities subjects at nine Northeastern universities. Reserve reading lists tend to emphasize secondary literature rather than original works; they are more likely to comprise supplementary texts that students are asked to read – a chapter in a book by a literary critic, for example – rather than original works of literature which students may be expected to buy in paperback, or rather than textbooks or anthologies which are adopted as the required text for a course and which, again, students may be expected to buy. The BYTES study does *not* show which publishers are most successful in publishing the books which are adopted as *required* texts for courses in history and literature and which students are expected to *buy*. To ascertain this, one would have to study the syllabuses for the courses rather than the reserve lists of the libraries, and this was not the remit of the BYTES study. On the other hand, the study does show that, in subjects like history and literature, the university presses make a major contribution to the material that professors actually use in their teaching and want their students to read, even if this material is not what we might conventionally think of as a 'textbook'.

The latter point is important. Our thinking about textbooks tends to be shaped by the model of the large, comprehensive textbook which covers all aspects of the subject in a cumulative fashion, designed in such a way that one chapter can be used in class one week and the following chapter can be used the next week – what I've called the 'core textbook'. Textbooks of this kind clearly have an important role to play in many subjects, especially but by no means exclusively at the lower levels of the curriculum. But it is also clear that in many subjects (especially in the humanities and softer social sciences) and at different levels of the curriculum (lower levels as well as upper levels), there are many professors who wish to use other kinds of books, as well as other kinds of teaching materials such as journal articles, newspaper articles, movies, video clips and documents of various kinds, in their classroom teaching. These other kinds of books are not 'textbooks' in the sense of the large, comprehensive textbook which covers all the main topics. Rather, they may be short introductory books on more specialized topics or themes; they may be seminal works and/or works by highly regarded scholars, such as Edward Said's *Orientalism* or Carole Gilligan's *In a Different Voice*, which are regarded by academics as path-breaking contributions to the field; they may be trade paperbacks which are written in a lively and engaging way, like Jared Diamond's *Guns, Germs, and Steel*; they may even be more specialized works of scholarship, such as case

Table 9.3 Publishers of fifty or more titles in the BYTES study, 2000

Rank	Publisher	Titles
1	Oxford University Press	743
2	Cambridge University Press	428
3	Harvard University Press	333
4	Penguin	330
5	University of California Press	309
6	Princeton University Press	272
7	University of Chicago Press	240
8	Cornell University Press	216
9	Yale University Press	215
10	Norton	214
11	Routledge	199
12	HarperCollins	158
13	St Martin's Press	153
14	Johns Hopkins University Press	133
15	Knopf	132
16	Vintage	130
17	Random House	121
18	Longman	109
19	Macmillan	109
20	University of North Carolina Press	99
21	Stanford University Press	98
22	Doubleday	98
23	Indiana University Press	95
24	Houghton Mifflin	92
25	Blackwell	90
26	Columbia University Press	88
27	Prentice Hall	86
28	Viking	84
29	University of Wisconsin Press	71
30	Scribner	64
31	University of Illinois Press	63
32	Basic Books	63
33	Duke University Press	62
34	Harcourt	61
35	Pantheon	60
36	Rutgers University Press	59
37	Methuen	57
38	McGraw-Hill	56
39	Little, Brown	53
40	Hill & Wang	50
41	New York University Press	50

Total number of titles = 6,143

Source: Reprinted with permission from *Library Journal*, 126/14 (Sept. 2001), a Reed Business Publication.

studies or books based on fieldwork and original research. As one university press editor, discussing the ways in which some of her anthropology books were being used in courses, explained, 'they're not textbooks in the standard use of the word but then so many people are eschewing textbooks. They would so much rather use other things. They're assigning movies, they're assigning books – things that will captivate their students, kids who have grown up in a television culture.'

These books are not standard textbooks but in the humanities and the softer social sciences (and sometimes in subjects like economics and business too) they are being adopted by professors and used in teaching at different levels of the curriculum, from the first-year introductory courses right up to graduate level. I shall use the term 'course-book' to describe these books – 'a book to be used in courses', as the same editor put it. In some cases they are being used *in addition to* a core textbook; the professor will adopt a core textbook and will also assign a number of other books and materials to enrich and broaden the learning experience. Hence they are sometimes described as 'supplementary' or 'supplemental' course adoptions. A coursebook in this sense doesn't necessarily try to map the content of a whole course on a chapter-by-chapter basis, as a core textbook does; rather, it can be a provocative and engaging text which will get students thinking and provide a good basis for discussion in class. From the publisher's point of view, the key issue is whether these additional books are *required* reading or merely *recommended*. If a book is required reading, students are much more likely to buy it and the adoption is much more likely to translate into sales. Bookstores will order accordingly: if a book is required reading, they will generally assume that a fairly high proportion of the students taking the course will buy the book and they will want to ensure that they have sufficient stock, either in new or used books, whereas they may stock only a handful of copies of a book that is merely recommended.

While in many cases coursebooks are used in addition to a core textbook, especially at the lower levels of the curriculum, there are other cases where professors eschew core textbooks altogether and build their courses around books and other materials which are more specialized in character. In a literature course, for example, they may use a selection of primary texts instead of an anthology (the equivalent of a textbook in literature) and they may require students to read a few books (or chapters of books) by key critics and commentators. In a history or a political science course, the professor may assign half a dozen books – a mixture of trade paperbacks and more scholarly works. In an anthropology course, the professor might require the students to read two or three key books based on fieldwork in addition to other things. These teaching practices vary from subject to subject, from institution to institution and from professor to professor, but they are more common in the humanities and the softer social sciences (and, of course, more common at the upper levels of the curriculum, though not restricted to the upper levels). There are many professors, especially in the humanities and the softer social sciences, who are sceptical of the value of the big, comprehensive textbooks and prefer to use materials which they feel provide their students with a richer and more engaging learning experience. 'Many are just not using textbooks at all,' commented the same university press editor. 'They're constructing their courses around monographs like this,' she said, pointing to an anthropological study based on fieldwork.

One of the motivations behind the BYTES study was to see whether there was a sufficient degree of overlap among the reserve lists in different university libraries to make

Table 9.4 Overlap of titles across schools in the BYTES study, 2000

Number of schools	Distinct titles	Total volumes
6	11	66
5	16	80
4	65	260
3	198	594
2	829	1,658
1	10,275	10,275
		Total volumes = 12,933

Source: Reprinted with permission from *Library Journal*, 126/14 (Sept. 2001), a Reed Business Publication.

a plausible case for creating electronic collections of frequently used books. The study revealed that there was a high degree of customization and individuality in the teaching of fairly standard undergraduate courses in history and literature – professors tended to have their own preferred texts which they used in their teaching. At the same time, the researchers found that there was a degree of overlap around certain authors and books. Seven of the nine schools had 17 titles by two authors (Shakespeare and Edward Said) on reserve; six schools had 59 works by four authors on reserve; five schools had 45 works by 13 authors on reserve; four schools had 164 titles by 47 authors on reserve; and so on.[3] Books by certain key authors frequently appear in the reserve lists – not only Shakespeare and Said, but also Harold Bloom, M. H. Abrams and Peter Brown. There was also a certain amount of overlap of titles across the schools, as table 9.4 shows. So, for example, 198 titles were on reserve at three of the nine schools, 65 titles were on reserve at four schools, 16 at five schools and 11 at six schools. The vast majority of titles (nearly 80 per cent) were on reserve at only one school during the two terms of the study, which attests to the high degree of customization involved in the teaching of history and literature at these schools. But the fact that there was some degree of overlap, especially with certain well-known authors and texts, does lend support to the view that, even in subjects like history and literature, there is some scope for the idea of creating electronic reserve collections, an idea advocated by the authors of the BYTES study. We shall return to this issue in chapter 14.

University presses in the field of higher education publishing

It's clear from the BYTES study (among other things) that university presses are producing books which are used for teaching purposes in colleges and universities, but to what extent do the university presses see themselves as active players in the field of higher education publishing? We have seen how, with the growing difficulties in the scholarly monograph market, many university presses migrated further into the field of

---

[3] Okerson, 'Wanted: A Model for E-Reserves', p. 57.

higher education publishing and sought increasingly to publish books which would secure adoptions on courses at both the undergraduate and graduate levels. Hence they were moving increasingly into territory that the commercial textbook publishers had claimed as their own. Were the university presses seeking to compete head-on with the commercial textbook publishers? How could they possibly win adoption struggles when their adversaries were able to send college travellers from campus to campus and were prepared to spend tens of thousands of dollars on ancillaries of various kinds?

The answer to these questions is that, for the most part, the university presses and the commercial textbook publishers did not compete directly with one another but tended to migrate into different sectors of the field. As the escalating costs of the package wars pushed the big textbook publishers down the curriculum, forcing them to devote more and more of their efforts to developing textbooks for the large freshman and sophomore courses in those subjects where the use of core textbooks was an accepted pedagogical practice, opportunities opened up at higher levels of the curriculum and in certain subjects for other publishers to provide materials which could be used in teaching. The university presses migrated into those levels of the curriculum that had been vacated by the commercial textbook publishers, that had become less of a priority for them or, indeed, that had never been their primary concern. The publishing programmes of the university presses (with a few exceptions) also tended to lean towards the humanities and the softer social sciences and towards interdisciplinary subjects like gender studies, ethnic studies and cultural studies where professors were less inclined to use standardized textbooks and more inclined to use other kinds of books and materials in the classroom.

With the partial exception of Oxford University Press, the university presses have never been conventional textbook publishers in North America. OUP is a partial exception because it has had a college division based in its New York office for a number of years. The division ran into financial difficulties in the 1980s, at which time OUP disbanded the college rep force and effectively closed down the division; in the mid-1990s the college division was started up again but without a college rep force. In those subject areas where OUP's college division is active, it publishes a number of texts which have the look and feel of a conventional core textbook, including four- or five-colour printing and packages of supplementary material. OUP is more like a textbook publisher than the other university presses but, even so, it is a small player in the field of textbook publishing. The textbooks it publishes are aimed mainly at the upper levels of the curriculum and it rarely competes directly with the big textbook publishers at the lower levels of the curriculum. OUP and the other university presses do not have the size and the resources to compete seriously in the core textbook market. They simply cannot afford to compete in a market where advances can reach $1 million, where the cost of packages can reach $250,000 and the costs of developing and producing the textbooks themselves can be very high, and where winning the big adoptions requires substantial investment in a dedicated sales force. They have tended instead to concentrate their efforts on publishing books which have adoption potential but which are not developed, designed and produced in the manner of core textbooks, and which do not require the same scale of investment. The university presses are able to do this with a degree of success because of (a) the level of the curriculum for which they seek to publish adoptable books, and (b) the subject areas in which they have tended to concentrate their activities. Let us briefly consider each of these factors.

Level of the curriculum   To the extent that the university presses are publishing books which are adopted for teaching purposes, it is primarily the upper levels of the under-graduate curriculum – the junior and senior years – and the graduate level where their books are being used. There are some subjects in the humanities and softer social sci-ences where university press books are occasionally adopted at the lower levels, as sup-plementary coursebooks for example, but this is rare; for the most part, their books are used at the upper levels of the curriculum. Adoptions at these levels are likely to gen-erate sales which would be regarded as quite satisfactory for most university presses, although they would in many cases be too low for the big textbook publishers. While many of the textbook publishers do publish texts for the upper levels of the curriculum, these upper-level texts do not usually receive the same degree of investment as the core textbooks aimed at the first and second years, nor are they generally given the same degree of attention by the college reps when they do their campus calling. Hence the upper-level texts published by the textbook publishers don't get marketed all that effectively; their sales and marketing operations are overwhelmingly oriented to the freshman and sophomore courses where the big numbers are, and the marketing of the upper-level texts tends to be hit-and-miss.

Subject areas   For reasons we examined in an earlier chapter, the university presses tend to publish in a wide range of subject areas. This is particularly true of OUP and CUP, which publish scholarly monographs in most academic subject areas from the humanities to the natural sciences. Nevertheless, apart from OUP, CUP and one or two of the American university presses, the university presses as a whole tend to be oriented particularly strongly to the humanities and the softer social sciences – to history, litera-ture, philosophy, theology, classics, sociology, anthropology, political science and a host of interdisciplinary subject areas such as gender studies, film studies, media and cultural studies, ethnic studies, environmental studies, etc. These are subject areas which tend to be less dominated by the big core textbooks, and where professors are more inclined to use a variety of different materials for teaching. In many of these subject areas, profes-sors will often put together their own courses rather than relying on a core textbook to define the syllabus of the course. Hence they will be more inclined to require their stu-dents to read a variety of books or chapters, including the kinds of books published by the university presses. So there are real opportunities in these subject areas for univer-sity presses to publish books which will be adopted for course use, mainly at the upper levels of the curriculum but even at lower levels in those cases where professors want their students to read paperbacks instead of, or in addition to, a core textbook.

　　Why have the university presses – especially the American university presses – tended to focus their efforts in the humanities and the softer social sciences? This is largely explained by two factors. The first factor is the historical interconnection of the university presses with the tenure system at American universities. It is primarily in the humanities and the softer social sciences where monographs – often based on Ph.D. theses – have served as key credentials in the tenure system. Hence there has been a substan-tial and increasing flow of scholarly content in these disciplines which has been available for university presses to publish, and an eagerness on the part of authors to publish schol-arly content in this form. The situation in the natural sciences and in subjects like math-ematics, economics and psychology has always been different, because these are subjects where the publication of papers in high-standing scholarly journals has tended to be more important for an individual's career than the publication of a scholarly monograph. The second factor that explains the disciplinary bias of the university presses is that many of their editors come out of the humanities and softer social sciences. Many are majors in English or history and they have an inclination to publish in areas with which they are familiar and comfortable intellectually. New editorial appointments also tend to have a background in the humanities and softer social sciences, and hence the disciplinary emphasis of the publishing programmes is reproduced over time.

Apart from OUP and CUP, there are a small number of the American university presses which have tried to break from the traditional emphasis on the humanities and softer social sciences and to develop programmes in economics and the sciences. As we saw in chapter 5, MIT Press was one of the university presses which moved in this direction in the late 1970s, axing some of its lists in the humanities and softer social sciences and developing programmes in economics, cognitive science, computer science, architecture and several other fields. More recently, Princeton University Press has also begun to develop its publishing programmes in economics and natural science, and Stanford University Press has launched a new list in business and professional publishing. Both MIT and Princeton have sought to publish textbooks and trade books as well as monographs in economics and natural science, but on the whole the textbooks they are publishing are pitched at a higher level of the curriculum than the level at which the commercial textbook publishers are aiming. Nevertheless, the more that some university presses move into subject areas like economics and seek to publish upper-level textbooks, the more likely it is that they will find themselves competing with the commercial textbook publishers, even if in practice this is relatively rare. As one commercial textbook publisher who is active in economics observed,

> We overlap a bit with the university presses and occasionally compete with them for textbooks, but they don't really come down into our bread and butter, which is the first, second, third year courses. By the time you get into that second course in econometrics or something like that, we commercial publishers might be just as willing to let a university press have the book if they think they can make something of it. And so the occasions when we've had overlapping interests have been rare.

So while both the commercial textbook publishers and the university presses are providing content for university teaching, they tend to occupy different regions of the field of higher education publishing. On the one hand, the conglomeratization within the world of textbook publishing and the competitive logic of the field has forced the big commercial players to concentrate their efforts on the lower levels of the curriculum, and above all on the big freshman courses and the gateway courses of the sophomore year. The downward pressure on the commercial textbook publishers creates opportunities for the university presses and other smaller commercial publishers to publish books that can be used for teaching purposes at the upper levels of the curriculum. At these levels the numbers tend to be too small for the big commercial textbook publishers to justify extensive development and dedicated sales and marketing, but for the university presses the numbers will look very attractive compared to their normal monograph sales. On the other hand, the American university presses have traditionally had very weak publishing programmes in those subject areas which are particularly important for the major textbook publishers, namely the hard side subjects like economics, psychology, the natural sciences, engineering and mathematics. Where the textbook publishers and the university presses do find themselves publishing in similar fields – in soft side subjects like history, literature, sociology, anthropology and political science and in some hard side subjects like economics – they are generally publishing different kinds of books and they are generally operating at different levels of the curriculum. So while the university presses and the commercial textbook publishers are both operating in the field of higher education publishing, they seldom find themselves competing directly with one another, either in the struggle to sign up authors or in the struggle to win adoptions. The main competitors for the university presses tend to be other university presses, and the commercial textbook publishers are most often competing against one another.

In addition to occupying different regions in the field of higher education publishing, the university presses and the commercial textbook publishers tend to operate in very different ways. The activities of the commercial textbook publishers have traditionally been shaped very strongly by the adoption system, and their textbook commissioning and development are closely geared to the aims of winning over the gatekeepers in the struggle for adoptions. Hence, in the big textbook publishing firms, acquisitions editors are generally recruited from the pool of college travellers: rising through the ranks of the sales force is the traditional pathway for promotion into editorial jobs. The activities of the university presses, on the other hand, have tended to be shaped by the concerns and procedures of scholarly publishing, which have gradually been supplemented and modified by some university presses as they have sought to give greater emphasis to higher education publishing. The recruitment path into editorial jobs in the university presses tends to be determined more by academic credentials than by sales experience: an editor in a university press is more likely to have a higher degree and to have been recruited out of college as an editorial assistant, rather than to have begun their career in publishing as a sales rep. The working methods and procedures used within these two types of organization also tend to be very different. We can see this by looking briefly at two areas: (a) content acquisition and development, and (b) sales and marketing.

Content acquisition and development   We have seen how the university presses have become more proactive in their commissioning in recent years, and how some have set in place internal systems to encourage editors to think more systematically about their acquisition priorities. Nevertheless these internal systems tend to be more relaxed and informal than the appraisal systems used by the commercial textbook publishers. The commercial textbook publishers place much greater emphasis on acquiring core textbooks with high revenue-generating potential, and acquisitions editors tend to be focused exclusively on this task. Their commissioning targets are revenue-based. For example, an editor at a major textbook publisher may be expected to sign each year textbooks that will generate between $1 million and $2 million of sales in their first year, and a good textbook editor may succeed in meeting these targets by signing a small number of core textbooks. An editor at a university press, by contrast, is generally expected to sign a variety of different kinds of books – some monographs, some trade or academic-trade books and some textbooks or coursebooks, perhaps some reference works too. They have a much more varied remit and are much less focused on the task of signing textbooks; and when they do seek to sign books aimed at course adoption, these are very rarely the kind of core textbooks that are sought after by the editor at a commercial textbook firm.

The commercial textbook publishers are able and willing to pay large advances for major new textbooks, and this is not something that the university presses are able to do. In highly competitive fields like economics and psychology, six-figure advances are relatively common; the university presses are simply not in a position to offer advances of this kind. Some of the larger university presses have been willing to offer advances in the tens of thousands for upper-level textbooks, but this still leaves them well below the levels which the commercial textbook publishers are able and willing to pay for core textbooks aimed at the lower levels of the curriculum.

The books published by the university presses do not generally undergo the same kind of development process as the textbooks published by the commercial textbook publishers – this is perhaps where the greatest differences lie. The commercial textbook publishers have a very clear sense of what they are doing: they are seeking to commission and develop textbooks that will be tailored to courses where the numbers are relatively large and that will be adopted by the professors – the gatekeepers – who teach these courses. Hence they invest a great deal of time, effort and expense in the development process – in extensive reviewing of chapters, in adding illustrative content and pedagogical features, in designing the text so that it is attractive and user-friendly, in developing companion websites and a welter of ancillaries aimed at facilitating use and at winning the adoption struggles. The development process is absolutely central to the editorial activities of the textbook publishers – it is one of the areas where they are able to add real value. All the major textbook publishers will employ development editors or even teams of editors who are dedicated to the task of developing the content of a new textbook or a new edition of a textbook, and who will work closely with IT staff to ensure that the development process is integrated with the production of ancillaries, companion websites, etc.

For the most part, the university presses are not accustomed to engaging in this kind of intensive development process. The university presses always review proposals and manuscripts before deciding whether to contract and/or publish them, and it has become increasingly common for editors to ask their external readers to address the question of whether the project under review would have course adoption potential – and, if so, at what level, for what courses, whether it would be required or recommended reading and so on. This feedback may be passed on to authors with a view to helping them revise the text, but this is nothing like the kind of intensive development process typically followed by the big textbook publishers. The university presses tend to see themselves as publishing high-quality books which may have adoption potential, rather than as publishing textbooks which are conceived of, developed and designed *as* textbooks. They don't see their books as having to compete for adoptions against other books, and hence they don't see the need to develop them in ways that will enable them to win out in the struggle for adoptions. As one university press editor put it, 'we don't think of our books as textbooks but as books to be used in courses. There's a development in textbooks that we tend not to do.' In other words, most university press editors see themselves as publishing what I've called coursebooks or supplementary (or supplemental) texts, not textbooks in the sense that this term is understood by the commercial textbook publishers, with all of the development and editorial input that this involves.

This is not true of all university presses. There are a few university presses that do see themselves as publishing textbooks in the same sense as the commercial textbook publishers, the only difference being that the university press's textbooks are generally aimed at the upper-level courses. These tend to be the larger university presses, and often they are presses where the director and/or some of the senior editors were once employed by the commercial textbook publishers and are therefore familiar with the methods used by them. Their background in the world of textbook publishing gives them an insider's knowledge of the workings of an industry about which most university press editors know relatively little. But these are the exceptions rather than the rule. For the most part, the university presses are not accustomed to investing substantial time and resources in the development of textbooks and, for the most part, they lack the expertise, the support systems and, indeed, the inclination to do so.[4] This is simply not a set of practices with which they are familiar and comfortable and towards which their editorial systems are geared.

Sales and marketing   The practices of the university presses and the big commercial textbook publishers also contrast sharply in the area of sales and marketing. The textbook publishers have traditionally relied on their sales forces of college reps who travel from campus to campus and call on the professors to try to persuade them to adopt their textbooks. In the case of the largest textbook publishers, these sales forces today number up to 400 reps, who between them cover all the major campuses across the country. The smaller textbook publishers will have fewer reps and will concentrate their efforts on certain regions and institutions – the Northeast, the West Coast (especially California), the 'big ten' of the Midwest and so on. However, it is very costly to maintain sales forces of this kind, and it is manageable financially only if the organization is relatively large and can carry substantial overheads of this kind, and only if it is concentrating its efforts on securing adoptions for core textbooks aimed at the first- and second-year courses.

The university presses, by contrast, do not use college reps to sell their textbooks. Like the commercial textbook publishers, the university presses work within the adoption system – that is, in so far as they are seeking to publish books which they believe to have adoption potential, they market these books to professors and hope that they will adopt them for their courses. But they use a variety of means to try to reach these professors without actually visiting them in their offices on the campuses. They attend academic conferences, where they display their books and distribute promotional material; they produce catalogues and leaflets of various kinds which are mailed directly to professors; they use various kinds of e-marketing; and they send out examination copies of books that are requested by professors. The aim is to produce an outcome similar to that achieved by the textbook publishers – namely, to secure adoptions – but without the expense involved in maintaining a sales force of college reps.

Most of the university presses do have sales reps (either their own or shared between several presses) who call on their major retail accounts, including both the major independent bookstores and the retail chains, but most are not in a position to maintain

---

[4] 'I've always felt that that is what a textbook editor does and that we are not textbook editors,' explained a senior editor at one of the larger American university press. 'It feels like it's formulaic, it's cookie-cutter. We are still editors that are trying to publish either original research or original and exciting syntheses of past research and to a certain degree the unique mind of that individual who is writing the book is going to provide the frame that is compelling enough that somebody is going to say, yes, I want to do this.'

even a small sales force of college reps. They simply don't have a sufficient number of low-level, high-selling textbooks to justify the level of expenditure that would be involved. However, some of the larger university presses are considering ways in which they might be able to do a limited amount of campus calling to improve their chances of securing adoptions – for instance, by asking their existing sales reps to shift the balance of their work so that they call on some professors as well as visiting bookstores. Some are also experimenting with the use of telemarketing, contacting professors by telephone and telling them about their textbooks. This may be more effective than direct mail because there is a degree of live interaction, but it is undoubtedly less effective than the kind of face-to-face interaction that takes place when the college rep calls on a professor in his or her office and takes them through the features of a textbook and its package.

While the field of higher education publishing has become increasingly important for the university presses, in some respects their systems and editorial approach are not well adjusted to the demands of this field and to the conditions of success within it. They tend to draw their publishing models more from the fields of academic publishing and, in some cases, trade publishing, and they are not always aware of the factors that matter greatly in the field of higher education publishing. Some bookstore managers complain, for example, that the university presses are very poor at delivering adopted books when they are needed – namely, at the start of the academic year, when students are begin-ning their courses and need to buy their textbooks. As the manager of one big college bookstore observed,

> The university presses have big problems. They can't deliver the product. They're used to delivering the product when they get around to delivering the product. If you're going to be in the textbook business and classes start on September 4th, the product has to be there on September 4th, and they're not good at it. They're very, very poor at it. And they're getting worse. We've had real problems with the university presses not getting it.

The commercial textbook publishers know very well when their textbooks and new edi-tions have to be published and when their stock has to be in the bookstores, and their systems – editorial, production and distribution – are well geared to ensure that these deadlines are met. The university presses, by contrast, tend to operate in a less concerted fashion and with less sense of urgency. They are publishing books for different fields – academic, trade and higher education – and their systems are not focused single-mindedly on the need to get their textbooks published and distributed in ways that will maximize their adoption potential and meet the needs of professors, students and booksellers.

Many in the university press world see higher education publishing as a field of untapped opportunities, and to some extent they are right to do so: as the big textbook publishers are forced by the logic of the field to concentrate more and more on the lower levels of the curriculum, there are real opportunities for the university presses and for smaller commercial publishers to publish textbooks which will meet the need for teaching materials at the upper levels of the curriculum. It is no doubt the case that the big textbook publishers will continue to take the lion's share of the revenue from the higher education market; as one senior editor put it, the university presses are like 'jackals nibbling around the edges of McGraw-Hill's feast'. But compared to the famine of academic publishing, even the leftovers look good. The university presses could do much more to take advantage of these opportunities. Relatively few university presses have invested significant time and expense in the commissioning and development of textbooks which are explicitly geared to the needs of professors and students, albeit at the upper levels of the curriculum. The university presses would also need to give more attention to the regular revision of successful texts – not just to keep them up to date but also to counter the effects of the used book market. Some university press directors and editors express surprise and alarm about the used book market and the rate of returns they experience from the college bookstores, but these are facts of life with which college textbook publishers have lived for many years. And the university presses would need to devote more of their marketing efforts to the task of securing adoptions in what is a highly competitive market for teaching materials. Given their close links to the world of higher education, the university presses are very well placed to expand their presence in the field of higher education publishing, especially at the upper levels of the curriculum. But in many ways they are held back by their rootedness in the field of academic publishing and by the attitudes, practices and mindsets that are part of that field, as well as by their limited understanding (with a few notable exceptions) of the principles and practices of higher education publishing. Small and medium-sized commercial publishers have in many cases moved more effectively into the field of higher education publishing than the university presses, partly because they are less tied to the practices and mindsets of traditional scholarly publishing.

The coursepack business

There is another aspect of the field of higher education publishing in the US that complicates the picture still further – the coursepack business. A coursepack is a collection of extracts, articles and other material, ranging from newspaper articles to course outlines and lecture notes, which a professor puts together for a specific course. The material is reproduced and sometimes bound or shrinkwrapped, and students taking the course are told to buy it. The coursepack is, in effect, an anthology of readings which is customized for a specific course on a specific campus. It is sold only to the students taking this course and has no sales potential beyond this highly localized market.

The task of assembling, reproducing and selling coursepacks is generally handled by campus-based service providers who are located on or near the campuses. Much of the business used to be done by so-called 'copy shops' – that is, by shops that provide essentially a photocopying service – but in 1991 the Association of American Publishers successfully sued Kinko's Graphics Corporation for infringement of copyright. Following the Kinko's ruling, many college bookstores and campus-based copy shops took on the role of coursepack publishers – 'custom publishing' as it is sometimes called – and became involved in copyright clearance. On some campuses, the role of coursepack production was taken on by the university itself, which set up an office to manage the assembling and selling of coursepacks for the various departments. Despite the Kinko's case, a great deal of illegal copying continues to take place, but subsequent law suits have reaffirmed the Kinko's ruling and increased the pressure on copy shops which reproduce coursepacks without clearing permissions. In 1992, Princeton University Press, Macmillan, Inc. and St Martin's Press brought a case against Michigan Documents Services, Inc., which was producing coursepacks for the University of Michigan without clearing permissions; MDS was found guilty of violating copyright law, a decision that was eventually reaffirmed by the Court of Appeals in 1996.

While the need to clear copyright and pay permissions fees added greatly to the complexity and cost of producing coursepacks, the business has continued to flourish on campuses across the United States. A study carried out in the mid-1990s estimated that total coursepack sales were more than $55 million in 1994–5 and that the volume was growing by about 30 per cent a year. The study estimated that coursepacks represented about 4 per cent of what was then a college textbook market worth $2 billion a year, and that this share was likely to increase.[5] Whereas sales in the traditional textbook business were generally flat (or growing only to the extent that prices were increasing year on year), the coursepack business was one sector of the college market that was genuinely growing. According to John Earl, director of publishing at Burgess International, Inc., a Minneapolis-based coursepack company that operates across the United States,

> Custom publishing is the only true growth segment in the college market. Traditional sales are flat or up a few points at best. It's the only part that is truly growing, and it is because:
>
> • Technology allows more on-demand publishing;
> • Students are resisting the prices of the huge textbooks, and
> • Professors want to be able to give students what they want, not extraneous material.[6]

There is a great deal of variation in the ways that coursepacks are used by professors depending on the subject, the level of the course and the personal preferences of the professor. In some cases, professors will put together a coursepack and assign it to their students *in addition to* a core textbook: students will be expected to buy both, and the coursepack will include primary material, such as documents, case studies and extracts from books and journals, that the student will not find in a textbook. In other cases, professors may structure a course around a coursepack and dispense with a textbook altogether. 'The textbook doesn't always cover everything you want,' said a sociology professor at Emory University. 'You feel bad making [the students] buy a book that can cost up to $40 or $50 if they only need to read two or three chapters. It's not a good use of their money.'[7] In fact, because of copyright fees, the cost of coursepacks is roughly comparable to the cost of textbooks. (Copyright costs represent about 60 per cent of the total cost of coursepacks, printing represents about 36 per cent and binding about 3 per cent.) But the usage rate of coursepack content is typically much higher than that of most textbooks, and hence coursepacks are perceived by many professors and students as better value for money.

New digital technologies have helped to streamline the coursepack business and make it more efficient. Some coursepack operators continue to use simple photocopy-

[5] *Custom Publishing on College Campuses: Marketing Research Report and Analysis* (Stamford, Conn.: O'Donnell & Associates, 1995), p. 5.
[6] Quoted in 'Course Packs Come of Age', *College Store Executive* (Mar. 1996), p. 12.
[7] Ibid.

ing technology, but others have digitized various aspects of the workflow, scanning texts, storing them on disk and using a digital printer to produce the coursepack. Digitization enables the coursepack operator to reduce the effort involved in preparing course-packs from one year to the next (since more than 70 per cent of material is reused) and reduce the risk of waste. Since unsold coursepacks cannot be returned to a publisher, overproduction is a serious problem for coursepack operators, a problem that is exac-erbated by the fact that the actual enrolment on many courses may not be known until after the course begins. Coursepack operators will commonly under-print and then print additional copies to meet actual demand, thereby minimizing the risk of leftovers. Digitization can also streamline some aspects of copyright clearance, which tends to be the most complex and time-consuming part of coursepack production.

One coursepack operator which uses a system of this kind is Cornell Business Services, which runs a custom publishing operation in the basement of the campus bookstore. The manager of the operation, Jim Lawrence, actively solicits requests for coursepacks from the professors on the campus and provides them with detailed instruc-tions about how to put together a coursepack, including guidelines on copyright fees and a detailed schedule to ensure that the coursepack will be available by the begin-ning of the semester. They provide coursepacks for courses at every level of the cur-riculum, from the large freshman courses to small graduate classes of only ten or fifteen students. The service began in 1989 and grew rapidly. In fall 1990 their gross sales from coursepacks were $42,000; by fall 2000 they were around $680,000, a more than sixteen-fold increase in ten years. In 2001 their gross annual sales from coursepacks were about $1.3 million; after deducting the costs of permission fees, printing, labour and operating costs, they were left with a healthy margin of around 17 per cent. Sales from course-packs represent about 14 per cent of the textbook sales in the bookstore. This does not appear to have damaged textbook sales, however, as textbook sales have increased 4–6 per cent each year since coursepacks were introduced. With no second-hand market for coursepacks (the store doesn't buy them back) and with content tailored to the course, sell-through is nearly 95 per cent of actually enrolled students – far higher than for con-ventional textbooks. By under-printing to begin with and filling additional orders by print on demand, leftovers can be kept to between 5 per cent and 10 per cent.

Coursepack operators based in campus bookstores are relatively common. Lawrence estimates that there are at least thirty other college bookstores across the country that do volumes of business comparable to Cornell, and at least two hundred college bookstores that do some level of custom publishing. However, these campus-based operators face growing competition from various players, including the big text-book publishers. McGraw-Hill launched Primis Custom Publishing in 1988, and Pearson developed its own custom publishing division around the same time. These and similar operations enable professors to design customized textbooks for their courses, which are then produced by the publisher in the quantity required by the professor and deliv-ered to a campus bookstore. We shall examine some of these initiatives in chapter 14, but for the time being it should be noted that the local coursepack operators have two key competitive advantages in relation to the publisher-based custom publishing projects. In the first place, in the case of the publisher-based projects, the material that can be used in the customized textbook is usually restricted to material for which the publisher holds the copyright. But for many professors who are trying to decide what they want their students to read, a limitation of this kind is unduly restrictive. For in many subjects, professors don't regard content as interchangeable; if they want their students to read a text by X, they don't want a publisher telling them 'we can't give you X but we can give you Y instead.' They're going to be much happier to work with a coursepack operator who is willing to clear copyright for any text that the professor wishes to include, regardless of where the text was originally published.

The second key advantage of the coursepack operators is that they are *local*. They are based on or near the campus and they have close relations with the professors they're serving. They see themselves as offering a personal service to professors and they do what they can to make things easier for them. As one coursepack operator explained,

> There is a high level of value based on personal service. When an instructor comes in with a variety of materials from magazines, books, journals, all different kinds of sources, I can basically walk them through that citation list and say, well, you can do this but you can't do that. Or this is going to cost you an arm and a leg, you don't want to do that. Now that's not the kind of service that any one publisher can provide. Wiley may not know what Prentice Hall does, or McGraw-Hill may not know that Simon & Schuster charges 20 cents a page for copyright. But this is something that a custom publisher will know since they deal with thousands of different publishers. So that's where the value is. There's a one-to-one interaction where we can resolve what can be done and what can't be done quickly so that they can get their materials published.

Coursepack operators or custom publishers are local service providers who are able to form personal relationships with the professors for whom this service is being provided. They can call on the professors and explain exactly what they need to do in order to ensure that their coursepacks contain the material they want and are available on time. If problems arise, they can get on the phone or meet face-to-face to resolve them. For busy professors who are already overloaded with commitments and demands on their time, the benefits of a local, personalized service of this kind, where the professor can hand over a set of materials that he or she would like to include in a coursepack and leave it to the operator to sort out everything else, are considerable. And this, together with the ability to include material from any source, gives the coursepack operators a real competitive advantage over the publisher-based custom publishing operations.

So despite the Kinko's ruling and the problems associated with copyright clearance, the coursepack business, and custom publishing more generally, has continued to grow in the US over the last ten years. One well-placed observer estimates that the custom publishing market in the US was worth about $600–700 million in 2004 – a twelvefold increase since 1994–5 – and was continuing to grow by around 25 per cent a year; about half of this total was accounted for by local and regional players. The legitimate coursepack operators who play by the copyright rules have found ways to streamline copyright clearance and are able to pass on the costs to the end users while still generating a healthy margin for themselves. No one knows how large the hidden economy of illegitimate coursepack production is, but those who work in the industry don't doubt that copy shops continue to thrive in college towns. 'There are, I would say, hundreds of custom publishers out there who don't ask permission. They just print. You want this? Sure. How many do you want? And they will print them out and never ask permission.' Moreover, some professors will give their students a copy of the material they want them to read and allow them to make their own copies. Whether the copies are produced by legitimate organizations which play by the copyright rules, by copy shops which are part of a hidden economy of content provision or by students themselves, the coursepack seems here to stay. It fulfils a real need in the field of higher education, enabling professors to provide students with materials that will enrich the learning experience and, indeed, to tailor the materials they use in the classroom to the ways they want to teach their courses rather than the other way around. It seems unlikely that the demand for customized pedagogical content of this kind will go away – on the contrary, the more standardized and homogenized the big textbooks become, the more likely it is that professors will want to supplement (or even, in some cases, replace) the textbook with material which matches their teaching needs more closely. The key question for the future of this activity is not whether it will continue to flourish (that seems indisputable) but rather who will provide it and how it will be transformed by the digital revolution – whether, for instance, it will give way at some stage to a web-based system of customized content provision. This is an issue to which we shall return in chapter 14.

The future of higher education publishing in the US

In this and the previous chapter I have analysed the logic of the field of higher education publishing in the US and explored some aspects of the stratification and differentiation of this field. I have tried to show that this field has a logic or dynamic that is peculiar to it, a logic that is very different from that which has characterized the field of academic publishing over the last couple of decades. I want now to draw this discussion to a close by looking to the future: how is the field of higher education publishing in the US likely to evolve in the coming years? It would of course be impossible to answer this question with any real certainty – there are too many unknown factors which could play a role in shaping the future. But let me highlight several trends which can be identified with some degree of confidence.

(1) In the first place, it seems likely that the trend towards increasing concentration in the industry will continue. There are currently three major players – Pearson, McGraw-Hill and Thomson – and a handful of others who remain serious players, including the Holtzbrinck group, Houghton Mifflin, Wiley and Norton. Most senior figures in the industry expect to see further concentration in the coming years as the smaller players struggle to keep a foothold in a market which is increasingly dominated by the large conglomerates. As one senior executive put it,

> The process is not finished because there are still some minor players that will get bought out. They will probably get bought out over the next decade, or even sooner than that because of this whole digital process. There is a lot of investment required. They can't necessarily keep up or don't have the finances to invest.

Anti-trust legislation in the US places limits on the extent to which any single publisher can be allowed to dominate in any particular field, and in some of the recent acquisitions (e.g. Thomson's acquisition of Harcourt's college division) the Department of Justice required the acquiring party to divest themselves of some titles in fields where they were judged to have excessive market share. But this still leaves the way open for the large conglomerates to acquire more lists in fields where they do not already have a dominant position, and some further concentration of this kind seems likely. So how many key players will there be in five years' time? 'It could be three or four, half a dozen on the outside,' commented one senior figure. 'That's on a global basis.'

(2) Given the size of the three majors and the importance of the blockbuster textbooks for each of them, we're likely to see intensified struggles for market share at the lower levels of the curriculum. In the big freshman and sophomore courses, it will increasingly become a battle of the titans. More and more resources will be poured into the big blockbuster textbooks – advances will continue to soar, the packages will become ever more elaborate, the incentives for winning adoptions will rise. In the big freshman and sophomore courses, market share is everything, and nothing will be spared in the struggle to win adoptions. The majors will leverage their resources – their financial resources, their technological expertise and their huge reserves of content – to offer more extensive and elaborate packages to the professors who make the adoption decisions. This doesn't mean that the smaller players will be automatically excluded from the lower levels of the curriculum, for some already have a stake in these fields with textbooks that are well known and well established. And it remains the case that winning adoptions is not just a matter of resources: it also depends on the quality of the textbook, which means that there will always be some room for smaller players to capture, retain or even increase their market share in selected areas. But in the struggles for market share at the lower levels of the curriculum, it is the big conglomerates who will increasingly define the rules of the game 'because only they can really afford it. It's a financial issue. The university presses aren't playing in that game and the little publishers are not going to survive it.'

(3) We're also likely to see greater market segmentation throughout the field. With the growth of student numbers in the two-year community colleges and the four-year state schools, the big players will increasingly target these sectors and will develop more textbooks which are specifically tailored for the needs of instructors and students in these institutions. They will develop a range of textbooks which are geared to different sectors of the market, so that they can win adoptions in each of these sectors while minimizing the extent to which they are competing against their own titles. With each title on a two- or three-year revision cycle, they can maintain a constant stream of newly revised textbooks which are in each case targeted at specific sectors of the market. At the same time, while the size of the large conglomerates and the overheads they carry force them to concentrate increasingly on the big freshman and sophomore courses, they will cede more and more ground at the upper levels of the curriculum to other players. In all likelihood they will continue to publish textbooks for those upper-level courses where the numbers are large enough to justify the investment, but these textbooks will not be their priority and they will not receive the attention and the resources that are devoted to the lower-level texts. Their ability to win the adoption struggles at the upper levels of the curriculum will be weakened by the increasing regearing of these organizations to the lower levels. This is likely to create more opportunities for smaller players and for the university presses to publish textbooks and other materials which are aimed specifically at the needs of professors and students at the junior, senior and graduate levels.

(4) These opportunities will also be created by the fact that pedagogical practices will continue to vary and there are many professors who will want to use material other than standardized textbooks in their classes. This is especially true in soft side subjects in the liberal arts colleges and the better state schools, but the wish of professors to use more varied pedagogical materials is unlikely to be restricted to these subjects and institutions. The growth of the coursepack business attests to a robust demand for a more varied diet of instructional materials. The extent to which smaller publishers and the university presses are able to cater for this demand remains to be seen. Undoubtedly they will be able to secure some adoptions for books and anthologies that are more specialized, original and idiosyncratic in character and which, for that very reason, will be preferred by some professors who want to steer clear of (or at least to provide some alternative to) the relatively bland and homogenized content of the standard textbooks. But here the smaller publishers and the university presses will also face stiff competition from the campus-based coursepack providers and other custom publishers who are able to provide professors with a product that is tailored to their individual needs.

(5) In some ways, the joker in the pack of the textbook industry is that party on whose dollars the whole industry ultimately depends – the student. As we've seen, the decision-making model which underpins the industry presupposes that students will buy the textbooks that they are told to buy by their professors, who are the gatekeepers in the marketing chain. The production of ever more elaborate textbooks and packages as a means of winning the adoption struggles is dependent on the ability to pass off the cost of developing these materials to the end users, who ultimately foot the bill for a struggle that is carried out in their name. That is precisely why many textbook publishers are so worried about what appears to be a growing problem of sell-through breakdown. If publishers begin to encounter serious resistance to prices, then the ways in which they have grown accustomed to waging their adoption struggles – ways which amount essentially to a form of non-price competition – will be called into question. If they were no longer able to increase prices routinely by 6–8 per cent a year, then their capacity to grow and achieve good margins would be threatened. Hence the problem of sell-through breakdown and price resistance is likely to be an issue of growing importance for the textbook industry in the coming years – though how serious it will become, and whether it will have any real impact on the practices of the big players, remains unclear.

(6) There can be no doubt that investment in new technologies will continue to be a high priority in the textbook industry. The principal reason for this goes back to the dynamic that lies at the very heart of the industry – namely, the struggle to win adoptions by producing ever more elaborate textbooks and packages. It would be misleading to say that the textbook industry is driven by technology, but it would be right to say that the dynamic that drives the industry is one that lends itself splendidly to technological innovation. The more elaborate and sophisticated the package you can offer to professors is, the better your chances are of winning the key adoption struggles. There may well be other ways – perhaps more profound ways – in which the digital revolution will transform the field of higher education publishing, and the big players have invested large sums of money in trying to figure out how this might happen (we shall examine this issue in more depth in chapter 14). But regardless of whether there is eventually some more radical transformation in the ways in which pedagogical content is delivered and used, the dynamic that

lies at the heart of the textbook industry will compel those publishers who want to compete at the lower levels of the curriculum to invest more and more in new technologies in order to remain serious players in the adoption struggles. Investment in new technologies is not a matter of choice: it is a condition of playing the game.

(7) As competition between the major players intensifies at the lower levels of the curriculum in the US, we're also likely to see the major players increasing their efforts to expand in markets outside the US. Given the sheer size of the US market and the prices they are able to charge, the US will remain the priority for them, but the majors will seek to increase their opportunities to expand in other markets as well, either by exporting products originally developed for the US market or by acquiring and/or expanding indigenous operations overseas. This process is already well underway and has been so for some time. Why global expansion is an attractive proposition for the large textbook publishers and how it tends to occur are questions which we shall address in chapter 11.

10

Higher education publishing in the UK

Higher education publishing is a field that varies significantly from one national context to another. There are, in fact, many different fields of higher education publishing, each situated in a particular national context and shaped by the institutions and practices of higher education in the country concerned. There is of course some overlap between these national fields, especially where there is a common language and where the content of courses is relatively independent of social and cultural contexts (as it is, for example, in subjects like mathematics, computing, engineering and the natural sciences). But even where there is a significant degree of overlap, the fields will always be differentiated by variations in curricula, pedagogical practices, student needs and methods of assessment, among other things.

In this and the following chapter, I want to examine the field of higher education publishing in the United Kingdom. In certain respects, my analysis of the nature of higher education publishing in the US applies equally well to the UK – the basic principles of the adoption system, for example, are just as valid in the UK as they are in the US. But in practice and in detail there are many differences, and I shall begin by examining the most important of these. Thanks to these differences, the field of higher education publishing in the UK has evolved in different ways from the US – in other words, the logic of the field is different. Whether higher education publishing in the UK is likely to move increasingly in the direction of the US, and in some ways to replicate the processes we highlighted in previous chapters, is one of the questions to which we shall return.

Differences between the fields of higher education publishing in the UK and the US

The fact that Britain and the United States share the same language means that there is considerable overlap between the British and American fields of higher education publishing, and indeed many of the same publishers are active on both sides of the Atlantic. But there are important differences too. Let me highlight five: (1) size, (2) pedagogical cultures, (3) used book market, (4) multiplicity of players at lower levels of the curriculum, and (5) marketing methods.

(1) *Size*   The most significant difference between the UK and the US fields of higher education publishing is the sheer size of the markets. The UK has traditionally had a relatively small higher education sector. Up until 1963, there were only twenty-four universities in the UK with a total of 120,000 students, 15 per cent of whom were at Oxford or Cambridge. The Robbins Committee, established in the 1960s, recommended a

Table 10.1 Students in universities in the UK, 1975/76 to 1993/94

	Full-time undergraduates	Full-time postgraduates	Total full-time	Total (including part-time)
1975/76	218,088	50,626	268,714	295,031
1976/77	228,269	51,052	279,321	306,658
1977/78	238,461	49,674	288,135	316,814
1978/79	245,933	49,990	295,923	325,476
1979/80	251,990	48,536	300,526	331,938
1980/81	258,175	48,439	306,614	339,325
1981/82	260,720	47,674	308,394	343,007
1982/83	257,733	46,232	303,965	338,907
1983/84	252,238	48,355	300,593	336,912
1984/85	254,819	50,189	305,008	345,760
1985/86	256,340	53,805	310,145	352,419
1986/87	260,091	56,199	316,290	360,809
1987/88	264,803	56,117	320,920	366,982
1988/89	275,193	58,354	333,547	383,644
1989/90	290,285	60,696	350,981	404,831
1990/91	304,972	65,282	370,254	428,858
1991/92	328,078	73,579	401,657	468,095
1992/93	357,127	78,490	435,617	511,123
1993/94	385,460	85,105	470,565	553,881

Source: Universities' Statistical Record, 1975/76–1993/94: Continuing Education (Colchester, Essex: UK Data Archive, March 1997); SN: 3501. The UK Data Archive cannot accept responsibility for any conclusions or inferences derived from the data by third parties.

massive expansion of higher education in the UK, and in the wake of the Robbins Report a number of new universities were built on greenfield sites outside cities. A range of 'polytechnics' was also created, mainly through the amalgamation of technical colleges that had been offering higher diploma and some degree-level teaching for many years. A binary system of higher education was established – universities on the one hand, polytechnics on the other – which continued until the division was abolished by the Conservative government in 1992 and polytechnics were integrated into the university system. In 1996 the government set up a major review of higher education under the chairmanship of Sir Ronald Dearing. The Dearing Report recommended that participation in higher education should be increased still further. At the time of the report, 32 per cent of school-leavers went on to higher education; Dearing recommended that this should be increased to 45 per cent. Under the leadership of Tony Blair, the Labour government has committed itself to ensuring that 50 per cent of 18–30 year olds should have some experience of higher education by 2010.

As a result of the policies of both Conservative and Labour governments, the numbers of students in higher education have increased dramatically since the early 1960s. Tables 10.1 and 10.2 and figure 10.1 show the numbers of students in higher education in the UK from 1975/76 to 2002/03. Table 10.1 is based on data gathered by the Universities' Statistical Record (USR), while table 10.2 is based on data gathered by the Higher Education Statistics Agency (HESA); the two data sets are not directly comparable because

Table 10.2 Students in institutions of higher education in the UK, 1994/95 to 2002/03

	Full-time undergraduates	Full-time postgraduates	Total full-time	Total (including part-time)
1994/95	817,790	128,895	946,680	1,567,315
1995/96	843,685	134,520	978,200	1,720,095
1996/97	997,660	140,910	1,138,570	1,756,180
1997/98	1,022,605	143,520	1,166,125	1,800,065
1998/99	1,032,895	146,365	1,179,265	1,845,755
1999/00	1,027,400	151,325	1,178,725	1,856,335
2000/01	1,036,055	159,505	1,195,555	1,902,350
2001/02	1,066,290	171,935	1,238,230	1,967,225
2002/03	1,106,035	190,565	1,296,605	2,061,370

Source: HESA Student Record, July 1994/95 to 2002/03. Reproduced by permission of the Higher Education Statistics Agency Limited 2004. HESA cannot accept responsibility for any conclusions or inferences derived from the data by third parties.

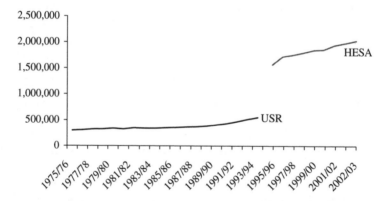

Figure 10.1 Students in higher education in the UK (full-time and part-time), 1975/76 to 2002/03
Source: Universities' Statistical Record, 1975/76–1993/94: Continuing Education (Colchester, Essex: UK Data Archive, March 1997); SN: 3501. *HESA Student Record July 1994/95 to 2002/03*; reproduced by permission of the Higher Education Statistics Agency Limited 2004.

the data was collected on different bases.[1] By 2002/03, there were 2,061,370 students in higher education in the UK, some seventeen times more than in 1962. However, even at two million, this represents a fraction of the total number of students in higher education in the US – it is about 14 per cent of the US total. In other words, in terms of sheer numbers of students in higher education, the US market is about seven times larger than the UK market.

[1] Prior to 1994/95, the Universities' Statistical Record (USR) collected data for the traditional universities that were funded by the Universities Funding Council (UFC) and the University Grants Committee (UGC); the data did not include students at the former polytechnics or at the Open

While the size of the UK market has grown significantly in recent years, in the sense that there are more students in higher education today than there were previously, there have also been important changes in student finances which have some bearing on the resources available for the purchase of books. In 1998 student grants were abolished and replaced by tuition fees and a system of student loans. In the new scheme, students are means-tested in order to determine how much they will contribute to their tuition fees, on a sliding scale up to £1,075 per academic year; students are also eligible for loans to cover their maintenance costs. These changes have led to a significant increase in student debt and a significant increase in the proportion of students who work part-time. There is some evidence to suggest that these changes have also deterred some students from buying some books. A study of student finances carried out for the Department of Education and Employment in 1998–9 found that 37 per cent of full-time students and 30 per cent of part-time students said that they had not bought some books they needed because they could not afford them.[2] A similar study carried out by the National Union of Students in December 1998 found that 35.5 per cent of full-time undergraduates said that they had not been able to meet the costs of books and equipment.[3] It is difficult to assess the extent to which the changing nature of student finances in the UK has actually altered the book buying behaviour of students (if indeed it has), but in a context where students are more hard-pressed financially than they used to be and are carrying substantial debts, it seems likely that they will be more cautious in their book buying behaviour and will look where possible for alternative ways of meeting their educational needs. It also seems likely that the pressure on student finances will be increased still further by the new measures contained in the government's 2004 Higher Education Bill, which will allow universities to charge students tuition fees of up to £3,000 per year, thereby increasing substantially the burden of debt carried by most students (the fees will be treated as a loan and recovered from students after they have graduated).

(2) *Pedagogical cultures* The differences between the UK and the US are not just quantitative: there are also very important cultural differences in the ways that lecturers and professors teach. Traditionally, many lecturers and professors in British universities teach by designing their courses and then providing lists of required or recommended readings, which may include textbooks as well as more specialized books and articles. They are less inclined than American professors to adopt one textbook and then structure their course around the text. As one textbook publisher in the UK put it, 'In the US the professors tend to teach the book. In the UK they tend to teach the course.' One consequence of this difference in pedagogical cultures is that in the UK

University. From 1994/95 on, data collection was handed over to the Higher Education Statistics Agency (HESA), which gathers data from all higher education institutions in the UK, including the former polytechnics (now upgraded to universities) and the Open University. This explains a large part of the gap between 1993/94, when the USR recorded 553,881 students in universities in the UK, and 1994/95, when HESA recorded 1,567,313 students in institutions of higher education in the UK.
[2] Claire Callender and Martin Kemp, 'Changing Student Finances: Income, Expenditure and the Take-Up of Student Loans among Full- and Part-Time Higher Education Students in 1998/9', Research Report RR213, Department for Education and Skills, London, Crown Copyright, 2000.
[3] *Student Hardship Survey* (London: National Union of Students, 2000), p. 12.

there tends to be much more heterogeneity in the syllabus from one university to another. Individual lecturers and departments are more inclined to structure their courses in ways that they regard as interesting and worthwhile, rather than follow a structure that is laid down by a particular textbook.

Another consequence of this difference in pedagogical cultures is that in the UK the match between the content of courses and the content of textbooks tends to be less than it is in the US. The standardized core textbook is based on the assumption that courses will be taught in roughly similar ways across a variety of institutions. But the more that lecturers and departments are inclined to structure their courses in ways they judge to be interesting and worthwhile, the less likely it is that the content of the textbook will map on to the content of courses across a variety of institutions, and the more likely it is that students will find that only part of the textbook will be useful to them. In a recent survey of student book-buying behaviour in the UK, nearly 60 per cent of students said they used 50 per cent or less of the contents of the last book they bought, and only one in seven said they used all or almost all of it; first-year students appeared to use less of their books than those in other years.[4] Another study found that around one-third of the students questioned claimed to use less than half of their textbook and that this was a significant source of dissatisfaction among students.[5]

A third consequence of the difference in pedagogical cultures is that, while the adoption system is just as important for textbook publishers in the UK as it is in the US, the adoption of a textbook by a lecturer in the UK is less likely to translate into sales – in other words, adoptions are less 'sticky'. In the US, many courses, especially at the lower levels of the curriculum, are structured around a core textbook, and both class assignments and exams are often based on textbook material. In a recent survey of students' usage of textbooks in the US, the student respondents report that 94 per cent of their classes require a textbook, 72 per cent of classroom reading assignments are from a textbook and 70 per cent of typical college exams come from a text; and the most important factors influencing the decision to buy a textbook are the extent to which class exams and class assignments are based on the material in the book.[6] In other words, in the US there tends to be a close integration between textbooks, class work and exams in many subjects and at some levels of the curriculum, and students' perception of the usefulness of textbooks for class assignments and exams is a key factor in ensuring that required textbooks are actually purchased by them.

In the UK, by contrast, the relation between textbooks and courses tends to be looser. Students are commonly given a reading list in which several books may be recommended; some books may be deemed essential or required, but it is common in many subjects for several books to be recommended without any particular textbook being required. Unlike the US, in the UK 'there are recommended books more often than there are required books', observed one publisher with experience on both sides of the Atlantic; 'there tends to be a selection of books and the purchasing decision is left to

---

[4] *Student Information Sources and Book Buying Behaviour 2000–2001* (London: Book Marketing Ltd, 2001), p. 51.
[5] *Student Market Today* (London: Book Marketing Ltd, 2000), p. 17.
[6] Student Watch, *Student Buying Habits: Textbooks and Course Materials II*, vol. 6 (Oberlin, Ohio: College Stores Research and Educational Foundation, 2000), pp. 11, 23.

the students.' The book buying practices of students in the UK are nevertheless strongly influenced by the recommendations of lecturers, and the most important factor in determining whether a student buys a book is whether it appears on the lecturer's reading list. In the words of one student, 'My choice is restricted to what is on the reading list or what the lecturer tells us to buy. I don't go beyond those – that is quite enough, thank you!'[7] According to one recent study, the top five factors affecting student book-buying choices in the UK were, in order of importance: (1) lecturers' recommendations, (2) price, (3) long-term use, (4) up-to-date content, and (5) clarity of language.[8] Students in the UK estimate that they buy seven to eight books a year, 70 per cent of which they describe as essential and most of the rest they describe as recommended – they buy very few books which do not appear on the reading lists.[9] But the fact that a lecturer has deemed a particular book 'essential' does not guarantee that every student (or even most students) taking that course will buy the book. Many students tend to be circumspect; they wait and see whether the book is really essential, whether they will use the book a lot over an extended period of time or merely for one or two essays, and whether they can get by without purchasing it. 'All of the time I am thinking – "do I need to buy this, or can I get the information elsewhere?" Most of the time I should be able to borrow the books, or go to the Internet for the information,' commented one student.[10]

One senior textbook publisher who has many years of experience in both the UK and the US estimates that the take-up of an adopted textbook in the UK is likely to be between 40 and 60 per cent. This relatively low take-up is, in his view, the most significant difference between the UK and the US: 'We don't have a problem with second-hand books. The used book market in the US is massive and I don't miss that at all. But what we do have is a growing problem of adoption: an adoption of any book for a hundred students will sell, on average, anywhere between forty and sixty.' In his experience, the level of take-up depends very much on what the lecturer actually says to the students in the classroom:

> It will be 60 per cent plus if the professor says, 'I'm going to be using this book. This is a tough course and you're going to need it.' They'll go to the shop and buy it. But usually what they say is, 'I know you've got very little money, you poor students' – which is sincere – 'so we'll make sure this book is in the library.' Once you've said that, that's the kiss of death for us because they won't buy the book. They'll go to the library. To me a library sale is not good news because that's not the market I'm in. For textbooks, a library sale is probably a lost multiple sale from the students.

So what can the publisher do to try to increase the take-up from adoptions? One thing it can do – and some of the larger textbook publishers try to do this – is to have someone, either a sales rep or an editor, there in the classroom when the adopted textbook is first mentioned to students, so that they can influence the way it is presented to them:

---

[7] *Student Information Sources and Book Buying Behaviour 2000–2001*, p. 46.
[8] Ibid., p. 48.
[9] Ibid., p. 38.
[10] Ibid., p. 46.

> We try as much as we can to get the reps and the editors or anybody to go into the classes and say to the professor, 'Can we come in there and say this is the book your lecturer has chosen? This is the study guide that accompanies it. It is for sale in the shop.' And the lecturer says, 'yes, you are going to need to use this because we will be testing based on this and this.' Then you sell almost 100 per cent. That's what they do in the US.

In other words, a publisher can try to counter the relatively low take-up by intervening directly in the process by which an adoption by a lecturer is translated into a recommendation to students, with the aim of ensuring that the recommendation is expressed in sufficiently strong terms to generate sales.

While there are important differences in the pedagogical cultures of higher education institutions in Britain and the US, there are some in the publishing industry who believe that these differences are declining. With the conversion of the former polytechnics into universities and the entry of more and more students into higher education, some believe that the traditional heterogeneity of British pedagogical culture is giving way to a more homogeneous culture. As one textbook publisher observed, the new universities

> will tend to use more similar elements in the course they teach. So they are moving slowly to the US model. They don't know it and they hate to hear it that way, but the reality is that they are. They are also tending to go to the lower common denominator more, which makes the publishing values and strategies in the US more relevant here both in style of production and in the similarities between what you are doing in different universities across the UK. We can see the way that the market is moving and it is moving in a good way for those introductory mass band courses that are taught across the curriculum.

The traditional universities like Oxford and Cambridge and some of the redbrick universities may well continue to design and teach courses in ways that reflect the interests and judgements of the lecturers and professors who teach them. These institutions have the advantage of being able to attract very able students, and they often pride themselves on the flexibility they have to design courses in ways they judge to be challenging and worthwhile. But at the newer universities, where lecturers often have to cope with large numbers of students on very modest resources, the use of a core textbook which covers the main topics may be an attractive option. And as the numbers of students entering higher education increases without proportionate increases in funding, the pressures on lecturers will only grow, making it more likely, one could plausibly argue, that lecturers will be inclined to use core textbooks and other pedagogical materials that will simplify their lives and make teaching easier and less demanding for them. In other words, pedagogical cultures in British higher education will move increasingly towards the US model, becoming increasingly homogenized in ways that will create a growing market for core textbooks at the lower levels of the curriculum – this, at any rate, is the view of some senior figures in the textbook publishing business.

(3)　*Used book market*　As one of the publishers quoted above indicated, one of the most significant differences between the UK and the US is the absence of a developed used book market in Britain. In an earlier chapter we saw how the development of the used book market in the US from the 1970s on had a profound impact on the business of college textbook publishing, greatly increasing the attrition rate from the first year to the second and third years in the life of textbooks and forcing publishers to speed up the revision cycle. In the UK there is a used book market for college textbooks, but it is not *institutionalized* in the way that it is in the US, where it has its own players – the used book jobbers and wholesalers – and where the retail chains are heavily involved. In the UK, of the seven to eight books bought on average by each student in 2001, only one was likely to be a used book; and when students bought used books, they purchased them mostly from other students – 71 per cent of used books bought by students in 2001 were purchased from individuals, and 29 per cent were purchased from bookstores.[11] In recent years some of the retail groups in the UK have entered the used book business and there is some evidence to suggest that bookshops and online retailers are becoming more important as sources of used books for students,[12] but these developments are still in their infancy and it's too early to tell if they will have a major impact on the purchasing practices of students.

Since the used book market for college textbooks is relatively undeveloped, textbook publishers in the UK have not experienced the high rates of attrition to which American textbook publishers have grown accustomed. Publishers in the UK can still publish textbooks with the expectation that the rates of attrition in years two and three will be relatively modest (if they exist at all), and hence with the expectation that they will be able to generate good margins and good revenues on reprints before the sales of the book begin to decline. Publishers in the UK have also not been obliged to speed up the revision cycle to two to three years in order to combat the used book market, with all the wasteful expenditure of time, energy and resources that this involves. It is still necessary for UK publishers to revise their successful textbooks at regular intervals in order to keep them up to date and to protect their market share, but the revision cycle is not driven by the used book market in the way that it is in North America. From the viewpoint of the publishers, the absence of a developed used book market is a very attractive feature of the field of higher education publishing in Britain. Whether it will continue to be a feature, and if so for how long, remains to be seen.

(4)   *Multiplicity of players at lower levels of the curriculum*   We have seen how, in most subject areas in the US, textbook publishing for the lower levels of the curriculum tends to be dominated by the big textbook publishers. Given the scale of investment required to produce large, four-colour, heavily illustrated textbooks and the elaborate packages that go with them, as well as the costs involved in maintaining a substantial sales force of college travellers, the costs of entry into this market have become prohibitively high for all but the largest players. The smaller higher education publishers have either been bought up by one of the large conglomerates or have been forced increasingly into the upper levels of the curriculum. In the UK, by contrast, the lower levels of the curriculum have traditionally been more open and have been catered for by a multiplicity of publishers, including some quite small publishers, which have been able to develop

[11] Ibid., p. 54.
[12] A follow-up study carried out in 2003 suggested that there had been a slight increase in the tendency of students in the UK to purchase used books from bookstores rather than from individuals. In 2003, 65 per cent of used books were purchased from individuals (compared with 71 per cent in 2001) and 34 per cent were purchased from bookstores (compared with 29 per cent in 2001), with 1 per cent purchased online. See *Student Information Sources and Book Buying Behaviour 2003* (London: Book Marketing Limited, 2003), p. 28.

textbooks that have secured substantial adoptions and sales. Given that the UK higher education market is much smaller than that of the US, the stakes are much lower, and the struggle for adoptions has not been waged as intensively. There have been no package wars, and the standards of production have generally been much lower – most textbooks for the higher education market in the UK are produced in one or two colours, for example, and the use of four colours in the internal design is the exception rather than the rule (though it is becoming more common at the lower levels of the curriculum, as we shall see). The prices of textbooks in the UK have also generally been much lower than in the US, since they have not had to bear the escalating costs generated by the package wars and the lavish standards of production characteristic of introductory textbooks in the US. Whereas a first-year textbook in economics or psychology in the US would typically be sold as cloth-bound and would commonly cost between $80 and $120 in 2003, a core textbook aimed at first-year university students in the UK would typically be issued as a paperback and would cost between £16 ($25) and £35 ($55), depending on the size of the book and the prices of competing texts – that is, between a third and half the price of a US textbook aimed at an equivalent level of the curriculum.

One of the issues I shall be exploring in this and the following chapter is whether this traditional pattern of higher education textbook publishing in the UK is in the process of changing. Are the lower levels of the curriculum becoming more competitive? Are the costs of entry rising, creating barriers in some subject areas that will prevent smaller publishers from being able to compete effectively? Are the dynamics of textbook publishing characteristic of the US field beginning to take hold in the UK? These are questions to which we shall return.

(5)   *Marketing methods*   The big US textbook publishers rely heavily on their sales forces of college travellers who call on professors in their campus offices and take them through the new textbook or latest edition, highlighting the key features, comparing it with the competition, demonstrating the package of print and electronic supplements and trying to persuade them to adopt it. The face-to-face interaction between the sales rep and the professor is a vital aspect of the sales and marketing strategy for core textbooks and a key tool in the struggle for adoptions at the lower levels of the curriculum. In the UK, by contrast, most higher education publishers have traditionally relied on indirect, mediated forms of marketing. Direct mail targeted at lecturers has been a principal means of informing potential adopters about new textbooks and new editions; lecturers are encouraged to request inspection copies if they are interested in considering a textbook for adoption. Some publishers have also used telemarketing methods to reach potential adopters and, increasingly, e-marketing. In addition to targeting potential adopters in these ways, most publishers have sales forces of reps who call on the bookstores and sub in the new textbooks and new editions. Some college bookstores try to open up channels of communication with the lecturers at the institutions they serve, in the hope of finding out which textbooks have been adopted and what the demand is likely to be, although in many cases the communication between lecturers and booksellers is erratic at best.

What is relatively new in the UK is the growing use of sales reps who call on lecturers, that is, the potential adopters, rather than on the booksellers – in other words, the growing use of college travellers. This development is being driven by the expansion of the large higher education publishers in the UK – Pearson, Thomson, McGraw-Hill, etc. – who are using in the UK the same kinds of sales and marketing methods they use in the North American context. The college rep structure has been present in the UK since at least the early 1970s, although in many cases the reps were not dedicated college travellers but rather sales reps who called on both bookstores and academics. In general, the college rep structure in the UK has been much less elaborate and less sophisticated than in the US – 'Quite honestly, the level of expertise and professionalism was at least ten years behind the US in 1995,' commented one senior executive. 'I'd like to think that now, with good training and transferring of skills and best practice, that some of our reps would compete and do well in the US. Not all of them; some of them would. We are probably three or four years behind.' Part of the problem is that college travellers are not viewed in the same way in the UK and Europe as they are in the US. In the US it is a profession with a long tradition. There are some college travellers who have been doing the job for decades and, as we've seen, many senior figures in college textbook publishing in the US began their careers as sales reps. But in the UK and Europe it tends to be seen as a short-term appointment. One senior executive in the UK who worked for many years in the US textbook industry put it like this:

> Culturally the reaction to sales people in Europe is different from that in the US. In the US it is an honourable profession. You'll see reps who have been around twenty-five to thirty years, who have been covering a territory for three decades and who have got tremendous relationships with the faculty. You never ever see that in Europe, anywhere. The reaction is, I'll be a rep for two years and, bang, I want to be a marketing manager, an acquisitions editor, and away I go because a rep is a bit of a dirty word. That's still a problem here. I don't know if it will ever go away. That means that it is a harder role in Europe to get to the same style of presentation. But we do exactly the same thing as they do in the States – same training, exactly the same sales cycle, same sales kit, same sales manuals. You name it, it is identical.

The changing structure of the field of higher education publishing in the UK

I mentioned earlier that, unlike the field of higher education publishing in the US, the UK field has traditionally been more open to a multiplicity of players, including some relatively small players who cater for specific subjects and market niches. This has been true even at the lower levels of the curriculum where, compared to the US, the market has been much less oligopolistic. However, over the last two to three decades, the field of higher education publishing in the UK has been changing in significant ways, and these changes are transforming the structure and dynamics of the field. Among the most important of these changes are (1) conglomeratization through mergers and acquisitions, (2) the growing presence of US-based college textbook publishers in the UK, and (3) the migration of academic publishers into the field of higher education publishing. Let me briefly examine each.

(1) *Conglomeratization through mergers and acquisitions* The trend towards conglomeratization which has characterized the field of higher education publishing in the US can also be seen in the UK, although the scale is smaller and the process has not

been as thoroughgoing (or at least not yet). The most important of the conglomerates now active in the UK field of higher education publishing is undoubtedly Pearson, which occupies a dominant position. Through the acquisition of Longman (acquired in 1968), Penguin (1970), Addison-Wesley (1988) and Simon & Schuster's educational operations (1998), Pearson has built a global higher education business which has a strong indigenous foothold in the UK as well as a major presence in North America, Europe and elsewhere.

While Pearson has grown through mergers and acquisitions to become the leading higher education publisher in the UK, the process of conglomeratization has not been restricted to Pearson. In an earlier chapter we noted that the Macmillan Group, which includes the imprint now known as Palgrave Macmillan, was acquired by the German conglomerate Georg von Holtzbrinck in 1995. Routledge also went through a complex process of being bought and sold by several parties during the 1980s and 1990s, until it was eventually bought by Taylor & Francis in 1998. Prior to that, Taylor & Francis was a relatively small scientific publisher. It floated on the London Stock Exchange in 1998 and, shortly after flotation, more than doubled its size by acquiring the Routledge Group, which included Routledge, Spon Press and Carfax. With this acquisition, Taylor & Francis emerged as a significant player in the British field of higher education publishing and, buoyed by support from the City, has indicated its desire to acquire more.

While Pearson is the largest of the indigenous higher education publishers in the UK, Palgrave Macmillan, Blackwell Publishing and Taylor & Francis are all significant players in the field. Of these four, only Blackwell remains a private independent company, which is still owned largely by the members of the Blackwell family.[13] The major British university presses, OUP and CUP, are also significant players in the field of higher education publishing in the UK. Their special status as university presses tends to place them on the margins of the mergers and acquisitions game; they are protected from takeover and, while they occasionally bid for and acquire specific lists in areas where they are seeking to grow, these acquisitions tend to be relatively modest.

(2)   *The growing presence of US-based college textbook publishers in the UK*   Conglomeratization in the field of higher education publishing in the UK has gone hand in hand with the growing presence of US-based college textbook publishers. This has occurred in two distinct ways. One way is the Pearson model: that is, a large UK-based or Europe-based media conglomerate acquires a US college textbook publisher (or publishers) and increases the flow of products, knowledge and expertise from the US division into the British and European fields. The second way is what one could call the McGraw-Hill model: a large US-based (or North American-based) media and/or publishing organization expands its operations in the UK and northern Europe and seeks to strengthen its position in these markets through a variety of means, ranging from the building up of sales and marketing teams to the development of indigenous editorial programmes. The ownership base is different in each case but the outcome is broadly similar: the increasing flow of products, knowledge and expertise from the US into the UK and northern European fields of higher education publishing.

---

[13] Whether Blackwell's independent status will continue has been a matter of much speculation in recent years, following a much publicized and, in the end, unsuccessful bid by Taylor & Francis in 2002 to acquire Blackwell Publishing for £300 million.

In the following chapter we shall examine in more detail the ways in which these large transnational media and publishing organizations strive to take advantage of the benefits of scale and accumulated expertise while at the same time seeking to meet the needs of local markets. Here it will suffice to say that through the interrelated processes of international expansion, corporate acquisition and organic growth, the conglomerates which have established dominant positions in the US field of higher education publishing – especially Pearson, Thomson and McGraw-Hill – have increased their presence in Britain and northern Europe and have, at the same time, increased the flow of US products, knowledge and expertise into the UK and northern European fields.

(3)   *The migration of academic publishers into the field of higher education publishing*
In an earlier chapter we saw how, with the decline in scholarly monograph sales throughout the 1980s and 1990s, many academic publishers began to reduce their output of scholarly monographs and sought to increase instead their output of textbooks and coursebooks for higher education – in other words, they sought to migrate into the field of higher education publishing. In the US, the patterns of migration were shaped by the fact that the large textbook publishers dominated the lower levels of the curriculum in the core textbook subjects. Hence academic publishers tended to migrate to the upper levels of the curriculum and tended to concentrate on the humanities and other soft side subjects. In the UK, by contrast, the field of higher education publishing was more open in the 1980s and early 1990s, and the lower levels of the curriculum, even in some hard side subjects like economics, business, psychology and the natural sciences, were less dominated by a few large textbook publishers. It was possible for small and medium-sized publishers to enter the field and to publish low-level textbooks that could become established as market leaders.

However, as more publishers migrated into the field of higher education publishing and as the large transnational corporations increased their presence in the UK, the relative openness of the field of higher education publishing in the UK began to change. The field became more competitive as more and more players entered it (or sought to increase their stake in it). The range of textbooks available in many subjects increased significantly, and the struggles for adoptions and for market share intensified. At the same time, many publishers experienced growing pressure to move their textbook publishing programmes down the curriculum, thus intensifying the competition at the lower levels of the curriculum. (We shall examine this process in more detail below.)

Taken together, these three processes – increasing concentration, the growing presence of US-based textbook publishers and the migration of academic publishers into higher education publishing – have shaped the structure and evolution of the field of higher education publishing in the UK over the last two decades. The higher education market in the UK was probably worth around £185 million ($300 million) in 2001.[14] Pearson is the dominant player by a significant margin and probably controls around a third of the market, but both Thomson and McGraw-Hill are becoming increasingly important players. McGraw-Hill's acquisition of the Open University Press in 2002 demonstrated

[14] This is an estimate of total student spend on books, based on data from the Publishers Association. Annual sales to higher education libraries amounted to another £48 million in 2001–2, although this figure would include monographs as well as textbooks.

its desire to increase its foothold in the UK and strengthen its indigenous commissioning base. Wiley and Elsevier are also significant players in the UK and northern Europe, especially in the natural sciences, medicine and engineering. The rest of the higher education market in the UK is accounted for by four indigenous publishers with significant stakes – Palgrave Macmillan, Taylor & Francis, Blackwell and OUP – and by a variety of other presses, such as CUP and Sage, with smaller stakes in the field. Unlike the US field of higher education publishing, which is now dominated by three big players who, between them, control more than two-thirds of the market, the UK field is more open and fluid; Pearson is in pole position with a significant share of the market, but the bulk of the remaining market is divided up between eight or nine other players which are struggling to protect their positions and to maintain or increase their market shares.[15]

Intensifying competition at the lower levels of the curriculum

We have seen that, throughout the 1980s and early 1990s, the logic of the field of higher education publishing in the UK differed in some important ways from that of the US – in the UK there were no package wars, the used book market was virtually non-existent and even very small publishers could enter the field at the lower levels of the curriculum. But since the mid-1990s, this situation has begun to change. As the process of consolidation has taken hold in higher education publishing, as the large conglomerates have sought to increase their presence in the UK and as more players have entered the field, the struggle has intensified among publishers for control of the lower levels of the curriculum. This has become the new battleground in the field of higher education publishing in the UK.

This struggle has been made all the more intense by another development which many UK publishers have experienced in recent years – namely, *the decline of upper-level textbooks and of supplementary texts*. Upper-level textbooks are textbooks aimed at and designed for second- and third-year undergraduate courses and graduate courses. Some publishers report that textbooks of this kind are selling less well than they used to. As one managing director of a major British firm observed,

> This is an area which is troubled. There are fewer purchases. There is a less strong recommendation from the lecturer, and the students are buying one of perhaps a list rather than going out to buy a particular book. So it is becoming more discretionary. It's an area which is threatened I think by photocopying, multiple library copies and all the rest – they've always been in there but it's probably getting worse. I don't think it's a great decline that we've seen but it is tougher, and the fact that the retail chains don't support that area makes it even harder.

[15] There are no published statistics on the market shares of different firms in the UK field of higher education publishing. One well-informed publishing analyst estimated that Pearson's sales in the UK higher education market were around £60 million in 2003, Thomson's were around £22 million and McGraw-Hill's around £18 million; this would give them market shares of around 32 per cent, 12 per cent and 10 per cent respectively. If these estimates are accurate, it would mean that the three players which are dominant in the US higher education market also control, between them, more than half of the higher education market in the UK. The market shares of the other significant players in the UK field – Wiley, Elsevier, Palgrave Macmillan, Taylor & Francis, Blackwell and OUP – probably range between 4 and 7 per cent each.

Some publishers have found both that initial sales of upper-level textbooks are lower than expected, and that the rates of attrition in the second and third years are significantly higher than they were in the past. The reasons for the decline in sales of upper-level textbooks are not entirely clear. It may be linked to the modularization of upper-level courses in most British universities. The increasing use of modular courses tends to mean that students study more subjects in less depth for less time, and hence they have to use a greater range of books rather than one core textbook. Moreover, since students are generally assessed at the end of the module, they have little need of the books once the module is finished. (The ability to use a book over a long period is one of the most important factors influencing a student's decision to purchase the book.) Hence students may be inclined to use library books for modularized courses, to rely on photocopying and to use other sources rather than to buy the recommended books. It may also be that students become more selective in the books they buy in their second and third years, more sceptical about the value of textbooks and savvier about how to get what they need in other ways. As one student remarked, 'I bought loads of books when I arrived – about fifteen or so – but I know better now. Most of them are just a waste of money and I will be far more careful in future.'[16]

The decline in the sales of supplementary texts is even more marked than the decline in the sales of upper-level textbooks. Supplementary texts are ones which may be recommended to students, either by being put on reading lists or mentioned in class (or both), but which are not adopted as the core textbook or as essential/required reading by lecturers. These books are often available in libraries and may, in some cases, be put in short-loan reserve collections. Since they are seen by students as supplementary reading and often pertain to particular topics rather than to the whole course, they are often regarded as optional purchases. Many students tend to restrict their book purchases to those textbooks which are essential/required reading and which can be used for more than a single topic – as one student said, 'On the whole I try to be sure that any book I buy will have some use beyond the immediate essay – preferably something I can use for the rest of the year or the course, or for different modules.'[17]

Whether it is because students are becoming more selective in their book buying practices or simply because they have less cash available to buy books (or are less willing to spend their available cash on books, given the other things on which it could be spent), the experience of many publishers is that the sales of books which could be regarded as supplementary texts are in decline. 'They are much weaker than they used to be,' commented one managing director. In the late 1980s and early 1990s, a UK publisher might print 1,500 paperback copies for the UK and rest of world (ROW) markets (excluding North America) of a book which was not a core textbook and would not be adopted as essential/required reading, but which was likely to be put on reading lists as a supplementary text. In some cases the print-runs were undoubtedly excessive and some stock would eventually be written down, but the expectation of being able to sell 1,500 paperback copies of a supplementary text in the UK and ROW was not unrealistic. By 2001–2, many publishers were finding that they were having to reduce quite significantly the print-runs of books of this kind, to somewhere between 700 and 1,000 copies for the UK and

---

[16] *Student Information Sources and Book Buying Behaviour 2000–2001*, p. 34. Second- and third-year students buy on average 1.5 fewer books per year than first-year students; see *Student Information Sources and Book Buying Behaviour 2003*, p. 19.
[17] Ibid., p. 35.

ROW – a reduction of between a third and a half from the print-runs that were fairly common a decade ago. As the print-runs fall, it becomes increasingly difficult to publish these books in ways that generate satisfactory margins. Publishers can put up prices to offset the decline in print-runs, and in recent years this tendency has become increasingly common, with prices on supplementary texts rising from the £12–15 ($19–24) range in the late 1990s to the £17–20 ($27–32) range today. But raising prices runs the risk of undermining still further the sales of supplementary texts. The result is a potentially vicious circle of declining sales, increasing prices and falling margins.

In some respects, this vicious circle has an uncanny resemblance to the vicious circle of scholarly monograph publishing which most academic publishers experienced in the 1980s and early 1990s, and there is serious concern among some publishers that supplementary texts will suffer the same fate as the scholarly monograph. Indeed in some respects the histories of these two types of books are intertwined. We have seen how, as the sales of hardback monographs declined, some academic publishers began to abandon the hardback-only publishing strategy and experimented with simultaneous editions, publishing books of a scholarly character in simultaneous cloth and paper editions. Part of the rationale for this was that the publishers believed that – and were encouraged by both their external readers and their authors to think that – these books would be recommended to students and would have sales in paperback as supplementary texts. But as we saw in an earlier chapter, in a significant proportion of cases these expectations turned out to be unwarranted, and the sales performance of these books in paperback was disappointing.

While some books treated by publishers as supplementary texts are in fact scholarly books which are being released in paperback in the hope that they will sell into the student market, it would be a mistake to think of supplementary texts exclusively in this way. Many supplementary texts are in fact commissioned by publishers as textbooks to be written explicitly for students, although it is recognized that these textbooks address a specific topic (or set of topics) rather than covering a whole course and hence are likely to be recommended as supplementary reading rather than as a core, required textbook. What is worrying for many publishers is that the sales of even this kind of supplementary text appear to be in decline.

Whatever the reasons for the declining sales of upper-level texts and supplementary texts, the result of these trends is that there has been a growing pressure on higher education publishers in the UK to move their publishing programmes down the curriculum – that is, to shift the primary focus of their efforts more and more to the first-year university courses (and even to A-level) and to try to commission core textbooks for these lower levels of the curriculum. But the more that publishers try to shift the primary focus of their efforts to the lower levels of the curriculum, the more competitive it becomes and the more difficult it is to succeed – both in terms of signing up new textbooks and in terms of winning and maintaining market share. While striving to increase their presence at the lower levels of the curriculum, most publishers accept that much of their commissioning activity will be geared to selected niches in the upper levels of the curriculum where they believe they can secure sufficient sales to make a go of it. One managing director put it like this:

> We have to balance the competing demands, which are, on the one hand, that the first-year courses are more reliable and get the full recommendations and so on, they're bigger. On

the other hand, we are competing against stiffer competition there. So it may be that we can carve out cleverly a bit of space for ourselves at the second- and third-year level. So we do both. We move down where we can but we also remain in that space where others are not yet entrenched or have not yet cottoned on to.

How far up the curriculum publishers are willing to go varies from one publisher to another and depends on the specific sales thresholds they set for themselves. One higher education publisher may be willing to publish textbooks for upper-level courses only in those cases where it is confident of being able to secure annual sales of at least 2,000 copies, while another publisher will be happy to settle for more modest sales – sales in the region of, say, 800–1,000 copies per year. But what most higher education publishers share in common is the desire – exacerbated by the decline of supplementary and upper-level texts – to commission and develop core textbooks which would be essential/required reading for the lower levels of the curriculum, for this is where the strongest and most reliable sales are to be found.

In this respect, the dynamic of the field of higher education publishing in the UK today is quite different from that of the US field. In the US, the struggles for the control of the lower levels of the curriculum were waged in the 1970s and 1980s, through the period of the package wars and the growing conglomeratization within the industry. When academic publishers tried to migrate into the field of higher education publishing in the 1980s and 1990s, they were generally obliged – at least in the core textbook subjects – to move up the curriculum and to concentrate their efforts on upper-level and graduate level courses. Given the sheer size of the higher education market in the US, the upper levels of the curriculum provided a reasonably comfortable home for many academic publishers, since the sales of texts adopted for upper-level and graduate courses in the US were generally a good deal higher than the sales they were accustomed to achieving for scholarly monographs. In the UK, by contrast, the struggles for the control of the lower levels of the curriculum are still very much underway. Some of the major transnational textbook conglomerates – Pearson, McGraw-Hill, Thomson, etc. – are certainly key players, but the UK-based higher education publishers are also fully engaged in these struggles. Moreover, since the size of the higher education system in the UK is much smaller than that in the US and since there are signs that the sales of upper-level textbooks and supplementary texts in the UK may be declining, there is growing pressure on UK higher education publishers – whether they are large, medium-sized or small – to move down the curriculum and to concentrate on trying to sign up core textbooks for first-year courses. The consequence of this dynamic is the intensification of struggles among higher education publishers at the lower levels of the curriculum. More and more publishers are moving into a particular region of the field where they are coming face to face with other publishers who are pursuing a similar strategy – namely, to sign up textbooks which will service the lower-level introductory courses.

The reorientation of UK publishers to international markets

Another important consequence of these developments is that many UK higher education publishers have sought to become less reliant on the UK market. They have looked increasingly to overseas markets as a way of generating higher sales. Scandinavia and northern Europe, particularly the Netherlands, have become increasingly important markets, since many lecturers and professors in universities in northern Europe are willing to use English-language books for their courses. But undoubtedly the real attraction has been the North American market, and over the last two decades many UK-based higher education publishers have sought increasingly to reorient their activities towards the US.

The extent to which UK-based higher education publishers have shifted the focus of their activities towards the North American market varies considerably from one firm to another – some have moved very strongly in this direction, others less so. Consider again the example of AC1 which we described in chapter 6. In the early 1980s and before, AC1 was a medium-sized UK-based academic publisher which was well known for its distinguished list of scholarly publications in the social sciences and humanities. In the course of the 1980s it began to migrate seriously into the field of higher education publishing in order to compensate for the declining sales of scholarly monographs. By the early 1990s, it had effectively exited the field of academic publishing and reinvented itself as a higher education publisher – in other words, AC1 metamorphosed into HE1. At the same time, HE1 began to reorient itself towards the US market. Reflecting on the evolution of HE1's publishing strategy in the late 1980s and early 1990s, one senior executive of the firm described the shift like this:

> Some of the rhetoric about the publishing policy that we were developing was about increasing revenue per title. One way of doing that was to publish more textbooks and reference books. Another way to do it, obviously, was to sell more copies in America. We guessed correctly that one good way of doing that was simply to commission more American authors. That we did mostly by operating from the UK. The difficulty we had was that it was very difficult to establish an editorial culture in America. It was only when we sent someone out on a long-term commitment who then appointed, trained and developed editors in the US that an editorial culture took root.

In the late 1980s and 1990s, HE1 invested heavily in expanding its presence in the US – both as a sales and marketing operation and as an indigenous commissioning operation. It increasingly oriented all aspects of its publishing operation to the US market, to such an extent that even the UK office became increasingly US-oriented. The UK–US axis became increasingly central to its strategic thinking and, more and more, the US became the centre of gravity. The managing director was proud of the fact that the UK operation was, as he put it,

> more US-centred than any other organization I know of in publishing. When we do our copy-editing, we do American copy-editing. When we think about the courses, the customers we are trying to reach, we think in terms of Americans. When we think who's the best author for this book, we actually have a prejudice in favour of the American market and the people in this office feel that they are directly responsible for the US success. So there is an obsession about America and the obsession that America is the gateway to the rest of the world.

> *So the orientation of people here in the UK is towards the North American market?*

> Absolutely. And I'd say that the people who actually happen to be there in the US are the avant-garde. The rest of us are helping them. They are at the cutting edge and they should

feel very excited about that. They are not at all in the frontier, off in Siberia. They are right there at the cutting edge and the rest of us are watching them intently and wanting to help, and many of us are wishing that we were right there at the cutting edge ourselves.

The reorientation of HE1 towards the North American market has had significant consequences for the *content* of the textbooks it commissions and publishes. The UK market is not ignored, but the needs of the US market tend to be given priority in the research and reviewing processes that are integral to the commissioning and development of textbooks. As the managing director explained,

> In the preparation for anything that's a textbook, the research will be conducted with a bias towards America. So if you've got a group of twenty reviewers, then I would have thought two-thirds of them were probably going to be based in America; some of them might be based out in Hong Kong or Australia as well. When you get the syllabus of what's being taught in some subjects like literature, you really, really know what's being taught in the States and you will say, I'm sorry, you know, there will be some sales in the UK but if I don't get it absolutely right for this 101 course in Introduction to Irish Literature for the American undergraduates, then there's not a hope, we'll never make it. So I've got to make that work and then I'll pick up some additional sales as well. But basically it's an enormous amount of information about the student numbers and course content in the States.

The importance attributed to the US market did not mean that HE1 was no longer interested in commissioning textbooks that were aimed primarily or even exclusively at the UK market. It was willing to do this, but only if the textbooks were aimed at the lower-level undergraduate courses in subjects like psychology or geography, or at professional courses like business or social policy where they could get some spillover into a market of professionals and practitioners. In other words, it would continue to commission textbooks that were tailored to the UK market only if it was confident that the UK market was large enough to generate good textbook sales on its own, without the additional revenue that could be generated from significant sales in the US; and this meant that the textbooks it commissioned primarily or exclusively for the UK market were focused increasingly on the lower-level (predominantly first-year) courses or on professional courses. In the managing director's words,

> If you want a book that is not going to have sales in the rest of the world or the US, and often the two come together, then you've got to be really sure of your market. So it has probably got to be one that is either a first-year undergraduate book and a course like psychology or geography and you say, right, I'm going after the UK market with this, or it's got to be a professional area like social policy where you think you can get a wider spillover audience of people who are actually practitioners, and that's a tricky one. But it does work and we do do those kinds of books.

What gets squeezed out of HE1's publishing programme are textbooks aimed at upper-level courses in the UK where the numbers are insufficient to generate good textbook sales and where the likelihood of achieving significant sales in the US is minimal. What also gets squeezed out are supplementary texts where the principal market is likely to be the UK and Europe. 'If you've got a higher-level book that is only going to sell in the UK and not the US, everybody will look at you and say, how the hell are you going to make this work?'

The evolution of HE1 is a striking example of how some UK-based higher education publishers have reoriented their publishing activities towards the US market, in such a way that the US market has become the key focus of their textbook commissioning programme. But not all UK publishers have become as US-centred as HE1. We can contrast HE1 with HE2 – a small, independent UK-based higher education publisher with a modest but well-respected list of textbooks in the social sciences. Like all UK higher education publishers, HE2 experienced the decline of supplementary text sales in the 1990s and, as a result, increasingly reoriented its publishing programme to the commissioning and development of textbooks that were designed for specific courses in the subjects where it had a presence – sociology, psychology, health, education, etc. As a small publisher with relatively low overheads, HE2 could do well with textbooks which were geared to first- or second-year courses in the UK or to professional courses like nursing and healthcare. It could compete with larger publishers in an increasingly competitive marketplace by being more nimble, by spotting the gaps and anticipating new developments rather than merely responding to existing needs, and by being able to provide the kind of personalized service to authors and a level of author care that was often missing in the larger publishing firms.

However, it was difficult for HE2 to achieve significant growth by relying on the UK market alone. Although the numbers of students going into higher education was increasing throughout the 1990s, sales in the UK tended to be relatively flat. Competition for low-level textbooks was intensifying, as more and more publishers were seeking to establish and increase their presence at the lower levels of the curriculum, and the sales of upper-level textbooks were not necessarily increasing. It was therefore important for HE2 to try to increase its international sales if it wanted to achieve significant growth and avoid getting stuck in a static market – or in what the managing director of HE2 described as 'a possibly declining market, not just a static market but declining, relatively at least'.

The problem for HE2 was that as a small, independent UK-based publisher, it had to rely on agency arrangements for international sales and it didn't have the resources to invest significantly in expanding its own presence overseas. In the US, HE2 had an agency arrangement with another UK-based publisher which had its own operation in the US, and which took HE2's books on consignment, marketing, selling and distributing them in return for a fixed percentage of sales. HE2 combined this with a selective practice of copublication, but in the early 1990s it decided to discontinue copublishing in order to keep the list together and build its brand in North America. The agency arrangement worked well but HE2 was never able to achieve significant growth in the US. Possibly this was because its books were not tailored with sufficient care to the US market, possibly it was because its books were not being marketed effectively enough, possibly it was a combination of both. In any case, the senior management of HE2 decided that they were more likely to achieve growth in overseas markets other than the US. As the managing director explained,

> We know that we are not in a position to let our editorial programme be led by the US textbook need. That may sound like lack of ambition, but it's deciding that the US market, the way it is currently structured, is only going to be so big for us. It is not going to be suddenly transformed. We are more likely to get growth in niche markets if there is a kind of parallel with the curriculum here. We are more likely to get growth in comparatively niche markets like South Africa or Australia or Canada than we are in the States.

HE2 built up a network of local agents in places like Hong Kong, Sydney, Cape Town and Vancouver who had a good local knowledge of the market needs in their respective territories – 'I think we very often get better on-the-ground knowledge from them than the big conglomerates get from their branches.' These agents were able not only to gain local sales, but also to visit campuses and talk to academics and feed back information about local needs. 'They do six-monthly or annual reports about the state of the market and all that stuff, and these reports might become more important than the actual sales. We might end up employing them on a fee basis rather than on a percentage of turnover basis because we need that local knowledge.'

In order to ensure that its textbooks would sell into these overseas markets, HE2 had to alter its editorial practices. Fifteen or twenty years ago, an editor at HE2 would have commonly allowed an author to write a textbook for the UK market only, where the implied reader was a student at a university in the UK, but now this is the exception rather than the rule. Now the editor will normally tell the author that he or she must write (or rewrite) the text in a way that will be both accessible and appealing to students in markets outside the UK:

> Fifteen years ago, I wouldn't be saying to the author, 'look, you're writing this as if it is just for the UK audience. You've got to reorient the material so that at least the reader in Taiwan or South Africa is not alienated by this. You can't necessarily use lots of examples from Taiwan but you've got to say, not "the government" but "the UK government"', things that are simple as far as I'm concerned and they should already know. I should've been saying it fifteen years ago but I wasn't. Now I am and all the editors are. So at the very micro level, we want the books to be accessible to all international markets. Overall, we see the company growing internationally. Gradually we are going to be increasing our sales in all overseas markets compared with the UK. So when I commission a book in higher education, I routinely explain to the author, 'look, we are expecting to sell at least 50 per cent of these books outside of the UK. Are you willing to write for a readership that is outside the UK?' I'm exaggerating that slightly – 50 per cent probably should have been 45 per cent, but it just brings the point across. Actually with some of those books we do sell more than half in international markets. So the orientation is much more to the international market than it was, both at the micro and the macro level.

So although the content of HE2's textbooks is not being tailored for the US market in the way that the content of HE1's textbooks is, nevertheless the content of HE2's textbooks is being 'internationalized' to some extent, as authors are urged or even required to write in ways that are more comparative and less contextually specific, so that the texts are less UK centred and are more accessible and appealing to students in higher education in Australia, South Africa, Hong Kong, Taiwan and other parts of the world.

While the strategies of HE1 and HE2 are very different and reflect their differing positions in the field and the differing levels of resources available to them, the strategies of both firms illustrate a common trend: in the context of a relatively static UK higher education market, UK-based higher education publishers have looked increasingly to overseas markets as a way of generating growth. The intensifying competition for lower-level textbooks for the UK market and the declining sales of upper-level and supplementary texts have tended to accentuate the importance of overseas markets for UK-based publishers, who have sought in various ways to reorient their editorial activities to ensure that the content they commission and develop will be either explicitly tailored for non-UK markets or at least accessible and appealing to readers in these markets. This development has important implications for the provision of content for higher education in the UK, especially at the upper levels of the curriculum, and we shall return to this issue in the next chapter. But there is another important issue that we need to consider at this stage.

We have seen how the dynamic of the field of academic publishing has led many academic publishers to move increasingly into the field of higher education publishing, and has led them to place less emphasis on the publication of scholarly monographs and more emphasis on the commissioning of textbooks – indeed in some cases, as we have seen, academic publishers have pulled out of monograph publishing altogether and reinvented themselves as textbook publishers. We have also seen how, in the UK field of higher education publishing, the limited size of the market and relative weakness of sales of many upper-level textbooks and supplementary texts have tended to push publishers down the curriculum, encouraging or even requiring them to concentrate more and more on trying to commission and develop textbooks for the lower levels of the curriculum. Hence the struggles for market share at the lower levels of the curriculum have become increasingly intense, as more and more players compete for adoptions in a crowded market. And yet at the same time as the competition for market share is intensifying, it is getting harder and harder for publishers to commission authors to write textbooks – that is, it is getting harder and harder to acquire new content. At the same time as UK publishers want increasingly to commission textbooks, academics in Britain increasingly don't want to write them. Why not? Why are the creators of textbook content increasingly unwilling to play the game? The answer to this question has nothing to do with publishing as such but with an altogether different dynamic that stems from the field with which higher education publishing is inextricably linked – namely, the field of higher education itself.

The impact of the RAE on higher education publishing

Publishers are not ultimately the creators of the content which they develop and sell. They are dependent on authors – and in the case of higher education publishers, this means primarily academics – whom they commission to create the content for them. But higher education publishers in the UK find themselves faced with a growing and very difficult problem: most academics in the UK don't want to write textbooks. They don't want to write them because they are part of a different field that has its own logic, and this logic has nothing to do with the kinds of books that publishers want them to write. Academics are under a great deal of pressure, stemming from the institutional constraints and demands of their own academic field, to concentrate their writing activities on the production of journal articles and scholarly monographs and to avoid writing textbooks altogether. Publishers and academics depend on one another but they belong to different worlds, to different fields, and the logics of their respective fields propel them in opposite directions. Let us examine this conflict in more detail.

British universities do not have the same kind of tenure-track system as American universities, and hence this has not become a source of growing tension between publishers and academics in the UK in the way that it has in the US. But the system of higher education in the UK has features of its own which have helped to ensure that the priorities and expectations of academics are increasingly at odds with the aims of publishers. One such feature is the Research Assessment Exercise (RAE), which was established by the Conservative government of Margaret Thatcher in the late 1980s as one of a series of initiatives aimed at providing some measure of accountability and external quality assurance in higher education. The RAE is one aspect of the proliferation of accounting practices which has swept through the public sector in recent years and which Michael Power has aptly described as 'the audit explosion'.[18] Since the late 1980s, the RAE has been carried out on a regular basis – every five or six years – by HEFCE, the Higher Education and Funding Council of England.

The explicit aim of the RAE is to assess the research output of university departments across the country. It does this by requiring each department (or assessment unit) to complete a dossier of the output of its research-active members of staff. Under the rules for the 2001 RAE,[19] each research-active member of staff was invited to nominate up to four items of output which he or she produced during the assessment period. The output was then subjected to an assessment process which was carried out by a series of subject panels whose members were drawn from a variety of institutions. Each department (or assessment unit) was given a score from 1 to 5* (where 5* means 'quality that equates to attainable levels of international excellence in more than half of the research activity submitted and attainable levels of national excellence in the remainder' and 1 means 'quality that equates to attainable levels of national excellence in none, or virtually none, of the research activity submitted'). The results of the RAE are published by HEFCE and widely reported in the press, which produces its own rankings of universities based on the scores attained by their constituent departments. The outcome of this process has consequences for the research funding received by the universities from government funding bodies, which use the RAE results to calculate the size of block grants for research which are allocated to individual universities. Universities and departments spend a great deal of time and effort in preparing themselves for the RAE. A good performance by a department can result in extra funding for research and new posts, while a poor performance can have serious consequences for a department – leading in some cases to the department being closed down – and for individual academics whose output is regarded as below par.

Given the importance that the RAE has come to assume in the academic field in the UK, the activities and priorities of individual academics have become increasingly shaped by it. Their careers in the academic field are determined with more and more force by the contribution they make (or would make) to the RAE performance of their department (or of departments which might be considering them for a post). Mobility within the academic field – both in terms of promotion within one's institution and movement between institutions – has become inextricably linked to assessments of one's likely contribution, based on actual and likely research output, in the RAE. What was introduced by the state as a mechanism of accountability and quality assurance – that is, a means of trying to ensure value for money in one sector of public service – has in practice become a core determinant of behaviour within this sector, generating a plethora of unintended consequences as institutions strive to improve their positions in

[18] Michael Power, *The Audit Society: Rituals of Verification* (Oxford: Oxford University Press, 1997).
[19] The rules for the next RAE, scheduled for 2008, will differ slightly.

the league tables, departments strive to improve their scores and individuals strive to accumulate the kinds of capital (in the form of suitable publications, research grants, etc.) that will strengthen their position in the field, maximize their mobility options and minimize the risk of sanctions that might be brought to bear if their performance is judged to be unsatisfactory.

Just as the RAE has come to play an increasingly important role in shaping the activities and priorities of individuals within the academic field, so too it has shaped these activities and priorities in ways that are in some respects at odds with the concerns of publishers. The logic of the academic field in the UK, heavily shaped as it is by the RAE, does not coincide with the logics of the fields of academic and higher educational publishing, which have been shaped by different sets of factors, and the non-coincidence of these logics is expressed in various forms of misunderstanding, disagreement, conflicting expectations and failed forms of cooperation. This can be illustrated most effectively by the differing attitudes towards textbooks and scholarly monographs. Let us focus for a moment on academic publishers. We have seen how academic publishers, for a variety of reasons specific to the field of academic publishing, have sought to shift the balance of their lists away from scholarly monograph publishing and to give greater emphasis to the commissioning and development of textbooks. Commissioning editors have been encouraged to reorient their activities increasingly towards the field of higher education publishing and towards the acquisition of textbooks which are geared to the teaching and learning needs of lecturers and students. But at the same time, these editors find themselves increasingly faced with the problem that the prospective authors of these textbooks – namely, academics who are employed by the universities – feel more and more obliged (and, in some cases, are strongly encouraged or even instructed by their heads of department and others) to concentrate on producing the kinds of publications that will be of most value for the RAE, and these are most definitely *not* textbooks. What matters above all in the RAE is the extent to which research outputs are perceived to be original, innovative and high-quality contributions to knowledge, both theoretical and empirical. The form of the output may vary, from articles in peer-reviewed journals to scholarly monographs, and the weighting given to different forms of publication and dissemination varies from subject to subject. But the key emphasis is on research excellence. Textbooks for students are not discounted by the assessment panels but they are not valued highly by them. Textbooks and other teaching materials are regarded as valid submissions in the RAE only if they can be shown to contain 'significant research effort'.

The weighting of different forms of output can be seen in the accounts offered by the different assessment panels of their criteria and working methods.[20] Let us consider, for example, the account offered by the panel for Politics and International Studies. The panel emphasizes that its primary aim is to assess the research merits of the items submitted by research-active members of staff. While recognizing that researchers may prefer different forms of dissemination, the panel indicates that it will generally observe the following rules:

[20] See 'Research Assessment Exercise 2001: Assessment Panels' Criteria and Working Methods', available at www.rae.ac.uk/pubs/5_99/.

Authored Books
3.31.10 Because they generally require greater effort the Panel will tend to place great weight on research monographs, depending, of course, on their quality.
Journal Articles
3.31.11 Articles published in journals which have high editorial standards will be taken as a strong indicator of research excellence . . .
Other Works
3.31.14 Other works may include textbooks, CD-roms, web-sites, conference papers and proceedings, annotated bibliographies, information guides, research guides and commentaries on, or introductions to, translated versions of existing works, if these can be shown to contain significant research effort . . .
3.31.15 The Panel wishes to make clear its attitude to the following types of evidence of research quality:
Textbooks
3.31.16 Whilst the Panel recognises that, in many cases, it is possible to distinguish clearly textbooks from research monographs, it also notes that textbooks frequently report the writer's research or provide an innovative synthesis of existing scholarship. The Panel is also aware that publishers often market a research monograph as a textbook to increase sales. The Panel will strive to judge the research merits of such works.[21]

The message conveyed by these guidelines is perfectly clear: in this subject area, research monographs are highly valued, as are articles published in recognized peer-reviewed journals; textbooks are valued less and will be considered for the purposes of the RAE only if they 'can be shown to contain significant research effort'. The panel acknowledges that it may not always be possible to draw a clear distinction between research monographs and textbooks, especially since publishers sometimes seek to present monographs as textbooks in order to increase sales. But it emphasizes that if it is called upon to assess what appears to be a textbook, it will do so by seeking to determine the extent to which it represents an original, innovative contribution to knowledge.

I have taken Politics and International Studies as an example, but the guidelines issued by other assessment panels convey a similar message. This is a message which filters down through the institutions of the academic field, since heads of department and other academics scrutinize the RAE guidelines and use them to structure their priorities, to shape their own research and writing activities and to inform the advice they give to others, including other members of staff within their departments.

Two fields, two logics, two contrasting and potentially conflicting sets of priorities: just as academic publishers are urging (even requiring) their editors to concentrate on commissioning textbooks for the student market, heads of department and others in the academic field are urging academics to concentrate on doing research and on publishing it in the form of scholarly monographs and journal articles. The result is that when the members of these two worlds interact and try to collaborate, they often do so (and do so increasingly) with opposing objectives in mind: editors want to persuade academics to write textbooks, while academics want to persuade editors to publish books based on their research. On the one hand, the changing conditions of academic publishing place growing pressure on many editors to commission textbooks, but as the RAE becomes

---

[21] Ibid.

more powerful as a structuring principle in the academic field, it becomes harder and harder for editors to persuade academics to write the kind of textbooks that they are being asked (or required) to commission. On the other hand, the RAE places constant pressure on academics to maintain an active research profile and to publish books and articles based on their research, but as the market for scholarly monographs deteriorates, it becomes harder and harder for academics to persuade editors to publish the kind of research monograph that is valued highly by the RAE.

I have focused here on the tension between academics and academic publishers, but the tension is all the more evident in the case of publishers who are engaged primarily or exclusively in textbook publishing: for these publishers, the RAE has become one of the most serious obstacles they face. It has created a structure of disincentives which strongly discourages academics at British universities from writing textbooks. As the managing director of one firm which is active in the field of higher education publishing observed, 'by comparison with those who, ten years ago, would have said "I'll have a bash at it" or "I'll do a sample chapter", my guess would be that 70 per cent of those would no longer wish to do so today.' The unintended outcome of the RAE is that many of the best academics at British universities are simply eliminated from the pool of potential authors for textbooks. Higher education publishers are obliged to search harder and harder for a dwindling number of British academics who are still willing to write textbooks; in many cases, these are academics who are retired (or near to retirement), or who are teaching at institutions or departments which do not aspire to perform well in the RAE. Alternatively they are obliged to broaden their author base and look beyond the UK, seeking to persuade academics in the US, Canada, Australia, Europe and elsewhere to write textbooks for them.

While the logics of their respective fields propel them in opposite directions, editors and academics continue to share one goal in common: they both want to publish books, even if the kinds of books they want to publish are increasingly dissimilar. This residue of common interest means that they continue to collaborate in many ways, but their collaborations are increasingly characterized by suspicion, misunderstanding and reluctant compromises. An editor approaches an academic and asks if she would be interested in writing a textbook on a particular subject; she responds by putting together a proposal for a book based on her research and suggesting that it would work as a textbook. Or an academic sends a proposal for a book based on his research to a publisher, who responds by saying that they could not publish a monograph of this kind but would be interested in seeing a proposal for a general textbook in the subject area. Or an author who was commissioned to write a textbook some years earlier eventually delivers a manuscript based on his research, only to find that the publisher sends it back and asks for it to be rewritten as a textbook. Or an author who has written a textbook balks at the editor's suggestion that the book be called 'An Introduction to . . .' for fear that the word 'Introduction' would disqualify the book as an RAE submission. And so the exchanges go on, like two dancers who are circling around the same camp fire but dancing to different tunes.

In these circumstances what publishers often end up with are hybrid books – an uneasy compromise between a research monograph and a textbook. They are books that the author, conscious of the demands of the RAE, wants to present as a work of original scholarship based on their research, while the publisher, wary of monographs and anxious to develop books that have some chance of being adopted for course use, wants to present it as a textbook. In the end, both parties often feel some degree of frustration and disappointment. Many academic authors feel frustrated and disappointed by the fact that publishers seem reluctant to take on their scholarly work and, while knowing very little about the actual economic conditions of academic publishing, they resent what they see as the transformation of publishers into commercial organizations interested only in making money. Publishers, on the other hand, often feel frustrated by the reluctance of academics to write textbooks that are genuinely geared to the needs of students, and they are often disappointed by the sales of books which they had wanted to market as textbooks but which turn out to be ill-suited, for one reason or another, to course adoption.

I have highlighted the ways in which the RAE has helped to generate a set of attitudes and expectations in the academic field which diverges in fundamental respects from the attitudes and expectations that have become increasingly prevalent in the fields of academic and higher education publishing. The RAE has encouraged academics in the UK to think of publishing first and foremost as a means of fulfilling their research obligations and has devalued the role of publishing as a form of pedagogy, that is, as a means of facilitating the educational process; hence it has increased the value they attribute to scholarly monographs and devalued textbooks at the very time when publishers, for reasons specific to the evolution of their own fields, have sought to reduce their monograph publishing programmes, to publish more textbooks and to concentrate more and more on the lower levels of the curriculum. But the RAE has also created other sources of tension between these fields. For example, the temporal structure of the RAE has meant that many academics, in some cases under pressure from their heads of department, have sought to get books out quickly in order to qualify for the RAE, and have in turn placed pressure on publishers to speed up their reviewing and production processes. This creates operational problems for publishers, who find that books tend to be bunched into a short period in the run-up to the RAE deadline. It also runs the risk of short-circuiting review and revision processes, and thus compromising quality in the interests of qualifying for the RAE. Sometimes this pressure takes an openly competitive form, as authors offer their books to more than one publisher and make it clear that they will work only with a publisher who can guarantee publication before the RAE cut-off date, or who will publish the book without revision. As one managing director of a UK-based university press remarked, 'We have lost some books to other publishers in this process, to our disadvantage and to the ultimate disadvantage of the books themselves. It would be an irony if it were an effect of the RAE that it lowered quality in the very attempt to measure it.'

The impact of the RAE on the publishing field in the UK is somewhat similar to the impact of the tenure system in the US, but long-term consequences of the RAE may be more profound. Whereas the operation of the tenure system has most impact on the attitudes and priorities of young academics at the beginning of their careers, the RAE affects all academics in the UK – from junior lecturers to senior professors. Hence, so long as the RAE continues in its current form, it will continue to exercise a profound influence on the shaping of the academic field and on the priorities and orientations of the individuals who wish to succeed within it. The divergence of interests that this produces between the academic field and the fields of academic and higher education publishing is therefore unlikely to disappear; on the contrary, it is likely to grow deeper with time.

11

Globalization and localization in the UK field of higher education publishing

In chapter 8 we examined the rise of large conglomerates in the field of higher education publishing and noted that these conglomerates tended to operate in an international arena, and in the previous chapter we commented on the growing presence of US-based college textbook publishers in the UK field of higher education publishing. What are the factors behind the transnational expansion of publishers that operate in the field of higher education? Why are they seeking to expand their activities beyond the domestic markets which were their original homes, and how are they seeking to achieve this expansion?

In this chapter I want to focus on these questions and explore the role of globalizing firms in the field of higher education publishing. I shall begin by examining some of the factors that lie behind the rise of globalizing firms in higher education publishing. I shall then focus on the UK and explore the interplay of globalization and localization within a specific publishing field.

The rise of globalizing firms in higher education publishing

The most important factor that lies behind the transnational expansion of higher education publishing is the fact that English has increasingly become the global language of higher education. Hence pedagogical content originally published in English will in principle be usable and adoptable in a growing number of national markets, whether or not English is the first language. The commonality of language between Britain, the US, Canada, Australia, New Zealand and various other countries created a basis for the diffusion of pedagogical content beyond the national boundaries of particular fields of higher education publishing, but the significance of English as the global language of higher education goes beyond this. Even in countries where English is not spoken as the first language, it is increasingly the case that students in some subjects will be expected to know English and will be able to use textbooks and other learning materials in English. This is particularly true of the Netherlands and the Scandinavian countries, for example, but the increasing use of English as a medium of higher education is a phenomenon by no means restricted to northern Europe.

Another factor that has facilitated the transnational expansion of higher education publishing is the fact that, in some subjects, the curriculum itself is becoming increasingly homogenized. The extent to which this is the case varies a great deal from subject to subject and country to country, but in subjects like economics, business, finance, the natural sciences, engineering and computer science, the structures of curricula in some countries have gravitated increasingly towards American models. This is partly due to the dominant role of the US in these subject areas, and partly because many young scholars go to the US for their graduate training and become familiar with the American curriculum, which they incorporate into their own teaching practices when they return to their home countries. This Americanization of the curriculum in some subject areas and some countries has helped to create and expand an international market for textbooks that were originally designed for US courses. One senior publishing executive put it like this:

> In Northern Europe, the curriculum is very much like the US. Basically it is an easy sell. If you are teaching corporate finance or you are teaching accounting or you are teaching marketing or chemistry or biology, you will use the US curriculum. In all of those instances in Northern Europe you will use the US books. In most of those instances in the UK, you'll use 50:50 a US- or a British-originated text. As you go to the Middle East, it's all US product. The curriculum is the same. Nearly all of the faculty, the Ph.D.s, are US-trained. Virtually anywhere you go in the business schools across EMA [Europe, Middle East, Africa], less so in the sciences and computer science but more and more they are US-influenced and they prefer the US type of textbook.

The increasing use of English as the global language of higher education and the growing Americanization of the curriculum in some subjects and some countries have helped to create conditions favourable to the international expansion of English-language based higher education publishers. These developments have helped to internationalize the field of higher education publishing, in the sense of creating a field that transcends national boundaries and is increasingly homogeneous in both linguistic and pedagogical terms – although one should be careful not to overemphasize the degree of homogeneity here, for reasons that we shall explore in more detail later in this chapter. But why do higher education publishers want to expand internationally? Why would the large textbook publishers who already have a strong foothold in the US market want to expand their presence outside the US? Why would the UK, Europe and other markets seem attractive to them as fields in which they could or should expand their activities?

There are essentially four answers to this question. First, the UK and Europe are large, mature markets where the demographics in terms of higher education are basically sound, and where English is widely used in higher education. Second, the indigenous competition is relatively undeveloped in terms of the standards of content development and production, in terms of the level of investment in supplementary materials and in terms of the methods of sales and marketing. Hence there are some senior executives who see an opportunity to carry over into the UK and Europe the skills and practices of textbook publishing which were honed in several decades of intense competition in the US, and which would give them a competitive advantage over local players. The third answer is that by expanding in the UK and Europe, they can exploit in new ways the content that was originally developed for the US market. They can do this either by selling units of the same textbooks that are being sold in the US market or by adapting this content in some way – either through customization for local markets or by translating into local languages. This gives them a way of increasing the sales of textbooks for which the bulk of the acquisition and development costs has already been paid. Given the intense competition in the US market and the difficulty of increasing one's market share within it, selling the same (or similar) content in over-seas markets provides one way of achieving growth. The fourth answer is that interna-tional expansion can also be a means of acquiring new content. For the most part, this new content will be acquired and developed for local markets. But there are also some subject areas – computer science being a good example – where new content acquired in the UK and Europe can be developed into textbooks that can be sold in the US market.

Three stages of global expansion

For the large corporations seeking to expand their international presence, there are typically three stages in the process of expansion. There is a logical sequence to these stages, in the sense that a corporation will typically begin with stage 1, move on to stage 2 and then possibly to stage 3. But stage 3 involves a great deal more investment and commitment, and hence some corporations tend to remain at the level of stage 1 or stage 2. The three stages are: (1) selling US-originated content; (2) customizing US-originated content for local markets; and (3) building an indigenous publishing pro-gramme. Let us examine each stage in turn.

Stage 1: Selling US-originated content   The most straightforward way of expanding in foreign markets is to set up a sales operation that will market and sell textbooks that were originally developed for the US market. This strategy can work well in certain subject areas, especially in the natural sciences, mathematics, engineering and computer science, but also to some extent in economics, business and finance. In computer science, for example, a good textbook on Java programming should be just as useful and adopt-able in the UK and northern Europe as it is in the US – the content is relatively neutral with regard to geographical locale. 'Programming is programming, biology is still biology and calculus hasn't changed in 500 years,' as one senior executive put it. Moreover, the quality of US textbooks – both in terms of content development and standards of production – is generally much higher than the quality of many locally produced text-books, and the range and sophistication of the supplementary materials are much greater. Hence many lecturers in the UK and Europe have been quite open to the idea of adopting these textbooks where they were available and in subjects where the content was neutral with regard to geographical locale.

If problems arise in terms of the marketing and selling of a US-originated textbook of this kind in the UK and Europe, they are more likely to stem from factors other than the pedagogical content as such. Two important problems of this kind are curriculum fit and pricing. The problem of curriculum fit arises because, despite the fact that there has been a certain amount of curriculum homogenization in some subjects in recent decades, the levels at which different kinds of material are taught tend to vary from one national context to another. Hence it cannot be assumed that a textbook which has been developed for freshman courses in economics or physics in the US will be equally suit-able for first-year economics or physics courses at most universities in the UK or north-ern Europe. In the UK, for instance, most students who do economics at university tend to have done economics at A-level, and much of what they have done at A-level would be covered by the core textbooks aimed at freshman courses in the US. A textbook publisher who covers several levels of the curriculum in the US will try to select those textbooks from their list which will be the best fit in terms of the content taught at different levels of the curriculum in the UK. So rather than marketing their freshman economics textbook to lecturers teaching first-year economics at British universities, they will market their sophomore microeconomics and macroeconomics textbooks to them – that is, they will try to achieve the best curriculum fit. To do this effectively, publishers have to have a good working knowledge of the educational systems and curricula in the countries where they are seeking to market and sell their textbooks.

The problem of pricing arises because, for reasons that we analysed in chapter 8, the big core textbooks in the US tend to be priced much higher than textbooks in the UK and Europe. Any corporation seeking to expand internationally by marketing and selling US-generated content must deal with the problem of how to price their textbooks in foreign markets, and solving this problem requires the development of suitable systems of internal trading. At one extreme, the corporation could adopt a policy of global pricing – that is, using the same price globally, converted into local currencies. In the field of academic publishing, global pricing has become the norm. But in the field of higher education publishing, it would be very difficult to adopt a policy of global pricing in most subject areas: given the high price of US-originated textbooks, it would mean in most cases that imported US textbooks would be priced far above the local competition and would, in effect, be priced out of the market. At the other extreme, the corporation could adopt a policy of pricing to market – that is, allowing the local sales and marketing operation to fix prices at levels that are comparable to the prices of local competitors.

In practice, the large corporations have found ways to deal with the pricing problem which position them somewhere between these two extremes. They generally steer clear of world pricing for fear that it would price them out of local markets, but at the same time they don't go as far as giving their local operations the freedom to price to market. They devise systems of internal trading which allow local operations to price well below the US selling price but which tend nonetheless to produce pressures for local operations to sell US-originated textbooks above the prices of local competitors. The system of internal trading varies from company to company, ranging from high discounts off US retail or net prices to a mark-up on unit cost (and various alternatives in between). The pricing latitude of local operations and their degree of profitability varies considerably depending on the terms of trade. But the overall impact of these arrangements is that the local operations are able to sell US-originated textbooks at prices that are well below US prices while still being significantly above – or at least at the top end of the scale of – the prices typically used by local textbook publishers. Within local markets, this has tended to produce an upward pull on the prices of textbooks, whether these are US imports or locally generated products. The prices used by the local operations of large corporations have tended to set norms towards which other publishers, including local competitors, tend to gravitate. The result is an overall inflation of the prices of the big core textbooks, whether imported or locally generated, which has tended to run well ahead of the rate of inflation.

The methods used by the large corporations to deal with the pricing problem are likely to come under growing pressure in the coming years. The corporations are faced

here with two complementary threats. On the one hand, by allowing their local operations to sell US textbooks at prices that are significantly lower than the prices for which
they sell in the US market, this policy runs the risk of generating a return flow: jobbers
can buy up US textbooks being sold in foreign markets at a fraction of the US selling
price and re-import them back into the US; even when they add on the cost of freight,
they can still undercut the price of the textbook in the US market. As we saw in chapter
8, there are signs that this risk is not merely hypothetical and that, with growing problems of sell-through breakdown in the US market, the large textbook publishers may
be forced to re-evaluate their policy of allowing their overseas operations to sell US-
originated textbooks at heavily discounted prices. On the other hand, if overseas operations are forced to put up their prices even further in order to stem the return flow,
they may price themselves out of their local markets and find themselves faced with
growing problems of sell-through breakdown (and, in the case of some markets in Asia
and elsewhere, growing problems of piracy).

Stage 2: Customizing US-originated content for local markets   While selling US-originated content in foreign markets is an effective strategy in some subjects, there is a limit
to how far a US-based corporation can grow its overseas business by pursuing a strategy of this kind. The problem is that even in subjects where the basic theoretical material is the same irrespective of where the teaching institution is located, there are
countless ways in which the content of a textbook tends to reflect its place of origin –
the examples and case studies used, the institutions discussed, the systems of currency
and measurement, the illustrations and artwork, the spelling, the grammar, etc. As one
senior executive put it,

> Imagine yourself studying economics and you're taking an introductory economics course
> and you're using a book that's full of examples of the Federal Reserve Bank and it is full
> of dollars, it's full of US macroeconomic data, it's full of examples of price theory and of
> applications in companies in Minnesota and Iowa, and you are in Cambridge [UK]: you'll
> understand it and it will sort of make sense, but these are not names you've heard of and
> it doesn't engage you as a student very well.

One way of getting around this problem is to adapt or *customize* a US-originated textbook for the UK and European market – and, indeed, for other markets too, if it seems
likely that the production of a customized edition would result in increased sales on a
scale that would justify the cost and effort involved. So in the case of a macroeconomics textbook, for example, one could keep the theory if it's very well done but adapt the
text for the UK and European market by replacing many of the American examples
with British and European examples, changing the currency, etc. The textbook is generally published with the same title and the same author on the cover, although the new
version is often distinguished from the US original in various ways (e.g. a different cover
design, perhaps a line indicating that this is a European edition or an international
edition, etc.) and the name of the person who adapted the text might be included as a
co-author. There are even some cases where the customized edition begins to take on
a life of its own, going through numerous editions that take it further and further away
from the original US textbook from which it began.

However, the customization of US-originated textbooks is not a panacea. The great advantage is speed – 'you've got the book, go and get someone to adapt it and you can get it out there.' But in other respects there are no great advantages. It doesn't necessarily cost any less to customize an existing textbook than to develop a new one – indeed, it can even cost more, because there are two sets of authors and that may mean paying higher royalties overall. It works well in some cases and in some subject areas, but the textbooks have to be picked carefully and the right person found to do the adaptation. For the big corporations that want to establish a real presence in the UK and Europe, customization is less important than the development of an indigenous publishing programme.

Stage 3: Building an indigenous publishing programme While importing and customizing US-originated content is an essential part of what the overseas offices of the large textbook publishers do, in the case of most large corporations it's only part of what they do, and in the eyes of some senior executives in these overseas offices it's not the most important part. For them, the key to being successful in overseas markets, and the real challenge they set themselves, is to build an indigenous publishing programme that is focused on commissioning and developing locally originated content for local markets. As one senior executive in a large international corporation put it, 'being local is the key.'

Why is it so important to build a local publishing programme? It is important because in many subject areas a publisher can only get so far by importing and customizing US-originated content. While the quality of US-originated textbooks is high in terms of both content development and production, it is not always easy to ensure that textbooks originated in the US, even when adapted to local conditions, will be able to compete effectively with the textbooks produced by local competitors. The production quality of the US-originated textbook may be much higher, but the pedagogical value of the text may be less than that offered by locally originated textbooks. There are two main reasons for this. First, in many subjects the content is not geographically neutral. It may be largely neutral in subjects like computer science, mathematics and natural sciences, but the degree of geographical neutrality begins to decline as one moves into other subject areas. In economics and finance the content can be relatively neutral (here the problems of geographical variability can be largely dealt with by customization), but the content is much less neutral in subjects like business and marketing, since these subjects generally rely on the extensive use of case studies and examples which are often more relevant to some national contexts than others. As one moves into the softer social sciences – sociology, anthropology, politics, geography, etc. – and into humanities subjects like history and literature, the geographical variability of the content increases significantly, and hence it becomes increasingly difficult to rely on a strategy of importing and/or customizing US-originated textbooks. The content of US-originated textbooks, even when it is customized by a local author, may simply be too far removed from the kind of content that is typically taught at universities in the UK, Europe and other parts of the world.

The other reason why it is difficult to rely on importing and customizing US-originated content is that, in many subject areas, locally originated content is likely to fit the local curricula better than imported material, even when the latter is customized for local needs. This is not just a matter of content but also of the structure of the curriculum – the levels at which different kinds of material are taught, the kind of background knowledge that can be taken for granted, the assessment procedures that are used, how best to prepare students for exams, etc. One can try to address these concerns by providing supplementary materials – either print or web-based – that relate the content of a US-originated textbook to the structure of local curriculae and assessment systems, providing guidelines for lecturers and students, sample exam questions and answers, etc. But even when supplemented in this way, a US-originated textbook may find it difficult to compete with a textbook written from beginning to end by a local author who knows the local curriculum very well and has pitched the text at the level that will meet the needs of lecturers and students.

So how does a US-based textbook publisher build an indigenous publishing programme? There are essentially two ways. One strategy is to build by acquisition – that is, it can buy one or more local publishing companies that will provide a foothold for an indigenous publishing programme. The key advantage of this strategy is that it's fast: the long gestation period of the commissioning and development cycle can be cut short. The main drawbacks are that (a) it can be costly, (b) there may not be suitable companies to buy, and (c) those companies that are potential purchases may not be an ideal match in terms of their organizational structures and the profile of their lists. Hence any purchase of this kind may require a great deal of restructuring before significant gains can be made. The second strategy is to build by organic growth. A publisher can invest in hiring acquisitions and development editors and thereby build up a locally based editorial team. The advantage of this strategy is that it can control much more directly the shape and development of the list – what is put under contract, how the content is developed, etc. The main difficulty with this strategy is that it requires a great deal of investment over a long period before it begins to pay dividends. It therefore requires a significant degree of patience from senior managers and shareholders, and patience of this kind is not always to be found in the large corporations.

These two strategies are not mutually exclusive, and some of the large international corporations have tried to do both. They have both acquired indigenous UK-based publishing firms which have provided them with a local foothold in the UK higher education market and, at the same time, they have sought to build up the editorial strength of the UK-based operation. But the opportunities for UK acquisitions at the lower levels of the curriculum are relatively limited, and the amount of restructuring that would be necessary to assimilate the rather diverse lists of most UK publishers tends to act as a disincentive. In the absence of serious acquisition opportunities, the large corporations that want to build an indigenous publishing programme are obliged to build their own. This is both a disadvantage and an opportunity – a disadvantage in the sense that the large corporations which are unable to acquire are deprived of the kind of UK foothold that others might have, thus putting them at a competitive disadvantage; but it is also an opportunity in the sense that they are faced with the task of building their own. The double-edged character of this challenge emerges clearly in the following exchange with a senior manager of a large corporation:

> *So you have a disadvantage here in the sense that you can't acquire a local publishing firm to give you a foothold to develop an indigenous publishing programme – is that right? You almost have to do it from scratch.*

Exactly. That's exactly it. Today it is a disadvantage, but it is a hell of an opportunity because we can't acquire. There really isn't anything to acquire, we are looking, believe me. There are nuggets here and there but nothing significant. There really isn't anything out there that would be a natural fit to give us growth. We have to do it organically.

The main focus of the indigenous publishing programmes of the large corporations is to commission and develop content for local markets, which in the case of UK-based operations means primarily the UK and northern Europe. Where it is felt that the content has potential in other markets, attempts will be made to realize that potential, but this is a secondary concern. 'The primary goal of our commissioning people is to publish a product which is justifiable almost completely on the basis of local revenues,' explained one senior manager in the UK office of a large corporation. There are some subject areas where textbooks commissioned in the UK and northern Europe will travel well to North America – computing is the subject area that lends itself most readily to this reverse flow, but there are examples in other subject areas too, such as the natural sciences. Apart from these isolated cases, however, the international flow of textbook content within the large corporations tends to be largely one way. This is partly because the US market is simply too competitive at the lower levels of the curriculum and is very well served by US-originated products. It is also because the UK and northern European markets tend to be more open to US-originated textbooks (whether unmodified or customized) than the other way around. 'There is more acceptance of American products here [in the UK] in general, not just books, than there is of British products in America,' explained one senior executive.

So there is a clear structural asymmetry in the flow of content within the large corporations. Local operations in the UK and northern Europe are concerned with importing and selling US-originated content, with customizing this content where appropriate and, in some cases, with developing and expanding indigenous publishing programmes. But with certain exceptions, the content originated in the UK and northern Europe is commissioned and developed primarily *for* the UK and northern European markets, and it is relatively rare for this UK-originated content to be imported or customized by the US side of the corporation for the US higher education market. As a general rule, the traffic in content within the large corporations tends to flow largely from the US to the UK and northern Europe (as well as to other parts of the world), while the reverse flow is relatively small and generally restricted to a few subject areas.

So far we've focused on the role of the large corporations in the UK and northern Europe, but these corporations are also very active in other international markets. They import and customize textbooks for other countries where English is either spoken as the first language (Canada, Australia, New Zealand, South Africa, etc.) or where English is used as a principal language of teaching in higher education (Malaysia, Singapore, etc.). Some of the large corporations have also developed separate operations in other linguistic regions – for example, in Spain and the Spanish-speaking world, which includes a large part of Latin America, in Portugal and Brazil, in Italy and so on. Broadly speaking, the same principles apply to these operations as apply to the UK and northern European operation, the only main difference being that imported content, whether taken as it is or customized, has to be translated before it can be used. This transforms the finances of importing content, since the cost of translation has to be factored in and the books have to be produced with the new text, but the basic principle of taking US-originated content and adapting it for local markets remains the same. In many cases these local operations are also charged with the task of building indigenous publishing programmes, commissioning and developing content that is specifically tailored to their local or regional market. The logical sequence in these foreign language markets is very similar to the sequence of development in the UK and northern Europe – initially translations of US-originated content, then adaptations, and then the development of indigenous publishing programmes, either through acquisition or organic growth (or both).

The competitive advantages of the global players

So what competitive advantages do the large global corporations have when it comes to developing indigenous publishing programmes? What features can they draw on in order to compete effectively with locally based publishing organizations? Their principal sources of competitive advantage include the following: (1) scale; (2) accumulated skills and expertise; (3) technology; and (4) sales and marketing.

(1)   *Scale*   Undoubtedly a major source of competitive advantage for the large corporations is their sheer scale. These are huge organizations with vast resources at their disposal, and this gives them tremendous power to invest in the development of indigenous publishing programmes, whether through acquisition or through the building up of local commissioning teams (or both). Their scale also gives them large pools of content in their core subject areas which they can draw on to build a major presence in the field. By importing and customizing US-originated content, they can quickly establish themselves as leading publishers in foreign markets without having to wait through the long gestation period of locally originated content. Scale gives them the resources to offer attractive advances to authors, to invest in the development of the content through extensive reviewing and to produce textbooks to high standards (including the use of four colours). Scale also gives them considerable power in the market when it comes to negotiating with other parties for the supply of materials and services and when it comes to negotiating discount terms with the major players in the retail sector. As the retail sector becomes increasingly consolidated and the balance of power begins to swing in favour of the chains, the larger publishing organizations are in a stronger position to counter the growing power of the retail chains and to negotiate better terms.

Being part of a large organization also offers economies of scale which are difficult to achieve in smaller organizations. As the publishing field becomes more competitive, it becomes more difficult to achieve significant growth in terms of sales. The market becomes more saturated as there are more and more textbooks competing for adoptions. But even when it is difficult to achieve growth in sales, large organizations can achieve cost reductions and scale benefits by combining forces and rationalizing tasks, and thereby maintain or even improve the bottom line. So they are able to maintain or improve their profitability even in conditions where it is difficult to increase their sales.

(2)   *Accumulated skills and expertise*   A second major competitive advantage of the large corporations is that they can draw on a wide range of skills and expertise acquired in the American textbook market and put these skills to work in the development of

their indigenous publishing programmes. In the American field of higher education, the textbooks aimed at lower-level courses are subjected to a much more intensive process of development than has traditionally been the case in the UK, both in terms of content development and in terms of the quality of production, the provision of supplementary materials, etc. The large corporations are able to transfer the methods, systems, skills and expertise used for textbook development in the US and apply these, through appropriate training of staff in their indigenous publishing operations, to the development of textbooks for the UK and elsewhere. The indigenous teams take the methods, systems and formats originally developed for the American style of textbook and use them in the commissioning and development of textbooks for their own markets. The careful development of content with the use of multiple readers, the emphasis on clarity and comprehensiveness, the use of pedagogical devices, a large number of illustrations and four-colour printing – these and other standard practices can be carried over into the UK market. The content of the textbooks originated in the UK will be different because they will be developed for and tailored to the UK and northern European market, but the development and production of these textbooks will benefit from the ability of the indigenous publishing team to use the methods and formats pioneered by the corporation in the American textbook market.

(3) *Technology* A third key source of competitive advantage for the large corporations is their capacity to invest in new technologies. For organizations active in the field of higher education publishing, this is important for several reasons. In the first place, it enables them to ensure that their back office systems are streamlined, efficient and up to date in terms of their capacity to handle the large quantities of information upon which the publishing process depends. The investment in IT – hardware, software and qualified personnel – is a substantial demand on the resources of most publishing firms, and the larger organizations are able to invest more heavily, to spread the costs more widely and to share the benefits across more operating units. A second reason why this is important is that it enables them to improve the quality and increase the flexibility of the product – i.e. the textbook – and to drive down the costs associated with textbook production. The more they are able to invest in technology to support the production process and to move to digital systems of content manipulation and storage, the more they are able to increase the quality of the product while at the same time driving down costs. It also greatly facilitates the process of bringing out new editions and of customizing textbooks for local markets.

A third reason why the investment in technology is important is that it enables these corporations to stay ahead in terms of the supplementary materials that are offered to lecturers and students to support textbooks. As we saw in an earlier chapter, the provision of supplementary materials played a crucial role in the struggles between the big textbook publishers in the US in the 1980s and 1990s – the package wars – and there are signs that this dynamic is becoming increasingly important in the UK and northern Europe. As the competition for adoptions at the lower levels of the curriculum intensifies, those publishers who are able to offer more elaborate packages of supplementary materials and more sophisticated companion websites to support their textbooks will have a competitive advantage in the struggle to win adoptions. The large global corporations are able not only to invest more heavily in the development and provision of supplementary materials and companion websites, but are also able to draw on the accumulated knowledge and expertise acquired by their US-based operations.

Finally, the large corporations are able to experiment with new technologies in ways and on a scale that smaller organizations cannot match. They can afford to take chances by investing in new ideas that may come to nothing, but from which they may learn something about how best to position themselves so that they will not be left behind if and when the market changes. Smaller organizations can be innovative too, but on the whole they tend to adopt a wait-and-see approach. They don't have the resources to experiment on the scale of the large corporations, and hence they tend to stand back and watch while others take the risks (and, as is so often the case in this domain, lose money). We shall return to these issues in later chapters.

(4) *Sales and marketing* The fourth source of competitive advantage for the large corporations is in the area of sales and marketing. As I mentioned in the previous chapter, the large global corporations which are active in UK textbook publishing tend to use the same sales and marketing methods used by their US-based operations, and this means above all the use of college reps who visit university campuses and call on lecturers in the attempt to win adoptions. Those who use college reps in the UK are convinced that it makes a substantial difference to their ability to secure adoptions and to translate these into sales. Here is the view of a senior manager in the UK-based operation of a large corporation:

> *How important is it, if you want to be a textbook publisher in the UK, to have a sales force that calls on lecturers rather than just calling on bookstores?*

> Crucial. In the past, before the late eighties, maybe in the early nineties, the publishers relied on selling their academic books through bookshops, paying 35–40 per cent discount, paying trade discount. Those bookshops don't determine the demand for textbooks. The demand is determined by the lecturer who decides to adopt or not. So you are talking to the wrong person.

> *Traditionally a lot of publishers in Britain rely on direct mail, sending printed material to those lecturers about their textbooks and then sending them inspection copies if they're interested. In your judgement, is it sufficient to rely on direct mail?*

> No. I'm convinced that if you don't have reps who are out there knowing what the market's doing, what courses are changing, which professors have moved from one institution to another, what your competitors are doing, showing material with some pretty complicated web support, you are not going to get those books sold in the same way. I am convinced of that 100 per cent and I love to compete against those who don't believe that because we always win out in the end.

But it is expensive to support a sales force of college reps and a publisher has to have a substantial number of core textbooks at the right level and clustered together in the same or similar disciplines to justify the expenditure. This tends to favour the large corporations which, in addition to their own indigenously generated content, can also draw on large pools of US-originated content for their reps to sell.

Some UK-based higher education publishers do a limited amount of campus calling, but for the most part they tend to rely on a mixture of direct mail, telemarketing and email to reach the academics who act as the gatekeepers in the adoption system. They are thus deprived of the direct, face-to-face contact which the college rep can achieve, and when it comes down to trying to persuade a lecturer of the merits of one textbook vis-à-vis its competitors, a telephone conversation with an anonymous telemarketer is no match for the kind of persuasive power that can be exercised through a face-to-face encounter. The visiting rep can take the lecturer through the chapters of the text, present the supplementary materials and demo the companion website. Just as importantly, the rep can build up a relationship of trust with the lecturer and provide a personal point of contact with an otherwise distant and anonymous organization. Even marketing managers at some of the larger UK-based publishing firms acknowledge that it may be difficult to compete against this by relying only on direct mail, telemarketing and email:

> With regard to intro textbooks, what strikes me is that it has just become so hugely competitive out there that it seems even more of a gamble now to launch an intro textbook in terms of the amount of time and resources that you have to put behind it. The Pearsons of this world have got themselves into such a strong position that a company of our size really does find it difficult to compete at that level with that sort of book. To a certain extent we just can't compete with the big guns ablazing, the army of reps doing the campus calling – as good and as lovely as our telemarketers may be, it's no substitute for the face-to-face contact and the regular contact that the reps can build up.

The importance of local knowledge

So how can UK-based publishing organizations compete with the large global corporations in the UK field of higher education publishing? Do they have any sources of competitive advantage – and if so, what are they? Among the sources of competitive advantage on which local publishing firms can draw are (1) local knowledge, (2) author loyalty, and (3) flexibility.

(1) *Local knowledge* Perhaps the most important source of competitive advantage is that local firms have substantial stores of local knowledge concerning the curriculum in the UK and the ways in which subjects are taught. In the field of higher education publishing, the importance of local knowledge cannot be overestimated: local knowledge is the key to success. Textbooks will be adopted by the gatekeepers only if they are seen by them as meeting their needs in terms of content provision for the courses they teach, and the strength of the adoption – whether recommended or required – will tend to reflect the gatekeeper's judgement concerning the suitability of the text for all or part of the course. Hence local knowledge of courses and of how they are changing is vital, and UK-based publishers who are successful in the higher education field have, either explicitly or implicitly, built up substantial stores of local knowledge which enable them to commission and develop textbooks which are suitable for courses in the UK. This local knowledge is one of their most valuable assets and a key source of competitive advantage for them. It is particularly valuable when it can be used to develop lists in subject areas which have a degree of geographical specificity, such as politics, social policy, healthcare and education, where the global corporations will find it more difficult to transfer content originally developed for the US market. As the managing director of a UK-based textbook publisher observed,

Teaching and learning are always a combination of local and global elements. A chemistry book can sell into the UK unaltered, but where there are differences of approach, of culture or whatever, there's going to be a local market. Now sometimes the Americans are good at doing that and sometimes they're not, and that's where you get the local publishers in different ways finding that they can get competitive advantage. We are a case in point. For instance, we are market leaders in politics because politics is a relatively small subject, mostly local in terms of UK/Europe, and it goes below their radar, so we can be there. We're market leaders in social work – same sort of thing. We have in the past tried to build a pure science list and we can't do it. We've given up on that.

Of course, UK-based publishers do not have a monopoly on local knowledge. It is perfectly possible for the UK-based operations of the large international corporations to build up similar stocks of local knowledge and to compete in subject areas which are relatively specific in geographical terms, and that is exactly what these operations seek to do. But UK-based publishers are deeply rooted in the pedagogical culture of British higher education, and this does give them a certain competitive advantage.

(2) *Author loyalty*   UK-based publishers also have some competitive advantages in the struggle to acquire content and to sign up local authors. These publishers are well known in the academic community and many of them have a high reputation among academics. Some authors who have published with UK-based firms may feel some loyalty to them and may wish to remain with them rather than publish with the UK branch of a large transnational corporation. They may value the personal contact with an editor whom they have known for many years and may attribute more significance to this than to the attractions – financial and otherwise – of publishing with a large corporation. Local publishers are able to provide a kind of *personalized service* to authors which the large corporations may find it difficult to match. Again, the managing director of a UK-based textbook publisher put it like this:

> There is one important issue here, which is that as a publisher you're making a service offering to an individual author in the textbook field. And for the same reason that people want to be published by Faber, they don't necessarily want to be published by HarperCollins – it's the great evil empire stuff. Actually, for the author, what matters is how they are being dealt with. And remember, many of our books are not going into the big development machine, which is where we can't compete very effectively, they are medium-sized books, and here the relationship with the editor and the relationship with the publishing company, given that a publishing company can do most things fairly competently, is enormously important. So we have to major on service and we have to make sure people want to publish with us, that it's a better experience. It's not just true in textbook publishing but I think it's true across the board. I don't think academics are impressed by pure commercialism – in fact, they're rather suspicious of it.

Moreover, some academics are attracted to the idea of publishing with an organization which has a varied list of publications – original scholarly works, trade books and upper-level texts as well as low-level textbooks – rather than with an organization that publishes low-level textbooks only. In the context of the RAE, this factor may be increasingly important for many academics, who may be increasingly reluctant not only to write textbooks but also to publish with organizations which are known above all else as textbook publishers. Some UK-based publishers have recognized the significance of this point and have sought to use the varied architecture of their list as a key resource in the struggle to acquire content and to attract the best authors. As one manager in a UK-based publishing firm explained,

> I wouldn't say that we are actively commissioning monographs in a lot of areas, but in two or three areas where we have been well known for some time we realize that we can't just go out to get textbooks and that we do need some substance as well for the research community.

Why do you need this substance? What's the concern that lies behind this change of policy?

> I guess the fear is not getting the right people on our list, whether it's to write textbooks or to write trade books. Word of mouth goes around in communities and various conceptions are born of publishers and their relative strengths, and we don't want to be seen as a publisher that won't give original research a chance. We want to get the top authors as much as anyone. Trying to get the best people to write the best textbooks is difficult if you don't have another channel to offer them.

We have seen how the logic of the field of academic publishing has forced many publishers to curtail their monograph publishing programmes and to migrate increasingly into the field of higher education publishing. It is one of the ironies of the publishing world that some of these publishers are beginning to realize that, in the intensely competitive field of higher education publishing, the possession of a varied list could provide them with some of the symbolic capital they need if they want to sign up the best authors to write textbooks for them.

(3) *Flexibility* A third source of competitive advantage for UK-based publishing organizations is that they can be flexible in terms of the kinds of books they publish and the levels of the curriculum they serve. The UK-based operations of the large corporations are generally obliged to focus their publishing activity on textbooks which will have an annual sale of at least 2,000 copies; anything less than that is difficult to justify in terms of the levels of investment and overhead costs involved. This means that they generally are obliged to focus their attention on the large introductory courses and on those selected upper-level courses where student numbers are big enough to support annual sales on this scale. These are the courses where competition for adoptions tends to be most intense, precisely because the numbers are relatively large. Small and medium-sized UK publishers are eager to publish textbooks for these courses too, but they don't have to be focused so single-mindedly on the courses with the big adoption potential. They can be more flexible and more nimble; they can publish textbooks aimed at more specialized courses and they can work with texts which have annual sales well below 2,000. With their knowledge of local markets and their networks of relations with the academic community, they can anticipate trends and take chances with texts which are more innovative and cutting-edge. The managing director of a small UK-based textbook publisher put it this way:

> We've got to spot the new areas before the others spot them. Now, not only will we be able to do that because I think we are nimble enough to. The conglomerate doesn't want that

area. It doesn't want to spot it beforehand. They only want it when it is established, when they know it is selling 3,000 copies a year or whatever. So what we've got to do is to continue to get in there early enough so that for a timeframe that may only be five years, that's our area. Then someone comes in and colonizes it and competes with us. In the meantime, we've got to have found three or four other areas.

In other words, despite the growing presence of the large transnational corporations in the UK field of higher education publishing, there are subject niches where small local publishers, who are close to the ground and knowledgeable about the new and emerging areas of study, can develop textbooks which anticipate developments rather than merely respond to existing demands. But given that the large players are likely to move in when the student numbers begin to look attractive, the small local publishers have to be able to turn flexibility and subject area innovation into an organizational trait, constantly searching out new and emerging subject areas in order to stay a step ahead of the competition.

The future of higher education publishing in the UK

What does the future hold for higher education publishing in the UK? Of course, it is difficult to comment on this with any degree of certainty, but at least six trends seem likely: (1) further consolidation; (2) polarization of the field; (3) the intensification of struggles for adoptions and market share; (4) the intensification of struggles for content; (5) the increasing localization of global corporations; and (6) the persistence but growing precariousness of indigenous higher education publishing.

(1) *Further consolidation*   As we've seen, there has been a substantial amount of consolidation among higher education publishers in the UK over the last twenty years and many imprints that were once significant and recognizable names in the UK field – names like Longman, Heinemann, Hutchinson, Edward Arnold, Harvester Wheatsheaf, Methuen, Routledge, Open University Press – have either disappeared or been integrated into other companies. Most senior figures in the field expect to see more consolidation in the coming years, although exactly what form this will take, and which firms will be bought and sold, is difficult to say.

Further consolidation does not necessarily mean that small textbook publishers will be squeezed out of existence. Given that the academic field itself is constantly changing, there will continue to be opportunities for small publishers to carve out niches for themselves, especially in subject areas which have a high degree of geographical specificity. However, it is likely that the smaller players will find it more and more difficult to compete at the lower levels of the curriculum. As the managing director of a medium-sized UK publishing firm observed,

I think there's always going to be scope for people who've got a burning wish to do their own small thing. I don't think that wish is going to be about getting rich. That wish is about trying to have a really good philosophy list or a really good list in a vocational area. And we've seen those develop and go on and then be sold. And I'm sure that process will continue. It's part of all publishing, not just academic publishing. They will not be able to do big blockbuster textbooks but they will be small and nimble with a low cost base.

(2) *Polarization of the field*   A second development which seems likely is the increasing polarization of the field of higher education publishing. What I mean by this is that the large transnational corporations are likely to become increasingly dominant at the lower levels of the curriculum in the core textbook subjects, where the scale of investment they can provide and their sales forces of college reps give them crucial competitive advantages. The small and medium-sized UK-based publishers are likely to find it increasingly difficult to compete at this level, and increasingly difficult to maintain the market share of low-level textbooks which have traditionally performed well for them. They will find themselves forced increasingly into the upper levels of the curriculum where the numbers are smaller, or into subject areas which have more geographical specificity and are less dominated by the big textbook publishers. The field of higher education publishing will become increasingly polarized: on the one hand, the large corporations will concentrate their efforts increasingly on publishing textbooks for the lower levels of the curriculum in the core textbook subjects like economics, business, finance, psychology, the natural sciences, mathematics, engineering and computer science, as well as some of the softer social sciences where the UK and northern European market is large enough to justify the investment, and, between them, they will probably succeed in taking a growing share of the market; on the other hand, the small and medium-sized UK-based publishers will find it increasingly difficult to compete head-to-head with the large corporations and will find themselves pushed into the upper levels of the curriculum and into subject areas such as the humanities and the softer social sciences, as well as interdisciplinary subjects like gender studies, media and cultural studies and regional studies.

This polarization of the field is similar to that which occurred in the US field of higher education publishing, where the large textbook publishers have come to dominate the lower levels of the curriculum in the core textbook subjects and where the university presses and smaller commercial firms have generally been confined to the upper levels of the curriculum and/or to subject areas where the big core textbooks are less entrenched as a pedagogical tool. But the fundamental difference between the US and the UK in this regard is that the higher education sector in the UK is much smaller than the US, and hence the numbers of students taking upper-level courses – both undergraduate and graduate – is much smaller. The real difficulty facing small and medium-sized UK-based higher education publishers is that they find themselves under pressure from two sides: on the one hand, the intensifying competition at the lower levels of the curriculum is making it increasingly difficult for them to compete at these levels and may erode the market share they already have; but on the other hand, the sales they can achieve for textbooks and supplementary texts at the upper levels of the curriculum in the UK (or the UK and northern Europe) are unlikely to be sufficient on their own.

If this analysis is correct, it raises some fundamental questions concerning content provision for higher education in the UK. It seems likely that the system of higher education in the UK will be well catered for at the lower levels of the curriculum in the core textbook subjects – the prices of core textbooks may be high and may get higher, but there are plenty of publishers who are keen to have a share of this market and who will continue to develop content for it. What is much less clear is who will provide the textbook content for upper-level courses in the UK, especially in those subject areas where the numbers are relatively small and where the content will not necessarily travel well to North America and other export markets – for example, upper-level courses in the softer social sciences, the humanities and interdisciplinary subject areas. The increasing numbers of students entering higher education in the UK will not necessarily translate into higher sales for textbooks and supplementary texts aimed at upper-level courses and publishers may find it increasingly difficult to publish books of this kind, especially when there is limited scope for developing the content in ways that would secure adoptions in markets outside the UK.

(3)   *The intensification of struggles for adoptions and market share*   At the lower levels of the curriculum, the struggles for adoptions and market share will undoubtedly intensify. The key players will increasingly find themselves competing head to head to win adoptions, and the ability to draw on sales forces of college reps and to offer lecturers ever more elaborate packages of supplementary materials will tend to favour the larger players. But the other side of this dynamic is that it tends to produce an inflationary pressure on prices. The investment in high-quality products (including the use of four-colour printing) and elaborate packages of supplementary materials is very costly, as are the teams of college reps. A publisher needs to grow the business substantially if it wants to recover these costs and generate some level of profitability. However, the higher education market in the UK and northern Europe is mature and very competitive; it is difficult to grow revenue by expanding market share and increasing the sale of units. The easiest way to achieve revenue targets in a context of relatively static unit sales is to increase prices. For this and other reasons, the large textbook publishers have tended to increase the prices of textbooks well ahead of the rate of inflation.

There are some in the industry who worry about this trend. They see the prices of their big textbooks being put up by two or three times the rate of inflation and, at the same time, they see a persistent and perhaps worsening problem of sell-through breakdown, and they fear – quite reasonably – that the two trends may be connected. Is there a danger that substantial increases in the prices of textbooks will place a growing strain on the adoption system, so that a declining proportion of students will actually buy the textbook even though it has been adopted? Will the cycle of increasing costs and increasing prices fuel the growth of the used book market in the UK, with all the consequences this would have for textbook publishers? Might it even create opportunities for competitors who are able to offer cheaper but equally effective alternatives? One textbook editor in the UK branch of a large global corporation expressed his concerns like this:

> The way that textbook publishers – our competitors and us – have put our prices up over the last five years invariably at least twice the rate of inflation every year, often three times the rate of inflation, you do wonder whether you're getting into easyJet territory. Are we becoming British Airways where we're offering a luxury product that does the job beautifully, that's immaculate? Are we opening ourselves up for easyJet to come in with easy-Books, at £19.99, that do essentially the same thing: they get you there, in other words the plane doesn't crash, and the price is a third less than the textbook? It seems like basic business to me. Where you've got poor sell-through and you've got an expensive product, it strikes me as likely that there's an opportunity there to publish cheaper books. And you can do it without necessarily compromising academic standards, because a lot of these elements can be removed. For example, four colour is significant – we could take a fiver off the price if we went back to two colour, let alone one colour. The supplementary materi-

als, the amount of development we do – we do a lot of development because a lot of it is market seeding, you don't necessarily need detailed academic comment from thirty people on a level one textbook, you do it so that you can compete to win adoptions. So you then think, well, if we don't spend all that money, and we don't spend all this money on production, we'd bring the cost down. Should we be thinking about that?

There is a more than an echo here of some of the debates that have characterized the American textbook industry in recent years – the vicious circle of intensified competition for the big adoptions leading to more and more investment in high-quality production and in the provision of ever more elaborate supplementary materials, leading to escalating prices and growing problems of sell-through breakdown. As in the US, it's unlikely that the big textbook publishers will adopt a radically different approach: their overheads are too high and they've invested too heavily in the development of their brands as high-quality content providers – as the British Airways in the field of higher education publishing. But it's quite likely that, as with their US counterparts, they will look for ways to make cheaper editions available and will review the pricing of some of their key textbooks in very competitive markets. With textbooks imported from the US, their hands may be tied by the terms of trade and by the overriding concern of the parent company to avoid the seepage of cheaper editions back into the US market. But the UK branches of the big textbook publishers may have some room to manoeuvre with their locally originated textbooks and customized editions, and they may offer price reductions or special offers in an attempt to sell more copies and increase market share.

(4)   *The intensification of struggles for content*   As the competition for adoptions at the lower levels of the curriculum intensifies, so too publishers are likely to find it more and more difficult to sign up authors who are able and willing to write new textbooks for the UK market. This is partly because the growing competition within the field is likely to produce an inflationary pressure on contractual terms, so that authors willing to write textbooks will be able to play one publisher off against another, but it is also because the author base within the UK is shrinking. Fewer and fewer academics in the UK are willing to write textbooks today because this kind of intellectual work does not contribute in any significant way to the assessment exercises upon which their career in the academic world, and the material and symbolic rewards they are able to derive from it, ultimately depend. Any academic who works at, or aspires to work at, a university in the UK which seeks to perform well in the RAE will be aware of the pressure to be, and the pressure constantly to remain, 'research active' and to publish the kinds of works which are highly valued in RAE terms. Since time for research and writing are limited, the idea of setting aside precious research and writing time for the purposes of writing a textbook aimed at students is likely to be viewed negatively by most academics who are still developing their careers, since the time spent writing a textbook will reduce the amount of time available to produce the kinds of outputs that are positively valued by the RAE. The result is that the pool of potential textbook authors tends to shrink. Many young academics at the beginning of their careers tend to exclude themselves (or are strongly discouraged from entering the pool by their heads of department); many established academics who are still aspiring to career advancement, either by being promoted within their own institutions or by moving to another institution, also exclude them-

selves from the textbook-writing pool. Publishers will have to search harder and harder to find a diminishing number of academics who are willing to write textbooks.

There are various ways in which publishers can try to cope with this situation – we examined some of these ways in the previous chapter. But unless the rules governing the RAE are changed in a significant way (or the RAE itself is discontinued at some point), it is difficult to see how the consequences for textbook publishing in the UK could be anything other than deleterious. As the pool of potential textbook authors diminishes, publishers are likely to invest more and more in the continuous revision of existing textbooks – not, as in the US case, because the used book market has under-cut the sales of new books, but because publishers are finding it increasingly difficult to commission good academics to write new textbooks. Publishers are also likely to look increasingly outside the UK to find authors who are willing to write textbooks – to the US above all, but also to Canada, Australia and elsewhere. The result is that more and more of the textbooks provided for higher education in the UK are likely to be written by non-UK authors, either because they are imported into the UK by the large trans-national corporations or because UK-based publishers or publishing operations have, for lack of suitable UK authors, turned increasingly to non-UK academics to write the books.

It is difficult to see how this situation can be beneficial in the long term to the UK publishing industry or, for that matter, to the UK system of higher education. After all, the ability of higher education publishers to provide high-quality pedagogical materials depends on whether they are able to persuade good academics to write high-quality content for them, and nothing does more to dissuade academics in the UK from doing this than a set of rules which effectively devalue the pedagogical output of academics and discourage them from devoting time and energy to writing textbooks. Faced with the formidable structure of disincentives created by the RAE, UK publishers are likely to find themselves struggling (mostly unsuccessfully) to persuade UK academics to turn their accumulated knowledge and expertise as teachers into the kind of content that can be developed as a successful and high-quality textbook. Those institutions which do well in the RAE may benefit from this rather severe administrative structuring of aca-demic priorities, as indeed may those academics whose research output gives them some leverage in the competition for academic promotion. However, it is not just the text-book publishers but also those involved in higher education in the UK – students as well as lecturers – who may be the losers in the long run.

(5) *The increasing localization of global corporations*   The global corporations that want to compete seriously in the UK and northern European market will continue to invest in their indigenous publishing programmes, since in many subject areas this is the only way they can develop content that is well tailored to local needs and can compete effectively against local publishers. While the ability to draw on large pools of US-orig-inated content is a great advantage for the global corporations, they are well aware that the development of indigenous publishing programmes is the key to successful expan-sion in the UK and northern Europe and in other non-North American markets. But expanding their indigenous publishing programmes in the UK and northern Europe is a costly business, especially since the opportunities for acquisitions in this area are limited. It requires long-term investment in organic growth, and given the long gesta-tion period involved in textbook publishing, the return on investment may be slow.

Managers of the UK-based operations of the large global corporations tend to express confidence that they have the long-term commitment of the parent company and that they will get the support they need to build an indigenous publishing programme. They set themselves the task of shifting the balance of their output so that they are relying less and less on imported products and more and more on indigenously commissioned or customized content, sometimes with ambitious targets. But at the same time they know that there will be intense pressure on them to deliver results and to show that the investment is paying off. In a mature and very competitive market, it is by no means certain that they will be able to achieve growth and profitability at rates and levels that will be acceptable to senior managers in the parent company. There is always the danger that the parent company may feel that the rate of growth and/or level of profitability are too low and may decide to reduce costs, and the easiest way to reduce costs is to cut investment in the editorial programme and to fall back increasingly on the sale of US-originated products. So this is the key dilemma faced by the large global corporations: on the one hand, to compete as a major player in the UK and northern European market you have to invest in the development of an indigenous publishing programme, either through acquisitions or organic growth (or both); on the other hand, in a mature and very competitive market it may be difficult to achieve rates of growth and levels of profitability that will satisfy senior managers in the parent company, who may at some point decide that they need to reduce costs, and that an expedient way to do this is to cut investment in the editorial programme. Building an indigenous publishing programme is an expensive gamble that requires long-term investment, and in the face of static sales and low levels of profitability the temptations of short-term cost reductions may be difficult to resist.

(6)   *The persistence but growing precariousness of indigenous higher education publishing*   Despite the trend towards consolidation and the growing role of the large transnational corporations in the UK and northern Europe, there will undoubtedly continue to be room for small and medium-sized UK-based publishers in the field of higher education publishing. There are subject areas and levels of the curriculum which the large organizations will find difficult to serve, partly because the numbers are too small and partly because these subject areas are less amenable to the standardized textbook format. Even in the core textbook subjects, there will be opportunities for smaller publishers to develop innovative texts which don't try to compete head to head with the big four-colour textbooks but which prove attractive to lecturers and/or students on other grounds.

The real difficulty facing small and medium-sized UK-based higher education publishers is whether they can generate sufficient levels of revenue and profitability if the sales they are able to achieve at the lower levels of the curriculum are seriously eroded. The more competition they face at the level of first-year introductory textbooks, the more difficult it will be for them to maintain market share for the textbooks that have traditionally performed well for them at this level. And the more their market share is squeezed, the less they are able to rely on their big-selling textbooks to bolster their financial position. They may find themselves pushed more and more into the upper levels of the curriculum and forced to depend more and more on upper-level textbooks where the sales are much lower and less reliable and where the margins are often less attractive. This in turn may render their financial position more and more precarious, with declining overall sales and with margins under pressure. As one senior manager at a medium-sized UK-based publishing house observed,

> We've found ourselves operating more and more at the higher levels of the curriculum for several years now. Partly we've been pushed and partly it's been a conscious decision. We knew that a lot of investment is required at those lower levels, whereas certainly a few years ago it did appear that there weren't that many players at the higher levels and that we had a real opportunity to carve a good profitable niche for ourselves if you got the right books for the right courses. It seems inevitable that publishers like us are going to be operating more and more at the higher levels of the curriculum in the coming years.

> *Does it also seem inevitable that, given the nature of competition in this field and the benefits of scale, there will be further consolidation within the UK higher education publishing business?*

> Yes, it looks very much that way. I think it's increasingly hard for smaller independent publishers to survive, it really is. It does seem that at one end of the scale monograph publishing is no longer viable, at the other end of the scale only a handful of publishers can do the big moneyspinners, and so the niche that we find ourselves currently occupying is probably the only niche we can be in and survive. The danger, of course, is what happens if this niche is squeezed.

Part IV
The Digital Revolution

12

The digital revolution and the publishing world

At various points I have mentioned the significance of the digital revolution and its impact on publishing, and indeed there are few topics that have generated as much interest and speculation in the publishing industry over the last two decades as this. Since the late 1980s there has been a widespread feeling within the industry that digitization is bound to have a profound impact on publishing, even if it was never entirely clear just what the impact would be. 'The digital future' has been the subject of countless conferences arranged by organizations which have an interest in publishing (for many years it has been a running joke in the industry that the only way to make money out of electronic publishing is to organize a conference on it), and many working papers have been produced on various aspects of digitization and publishing (of which the series organized by Mark Bide and Mike Shatzkin in the 1990s is perhaps the most innovative and worthwhile[1]). But the interest in digitization has not been merely speculative: a great deal of money has been invested in digitization and computerization by publishing firms themselves and by a variety of other organizations with an interest in publishing, including technology firms, private investment firms and various charitable foundations. The world of book publishing has become an arena of active and ongoing experimentation by organizations which have, or would like to have, a stake in a digital future.

With some fifteen years of speculation and experimentation behind us, this is a good time to take stock. The inflated expectations of the mid-1990s are now in the past and we can reflect with a more sober sense of reality on what kinds of changes are likely to occur (and which are likely to endure) in this domain. It is helpful at the outset to distinguish three broad phases in the debates surrounding digitization and publishing. In the mid-1990s, there was much feverish speculation about the impact of digitization on the publishing industry and the imminent demise of the printed book. With the internet rapidly establishing itself as a major communication network, there were many who thought that it was distinctly possible, if not likely, that the printed book would soon go the way of the vinyl LP and become little more than a collector's item, eclipsed by the emergence of new technologies that would enable book content to be delivered online. It would, it was thought, be much cheaper and quicker to deliver book content in this way, and the legion problems of the book supply chain – the cost of inventory, the cost and the delays involved in shipping and the problem of returns, to mention just a few – could be resolved at a stroke. Looking over their shoulders at what happened in the music industry and elsewhere, some senior executives in the large publishing firms argued in favour of substantial investment in order to experiment with new technolo-

[1] See Vista 1995, 1996, 1997, 1998, 1999.

gies, fearful that if they were not willing to experiment early on, they would run the risk of being left high and dry when the new technologies invaded the market and took off. The message of Bower and Christensen's 1995 article on 'Disruptive Technologies'[2] – with its blunt warning of the dangers faced by leading companies who resist new technologies because mainstream customers don't want them and projected profit margins aren't big enough, thereby leaving the field to smaller companies who are able to create a market by experimenting with new products – was not lost on some corporate chiefs. (One senior executive of a large publishing corporation explicitly referred to this article in our interview.) And indeed, a good deal of the investment in experimentation and new technologies in the mid to late 1990s did come from outside the publishing field, from new technology firms backed by private investors who saw commercial opportunities opening up in areas where the traditional world of publishing intersected with the new world of digital information and the internet. There was much talk of 'disintermediation' and much scratching of heads, as publishers and other players in the traditional publishing supply chain tried to figure out how they could position themselves and secure their futures in a world where more and more content would be managed and delivered in digital formats.

By late 2000 the inflated expectations of the mid to late 1990s had begun to give way to a mood of growing scepticism about the capacity of the digital revolution to transform the publishing world. Some of this scepticism was an understandable reaction to the bursting of the dot.com bubble and the economic downturn of 2000–1, which brought the long period of growth in the 1990s to an abrupt end. For many of the new technology firms which were relying on speculative investment funds to cover their start-up costs, sources of new finance suddenly became very hard to come by and major cost-cutting measures became the order of the day. For many of the publishing firms which had invested significant sums in experiments with new technologies, in some cases developing substantial ebook programmes and launching separate ebook imprints, a new mood of caution prevailed. Static or declining sales tended to produce a sharp readjustment of priorities, and many publishing firms curtailed their electronic experiments in order to focus on their core revenue-generating businesses. A period of retrenchment set in and both publishing firms and private investors began to count their losses.

Underlying the new mood of scepticism was the fact that the actual performance of many of the new electronic publishing initiatives was falling far short of what many had expected. In the late 1990s a variety of consultancy firms had predicted that in a few years' time, electronic books would comprise a substantial and growing part of the market. Among the most frequently cited was a report published in 2000 by PricewaterhouseCoopers which forecast an explosion of consumer spending on electronic books, estimating that by 2004 consumer spending on ebooks would reach $5.4 billion and would comprise 17 per cent of the market. A study by Arthur Andersen, commissioned by the Association of American Publishers and published around the same time, predicted that the ebook market would be anywhere from $2.3 billion to $3.4 billion by 2005 and would represent up to 10 per cent of the market. Expectations were also raised by the startling success of one of Stephen King's experiments with electronic publish-

[2] Joseph L. Bower and Clayton M. Christensen, 'Disruptive Technologies: Catching the Wave', *Harvard Business Review* (Jan.–Feb. 1995), pp. 43–53; available at www.hbsp.harvard.edu/products/articles/hbronpoint.html.

ing. In March 2000 he published his novella *Riding the Bullet* electronically, available only as a digital file that could be downloaded for $2.50: there was an overwhelming response, resulting in about 400,000 downloads in the first twenty-four hours. Notwithstanding Stephen King's good fortune, it quickly became clear that the kinds of predictions made by PricewaterhouseCoopers and others were wildly optimistic. Publishers who experimented with making books available in ebook formats in the general retail market were invariably disappointed by the very low levels of take-up. This comment, from the managing director of a small publishing firm interviewed in May 2001, conveys very well the mood of that time:

> About eighteen months ago it looked like it was all going to accelerate, particularly with the development of ebooks, but it has become rather calm. We've got Microsoft backing to convert some of our titles and put them up on the Barnes & Noble website. We deliberately chose books that were more on the tradey side of the list because that was what Microsoft wanted. But they haven't done an awful lot – I think they generated less than $2,000 since last August when they were put up there. Since last October, the whole ebook revolution seems to have slowed down. There is a lot of scepticism about it in trade publishing. There is a fair amount of scepticism in academic publishing too. I genuinely thought last October that if we didn't have 200–300 ebooks available within a year, by this October, then we'd be at some kind of disadvantage. It doesn't appear to be the case at the moment.

By 2002 many of the new electronic publishing divisions and ebook programmes – some of which had been announced with much fanfare and at considerable expense only a year or two earlier – were being either closed down or radically scaled back. The ebook revolution had certainly stalled, possibly failed and in any case had definitely been postponed.

The third phase of the debates surrounding digitization and publishing is one that we could describe as cautious experimentation. The hype that was so pervasive in the late 1990s and the huge sums of money that were being poured into massive digitization projects are now long gone – they seem like the fanciful and extravagant whims of another age. A new mood of caution and austerity has set in, driven partly by the disappointments of the last few years, partly by the drying up of venture capital and partly by the increasingly difficult economic conditions faced by many publishing firms. Experimentation has certainly not come to an end – on the contrary, there are many ambitious projects that are still underway or about to be launched, and it will be some years yet before the outcomes are clear. But today the experimentation is much more cautious, focused and considered. The areas where electronic delivery of book content has failed to live up to expectations (such as general trade books) have been sidelined and attention has focused increasingly on those areas (such as reference, professional and scholarly publishing) where the prospects for electronic delivery seem more promising. Today there are few who believe that electronic delivery is going to provide a quick fix to the financial woes of book publishers – if anything, the costs associated with building systems and managing content in digital formats are much higher than many people assumed in the 1990s, and in most cases the revenues have come nowhere near to covering the costs. The phase of cautious experimentation is generally premised on the assumption that printed books will remain the principal source of revenue for most book publishers for the foreseeable future. The key challenge faced by publishing firms who wish to experiment in this domain today is how to protect their existing print-based revenue streams while at the same time exploring ways in which digital technologies can be used to enhance existing revenue streams and create new ones, whether by enabling them to produce and deliver print-based products more efficiently or by enabling them to make their content available in alternative formats.

In the following chapters I shall examine some of the experiments undertaken and the challenges posed by the digital revolution in the two fields of publishing that are the focus of this study, academic publishing and higher education publishing. In many ways these fields are ideal terrains for experimentation: there are good prima facie grounds for thinking that content could be delivered electronically instead of (or perhaps in addition to) being delivered in the traditional printed form; the transition to electronic content delivery has occurred very successfully in some neighbouring fields (most notably in the field of scholarly and scientific journal publishing); since the late 1990s substantial sums have been invested – by publishing firms, venture capitalists and philanthropic organizations – to experiment with electronic content delivery in these fields; and even in this phase of cautious experimentation, some bold new initiatives are underway. However, it would be misleading to focus this discussion exclusively on the issue of electronic content delivery. It is undoubtedly the case that this is the issue that has captured the public imagination and dominated the headlines – the idea that the printed book, this most familiar object that has been with us since the days of Gutenberg, is about to disappear has a dramatic, almost apocalyptic feel. But to focus our attention exclusively on this issue would be to lose sight of a whole series of trans-formations which have been wrought in the publishing industry by the digital revolu-tion. These transformations are well underway and their implications are far-reaching. They have affected everything from typesetting and design to the principles which for centuries have governed the basic risk-taking decisions of publishers, such as how many copies of a book to print and how long to keep it in stock. Irrespective of whether ebooks ever emerge as a significant medium for delivering content to readers, the digital revolution will have transformed the business of book publishing in a profound and irreversible way. This 'hidden revolution' will be the focus of the final chapter.

The impact of digitization on publishing

Before we turn our attention to the issue of electronic content delivery, I want to situate this issue within a broader analytical and conceptual framework. In order to make sense of the impact of digitization on the publishing industry, we need to distinguish at least four different levels at which digitization can affect the business of publishing: (1) the level of *operating systems*; (2) the level of *content management and manipulation*; (3) the level of *marketing and service provision*; and (4) the level of *content delivery*. Let me comment briefly on each.

(1) *Operating systems*   The most immediate respect in which digitization has affected the publishing industry is in terms of operating systems and information flows. Like many sectors of industry today, the management systems in all major publishing houses are now computerized and management information is compiled and circulated in digital forms. Most publishing organizations have built or installed back office publish-ing systems which store bibliographical and other data on each title and which can be

accessed by anyone in the organization who can log onto the network. Financial data and information on production is commonly held in dedicated IT systems; calculations of prices, print-runs and gross profit margins are automated; and royalties and other transactions are handled by computer. A high proportion of the communication within organizations, and communication with clients and customers outside the organization, now takes place electronically. The use of computers and IT is now so pervasive in most publishing houses that it's almost difficult to remember how different it was only twenty years ago, and how much has changed in such a short period of time. In the early 1980s, many publishing organizations were not computerized and the typewriter was the most common piece of office equipment. 'In 1985,' recalled one senior manager,

> there wasn't even a spreadsheet. When I came here [in 1983] we were just beginning to think about how you can create a simple modelling system for book pricing – if I sell so many copies at this price and at this discount, how much money will I get? And if I put the price up to this, what will the outcome be? It was a million miles away from the kinds of things you do today.

From the mid-1980s on, most publishing firms have been engaged in a continuous process of investing in the computerization and digitization of their offices and operating systems. This investment has undoubtedly generated efficiencies and has enabled some costs to be eliminated or reduced (many editors and other staff are now routinely responsible for their own correspondence in a way that was simply not the case twenty years ago, for example). But the costs involved in building, maintaining and constantly updating the IT infrastructures of publishing organizations, and the effort and costs involved in constantly training and retraining staff, are very substantial indeed. In the decade from the mid-1980s to the mid-1990s, most publishing firms switched over from a paper-based office culture to a screen-based culture and have incurred the costs associated with building and maintaining the IT infrastructure upon which a screen-based culture depends. This has transformed their working practices and information flows, but this transformation has come at a hefty price.

It is not just the working practices and information flows within firms that have changed: the digital revolution has also led to the digitization of the supply chain. The systems for managing stock and transferring it between different organizations within the supply chain have become increasingly computerized. More and more bookstores introduced electronic point-of-sale (EPOS) facilities to track the sales of individual titles and manage stock flows, and the ordering of stock from wholesalers and publishers was increasingly handled through dedicated electronic ordering services like PubNet, Tele-Ordering and First Edition. The use of increasingly automated EDI (Electronic Data Interchange) systems has become a pervasive feature of the supply chain. The development of sophisticated computerized systems for stock management and control has also become an important source of competitive advantage for the large retail chains and for the large wholesalers, such as Ingrams and Baker & Taylor in the US and Bertram's and Gardner's in the UK. By expanding their inventories and developing computer-based information systems that enabled them to fulfil orders in one or two days, the large wholesalers could provide a highly efficient, one-stop service to bookstores, who could reorder stock on a daily basis in the light of their computerized point-of-sales data.

(2) *Content management and manipulation* The computerization of operating systems is not of course unique to the publishing industry – most sectors of industry have experienced similar transformations during the last two decades. But digitization has the potential to transform the publishing industry much more profoundly than this, precisely because the publishing industry is concerned fundamentally with symbolic content that can be codified in digital form. The digital revolution has made it increasingly clear to many in the publishing industry that the *content* they acquire and develop is one of their principal assets. Indeed, in many ways it is their most fundamental asset, since the value of the printed book depends on the content that is embedded in it. In essence, publishing firms are engaged in the business of acquiring content, adding value to it in various ways and selling it in whatever form they can. The printed book is the most tangible output of the publishing business and it remains the predominant medium through which book content is exchanged in the marketplace. But in essence, as many in the industry have reminded us in recent years, 'content is king'.

When I say that the digital revolution has made it increasingly clear to many publishers that their content is one of their principal assets, I don't want to suggest that publishers were altogether unaware of this before digitization became widespread. But one of the consequences of digitization is that it has encouraged and indeed forced publishers to think hard about what their distinctive contribution to the value chain actually is. Publishing organizations do not for the most part create the content (authors do), nor do they print the books they publish (with the exception of Cambridge University Press). Many functions in the production process, from copy-editing and design to typesetting and production, are increasingly outsourced to freelancers and specialized firms. So what do publishers do at the end of the day? What do they add to the value creation process? They add capital, expertise and management skills, among other things, and this enables them to add value to the content which originates with the author but which is selected, elaborated, revised and transformed by the editorial and production processes. The key activity of the publisher lies in the acquisition, development and manipulation of content, and it is this content, suitably revised and transformed, which is one of the publisher's principal assets. The decision about how to make this content available – whether to publish it as a printed book at such-and-such a price or to make it available in some other form – is a decision about how best to exploit the publisher's asset in the marketplace in order to realize its value.

In so far as publishers are in the business of acquiring and transforming content, their business is particularly susceptible to digitization, for the simple reason that the content publishers are dealing with – both text and images – is the kind of content that can be digitized. Hence the whole process of creating, managing, developing and transforming this content is a process that can in principle be handled in a digital form – from the writing of the text to the production of the final file in a format that can be used by a printer. A central part of the history of the publishing business over the last twenty years has been the progressive application of digitization to the various stages of the content transformation process, leading to the gradual rise of what could be called 'the digital workflow'. In most publishing houses, the digitization of the workflow process is far from complete, and some stages (such as copy-editing) continue to be handled mostly in a non-digital way. But the progressive digitization of the workflow process is an unmistakable and irreversible trend. It is part of the hidden revolution in publishing that we shall examine in chapter 15.

(3) *Marketing and service provision*   Another area of the publishing process that has been deeply affected by the digital revolution is marketing, and more generally the relationship between publishers and their customers. With the development of the internet, many publishers invested in the development of websites to give themselves an online presence. Initially the website was regarded by most publishers as little more than an online catalogue – an environment in which their books could be listed and, for those who developed e-commerce capabilities on their website, sold. But increasingly the internet came to be seen as something more: as a medium which could provide a range of support services for customers and which could be used more proactively to market books and to carry out market research. The rise of e-tailers like Amazon also created important new channels to market, as we have seen.

More generally, electronic communication has increasingly become the central medium through which publishers interact with their actual and potential author base, on the one hand, and their actual and potential customer base, on the other. Publishers have always had close and direct relations with authors, but increasingly the interactions between authors and publishing staff – from commissioning editors and copyeditors to marketing staff – have become mediated electronically: email has largely replaced the physical letter. Increasingly, prospective authors contact publishers via their websites, and increasingly editors use the internet to search for potential authors. Publishers' links with readers and end users have traditionally been much more attenuated, since their immediate customers in the book supply chain are wholesalers and retailers rather than readers and end users, but here too electronic communication has facilitated more direct forms of market research and feedback. In higher education publishing, for example, it is much easier in an online environment for editorial and marketing staff to contact a range of potential adopters of a textbook and solicit their views on the suitability of the text for the courses they teach. Many higher education publishers build up databases of contacts in the world of higher education which they can use for both editorial and marketing purposes. These contacts become networks of users and potential users which enable publishers to reach out to their customer base more quickly, more directly and more comprehensively than they were able to in the past. They also enable them to create marketing channels that are well targeted and customized for the specific titles they are publishing. To some extent, publishers can be seen as service organizations embedded in networks of communication which are increasingly electronic in character and within which they are seeking, among other things, to coordinate the creation and development of content (generated in part by authors) with the needs and desires of readers, end users and relevant intermediaries.

(4) *Content delivery*   The level at which the impact of the digital revolution on the publishing industry is potentially the most profound, and yet at the same time the most difficult to fathom, is the level of content delivery. It is potentially the most profound because the delivery of content to the end user electronically, rather than in the form of the physical book, would transform the whole financial model of publishing. It would no longer be necessary to lock up resources in physical books (with the attendant costs of paper, printing and binding), store the books in warehouses, ship them to bookstores and wholesalers, accept them as returns if they were not sold and ultimately write them down if they turned out to be surplus to requirements. In the dream vision of electronic content delivery, publishers could bypass most if not all of the intermediaries in the tra-

ditional book supply chain and supply content either directly to the end user through their own website or via an online e-tailer. The costs associated with producing, storing and shipping physical books would be eliminated and the problem of returns would disappear.

This dream vision of electronic content delivery has underpinned many experiments in electronic publishing which have been undertaken since the late 1980s. The term 'electronic publishing' is a broad term which comprises at least three different forms of computer-based media: diskette, CD-ROM and the internet. There was some publishing of texts on diskettes in the 1980s but this was never a significant development. CD-ROM was more important as a medium for electronic publishing, and some publishers invested heavily in CD-ROM development in the late 1980s and early 1990s; many also lost substantial amounts of money, and this experience has served as a cautionary tale for some in the publishing industry who lived through what is sometimes referred to as 'the great CD-ROM fiasco'. But it was above all the rise of the internet in the 1990s which opened the way for a much more radical vision of electronic publishing, since now it was possible not only to *store* content in a digital format but also to *deliver* it to the end user via the internet, bypassing all the usual intermediaries and dispensing with the need to ship a physical product (whether a printed book or a CD-ROM). The idea of the ebook as a digital reproduction of the traditional printed book, delivered directly to the consumer from the publisher's or author's website or via an e-tailer like ebooks.com or b&n.com, was only one of the many new scenarios opened up by the rise of the internet. But it was undoubtedly an alluring scenario, and one to which a great deal of significance was attached by those who were commenting on the transformations taking place in the publishing industry at the turn of the millennium. So why did the ebook revolution falter, and what significance should we attach to this?

Among those who work in the ebook business, four reasons are commonly put forward to explain why ebooks did not take off as quickly as many expected. First, there is the problem of *hardware*: the reading devices that have been developed so far are expensive and awkward to use. Few people like reading extended texts on small screens with low resolution, and many are reluctant to spend several hundred dollars on dedicated reading devices which they may not use a great deal. 'The devices have to be multifunctional, they have to have larger screens and most of all they have to be priced correctly,' commented one industry insider. Second, there is the problem of *formats*: there is a bewildering array of proprietary formats which are not interchangeable across different reading devices. This is confusing and off-putting for consumers, who may be inclined to wait until a standardized format emerges before investing in something that may be eclipsed by technological change. Third, there is the problem of *rights*: there is often considerable confusion about who owns the rights to exploit the content of a particular book in an electronic format. Is it the publisher? The author? And what should be paid to whom? Most contracts between authors and publishers were drawn up at a time when the idea of exploiting content electronically was not even imagined, so there is no provision in the contract to indicate who controls the rights and how revenue is to be distributed. The problem is rendered even more complex by the problem of embedded rights – that is, the copyright on material which is embedded in the text, such as quotations or illustrations. The publisher may have cleared permission to use this material for the print edition of the book, but can it be assumed that this permission can be transferred to an electronic edition? 'No one knows for sure who really owns the rights,' commented the same industry insider; 'this is a big question mark that is causing people to hold back.' Finally, there is the question of *price*: on the whole, publishers and retailers chose to price ebooks at levels that were roughly comparable to the price of print books. This was partly experimental, and partly in recognition of the fact that the savings involved in delivering book content in electronic formats were not as great as some of the early champions of ebooks had suggested – all the development costs were still there, as were the royalties, the marketing costs, the publisher's overheads, etc. But this does not go down well with consumers, for whom the perceived value of an ebook is significantly lower than that of a print book. So the prices of ebooks would have to come down significantly before there would be any substantial increase in sales.

For some who work in the industry, these four factors – the hardware, the formats, rights and prices – go a long way to explaining why ebooks failed to take off as many had expected. The upshot of this perspective is that if these problems can be solved, then the way will be clear for further progress: the revolution may have faltered but it hasn't failed, and ebook sales will grow once the technical, legal and financial issues have been sorted out. But there are others who take a more sceptical view. The fundamental problem, in their view, is that many in the industry have failed to think carefully about the relation between technologies and markets. Too many people in the industry were swayed by the rhetoric and prone to adopt what one could describe as the 'technological fallacy': the idea that because the technology exists to do something, consumers will invariably use that technology. This is a mindset that is promoted by a technological view of the world, a view that is preoccupied with the latest developments in technology and tends to assume that technology is the pacesetter of social change. But the problem with this view is that it doesn't give sufficient attention to the nature of markets and to what end users actually want. It doesn't see, for example, that there might be all sorts of reasons why most readers remain deeply attached to the physical book – not just because they are put off by certain technical features of the ebook devices currently available, but because they have a genuine preference for the book as a physical and cultural artefact and they believe that for certain kinds of reading experience, such as reading an extended text like a novel or a biography, the physical book has a value which an electronic reading device, however elaborate it may be, cannot match.

So is there a different way of approaching these issues which will enable us to avoid the technological fallacy? We can approach these issues differently by emphasizing that *technologies must always be contextualized* – that is, they must always be analysed in relation to the specific social contexts in which they are developed and used, and hence in relation to what users actually do with these technologies, what they want and what they are willing to pay for. One senior figure in the publishing world expressed this point very well:

The key thing is not the technology, it is the market. That's what you have to keep your eye on. What do your customers want? The great danger of technological change is people look at the technology and use it because it is there . . . There is pressure to be progressive, i.e. to use the technology because that is part of being modern. That is one of the reasons why so many publishers lost a fortune during the great CD-ROM fiasco. So our task really is to look at the market and say, where is it that there are going to be market demands which this new technology can satisfy more effectively than the old? In other words, where can we actually add value?

This approach, which analyses new technologies in relation to social contexts of use, to markets and ways of adding value, is the approach that I shall adopt here. It encourages us to be more analytical and contextual in our thinking, to examine the uses of new technologies in relation to specific types of content and specific fields of publishing and to avoid the temptation to generalize from the experience of one type of content in one publishing field – *content and context are crucial*. The disappointing performance of ebooks in the field of general trade publishing is a sober reminder of how easy it is to overestimate the take-up of new technologies and to be carried away by the bells and whistles of technological innovation, but it does not by itself tell us a great deal about what is happening (and what is likely to happen) in other fields of publishing where the problems, the needs of users and the structure of markets are different. My approach will be to situate the question of new technologies and their uses for content delivery within the general framework of the theory of publishing fields, and then to look in detail at some of the initiatives that have been undertaken in the fields of academic and higher education publishing, where the problems and the opportunities are different from general trade publishing. But before immersing ourselves in the detail, we need to examine further some of the broader conceptual issues.

Technologies, markets and added value

In trying to think through the ways in which the digital revolution is likely to play itself out at the level of content delivery, it is essential to think carefully about the interplay between technologies, markets and types of content. Which types of content lend themselves to being delivered to end users in electronic formats and why? Where does the use of new technologies enable content providers to add real value to their content, value which is sufficiently important for end users (or for intermediaries like libraries) that they are willing to pay for it? We can begin to answer these questions by distinguishing six respects in which new technologies can enable content providers to add real value to content: (1) *ease of access*, (2) *updatability*, (3) *scale*, (4) *searchability*, (5) *intertextuality*, and (6) *multimedia*. These features are not unique to the online delivery of content; they are also found in other forms of electronic publishing, such as CD-ROM. But here I shall focus on the online environment and comment briefly on each.

(1) *Ease of access* One of the great advantages of delivering content in an online environment is ease of access. In traditional systems of content provision, access to content is generally governed by certain spatial and temporal constraints – libraries and bookstores, for instance, are located in specific places and are open for certain hours of the day. But content delivered in an online environment is no longer governed by these constraints: in principle it is available twenty-four hours a day, seven days a week, to anyone who has a suitable internet (or intranet) connection and the right of access. There is no need to go to a library to track down a book or a journal article if the content can be accessed from one's office or home. The personal computer, located in a place

or places which are convenient for the end user, becomes the gateway to a potentially vast body of content which can be accessed easily, quickly and at any time of the day or night. Moreover, unlike the traditional printed text, an electronic text available online can in principle be accessed by many users simultaneously.

(2)   *Updatability*   Another key feature of the online delivery of content is that it can be updated quickly, frequently and relatively cheaply. In the case of content delivered in the form of the traditional printed text, making changes or corrections is a laborious process. Changes can be made to the text at any point up to the typesetting stage, but once the text is typeset it is costly to alter it. Printed texts cannot be changed: once they are printed the content is fixed. But content delivered online is not fixed in a printed text, and hence it can be altered and updated relatively easily and cheaply. This is a particularly important feature in cases where the content is dealing with material which is in a state of continuous flux, such as financial data. But there are many other contexts where the capacity to update content quickly, frequently and cheaply is an important trait and can add real value.

(3)   *Scale*   Undoubtedly one of the most important features of the online delivery of content is scale: the capacity to provide access to large quantities of material. The internet economy is an economy of scale – it offers the possibility of providing access to collections of material which are extensive and comprehensive, of providing a range of choice and depth which is simply not possible in most physical collections. It is this scalability of the internet economy which has driven the online aggregation business. Numerous intermediaries have emerged with the aim of aggregating large quantities of content and selling this on to libraries and other institutions. Part of what is attractive to libraries is the ability to gain access to large quantities of content at relatively low costs, or at costs that are significantly lower than they would have to pay if they were to acquire the same content in a piecemeal fashion. Part of what is attractive to end users is the knowledge that they can find what they are looking for at a single site – that it is a one-stop shop. By providing scale, that is, access to very large quantities of data or content, the content providers (or intermediaries) can add real value. In the internet economy, the whole is more than the sum of its parts, precisely because the comprehensiveness of a collection is valued for its own sake. However, it is important to add a proviso here: it is not quantity alone which is valued, but rather quantity that is perceived as relevant to what the user wants and needs – what we could call *pertinent scalability*. As we shall see, intermediaries that set about aggregating large quantities of content while paying relatively little attention to what end users actually wanted would soon find that quantity alone does not suffice. What end users generally want is not scale as such but rather pertinent scale.

(4)   *Searchability*   A fourth key feature of the online delivery of content is the capacity to search a database. The traditional printed text offers its own means for searching the content – the table of contents provides a guide to the content of a book, and the index is effectively a search mechanism for the printed text. But the capacity to search a digitized corpus of material using a search engine based on keywords or names is infinitely quicker and more powerful than the traditional search mechanisms employed in printed texts, and the search capacity can be extended to much larger quantities of

content. Search capacity can be provided both within corpora and across corpora, thus providing the end user with a powerful means of searching for and accessing relevant content. This way of adding value is complementary to, and in some ways required by, the provision of scale. For the end user, there is not much value in having scale – even pertinent scale – unless you have an effective means of locating the content that interests you. The greater the scale, the more valuable it is to have an effective means of searching the database.

(5) *Intertextuality*   A key feature of the online environment is that it is able to give a dynamic character to what we could describe as the referential function of texts. In the traditional medium of the printed text, the capacity to refer to other material is realized through conventional literary devices such as references, footnotes (or endnotes) and bibliographies: these are mechanisms for referring the reader on to other texts upon which the author has drawn or which the author regards as important, interesting and/or worthwhile. In the online environment, the referential function of the text can be made much more dynamic by using hot links to enable the reader to move to other pages and other sites. These links can be of various kinds – links to other pages, to other texts, to other sites and resources of various kinds, to bibliographies, to biographies, to online bookstores, etc. The links can be internal to the publisher's own site or can be to external sites. Through the use of hypertext links, the content provider can enable the end user to access referred-to texts quickly and easily, without having to locate the text physically. Moreover, whereas references in printed texts can be updated only when there is a new edition of the work, hot links can be updated incrementally and at any time. The drawback with external links is that it can be costly to keep them up to date, since external sites can die or be moved to new locations.

(6) *Multimedia*   The online delivery of content also enables the content provider to use a variety of media and to supplement text with content delivered in other forms – including visual images, streaming video and sound. There are contexts in which this can enable content providers to add real value – for example, where it enables them to use colour illustrations that would be too costly to reproduce on the printed page, or to use streaming video to reproduce a speech or to illustrate a complex process. Of course, there are costs associated with the provision of multimedia content – it may be costly to produce and permission fees may be high. It may also be difficult to use, in the sense that the files may be large and slow to download. But it does offer at least the possibility of adding a kind of value to content which would not be possible in traditional print formats.

Technologies and forms of content

I have identified some of the ways in which the use of new technologies can enable content providers to add real value to content. But the extent to which value can be added also depends on the nature of the content – some forms of content lend themselves more readily to delivery in an online environment than others. In order to explore this issue further, I shall distinguish four basic forms of content, though I shall subdivide two of them so that there are eight forms in total, as shown in figure 12.1. In

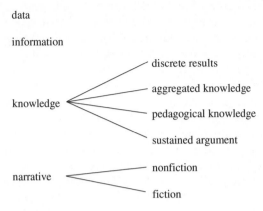

Figure 12.1 Forms of content (1)

distinguishing between these various forms of content, I do not wish to suggest that this schema is comprehensive – of course it is not. I have concentrated on forms which are particularly relevant to our concerns here and have neglected others. Nor do I wish to imply that the distinctions between the various forms and subforms are always clear and easy to draw – on the contrary, they often blur into one another, as we shall see. Nevertheless, it is helpful to draw some distinctions between forms of content if we wish to understand how and why different kinds lend themselves (or don't lend themselves, as the case may be) to being made available in electronic formats.

By *data* I mean content which is essentially a compilation of numbers presented in varying degrees of orderliness. Financial data on the prices of stocks and shares are a good example of data in this sense: they are numbers compiled and ordered in certain ways so that someone who knows how they are gathered and presented will be able to interpret the numbers. Data of this kind – like share prices – may be time sensitive, and hence may lend themselves particularly well to being made available online, where they can be continuously updated in real time. Financial services companies like Reuters and FT.com have built successful online businesses out of making data of this kind available in an online environment.

Data can be distinguished from *information*, by which I mean basic descriptive content which is generally articulated in a discursive form. Examples would be the records of court cases (pleas, judgments, sentences, etc.) and basic information about businesses (history, ownership, size, turnover, etc.). Again, information of this kind lends itself to being made available in an online environment because it can be easily accessed, quickly updated and searched. Hence there is a second level of online publishers such as Thomson, Reed Elsevier and others who are building online businesses by making legal information, business information, medical information and other types of information available online, primarily but not exclusively for professionals. Lexis-Nexis – the online legal and financial service, now owned by Reed Elsevier, which began in 1973 as an electronic database of codes and cases for lawyers and legal researchers – is a good example of an online information system of this kind.

The third level is what could be broadly described as *knowledge*: this is not just ordered data or descriptive content, but rather a form of discursively articulated content which helps us to make sense of the world. Knowledge is more than data or information; it involves an effort of interpretation or analysis, an attempt to provide some kind of theory or argument or interpretative framework which will help us to make sense of data or information. But this effort of interpretation or analysis can be articulated in different ways and we need to distinguish several different types of knowledge.

First there is what we could call *discrete results*. By this I mean the results of particular scientific experiments or other knowledge claims that can be expressed in a concise form. Within the scientific and academic world, the commonly accepted format for the publication of discrete results is the journal article. One of the most dramatic developments in the publishing world over the last decade is the speed with which journal publishing has moved into the online environment. All the major journal publishers – Elsevier, Blackwell, Taylor & Francis, Wiley, OUP, CUP, etc. – have increasingly shifted their journal programmes from print-only to print plus electronic, and in some cases to electronic-only. This shift to electronic journals has been led by the scientific journal publishers, but journals in the social sciences and humanities have moved increasingly in the same direction. There are a number of factors which help to explain why journal publishing lent itself to online delivery:

- Journal articles are generally very short (from two or three pages to twenty pages), and hence they can be either read onscreen or printed with relative ease.
- Particular issues of journals are for the most part arbitrary collections of articles which bear no intrinsic connection to one another (with the exception of themed issues), and hence the end user is likely to read only a specific article rather than a series of articles.
- Since users are generally looking for specific articles on specific topics, the capacity to search for relevant material across a corpus of content is a highly valued feature. Cross-referencing to other relevant work is also highly valued.
- Scientists and academics are accustomed to working onscreen and they value the ability to access journals from their desktops without having to visit a physical library.
- Since the subscription model for journals already existed, it was relatively easy to move to a site licence model for journals delivered online. Librarians were familiar with the business model and were generally keen to be able to provide an additional service to their users.
- The move into an online environment provided new opportunities for the aggregation of content. Journal publishers with large numbers of journals could offer special deals to libraries and library consortia for access to the whole corpus (e.g. Elsevier's ScienceDirect), and third party aggregators could offer packages of content assembled from a variety of different publishers (e.g. Gale).

For these and other reasons, the publication of discrete results in the form of journal articles has moved rapidly into an online environment. It has moved rapidly but not *exclusively* into this environment. Librarians are keen to be able to offer their users the ability to access journals online, but many librarians remain concerned about what they call the 'archiving problem' – that is, how can they ensure perpetual access to journal content for which they have already paid? What happens if at some future date they cancel the subscription, or if at some future date the journal folds or the publisher goes out of business? How then will they be able to ensure access to back issues unless those issues are sitting physically on their shelves? If the electronic content is to be held in escrow by a third party, who will bear the costs of doing so and manage the collection? Until librarians are convinced that the archiving problem has been satisfactorily solved, many will continue to insist on receiving hard copies of each issue as well as access online and the economies that could be achieved by moving entirely into an online environment – both in terms of production costs and in terms of shelf space – will not be realized.

A second type of knowledge is what we could call *aggregated knowledge*. By this I mean those forms of knowledge that involve the accumulation of discrete results into an extended text that provides a sustained treatment of a particular topic or theme. Reference works are the classic examples of accumulated knowledge in this sense – from the reference work on a specific topic (breast cancer, for example, or the structure of the brain) to comprehensive reference works like dictionaries and encyclopaedias. Once again, there are various reasons why reference works lend themselves to online delivery:

- Reference works are an accumulation of discrete pieces of knowledge.
- Users do not generally read a reference work from cover to cover but rather consult it in order to answer a specific question or gain a specific piece of knowledge.
- The capacity to search quickly for a specific piece of knowledge is therefore a valuable feature. Similarly, cross-referencing to related material is valued by users.
- Scale is important in reference works: in many cases, the more comprehensive they are, the more useful they're likely to be for the user. (Although this is not always the case: sometimes a concise reference work may be quite adequate for the purpose at hand – e.g. a dictionary.) Large reference works, like comprehensive encyclopaedias and dictionaries, are very costly and unwieldy in print.
- Reference works need to be regularly updated. It is very costly to do this in the print medium, but a reference work can be continuously updated and expanded in an online environment relatively easily and cheaply.
- For some reference works, the use of multimedia – colour illustrations, sound and streaming video – can add real value.

While there are a number of good reasons why reference works lend themselves to being made available in an online environment, there are also good reasons why the transition to the online environment has been much more uneven for reference works than it has been for journals. One reason is the absence of suitable business models which would enable publishers to recover the substantial costs involved in preparing reference works. In the case of journal publishing, the business model already existed: the principal market for scholarly journals is the institutional market of research libraries, and libraries were already accustomed to purchasing journals on a subscription basis. But many reference works were traditionally sold to individual consumers on a transactional basis – one copy, one sale, end of transaction. It is not at all clear that individual consumers would be willing to sign up to a subscription for access to a reference work which they may wish to consult only from time to time.

That leaves the institutional market, but here the problem is one of scale. Many reference works are single volume works: they simply do not have the kind of scale that would make them attractive to librarians as works that would be suitable for online delivery on a subscription basis. Those reference works that are attractive to librarians tend to be the large, highly valued reference works that would previously have been available only as a large and relatively expensive volume, like *Granger's Index to Poetry* published by Columbia University Press, or as a multi-volume series, such as the *Oxford English Dictionary*, Elsevier's multi-volume *International Encyclopaedia of the Social and Behavioral Sciences* or Taylor & Francis's multi-volume *Encyclopaedia of Philosophy*. Librarians are willing to purchase site licences for large reference works of this kind for several reasons: first, they have the kind of scale that makes online access attractive and worthwhile; second, they have other facilities, such as search mechanisms and the ability to be continuously updated, that can be provided relatively easily in an online environment; and third, many of the reference works already have a reputation among librarians that was established by the print version – in other words, to librarians these are known quantities, and the brand precedes the new technological medium in which the content is being delivered.

One reference publisher has recently come up with an innovative solution to the problem of scale: in 2002 Oxford University Press launched Oxford Reference Online. The key idea behind this initiative is what we could describe as *the aggregation of aggregated knowledge* – that is, OUP is making available, as a single, integrated resource, a cluster of reference works that can be accessed online. Access is sold primarily to libraries on a subscription basis. OUP is able to build a site of this kind precisely because it is already a major player in the field of reference publishing and has a large quantity of copyrighted reference material which it can digitize, customize and aggregate on a single site. It also has an established reputation with librarians as a high-quality reference publisher which has successfully delivered reference material in an online environment (OED online was launched as a subscription-based service in March 2000).

A third type of knowledge is what I shall call *pedagogical knowledge*. By this I mean a type of knowledge which is oriented essentially to the pedagogical goal of conveying content to students who are seeking to learn a body of knowledge and who will be assessed in some way to determine the extent to which they have successfully acquired this knowledge. Pedagogical knowledge is structured in a different way from other forms of knowledge and is designed to fulfil different aims. This is not the kind of knowledge which claims to make original discoveries about the world or to present new findings to the scientific or scholarly community, but rather the kind of knowledge that seeks to impart theories, concepts and facts to individuals who are not already part of this community. The textbook, used in the context of a structured course in an educational institution, is a common form in which pedagogical knowledge is conveyed.

A fourth type of knowledge is what I shall call *sustained argument*. By this I mean a form of knowledge which involves the development of a sustained argument or analysis in an extended text. This kind of knowledge is particularly common in the humanities and social sciences, which are less experimentally based than the natural sciences and hence are less dominated by that form of knowledge that I have called discrete results. The development of a sustained argument or analysis can be published in the form of a journal article, and indeed journals play a vital role in the humanities and social sciences both for the publication of discrete results and for the presentation of sustained arguments or analyses. But the fact that journal articles tend to be short – usually a maximum of twenty pages – has tended to limit the capacity of journals to provide a suitable format for this type of knowledge. This is where the book or scholarly monograph has come into its own: it provides a suitable format for the publication and dissemination of sustained arguments or analyses which cannot be readily compressed into the limited confines of the journal article. Moreover, the book or scholarly monograph has become an accepted part of the culture of knowledge and research of many disciplines in the humanities and social sciences, in a way that is less so in the natural sciences and in those social sciences (such as economics and psychology) which are more empirical in character and closer in terms of their methodological self-understanding to the natural sciences than the humanities.

As we have seen, discrete results and aggregated knowledge lend themselves to some extent to being made available online, but a question that remains very unclear is the extent to which pedagogical knowledge and sustained argument also lend themselves to online dissemination. This is the question to which I shall devote the following two chapters. In addressing this question I shall not remain simply at the level of speculative possibilities – there has been a great deal of speculation about what is technologically possible, but very little of this speculation has been borne out in terms of concrete and sustainable developments. So I shall concentrate above all on a careful analysis of what has actually been attempted and achieved in these domains – the initiatives, the successes and the failures – and I shall try to draw some general lessons from these undertakings. For although the experiments to date are limited in many ways, they nevertheless provide clearer insight into the interplay of technologies, content and markets than one would gain by merely speculating on the possibilities inherent in new technologies.

There is a fourth basic form of content that I have not yet discussed – what I have called *narrative*. This is a form of content that is articulated as an extended story with a beginning, a plot of some kind and an ending of sorts. The narrative form is not a clear-cut and definitive mould but it is a structure with which we are all intuitively familiar. It is a structure commonly used in fiction but it is not restricted to the fictional realm: it is also used in nonfiction, for example in biographies and autobiographies, or in the kind of historical writing that tells a story about the past, about specific events or characters or about a more general historical development. There is not a clear distinction between narrative nonfiction, on the one hand, and the form of knowledge that I've called sustained argument, on the other. These forms of content overlap and in some cases could be said to coincide (a serious and sustained analysis of a specific topic could be written as a kind of narrative with the overall argument providing the plot). But not all works of sustained argument are written in a narrative form, and hence it is helpful to distinguish between them.

If the question of the extent to which pedagogical knowledge and sustained argument lend themselves to electronic dissemination is unclear, the uncertainty is even greater in the case of narrative content. Partly this is due to significant differences in what we could describe as the 'bittiness' of content. Data, information, discrete results and aggregated knowledge are, by their very nature, bitty forms of content: they are constituted as discrete pieces of data or text which can be aggregated into corpora of various kinds, and where functions such as scale, searchability and intertextuality can add real value. By contrast, narrative content (both fiction and nonfiction) is less bitty in this sense. Narratives tend to be extended pieces of text which have a progressive, cumulative character; they require time and patience to read and they have to be returned to again and again if the reader wants to follow the story to the end – rarely will a novel be finished at one sitting. The same is true of sustained argument and (perhaps to a lesser extent) of pedagogical knowledge: these are forms of content that have a gradual, progressive character to them, you cannot enter them at any point but you begin at the beginning (more or less) and finish at the end (more or less), and they generally require an extended period of time to complete. There are ways in which an online environment can add value to content of this kind (for example, by building in search facilities and multimedia components). But whether these are features that end users really want and are willing to pay for is another matter, and whether the kind of value that can be added in an online environment would be sufficient to outweigh the disadvantages and inconveniences involved in accessing extended texts online is by no means clear.

What kinds of disadvantages? The most obvious and much discussed disadvantage is that it is simply very inconvenient to read extended texts online or onscreen, whether using a desktop, a laptop or a handheld device. For checking data, getting information or reading a short text, the computer screen is perfectly serviceable, but there are very few people who enjoy the experience of reading an extended text on a screen. Most people will print out an extended text if they want to read more than a limited number of pages. People rarely read web pages word by word – they tend instead to scan the page.[3] It may be that further developments in screen technologies will help to alleviate this problem. Certainly, intensive efforts are underway to develop 'e-ink' and 'e-paper' that will enable screen designers to replicate more closely the experience of reading ink on paper, and various manufacturers (including Philips and Sony) have announced their intention to release handheld devices incorporating e-ink technology in 2004 or 2005. The distinctive feature of e-ink and e-paper is that they rely on reflected light rather than illuminated screens; hence they are able to replicate some aspects of the experience of reading print on paper and to do so in an energy-efficient manner (since energy is used only when the page is changed), while also delivering the advantages of online access and electronic storage of content. But whether these new initiatives will be any more successful than their predecessors remains unclear, as the obstacles to moving extended texts into an online environment are not just technological: they are also social and cultural.

As I have shown in earlier chapters, books are embedded in social contexts of varying kinds and the use of books is bound up with institutions and clusters of social practices. In the case of scholarly and pedagogical books, the institutions and social practices are those involved in research and teaching; in the case of narrative books, the institutions and social practices include those associated with free time and leisure, when individuals have the time and opportunity to read extended texts for pleasure or for their own personal interest. Books are not merely objects which will be swiftly and automatically replaced by technologically more efficient modes of content delivery, for they are bound up with forms of life and social practices which change only slowly and gradually. If we wish to understand how the relations between print and electronic forms of content delivery are changing and will change in the future, then we have to pay attention not just to technological innovations, but also to the forms of life and social practices in which this content is embedded and used.

[3] See Jakob Nielsen, 'How Users Read on the Web' (1997), available at www.useit.com/alertbox/9710a.html.

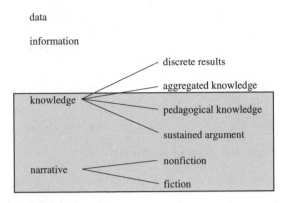

Figure 12.2 Forms of content (2)

In the light of this analysis, we can see that there are certain forms of content that lend themselves to online environments, partly because the content has a bitty character and is readily amenable to the value-adding functions characteristic of online environments, and partly because of the ways in which this content is typically used. On the other hand, there are other forms of content where there is real uncertainty about the extent to which it lends itself to being distributed and used in online environments: in these cases, we simply do not know whether, or to what extent, online environments will turn out to be suitable media for dissemination. Is the value that can be added by making this content available online the kind of value that the users of this content want and are willing to pay for? Or, given the uses to which this content is typically put, would users prefer to access the content online or in traditional print formats? Should the making available of this content in online environments be seen as a replacement of the printed text or as supplementary and complementary to it? What kinds of business models would enable content providers to generate revenue from the sale or licensing of content online? Would the revenue generated thereby ever be sufficient to cover the costs incurred in producing the content and running the organizations involved in producing and disseminating it, while at the same time enabling them to generate an operating profit? It is these kinds of questions – which are primarily social, cultural and economic rather than technological – that are the key questions, and it is these questions that remain unanswered.

The shaded box in figure 12.2 calls attention to the uncertainty that surrounds the suitability of some forms of content for dissemination in online environments. At this stage we simply don't know the extent to which the forms of content in the shaded box will turn out to be suitable for dissemination in online environments, or whether they will be suitable at all.

Technologies and types of publishing

In the previous section we looked at the suitability of different forms of content for online environments, but we can analyse different types of publishing in a similar way. Since different types of publishing tend to work with different types of content, we can

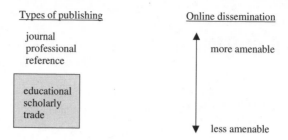

Figure 12.3 Technologies and types of publishing

use figure 12.2 as a basis to produce a very rough and preliminary schema of the amenability of different types of publishing to online dissemination. This schema is presented in figure 12.3. Once again, this schema is not intended to be comprehensive – there are many types of publishing which are not represented here. I am concentrating only on those types of publishing which bear directly on our concerns here.

The schema highlights the fact that journal publishing is highly amenable to online dissemination for the reasons indicated earlier: journals publish discrete results in the form of short articles which are generally consulted and read on a one-off basis; ease of access, searchability and cross-referencing are highly valued by end users; the business model of institutional subscriptions already exists; and there are economies of scale to be achieved by providing access to multiple journals online, either within the framework of a single journal publisher who has a large stable of journals or through the intermediary of a third-party aggregator. Some sectors of professional publishing also lend themselves to online dissemination, especially in those areas which involve the supply of data and information which need continuous updating, such as financial data and legal information.

It is becoming increasingly clear that some kinds of reference publishing also lend themselves to online dissemination, since reference publishing deals with what I have called aggregated knowledge and the online environment enables reference publishers to add real value in terms of scale, updatability, searchability, intertextuality and multimedia. The main problems facing publishers who want to make reference material available online are twofold: scale and business models. The question of scale arises because many reference works issued in print form are relatively small works, and hence they don't have the kind of scale you need if you want to add real value in an online environment. The principal way that reference publishers have dealt with this problem is to concentrate on those reference works that do have real scale, like encyclopaedias or multi-volume dictionaries, or to aggregate reference material along the lines of Oxford Reference Online. In terms of business models, most reference publishers have used the site licence model which is aimed primarily at institutions like libraries. End users gain access to the reference material by virtue of their membership of these institutions. Whether there is any scope for selling access to reference material directly to individual end users, who would purchase an individual subscription to access the material, is much less clear.

The schema highlights the fact that educational, scholarly and trade publishing are less amenable to online publishing, partly because they are dealing with forms of content (pedagogical knowledge, sustained argument and narrative) which lend themselves less readily to online environments and partly because of the nature of the institutions and social practices in which the uses of these forms of content are embedded. The aim of the next two chapters is to examine some of the ways in which the output of scholarly publishers (chapter 13) and higher education publishers (chapter 14) has been made available in online environments, and the extent to which the attempts to do so have been successful. One of the reasons why this is interesting is that it is still very much an open terrain. Much of the material I shall discuss in the next two chapters is experimental. There are a few success stories, many failures and some cases where the outcome is still unclear. The overzealous optimism of some of the ebook advocates of the late 1990s was undoubtedly misplaced, but it is too early to say exactly how the developments in the fields of academic and higher education publishing will play themselves out. What I try to do in the next two chapters is to analyse some of the initiatives that have been made in these fields and assess their implications, but at this stage in the history of the digital revolution, this analysis can be at best a very partial and preliminary assessment of a development that is still underway.

I shall be concentrating here on scholarly and higher education publishing and I shall not discuss any further the many initiatives that have been made in other fields of publishing, including trade publishing. It is one of the many ironies of this unfolding story that the field of publishing which – if my analysis is correct – is least amenable to online dissemination has been the very field where the experiments in ebooks have received the most attention in the press. This has tended to skew a proper understanding and accurate assessment of the implications of the digital revolution for the publishing industry. For not only are the implications much wider and more profound than the focus on online dissemination of content would suggest, but there are also fields of publishing where the shift to online dissemination has been quick, dramatic and irreversible (most notably, journal publishing). In the light of the analysis developed here, it could be argued persuasively that trade publishing is likely to be one of the *last* areas to be affected in a significant way by the online delivery of content, if it is affected significantly at all. Those publishing firms and entrepreneurs who in the late 1990s poured many millions of dollars into preparing themselves for the online delivery of trade books aimed at the general consumer market were, in all likelihood, backing the wrong horse.

13
Academic publishing and the digital revolution

Academic books as digital content

In 1994 MIT Press decided to make one of their books, *City of Bits*, available for free on their website. The author, Bill Mitchell, was interested in how computer technology was affecting urban design, and *City of Bits* was an exploration of what the wired city of the future would look like. Mitchell was keen to experiment with the idea of putting the whole text up on the press's website, with lots of hot links in the text to other websites so that readers could follow up ideas. There was considerable anxiety among the marketing staff at the press, who feared that making the text freely available online would cannibalize the sales of the printed book. Who's going to buy the book if they can go to the website and get if for free? On the other hand, there were some on the editorial side at the press who thought that making the text available online for free might actually enhance the sales of the book, because people don't like to read long texts on screen. If readers scrolled through a few pages of text and liked what they saw, they would be more inclined to hit the 'buy me' button and purchase the book – in other words, making the text available on the website might serve to promote the book rather than to undermine its sales. To put these ideas to the test, the marketing department was asked to estimate how many copies of the book they thought they would sell if the text was *not* made available on the website. They estimated between 6,000 and 8,000 copies. The text was put up on the website, with hot links to other websites and access to the author, and *City of Bits* was published as a printed book. The press sold 10,000 copies and is still selling the book today.

MIT's gamble was one of many experiments in electronic publishing that academic publishers and third parties of various kinds have undertaken since the mid-1990s – *City of Bits* was one of the earlier experiments and, as it happens, one of the less risky and more successful experiments, but there have been countless others. The terrain of the late 1990s is littered with the remnants of experiments in electronic publishing that have either failed outright or have limped along from one year to the next, gradually metamorphosing from one model into another in search of the ever elusive revenue stream. Why this restless search? Why have so many academic publishers, third parties and funding bodies been so eager to invest in electronic publishing experiments for scholarly books?

Undoubtedly the speed and success with which journal publishing has shifted into an online environment played an important role here. Many academic publishers are also active in the field of scholarly journal publishing and they were acutely conscious of the enormous change that was taking place in this field. Since scholarly journals were publishing the results of research for use primarily by the academic community, why shouldn't scholarly books move in the same direction? To some, the process seemed inevitable – it was only a matter of time. Others were (and remain) more sceptical. But even the sceptics were bound to wonder whether the transformation that was revolutionizing journal publishing could simply bypass the world of scholarly book publishing and leave it unscathed – maybe it could, but you had to wonder.

Undoubtedly the bandwagon effect has also played some role here. When other publishers are actively experimenting with new technologies it is hard to resist the temptation to do the same, for fear of being out of step with the key issues and debates in the field or, worse, of being left behind like a beached whale if and when the new technologies suddenly take off. The temptation to experiment was accentuated by the proliferation of third-party organizations which were springing up in the publishing field throughout the second half of the 1990s. Well funded by venture capitalists who were temporarily infatuated with the internet boom, these third parties were knocking on the doors of publishers in search of content which they could license for use in their prospective web-based businesses. The approaches were often linked with financial incentives to participate – for example, a significant amount of content would be digitized free of charge if publishers were willing to commit to an as yet untested business venture. The third-party initiatives affected all publishers, but the university presses and other academic publishers were specifically targeted by a number of initiatives that were seeking to tap new markets in the sphere of higher education. Many publishers reacted with a mixture of interest, bewilderment and caution. Some experimented – a few threw caution to the wind and committed a substantial amount of content to one venture or another, but mostly they experimented cautiously, offering a selection of older and slow-selling backlist titles, just enough to enjoy the benefits of early participation without exposing themselves too seriously to the dangers of cannibalization or taking too many risks in case the venture failed (as indeed many did).

But apart from the wish to experiment and the fear of being left behind if they didn't, there were other reasons why many academic publishers were interested in electronic publishing. Let me mention three. First, there was (and still is in some quarters, though now in a more tempered form) the hope that publishing scholarly books in online environments would become a new source of revenue, and eventually a profitable and financially self-sustaining operation. In principle there are various ways in which revenue could be generated by making the content of scholarly books available in online environments, either as entire books or as bits of books, and many academic publishers have been keen to explore these possibilities. After all, if new revenue streams could be generated, this could help to expand the market for scholarly content; it would not necessarily spell the demise of the printed book but might simply create new sources of incremental income – much like subsidiary rights income – which would improve the overall financial position of the firm. So why not experiment with various possibilities to see if real revenue streams could be generated from the dissemination of scholarly book content online?

A second reason why many academic publishers were interested in electronic publishing had to do with the growing difficulties of scholarly monograph publishing. As the sales of scholarly monographs continued to decline throughout the 1990s, there were many in academic publishing who looked to the world of the internet in the hope of finding – to borrow a phrase that has been used often in this context – 'an electronic solution to the problems of monograph publishing'.[1] From the viewpoint of the publisher, the attractions were not difficult to see: if scholarly monographs could be made available online, then the costs involved in producing them could be reduced, the dangers of excess stock could be avoided and the problem of returns could be eliminated. Electronic dissemination offered publishers the prospect of being able to continue publishing scholarly work in book-length formats while extricating themselves from the seemingly inexorable economic logic of the field which was making the publication of printed monographs increasingly unattractive. Of course, there were significant technical and legal obstacles to turning this dream into a reality – problems of format, standardization, metadata and copyright, to mention only a few, problems that continue to preoccupy those who work in this area. Moreover, the amount of savings that publishers were able to make by publishing in an electronic medium were often overestimated by the early proponents, both because the cost of printing, paper and binding was only a relatively small part of the overall cost involved in publishing a book and because it's not cheap to convert or mark up texts and to put in place the kind of hardware and software needed to publish electronically (together with suitably qualified technical staff). But the fundamental problem that faced any publisher who thought that there might be an electronic solution to the problems of scholarly monograph publishing was that no one had demonstrated that there was a viable market for monographs delivered in an electronic form, and no one had come up with a business model which showed that the electronic publication of scholarly monographs would be a financially viable, let alone profitable, concern.

A third reason why some publishers and others have been interested in the electronic publication of scholarly monographs is that the electronic medium has the potential to liberate the scholarly work from the constraints imposed by the medium of the printed book. While the printed book is in many ways a very convenient medium for the dissemination of scholarly work, it has obvious limitations: length is costly, so most publishers are reluctant to publish scholarly books which are more than 300 pages in extent; illustrations are costly (and colour is prohibitively expensive), so illustrations are usually kept to a minimum; and the addition of multimedia supplements is not practicable. Faced with such limitations, there are some who have seen electronic publishing as a way of liberating scholarly work from the constraints of the medium of print. A scholarly work that was created for dissemination in an online environment – 'born digital', as it is sometimes called – could be conceived of in an entirely different way. Length would no longer be a critical issue, illustrations (including colour) could be used in abundance, archival material could be added and the written text could be supplemented with sound and streaming video. In short, the scholarly work could be reinvented for the digital age.

The most prominent proponent of this new conception of the scholarly work is the American historian Robert Darnton. In a series of articles he has advocated what is sometimes described as the 'pyramid model' of the electronic book.[2] The central argu-

---

[1] See C. J. Armstrong and Ray Lonsdale, *The Publishing of Electronic Scholarly Monographs and Textbooks* (1998), available at www.ukoln.ac.uk/dlis/models/studies/elec-pub/elec-pub.htm; Anthony Watkinson, *Electronic Solutions to the Problems of Monograph Publishing* (London: Resource, the Council for Museums, Archives and Libraries, 2001), available at www.publishers.org.uk/paweb/paweb.nsf/pubframe!Open.

[2] Robert Darnton, 'A Historian of Books, Lost and Found in Cyberspace', *Chronicle of Higher Education*, 12 Mar. 1999, available at www.Theaha.org/prizes/gutenberg/rdarnton.cfm; Robert Darnton, 'The New Age of the Book', *New York Review of Books*, 18 Mar. 1999.

ment of a scholarly work could still be developed as a relatively concise narrative –
there are undoubtedly virtues in conciseness which are intellectual as much as economic.
But in an online environment the work could then be developed further at different
levels, so that the reader who was interested in pursuing particular issues could do so
in more depth. The scholarly work could therefore be structured in layers like a pyramid:

> The top layer could be a concise account of the subject, available perhaps in paperback.
> The next layer could contain expanded versions of different aspects of the argument, not
> arranged sequentially as in a narrative, but rather as self-contained units that feed into the
> topmost story. The third layer could be composed of documentation, possibly of different
> kinds, each set off by interpretative essays. A fourth layer might be theoretical or historio-
> graphical, with selections from previous scholarship and discussions of them. A fifth layer
> could be pedagogic, consisting of suggestions for classroom discussion and a model syllabus.
> And a sixth layer could contain readers' reports, exchanges between the author and the
> editor, and letters from readers, who could provide a growing corpus of commentary as the
> book made its way through different groups of readers.[3]

Just as the scholarly work in an electronic medium would be written differently, so too
it would be read differently. Some readers would stay on the surface and content themselves with the concise narrative that laid out the central argument. Others would click
down to layers which offer more detail and supplementation – extended discussions
of particular points, empirical data, archival material such as documents or letters,
bibliography, iconography, recorded speeches or music, and so on. 'In the end, readers
will make the subject theirs, because they will find their own paths through it, reading
horizontally, vertically, or diagonally, wherever the electronic links may lead.'[4]

Darnton's hope is that his vision of the scholarly work reinvented for the digital age
would enable two problems to be solved at once: it would enable the scholar to take
advantage of the new opportunities brought into being by electronic media, and at the
same time it would enable academic publishers to continue publishing scholarly work
despite the declining sales of the traditional printed monograph. This vision has helped
to inspire a number of experiments in electronic publishing in the United States – most
notably the Gutenberg <e> project funded by the Andrew W. Mellon Foundation and
run by the American Historical Association (I shall discuss this project in more detail
below). But as with so many ideas and experiments of this kind, the key question in the
end is whether the publication and dissemination of scholarly content in this way can
be transformed into an economically viable proposition for publishers and/or other
organizations. For however compelling the idea may be from a purely scholarly point
of view, the ability to turn this idea into a sustainable form of publication presupposes
that sufficient resources are available to cover the costs of doing so. The initial resources
may be provided by grants or venture capital, but unless a project can generate
sustainable revenue streams in the marketplace it is unlikely to continue beyond an
experimental phase.

In fact, the period from around 1995 to the present has been one of considerable
experimentation with the electronic publication of scholarly monographs. Some of the

---

[3] Darnton, 'The New Age of the Book', p. 7.
[4] Darnton, 'A Historian of Books'.

funding for this experimentation has come from venture capitalists (especially in the second half of the 1990s, before the bursting of the dot.com bubble), some has come from philanthropic organizations with an interest in scholarly communication (the Andrew W. Mellon Foundation in New York has been a particularly generous and forward-thinking benefactor) and some has come from publishers themselves, who have been prepared in some cases to use their own resources to experiment with new formats. (Self-funded experimentation of this kind was more common in the late 1990s, before the worsening climate of 2001–2 forced many publishers to tighten their belts, but it continues today.) In this chapter I shall examine some of these experiments. I shall not attempt to be exhaustive – on the contrary, I shall be very selective and shall examine only a handful of experiments which have been particularly significant, which seem particularly promising and/or which highlight broader themes. My interest is not so much in the strictly technical issues of how to make scholarly content available in an online environment; I shall not ignore the technical issues, but this is not my primary concern. For as I stressed in the previous chapter, the really key questions are not technical – rather, they are about the market, the take-up and the actual usage of this material, as well as the business models that would enable publishers to generate sufficient revenue to make the electronic publication of scholarly monographs a viable, ongoing concern.

There are a range of possible models that could be used for the publication and dissemination of scholarly book content in online environments. For the purposes of this discussion, I'm going to distinguish between four basic models – what I shall describe as (1) the virtual library model, (2) the digital warehouse model, (3) the scholarly corpus model, and (4) the scholarly community model. Although I shall distinguish between these four basic models, it must be emphasized that in reality the distinctions between these models are very blurred. Each model admits of numerous variants or subtypes, and there are some initiatives which could easily be treated as a variant of more than one model. Nevertheless, by distinguishing between these models we can give some structure and coherence to the discussion of what might otherwise appear to be a very cluttered and confusing domain. In the following sections I shall examine each of these models in turn, using various experiments to illustrate the pros and cons of each. In the final section I shall step back from the detail and offer a broader assessment of the prospects for the publication and dissemination of scholarly book content in online environments.

The virtual library model

One model for the electronic dissemination of scholarly book content which has been extensively explored in recent years is the virtual library model. The term 'virtual library' has been used in many different contexts; here I shall use it to refer to the creation and maintenance of a collection of electronic books and other content in a manner which allows it to be consulted and read by end users without being purchased by them. The creation and maintenance of this collection typically involves a number of institutional intermediaries. The intermediaries often include (a) third parties which acquire the right to use the content from publishers and which may undertake to convert the content into suitable electronic formats, and (b) existing libraries or other institutions (such as research institutes or corporations) which purchase the right for members of their institutions to access the content under certain conditions. The third parties that constitute themselves as virtual libraries generally do not own the content with which they build up their collections; rather, they license this content from the publishers who own or control the copyright (unless the material is out of copyright, or unless the copyright has reverted to the author). The costs involved in licensing content and, in some cases, converting it into suitable formats have generally been met by substantial investments from venture capitalists or other interested parties. The virtual libraries themselves were generally set up as commercial concerns which would seek to recoup their set-up and running costs and eventually generate a profit by selling licences to access the material in their libraries. They conceived of their principal customers either as other institutions, such as university libraries or private corporations which would buy a licence to allow their members to access the material, or as individual end users, who would purchase the right to access the material directly via the web. The content itself is generally held on the third party's server, and access to it is governed by a password or a user identification system (such as IP or Referring URL authentication).

Different third parties have used different means of acquiring content and different methods of charging for the right to access it, and these methods have generated a number of variants or subtypes which differ in important ways from one another – indeed, it would be more accurate to speak of 'virtual library models' in the plural. We can explore these variants in more detail by examining the three virtual library experiments which gained most prominence in the late 1990s – netLibrary, Questia and ebrary.

netLibrary

netLibrary was founded in Boulder, Colorado in August 1998, although the technology had been in development for several years prior to that. Its aim was to create a large collection of books and other content in a digital format which could be sold on to academic libraries and corporations. Its development plan was to acquire content from publishers, convert it into a suitable digital format, add some functionality such as full search facilities, and then sell it on to libraries and other institutional customers. In the course of 1999 netLibrary succeeded in raising $110 million from venture capitalists and strategic partners to implement its plan. In order to induce publishers to license content to it, netLibrary initially offered to digitize content for free. Books were shipped to netLibrary's facilities in Boulder, where the spines were sliced off and page images created. The production of files was then outsourced to overseas production facilities in India, the Philippines, Indonesia and elsewhere. In many cases books would be rekeyed. The files would be checked for quality and then returned to Boulder, where they would be manipulated according to a house style guide to produce a proprietary format – a netLibrary edition ebook.

The netLibrary model was based on the idea that the books held in its collection would be sold on a title-by-title basis to academic libraries and other institutions. The librarian would purchase a range of individual titles from netLibrary at the price of the hardcover editions. The ebooks would be held on netLibrary's server and legitimate library users would be able to access them via a user identification system. The library would pay a management fee of 9 per cent per annum of the purchase price of the book (or 50 per cent in perpetuity) for the book to be held on netLibrary's server, but the library would save the cost of having to catalogue, shelve, manage, repair and/or replace the physical book. netLibrary would pay a royalty or fee to the publisher of somewhere in the range of 30–50 per cent of the sale price (the precise figure was negotiated separately with each publisher). From the publisher's point of view, a fee at the upper end of this scale would be somewhat similar to the net price it would receive if the book had been sold as an ordinary printed book at a high trade discount.

One controversial aspect of the netLibrary model was that it restricted the usage of ebooks to one user at a time. Of course, the one-user-at-a-time model is how libraries traditionally operate with the printed book, but in the online environment there is no technical reason to restrict usage in this way – indeed, from the viewpoint of the librarian or the end user, this restriction seems absurd. It undermines one of the key respects in which the online environment can add real value to content by making it easily accessible to multiple users. So why did netLibrary adopt this restrictive model? It adopted it largely because it thought it would help allay the anxieties of publishers, upon whom it was dependent for the acquisition of content. The model of selling ebooks to libraries at the same price as hardcover editions and restricting access to one user at a time was a model with which publishers were already very familiar, since it was the same as the model that had been used for centuries with physical books. There was no radical change here. If publishers were worried about cannibalization (and many were), then there was no reason for them to be a lot more worried about the loss of sales when netLibrary sold an ebook to a library than when Baker & Taylor sold a hardcover edition to a library: any library sale has the potential to damage sales to individual readers, but there is no reason to be a lot more worried about the sale of an ebook when access is restricted (as it is in practice with physical books) to one user at a time. Moreover, this model also makes it much easier for publishers to fulfil their contractual commitments to authors. Publishers can treat the sale of the ebook to a library as equivalent to the sale of a hardcover book to a library and can treat the remittances from netLibrary as equivalent to the net receipts from these sales; and they can then pay royalties to authors as a percentage of these net receipts, just as they would with the sale of a hardcover edition. Although many librarians complained about the one-user-at-a-time model, netLibrary believed that it would appeal to many publishers precisely because it replicated the model with which they were already familiar, and hence it would reduce the uncertainties and fears surrounding the idea of making book content available in an online environment.

netLibrary launched its service in February 2000 and generated a significant level of sales in the first year of operation. Its customers were largely university libraries and public libraries in the US; it also sold books to various corporations and to some libraries overseas. The books were generally bought in collections in specific subject areas such as history, women's studies, business, science or law, reflecting the priorities and acquisitions policies of the institutions concerned. Many librarians were open to the idea of building electronic collections of scholarly books and were willing to experiment with netLibrary. By 2001 publishers were receiving cheques from netLibrary; in most cases the sums were very modest, though some publishers who had licensed a substantial number of titles to netLibrary reported earnings that were not insignificant. But the rate of growth of netLibrary's sales was not sufficient to cover its costs. Already in 2000 it had reduced its staff and slashed its sales force to reduce costs; it had also changed its policy on digitization, phasing out the arrangement whereby it covered the cost of digitization and shifting the cost on to publishers. But the gulf between costs and revenues, and the difficulty of raising fresh finance for new technology ventures in the aftermath of the dot.com collapse, eventually forced netLibrary into receivership. In September 2001 netLibrary filed for Chapter 11 bankruptcy and was bought by OCLC (the Online Computer Library Center) for $2 million – a small fraction of the total sums that had been invested in the venture a few years earlier. netLibrary continues to trade now as a wholly owned subsidiary of OCLC.

The great strength of netLibrary's model is that it was and remains firmly rooted in the institutional library market. The founders and managers of netLibrary perceived early on that university libraries were likely to constitute the most robust market for electronic books in the scholarly domain, and they worked hard to cultivate their relations with the librarians and acquisitions staff. They didn't try to develop a model that would be oriented to the sale of individual ebooks to individual end users but concentrated instead on institutions which had substantial budgets for the acquisition of content and which were already accustomed to working with new technologies. As one senior manager explained, 'we start with institutions for a simple reason: they have budgets. We had to build a business and find someone who had the money, and the fact is that consumers have not once indicated the desire to buy a device or to buy ebooks privately.' However, while netLibrary's focus on the institutional market was undoubtedly sensible and far-sighted, there were certain weaknesses in its model and its overall approach. There were also certain constraints that limited its ability to build a virtual library which would meet the needs and wishes of its principal customers. These weaknesses and limitations can be summarized as follows.

(1)   As a third-party aggregator of content, netLibrary was dependent on the supply of content from publishers – in this case, mostly academic publishers. Given uncertainties about the market for electronic books and worries about the possible cannibalization of sales of printed books, many publishers were reluctant to license their most recent books and their strong-selling titles to netLibrary (and, indeed, to other third-party aggregators). They were inclined to take a more cautious approach and to license older backlist titles where the risks of undermining revenue streams from the printed book were minimized. But the result is that the content acquired by netLibrary did not match very closely the needs and purchasing preferences of librarians. Not only were most of the titles on offer by netLibrary older books, in many cases they were also books that the large research libraries had already bought in cloth editions. Many librarians complained that when they looked through the list of books on offer from netLibrary, they found very little, if anything, that they wanted to buy ('not-library', as some librarians began, rather uncharitably, to call it). netLibrary built its collection largely on the basis of what publishers were willing to supply rather than on the basis of what their principal customers, the librarians and acquisitions staff, wanted to buy. The result was that netLibrary invested large sums of money in converting content that was poorly matched to the needs of the institutions that it had identified as its core market.

With time, netLibrary was able to counter this problem to some extent and to persuade some publishers to make more of their frontlist content available. Once it began sending royalty cheques to publishers, it could redouble its efforts to acquire more recent books – 'in return for those royalty cheques, we then assumed the leverage to ask for the frontlist content,' explained a senior manager. But in the eyes of many of the librarians, the damage was already done: netLibrary had gained the reputation for having a catalogue of ebooks that was made up largely of older, backlist titles that did not feature high in their list of priorities for acquisition.

(2)   If the range of titles on offer was unattractive in the eyes of many librarians, the usage model was viewed by all librarians as deeply flawed. As we have seen, the one-user-at-a-time model was adopted by netLibrary in order to placate the content suppliers. netLibrary sought to allay publishers' anxieties by using a model that replicated the traditional library practice: only one person could access the book at any particular point in time. But while this may have allayed the fears of some publishers, it was anathema for librarians. One of the great advantages of the online environment, and one of the key respects in which it enables value to be added, is that it can allow for multiple users at the same time. Librarians had become accustomed to this feature from their experience of acquiring journals and databases online and they complained bitterly about what they saw as netLibrary's unacceptably restrictive usage model.

(3)   A third major problem with netLibrary's approach is that it set out to build a virtual library in which all of the content would be converted into a proprietary format with a consistent appearance and high levels of accuracy and functionality. It set itself high standards in terms of text conversion and quality; it worked in XML (which is not a file format traditionally used in the book publishing industry), it did a substantial amount of rekeying (mostly outsourced to India, the Philippines and elsewhere) and the files were then adapted to the proprietary netLibrary format by its own in-house staff in Boulder, Colorado. Since it was eager to acquire content from publishers as quickly as possible, netLibrary offered packages to early adopters in which netLibrary committed itself to digitizing large numbers of books at its own expense – it was this commitment to free digitization, together with the advances paid, that encouraged many publishers to experiment with netLibrary and offer it some of their content. But by early 2000 it was becoming clear that the digitization commitments were draining netLibrary's resources at a rate that would soon become unsustainable. It had to change course and put an end to free conversion. So it went back to publishers and explained that it could no longer offer to digitize content for free; publishers would either have to provide their content to netLibrary in a suitable format or pay for the cost of digitization. To facilitate this process, netLibrary eventually abandoned its proprietary format and adopted the OEB (Open Ebook) standard. It threw away its 700-page in-house style guide and replaced it with a fifteen-page guide for publishers.

In retrospect, it seems clear that netLibary's attempt to build a virtual library was based on a series of miscalculations about costs and revenue streams. It did succeed in generating real revenue streams, but given the kind of library it built and the way it went about building it, it would eventually reach a point when the revenue streams would fall well short of the levels it needed to keep the operation going in its existing form. That point was reached in the autumn of 2001.

Despite the difficulties encountered by netLibrary, it has demonstrated that there is a real market among university libraries for scholarly book content delivered in an online environment. By the time netLibrary went into receivership, it had over 6,000 library customers. The fact that netLibrary was bought by OCLC is itself significant. Based in Dublin,

Ohio, OCLC is a non-profit consortium of 41,000 libraries around the world which provides a range of services and databases, including an online cataloguing system, to its constituents in return for a membership fee. Ownership by OCLC locks netLibrary firmly into the library world which always was its primary market; it also gives netLibrary greater credibility in the eyes of librarians, since it is now backed by its own membership organization. netLibrary was a pioneer that demonstrated that there is a significant institutional library market for books delivered online, even if in the end netLibrary's costs greatly outstripped its revenues, eventually forcing it into receivership and obliging it to make fundamental changes in its procedures, its business model and its working practices. Among other things, netLibrary is now accepting files in PDF format and seeking to renegotiate contracts with publishers to allow multiple users at a time.

Questia

Questia was the brainchild of a Harvard law student, Troy Williams. While working as an editor at the *Harvard Law Review* in 1997, he was struck by the fact that although one could search the full text of any law case online, one could not search the full text of books. So he came up with the idea of creating a massive online library of books that would be interlinked through their footnotes and bibliographies. The library would be aimed directly at students and would be designed in a way that would enable users to create their own personal workspace, to highlight and annotate books and to create their own links between pages of different books. In June 1998 Williams graduated from Harvard Law School and went back to Houston, where he had been an undergraduate, to see whether he could raise enough capital to get the venture underway. In April 1999 Rod Canion, the co-founder of Compaq, provided some initial seed capital, and Troy Williams and his colleagues subsequently raised more than $130 million in venture capital from OppenheimerFunds, TA Associates and other investors. They set about contacting both publishers and authors with a view to persuading them to license content to Questia. In January 2001 they launched Questia Media, Inc. with around 30,000 titles in the humanities and social sciences, aiming to expand the service to 250,000 titles by 2003.

Since the aim of Questia's founders was to develop an online resource that would be useful for students in higher education, they took advice from librarians and professors. They hired a librarian who put together a team of librarians to help them select titles for inclusion, they used the OCLC database to try to determine which books were used most frequently in a range of liberal arts colleges, they looked at reserve lists at libraries and they scrutinized the recommended reading lists of professors – in these and other ways, they built up lists of books for which they thought there would be a demand from students in the arts and social sciences. This enabled them to draw up a shopping list of titles which they could use in their efforts to acquire content from publishers. As one manager explained,

> One of the things that distinguished us from a number of internet companies that were simply going to publishers and saying, 'give us your content, whatever content', we were going in with a very specific list. Then the publishers might respond to that and they might say 'why do you want this book? We sold fifty copies of it. Why aren't you selecting this book instead?' So there was a fairly vibrant give and take. But it was always very focused.

Acquiring content was not easy, however. 'There was a lot of anxiety, a lot of fear of cannibalization, a lot of confusion because there were a lot of internet companies coming to publishers and they were confused about our business models and how we were different and what we wanted.' If publishers were willing to license content to them, Questia covered the cost of digitization, including the cost of marking up the text in XML and adding search functions and referencing and citation tools. At the outset Questia also contacted authors directly if it thought that rights had been reverted to them, but it quickly discovered that this was not going down well among publishers and it subsequently modified its approach.

Questia's business model consisted essentially of two elements: on the one hand, publishers would share in a royalty pool that would be based on page views, and on the other hand, revenue would be generated by selling subscriptions to students. The calculation of publishers' royalties was based on a simple principle: all publishers would be treated equally and would receive a share of the royalty pool that was proportional to the number of times that the pages of their books had been viewed by users. So if publisher A's books generated X per cent of the page views, then A would receive X per cent of the royalty pool.

Questia's proposed method of generating revenue was much more problematic. The method was shaped fundamentally by its aim of providing a direct service to students. It saw its potential market as the 12.3 million undergraduates and 1.7 million graduate students in higher education in the US, and its goal was to design a service which would provide real value to students, making it easier for them to get the resources they needed for their courses and write their papers. Its gamble was that students would be willing to pay for a service that was tailored to their needs. Hence Questia's business model was based on the idea of selling subscriptions to individual students. A three-tier subscription model was created to provide flexibility: users could take out an annual subscription (initially set at $149.95), a monthly subscription (initially set at $19.95) or a short-term forty-eight-hour subscription aimed at students who had to meet a deadline for a paper (initially set at $14.95). Questia invested substantial sums in promoting the service to students, including campus calling, stuffing mailboxes with brochures and launching a series of television ads that were broadcast during the college basketball season.

By the summer of 2001 it was already clear that Questia was going to have difficulty meeting its revenue targets. It announced substantial staff reductions and began to cut back its digitization programme. It was hoping for a surge in subscriptions at the beginning of the new academic year but this did not materialize on the scale it needed to continue with its ambitious expansion programme. The operation was scaled back and Questia began to search for other methods of generating revenue.

What went wrong with Questia? There were many problems with its approach but the most significant were probably the following.

(1)   Questia's acquisitions programme was very costly to implement, since it committed itself to digitizing content, marking it up in XML and adding search and referencing functions. This approach consumed a substantial proportion of the venture capital it had raised, draining its resources at a rate that greatly exceeded its capacity to generate revenue from the sale of the service to users. The burn-rate was exacerbated by the high marketing costs associated with trying to recruit individual subscribers

(especially when the marketing included campus calling and television advertising campaigns). As the dot.com bubble began to burst, it would prove difficult to raise new finance for a venture of this kind. It was only a matter of time before the directors would be forced into substantial cost-saving measures and would be obliged to scale down their ambitions.

(2)   The most significant problem with Questia was undoubtedly the fact that its business model was based on the assumption that individual students would be willing to subscribe to the service. It was designed as a service for which the individual user would pay; student surveys had apparently convinced Troy Williams that there was a viable market here – 'we've found that there is a tremendous willingness for students to pay,' remarked Williams in April 2000.[5] But by designing the service in this way, Questia was competing directly with other demands on students' resources. Troy Williams's confidence notwithstanding, there were many observers who doubted whether Questia would come out ahead if it was thrown into a head-to-head battle with beer and pizza. True, some students might like the convenience of being able to find texts on their desktops any time of the day or night, without having to leave the comfort of their dorm rooms. But would they actually be willing to dig into their own pockets and pay for this convenience? Many observers were sceptical, and in the end their scepticism proved justified.

As it became increasingly clear that Questia would find it difficult to meet its revenue targets on the basis of individual subscriptions, it began to look for other methods of generating revenue from users. One strategy was to shift the main target of its promotion campaign from students to their parents: after all, if parents were paying tuition fees and other costs associated with their children's education, why not ask them to pay the subscription to Questia as well? Another strategy was to explore the possibility of selling site licences to institutions – that is, to universities, university libraries or even individual departments. But the difficulty with this strategy is that it would conflict with the terms under which it had licensed content from publishers, since the licences assumed that subscriptions would be sold to individual users rather than to institutions.

The fundamental flaw in Questia's business model was that it looked to individual end users (i.e. students) rather than institutions as the source of its revenue. All the evidence points unswervingly to the conclusion that this basic strategic decision was a mistake. The error was then compounded by the marketing strategy used by Questia, which was a very traditional and very costly strategy of trying to persuade students to buy its service by marketing it directly to them. Had it looked more carefully at what happens in the field of textbook publishing, it might have realized that textbook publishers very rarely try to market their books directly to students. They rely on the professors, the gatekeepers, and they direct their marketing efforts at them, because they know that students' book purchasing decisions are largely determined by what their professors tell them to buy. To assume that students would suddenly be willing to purchase access to educational content in a fundamentally different way was an excessively optimistic (and, one might say, ill thought through) assumption. It took no account

[5] Quoted in Gary McWilliams, 'Questia's Aim: The Big Database on Campus', *Wall Street Journal*, 13 Apr. 2000.

of the basic structures of the field within which Questia was trying – in the end unsuccessfully – to intervene.

(3)   The third problem with Questia was the very broad and unfocused character of its collection. By seeking to offer a service in the humanities and social sciences, it was aspiring to cover a very large range of subjects at different levels of the higher education curriculum; it would be difficult to do this and at the same time provide a collection that met the needs of students in any particular subject area. Moreover, while Questia did try to exercise selectivity in building its collection, it is difficult to build a general collection of this kind that will meet the needs of students in diverse institutions. As we saw in our discussion of the BYTES study in chapter 9, there is a great deal of variation across institutions in terms of the books that professors recommend to their students in subjects like English literature and history. A centralized resource like Questia, seeking to cater for a wide range of disciplines across all levels of the higher education curriculum with a limited number of volumes, is bound to fall short of what students in different institutions across the country are likely to need.

Questia continues to trade (as of 2004) and claims to offer 'the world's largest online library of books' with around 50,000 titles available (as well as over 390,000 journal, magazine and newspaper articles), but its staff has been slimmed down to a minimal core. At the end of the day, it simply could not generate a revenue stream to sustain a more substantial operation. It spent excessive amounts of money on conversion and marketing and the uptake in terms of subscriptions was disappointingly low. The business model was deeply flawed from the outset, but Questia did not help its case by targeting students in the liberal arts, who would probably be even less inclined to subscribe to such a service than students on professional or vocational courses. It was a daring idea but most observers would now agree that its ambitions exceeded its actual performance by a considerable margin.

ebrary

ebrary was invented by Chris Warnock, the son of John Warnock, founder of Adobe. Chris Warnock received a Mellon grant when he was at Stanford University to digitize the university archives, and while working on this project he came up with the basic idea of ebrary. In the course of 2000, Chris Warnock and a colleague, Kevin Sayer, raised seed money from John Warnock, from three publishing firms (Random House, Pearson and McGraw-Hill) and from a venture capitalist. They began building up a team to design the software and acquire content for a virtual library that differed in certain fundamental ways from netLibrary and Questia.

    The basic idea behind ebrary was to allow anyone to browse the full text of books free of charge, as they would in an ordinary bricks-and-mortar library or bookstore, and to charge them only when they bought the book or parts of the book. Unlike netLibrary, which sold ebook collections to libraries and other institutions which then entitled members of the institution to access the ebooks that were purchased, ebrary would allow anyone to have full text access to any book in the library free of charge. And unlike Questia, which targeted students and required them to subscribe to the service in order to gain access to content, ebrary would charge end users only when they wanted to perform some function such as copy and paste or print part or all of the text. It was a model based on the principle that end users should be able to browse the full text free of charge and should pay-as-they-use.

The other key respect in which the ebrary model differed from netLibrary and Questia is that ebrary used PDF rather than XML or a proprietary format (like netLibrary). This decision was no doubt influenced by the Adobe connection, since PDF is the format developed by Adobe, whereas XML is a mark-up language used by one of Adobe's major rivals, Microsoft (the differences between these formats will be explained in more detail in chapter 15). But the decision to use PDF also had a certain logic which dovetailed nicely with the publishing world, since most publishers already used PDF in their production processes. This had both aesthetic and economic advantages. A book made available online in PDF will look exactly like a physical book – the pages will be the same, with the same layout, the same page numbering, and so on. It also meant that ebrary didn't have to invest huge sums in the conversion of content, since in principle publishers should already have PDF files for most of their recent titles. 'One of the ways we are different from netLibrary and Questia', explained one ebrary manager, 'is that we are not converting titles.'

> We are not out there willy-nilly taking titles from publishers and converting them for $400–600 a file in the hope that we make it back. We think that is completely insane and the return on investment is a huge question mark, because if you are going to spend that kind of money up front you better be darn well sure that those are the right titles that you are converting or you are in big trouble. So what we are doing is simply working in PDF because it is one of the workflow formats of choice for publishers. It happens to represent the print book accurately so there is an aesthetic quality to it and there's no incremental cost to the publisher or us to participate.

While in principle publishers should have PDF files for their recent books, in practice it was not always easy to track these down. Most publishers were simply not accustomed to keeping track of the PDF files for their books – sometimes they were left with type-setters and pre-press houses, sometimes with freelancers, sometimes on a disk in the bottom of a drawer in the production department. So while using PDF made a good deal of sense, it turned out to be more difficult in practice because most book publishers did not have systems in place for managing their digital assets.

ebrary saw itself as acquiring content for three different user groups: the academic community, ranging from undergraduate and graduate students to professors and researchers; professionals in the areas of healthcare, medicine, engineering, etc.; and general consumers looking for reference content, such as travel guides and cookbook recipes. Rather than trying to market directly to these end users (as Questia had done), ebrary adopted a channel strategy. It developed partnerships with other online businesses to channel traffic to its content. In other words, it adopted a business-to-business (B2B) rather than business-to-customer (B2C) approach, situating itself as a content service provider for online businesses with an existing customer base. So, for example, it developed a partnership with the Learning Network, whose education-oriented customer base might be interested in ebrary's academic content; and it developed a partnership with Expedia, whose travel-oriented customer base might be interested in ebrary's collection of travel guidebooks (which included the Fodor's guides and the Let's Go guides). The B2B partnerships served to channel users to the ebrary site where they would have access to content that might be valued by them.

ebrary's content acquisition programme was shaped by the channel strategy. It was seeking to aggregate content in areas that would be particularly attractive to the customer bases it could access via its B2B partnerships. Its general fields were academic, professional reference and trade reference, and it used methods very similar to an ordinary bricks-and-mortar bookseller to select content: it identified the nonfiction categories that were of interest, and then identified the publishers who were major players in those categories and the titles that were strongest in terms of revenue and units sold. This enabled it to generate shopping lists of titles it wished to acquire. Many publishers were willing to license content to ebrary, though some were worried that free full-text browsing would cannibalize sales and others were put off by ebrary's unwillingness to pay advances.

ebrary's business model was simple: users would be free to browse but would be charged if they chose to copy and paste or print any part of the text, and the revenue generated in this way would be split on an agreed percentage (say 50:50 or 40:60 or some other agreed figure) with the publisher. The publisher would treat this as rights income and would pass on a share to the author in accordance with their existing contracts. The charges for copy and paste or print would vary from text to text and would be determined ultimately by the publisher; the range was from 15 to 50 cents per page, with 25 cents per page being a typical price. 'We wanted to approximate the price that somebody would pay at Kinkos or a photocopier machine, with a premium,' explained a manager. 'So obviously the premium is for the convenience – you're in your dorm, you're in your home office, your printer is sitting next to you.' The user who wanted to copy and paste or print would open an account with ebrary – say for $5 – and the account would be debited with each transaction. The pay-as-you-use, micro-transaction approach was the core of ebrary's business model, but it also sought to generate revenue through the licensing of both the content and the technology to third parties and channel partners.

ebrary went live in July 2001. This was essentially a consumer-oriented launch which included a site on the Learning Network for e-learning support. However, it quickly became clear that the micro-transaction approach was not going to generate the revenue streams it needed. By September 2001 ebrary had changed direction and reoriented the business towards the library market. In January 2002 it launched its library programme, offering libraries the opportunity to purchase annual subscriptions to a full-text database of books. The subscription charge was based on an FTE (full-time equivalent) pricing model, and the revenue generated would be split with publishers depending on the number of books they had in the database. ebrary had effectively metamorphosed from a micro-transaction based service aimed at individual consumers to a subscription-based database service oriented to university libraries and some corporate clients. It was now competing on the same terrain as netLibrary and other third parties who were supplying databases to libraries, such as ProQuest, EBSCO and Gale. But unlike netLibrary, ebrary was selling access to a full-text database of books on an annual subscription basis, rather than selling individual ebooks (or collections of ebooks) on a title-by-title basis. ebrary's database service also allowed multiple simultaneous users, and hence avoided the restrictive model of usage which had made netLibrary so unattractive to librarians.

The metamorphosis of ebrary tends to confirm the lessons that emerge from the experiences of netLibrary and Questia – namely, that the institutional library market is likely to be far more robust than the individual consumer market when it comes to generating revenue streams from the delivery of scholarly book content online. ebrary's original pay-as-you-use, micro-transaction approach simply didn't pan out; 'it was a good idea on paper, but getting people actually to behave in that way was a different story,' reflected one ebrary insider. Individual consumers simply could not be channelled to the site in sufficient numbers and be persuaded to carry out micro-transactions in sufficient volume to keep the business afloat. In essence, ebrary had misunderstood the real market for the content it had aggregated. It thought its content would have real value for individual consumers, who would be motivated to carry out micro-transactions by virtue of the sheer convenience of being able to copy and paste or print from home or from their place of work, but in fact it was not individual consumers but rather librarians who were much more likely to appreciate the value of being able to access high-quality book content online. It is to ebrary's credit that it came to see this very quickly after it had launched its ill-fated consumer-oriented service and that it managed to reinvent itself as a library-oriented subscription-based service in a matter of months. One of ebrary's staff expressed this point of recognition very clearly: 'Where the value of the content really lies is in the minds of librarians and what they're willing to pay.'

However, the fact that ebrary began as a consumer-oriented virtual library aimed at three different user groups (academic, professional and general consumers) is a mixed legacy when it comes to persuading university librarians to sign up to the service. For a consumer-oriented service, having thirty-eight categories of content which include high-profile travel guides and cookbooks may be an asset, but in the eyes of academic librarians this is likely to be perceived as a liability. The database looks like a general collection of books with insufficient focus and scholarly depth. This is a perception that can be overcome only by reshaping the content of the database itself so that ebrary is able to build up a critical mass of high-quality content in selected subject areas that will be valued by librarians. 'We have to take a market leadership position and be *known for* business and economics or be *known for* computers and technology or both, and then also *just happen to have* thirty-eight other categories that you can show to someone and say "hey, look, you also get these",' explained one member of ebrary's staff who was partly responsible for managing the transition. In other words, ebrary will have to prioritize certain subject areas and build a reputation for having a high-quality, in-depth collection of titles in these subject areas – a process which by its very nature takes time because it means one has to go back to the very beginning and redirect the activity of content acquisition, identify new titles that need to be added and open discussions with different publishers. The big question mark over ebrary is whether, in the context of budget cuts and tightened fiscal policies in libraries, it will be able to buy the time it needs to transform its database into a sufficiently rich and well-focused collection of scholarly books to make it a highly valued asset in the eyes of librarians. The ability to license its technology will help it to buy some time, but eventually it will have to be able to generate sufficient revenue through library subscriptions to cover the bulk of its operating costs.

While netLibrary, Questia and ebrary have been the most visible players in the virtual library marketplace, they are not the only ones. Another significant player is Books

24 × 7, a Boston-based organization which has built up a well-focused collection of ebook content in computer science and business aimed primarily at the corporate market. Unlike the other virtual libraries, Books 24 × 7 built a collection that was tailored to the needs of technical and professional staff working in an institutional (and largely corporate) environment. It selected content carefully to meet the needs of this clientele. Books 24 × 7 bore the cost of digitization, but costs were kept down by a highly selective acquisitions programme. Revenue was generated through the sale of annual subscriptions – primarily to corporate clients but also to some government departments and a relatively small number of individuals. This approach proved to be relatively successful, demonstrating that there was an institutional market among private corporations for collections of technical and professional ebook content that were carefully tailored to the needs of their staff. In January 2002, Books 24 × 7 was acquired by Skillsoft, an e-learning organization that specializes in developing professional and technical courses for Global 2000 companies. The acquisition was a natural fit: Skillsoft provided web-based e-learning solutions and resources for the corporate training market and Books 24 × 7 was the leading virtual library of IT and business reference content that was specifically tailored to corporate needs.

The virtual library marketplace is still evolving and the future of some of the key players, such as Questia and ebrary, is at this stage unclear. But there are a number of clear lessons that emerge from the brief and rather turbulent history of this sector, the most important of which are the following two.

(1)   *The market for virtual library collections is overwhelmingly an institutional market.* It consists primarily of university libraries but also includes, for certain kinds of collections, corporations, government departments and other institutions. Institutions have budgets and the institutional gatekeepers, such as the librarians, are empowered to spend these budgets without incurring any personal cost. Of course, these budgets are under pressure and virtual library vendors must compete with other demands on limited resources, but the budgets do exist and a virtual library vendor with a compelling case does stand a chance of securing a slice of the cake. On the other hand, all the evidence suggests that a virtual library based on a business model that seeks to generate revenue from individual end users – whether through subscription or a pay-as-you-use approach – is likely to fail. Individual end users are not accustomed to pay for online services of this kind and are not easily persuaded to do so. It seems very unlikely that a virtual library could ever persuade enough individual end users to part with enough cash to cover its overheads, let alone to become a profitable venture, as both Questia and ebrary discovered to their cost.

(2)   *Acquiring content which is well focused and highly valued by institutional clients is a key to success.* Most of the early pioneers in the virtual library world were wildly ambitious in their aims and aspirations. They were hoping to create vast libraries of digitized book content, the more the better – the sheer ambitiousness of the projects was part of their appeal. This was the modern equivalent of the library of Alexandria – the dream of creating an expanding and potentially limitless collection of books in an online environment, so that anyone anywhere could in principle have access to large reserves of scholarly and literary content. But ambitiousness in this domain had two dangerous consequences: first, for those organizations that initially undertook to bear the cost of con-

version, this cost turned out to be much too high, creating a burn-rate that exhausted the investment capital well before the business was up and running; and second, the acquisitions strategy was too indiscriminate (what one observer described as the 'back-up-the-dump-truck approach'), and the library found itself building up a collection of content (and in some cases paying out substantial sums of money to acquire and convert it) some of which was not highly valued by institutional clients. In their differing ways, both netLibrary and ebrary found themselves in this position, and both are struggling to cast off the image of having many thousands of titles in their collections which are of little or no interest to librarians. Books 24 × 7 adopted a very different approach, building a highly selective collection of IT and professional business titles which was carefully tailored to the needs of its corporate clients and highly valued by them.

While the history of the virtual library world suggests that there are institutional markets for high-quality, well-focused collections of ebook content, what is much less clear is how robust the library market for scholarly book content delivered in online environments is likely to be in the future and what organizational forms are likely to prove viable and durable as a means of delivering this content to libraries. The virtual library model pioneered by netLibrary, Questia and ebrary was that of a third-party intermediary who acquired content from a variety of publishers and sold it on or licensed it to users, occupying a position in the value chain that is somewhat similar to the role of the wholesaler in the world of the printed book. There are of course many differences between virtual libraries and wholesalers – the wholesaler effectively acquires stock on consignment and delivers a service to booksellers and librarians but does not get involved in content conversion or adding value to content through the addition of search and other functions – but wholesalers occupy a somewhat similar position as intermediaries between publishers and institutional clients located further down the value chain. Hence it is not surprising that book wholesalers are beginning to take an active interest in offering digital content services to their institutional clients. Baker & Taylor, the largest library wholesaler in North America, has recently announced that it will offer a new service – known as ED, short for eContent Delivery – to supply ebooks to libraries, and other wholesalers are considering similar schemes. The book wholesalers recognize that if they want to protect their long-term position as intermediaries who channel and manage the provision of book content to libraries, then they must try to ensure that they are not cut out of the loop if and when the content migrates into digital formats; and given that the wholesalers already have an established relationship with libraries, they are in principle in a good position to extend their services into the digital domain.

What we're likely to see in the future, however, is more attempts by *publishers themselves*, operating either on their own or in collaboration with other publishers, to deliver collections of ebook content directly to institutional clients. If there is an institutional market for ebook content, why should publishers rely on third-party intermediaries to cater for the needs of this market? When the third parties were able and willing to pay substantial sums of money to convert content and pay advances, the case for collaborating with them may have been strong, but with the demise of free conversion and the evaporation of significant advances the case is less compelling. Why shouldn't publishers supply the content themselves, cutting out the intermediary and delivering the content directly to libraries or other institutional clients, as the large journal publishers already do? The launching of Safari Books Online in July 2002 – a joint venture between

O'Reilly and Pearson to create an online, searchable database of books in IT and computer science – is one example of publisher-driven initiatives of this kind. They represent a potential threat to intermediaries, whose existence depends on their ability to acquire high-quality content from publishers. But whether publisher-driven initiatives of this kind are likely to displace third-party intermediaries or merely occupy a space alongside them remains unclear at this stage. The success of publisher-driven initiatives is likely to depend on certain conditions (such as scale and the ability and willingness to collaborate with other publishers) which may not be easy to fulfil (and which, in any case, may apply more to some publishers than to others). There may well continue to be space for third-party intermediaries who are able to distinguish themselves from publisher-driven initiatives by their ability to aggregate content originating from a variety of different sources, although this space may become more crowded and the third parties may find it increasingly difficult to acquire material from publishers who hold some of the most highly valued content.

In this section I have concentrated on the virtual libraries which established themselves as third-party intermediaries. In the following sections I'm going to examine some of the initiatives in the area of scholarly publishing which have been taken either by publishers themselves or by funding organizations acting in tandem with academic publishers. I shall begin by looking at some attempts by publishers to create a publisher-run ebook service for their customers.

The digital warehouse model

The virtual libraries are third-party intermediaries who license content from publishers and then attempt to generate revenue by charging in various ways for access to and/or use of this content. But a number of academic publishers have sought to create alternative ways of generating revenue through the sale of their own content in digital formats. One way of doing this is to create a 'digital warehouse', either on one's own or in conjunction with a technology partner, and then use this as a means of supplying ebook content to customers who can place orders through an e-bookstore hosted on the publisher's website and/or on the websites of various e-tailers. This model, which has been adopted by some academic publishers, is summarized in figure 13.1.

In this model, the digital warehouse functions in the same way that a physical warehouse functions for printed books: it holds the publisher's content, although the content is now held in the form of digital files rather than bound and printed books. The digital warehouse may be housed in the publisher's own server but in many cases it is hosted by a third-party technology partner (like Overdrive, Reciprocal or Digital Publishing Solutions). In some of the early initiatives in this area, there were major incentives for publishers to work with third-party technology partners, including the offer to convert a substantial amount of content either free of charge or in an arrangement whereby the cost of conversion would be earned back as a charge on later sales of the converted title. But even where the digital warehouse is hosted by a technology partner, the content is still owned by the publisher; it is not licensed to the third party, as it is in the virtual library model.

The digital warehouse is a back-office technology support system: the customer does not interact with it directly, any more than he or she interacts directly with the physi-

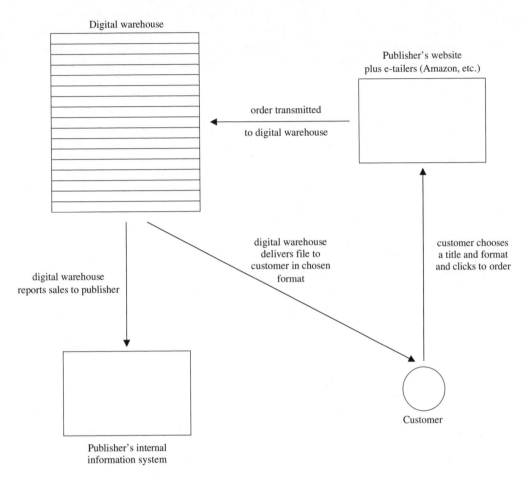

Figure 13.1 The digital warehouse model

cal warehouse in which printed books are stored. The customer who wants to buy an ebook goes either to the publisher's website or to the website of an e-tailer like Amazon or b&n.com. There the customer will find a menu of options: do you want to buy this book as a printed book or as an ebook? And if you want to buy it as an ebook, which file format do you want – Adobe or Microsoft Reader or Palm Pilot? If you choose the ebook option and select an appropriate format, you can then click to purchase the ebook. You'll be asked for your credit card number and charged at whatever price is indicated. Your order will then be automatically relayed to the digital warehouse, which will supply the ebook directly to the customer in the chosen format – with a normal internet connection speed, the download takes about a minute. The content may be encrypted so that it cannot be passed on to another user or viewed on another computer. (There are various digital rights management (DRM) systems available to minimize the risks of piracy and unauthorized dissemination, although these often involve some inconvenience to the user.) If the digital warehouse is hosted by a third-party technology partner, it will relay information on sales to the publisher. The technology partner will charge the publisher a fee to provide its service; all or part of this fee may be calculated as a percentage of sales (the specific arrangements vary from publisher to publisher and from partner to partner). If the sale comes via an e-tailer like Amazon, the e-tailer would normally be charged by the publisher at a discount of around 20 per cent.

The digital warehouse model also enables the publisher to introduce a variety of micro-transactions so that the customer can purchase less than a whole ebook – what is sometimes described as 'slice and dice'. For example, customers could be allowed to download a single chapter rather than a whole book, or to print off a specific number of pages. They might be charged at a pro rata cost per page, marked up by a factor of two or three. So, for example, if they chose to print off five pages, they might be charged at three times the pro rata rate; if they chose to print off a chapter, they might be charged at twice the pro rata rate. Although the charge is a mark-up of the pro rata rate, it may still be cost effective for customers to slice and dice, because instead of paying £15 ($24) for the whole ebook, most of which they don't need, they may end up paying £1.20 ($1.90) for the five pages they do need. And it may still be economical for the publisher because it is likely to be an additional sale, incremental income that would not have been earned if the slice and dice option had not been available, and because the publisher receives more than the pro rata rate.

Among academic publishers, one of the best publicized ebook initiatives based on the digital warehouse model is that of Taylor & Francis. In spring 2000 it entered into an agreement with a technology partner named Versaware to create a digital warehouse that would be hosted by Versaware. As part of the deal, Versaware undertook to digitize Taylor & Francis's entire backlist of 17,000 titles at its conversion facilities in India. Taylor & Francis would retain full control of the content while Versaware would provide the technical services of converting the titles and creating and maintaining the digital warehouse; Versaware's costs would be recovered through a revenue stream that would be calculated as a percentage of subsequent sales. Taylor & Francis would create its own e-bookstore but it would also encourage e-tailers like Amazon and b&n.com to list its ebooks on their websites. The site was due to be launched in June 2001 but – with the kind of misfortune that is all too symptomatic of this high-risk new technology sector – Versaware went bust at the beginning of 2001, leaving Taylor & Francis with a fraction of its 17,000 backlist titles in a suitable digital format. With the help of Versaware's successor company, a firm called Digital Publishing Services, Taylor & Francis did manage to launch its digital warehouse and e-bookstore in July 2001 with 450 titles, adding another 50–100 titles a week in the following weeks so that it had reached over 900 titles by September.

The digital warehouse model has some attractive features for publishers. It enables publishers to retain control of their content and to pay e-tailers and technology partners in ways that are roughly comparable to the fees they would pay to booksellers and distributors in the traditional supply chain for printed books. In the virtual library model, publishers hand their content over to third parties who are licensed to sell access to it, and the publishers generally receive a modest percentage of the revenue generated by the third party. In the digital warehouse model, by contrast, publishers retain control of the content; they may work with a third-party technology partner, but they do not license their content to this partner. The publisher decides how to price the content and receives the bulk of the revenue generated, less any fees payable to the technology partner and any discount retained by the e-tailer. The publisher also retains control in terms of the quality of the final product, its security, the ways in which it is aggregated with other content, the assignment of rights and so on. If it was an early player in the ebook game, a publisher might also be able to work out very favourable terms with a technology partner which would enable the publisher to digitize a proportion of its backlist at little or no cost to itself (although agreements of this kind were largely a feature of the late 1990s when new technology firms were flush with capital and keen to attract content providers, and it is unlikely that any publisher would be able to secure such an agreement today). So for early players like Taylor & Francis, the digital warehouse model provided a low-cost, low-risk way of entering the ebook marketplace, while at the same time enabling the publisher to retain control over its content and the ways in which it could be aggregated and sold.

However, there are also problems with the digital warehouse model. Here I shall concentrate on what seems to me to be the most important issue – namely, the business model which underlies this approach and the revenue that is likely to be generated by it. The business model generally associated with the digital warehouse approach is a consumer transaction model aimed primarily at the individual – in this case, the academic, the student or the professional who wants to purchase the ebook or part of the ebook, or to print off a number of pages. The model assumes that there will be sufficient demand from individual consumers to drive the business forward. The evidence to date suggests, however, that the actual level of demand from individual consumers for ebooks (in whole or part) is very low and is likely to remain low for the foreseeable future. This is true not just for trade books aimed at the general reader of fiction or nonfiction, but also for books of a more scholarly kind. Those academic publishers who have launched digital warehouses and have offered a range of their titles for sale as ebooks have generally found that the revenue generated through ebook sales was minimal and well below their original expectations. Where sales did occur, they tended to be in more professional areas rather than in purely academic subjects. The most active customers also tended to be overseas, suggesting that the ability to download an ebook was valued most by some individuals who were not able easily, quickly and cheaply to acquire the printed book.

The slice and dice approach provides an interesting variation on the consumer transaction model but it encounters the same difficulties and raises new problems of its own. Again, the evidence so far suggests that the uptake of slice and dice by individual consumers is likely to be very low – it is attractive in principle but in practice the usage of this facility is minimal. Slice and dice also runs the risk of creating a situation where there are many micro-transactions that add up to very small amounts in terms of overall revenue, and where the transaction cost involved leaves a publisher with very little net return. This danger has tended to force publishers offering slice and dice facilities to set a minimum transaction charge of, say, £3 (or $5). Undoubtedly this helps, but in the end the low levels of revenue combined with the relatively high transaction costs make this a rather unattractive business proposition.

The fundamental problem with the digital warehouse approach is that it tends to be based on a business model – what I've called the consumer transaction model – which is oriented primarily to the individual consumer. However much the business model is refined and revised, its effectiveness will depend ultimately on the willingness of the individual consumer to purchase the ebook (either in whole or in part) or to initiate some other transaction (such as printing off a number of pages). But it may well be that the demand for ebooks from individual consumers – whether these are academic books or trade books – will remain very low for the foreseeable future, and that the kind of revenue generated from a consumer transaction model will be extremely modest. The evidence so far tends to point to this conclusion. It could be argued – persuasively in my view – that if there is a significant market for scholarly book content delivered in a digital format, then it is more likely to be an institutional market rather than an individual consumer market. The experience of the virtual libraries and of those publishers who have experimented with digital warehouses tends to lead inexorably to the conclusion that it is institutional gatekeepers like university librarians, rather than individual consumers (be they academics or students), who are most likely to be interested in and willing to disburse resources for access to scholarly book content delivered in a suitable digital format. In short, the academic publisher who created a digital warehouse with a view of selling ebooks to individual consumers was, in all likelihood, barking up the wrong tree. It is significant that Taylor & Francis, whose ebook initiative was originally aimed primarily at individual consumers, has subsequently reoriented the project towards the library market, which now accounts for the majority of the modest revenues generated by it.

Publishers who have gone down this path might nevertheless argue that the experiment has been, and continues to be, worthwhile. It has enabled them to enter the ebook marketplace at relatively low cost and to gain valuable knowledge and experience of digital content management. They can argue that building a digital warehouse to hold the content of their books in digital formats is a worthwhile activity in itself, because it will 'future proof' them even if the market for ebooks remains very uncertain. This line of argument has some plausibility, as we shall see. A strong case can be made in support of the view that publishers should be building some kind of digital asset store or archive in which they can hold their book content in a suitable digital format. Of course, this does not necessarily mean that they should be investing in a digitization programme that would involve converting all or most of their backlist content, or that they should be incurring the extra expense involved in marking up their content in XML. Nor does it mean that they should be going to the trouble and expense of building a customized e-bookstore for the sale of their own ebooks, or buying an e-bookstore template from a technology partner to achieve the same end. The building of a digital asset store may have more important uses for a publisher, and greater value for them, than that of servicing the sale of ebooks to individual customers. We shall return to these issues in chapter 15.

The scholarly corpus model

Another way of delivering scholarly books in an online environment is to create a corpus of scholarly book content and to charge for access to this corpus on a subscription basis. How does this approach differ from the virtual library model and the digital warehouse model? The models do overlap in some respects, but I want to distinguish between them on the following grounds. In the way that I'm conceptualizing the issues, the virtual library model is based on the idea of a third party which does not own content but functions as an aggregator of the content of others. The virtual library is effectively a third-party licensed aggregator of content: it licenses content from publishers and then sells access to it in various ways – either by the sale of collections of ebooks (netLibrary) or by selling subscriptions to individuals (Questia) or institutions (ebrary, Books 24 × 7). The scholarly corpus model, on the other hand, is based on the idea that the publishers themselves, acting either as single organizations or in some kind of association or collaboration with other publishers, seek to create a corpus of scholarly book content to which they can sell access. It is essentially a publisher-driven model in which the publishers retain control of their content, although they may supplement their own content with content acquired from other publishers or other sources. If publishers were successful in creating and running their own scholarly corpora, they could find themselves competing with the virtual libraries, and the latter could find it increasingly difficult to license new content from publishers in subject areas where publishers were active themselves. While the creation of a scholarly corpus of this kind requires the publisher or publishers to build a digital repository for the content, the repository is not treated as a warehouse which supplies orders on an ebook-by-ebook (or chapter-by-chapter) basis (as in the digital warehouse model). Rather, in the scholarly corpus model, the content forms a corpus, an online searchable database, to which access is sold on a subscription basis. Subscriptions are sold primarily to institutions such as university libraries, but in some cases they may be sold to individuals as well.

The scholarly corpus model assumes that the publisher creates the corpus, but in practice there are various subtypes or variants of the model, depending on who exactly is involved in creating the corpus and whose content is used. We can distinguish between the following subtypes (and there are others):

(1) *The publisher-based corpus* In this case, a single publisher builds a corpus of content using material for which it holds the copyright. The advantage of this approach is that the copyright problems are minimized and the revenue streams are simplified, since the publisher holds the copyright on all of the content. The disadvantage is that the breadth and/or depth of the corpus may be limited, since very few publishers have sufficient content in any subject area to create a comprehensive database on their own. The most significant current example of this approach is Oxford Scholarship Online.

(2) *The cross-publisher corpus* One way to overcome the limitations of the publisher-based corpus is to collaborate with one or more other publishers to create a joint database. The attraction of this approach is that it enables publishers acting together to create a database that is much more comprehensive than anyone of them could create on its own. The main problem with this approach is that publishers traditionally find it very difficult to collaborate with one another. They compete with one another in many ways and they don't find it easy to set aside their competitive rivalries. A good example of the cross-publisher corpus in the area of scholarly publishing is the new initiative which is being developed by OUP-USA with the help of a grant from the Mellon Foundation, provisionally called The Online Resource Center in the Humanities or TORCH.

(3) *The publisher-linked, grant-funded corpus* This hybrid model is largely a product of the innovative and far-sighted funding policies of a few philanthropic foundations,

most notably the Andrew W. Mellon Foundation. The Mellon Foundation has made substantial grants available to experiment in various ways with the creation of corpora of scholarly book content. The projects often involve the participation of university presses, although the funding, at least initially, is provided by the Foundation. The main difficulty faced by initiatives of this kind is whether they can secure a sufficient subscription base to continue to survive after the initial funding has been exhausted. Examples of this approach include CIAO (Columbia International Affairs Online), the Gutenberg <e> project and the History Ebook project.

(4)   *The publisher-based, content-aggregating corpus*   This is another hybrid model, situated somewhere between the publisher-based scholarly corpus model and the third-party virtual library. Like the virtual library, this hybrid model involves the aggregation of content from other sources, either from other publishers and copyright holders or from the public domain. But like the publisher-based scholarly corpus, this hybrid model is rooted in the initiatives of a publisher who adds real value to the corpus by creating new content for it, integrating, cross-referencing and hyperlinking it, and adding functions such as search facilities. In the field of scholarly publishing, a prominent example of this hybrid model is the work of the Cambridge-based electronic publisher Chadwyck-Healey (now renamed ProQuest, following the sale of the company to the American firm Bell & Howell). Chadwyck-Healey's Literature Online and History Online, as well as its more specialized databases like the Patrologia Latina and the Acta Sanctorum, are online, searchable databases of texts which have been aggregated into corpora and to which significant value has been added by Chadwyck-Healey's own editorial teams.

In this section I want to examine some of these initiatives in more detail. Since some are very recent (and some still in a state of planning and development), it is not possible at this stage to offer a conclusive assessment of their strengths, limitations and prospects. However, in at least some of these cases, the projects have been going for long enough to offer at least a preliminary assessment. I shall begin by looking at three projects which fall into the third category of Publisher-linked, grant-funded corpora: CIAO, the Gutenberg <e> project and the History Ebook Project. I shall then consider an initiative which falls broadly within the second category of a cross-publisher corpus, namely, the TORCH project (although this initiative is also facilitated by a Mellon Foundation grant). Finally, I shall examine OUP's important new initiative, Oxford Scholarship Online, which falls within the category of a publisher-based corpus. I shall defer the discussion of Chadwyck-Healey's Literature Online and History Online until the next chapter, for reasons that will become clear.

CIAO

Columbia International Affairs Online was initiated in 1997 with the help of a three-year grant of $360,000 from the Mellon Foundation. The aim was to create an online database of searchable content in international affairs and to sell site licences to libraries and other organizations on an annual subscription basis. A major part of CIAO's activity consists of aggregating 'grey literature' – that is, working papers, research reports, conference proceedings, policy briefs and other material produced by a wide range of organizations and research institutions. There are currently over 190 organizations from which CIAO acquires various kinds of content. CIAO has an advisory board of scholars in political science and international relations who help to provide some guidance in the selection process. It seeks to add between 2,500 and 3,000 pages a month to the site, largely by aggregating grey literature produced by others. The site also includes a collection of books, a selection of journals and some original content. CIAO recently launched a new series of case studies, each with between fifteen and thirty-five pages of text together with documents and multimedia supplements, on key episodes and issues in international affairs, such as the Cuban missile crisis, Iraq and the Gulf War, weapons of mass destruction, America and Europe in a post-9/11 world, and so on. The case studies were developed with the aim of making CIAO useful as a teaching resource, not just as a resource for scholars and researchers.

From the perspective of electronic publishing, one of the most significant features about CIAO is that it is one of the few sites in the area of scholarly online publishing which is financially self-sustaining. By the time the Mellon grant expired in 2000, CIAO had built up a subscription base among libraries and some governmental and other organizations that was generating sufficient revenue to keep the operation going. CIAO enjoys certain benefits from being linked to Columbia University and to Columbia University Press – the site is hosted on the university library's server, for example, and not all staff and overhead costs are fully costed to the project. But the revenue generated from subscriptions is now sufficient to cover the core running costs and enable the staff to continue expanding and developing the site. So what are the keys to CIAO's success? Three aspects of CIAO have been particularly important:

1   First, CIAO is focused on a particular subject area in which it has been able to establish a reputation as a leading online resource. By focusing sharply on international affairs, it has been able to build some depth and critical mass. It was also the first major online resource in this area, which enabled it to stake a claim before any significant competitors came on the scene.
2   A second key feature underlying CIAO's success is that it saw there was a need for someone to function as an aggregator of grey literature in this area, and it shaped its acquisition strategy to meet this need. The working papers comprise the largest and most heavily used part of the CIAO site. Much of this material is freely available elsewhere, on the websites of different organizations and research centres, but by selecting and bringing together in one place some of the most important of this material, CIAO provides a service that is valued by librarians and end users.
3   The third key to CIAO's success is that it clearly targeted the institutional market and it worked hard to build up its subscriptions among libraries and other organizations. The vast majority of the subscriptions are with libraries, mainly university libraries but also some public libraries, and most of the remaining subscriptions are with government organizations and NGOs. Individuals can subscribe but individual subscriptions constitute a tiny fraction of the total.

While CIAO's reliance on grey literature is one of the keys to its success, it is also a potential source of weakness for an organization of this kind. As an aggregator of grey literature, CIAO does not own this content, nor does it have an exclusive licence to make it available online. Hence it will always be faced with a twin danger. On the one hand, it could find itself faced with a competitor who is much larger and better resourced, and therefore able to create a similar site on a much larger scale. The aggregation business is fundamentally a business of scale – how much content can be aggregated and made available at what price – and any aggregator who has found a viable niche is always going to face the danger that someone else could aggregate more content and make it available more cheaply. On the other hand, it could also find that what it has to offer, being largely aggregated content much of which is freely available elsewhere, is not valued sufficiently highly by libraries and other organizations to ensure that subscriptions are renewed when institutional budgets are squeezed. Small players like CIAO are always vulnerable when institutions are looking for ways to cut expenditure. CIAO is a success story: so far it has managed to secure enough subscriptions and ensure that they are renewed from one year to the next to cover their running costs. But at a time when institutional budgets are being squeezed, the renewal of subscriptions cannot be taken for granted.

The centrality of grey literature to CIAO's success also means that, as a model for the publication of scholarly *book* content in an online environment, CIAO may be of limited value. The CIAO site does include a collection of electronic books but this collection is relatively small and the books are not heavily used. Scholarly book content is not the core of CIAO but a relatively marginal feature of it; the real driver of CIAO is the aggregation of grey literature, and it is to this primarily that it owes its success. Hence, taken by itself, CIAO does not tell us all that much about the prospects for the publication and dissemination of scholarly book content in an online environment.

Gutenberg <e>

Columbia University Press and the American Historical Association launched the Gutenberg <e> project in 1999 with the help of a substantial grant from the Mellon Foundation. The aim of the project was to select a small number of high-quality Ph.D. dissertations in particular fields of history and to publish them as sui generis ebooks without a paper equivalent. So the aim was effectively twofold: first, by selecting dissertations in fields where it was becoming increasingly difficult to publish scholarly monographs, the project would explore whether the electronic medium offered a viable alternative means of publishing and disseminating high-quality scholarly work in so-called 'endangered' subject areas; and second, by publishing the works as sui generis ebooks, the project would provide an arena to experiment with the *form* of scholarly output and to push scholarship in new and largely unexplored directions. The project was influenced by Robert Darnton's conception of the ebook as a new medium which made possible different kinds of scholarly output, and indeed Darnton was in many ways the intellectual inspiration behind the project.

Gutenberg <e> was launched in 1999 for three years in the first instance, although the grant from the Mellon was subsequently renewed for another three years. The idea was that each year a special committee of the American Historical Association would select six dissertations in a chosen field. Each author would be offered a prize of $20,000, in return for which they would sign a contract with Columbia University Press to publish their dissertation as an ebook on a dedicated website. In 1999, six dissertations were chosen in the fields of African, colonial Latin American and South Asian history; in 2000, six dissertations were chosen in the field of European history before 1800; and in 2001, the field was diplomatic and military history not primarily of the United States. Once the author had accepted the prize, he or she would be invited to New York to talk with the technical staff at Columbia University Press about how they could develop their work to take advantage of the electronic medium. They could add photographs, streaming video, audio files and archival material; they could play with the narrative form, running two or more narratives alongside one another; they could add hot links to other web-based resources; or they could stick with the traditional format of the scholarly work if they wished. When they submitted the final files, the text would be copy-edited on screen, marked up in HTML or XML, designed as an ebook and then put online. The site went live with the first six titles in spring 2002.

While the aim was to publish scholarly work as sui generis ebooks, the organizers soon found that some of their authors were anxious about the fact that their work would be available only in electronic form. As young scholars concerned about getting academic jobs and securing tenure, they worried about whether the publication of an ebook would have the same value for appointment and tenure committees as a traditional printed monograph. Partly in order to assuage this concern, the Gutenberg <e> staff agreed to produce fifty copies of a printed version of the text. The print version is effectively a set of galleys which is printed from the electronic file, bound and jacketed with a basic cover. The galleys are given to the authors free of charge so that they can distribute them as they wish. The quality of these galleys is significantly inferior to the ebook, since the galleys lack the multimedia supplements of the ebook; it is also inferior to the quality of a traditional printed monograph. But the galleys provide the authors with something in print that they can use for the purposes of advancing their own careers. They are a concession to the printed word in a world which continues to place value on the physical product of scholarly work.

The funding for Gutenberg <e> comes from a Mellon Foundation grant, but the aspiration of those involved in the project is to generate a significant revenue stream by selling site licences to research libraries on an annual subscription basis. The subscription fee is modest – $195 per year (in 2002) for access to the collection, which will increase by four to six works each year. However, whether they will be able to generate sufficient revenue to cover their running costs is very much an open question. This is not an inexpensive project to run – the annual prize money alone comes to $120,000, before taking account of the salaries of technical staff, the costs of running the website and the costs of publicizing the website and marketing it to librarians. While producing ebooks involves some savings in terms of printing, paper, binding, warehousing and distribution costs, it also creates new costs in terms of technical support staff, multimedia development and mark-up and design costs, as well as the costs of running and maintaining the website. 'I don't think we've ever done a cost comparison counting all our salaries,' commented one staff member, 'but I think what you'd find is that the ebooks probably are more expensive than traditional print monographs.' Is it conceivable that an operation of this kind could generate sufficient revenue through the sale of site licences on an annual subscription basis to be self-sustaining when the grant from the Mellon runs out? Of course, it is too early to offer a definitive judgement, but even at this early stage it would not be unreasonable to suggest that this outcome is unlikely.

Why? What are the characteristics of this project that would lead one to doubt whether it would be financially viable without a substantial grant? The relatively high costs are undoubtedly an issue, but the fundamental problem with this project is that it is small-scale, niche publishing – six monographs a year in specialized, relatively peripheral fields of history. Many librarians are interested in experimenting with scholarly content in electronic formats, but this is a very small item for them and it's unlikely to feature high on their list of priorities. Gutenberg <e> is a highly innovative experiment in electronic scholarly publishing, and for this reason alone it is undoubtedly a worthy project. But as a business proposition it lacks one of the crucial features that enable value to be added in an online environment: scale. As one participant remarked, it suffers from the problem of the 'boutique website' – the small, specialized site that finds it hard to get a seat at the table when librarians are dishing out their budgets, and hard to keep a place at the table when the budgets are getting squeezed. Sites of this kind may have novelty value and may attract the attention of librarians who are sympathetic to the aims of the project, but they are not 'must-have' content. So it seems unlikely that Gutenberg <e> will be able to generate sufficient revenue through subscriptions to continue in its current form as a self-sustaining operation in the absence of a grant. If the project has a future beyond the period of its grant, it will in all likelihood be a future in which it will be merged together with other resources to provide it with the kind of scale that it currently lacks.

The History Ebook Project

In 1999 the American Council of Learned Societies (ACLS) was awarded a grant of $3 million from the Mellon Foundation to set up an electronic publishing project in the field of history. The ACLS is an umbrella organization comprising numerous learned societies, and the idea was that five of these societies would collaborate with a select group of university presses to explore the possibilities for publishing high-quality historical work in an electronic environment. Ten university presses were eventually selected – California, Columbia, Harvard, Johns Hopkins, MIT, Michigan, New York, North Carolina, Oxford and Rutgers. After a rather bumpy start, Eileen Gardiner and Ron Musto joined the project in October 1999 and helped to give it a clear focus and direction. Under their guidance, the project developed along two parallel tracks. On the one hand, working together with the university presses, the project would seek to publish 85 new books in an electronic format; on the other hand, it would also digitize around 500 key backlist titles which would be selected to form subject-based clusters of high-quality book content to complement and supplement the new books and give greater depth and scale to the project as a whole. The two sets of books – new and backlist titles – would be aggregated into a single searchable database which would be hosted by the Digital Library Production Service (DLPS) at the University of Michigan. Access to the database would be via site licences that would be sold to libraries on an annual subscription basis.

The project was oriented towards four broad fields within history (reflecting in part the learned societies involved): American history, European history, Middle Eastern history and the history of technology. Within each of these fields, the project organizers and the publishers would identify new books that they would like to include in the project; in some cases these would be books already under contract with one of the university presses, while in other cases they would be new books that had yet to be commissioned. The arrangement was that one of the university presses would sign up the book and undertake to publish it as a printed book. The History Ebook Project would then license the electronic rights from the press and pay it a fee – both a licence fee of $2,000 for the electronic rights and a 'materials fee' of $12,000 to facilitate the process of creating an ebook and producing a file in the appropriate format, so that the content could be integrated into the project's database. The project developed a tagging system – a DTD or Document Type Definition – which was shared with all the participating presses and specified the format in which the files had to be delivered. Authors were encouraged to experiment with the form of the text – to use illustrations (including colour illustrations), to add archival material and to include hyperlinks, among other things. Here again, Darnton's ideas about how electronic media could be used to transform the nature of scholarly writing played an influential role. But unlike Gutenberg <e>, the new books destined for the History Ebook Project were conceived of as dual-format publications: they would be published as traditional printed books by the university presses while also appearing as ebooks (in some cases with additional illustrations and supplementary material) in the database of the History Ebook Project.

The backlist titles were selected with the help of the learned societies, which produced lists of books which they regarded as works of lasting merit in their fields, and with the help of a committee of scholars who scrutinized the lists and recommended additional titles. The project staff then sought to acquire non-exclusive electronic rights for the selected titles and covered the cost of conversion. While the new books were marked up according to the tagging system worked out by the project's technical staff, the backlist titles were scanned and converted using OCR (optical character recognition), with a minimal amount of coding (e.g. of the table of contents) to facilitate navigation through the site; this helped to minimize the conversion costs, which were about $1 per page. The idea of adding backlist titles wasn't part of the original idea of the History Ebook Project, but as the project developed it took on more and more importance. In the eyes of the project directors, the backlist was crucial. It provided a context for the new books, 'so we won't be putting these isolated books out into cyberspace', and it gave some critical mass to what would otherwise be a very small quantity of scholarly content.

While the funding for the project has been provided by the Mellon Foundation, the aim is to generate a revenue stream by selling site licences to libraries on an annual subscription basis. The subscriptions are very modest, ranging from $300 for the smallest institutions to $1,300 for the largest. Half of the revenue generated is channelled into a royalty pool for the publishers, and each publisher is paid according to the proportion of hits on its titles. The site was launched on 1 September 2002 with 500 backlist titles and half a dozen new titles. By the end of December 2002, just over 100 institutions had signed up; by April 2004, 160 institutions were on board. The project directors still have some way to go; they will need to increase the institutional subscriptions sixfold to become self-sustaining. The funding from the Mellon Foundation expired in 2004 but the project directors hope that bridging funds will be made available while they continue to build the subscription base.

As an electronic publishing venture, the History Ebook Project has many attractive features. It is well focused on certain subfields of history and it uses rigorous selection procedures to aggregate content – features that are likely to appeal to many librarians, who tend to value the quality of collections as well as the quantity of content. The decision by the project directors to add backlist titles of 'lasting merit' also helped to give some scale and depth to the collection. And the collaboration with university presses to adopt a dual-format approach to publication – publishing new work in print with a university press as well as electronically with the History Ebook Project – provided a clever way of overcoming the reservations that many academics would have about publishing their work as an ebook only, given the extent to which scholarly culture in subjects like history is still wedded to the printed book. But it is doubtful whether the financial inducements used to facilitate the participation of the university presses – the $12,000 materials fee – could be maintained without the generous funding of Mellon, and hence it remains unclear whether the dual-format approach could be sustained without a grant. The dual-format approach also meant that the extent to which authors would be inclined to experiment with the form of scholarly output would, in all likelihood, be limited in practice. While authors would be encouraged to add illustrations, archival material, hyperlinks and other features that could not be included in the print version, the text for the ebook would be essentially the same as the text for the printed book. There was room to experiment, but there was also a danger inherent in this approach that the ebook would turn out to be, to all intents and purposes, an electronic version of the printed book.

However, the big question facing the History Ebook Project, as with so many of these undertakings, is whether it will be able to generate sufficient revenue through library subscriptions to become self-sustaining. Given the current pricing structure, the project needs over a thousand institutional subscriptions to break even, and closer to two thousand subscriptions to continue to expand the database by adding new and backlist titles. With subscriptions standing at 160 in April 2004, these seem like ambitious goals. The fact that its subscription fees are very modest will be attractive to many librarians, but it might have been wiser for the project directors to have set the fees higher and aimed for fewer institutions in order to achieve their revenue targets. There is much goodwill among the library community towards a non-profit venture of this kind which has the backing of Mellon, the ACLS and the university presses. But in a tough economic climate when many university libraries are being forced to look for savings, taking on additional recurrent expenditures of this kind, however modest, is not easy for librarians. While they may be sympathetic in principle, their budget constraints may force them to the conclusion that this is not a must-have acquisition. The harsh reality of budgets has a way of overriding ideals. And despite the project directors' very sensible decision to add high-quality backlist titles as a way of giving some critical mass to the site, it is still a very small database – a 'boutique website', to borrow the term used earlier to describe Gutenberg <e>. In the end, the History Ebook Project, like Gutenberg <e>, may find itself obliged to merge with other similar ventures in order to achieve greater scale and to present librarians with a simplified one-stop shop that might stand a better chance of securing their ongoing support at a time of financial stringency.

TORCH

With the support of the Mellon Foundation, the New York branch of Oxford University Press embarked on a feasibility study in 2002 for the development of a subject-based online resource centre in the humanities that would make scholarly monographs available electronically to university libraries for the purposes of research. The idea behind this project was to see whether it would be feasible to create a publisher-based distribution service that would aggregate high-quality scholarly content from university presses in specific subject areas. The aggregated content would form a set of searchable databases, access to which would be regulated by site licences sold to university libraries on an annual subscription basis.

The overall aim of TORCH is to try to create a business model and distribution platform for scholarly corpora which have (a) focus, (b) scale, and (c) selectivity, and which remain within the control of the publishers who hold the copyright on the content. The focus is provided by concentrating on specific academic subject areas. The subject chosen for the feasibility study was American history; a prototype, restricted to slavery in the antebellum South, was developed for testing and research. Scale would be achieved by aggregating content from a plurality of publishers. Although OUP would provide some of the content, the aim was to develop a framework that would allow for and encourage the participation of other presses. In the original plan, selectivity was to be achieved by including content which was put through two stages of vetting: content which had already been vetted by the university presses would be subjected to a further stage of selection by a panel of scholars in the subject. The project director put it like this:

> The premise is that a true scholarship-driven, distributed project will have greater market impact than 'licensed aggregator' distribution models. By creating a 'best of the best' service, the hope is that librarians and scholars will respond most favorably. Furthermore, by focusing only on single subjects, the service can provide depth and range within a topic that is not possible in current library market aggregation products.

Many projects of this kind have invested a great deal of time and effort in building a platform, often in XML, and in grappling with the technical problems involved in marking up content in new formats. The director of TORCH very sensibly decided to short-circuit this process by licensing the platform developed by ebrary and working with PDF, which is the accepted format of the publishing business. This enabled TORCH to minimize conversion costs and concentrate on developing the distribution system and the business model and on doing a market analysis and usability study of the prototype.

In the course of carrying out the feasibility study, the original plan was modified in various ways. While the idea of aggregating content from a variety of publishers and sources was an attractive way to achieve scale and comprehensiveness in a subject area, it also presented many problems in terms of rights and costs, and the project director therefore decided to focus exclusively on the university presses. The idea of putting books through a two-stage vetting process was also abandoned, since scholars were not enthusiastic about the idea; the fact that the books were published by university presses was deemed a sufficient guarantor of quality. Moreover, while scholars and librarians made it clear that they would like corpora of this kind to include new works and all titles that they regard as 'key', it soon became clear that this would present difficulties for the university presses. The presses rely heavily on revenues from the sales of new monographs and books adopted for course use and they would be unlikely to offer these titles for inclusion in TORCH, since they would not wish to risk the possibility of cannibalizing the sales of the print editions. In order to overcome this problem, the direc-

tor of TORCH decided to restrict the corpora to backlist and out-of-print titles, in much
the same way that JSTOR was restricted to backlist journals.[6] The hope is that TORCH
might be able to achieve, in the world of the scholarly monograph, what JSTOR has
achieved in the world of the scholarly journal – namely, to revive older, backlist material by making it available in a coherent and searchable database that was made available to research libraries on an annual subscription basis.

TORCH is still at an early stage of development. The feasibility study was completed
in July 2003 and Mellon has given the project another one-year grant to develop a business plan. It is of course too early to say whether this will turn out to be a viable
approach, and whether the kind of collaboration between university presses that would
give scale and scholarly depth to the databases can be realized in practice. It has generally been very difficult to build genuinely collaborative ventures between university
presses: while they are all not-for-profits and the problems they face are similar in many
ways, the presses themselves are very different in terms of scale and organizational
culture, and the interests they share in common can easily be overshadowed by competitive rivalries, suspicions and fears. And of course, it is much too early to say whether
a project of this kind would prove sufficiently compelling to persuade librarians to part
with a slice of their hard-pressed budgets – it is upon this that the long-term viability
of the project would ultimately depend. But this is a bold and ambitious project, and
there is much to be said in favour of the idea of creating cross-press scholarly corpora
which have focus, scale and selectivity, which involve a collaborative effort among the
university presses and therefore remain within the not-for-profit sector, and where
control of the content is retained by the publishers who have acquired and developed
it.

Oxford Scholarship Online

Quite separately from the Mellon-funded project being undertaken by its New York
branch, Oxford University Press in the UK has developed a self-funded project of its
own for delivering monographs to libraries in an online environment. This project, called
Oxford Scholarship Online (OSO), aims to create subject-specific corpora of scholarly
content which will form searchable databases, to which university libraries can purchase
access on a renewable subscription basis. While there are evident similarities between
OSO and the Mellon-funded project, there are also three key differences. First, OSO is
conceived of as a single-publisher initiative: the monographs in OSO will consist exclu-

---

[6] With the assistance of a grant from the Mellon Foundation, JSTOR was established in 1995 as
a not-for-profit organization dedicated to creating an electronic archive of the back issues of journals which could be made available to university libraries at a relatively modest cost. JSTOR's
licence agreement with journals publishers is based on the notion of a 'moving wall' of between
one and five years (typically it is either three years or five years). This ensures that current and
recent issues are excluded from the archive and thus protects the publisher's subscription revenue.
For a brief account, see Kevin M. Guthrie, 'JSTOR: The Development of a Cost-Driven, Value-
Based Pricing Model', in Richard Ekman and Richard E. Quandt (eds), *Technology and Scholarly Communication* (Berkeley: University of California Press, 1999), pp. 133–44. For a detailed
account of the origins and development of JSTOR, see Roger C. Schonfeld, *JSTOR: A History*
(Princeton: Princeton University Press, 2003).

sively of monographs published by OUP; it does not aim to aggregate scholarly content from a plurality of university presses (or at least not in the first instance). Second, while TORCH decided to concentrate on aggregating backlist material only, OSO will make available a range of new OUP titles in selected subject areas. Third, the thinking behind OSO is shaped fundamentally by the experience of publishing scholarly journals online. The latter point is particularly important – let us examine it further.

OSO is premised on the idea that there are certain affinities between scholarly journals and scholarly monographs, and that some of the benefits achieved by making scholarly journals available online can be replicated in the world of scholarly monographs. As one senior manager involved in the project explained,

> What you have at the moment in the scholarly community is the rather odd situation whereby a lot of journals are online but none of the monographs are. But they both consist essentially, as you know, of the same thing. It is just the length of the articles. A monograph, after all, is only a fat journal. It is just that the articles are called chapters and they are linked together in a coherent way. So you could argue that as products they are more attractive than journals because they are coherent, whereas journals aren't; there's not usually very much in one journal that you actually want to read. Yet, for various curious reasons, journals are online and the monographs aren't. So our basic idea is to try and link the two. So this won't just be therefore monographs online, it will be monographs online with the metadata, things like the chapter headings, list of contents, abstracts of the books, abstracts of the chapters, links to the same metadata you get for journals.

The methods that have been used very successfully to shift scholarly journals into an online environment will be applied to scholarly monographs – in effect, monographs will be treated as if they were journals, and each chapter will be treated as if it were a journal article. So new monographs will be marked up in XML, tables of contents and chapter headings will be treated as the same kind of metadata as the titles of journal articles, authors will be asked to provide abstracts of the book and abstracts of each chapter, and so on. The monographs will form a corpus of scholarly content which can be optimized in terms of searchability and cross-referencing, and which replicates the kind of system that academics already use in the online environment of scholarly journals.

But can a single publisher create a corpus of this kind that has the kind of scale that librarians may want? Should the publisher aggregate the content of scholarly monographs across all of the disciplines in which it publishes, or concentrate on specific subjects so that the corpus has disciplinary focus? OUP reckons that it is large enough to get a project of this kind off the ground and that, given the volume of its monograph throughput, it will be able to create a corpus that will have sufficient scale to be attractive to librarians. OUP also believes that a subject-based structure would maximize the chances of meeting the needs of librarians and end users, providing both disciplinary depth (which will appeal to end users) as well as some spread of disciplines (which is likely to appeal to librarians, since it will enable them to get more support from their university rather than spending a lot of money on one department). To begin with, OSO will comprise four disciplines: economics and finance; philosophy; political science; religion and theology. These are disciplines where OUP has considerable strength in terms of its scholarly output and where the academic community is accustomed to working online.

OSO was launched in November 2003 with over 700 titles. Access to the content is regulated by a site licence sold to libraries on an annual subscription basis; 200 new books are added each year as part of the annual subscription. The business model allows for the possibility that an institution might wish to purchase access to the entire collection or to one or more subject modules, depending on the needs of their institution (they might offer courses in economics and business, for example, but not in philosophy or politics).

OSO is an exciting and imaginative project. OUP is taking a leading role in exploring the possibilities for the dissemination of scholarly monographs in an online environment. As the largest of the university presses with a high volume of monograph throughput, OUP has the kind of scale a publisher needs if it wants to create a substantial corpus out of its own copyrights. It is able to take advantage of the experience it has gained in making its scholarly journals available online, in making the Oxford English Dictionary available online and in creating an online reference site, Oxford Reference Online. It is also able to draw on the Oxford brand, which is recognized by librarians as a mark of quality and distinction in the field of scholarly publishing. If it is possible for a single publisher to make a success of disseminating scholarly monographs in an online environment, then OUP is very well placed to do it. Of course, what kind of revenue streams it will be able to generate remains to be seen. Like all online projects targeted at university libraries, OSO will have to compete for a slice of librarians' budgets at a time when these budgets are under renewed pressure, and it may be difficult to secure a substantial number of firm subscriptions. Whether OSO will have any impact on the sales of the printed version of the monographs included in the scheme also remains unclear at this stage. If the online availability of monographs were to diminish still further the sales of the printed version (although there is as yet no clear evidence to suggest that this would be the case, and indeed it could even stimulate sales), then this would increase the pressure on OSO to generate revenue through the sale of subscriptions. Only time will tell whether the dissemination of monographs online will alter the value placed on the print version by libraries and end users, and whether the revenue stream generated by institutional subscriptions will be sufficient to make up for any further deterioration in the sales of printed monographs. The academic publishers who are experimenting in this area may find new ways of combining the revenues generated from annual subscriptions, from the sales of books printed in the traditional way and from short-run digital printing and print on demand. At this stage it's too early to say just how the revenue mix will pan out in different areas and whether, in the long run, it will be sufficient to cover costs and generate a positive financial contribution.

The scholarly community model

The various models considered so far consist essentially of collections of digitized content to which various functions such as searchability, cross-referencing and citation have been added. Some or all of the content is drawn from scholarly books which are digitized and incorporated into a database, and access to the content is regulated by charging mechanisms of various kinds. We can distinguish these models from another way of conceptualizing the dissemination of scholarly content in an online environment

– what I shall describe as the scholarly community model. This model is based on the idea of building an interactive community of scholars and making certain services, including access to scholarly content, available to them. In the scholarly community model, it is the building of the online community – the e-community – that matters above all; providing access to scholarly book content is only one of a range of services which are made available to members.

One of the most significant attempts to build a model of this kind in the field of scholarly communication emerged from the experiences of MIT Press in the 1990s. The success of the publication of *City of Bits* online helped to create a climate of experimentation at MIT Press in the mid-1990s. The press created one of the first online catalogues in 1994 and began experimenting with making more books available online. A visit from Vitek Tracz, who had founded a company in the UK called Current Science and had been involved in the creation of an online community in the biomedical sciences called Bio-MedNet, introduced the idea of online communities into the context of a university press which was willing to try out new ideas. At about the same time, MIT Press was beginning to receive submissions from the contributors to the MIT Encyclopedia of Cognitive Science, which it had commissioned some years before. The press saw an opportunity to link the development of a traditional print-based product with the new idea of creating an online community. It decided to use the Encyclopedia to provide the lexical architecture for a community-based site that would replicate in cognitive science what Tracz and his colleagues had achieved in biomedical sciences – thus CogNet was born.

CogNet became one of the core projects of the new Digital Projects Lab that was set up at MIT Press in the fall of 1996. The basic idea behind CogNet was to build a branded, subject-based community of scholars which would evolve through interactive consultation with the members.[7] The architecture of the site as well as some of the initial content was provided by the Encyclopedia project, though the intention was to add other relevant content from MIT's list in the cognitive and brain sciences, including reference works, monographs and journals, to build an archive of grey literature (such as working papers and conference proceedings) and to create a range of customized services. When the site was launched in October 1998, it comprised a digital library containing material from the Encyclopedia and 150 digitized MIT Press titles in cognitive science, and it offered various services to members including HotScience (an editorial with threaded discussions), a discussion forum, job listings, members' profiles and individual workspaces where members could lodge CVs, assemble bibliographies, etc. Members had to register in order to gain access, but registration at this stage was free. Registered members were allowed free access to all content on the site and were encouraged to interact with the development team, so that the members were actively involved in shaping the evolution of the site. 'What we're trying to do', explained one of the managers on the development team, 'is to let the customer, the reader, the scholar, lead us into what the developments should be.' A great deal of effort was invested by the development team in responding quickly to requests and inquiries from members, since it was felt that in order to build a successful user-community in an online environment, members had to feel confident that there was a responsive layer of human administration behind it.

[7] See Marney Smyth, 'The Community *is* the Content', *Publishing Research Quarterly* (Winter 2001), pp. 3–14.

The number of registered members built up relatively quickly and largely by word of mouth. By the end of 1998, around 550 members had enrolled, and by the end of 1999 there were over 5,000 members. However, up to this point CogNet was being funded largely by MIT Press (it had also received a grant of $150,000 from SPARC, the Scholarly Publishing and Academic Resources Coalition, in October 1999, but this covered only a portion of the start-up costs); and given the strong commitment to service and responding to queries, the running costs were significant. The press had to see whether CogNet could be run as a self-financing operation. In October 2000, free membership was replaced with fee-based access and CogNet began to sell site licences to institutions (primarily libraries) and individuals. It estimated that it needed between $150,000 and $200,000 a year to sustain the operation. An additional problem faced by the press was that by 2001 the technical architecture of CogNet needed to be upgraded, and to do this would cost around $200,000. When fee-based access was introduced in October 2000, there were more than 10,000 legacy individual registrations, but most of these were lost when the fees were introduced. Building a new membership list on a subscription basis was a slow and difficult task. By the middle of 2001 CogNet had signed up 145 libraries, about a third of which were fee-paying (the others were on trials), and it was about halfway to achieving its revenue target. By the middle of 2002 it had around 80 paid site licences and was getting close to a break-even point. Unfortunately the economic climate for academic publishers had worsened in the meantime and, like most of the university presses, MIT Press's sales were below budget. Difficult decisions had to be made. The Digital Projects Lab was closed down in June 2002, staff were laid off and CogNet was moved over to the journals division of MIT Press, where it is currently lodged. The technology was upgraded and the number of subscriptions was raised to a level that enabled CogNet to operate on a break-even basis.

The fact that CogNet was able to generate a significant revenue stream through institutional site licences does suggest that there is some scope for the development of gated scholarly communities in an online environment. CogNet was a pioneer in this domain and, like CIAO, it eventually managed to raise sufficient revenue through library subscriptions to cover all or most of its running costs. So what is it that enabled CogNet to succeed as an online community? Undoubtedly part of its success derived from the fact that cognitive science was an emerging field of research that had a certain cohesiveness to it. The field was sufficiently distinctive and well defined to provide some sense of identity and shared concern among those working within it. As one of the CogNet managers put it, 'the community is clubbable. It's pretty well defined and it's about the right size to be manageable without being so large that it's diffuse. General psychology for instance wouldn't work.'

But the need for the community to be 'clubbable' is also a potential drawback when it comes to trying to generate revenue, because cognitive science is not a subject taught at all universities and CogNet may be seen by many librarians as too specialized for their needs. Indeed, the experience of CogNet shows how difficult it is to generate a revenue stream of sufficient volume to establish and sustain a niche online venture of this kind. Although MIT Press was able to raise some development money from SPARC, most of the start-up costs were borne by the press itself, and four years after the site had been launched the press was still struggling to generate sufficient revenue through the sale of site licences to cover the running costs. The press was undoubtedly right to assume that institutional subscriptions were likely to be the only significant source of recurrent income for the site, but the experience of CogNet shows just how hard it is to reach a break-even point. These difficulties may be exacerbated in the case of an online community such as CogNet simply because the commitment to customer service does not come cheap, and the cost of providing this support must be factored into the equation.

Of course, the capacity to become self-supporting is not the only financial criterion for evaluating a venture of this kind, as there may be other, more indirect benefits. By helping to create a virtual community of scholars who share a common interest in a particular subject area, the development of a site of this kind may serve to strengthen the position of a publisher as a leading player in the field, just as CogNet has undoubtedly helped to consolidate MIT Press's reputation as a leader in the field of cognitive science. It may help a publisher to keep in touch with current developments and may provide an excellent way of building up the kinds of subject-based networks upon which good commissioning depends. It may also help to give greater visibility to book titles – both new books and backlist – among a self-selecting set of individuals who have a particular interest in the subject, and may even stimulate the sales of the printed editions. In these and other ways, the development of online communities may produce less tangible benefits for publishers who invest in them.

However, the question that remains is whether the intangible benefits of online communities are of sufficient value for scholarly book publishers to justify the costs and the effort involved in establishing and maintaining them, and indeed whether online communities established and managed by publishers are the kinds of communities that scholars are going to value and encourage their institutions to support. It is also not entirely clear whether it would be sensible for publishers who are primarily concerned with scholarly book publishing to become involved in the running of online sites which are so strongly oriented to customer service, with all the costs in terms of support staff which that entails. In the final analysis, while the model of the online scholarly community clearly has some relevance for the world of scholarly book publishing, it may well be of more interest and more value for other purposes. CogNet has the potential to provide a template for the creation of interactive communities which may be perceived as valuable or worthwhile by organizations which are not directly related to publishing (and in fact CogNet has already been used in this way: in 1999, the Aga Khan Trust for Culture in Geneva initiated a collaboration with the MIT School of Architecture and Planning and MIT Press to develop and fund ArchNet, an online community for architects and urban planners with a particular interest in the Islamic world). Moreover, the decision to move CogNet into the journals division was based partly on the view that the model of the scholarly virtual community may have more potential in the sphere of scholarly journal publishing – where the readers of a journal already constitute a kind of virtual community, although the levels of interaction are generally very low, and where the issue of providing a service to scholarly societies is often crucial – than in the sphere of scholarly book publishing per se. Of course, it may well be that the distinction between scholarly books and scholarly journals will become increasingly blurred in the online environment, and that services that are organized initially around journal content may eventually become effective vehicles for the dissemination of book content as well. But for the time being, the model of the online scholarly community may be of more immediate interest and value for purposes other than the dissemination of scholarly book content online.

Lessons, problems and prospects

The terrain surveyed in this chapter is in a state of flux: it is a domain that is changing rapidly as new ventures are undertaken and some older ventures evolve into new forms or fall by the wayside. It would be not just difficult but foolhardy to try to draw firm conclusions about a domain that is likely to look different in a year or two, by which time some of the players who are currently active may have disappeared and new initiatives may have emerged, and by which time we shall know more about the actual experiences of those ventures currently underway. Nevertheless, it is possible to draw some lessons from the experiments of the last decade and to offer some tentative conclusions about the prospects for the dissemination of scholarly book content in an online environment. It would be unwise to be too sanguine about the prospects for success – there are too many examples of failed dreams in the dot.com world to be anything other than cautious. But the fact that both librarians and academics have adjusted remarkably quickly to accessing journal content online does lend some support to the views of those who believe that the content of scholarly monographs will be made available in an online environment in some form, either in addition to printed monographs or as an alternative to them. So let me conclude by highlighting a number of lessons and issues that have emerged so far from the brief history of experimentation with the publication of scholarly books online.

(1)   The key problems that have to be solved in any attempt to make scholarly books available online are more economic than technical: they have to do with the nature of the markets that may or may not exist for the delivery of scholarly book content online, with the kinds of business models that are most appropriate for generating revenue in these markets and with the size of the revenue streams that can be generated. The key issue is for scholarly content providers to understand better the markets that already exist or are likely to emerge for the delivery of scholarly book content online. Too much of the early experimentation was driven by a preoccupation with technological possibilities and by very speculative assumptions about market uptake and consumer behaviour. And if the brief history of experimentation in this domain has taught us anything, it is this: *the principal market for scholarly book content in electronic form is likely to be institutional rather than individual.* The attempt to generate revenue by selling scholarly book content to individuals, either through a subscription to a virtual library (as in the Questia model) or through the sale of individual ebooks or parts of ebooks (as in the digital warehouse model), seems unlikely to succeed, at least for the foreseeable future. By contrast, many institutions have budgets to spend for the acquisition of content, and even if these budgets are under pressure, they are likely to be a more reliable source of revenue than the personal resources of individuals. As with scholarly journals, the main market for the delivery of scholarly book content online is likely to be the institutional market of university libraries. Librarians are accustomed to purchasing content in electronic form, and many are receptive to the idea of acquiring scholarly book content online. In the case of scholarly content which has a professional orientation (such as business studies, law, medicine, international affairs, computer science and IT), the institutional market may also include organizations other than university libraries, including corporations, research laboratories, professional bodies, government agencies and

NGOs. In general, the ventures that seem most likely to succeed are those which have clearly targeted an institutional market and have cultivated close relations with the institutional gatekeepers, so that they are able to tailor their product and their service to the needs of their institutional clients.

(2)   The best way to maximize the added value of delivering scholarly book content online is *to treat individual books as part of a scholarly corpus or database which has scale, selectivity and focus*. The corpus is important because it enables end users to make the most of the functions of searchability and cross-referencing. Scale is important because it provides end users with the richness and depth of a collection, and it provides the institutional intermediaries with value for money. Selectivity and focus are important because they ensure that the end users and intermediaries are getting quality as well as quantity, that the content is relevant to their needs and that the corpus is not filled with low-quality content that is dated, marginal and of little interest – the online equivalent of 'white noise'. One of the great mistakes of the early virtual libraries was to be wildly ambitious, to try to acquire and digitize vast quantities of content across many subject areas in the hope that the sheer scale of the undertaking would ensure a place in the market. Not only were these ambitious plans extraordinarily expensive, but the resulting corpora tended to lack focus and selectivity and often contained a good deal of dated material that was of little interest to anyone. Scale is undoubtedly important in the online environment, but *pertinent scale* is more important than scale for the sake of it. More modest undertakings, such as Books 24 × 7, grasped this point well and reaped the rewards. On the other hand, very small-scale electronic publishing ventures, such as the Gutenberg <e> project, seem unlikely ever to achieve the kind of scale needed in the online environment to become an attractive acquisition for institutional gatekeepers; they seem destined to remain boutique websites that will either require grants or other subsidies to survive or will be folded into larger aggregations of content. One experiment which has proved to be successful, CIAO, has effectively combined scale, selectivity and focus: it has a clear focus (international affairs), it achieves selectivity by drawing on a board of academic advisers, and it achieves pertinent scale by aggregating a large quantity of grey literature in a way that is valued by users. CIAO is a model from which others could learn a good deal.

(3)   Whether the development of scholarly corpora is best handled by publishers themselves, acting either on their own or in collaboration with one another, or by third-party aggregators of content remains an open question. There are advantages and limitations both ways. For publishers, the advantage of developing scholarly corpora themselves is that they retain control of their copyrights and the revenue streams. The disadvantages are that (a) it is costly and the publishers are often carrying the risk, (b) it is difficult for a single publisher to achieve scale and comprehensiveness by relying on their own copyrights, and (c) publishers find it difficult to cooperate with one another in ventures of this kind. From the point of view of the end user, there is little advantage in having corpora that are restricted to a single publisher's output. Part of the value of corpora of this kind is their scale and comprehensiveness in particular subject areas, as well as the ability to search across the corpus and access other relevant material, and it doesn't matter to the end user whether this material originates from one publisher or from several. Given that there are pros and cons for both the publisher-driven and the third-

party aggregator approaches, it is likely that we'll continue to see experiments with both approaches in the coming years, as well as experiments with hybrid versions (such as single-publisher-based initiatives which license content from other publishers, or grant-based initiatives which rely on a degree of collaboration from affiliated publishers). The needs of end users are likely to be met most effectively by an approach that is able to aggregate content from a variety of publishers, but whether this is handled by third-party aggregators or by publishers collaborating together and/or licensing content from others (or both) remains to be seen.

(4)   There has been a great deal of anxiety among publishers over the issue of canni-balization. In the mid to late 1990s, many publishers were reluctant to license their copy-rights to digital libraries for fear of undermining the sales of printed books, and some publishers were willing to license only the older backlist titles. However, after several years of experimentation in this domain, there is no conclusive evidence that digital dis-tribution cannibalizes the sales of hard copies. Indeed, there are many who express the view that making the contents of books available in on online environment may actu-ally help to increase the sales of printed books – as *City of Bits* demonstrated in the early 1990s. In other words, even if the distribution of book content online does not create a significant new revenue stream, it may play some role as a marketing tool for the printed book, helping to stimulate interest in the book and induce readers to buy a printed copy, much as browsing in a bookstore does.[8] However, the extent to which this argument applies in the case of scholarly monographs, where the principal market con-sists of research libraries and where the cost of the print edition is relatively high, is less clear; hence the anxiety of academic publishers, who have seen the sales of monographs decline to perilous levels over the last decade, is understandable. While there is as yet no clear evidence to demonstrate that the sales of printed books are cannibalized by the online availability of book content, it is likely that publishers faced with the seem-ingly inexorable decline in the sales of scholarly monographs will continue to proceed cautiously, particularly with regard to their frontlist titles.

(5)   There has been much debate within the industry about the most suitable techni-cal format for making scholarly book content available online. The main line of division

---

[8] This idea has encouraged some publishers to participate in schemes such as Amazon's 'Search Inside the Book' and Google Print. These schemes make available book content in low-resolu-tion page images which readers can search and view online. The amount of text which the reader can view is restricted and security measures are put in place to prevent readers from download-ing and printing text. 'Search Inside the Book' enables users of Amazon to browse an excerpt from the book before deciding whether to buy it; once they've viewed the pages, they can order books from Amazon in the normal way. 'We developed Search Inside the Book to help customers find the perfect book to buy,' explains the Amazon information page. Google's aim in develop-ing Google Print is to strengthen its position as the pre-eminent search engine and increase its advertising revenue by adding book content to a database that its spiders can comb when carry-ing out a search. Someone using Google for a normal search will find books in the Google Print scheme coming up in the results; clicking the relevant link will enable the user to browse a short extract from the book. The browse page has further links to the publisher's website and to the book's description pages at Amazon, b&n.com and Books-A-Million, so that the user can buy the book. 'By and large, most publishers have come around to the idea that browse leads to buy, and more browse leads to more buy,' observed a manager at Google Print.

has been between those who argue, on one side, that scholarly book content should be marked up in XML on the grounds that this gives maximum flexibility and optimizes searchability, and those on the other side who argue that PDF should be used, primarily on the grounds that it is already the standard format used in the publishing industry and therefore the cost of conversion is minimal. There is considerable force to the latter argument, and with the benefit of hindsight one can see that the early decisions by netLibrary and others to invest substantial resources in the conversion of texts into XML or into proprietary formats was misguided. ebrary's much more pragmatic approach, developing a platform which used the PDF format that was already being used by most publishers, was prescient. We shall examine the technical issues concerning PDF and XML in more detail in chapter 15. Here it will suffice to say that, until it has been demonstrated that the delivery of scholarly book content online is capable of generating appreciable revenue streams, the case for converting backlist titles into structured XML files, or modifying workflows to build XML tagging into all new books, is not overwhelming. At the current stage of technological development, it may make more sense for publishers to continue to use PDF for the bulk of their book throughput and to build XML tagging only into those files where they see a well-defined opportunity to make the content available online.

(6)   One issue that has plagued developments in this area is the issue of rights. There has been a great deal of uncertainty among publishers about whether they actually have the rights to disseminate their content electronically or to license it to third parties. To a large extent, this uncertainty stems from the fact that earlier contracts with authors simply did not envisage the possibility of electronic dissemination, and hence contained no clause relating to it. Most publishers have dealt with this situation by writing to authors and requesting their permission to disseminate their work electronically or license it to others. In the vast majority of cases, authors have been happy to grant permission. But this is an enormously time-consuming and, indeed, costly business, and not infrequently it leads to delays and dead-ends. There is the additional problem of how to deal with 'embedded copyrights' – that is, copyrighted material which appears in a book but which is not the author's own work, such as quotations, illustrations, etc. Many publishers have found that their records about who has cleared permission for embedded copyrights and under what conditions are incomplete at best (non-existent at worst), and a good deal of uncertainty remains about whether permission needs to be cleared again if this copyrighted material is reproduced when the book is made available in an online environment. Some publishers have taken the cautious view that all copyrighted material has to be cleared again before the book can be made available online, while others have taken a more relaxed view and have allowed books to be made available online without seeking to gain fresh permissions for embedded copyrights. The uncertainty, complexity and lack of clarity concerning copyright issues in the electronic environment have seriously delayed developments in this area, and the establishment of clear and accepted guidelines would help enormously to facilitate experimentation and calm the nerves of anxious publishers. Ultimately it would be a significant advantage for publishers to have a sophisticated system for recording and tracking the copyright status of all their content, including the status of the embedded copyrights, so that they are in a position to determine quickly and easily whether the content of a particular book can be made available online.

(7)   Several years of experimentation and debate have also made it very clear that the costs associated with publishing and disseminating book content in an online environment are much greater than many people once assumed. There were many people who thought (and some who still think) that the dissemination of book content online would greatly reduce costs for publishers: there would be no need to print and bind the books, no paper costs, no need to store and ship books from the warehouse to the bookstore, etc. It is of course true that there are some savings here, but in fact this represents a modest proportion of publishers' overall costs – all the development and overhead costs are still there, and editorial and other staff still have to be paid. Moreover, the additional costs involved in developing software platforms, digitizing content, employing technical staff, clearing copyright permissions, dealing with licence agreements, etc., often exceed any savings made, and the additional costs often have to be borne by publishers in the absence of any significant new revenue streams. For many publishers, the experience of preparing themselves for a digital future has been one of increased expenditure with no significant new income streams to ease the pain. It has been an investment and an additional cost, and in some cases a very substantial additional cost; it has not (or at least not yet) become a significant and reliable source of income. The balance of the equation between costs and revenue has been tipped very heavily towards the former. Academic publishers have often been criticized for their reticence in experimenting with new technologies, but in fact their willingness to experiment has in many cases gone well beyond what could be justified by a strict cost–benefit analysis. From the viewpoint of the publishers, the key question for the future is whether the markets for the dissemination of book content online will ever be sufficiently robust to generate a revenue stream that will redress the balance.

(8)   Another key issue that has shaped the debate so far is what we could describe as the legacy of print. There is a tension here between two different ways of thinking about the nature of scholarly monographs delivered in an online environment. One approach is to think of scholarly monographs delivered online as effectively the same as print monographs. The content is the same, even though the medium of delivery and the mode of access have changed – the ebook is a replica of the p-book, although the index may be replaced with a search engine. Another approach is to think of the electronic medium as offering radically new opportunities for the way in which scholarly work is carried out, published, disseminated and read. This is the kind of approach advocated by scholars like Darnton. It is also the kind of approach exemplified by some of the more adventurous experiments in online scholarship, such as the Gutenberg <e> project and the Valley of the Shadows website (an innovative site which gathers together original documents from two communities during the American Civil War),[9] where the content is 'born digital' rather than being the replica of a print product. While there is much to be said in favour of these more radical experiments with online scholarship and their potential for redefining the nature of scholarly work, they face serious difficulties both in terms of financial viability and in terms of the cultural value which continues to be placed on the printed book in the academic community. They face financial difficulties for all the reasons outlined above – what can be said at best is that, with one or two

[9] See valley.vcdh.virginia.edu.

notable exceptions, most experiments in the online publishing of scholarly book content have yet to demonstrate their financial viability. They also face difficulties in terms of the cultural value of the printed book, in the sense that the printed book remains a keystone for the advancement of careers within many disciplines of the humanities and the social sciences. Academic professions are slow to change, and appointment and tenure committees in many disciplines continue to regard the printed book as a key credential for selection and promotion. For these and other reasons, many academics are likely to be very hesitant about the idea of publishing their books in an online environment only. Academic authors in the humanities and social sciences are deeply attached to the printed book as an expression of their research effort and creativity, and the printed book is deeply embedded in the culture of the academy and in what I earlier described as the cultural economy of research. It may be that the growing significance of journal articles as a principal form of research output will gradually erode the cultural value of the printed book as a keystone for career advancement in the humanities and social sciences, but it may need a change of generations before books published exclusively in an online environment acquire the same value as a printed book within these academic disciplines (if they ever do). While the ideas of Darnton and others may have considerable appeal in abstract terms, they are rather distant from the practical realities and pressures faced by publishers and from the concerns and preferences of academics.

(9) There is an area of potential overlap between scholarly journal publishing and scholarly monograph publishing that deserves to be explored in further detail. There are significant differences between scholarly journals and scholarly monographs (some of which I explored in the previous chapter), and there are also significant differences between academic disciplines in terms of the relative importance of journals and books for scholarly communication and research. Nevertheless, for those publishers who are active in both fields of publishing, there may be real opportunities to create synergies between scholarly journals and scholarly monographs in an online environment. Oxford Scholarship Online is one very imaginative attempt to do exactly this: to treat monographs as if they were journal issues, each made up of discrete chapters for which metadata is produced. The next step might be to create even more integration between journals in particular subject areas and scholarly collections in the same subjects – producing, in effect, integrated subject-based corpora which combine the content of scholarly journals and the content of scholarly monographs, with the capacity to cross-reference and to search across both. This would not preclude the possibility of printing specific monographs in limited quantities if there was sufficient market demand for them; with the advent of digital printing, short print-runs have become feasible in a way that wasn't possible several years ago, a point to which we shall return. But if at least a proportion of the revenue publishers need to cover their costs could be generated through a subscription-based model similar to that used in journal publishing, then it would reduce publishers' dependence on the sales of individual printed copies. The outcome of experiments like OSO is therefore of real significance for both academic publishers and the academic community.

(10) It is often argued that scholarly monographs do not lend themselves to electronic formats because most people don't like to read extended texts onscreen, and there is

unquestionably some truth in this. However, this argument points to a deeper problem which is crucial to further developments in this domain: we know relatively little about how monographs are actually used by the academic community and how they are incorporated into the research process. No doubt scholarly monographs are used in a variety of different ways – sometimes consulted, sometimes read, sometimes left on the shelves untouched for months or even years. It may well be that some uses could be served very well by electronic access – for example, scholars could search a variety of texts quickly and efficiently from the comfort of their homes or offices without having to traipse around the stacks – while other uses, like the close reading of a substantial part of the text, would be better served by the traditional printed book. This would suggest that the needs of scholars and researchers might be best met by a dual-format approach which treats print and electronic versions as complementary rather than mutually exclusive, since they are likely to be used in different ways.[10] If we knew more about the actual patterns of usage and how these are changing, and about what end users as well as institutional intermediaries want and expect from scholarly monographs, then we could form a clearer picture of future scenarios.

(11)   So let us return to the question asked by many: is there an electronic solution to the problem of scholarly monograph publishing? Although the issues are still very much open and some of the most interesting experiments are still at an early stage of development, there are two points that can be made in response to this question. First, there is no *obvious* solution. There are numerous ways of addressing the issue of how the content of scholarly monographs can be made available in online environments, but it is by no means clear that any of these ways of distributing them online will be capable of generating the levels of revenue required by publishing organizations in order to select and develop the content to the point at which it can be published. New technologies have been and will continue to be enormously helpful in the field of scholarly publishing, but they are not a panacea. The second point is that the question is to some extent misconceived. Rather than asking whether there is an electronic solution to the problem of scholarly monograph publishing, we need to address the more fundamental issue of why this problem has arisen in the first place, what roles scholarly monographs play in the process of research and scholarly communication and in the academic world more generally, and whether these roles continue to make sense today. The problems of scholarly monograph publishing do not admit of a quick technological fix; they run much deeper and require us to ask questions of a more profound kind about the nature and structure of the fields within which monographs have come to play their current roles.

---

[10] The Columbia Online Books Evaluation Project – probably the most systematic attempt to date to look at the actual usage of scholarly books online – lends some support to this dual-format approach. It found that scholars read relatively little of the books they review for their work and that only a small number of books are read at length. Most scholars were strongly disinclined to read more than a few pages onscreen and they felt passionately about the need to have a printed copy of a book if they wanted to read it at length; at the same time, they could see some advantages in doing the initial reviews of books online with a flexible search engine and a collection that contained a substantial proportion of the current publications of the major academic publishers in their fields. See the various papers and reports available at www.columbia.edu/cu/libraries/digital/texts/about.html.

(12)   In the longer term, what happens in this domain will be shaped by broader developments in the academy, in the world of research libraries and in the nature of scholarly communication. The traditional scholarly monograph has come to assume certain deeply entrenched roles in the academy and in the intellectual life of particular disciplines, as we've seen. But the growing economic difficulties of monograph publishing, coupled with the fact that other forms of scholarly communication such as journals have moved increasingly into an online environment, could lead to a gradual transformation of scholarly communication itself. The value of the printed monograph as the gold standard of academic achievement in certain disciplines and as the principal currency of tenure, promotion and scholarly recognition could diminish over time and be increasingly supplemented or even eclipsed by other forms of scholarly output. The growing role of the internet as a means of communicating with other scholars and disseminating the results of research could give rise to new patterns of scholarly communication which, while not necessarily supplanting the traditional printed monograph, could become more important to scholars as a means of disseminating their work, at least in certain disciplines or subdisciplines. The growing emphasis on electronic resources within research libraries, and the metamorphosis of libraries from repositories of books to providers of a range of information services and resources, could contribute to a gradual shift from print-based to electronic forms of research and communication within the academic community. These are real possibilities and, if they were to materialize, they would have major implications for the nature and future of academic publishing. Some of the smaller university presses could find themselves increasingly integrated into the administrative structures of the research libraries, which would become increasingly important players in the system of scholarly communication (a trend which can already be discerned in some quarters). But at this stage in the history of scholarly communication, it is too early to say with any certainty how these developments will unfold.

(13)   Given the unsettled state of the debate, how should academic publishers prepare themselves for an uncertain future? The real difficulty that publishers face is that they have to struggle constantly to keep their heads above water financially, in a world where the only significant revenue stream they can see is based on the traditional model of selling printed books, while at the same time they have to try to keep abreast of new developments so that they're not left behind if the electronic dissemination of book content becomes a serious alternative. How can they reconcile these two rather different, if not conflicting, imperatives? The larger and more adventurous publishers have experimented and will continue to do so – although there is nothing like a downturn in book sales to dampen the enthusiasm for experimentation and readjust publishers' priorities in favour of known and reliable revenue streams. Other publishers with fewer resources to spare will tend to experiment in ways that involve little outlay on their part, preferring to license content to third parties who are willing to invest in conversion and carry the risks. What all publishers should be doing at the very least, however, is two things. First, they should be thinking hard about what they are publishing and why. For when all is said and done, the viability of a publishing firm depends on the value of the content it acquires and develops, and this fundamental principle will remain just as valid in the online world as it is in the world of print. Second, they should also be developing systems and workflows which enable them to prepare, gather together and store their content in suitable digital formats. This includes the building of digital

archives that will enable them to make the most of the content they have, whether this will be by disseminating it online in ways that have yet to be fully worked out, or by using new methods of digital printing to gain sales that would otherwise have been lost because of the prohibitive costs of reprinting scholarly works in low print-runs using traditional offset methods. We shall return to this issue in chapter 15.

14

Higher education publishing and the digital revolution

The impact of the digital revolution has been a subject of intense discussion within the world of higher education publishing as well: since the early 1990s, there has been a great deal of speculation about and experimentation with the use of new technologies for the delivery of pedagogical content. Here, too, the debates have tended to evolve over time. In the mid to late 1990s there was much feverish speculation about the demise of the traditional textbook and rise of the 'bookless campus' in which the electronic delivery of pedagogical content would, it was thought, become increasingly widespread. A report by Forrester Research in December 2000 predicted that by 2003 digital text-book sales would grow to $1.3 billion and would account for 14 per cent of all textbook sales. The large textbook publishers invested heavily in the development of new products, and a variety of new technology players, such as Thinkwell, WizeUp, MetaText and XanEdu, began to enter the higher education field.

By 2001–2, however, it was becoming increasingly clear that the traditional textbook was not about to disappear in the near future and the impact of new technologies in the field of higher education publishing was likely to be more complex than some of the earlier commentators had envisaged. The e-textbook simply did not take off as some had predicted. Many of the big publishers experimented with e-textbooks but the demand simply wasn't there.[1] Today the debates within the field of higher education publishing are much less about whether the traditional printed textbook will be phased out and replaced by an electronic-only product and much more about exactly how print and electronic materials can be developed together to take advantage of the opportunities offered by new technologies and to strengthen the competitive position of the firm. There are many players, both large and small, who continue to experiment actively with new technologies and new modes of content delivery; but for the major textbook publishers, the printed textbook remains the cornerstone of the business. The printed textbook is the principal revenue-generating mechanism for the firm and is likely to remain so for the foreseeable future.

This is not to say that there is a clear consensus of views within the world of higher education publishing – there isn't. There are sharply dissenting views, but the differences have attenuated somewhat over time. There are some senior figures in the field of higher education publishing who were always deeply sceptical of the claims of the e-textbook proponents, and with some justification they see the failure of e-textbooks to take off

---

[1] 'E-books were a non-event,' said one senior executive at a large US textbook firm. 'We had 500 textbooks that you could pay for and download online. We sold 2,300 units. That's nothing. I don't think that means it's a failed or a bad idea. I just mean it is a non-starter so far and nothing's happening.'

as confirmation of their view. There are others who are firmly convinced that the business of higher education publishing will become increasingly web based – it's just a matter of time. The big 1,000-page, four-colour, highly illustrated textbook will gradually give way to a slim 200-page printed manual and most of the content, including all the bells and whistles, will be delivered online. 'It's already evolving,' said one senior executive in a large US-based textbook firm. 'From A to Z, it's still at B. But over the next decade it will happen, without a doubt.'

And it's not difficult to see why some of the large textbook publishers would *like* things to move in this direction. It's very costly to produce big, four-colour, highly illustrated textbooks. If these could be replaced by a slender 200-page manual printed in black and white with all of the pedagogical content and illustrations delivered online, this would greatly reduce the investment in physical stock sitting in a warehouse. It would also open up exciting new possibilities in terms of the way that content is presented. There are new kinds of functionality that are possible in an online environment that are simply not possible in a printed book. Text and static images could be supplemented or replaced by moving images and audio files, and the learning experience could be made more dynamic, interactive and multimedia. What happens when a muscle tears? Instead of simply describing it, you can show what happens in a dynamic sequence of images. The content could be updated regularly and relatively easily, returns could be eliminated and the used book market could be wiped out at a click. Students taking a particular course would buy a subscription to the online material for the duration of the course, accessed by a PIN or a password; they wouldn't end up with a textbook at the end of the course which they could sell back to the bookstore. Indeed, the bookstore, and much of the traditional book supply chain, would simply be cut out of the loop. Although the development costs would be high, the savings that could be achieved by delivering pedagogical content online would enable the big publishers to bring down the costs, thus bringing to an end the spiral of escalating costs that have driven the prices of textbooks ever upwards in recent years. It's a big textbook publisher's dream.

There are also educational grounds for arguing that an online environment would have certain advantages over the traditional printed textbook. The traditional textbook is a standardized product: it is generally developed in a way to maximize its adoption potential in the course markets for which it has been designed. The range of topics covered often greatly exceeds what any particular professor or instructor will actually teach on his or her course, and exceeds what the students on that course will actually use. The range is there to ensure that a professor who wants to teach a particular topic will not decline to adopt the textbook because that topic is not covered: breadth of coverage maximizes adoptability. But the result is further upward pressure on costs, since large textbooks – commonly 1,000 pages or more – are costly to produce. Many professors feel that the textbooks have become too standardized, and many students feel that they are paying too much money for a textbook of which they are only using part. If publishers were able to deliver the content in an online environment, they could enable professors to customize the content so that it was tailored to the course they wanted to teach. The standardized, comprehensive textbook could be replaced by a web-based delivery of content tailored to the needs of individual professors and their students, and students would pay for access only to the content they actually needed for their course. Moreover, the kinds of functionality characteristic of the online environment – interactivity, searchability, the use of rich multimedia content like animations, sound and streaming video – could be built into the design of the material.

Of course, if traditional textbooks were to be replaced by the online delivery of pedagogical content, there would be losers. The typesetters and printers for a start: no more big, highly illustrated textbooks to produce, no more new editions coming through with ever increasing frequency. The college bookstores and other intermediaries in the textbook supply chain, including the used book jobbers and wholesalers who have built a thriving business on recycling second-hand textbooks, would also be out of a job. And the smaller and medium-sized textbook publishers would also probably find that life in this brave new world would be very tough, since the scale of investment required to develop and maintain online multimedia products of this kind would tend to favour the big players. In all likelihood it would drive further consolidation in the industry and the lower levels of the curriculum would become increasingly dominated by a small number of large firms – perhaps three or four large global corporations. The smaller and medium-sized publishers who survive would probably be pushed increasingly into the upper levels of the curriculum where print products would continue to be used for some courses and where the levels of investment – and the levels of reward – would be much smaller.

There are some senior figures in the industry who are convinced that this scenario will eventually come to pass. 'Could it take eight years? Yes. Could it take fourteen years? Also possible. But it will happen. In, let's say, 2020 if you like, the world will have changed.' Whether they are right is, at this stage, anyone's guess. Digital optimizers of this kind are not hard to find, but their voices have become a little lonelier in recent years as the mood of caution has gained ground. Some senior figures in the industry were always deeply sceptical about the claims of the digital optimizers, and they remain so. Others are openly agnostic about the future: they simply don't know what is going to happen in the next five to ten years, and in the meantime they get on with the business of developing and selling textbooks while keeping their eyes on the trends.

But this is not to say that things aren't changing: they are, and the digital revolution is transforming the industry in certain fundamental ways. This transformation is happening and will continue to happen regardless of whether the radical scenario sketched above ever comes to pass. To understand this transformation, we have to return to the basic logic of the field of higher education publishing, for it is this logic that provides the context within which new technologies have been energetically – and, one could say, unavoidably – taken up by the major textbook publishers.

Textbooks, companion websites and e-supplements: the evolution of the package

As we saw in chapter 8, the development of the field of higher education publishing since the late 1970s has been characterized by an ever intensifying cycle of providing more and more elaborate packages of material to accompany textbooks – the so-called package wars. Publishers found themselves locked in a struggle to produce ever more elaborate packages of supplements and ancillaries which were produced primarily for the purposes of persuading professors – the gatekeepers in the adoption system – to adopt their textbooks. In this context, the new possibilities opened up by the digital revolution were seized upon by textbook publishers as a new way of producing supplements and ancillaries that would be better, more attractive and more compelling than anything they had been able to produce by means of print. As the digital revolution took hold in the 1980s and 1990s, it did not fundamentally alter the competitive dynamic of textbook publishing – on the contrary, it was grafted onto the logic that already structured the field.

From the early 1980s on, the major textbook publishers began to use new technologies to produce more elaborate supplements and ancillaries to support the printed textbook. Initially it was test files supplied in digital formats, then a whole range of electronic supplements was added – floppy disks, laser disks, videos, CD-ROMs, etc. As the internet emerged in the early 1990s, the textbook publishers began to develop their websites. First they created one general website and used it primarily for marketing purposes, but then they began to develop specific websites for specific textbook titles – the 'companion website' became an increasingly important feature of the package of supplements. As one senior manager in the digital division of a large textbook publisher explained, 'it kind of evolved over the years to be a useful supplement. Right now you pretty much can't have a title without a website. In fact, it is assumed that if you have a title, you have a website.' Initially it was only the major titles, where the expected sales were above a certain threshhold, which had dedicated websites. But gradually the threshold moved down so that today, in the large textbook publishing firms, many of the middle-range textbooks will have their own companion websites.

In large publishing organizations which have many textbooks – either new books or new editions – going through the system at any one time, the development and maintenance of companion websites and other electronic supplements has become a major undertaking. In the early 1990s, many of these organizations set up special technology teams or divisions to work directly with the editorial groups in developing suitable kinds of electronic ancillaries and web-based supplements for each major textbook going through the system. A budget is agreed for each title – anything from $10,000–15,000 to, in exceptional cases, $250,000–300,000 – and the technology team works closely with the editor and with the sales and marketing staff to decide what supplementary materials would be appropriate in each case and then to develop and produce them. 'So it is a collaborative effort,' explained the manager of one technology team. 'Everybody has their own defined responsibilities but as a product idea is created, it is pretty much a team effort. When the plan is in place and everyone knows what needs to be done and how, then the producer from my team takes it over until it is done.'

The development of the supplements often takes place as a process parallel to the production of the textbook itself – these are two workflows which overlap in certain respects but which are organizationally distinct. However, there are good reasons for trying to ensure that the content of the textbook itself is marked up and stored in formats that are consistent with those being used by the technology teams: this creates more flexibility and enables a single, integrated database to be produced so that content from textbooks can be used in the supplements and vice versa. For this and other reasons, textbook publishers have moved increasingly in the direction of digitizing the workflow of textbooks and developing links with the workflow of supplement production – 'we are building bridges between them but they are still parallel paths . . . I guess through this approach we will get closer to integrating them perhaps in one process when the time is right.' The ultimate aim would be to develop a single content management system in which the workflows were integrated into a single production process, yielding content in a consistent digital format. They may not be there yet – 'for many people here, it's "we'll get there one day", but for now it's too big a task' – but this is the direction of change.

In most subject areas, web-based materials have now become the most common form of electronic supplement – 'every major title has an online learning centre website,' the manager explained. But CD-ROMs are still used, especially in subject areas where audio and video supplements are important, such as learning foreign languages. 'When you're teaching a new language, you have to be very, very clear and precise, and people cannot deal with technology problems when they're dealing with a new language. Those types of applications are still much better in the CD-ROM world.' In other cases, CD-ROMs are produced simply to make life easier for the professor. 'We have all the supplements available in our instructor area for each title on the web, but some instructors prefer CD-ROM. So we still do dual versions and if the instructor wants CD-ROM, they get an instructor-only CD-ROM.'

As part of the development process, the technology team creates content in a uniform digital format so that it can be used in different places – on the website, on CD-ROMs, etc. It builds up libraries of digital content in different subject areas and looks for ways in which content can be shared between different textbook projects. 'So, for example, for chemistry we build libraries of animations, similarly for biology, anatomy, physiology and so on.' The more that the company is able to build up its own internal libraries of digital content in particular subject areas, the more it can achieve some economies of scale by using this as a database that can be used for different projects and purposes.

The supplements, whether web based or CD-ROM, are developed both for instructors and for students. Companion websites typically have password-protected (or PIN-protected) regions which are aimed either at the students who have purchased the textbook or at the instructors who have adopted it. The instructors' regions include contents like instructors' manuals, PowerPoint slides, test files and specially designed instructional materials that can be used in the classroom. The textbook publishers have developed their digital resources in ways that can be integrated with course management systems like Blackboard, WebCT and eCollege: when a textbook is adopted, the instructor is provided with a cartridge of supplementary material that can be plugged into whichever platform is used in his or her institution. The larger publishers have also developed their own course management systems, such as CourseCompass (developed by Pearson) and PageOut (developed by McGraw-Hill). Among other things, course management systems enable instructors to combine content drawn from the publisher's databases with their own materials, such as lecture notes, assignments and reading lists, to create a customized set of course materials for students.

Why do the large textbook publishers invest so much money and effort in developing electronic supplements and support systems of this kind? Of course, there are good educational arguments in favour of developing web-based supplements – undoubtedly they have the potential to enrich the educational experience by providing both instructors and students with a wider array of materials that can be displayed more dynamically, that are more interactive and that can be tailored to some extent to the needs of particular instructors and students. But you can understand why the textbook publishers were prepared to invest so heavily in the development of electronic supplements of various kinds only if you see that it was an intrinsic part of the struggle for adoptions. These developments were made possible by the digital revolution and were cloaked in the language of educational enrichment, but they were driven by the competitive dynamic built into the adoption system. 'Publishers did it because it was expected and everybody was doing it,' explained one manager. 'You had to play the game. The rep basically would not get the attention of the instructor if they were asked "Do you have a website" and the answer was "no".' A publisher who had invested heavily in the commissioning and development of a textbook simply could not afford to take the risk of losing adoptions because it had not invested in a companion website. For a major textbook, not investing in a website was simply not an option. And the more common websites became, the higher the stakes were raised. Initially instructors wanted simply to know whether the textbook had a website; now they want to know what is on the website, what features it has, etc. 'Now they pay more attention to the content. It's not good enough to say I have a website. So just as reps talk to instructors about the features of the book, now they have to talk about the features of the website and have to be able to demo that website.'

As with earlier kinds of ancillaries, the cost of developing web-based supplements is treated as part of the development cost of the textbook. The materials are made available to the instructor at no cost to the instructor: for the publisher, this is simply part of the price of doing business within the adoption system. The development costs are passed on to the students in the form of higher prices for textbooks. While students also have access to a range of resources and learning materials on the website, they do not pay separately for this: they gain access by purchasing the textbook. Despite the substantial investment in ancillaries and online supplements of various kinds, it is the sale of the physical textbook that remains the core revenue generator.

Will this ever change? 'I don't know if I have the right answer,' confessed one manager who has followed these developments closely since the early 1990s:

> I think it will change and will evolve over time. It's not going to be a revolution, it's going to be an evolution. Some people believe that print will disappear but in my mind, I think print will be transformed. You will have a print component and you will have extensions of it. Students and instructors will be making choices – I prefer to read this part here or I prefer to do this online, or I prefer to use my PDA to do certain things. So I think it is going to be a package of knowledge and tools that instructors and students will have, and they will be able to access this integrated package as they go through the semester and make a decision about what is printed, what is electronic, what is on their PDA or some other device they choose to use.

In short, the package will evolve, and the balance between print and web-based content will gradually change over time. There will undoubtedly be more investment in the development of elaborate web-based content, such as animated sequences, interactive materials and self-testing exercises. But what is by no means clear at this stage is whether the basic business model that is built into the existing adoption system – whereby revenue is generated by the transaction that takes place when the student buys the physical textbook – will change in the near future. Of course it *could* change at some point. It may be that the quantity and quality of the material delivered online will eventually overshadow the printed text, and that adoption decisions by professors will be translated into student subscriptions to online resources rather than student purchases of printed textbooks. Or perhaps special web-based content and services developed by publishers, such as homework or test supplements, will be seen to have sufficient added value that students will be willing to pay for it in addition to the printed textbook. But at the moment there is no real sign that developments of this kind are likely to provide a significant revenue stream for publishers. What seems most likely for the immediate future is that the principal revenue generating mechanism will remain the purchase by students of the printed textbook, in some cases bundled together with ancillaries of various kinds, and that through this transaction the student will gain access, via a password or PIN, to an increasingly elaborate range of dedicated web-based content that will supplement and augment the printed text.

While much of the activity in terms of new technologies has been focused on the development of ever more elaborate web-based supplements for traditional textbooks, the major textbook publishers have also looked for innovative ways to generate new revenue streams. Two kinds of initiatives are of particular interest in this regard: the development of customized textbooks, and the establishment of business-to-business partnerships with institutions of higher education. Let us consider each in turn.

The rise of the customized textbook business

The rise of the customized textbook business began in the late 1980s and early 1990s, as a number of publishers began experimenting with ways in which the contents of textbooks could be tailored to the needs of particular adopters. While the development of the large standardized textbook had many advantages in terms of the comprehensiveness of the coverage and the quality of the presentation and production, it also meant that most textbooks contained much more material than was actually needed and used by most professors and students. Many professors would find that most textbooks contained some chapters they would regard as essential reading, while other chapters dealt with topics that were not covered in their course, and many students resented paying for material they didn't actually use. It was partly in order to deal with this problem that some textbook publishers began experimenting with ways in which digital technologies might enable them to customize textbooks to the needs of particular instructors.

The rise of the customized textbook is part of a broader domain of what we characterized in chapter 9 as 'custom publishing' in the field of higher education publishing. We could define custom publishing in higher education as the development of instructional materials which are specifically tailored for particular courses. They are not designed for maximum adoptability but, on the contrary, they are designed to be adopted and used by a professor teaching a particular course. The term 'custom publishing' covers a wide range of different products, from photocopied coursepacks produced by a local copy shop to digitally printed textbooks where the chapters have been selected, reordered and perhaps supplemented with other materials by the professor who adopts it for his or her course. In overall sales terms, custom publishing is still a relatively small part of the overall higher education market, but it is a thriving and expanding sector. While the development of custom publishing has been driven primarily by small, local, campus-based organizations which assemble coursepacks for professors, since the late 1980s some of the traditional textbook publishers have also entered this market and sought to increase their stake in it. A survey carried out in 1995 suggested that textbook publishers accounted for around 10 per cent of the custom publishing market in the US, whereas local operators (including campus-based bookstores, independent copy shops and university copy centres) accounted for around 78 per cent; the remaining 12 per cent was accounted for by dedicated custom publishers who operate on a regional and national basis (see figure 14.1).

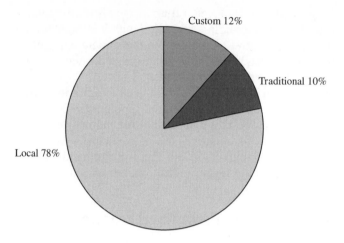

Figure 14.1 Market share of custom publishers in the US by number of products, 1995
Source: Custom Publishing on College Campuses (Stamford, Conn.: O'Donnell & Associates, 1995).

The traditional publishers who were early entrants into this field include educational publishers such as Kendall/Hunt and Ginn, but McGraw-Hill also moved into this field at an early stage with its Primis Custom Publishing project. Primis began to take shape in 1988, when an editor at McGraw-Hill initiated the idea of using computer software and digital printing to produce customized textbooks and supplements. Primis was launched in January 1990. 'Our market was for those customers who kept telling us, "I want to be able to have these chapters from this book" or "I want to be able to combine this supplement with this thing and I want it bound together",' explained a senior manager at Primis. Custom publishing was also seen as a way of being able to control the content at a local level and bring down prices by eliminating material that students didn't use. Students were often buying two books, a textbook and a reader or anthology, but they might use only 60 per cent or 70 per cent of both. If the publisher was able to produce a single customized volume which included only the material that the students would actually use, then the price of the customized volume might be significantly less than the total price of the two standardized texts.

Primis Custom Publishing has evolved over the years into a range of services offered to instructors. One service is the adaptation of existing textbooks: an instructor can take an existing textbook and adapt it to his or her needs by reorganizing the chapters so that they match the course syllabus more closely, deleting chapters that are not used, adding special readings or lecture notes, and/or combining the textbook and the student study guide together in one volume. The adapted textbooks are generally printed digitally in black and white, but they may be printed in colour if the enrolments are high enough. Adaptations of this kind are generally handled by the sales reps who call on instructors and try to persuade them to adopt textbooks. The ability to offer customized adaptations provides the rep with another tool to use in the struggle for adoptions. For some instructors, the ability to adapt an existing textbook so that it matches his or her needs more closely might make a difference when it comes to deciding whether or not to adopt the textbook; hence it may influence a decision about whether to adopt

McGraw-Hill's textbook or a textbook offered by one of its competitors, or indeed whether to adopt a textbook at all. In this respect, customization is a service aimed at supporting existing textbooks by enhancing their adoptability. It is intrinsically linked to the competitive dynamic built into the adoption system.

Primis also enables instructors to create a textbook which is tailored to their needs by selecting material from an online database of content – a service that is called Primis Online. The database is created by uploading the content of existing McGraw-Hill textbooks into subject-specific collections. Each textbook is broken down into chapters which are treated as discrete units. An instructor can create a customized textbook online by selecting the appropriate discipline, reviewing the range of materials available and clicking on the chapters he or she wishes to include. The instructor can select chapters from any of the textbooks available and arrange them in any order. The customized textbook is given a separate ISBN, outsourced to specialist printers to be printed digitally and shipped to the local campus bookstore, which places an order depending on the number of students on the course. The price is calculated on the basis of a standard per-page charge, with an additional charge made for a simple one-colour cover. In 2001, a 700-page customized textbook was likely to cost around $67 net, which was less (though not substantially less) than the price of many of the large standardized textbooks.

In 2000, Primis Online introduced a variant on this model which allows the instructor to order the book as an e-textbook rather than as a digitally printed text. The instructor goes through the same procedure to create the textbook but then chooses to have it delivered as an ebook. The students on the course pay by credit card and download the ebook onto their own computer. Since the files are stored in PDF, the ebook can be read with Adobe Acrobat Reader software. Primis uses a recent version of the Acrobat Reader which locks the ebook to the student's computer, so that it can't be shared. The per-page charge for the electronic version of the textbook is about 15 per cent less than for the printed version.

McGraw-Hill's Primis project was one of the early innovators in the field of customized publishing, but other major textbook publishers such as Pearson and Thomson have developed their own customized publishing programmes and have sought energetically to expand them in recent years. The services offered by other textbook publishers are similar to those offered by Primis and include adaptations of existing textbooks, the publication of original course material and the creation of textbooks and coursepacks online from databases of content. The adaptations of existing textbooks are by far the most successful of these operations, partly because this process is driven by sales reps who interact directly with instructors and have an interest in persuading them to adopt the textbook, and partly because the reps do the necessary work to ensure that the customized textbook is produced and delivered on time. The creation of customized textbooks and coursepacks online by professors themselves is a much smaller business; sales have tended to be modest for both print and electronic versions and, although it is still early days, the delivery of customized textbooks as ebooks is not at this stage a financially significant activity.

Custom publishing provides textbook publishers with ways of generating new revenue streams and protecting existing ones. It protects existing revenue streams by enabling them to secure adoptions which they might otherwise have lost, and it generates new revenue streams by enabling them to repackage their copyrighted material in ways that are tailored to the needs of individual professors. This is one of the areas where the big textbook publishers have been able to generate some modest but real growth in recent years. Moreover, given the growing resistance to the prices of the big textbooks, there are many in the industry who expect customized textbooks to become increasingly attractive to professors, since the customized versions are generally cheaper than the standard textbooks. However, customization does require the professor to do some work, to decide which chapters to include and which to leave out, and this will undoubtedly deter many professors from going down the customization path. The quality of the final product – in terms of the use of colour, etc. – is also significantly lower, and many professors may feel that the modest reduction in price is not sufficient to justify the extra work involved and the decline in the quality of the final product.

One of the key questions at this stage is the extent to which the traditional textbook publishers will be able to compete effectively against local, campus-based operators in the market for customized course material. When it comes to adapting textbooks, they are not really competing with local suppliers, since in these cases the publisher is simply modifying the contents of an existing text. But to the extent that the traditional publishers seek to offer professors the opportunity to create their own textbooks or coursepacks from scratch, as in Primis Online, Pearson's database publishing programme and Thomson's eCoursepacks, they are moving onto terrain which is largely controlled by a diverse array of local, campus-based operators. And as we noted in chapter 9, the local operators have two key competitive advantages over the traditional textbook publishers: first, they are *local* and they are able to provide a convenient, campus-based service to professors and instructors; and second, they are able to assemble coursepacks using material from any source that the professor wishes to include – articles, book chapters, extracts from newspapers and magazines, etc. – and they take over the task of clearing copyright for this material, whereas the database of a textbook publisher consists to a large extent of that publisher's own copyrighted material. 'Professors don't want one source,' explained one local coursepack operator, 'they want eighty sources.' Professors want to be able to put together a collection of pieces that they regard as important and worthwhile for their students to read, regardless of where the pieces were originally published and who owns the copyright.

Given these competitive advantages, it seems likely that the local operators will remain the principal suppliers of customized coursepacks and that the big textbook publishers will find it difficult to take a substantial share of this market (although there are other areas of custom publishing where they will be able to achieve real growth). In the longer term, it is quite possible that the provision of certain kinds of customized course materials will migrate increasingly into a web-based environment. This is already happening in practice on many campuses, as the texts and extracts assigned by professors for particular courses are scanned and made available to students online along with the course outlines and reading lists – 'e-reserves', as they are sometimes called. Professors need only a single copy of the article or chapter to have it scanned and made available to all the students taking the course, who can access it anytime and free of charge from the comfort of their dorm or home. Apart from scanning the texts into the system, librarians don't have to manage physical reserves and deal with student requests. Whether it is legitimate to do this without clearing copyright permission is another matter – e-reserves have become one of the new grey areas of copyright law. Professors tend to believe that this counts as 'fair use' and is little different from putting the material on reserve in the library, and many librarians may be inclined to agree. Publishers, on the other hand, are concerned by this development; they are worried that e-reserves could become an alternative to basic text materials and could begin to replace coursepacks, for which publishers do, at least in principle, receive copyright fees.[2]

To the extent that the provision of customized course materials does migrate into an online environment, it will become increasingly important for librarians and publishers to work out a mutually acceptable framework for e-reserves. Currently there are no clear guidelines about how much material can be used, to whom it can be made available and for how long, and there is no accepted business model that clearly defines who should pay for what. It is not just the big textbook publishers and the local coursepack operators who stand to lose out here, but perhaps even more the university presses whose books feature prominently in reserve collections, as the BYTES study demonstrated. The predominantly local business of assembling and producing customized coursepacks may gradually evolve into the increasing use of locally managed web-based electronic reserves assembled for specific courses, and publishers may find that, in the absence of a mutually agreed framework concerning the use of copyrighted material, this emerging pedagogical practice takes place without them.

B2B partnerships with higher education institutions

The development of companion websites and customized textbooks are important features of higher education publishing, but to a large extent they supplement and support the traditional business model of textbook publishing which is based on the adoption system. This is a model in which the decision flows from professor to student and the revenue flows from student to bookstore to publisher, as illustrated by figure 14.2. In this model, the publisher deals directly with individual professors and in some cases with committees of professors, but not with the university as a whole. However, the possibility of delivering substantial databases of content or even courses in an online environment has opened up the possibility of publishers dealing directly with universities in ways that would bypass the traditional business model of textbook publishing. Rather than trying to persuade individual professors to adopt particular textbooks, publishers

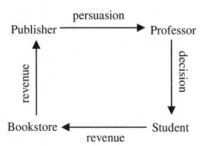

Figure 14.2 The traditional business model of textbook publishing

[2] See Lois S. Wasoff, 'Back to the Future . . . Are E-Reserves the New Course Packs?', *Professional/Scholarly Publishing Bulletin*, 4/1 (Spring 2003), pp. 1–3.

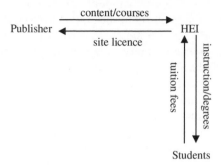

Figure 14.3 Site licence business model for B2B partnerships between publishers and higher education institutions

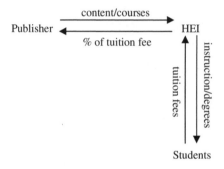

Figure 14.4 Tuition fee business model for B2B partnerships between publishers and higher education institutions

could form business-to-business partnerships with higher education institutions (HEIs) to develop and provide them with pedagogical content.

There are various ways in which this new kind of relationship could work depending on the kind of content that was being provided and the uses to which it was being put. A publisher could simply license some of its online databases or courses to an HEI using a site licence model, as in figure 14.3. On this model, the publisher provides the content or course to the HEI and, in return, the HEI pays a fee to the publisher based on the number of students taking the course. Students have access to the content as part of their course and do not pay separately for it: the cost to the HEI is part of its educational outlay and may be recovered from the students' tuition fees. The site licence model may be particularly appropriate in cases where the content or course is developed independently by the publisher and then marketed to different HEIs. Alternatively the publisher could work with a particular HEI to develop content and/or courses which would be a core part of the instructional materials delivered to students. In this case, the publisher becomes not just a supplier of pedagogical content but a partner in the pedagogical process, working with the teaching staff to develop content that is tailored to the aims of the course. Here the publisher could use a different business model in which the revenue is generated by taking a share of the tuition fees paid by students, as in figure 14.4. In this model, the publisher works together with the HEI to develop and provide content and courses; the HEI collects tuition fees from students in return for providing instruction and awarding degrees; and the HEI passes on an agreed percentage of the tuition fees to its publishing partner.

Why would HEIs be interested in acquiring pedagogical content from publishers on the site licence model? Different factors come into play here. In some cases there is pressure from senior administrators in the university, or even political pressure from state or federal governments, to include an online component in courses. This is one of the factors that has helped to drive the development of companion websites. But the problem with companion websites is that the costs cannot be recovered by charging directly for the online content. The costs have to be recovered by raising the price of the printed textbook, and in contexts where the price thresholds for textbooks are relatively low, such as the UK, it is difficult to develop a significant online component using the traditional textbook model. 'So we were in a position where we were limited in what we could offer in a companion website because it wasn't profitable to do that,' explained the director of an online course programme at one higher education publisher in the UK:

> So what we started doing with the online courses was actually selling them to the universities. We started having conversations at the Vice-Chancellor level. So we identified universities that were requiring this online component to a course, or requiring lecturers to deliver part of their course online. At the same time, our sales reps were talking to the lecturers about the online courses. Where we have actually made sales is where those two have met. Lecturers that really wanted to use our courses had trouble getting funding unless we'd prepped the Vice-Chancellor ahead of time, or the Dean. So, where people are using our online courses is where those parties have met up and started to communicate.

If the university decides to purchase a prepackaged online course of this kind, then it is installed on the university's server and it is free to customize it for its own needs. In return, it pays the publisher a licence fee based on the number of students on the course – say £10 ($16) per student × 300 students = £3,000 ($4,800).

A key part of this model is that the online courses are acquired by HEIs to be used within the context of an existing pedagogical process – that is, on an existing course for which students are already enrolled and which is part of their degree programme. For the most part, they are on-campus courses where students are attending lectures and classes and using traditional printed textbooks as well as online materials. 'It's coupled along with the adoption market,' explained a manager. 'They tend to be used in big introductory courses where there are so many students that the lecturer is feeling overrun.' By treating these online courses as the web-based components of courses that already exist in colleges and universities, the publisher can tie their content into existing courses, in much the same way that it does when it seeks to get adoptions for its textbooks.

Despite the fact that these online courses are designed as supplements for existing courses, the take-up has so far been relatively modest. One director of an online course programme at a major higher education publisher sees several reasons for this. Partly the problems are political in the sense that 'just selling to the institution is quite difficult because by nature you get more decision-makers and so the funds have to be freed up and it's quite a hassle for the lecturer. So it's just very time-consuming.' In most institutions of higher education, the competition for resources is intense, and it's not easy to persuade those who control the purse-strings to pay for experimental material of this kind. Moreover, it's not always clear which part of the institution should pay – is it a departmental expenditure, or should it be part of the library budget? There may also be a certain reluctance on the part of professors and lecturers to be dependent on content from a single commercial publisher – 'some people have a lot of concern about that.' This is one of the reasons why publishers let the universities host the course themselves, add their own content and customize it for their own purposes. And of course, the extent to which teaching staff and students actually wish to use content delivered in this way, especially when they are teaching and studying in a campus-based environment and using traditional printed textbooks as well, remains unclear.

So are initiatives of this kind likely to expand in the near future? 'I don't think it's going to expand so much as just blur,' explained the director of this programme:

> At the moment we have a huge amount of our business in textbooks and a small amount in online courses and a fraction in companion websites. I'd expect that the balance between books and web for different subjects will start to shift and differentiate themselves. So we can have an editor who is working on the geography list who is focusing an online course on collecting real data or something, whereas an editor on a business list, for a really fast-changing area like business information systems, might have much more of an online component because they can stay much more current that way. So I hope we stop making the distinctions that we are making at the moment. That's what I think will happen because I think that's what the market is starting to say.

While the sale of online courses to HEIs is still an extremely small part of the business of higher education publishers, it is possible, as this programme director suggests, that online course content of this kind will become incorporated into the evolution of the package of educational materials that the publisher makes available to the higher education sector and that the nature of these packages will vary from one discipline to another.

So far we've been examining prepackaged online courses that are sold to HEIs on a site licence basis and are used primarily in a campus-based teaching context, but there are other scenarios which are beginning to emerge. One possibility, alluded to above, involves the publisher working directly with the HEI to develop a customized online course which can be used to structure the pedagogical process of the students who are enrolled in this institution, and where the publisher takes a percentage of the tuition fee. For example, a publisher could work with an HEI to develop an online course based on a course actually taught on its campus, and then work together with the HEI to build a distance learning programme that would be organized around the online course. This would enable the HEI to enlarge its enrolment by recruiting students at a distance, and it would enable the publisher to develop an online course that would be closely tailored to the needs of the teaching staff and students on a particular degree course. For both the HEI and the publisher, this partnership would open up new revenue streams that would simply not be available otherwise, since the online approach would enable the HEI to recruit a new set of students that they could never get on campus but could get through distance learning.

Why would an HEI wish to involve a commercial publisher in developing a distance learning programme of this kind and give it a share of the tuition fees when, with some

specialist help, it could do it on its own? 'Well, because I think that they think they can't
do those things on their own,' replied a senior manager in a large publishing firm which
is a leading player in this field:

> They can't generate content that customers want to buy on their own, otherwise why don't
> universities publish their own textbooks or at least just farm them out to a printer? They
> can't do it actually. There is an issue to do with positioning yourself in a way that you under-
> stand the global market and no one institution is going to have that handle on the global
> market in the same way that we do. There are also some operational things that we can do
> more effectively – customer service and marketing and what-have-you. So there are other
> reasons why they can see the benefits in working with someone else. Our experience actu-
> ally is that universities are very keen to work with us and are not saying, oh, we'd rather
> do it all on our own. Quite the reverse.

For this senior manager, the development of distance learning programmes in partnership with HEIs is one of the key priorities in terms of new initiatives – 'in terms of
getting continued dramatic growth in the future, I think it's the area to look at.' The
development of distance learning programmes has real advantages for HEIs, for it
enables them greatly to extend their recruitment net and to increase their enrolment
without the high costs involved in the physical relocation of students to a campus-based
environment. By forming partnerships with HEIs, publishers can provide value-added
content and services that will form an integral part of these distance learning programmes and can participate in what some think is likely to be a growing trend in higher
education.

One higher education publisher – let us call it HE3 – has developed a number of partnerships of this kind with HEIs. HE3 takes the initiative by approaching universities
which have successful campus-based courses up and running in areas where it thinks
there is potential for developing a distance learning programme. These tend to be practical, career-oriented courses – business and IT are head of the list, but it also looks for
other practically based courses like engineering, healthcare and tourism. 'All of the
courses we would think of as viable', commented one manager, 'are career-related.
The sort of education-as-leisure angle is not one that we think is worth exploring at the
moment. It's very much driven by the students' need to increase their skills and get a
qualification relevant to their work on their CV.' If the teaching and administrative staff
at the university are interested in pursuing the idea of developing a distance learning
programme and see it as a potentially cost-effective way to increase their enrolment,
then distance learning staff at HE3 meet with the teaching staff in the relevant department and work out a plan for the development of the course. This typically involves a
division of labour between the two partners: the teaching staff are usually responsible
for writing any new material for the course and for assessing and examining students,
while the publisher develops the content management system and adds content from
its existing course materials (including its textbooks), designs and manages the website
and may also take responsibility for some or all of the marketing and recruitment. The
fact that the distance learning programme is part of an existing degree course at an
established university is crucial. From the viewpoint of the staff, it means that the programme does not have to be developed from scratch but can be built on, and integrated
with, an existing course. From the viewpoint of potential students, it provides some

quality assurance and means that, if they complete the course, they will end up with a formal qualification from an established university which they can add to their CV.[3]

The course materials for the distance learning programme are not necessarily all online – on the contrary, they can range anywhere from 100 per cent print-based to 100 per cent online, though a mixture of print-based and online materials is common and preferred by the management at HE3. 'There are some universities that are running distance learning programmes that require no print. My view is that this is a big limitation,' commented one senior manager. 'Why would you limit yourself only to online? Surely you would want to maximize your learning opportunities. I think that some sort of multimedia approach is almost certainly the right way to go.' The courses also vary in the extent to which they rely on distance learning materials – whether print-based or online – and the extent to which they rely on face-to-face tuition. One of the traditional problems with many distance learning courses is that they lack a face-to-face component. This can give rise to difficulties for some students, especially if they come with varying degrees of background knowledge and preparation. One way that HE3 has tried to cope with this problem is to develop a hybrid model which combines distance learning with a limited amount of face-to-face tuition, in a way that is somewhat similar to the UK's Open University model. In one of its distance learning MBA programmes, for example, HE3 sets up support centres in the countries where the students are located, and these centres recruit local tutors who meet students in face-to-face settings at regular intervals. In this particular instance, about 80 per cent of the student's work is based on distance learning materials (both web-based and hard-copy materials like textbooks) and about 20 per cent is based on face-to-face interaction with local tutors. Many of HE3's distance learning programmes are aimed at students in South East Asia, South Africa and elsewhere, and local tutors will have a much better understanding of their background knowledge, the kind of educational system they've been through and how accustomed they are to thinking analytically.

The setting up and running of distance learning programmes of this kind is a costly and time-consuming undertaking, both for the publisher and for the teaching staff, and success is by no means guaranteed. HE3 is able to save time and money by using some of its existing course materials – that is, by taking content from some of its existing textbooks and related course materials and adapting it to particular distance learning programmes. It can also save time and money by developing standardized templates and procedures for producing new content. Nevertheless, writing new material is time-

[3] This is one of the respects in which HE3's initiatives differ from some of the other e-learning courses that proliferated in the late 1990s and early 2000s, such as those offered by Fathom. Fathom Knowledge Network, Inc. was founded by Columbia University in 1999 and launched its website in April 2000 with the aim of providing high-quality educational resources to a global audience through the internet. With start-up funding from Columbia, Fathom put together a consortium of institutions – including Cambridge University Press, the London School of Economics and the New York Public Library – which contributed content of various kinds. However, the courses offered by Fathom were not tied into any degree-granting body, and completing a course did not provide a student with a qualification of any kind. Fathom was relying on an excessively optimistic set of assumptions about the extent to which ordinary members of the public would be willing to pay for short online courses which would be pursued for their own sake and would contribute to what one senior manager at Fathom described as their 'intellectual wellness'. Fathom ceased operations in March 2003 after consuming more than $30 million.

consuming for teaching staff, who in many cases are already overburdened with teaching and administrative duties. Moreover, given that university teachers remain responsible for assessing students and interacting with local tutors and/or students, and given that course materials need to be continuously updated, the running of a distance learning programme makes ongoing demands on teaching staff. For a programme of this kind to be successful, the demands on teaching staff have to be formally recognized by their own institution and they have to be given some credit – for instance, in terms of their teaching stints – for the time and effort they invest.

So is it worth all the time and effort? Are distance learning partnerships of this kind likely to be successful, or will they go the way of so many of the online ventures that were part of the dot.com boom? HE3 can point to the example of a successful distance learning MBA which it developed some years ago with a business school and which now has several thousand students – certainly more than enough to make it financially worthwhile. This particular programme was developed initially as a correspondence course using print-based materials, but an online component has since been added. HE3's other initiatives are still at various stages of development and it is too early to say how successful they will be, but senior managers feel confident that there is a real market for distance learning courses and that, by forming partnerships with HEIs, they will be able to tap into this market in new and innovative ways. The key point is that initiatives of this kind are not conceived of primarily as online businesses, but rather as distance learning courses that use online materials as one of a range of pedagogical resources. 'We don't see ourselves primarily as an online business,' explained one manager:

> We see ourselves as a business that enables universities to offer distance learning courses and there are a number of very mature markets for those sorts of courses already. You only have to open an education supplement at the moment to see predictions about the growing importance of distance learning as lifelong learning becomes more important, as people want to update skills, particularly in the IT sector, that become outdated in two or three years. So it's not really about the success or otherwise of the medium. There are good reasons for thinking that distance learning is going to become an increasingly important feature of the educational experience over the next five, ten or fifteen years. Let's have a look at that opportunity and work out the best ways of delivering that kind of distance learning experience. The key question for us is how do we deliver effective distance learning, not how do we make an online business work.

HE3 sees itself as a commercial partner that can work with institutions of higher education to tap what it believes will be a growing market for distance learning courses. It is not trying to create an online business but rather to develop distance learning programmes in collaboration with existing campus-based universities in which the delivery of course materials in an online environment will play an important but by no means exclusive role, and in many cases will be used in conjunction with traditional print-based materials and face-to-face tuition.

I have focused here on a particular example of how higher educational publishers have sought to form partnerships with HEIs, but there are many other examples of how publishers have become increasingly active in the expanding markets of distance learning, corporate learning and what is sometimes called 'lifelong learning'. In the US, a number of the major higher education publishers have entered into agreements with the University of Phoenix to supply pedagogical content. Founded in 1976 as an institution aimed at meeting the educational needs of the adult working population, the University of Phoenix had more than 160,000 students in 2003, including more than 70,000 attending via the internet through the university's online campus. It claims to be the largest private university in the US, and with enrolment increasing from around 100,000 in 2001 to over 160,000 in 2003, it is among the fastest growing. Some of the large higher education publishers have also developed corporate training divisions in which they draw on their existing copyrights to develop web-based courseware aimed at professional development programmes within corporations. Initiatives of this kind have had varying degrees of success; some have generated new revenue streams for publishers and HEIs, while others – especially some of the more ambitious 'e-universities' – have turned out to be costly failures.[4] Nevertheless, there are good reasons to believe that non-campus-based higher and further education is an area that is likely to expand in the coming decades, and this expansion may open up some opportunities for higher education publishers to generate new revenue streams by developing and supplying pedagogical content to non-traditional markets.

The development of pedagogically oriented databases

So far we have been considering some of the ways in which the major higher education publishers have used new technologies both to support their existing textbook business and to open up new business opportunities, whether through custom publishing or through distance learning and lifelong learning programmes. But there are other players who have sought to enter the higher education market by making content available online for pedagogical purposes. Some of the initiatives examined in the previous chapter would fall into this category – for example, some of the virtual libraries, such as Questia, are explicitly aimed at the student market, and many of the other initiatives were developed in the expectation that students in higher education would comprise at least part of the user population. However, there are also a number of organizations which have traditionally been active in the content aggregation business and which have sought in recent years to develop innovative online projects in the educational field.

In this section I want to consider one example of how a content aggregator has sought to develop its databases into pedagogically oriented content that can be marketed to educational institutions. Literature Online (LION) was developed in the 1990s by the Cambridge-based electronic publisher Chadwyck-Healey (now part of ProQuest Information and Learning, following its acquisition by the US company Bell & Howell in 1999). One reason why this project is interesting is that, unlike many online initiatives, LION has succeeded in generating a significant revenue stream over a number of years. It has demonstrated that there are viable markets for pedagogical content delivered in an online environment and that well-designed online products of this kind can be successful in both pedagogical and commercial terms. A little later we shall try to uncover some of the reasons for LION's success, but first let us briefly recount the development of the project.

---

[4]The collapse in 2004 of the UK e-University (UKeU), which was funded by the British government to the tune of £62 million, is only the most recent in a long series of spectacular failures in the field of e-learning. See Donald MacLeod, 'E is for error', *Education Guardian*, 8 June 2004, pp. 18–19.

LION emerged from a series of CD-ROM databases in English literature that had been put together by Chadwyck-Healey in the early 1990s. Since the early 1970s, Chadwyck-Healey had built a business that was based on aggregating and indexing large quantities of content and converting it into a medium in which it would be valued by libraries and other institutions. In the 1970s and 1980s, this medium was primarily micro-form (microfilm and microfiche), but in the 1990s it began creating databases by keying large bodies of text and storing them on CD-ROM. One such project was to produce a comprehensive collection of English poetry, which was digitized and stored on CD-ROM and sold to university libraries in the UK, North America and elsewhere. This was followed by a number of other CD-ROM databases in English and American literature, including databases on English verse drama, prose drama, novels and twentieth-century poetry – there were nine separate databases altogether, all available on CD-ROM. These databases were targeted exclusively at the institutional market. Chadwyck-Healey worked closely with librarians and knew what kinds of collections they would be interested in acquiring, and the financial model was based on the assumption that a certain number of libraries would purchase the databases. So, for example, if a project cost £1 million to produce and it thought that fifty libraries would acquire the database, then it knew its break-even price was £20,000; if it sold it for £25,000, it stood a good chance of recovering its costs and generating a margin, and every sale above fifty would be highly profitable.

However, as American university libraries began to move online around 1995, Chadwyck-Healey faced growing demands from librarians to make its databases available online rather than on CD-ROM. Literature Online was initially conceived of as an umbrella site to make the various literature databases available in an online environment, but it quickly evolved into something else: into a large body of digital content in literature that could be integrated, continuously augmented and tailored for different institutional markets. The business model also changed: rather than selling discrete databases to libraries on CD-ROM, Chadwyck-Healey now had to persuade librarians and other institutional gatekeepers to pay an annual subscription fee for access to LION. It strengthened its case by thinking about the needs of different institutions and creating different versions that were tailored to them. For the big research libraries which are relatively well endowed and which cater primarily for academics and post-graduate students, there is a full version of LION which contains all the primary texts – it is designed primarily as a research-oriented database of primary and secondary literature. But for the colleges and universities that are oriented primarily towards under-graduate teaching, Chadwyck-Healey developed a different version of LION, called LION Select, which is tailored to the needs of undergraduate students. 'It takes a lot of the content and presents it in a very different way,' explained a senior manager:

> It effectively presents it in what we call study units. So what we've done is look worldwide at the undergraduate curriculum in English and American literature and said, who's studied, what works are studied, what genres are studied, and we've stripped out some of the content and we've organized the content that's left into study pages. So, the study page on Yeats will get you to all of Yeats's poetry and whatever other writings of Yeats we have, will get you to journal articles on Yeats, criticism on Yeats and so on. Likewise they can go to a study unit on the Romantics or whatever and they will find everything that is in Literature Online that is relevant to that author or set of works or genre accessible from that study page. So rather than coming to this absolutely vast warehouse of content, very well

indexed but nonetheless vast, and having to search for things themselves, they'll be able to go straight to it. There is twice as much onscreen help for the student and the structure of the thing is organized around the needs of the undergraduate.

So whereas the full version of LION is marketed to the research libraries, LION Select is marketed to the undergraduate-oriented colleges and universities, from some of the big state universities and liberal arts colleges in the US down to the two-year community colleges. Another reference-only version has been developed for universities – especially those outside the English-speaking world – who want the biographies and reference works but don't want the primary texts since 'their students are not doing the kind of analysis where they would need that'. And another two versions have been developed for schools, one for schools in the UK and one for schools in the US.

By treating LION as a digital resource that could be tailored for different institutions depending on the needs and interests of the end users, Chadwyck-Healey was able to produce a set of pedagogically oriented databases that were geared to different types of students, from college undergraduates to school students, and was able thereby to open up markets that would not otherwise have existed. 'So what I've tried to get our publishers to do', explained a senior manager, 'is to think about overall publishing streams and portfolios of products whereby we exploit our content in more than one way or more than one product.'

> What drives the whole business is something much closer to traditional publishing than has normally been associated with large aggregators or digitization businesses. So we are taking a customer-focused view. We are saying, there are all these sectors of the market. What does each sector want? In the case of Select or the schools product, sure, they want the content, but actually the organization of the content, the way into it, is probably more important than having all the content.

In fact, the school version may turn out to be the most successful in financial terms. Although the full version is more expensive, it is also heavily discounted since many of the universities had already bought some of the constituent databases, and the market for the full version is small – probably only fifty or sixty institutions worldwide. But there is a potentially large market for LION in secondary schools and further education colleges, where the take-up has been very encouraging.

Having established LION as a portfolio of products tailored for different institutional markets, Chadwyck-Healey can now concentrate on strengthening the database by adding new content, improving the functionality and service component, and developing new products for different market sectors. It can also use LION as a model for developing new ranges of products in other subject areas such as history. The problem with a subject area like history, however, is that the quantity of primary material is potentially huge, and hence a potentially massive investment is required to build up a database of content:

> Digitize a back-run of a British newspaper to its beginnings – well, you are probably looking at an investment of between $3 and $5 million just to do that. Digitize the whole of the parliamentary papers, fantastic resource, but again an investment that would run into the millions of pounds or dollars. You look at all the other stuff around that and it is almost impossible to know where to start.

So how did Chadwyck-Healey move forward with History Online? Essentially it followed the model it had used in developing LION for the undergraduate and schools market – that is, the study unit model:

> For history we've identified around 500 study units that will cover broadly the undergraduate curriculum in British and US history. For each of those study units what we're doing is identifying key primary documents. It could be a report in a Parliamentary committee, it could be some articles from *The Times*, it could be a primary document like the Magna Carta, it could be a decree or whatever. So we are identifying the key primary documents and putting those together with key secondary documents, with reference material, criticism, journal articles and so on to create a unit of maybe forty to fifty items. So enough not to restrict the undergraduate to a very tight selection of material but sufficient for that undergraduate to find some things that other undergraduates doing the same study won't necessarily find. We are building History Online out of those study units.

Whereas Literature Online evolved from a research-oriented set of databases into a set of online products aimed at undergraduate and school students, History Online started life primarily as a set of pedagogical tools designed for students with some databases developed in parallel for the researcher. 'The model that probably best describes how we are approaching it might be one of intersecting circles. If you imagine a large circle in the centre, which is the undergraduate product content, and then some smaller circles that intersect with that larger circle which are the research collections.' So, for example, the Annual Register is a series of annual reviews of events which go back to around 1750. The whole series is being digitized and will form a discrete database, and some of the content of this database will be incorporated into study units in the History Online site. History Online will be sold on a subscription basis to university libraries for undergraduate use, while the discrete databases will be sold either on an outright basis or by subscription. The institutions that purchase both History Online and the databases will be able to move freely between them. A student can start with a study unit and then move into the larger collection of primary material to do some original research. 'What we're trying to address here, one of the needs that we're trying to meet, is the increasingly project-based approach to the teaching of history, one which attempts to get the students doing some original research in their undergraduate period and not just when they go on to do a Ph.D. or whatever.'

History Online is an ambitious project and it is too early to say how successful it will be. Undoubtedly it has the potential to be used as a pedagogical resource at both the undergraduate level and at the level of secondary schools, but it will be some while before it's clear how widely it will be taken up. Literature Online, however, has already established itself as a commercially successful online resource in higher and secondary education. LION's running costs are around £500,000 per year and it generates a revenue stream well in excess of that, enabling the site to be maintained and developed while at the same time producing a profitable return.

So what are the keys to LION's success? No doubt there are several reasons – let me mention six. In the first place, Chadwyck-Healey was never a conventional book publisher, and hence its way of thinking about electronic media was not shaped by the priorities and constraints of printed book publishing. 'We had no hang-ups about print,' commented one senior manager. 'We had no print heritage. We didn't worry about whether we were cannibalizing our print sales by going electronic. We were wholly dedicated to being electronic publishers. There was no baggage to hold us back.' Second, and related to this, it was accustomed to working with scale. Given its background in microform and its experience in aggregating large quantities of material for the institutional market, it was not daunted by the prospect of building large repositories of digitized content:

> 'Small is beautiful' has never been Chadwyck-Healey's catchphrase. We're comfortable with scale and we're comfortable with projects that may cost us half a million or a million pounds or more to develop, which most print publishers would be far less comfortable with. They wouldn't put all their eggs in that one basket as we have done.

But scale alone is not enough: it also invested a great deal of editorial thought in deciding what kind of content to acquire and how to present it in order to maximize its usefulness for the targeted end users – this is the third point. 'So it is not scale alone, but it is scale combined with having the right content and then the right editorial and technical skills to deliver that content in the right way in this portfolio of products.' In short, it sought to create *pertinent scale*.

A fourth reason why Chadwyck-Healey was successful with LION is that it saw from the outset that its main market would be the institutional market and it worked hard to cultivate its links with the key institutional gatekeepers. In this respect, it was able to build on a history of working with librarians that extended back to the 1970s. Over a period of some two decades, it had built up relations of trust with librarians in the UK, North America and elsewhere, and it was known to librarians as a reliable provider of high-quality aggregated content. Indeed, many librarians were already familiar with some of the databases, such as English poetry, that eventually became constituent parts of the online product, since they had already acquired these databases on CD-ROM. By clearly targeting the institutional market and developing LION for it, Chadwyck-Healey avoided the pitfalls of thinking that ambitious projects of this kind could be sustained by selling subscriptions to individuals. 'I don't believe the consumer market for this kind of product truly exists. But if it did we'd be the wrong people to develop and sell it to that market. We are absolutely institutional publishers and I think we'd be going down completely the wrong track if we thought we could take what we are doing and apply it to the private individual.' This is one of the reasons why, in the early 1990s, Chadwyck-Healey was successful with its CD-ROM publishing programme, while most of the traditional book publishers who experimented with CD-ROMs lost their shirts. Unlike those publishers who thought they could develop CD-ROMs profitably for the consumer market, Chadwyck-Healey's CD-ROM publishing programme was directed exclusively to the institutional library market. ('I've lost track of the number of letters we had from academics who said, "Oh, if you'd published English poetry or the Patalogia at £100 a time, you'd have sold a lot more." Well, yes, but not 250 times more, which is roughly the multiple we're looking at here.')

A fifth reason why Chadwyck-Healey was successful with LION is that it was an early entrant in the field of online publishing. The fact that it had already built up large databases of content in literature that were being sold into libraries on CD-ROM gave it a head-start when the libraries began to move to online around 1995. It already had large digital repositories of relevant content and, in many cases, it already had a foot in the library's door. Being an early entrant was important not only in terms of persuading librarians to sign up to the project: it was also important because the development of online resources of this kind may be governed by a 'winner takes all' logic. That is, given the importance of scale and given the constraints on librarians' budgets, it may turn out that one site will come to dominate a discipline over time:

> Another thing to take into account in the development of these sites is our belief that in general one site will come to dominate a discipline and if you can make it your site that dominates that discipline, then you will certainly get your investment back. I think it's a winner-take-all environment. There will be room probably in some areas of the humanities, and maybe in some areas of the sciences, for more than one player, but I think in general if you are looking at a product that is bound by its nature, because of its size and other factors, to sell for several thousand pounds a year, it is very, very unlikely that a library is ever going to justify buying more than one of those products. So you have to be the winner.

By building on its established products and reputation in the field and launching LION at the very beginning of the online revolution in the library world, Chadwyck-Healey was able to put itself in a strong position to fend off the competition that would soon begin to appear.

A sixth and final reason why LION has been successful is that Chadwyck-Healey saw the need to tailor its digital resources to different types of end users. It has taken a market-oriented, customer-focused view and asked, 'how can we adapt the content we have to different sectors of the educational market?' While LION was built on the basis of databases that were originally designed primarily for the purposes of research and originally sold primarily to the major research libraries, the project was increasingly seen as a repository of digital content from which a range of different products, aimed at meeting the needs of teachers and students at different levels of the curriculum, could be developed. By segmenting the market it was able to make the most of the content. The full version of LION is still sold to research libraries as a resource for scholars and graduate students, while the versions aimed at undergraduates and school students are designed as pedagogical tools tailored to different levels of the curriculum. This flexible, customer-focused view enables Chadwyck-Healey to generate new revenue streams in different sectors of the educational market and reduces its dependence on the research libraries. 'If we were only doing Literature Online, the flagship product for the top tier of the HE sector, I don't think it would be very profitable,' commented a senior manager.

I have examined Literature Online in some detail because it provides an instructive example of how the online environment can be used creatively and successfully for the development of pedagogical content that is tailored to the needs of teachers and students. We shall draw some lessons from this example in the final section of this chapter.

Lessons, problems and prospects

The digital revolution has not led to the wholesale transformation of the field of higher education publishing, as some commentators in the late 1990s were predicting. The idea that the traditional textbook, piled up in the aisles of college bookstores at the beginning of the academic year, would be eclipsed by web-based content delivery systems has not – or at least not yet – materialized on any significant scale. But the digital revolution has had a much more profound impact in higher education publishing than in some other publishing fields, such as trade publishing, partly because the logic of the field of higher education publishing had created a context in which new technologies could be effectively used in the struggle for competitive advantage. New technologies, and especially web-based support systems of various kinds, were quickly seized upon by the textbook publishers as a way of enriching the packages they developed for the purposes of persuading professors to adopt their textbooks – in other words, the digital revolution provided an array of ever more elaborate materials to be used in the package wars. Given the competitive dynamic built into the adoption system, the increasing investment in new technologies to support the printed textbook was not an option for those publishers who wanted to win big adoptions at the lower levels of the curriculum: it was a condition of playing the game.

The digital revolution has not fundamentally changed the rules of the game but it has altered the stakes. The field of higher education publishing is still governed by the logic of competition built into the adoption system, but the cost of competing in this field today is much higher than ever before – it's not exactly 'business as usual'. It was always costly to compete at the lower levels of the curriculum in the US, especially given the costs associated with maintaining a college sales force, but the ever increasing investment in new technologies and support materials of various kinds has significantly escalated the cost. It has raised the barriers to entry, making it more difficult for new players to enter the field, and it has further strengthened the positions of the largest players, who are able to support dedicated technology teams and to spread the costs associated with developing new products across a wider range of textbooks. The large textbook publishers who have developed a wide array of support materials are able to bundle together more and more contents in their packages, offering professors and instructors access to an ever increasing range of products and services. This makes it harder and harder for the smaller publishers who remain in the field to compete at the lower levels of the curriculum and increases the pressure towards further concentration.

While the use of new technologies to support the printed textbook is undoubtedly the most significant impact to date of the digital revolution in the field of higher education publishing, there are other ways in which the digital revolution is affecting the field and opening up new opportunities. I shall draw this discussion to a close by highlighting nine general points that emerge from my analysis of recent developments in this field.

(1) The traditional printed textbook is not about to disappear in the near future. Various publishers and third parties have experimented with e-textbooks of various kinds – for example, by digitizing textbooks and making them available as ebooks with various kinds of functionality added, such as the ability to add notes in the margins. But experiments of this kind have resulted in minimal sales and e-textbooks understood in this way – as digital replicas of printed textbooks with added functionality – seem unlikely to take off in the near future. There are many senior figures in higher education publishing today who are relatively sanguine about the future of the printed textbook – it will remain, in their view, a key component of the higher education curriculum

and the principal source of revenue for higher education publishers. However, even with increasing student numbers, it is extremely difficult to achieve significant growth in the textbook market, given the intense competition that exists at the lower levels of the curriculum in mature markets like the US. Hence, the investment in new technologies provides the major players both with a means of increasing their competitive advantage in the struggle for market share and with a way of opening up new opportunities for generating revenue and growth on the margins. 'The printed text is not under threat in my view,' explained the managing director of a large publishing firm. 'The issue with the printed text is more to do with how much opportunity there is to keep selling more, with how much more growth is available in the printed text. It's not that it is about to die. I don't think it is about to die at all.' While there is not a consensus on this issue, the view that the printed textbook will remain a key component of the higher education curriculum for the foreseeable future is the dominant view among senior figures in higher education publishing today.

(2)   While the printed textbook may not be about to die, what we are likely to see is the continuous evolution of the package of which the printed textbook is part. This evolution is rooted in, and driven forward by, the competitive dynamic built into the adoption system. In order to win adoptions, the big textbook publishers will invest more and more in producing ever more elaborate packages, and more and more content, as well as practical exercises, tests and other forms of self-assessment, will be delivered online. Gradually the balance between content delivered in the printed textbook and content delivered online may shift more and more towards online delivery, especially in subjects where up-to-date content and dynamic visual representations are particularly important. However, whether the point will be reached when the printed text becomes little more than a manual to guide instructors and students through the resources available online, and when students pay by credit card for a PIN or password to gain access to the online resources, is much less clear. It could happen, and perhaps some subject areas will lend themselves to this kind of transformation more readily than others, but this is largely a matter of speculation.

(3)   The increasing use of course management systems in colleges and universities could have an impact on the provision of teaching and learning materials in the medium to long term. Course management systems, like Blackboard and WebCT, provide a common, cross-campus platform which enables staff and students to organize courses and share materials online. Already the big textbook publishers take care to ensure that the supplementary materials for their key textbooks are available in cartridges that can be plugged into the various course management systems that are in common use. At this stage, course management systems are used primarily for the purposes of administration – posting the syllabus, communication from faculty to students, communication between students, etc. At some point, however, course content could also migrate onto the course website – 'it's not hard for me to believe that content will start pouring through there at some point,' remarked one senior executive. For many courses, the course website could become increasingly important as the place to which students go for materials relating to the course, including teaching materials. How exactly this will affect the ways in which textbook publishers provide pedagogical content and whether

it will have any long-term impact on the sales of printed textbooks is at this stage unclear, but these are developments which the big textbook publishers are watching closely.

(4)   If we wish to understand how the provision of teaching and learning materials is changing and is likely to change in the future, we have to study these changes in the context of the pedagogical process itself. It is in the context of what I described earlier as the study space that the content provided by higher education publishers is actually taken up and used by students (or not used by them, as the case may be). And yet we know surprisingly little about what actually happens in the study space – how students study in different subject areas and in different kinds of institutions, what kinds of materials they use, how they use them and how these patterns are changing. On the whole, this is a topic that publishers have tended to neglect, because their reliance on the adoption system has generally meant that they have focused their interest only on what the professors want and they have assumed that students will buy what the gatekeepers tell them to buy. To a large extent, this traditional textbook model has worked, but there are many reasons why, in this rapidly changing information environment, it would be sensible to look more carefully at what students actually do and how their study practices are changing. The growing problem of sell-through breakdown suggests that in the context of escalating textbook prices, students may be finding other ways to do the work required of them, and in any case the adoption system has always operated with greater laxity in the UK. We simply don't know the extent to which students are relying on textbooks, whether purchased, borrowed or shared, or are availing themselves of other resources (including resources available, often for free, on the internet), and we know relatively little about how students actually use the materials on which they draw in their day-to-day study practices.

(5)   While the adoption system has never operated in a watertight fashion, it nevertheless remains a powerful factor shaping student decisions concerning the content they are likely to use within the pedagogical space. We may know relatively little about what students actually do in their day-to-day study practices, but we do know that they are in a position of knowledge dependency on their professors and instructors – they rely on them to a large extent for guidance through the subject they are studying and they trust them to provide sound advice about which literature is worth reading. Reading books is very demanding work, especially if they are long and the material is difficult, and most students don't wish to waste time and money buying and reading books which are not essential to the specific tasks they face within the study space. It would be unwise for those who wish to experiment with new technologies in the field of higher education publishing to ignore these powerful structures and constraints. Simply making content available in new media, without working closely with the professors and instructors who are the gatekeepers in the adoption system, seems unlikely to succeed, for students are likely to purchase access to content, regardless of the medium in which it is made available, only if they are required or strongly advised to do so by those upon whose guidance they depend. Trying to market pedagogical content directly to students, whether it is a traditional printed textbook or content made available online, is both extremely costly and unlikely to be effective, as Questia among others discovered to its cost.

(6)   While the traditional printed textbook is likely to remain a key component of the curriculum for the foreseeable future, there is a vibrant and expanding market for customized course materials which are tailored to the syllabuses of specific courses. In some respects, the growth of this market is both complementary to and a reflection of the limitations of the traditional textbook. As the competitive logic of the field has driven publishers to produce ever more comprehensive and standardized textbooks, many professors feel inclined to supplement (or even replace) these textbooks with materials that are tailored to the specific course they intend to teach, and many students resent having to pay high prices for large textbooks which contain a good deal of material they will never use. Sentiments of this kind have fuelled the growth of the custom publishing business and there is every reason to believe that this business will continue to grow. What is less clear at this stage is how the business will evolve and who the key players will be. The major textbook publishers have developed custom publishing divisions and have experienced some growth in this area, but the custom publishing business in the field of higher education in the US has hitherto been dominated by small local and regional players who have certain competitive advantages over the traditional textbook publishers. A key question for the future is how the custom publishing business will change, and how the small local players and traditional textbook publishers, as well as those involved in teaching within higher education institutions, will seek to use new technologies to provide pedagogical materials which are tailored more closely to the courses that professors want to teach.

(7)   One aspect of this is the extent to which electronic reserves – 'e-reserves' – will emerge as a significant component of the teaching materials used in higher education. There are parties in the field of higher education who have an interest in making course materials available online through local, campus-based intranets. For librarians, this would in principle reduce the costs involved and space required to manage their reserve collections. For professors, it would enable them to assemble materials from different sources and ensure that they were easily accessible to all students taking the course. And for students, it would enable them to access the course materials quickly and perhaps cheaply from the convenience of their home or dorm. On the other hand, in the absence of an agreed business model, e-reserves represent a real threat to publishers and authors who have invested time, effort and resources in developing and producing the materials which may find their way onto e-reserve lists. Publishers and librarians need to devise a new model which allows parts or chapters of books to be held electronically and accessed simultaneously for a limited period of time by the students taking a particular course, and which reimburses publishers with an appropriate fee. Unless their copyright is formally recognized and reimbursed in some way, publishers have no interest at all in allowing their content to appear in e-reserve collections. For publishers, unauthorized e-reserves are no different from backstreet copy shops which reproduce their content without permission – and, indeed, may even be worse, since the content made available in e-reserves can be accessed more easily and more cheaply than content reproduced by photocopying. While new technologies open up the possibility of developing much more efficient systems for making available customized course content via e-reserve collections, there is a deep-rooted conflict of interests here which can be resolved only by establishing an agreed framework for reimbursing copyright holders.

(8)   Another area where there may be some scope for growth is in the area of non-traditional, non-campus-based higher and further education. The success of the Open University in the UK and the growth of institutions like the University of Phoenix in the US suggest that non-campus-based higher and further education using distance learning models has the potential to expand access without incurring the costs and the relatively rigid time-space constraints associated with traditional campus-based education. These models are likely to prove particularly attractive to individuals who fall outside the 18–22 age group, who may be working and are keen to acquire or extend their qualifications; they may also prove to be attractive to individuals overseas who are keen to acquire qualifications from a British or American university without incurring the high costs associated with long-term residential courses. Some higher education publishers have collaborated with institutions of higher education to develop new business models for providing the pedagogical content and support services needed for distance learning courses of this kind. By working with HEIs to provide materials for accredited, degree-bearing courses, they have sought to expand the market for pedagogical materials while at the same time remaining within the framework of a formally recognized pedagogical process. Rather than relying exclusively on online resources, many of these initiatives have tried to achieve a balanced mix of pedagogical materials, both printed and online, and have combined distance learning with some degree of face-to-face tuition. The optimal mix of print versus online media, and of distance learning versus face-to-face tuition, is likely to vary from course to course depending on the subject matter and the nature and background of the student body, among other things. The cost of providing face-to-face tuition may be significantly higher than a course that relies on distance learning alone, but the pedagogical outcomes may be significantly enhanced as a result.

(9)   There are also opportunities for non-traditional publishers to play an innovative role in making pedagogical resources available online, as shown by the success of Literature Online. The fact that Chadwyck-Healey was not a traditional book publisher and had no stake in the medium of print undoubtedly increased its willingness to experiment with the online environment, and the fact that it was accustomed to working with large databases meant that it was in a good position to exploit the value-added features of online dissemination. But it took real insight to see that the databases it had built up had the potential to be used for pedagogical purposes, and it took a great deal of editorial effort and flair to adapt the content for different levels of the curriculum. One of the reasons why LION has succeeded is that it was not modelled on the structure and format of the traditional printed textbook but rather took advantage of the distinctive features of the online medium to create a rich but well-structured pedagogical environment. Another reason why it succeeded is that it was developed in consultation with gatekeepers at different levels of the curriculum and it was marketed and sold to institutions rather than to individuals. Literature Online is only one model for the development and dissemination of pedagogical content in an online environment, but it is a modest and instructive success story in a domain where success is rare.

15
The hidden revolution: reinventing the life cycle of the book

Much of the discussion concerning the impact of new technologies on the publishing industry has been focused on the question of whether the traditional printed book will be eclipsed by the delivery of content online, whether in the form of ebooks or by the development of more elaborate databases of electronic content. The fact that ebooks have failed to take off in the way that many predicted in the late 1990s has led some to believe that the digital revolution in the publishing industry has failed, that the promise has not been fulfilled and is likely to remain unfulfilled for the foreseeable future and that, so far as the book publishing industry is concerned, it's business as usual. But this would be a mistaken view. In fact, thanks to digitization, there is a revolution taking place within the publishing industry, but it's not exactly the kind of revolution that the ebook champions of the late 1990s had in mind. It's a quiet revolution, a hidden revolution, one which doesn't grab the attention of journalists and doesn't make dramatic headlines but which is steadily and profoundly transforming the working practices and business models of the publishing industry, indeed transforming the life of the book itself. It's not so much *a revolution in the product* as *a revolution in the process*: while the final product may look the same as the old-fashioned book, the process by which it is produced has been, and is being, radically transformed. The ebook is merely a symptom of a much more profound transformation which has taken place behind the scenes and which has reconstituted the book as a digital file – that is, as a database. And this hidden revolution has an ironic twist, for in some respects it has turned the prophecy of the ebook champions on its head: so far from spelling the demise of the printed book, the reconstitution of the book as a digital file has enabled publishers to bring old books back to life and to keep slow-selling titles in print in perpetuity.

In this final chapter I want to explore this hidden revolution in the publishing industry. I shall do so primarily with reference to the field of academic publishing, but most of the developments I discuss here have occurred, with various permutations, in other fields of publishing. I shall begin by examining the rise of the digital workflow and the development of digital content management systems. I shall then focus on the development of digital printing and the emergence of print on demand – developments which are of particular significance in the field of academic publishing, where print-runs tend to be low and where the economics of traditional offset printing make it difficult to keep many backlist titles in print. These developments have far-reaching implications for the very nature of book publishing as a business and for the very nature and life of the book itself, as we shall see.

The rise of the digital workflow

The hidden revolution in the book publishing industry began in the late 1980s and early 1990s, as digitization began to transform various aspects of the production process. Through a series of incremental changes that affected different aspects of the production process, a new workflow emerged that was increasingly digital in character. That is, the process of producing books, from the point at which the author's creative output is fixed in a durable medium to the point at which final printed books are delivered, was increasingly transformed into a process of capturing and manipulating content in digital formats. It is this transformation that I describe as the rise of the digital workflow.

The hidden revolution in the publishing industry began, to a large extent, in the sphere of typesetting. In the course of the 1980s, the typesetting business went through a series of dramatic changes as the old linotype machines, using hot metal, were replaced first by big IBM mainframe typesetting machines and then, in the early 1990s, by desktop publishing. These technological changes greatly reduced the costs of typesetting and, at the same time, led to a continuous redefining of the tasks of typesetters and of the organization of typesetting as a business. As one production manager at an American university press explained,

> When I got into the business in the 1970s, you would expect to pay $10 a page to get a book typeset from manuscript. It was set on a linotype machine, it was hot metal. Today we're doing that same page for somewhere between $4 and $5 a page – and you know where the dollar's gone in the last thirty years. So I always tell everybody, don't ever let your sons and daughters grow up to be typesetters. That is not the business to be in because that is a business that has totally changed in every manner that you could look at from an economic perspective. For one, it used to be very difficult to enter because it was heavy capital investment to buy these big cluggy metal machines. Then you reached a point where more people could get into it because you could rent an IBM machine from one of the bigger companies and you could set it up if you had the space and you knew how to run it. Now you can buy off-the-shelf software and you can run it in your home. So it's very easy entry and there's no capital expense of any consequence to speak of. Today anybody can present themselves as a typesetter. It's not like the days when you had journeymen line operators and people who did page make-up and it was highly organized and unionized. Now it's easy entry, anybody can get into it. The technology just drove the price down.

In retrospect, the transition from traditional typesetting to desktop publishing may look like a relatively quick and straightforward process, but at the time it was confusing for people in the industry as they tried to keep up with the changes, to adapt their working practices and to make sure that their systems meshed with those being used by their suppliers. Adapting to a constantly changing technological environment while at the same time maintaining quality was not always easy, especially because some of the new players who entered the field did not have the same skill sets as the traditional typesetter. 'You were giving up a lot that you got from a traditional typesetter – proofreading, three hyphenations in a row, widows, that kind of stuff,' recalled one production manager. 'Everybody was dabbling in desktop but I think in many ways floundering. They weren't making good books. I had one book where huge chunks of pages were missing, they just disappeared, nobody knew how or why. Everybody in the industry was

floundering but everybody was talking about the buzzwords – "yes, we're doing it."'
Lines of responsibility also became blurred. When a publisher paid the old-fashioned
compositor $10 or $12 a page, it knew exactly what it was getting, but what exactly was
it getting for $3 or $4 a page from the new typesetter? And if something went wrong,
whose responsibility was it? 'The rules were not defined anymore. So from a publisher's
production point of view, it was a very stressful time.'

The transformation of typesetting was fuelled by the development of word processing, which added a crucial new dimension. Up until the mid-1980s, authors always
worked on typewriters or pen on paper, and what they delivered to the publisher was
a typescript. The development of word processing software and the proliferation of PCs
in the late 1980s and 1990s opened up the possibility for authors to deliver something
quite different – namely, *keystrokes captured in a digital file*. In principle, this meant that
what the author had produced would not necessarily have to be rekeyed. As it turned
out, many publishers found that they did have to rekey after all, because authors didn't
follow publishers' instructions and didn't follow the instructions in the word processing software, and many authors who had grown up on typewriters didn't differentiate
between the letter O and zero 0, between hyphens and en-dashes, and so on. Moreover,
authors sometimes made further changes to the disk after they'd already printed out
the text, so the disk version and the printed version were sometimes not exactly the
same. For these and other reasons, it was often necessary to make many corrections to
the author's file, and it could be more expensive to make the corrections than to rekey
the text. 'The rule of thumb was that if you had more than eight or ten corrections on
a page, it was more cost-effective to actually rekey the entire page than to find the
correction, see where it is, make sure you're in the right spot and key it in.' However,
publishers found ways to overcome these problems and to streamline the process. For
instance, in the early 1990s one production manager contracted an outside firm to
develop a set of macros that would iron out the basic errors in the file and mark up the
text in a preliminary way before it went to the copy-editor:

> So basically what happens is they convert everything over from whatever the author's file
> had been. Then they dumped this out into a typeface design so you can clearly tell the dif-
> ference between O's and 0's and that sort of thing. Then they show what all the coding is
> – so that's a preface, that's a title and so on. It guaranteed the integrity of the file and the
> structure of the file for the typesetter. So it didn't matter who we sent the typesetting to,
> the files went the same way.

By outsourcing the author's file to a client who would run it through a set of macros,
the production department was able to clean up the file and make sure that it could be
used in the production process so that the text would not have to be rekeyed – 'we're
cleaning up the messes the authors leave with their work, that's essentially what we're
doing.' This was a somewhat unusual step because it altered the traditional workflow of
the production process. Normally a manuscript would go straight to copy-editing and
then on to production, but now the text was being put through a preliminary cleaning-
up process – 'initial prep', as some production managers called it – to ensure that the
file was usable and to do some preliminary coding. 'What we were saying was, if we get
this work done ahead of time, it was going to save us a ton of money. Not only that, it
was going to save us copy-editing time because the copy-editor doesn't have to mark

these things. It's already done. The only thing they have to mark is if they get it wrong, or if they want to change it.'

Copy-editing is traditionally an ink-on-paper activity: the copy-editor takes the manuscript, works on the style, corrects the grammar, checks to ensure that references are complete, etc., and marks up the text for the typesetter. Good copy-editors can transform the quality of a text by improving the style, eliminating repetition and spotting errors that the author had overlooked. But it is costly for a typesetter to key in all the changes and corrections made by the copy-editor, and these costs could be reduced significantly if the copy-editing could be done directly on screen. So in the early to mid 1990s, some production managers and managing editors began to press for onscreen editing. 'Basically we had to take editors who had been doing this the same way for whatever number of years and get them to change this,' explained one production manager. 'We had to show them the benefits of doing this.' The transition wasn't easy, however. Many copy-editors were accustomed to working on paper and were reluctant to change. Many worked as out-of-house freelancers and were not equipped or trained to edit onscreen, and in the early 1990s the available software was not user-friendly. As one managing editor at an American university press recalled,

> Initially we just experimented with a few books and a very esoteric, un-user-friendly software called Zywrite 3+. It was DOS-based – no Windows, no interface, it was just the flashing cursor and command driven, etc. It was like trying to remember the five hundred Chinese characters you need to read a newspaper – if you didn't do it every day, you'd forget. The advantage for typesetters was that it was almost pure ASCII, so when you sent the disk to the typesetter they didn't have to strip out all sorts of unneeded formatting and so on. So from the typesetter's standpoint, it was great. But in terms of its interface with non-technical, textually based people like editors, it wasn't fun.

When Zywrite 3+ was replaced by Zywrite 4, the press moved over to Microsoft Word, which was becoming more widely used. 'We developed an EMS [Electronic Manuscripts System] in Word and many copy-editors that we worked with already owned it and already knew how to use it. So it was just a matter of us developing our own customizations that would facilitate certain kinds of editorial changes so that fewer keystrokes would be involved.' Editors already used coding systems when they edited on paper, but the coding requirements on disk are more elaborate and more precise.

> So things that we had previously not coded had to be coded. For example, you could code a level 1 subhead H1 as we had always done, and a level 2 subhead H2 as we had always done, whether it was on paper or on disk, but if you had stacked subheads like a level 1 subhead immediately followed by a level 2 subhead, you also had to code the space in between because the space below a level 1 subhead would be different if it was immediately followed by an H2. We had to code that on the disk because we were supplying the disks to the typesetter. So there were additional coding requirements.

The copy-editors use the red-lining feature of Word which shows editorial changes both onscreen and in a printout. The comment function of Word can be used to query authors on specific points. The author is then sent the printout which shows the editorial changes and is asked to respond to the queries. The copy-editor takes account of the author's responses and produces a final, cleaned-up file.

Once editors got used to it, many saw the advantages of onscreen editing and realized that much of what they'd been doing was a waste of their time, but the transition wasn't easy. 'It was a rather long haul,' recalled one production manager. 'Some came kicking and screaming.' It was generally easier with in-house editors who could be properly equipped and retrained on site, but with more and more manuscripts being put out to freelancers, managers had to look for ways of encouraging and persuading individuals who were not on the publisher's payroll. 'Initially when we introduced onscreen editing to our freelancers, some were resistant, some were willing to try it, some were sceptical but tried it anyway, and so forth,' said one managing editor. 'With a few exceptions of people who decided to quit editing altogether, most of our editors, even ones who had worked for twenty-five years with a pencil, eventually came to say "This is a very powerful editorial tool. I actually prefer working onscreen."' The advocates of onscreen editing argue that it actually empowers editors to do highly accurate work. Editors are able to use the search function to increase accuracy and consistency. They are able to query more extensively 'because they are typing queries and they don't have to fit queries onto little yellow slips of paper and write and rewrite them and make them smaller and more legible and so on.' And they have the capacity to generate a clean printout of the edited version of the manuscript even though the red lining is still present. Moreover, editing onscreen reduces the need to key in editorial changes from a corrected manuscript, which can introduce new errors.

On the other hand, there are trade-offs in terms of editorial quality and ease of work that many editors will point to. If the text needs a lot of structural or developmental editing, such as substantial rewriting, cutting or reorganization, it can be difficult to do this onscreen. As one editor explained,

> Even on a large screen, you can only see about a paragraph and a half of text. It is just very hard somehow, at least for old horse-and-buggy editors like me, to work in that kind of visual environment. The visual memory seems to be so weak that you tend to think in terms of the paper presentation of a document. So, for example, if you've got a twenty-page chapter with a six-page digression, on paper you know that's too long a digression. When you are onscreen, you just keep scrolling up and down and saying 'will the readers remember or will they get confused?' You can't make that judgement somehow. So I find substantive editing – structure, organization, that kind of thing – very difficult to do on the screen.

For manuscripts that have a lot of non-Roman characters, such as Greek or Chinese characters, it may also not be practical or cost-effective to try to edit them onscreen. Nevertheless, many of the university presses have moved to onscreen editing, and some are editing 80–90 per cent of their manuscripts onscreen. This is not true of all publishers, however. Different publishers have different practices and workflows, and different types of publishers tend to work in different ways. Many trade publishers, for instance, continue to pencil edit and then input the edits on the author's disk at a later stage in the workflow.

Once the final copy-edited file has been produced, a version of this is given to the typesetter with instructions from the designer about how to produce the pages. Some books are individually designed, but many books are typeset according to standard designs which have been developed by the publisher. So what the publisher gives the typesetter is a final edited file, a list of any oddities in the manuscript and a set of style sheets that say this is in this size, to this measure, etc. The typesetter may already have a template set up for that design, often in Quark, which is a page make-up programme often used by typesetters for paging books. So it takes the files and converts them into a page layout. It then generates a set of page proofs which are returned to the publisher for correction. Since it is not rekeying, the typesetter can generate the page proofs much faster and more cheaply than in the past. However, since the publisher is supplying supposedly consistently and correctly prepared disks, almost every error that turns up in page proofs is the publisher's responsibility. 'There is hardly anything called a PE, printer's error, anymore,' explained one managing editor. 'They are almost all editorial errors. So whereas our direct per-page costs have gone down, our alteration bills have gone up. When you start adding those up, the savings diminish somewhat.' What has happened, in effect, is that the publisher has taken in-house a lot of the functions previously performed by composition vendors. 'So it is not a pure savings, from like $12 a page to $5 a page or something like that, because we have brought into the house additional work and responsibility.'

Given that the functions performed by the typesetter have changed so significantly, it is no longer necessary for publishers to work with high-end composition vendors. Once it has the disks, a publisher can hire a desk-topper working in Quark to page the book for it. Some smaller organizations have the designers paging books. 'So they are actually doing their own composition or they are outsourcing composition to cottage industry desk-toppers.' But many of the larger publishers continue to use high-end composition vendors. Why? Partly because larger publishers can get a volume discount. Smaller presses can get lower costs using desk-topping or cottage industry composition than by going to the high-end vendors because they can't get the kinds of discounts that the larger presses can get. Another reason is that by using high-end vendors, the responsibility for technology upgrades is the vendor's. As the managing editor at a large American university press observed,

> If we were just contracting job by job with individuals, then the next time this preparation has to be different because the printers are now doing this rather than that, we would have to figure that out and we would have to help our cottage industry people get up to speed with the new technology, whereas at present our composition vendors basically do that aspect of R&D for us. They invest in the new equipment and they invest in the new software and they figure out how to use it and they debug it. You know, technology is really expensive.

While new technologies have fundamentally transformed the role of the typesetter and have made it possible for typesetting to be done in-house or by freelance desk-toppers, most publishers still prefer to use composition vendors who will give them volume discounts and take responsibility for technology upgrades.

In the traditional workflow, the correction of page proofs was followed by camera-ready copy or CRC, but desktop typesetting applications enabled one to move to Post-Script and subsequently to PDF. Using PostScript was a huge step forward because it meant that the files could be sent to the printer and the printer could output directly to film, as opposed to outputting to CRC and then sending that to be photo-mechanically prepared. But the problem with PostScript was that it wasn't particularly stable. As one production manager explained, 'it was very easy for someone to make a mistake creating a PostScript file because they didn't load the right font or they didn't do this. So when you went to output it, sometimes you had problems. And because the files were so big, some of the imposition software choked on it. They didn't have the horsepower in their machines sometimes to output these things.' So around 1995 Adobe introduced what it called PDF – Portable Document Format – which is essentially a PostScripted file distilled down to eliminate all the extraneous information not needed to print or to output to some other device. 'Basically it cut the file structures by anywhere from 90 to 95 per cent and allowed you to run them on simpler machines. They were much more stable, but more importantly, they were page independent.' PostScript was a chapter or whatever size file you put it together with; the PostScript file covered everything in the whole chapter and you couldn't extract single pages from it. But PDF was page independent, which allowed you to output just one piece – e.g. one page – of a document if you wanted to. Another feature of PDF is that the font is embedded into the document that has been created. Hence anyone can view it or print it without having to have that font on their PC.

> That saved our butts a lot because printers would look and say 'Times Roman, we have Times Roman', but we would have to say 'No, put our Times Roman on because there are twenty-five versions of Times Roman out there.' If ours is not the same as theirs, hyphenation and justification rules don't apply because you might have a difference in the width of a character.

PDF quickly established itself as the de facto standard in publishing and in the graphic arts. 'PDF has really revolutionized how we work,' explained one production manager. It became an intrinsic part of the workflow process. The typesetter creates a PDF of the final corrected page proofs and writes it to a CD-ROM. (At an earlier stage in the workflow, the typesetter might also be asked to create a PDF of the uncorrected page proofs and load that onto an FTP site so that a bound galley printer can download it and do a short print-run of, say, a hundred copies. It used to take six weeks to produce bound galleys; now it can be done in five days.) The printer uses the PDF files to create film, from which it produces the plates to be used in offset printing in the traditional way.

While the basic techniques of offset printing have remained unchanged for several decades, there are at least three important changes that are taking place in the printing industry today. First, it is becoming increasingly common for printers to use new technologies which enable them to generate plates directly from PDF files – 'computer-to-plate' or CTP as it is commonly called. Once the PDF has been through a pre-press screening process, it can be used to produce directly the aluminium plates which are used in offset printing, thereby bypassing the traditional photo-mechanical process of producing plates through film. This simplifies and greatly speeds up the production of plates: using CTP, it takes just over half an hour to produce the sixteen plates needed for a typical 256-page book, whereas with the old system of film making, it would have taken around four hours.

Second, the litho printing presses themselves have been revolutionized by the application of computer technology. (This is also true of other aspects of book manufacture, such as the binding process.) The latest generation of litho presses incorporates sophis-

ticated digital technologies which improve the quality of the printing and further auto-
mate the printing process, thus reducing significantly the make-ready time and speeding up the rate at which sheets are printed. Five years ago, the average make-ready was
22 minutes; now it takes 7 minutes on average to prepare the press for printing.

The third major development in printing technology was the emergence of digital
printing and print on demand, which have created an alternative to traditional offset
printing. This is a development which has far-reaching implications for the publishing
business (and for academic publishing in particular), and I shall devote a section to it
below. But first we should examine another important development in the rise of the
digital workflow.

The management of digital assets

As the production workflow became increasingly file-based, production managers
became increasingly conscious of the need to develop reliable and secure methods of
storing their digital files. The traditional practice was that when publishers wanted to
reprint a book, they contacted the printers who went into their warehouse and pulled
the film flats. Publishers hoped that the printers were still holding the film, although in
some cases – especially with older titles and books that had been put out of print – they
could find that the printer had gone through their filing systems and got rid of the film.
With the rise of the new digital workflow in the 1990s, many publishers were generating files but they had not developed any systematic way of storing them. 'You would
have boxes and boxes of big 5^1/$_2$-inch floppies lying around everywhere,' recalled one
production manager. 'So we began asking "How are we going to store all this stuff?"
Printers, pre-press houses, jacket people started investigating ways, on-site and off-site,
to store all this.'

There was another reason why, in the late 1990s, many publishing houses became
increasingly conscious of the need to gather together the digital files for the books they
had published: speculation about ebooks was gathering pace and various ebook vendors
began knocking on their doors. They were looking for content and, while many of the
ebook vendors were willing to shoulder the costs of conversion in the early days, this
development heightened the sense among publishers that their content was an asset
that could potentially be exploited in different ways, not just in the traditional format
of the printed book. Publishers began to see that their content – the data that were the
outcome of the digital workflow process – were themselves an asset that needed to be
managed. 'The key is treating your data like an asset, not treating the book that is in
the warehouse as the asset,' explained one senior manager. 'The book is an asset, it is.
But the data are an asset too and the data are of a higher value.' Depending on the
format in which the data are stored, the publisher may be able to generate new revenue
streams by, for example, licensing the content to virtual libraries, ebook vendors or other
third parties. So if publishers could develop a secure and reliable way of storing their
content in a suitable digital format, then they would have more control of their core
asset and would be able to make it available in different ways depending on the opportunities that arose.

For these and other reasons, many publishers became increasingly concerned in the
late 1990s to develop an integrated content management system with a central archiv-

ing database. The idea was to incorporate the archive into the digital workflow, as illustrated by figure 15.1. At the same time as the final PDF was sent to the printer, a copy could be stored in a central archive which could be located either on-site or off-site, and which would provide an accurate and up-to-date repository for the publisher's digital content. If in future the publisher wanted to reprint the book and the printer no longer held the film, or if the publisher wanted to do a digital reprint or put the book into a print-on-demand scheme, the PDF would be available. If opportunities arose to exploit the content electronically through an ebook vendor or some other channel, then the publisher would at least have the content stored digitally, even if it required further conversion before it could be used by a particular vendor. The publisher would also have files which could be used for future editions if necessary, as well as jackets and other artwork that could be used for marketing purposes.

While the idea of a digital archive emerged as a key component of an integrated digital workflow, there were many difficult tasks and complex issues that had to be addressed. Here I shall briefly consider three: (1) file collection, (2) the PDF/XML dilemma, and (3) the recovery of legacy content.

(1) *File collection*   In the first place, publishers had to figure out what digital assets they actually had. This was more complicated than it might at first seem. Although many publishers began producing from files in the early to mid 1990s, initially from PostScript and subsequently from PDF, they generally didn't keep the files – they sent them off to the printer and that was it. Once the printer had used the PDF to create the film, it often disposed of the file. So in the late 1990s, when publishers began to think about working with ebook vendors, reprinting books digitally or putting older titles into print-on-demand schemes, they had to look around to see whether they still had a file and, if not, they had to scan the book to generate a new PDF – a process that not only added cost but also resulted in a lower quality product. Some production managers went back to the compositors to see whether they kept copies of the original files – sometimes they did, sometimes they didn't, and, in any case, it wasn't always clear whether the older files could still be used, since in older systems the illustrations were stripped in conventionally rather than incorporated into the files. But such was the scale of the change taking place in the industry in the 1990s that inquiries of this kind generated anxiety among typesetters, who feared that they might lose work. 'Compositors started getting frightened, "Why does she want this?",' recalled one production manager. 'I made a firm statement that it would not jeopardize the work you do for me, it would only enhance it. I explained that we were thinking of doing ebooks, so please don't be frightened, but a lot of people were very frightened by this.'

On the whole, publishers discovered that they had a lot less content held in digital files than they would have liked. Some discovered that they had no files at all for books published before 1997 or 1998, for example, while others found that the files they did have were corrupt or unusable for some reason. They soon realized that if they wanted to recover older content and make it available again, they would have to develop a conversion programme to create new files from printed books. Since some of the virtual libraries and other ebook vendors were at that stage offering to do free conversion in order to acquire content, some publishers tried to negotiate deals which would enable them to acquire the files in return, either as part of the original deal or subsequently as a buy-back. As one production manager recalled,

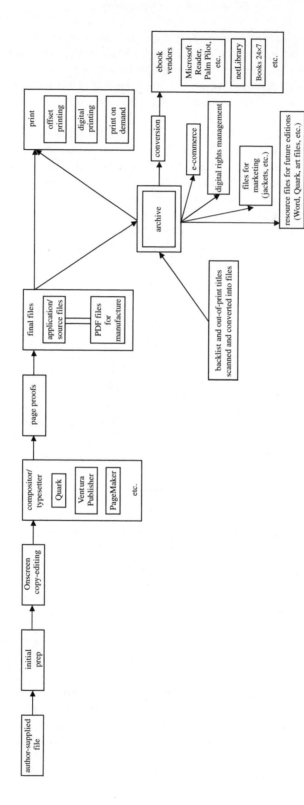

Figure 15.1 The digital workflow

I remember going to netLibrary at one point and saying, 'Could I buy back my files?' and they're like, 'Why would you want to do that?' I'm thinking, we're going to put them in this big database and we're going to save our stuff like I save everything else, but I was also thinking we could do things with them. 'No, no, that's not in our plan, we're not doing that', at least that's what the woman told me. But she said, 'let me think about it', and then I never heard a word from them, nothing. A year later they had a whole new division selling back files.

If publishers were unable to buy files back from the virtual libraries or other ebook vendors, they would have to look for other ways of converting texts into files. Some of the third parties involved in digital printing and print on demand were offering free conversion to PDF under certain conditions, and many publishers took advantage of this. Others developed their own programmes to digitize their backlist, funding this either from their own resources or from external grants or partnerships with technology firms.

Once a publisher had collected whatever files it was able to find, it had to decide how and where to store them. Some opted to build a digital repository in-house, while others opted to lodge the archive in an off-site facility. The advantage to a publisher of building its own repository in-house is that it keeps full control of its resources, but some publishers preferred to hand this over to a technology partner who could take responsibility for building and maintaining the archive. While outsourcing the archive came at a price, it meant that the publisher could leave the technical issues to others and didn't have to tie up the time of its own staff. ('Why do I want three people sitting in here doing that?' commented one production manager. 'It's a hassle. The bottom line is, if I'm going to pay someone to work in production, I want them producing books out the door.') Outsourcing the archive also meant that someone else would be responsible for keeping on top of technical updates and converting files to the latest versions when necessary.

(2)   *The PDF / XML dilemma*   If publishers wanted to store their digital assets in PDF, then the digital workflow that emerged in the course of the 1990s was well tailored for this end. In the late 1990s, PDF became the de facto standard in the publishing industry and the final files prepared by the typesetter were in this format. The publisher could simply ask the typesetter to produce two copies – one for the printer and one for the archive. The new digital workflow would ensure that for all frontlist titles, there would be a PDF in the archive, and the only issue for the publisher then was whether it needed to create a PDF for those backlist titles where no PDF existed. However, this picture was rendered much more complicated by the issues surrounding SGML and XML.

SGML (Standard Generalized Markup Language) and its sequel, XML (the Extensible Markup Language), are metalanguages that enable the creation of unique mark-up schemes for tagging particular kinds of content. SGML was developed in the early 1980s as a non-proprietary generic mark-up language and adopted as an international standard in 1986.[1] XML was developed as a subset of SGML that was simpler and easier to implement on the web; it was released in 1998 and was quickly accepted as a stan-

[1] See William E. Kasdorf (ed.), *The Columbia Guide to Digital Publishing* (New York: Columbia University Press, 2003), pp. 74ff.

dard. Documents marked up in SGML or XML can be converted into HTML (Hyper-Text Markup Language), which is the mark-up language used to display documents on the web. XML has also become a basis for other standards. For example, the Open eBook Publication Structure (OEBPS) is an XML-based standard for tagging files to be used in ebooks. It was devised by an industry-based group called the Open eBook Forum that was convened to try to create open, non-proprietary standards for ebooks.

In the course of the 1990s, SGML and XML were widely used in journal publishing, reference publishing and other areas where it was clear that there was real potential for electronic publication. Among book publishers, debates raged about whether the content for books, too, should be marked up in SGML, and later XML. If this is going to be done, the most efficient and cost-effective way to do it is to mark up the text early on in the production cycle, before the final file is created by the typesetter. This requires the marking-up process to be built into an early stage of the workflow. But this adds complexity and cost, and the question publishers had to ask themselves was whether the benefits to be gained by marking up texts in SGML or XML were sufficient to justify the additional effort and expense.

Publishers took different views on this question, but they fell essentially into two camps. On the one hand, there were those who argued that the workflow should be re-engineered so that all books going through the system would have SGML or XML built into them. In essence, books would be built as databases that incorporated SGML or XML tagging, so that the final files could be used both for printing books in the traditional way and for delivering content in different electronic formats. This would maximize the potential of the content and enable the publisher to exploit it in both print and electronic media. On the other hand, there were those who argued that this was overkill and that, if SGML or XML tagging was going to be built into a text, it should be done very selectively and only in those instances where there was a clear revenue-generating opportunity for electronic exploitation – for example, in the case of a major reference work. The proponents of the comprehensive approach argued that by building SGML or XML into all new books, the press would be putting itself in a position of maximum flexibility with regard to the future, even if it was not entirely clear at this stage how the opportunities for electronic exploitation would evolve. It was like taking out a technological insurance policy on an uncertain future. The proponents of the selective approach argued that it was a waste of time and resources to build SGML or XML into all new books when it was still very unclear whether ebooks and other forms of electronic dissemination would take off. It would be much better, in their view, to invest the extra cost and effort only in those cases where there were concrete plans for marketing the content in an electronic format as well as in print.

Some of the early attempts to implement the comprehensive approach turned out to be costly failures. In the mid-1990s some presses tried to re-engineer their workflows so that they could build in SGML up-front, as part of the initial preparation of the files. It turned out to be enormously complicated; every manuscript came in with new elements, and the coding list kept changing and getting longer. Project editors and freelance copy-editors just couldn't cope – 'it was like being asked to run laps while they were performing open heart surgery on you,' recalled one editor. In some cases, these early experiments had to be abandoned and they left a bitter legacy that persists to the present day. 'It finished badly and the whole system fell apart. It was a very dark era of our history.'

More recently, however, some presses have successfully re-engineered their work-flows using XML, which is much simpler than SGML and easier to use. In the case of one large university press, for example, the author's file is sent to an outside client who does a first round of XML tagging before the copy-editing begins. The copy-editor then works on a text that has already been marked up. The workflow results in an XML-tagged file which is, in effect, a database that can be lodged in the archive. One output of this database is a PDF which can be sent to the printer, but other outputs can be generated – it can be turned into a file for Microsoft Reader or Palm Pilot or anything else. In other words, the creation of the PDF is not the outcome of the structured workflow but is simply one of the outputs of the XML file – 'it is just an on-the-fly output of the database which you've created,' explained a senior manager. The XML file is a versatile file which can be used for different purposes – even if, in practice, it is used at present primarily to generate a PDF for the printer. Moreover, if the workflow is structured properly, producing XML files may not cost any more – indeed, it could even cost less. And if a publisher can make it cost less and at the end of the day get a better and more versatile file, while at the same time increasing the quality and the speed of the whole process, then a comprehensive solution of this kind seems to make a good deal of sense.

However, there are many in the publishing industry who doubt whether it is worth-while to try to restructure the workflow across the board so that all books are produced as XML files. They can't see the point in investing the extra time and effort (and perhaps the extra cost) in producing an XML file when the only revenue-generating output they can envisage at present is the use of a PDF to print books. Many production managers are particularly sceptical. They have been trained in the graphic arts and they are comfortable working with PDF; to them, it seems pointless to get involved in XML tagging if there is no discernible benefit in the foreseeable future. 'I just think PDF is the way to go,' explained one production manager at an American university press:

> There are other people here who want to go to XML. Twenty-five years ago they wanted to go to SGML – there's a very funny definition of SGML, not Standard Generalized Markup Language, but Sounds Good Maybe Later – and XML is really a derivative of that. But it's still a highly complex coding system that you've put into your document and if you haven't made it up into pages you still can't print it out as a book. So if we have this extra level of XML, I think we're just adding cost to what we're doing. So I've been very resistant about going the XML route. If I were in the scientific journal business or if I was in an elementary schoolbook division where I was reusing stuff all the time, that might be a different story, but our books are our books. We don't make many hybrids and we don't do a lot of crazy things with them and reissue them in different formats and things. I think we're better off where we are, just with PDF.

For this production manager, it makes more sense to archive the PDF because the press is primarily and fundamentally a print business and is likely to remain so for the fore-seeable future. If an ebook vendor wants to use the file, then it can give the PDF to a subcontractor to convert, and the conversion cost can then be weighed against the likely revenue. 'I think that's better because then it's pay as you go. Then we can figure out how many ebooks we'll have to sell to get our money back, as opposed to how many ebooks we have to sell to pay for XML files on every single manuscript that comes through here.'

The issues are made more complicated by the fact that PDF is not restricted to a print-based environment: a text in PDF can also be used in an electronic environment and read onscreen with the Adobe Acrobat Reader, which is freely available. Some of the virtual libraries – notably ebrary – have taken advantage of this and have built their services around PDF, thus enabling them to minimize the cost and effort involved in converting publishers' files. In an online environment, PDF files have some disadvantages – for example, they tend to be much larger than XML files in terms of memory since they capture the visual layout of the page, and hence they take longer to download. Moreover, although structure can be added to a PDF so that the file is searchable, the degree of functionality is generally lower than it would be if XML tagging were built into the file. Nevertheless, the question that publishers (and others like ebrary) had to ask themselves was whether the disadvantages of using PDF in an online environment were outweighed by the advantages of using a file which was already the standard format used in the publishing industry.

While the PDF/XML dilemma has divided the publishing community, this is one area where advances in software are likely to reduce or even eliminate the gulf between the two sides. Already Microsoft Word provides a pull-down menu which enables a word document to be converted into an HTML file which can be posted as a web page. It is possible that, before long, something similar could be done with XML. If so, then the task of building XML tagging into an author's file would be essentially an automated process – the file could simply be saved as XML. It is also likely that new developments in software will make it increasingly easy and cost-effective to convert typesetting files into structured XML content. In the meantime, it is perfectly understandable that many publishers who see their businesses as fundamentally print-based, and who have yet to see any significant new revenue streams emerging from electronic dissemination, should stick with a digital workflow that, for the vast majority of their books, results in a PDF that can be both sent to the printer and stored in the archive. If they have particular projects, such as a large reference work, or if they are developing an electronic publishing programme for all or part of their list and have a clear sense of how the programme will be implemented and how a revenue stream will be generated, then they could modify the workflow for these projects or parts of the list to ensure that XML tagging is built into the texts. But at the current stage of technological development, there is an understandable reluctance on the part of many production managers to re-engineer the basic workflow so that all books, rather than simply the exceptional books, are produced with XML-structured content. Given the limited opportunities currently available for electronic exploitation of book content, there is a risk that one would be investing considerable time and effort (and perhaps extra expense) to produce a fleet of Rolls-Royces when Toyotas would do.

(3) *The recovery of legacy content* The above discussion was concerned with frontlist titles – that is, with the kind of workflow a publisher needs in order to ensure that for its new titles, it ends up with files of a certain kind that can be stored in a digital archive. But a great deal of a publisher's content lies in its backlist – in the hundreds or even thousands of titles that were published in previous years and decades, many of which may be long out of print. With the coming of the digital revolution, publishers have begun to see this legacy content in a new light. In the 1980s and before, once the sales of a book had fallen below a certain level – say 200 or 300 copies a year in the case of

an academic publisher, higher in the case of a trade publisher – the book was often put out of print when the stock ran out (or even, in some cases, before the stock ran out). Given the economics of offset printing, it was often too expensive to reprint a book that was selling slowly, and it was often wiser to put the book out of print than to reprint more copies than were needed in order to get a decent margin and then find that stock had to be written down in two or three years' time. In some cases when books were put out of print, the publishers wrote to authors and formally reverted the rights to them. But in many cases, older titles were simply left to languish on the backlist, sometimes continuing to sell a few copies each year or to build up mythical back orders that would never be fulfilled.

But in the 1990s, this traditional view of legacy content underwent a fundamental transformation. Two factors drove the change. First, as the virtual libraries and ebook vendors began knocking on doors, publishers realized that their legacy content could in principle be repurposed in an electronic medium and might even be capable of generating an additional revenue stream. However, to take advantage of this possibility, the content had to be converted into a suitable format. The second factor which drove the re-evaluation of legacy content was the development of digital printing and print on demand, which became increasingly important in the book publishing world from around 1998 on. The emergence of print-on-demand fulfilment operations like Lightning Source enabled publishers to see that their legacy content could remain an asset even if it was only selling at a snail's pace. Slow-selling titles could be maintained in a state of permanent availability even when the existing supplies of stock ran out, and older titles that had run out of stock or even been put out of print could be made available again, thus generating revenue streams that would otherwise have been lost. But once again, to take advantage of this possibility, legacy content that existed only in the form of a printed book had to be converted into a suitable digital format – and in some cases, the book itself had to be found.

As it happens, the two factors that drove the re-evaluation of legacy content required different kinds of conversion. For the purposes of digital printing and print on demand, it is sufficient simply to scan the text and produce a PDF. The book is usually destroyed in the process, since the spine is sliced off so that the pages can be fed through a scanner. The scanning process results in a bitmapped file known as a TIFF (Tag Image File Format) file which captures the image of the page in pixels. The image may need to be realigned (scanned pages are often not entirely straight) and cleaned up (removing marks or smudges, for example), but the text is not altered in any way and no functionality is added; the file is simply an image of the printed page. The TIFF file can then be enclosed in a PDF wrapper and used for digital printing and print on demand. The whole process is relatively simple and cheap – as little as 15 or 20 cents a page, or around $30–40 for a simple 200-page book. However, if one wishes to convert a printed book into a digital file which enables the text to be altered and/or which enables it to be used by a range of ebook vendors, then the conversion process is more costly and complex. The text either has to be rekeyed or scanned and processed using OCR (Optical Character Recognition) software. Both rekeying and OCR introduce the possibility of errors, so the digitized text generally has to be proofread and corrected (perhaps several times). And if the text is to be marked up properly in XML, this tagging has to be added. All of these operations add cost, and the total cost varies depending on the amount of work, on where the work is done, the size and complexity of the text, the level of accuracy required in the data capture and the thoroughness with which the file is tagged. A typical cost from a conversion vendor is around $1.50 per page, or around $300 for a 200-page book – in other words, it is about ten times the cost of a simple scan. The $1.50 charge would be for a no-frills conversion of a straightforward text; it would cost more if the book was longer or more complex, if it contained figures, tables and mathematical formulae, if there was a need for more elaborate tagging, hyperlinking with the index, etc. The conversion work is usually done overseas, in countries such as India, China, Malaysia or the Philippines, where the labour costs are much lower than they are in the West.

For the most part, publishers have adopted an ad hoc, piecemeal approach to the recovery of legacy content and have sought where possible to defray the costs of conversion onto third parties. In the late 1990s, when the virtual libraries and ebook vendors were eager to acquire content, it was possible for publishers to negotiate deals for the free conversion of backlist titles. However, as the venture capital funds which got the virtual libraries off the ground began to dry up, the resources available for free conversion became much harder to find. Some of the university presses were able to secure funding from charitable foundations, such as the Mellon Foundation, to help defray the costs of conversion for some of their backlist titles, and one university press – MIT – worked out a deal with Hewlett-Packard to share the costs and work involved in converting its backlist. The days of free and subsidized conversion may be over, but the questions that publishers need to ask themselves about their legacy content remain. The key questions are: (1) how much of the backlist do they need to convert, (2) for what purpose, (3) to what level of sophistication, and (4) at what cost?

Publishers have tended to respond to these questions in one of two ways. On the one hand, some publishers have taken the view that all or a significant part of the backlist should be reconstituted as XML files. In other words, the sausages should be put back into the meat grinder and churned out again in a versatile digital format that would enable the content to be repurposed in a variety of ways – sold as ebooks, incorporated into web-based databases, made available again as printed books through digital printing or print on demand. But the issue here is whether publishers can justify the cost and effort involved in reconstituting the backlist as XML files if the uses to which these files may be put remain at this stage very unclear. And if publishers don't know what uses the files may have at some future date, can they be sure at this stage that they know how best to reconstitute the files, how much functionality to add, what level of granularity (or level of tagging) is necessary and so on? As one senior manager observed, 'if you are going to take a book out of the warehouse and make it into something electronic, you only want to do that once and you want to do it properly. Do we know how to do that now?'

On the other hand, many publishers have adopted a more pragmatic approach to their legacy content. If the purpose of converting backlist titles is simply to keep them in print or make them available again by reprinting them digitally or putting them into a print-on-demand scheme, then there is no real point in going to the extra cost and effort involved in converting the book into a fully functional digital file – it is sufficient simply to scan the book and produce a PDF that can be used by the digital printer. It is much cheaper and the cost of conversion may be covered by the digital printer or print-on-demand service. It will not give the publisher the kind of flexibility offered if the text had been rekeyed or put through OCR software and tagged in XML. But if the publisher does not foresee any use for the file apart from digital printing or print on demand, then the basic scan and PDF may be quite sufficient.

Digital printing and print on demand

While the future of ebooks and other forms of electronic dissemination may be shrouded in uncertainty, there is one development which has had a growing impact on the book publishing world since the late 1990s: digital printing and print on demand. The basic technology for digital printing has been around since the late 1970s, but it was not until the 1990s that the technology was developed in ways that would enable digital printing to become a serious alternative to the traditional offset presses. The advantages of offset printing are that the quality of reproduction is generally very high and, once the printing job has been set up, the cost per page is low. Hence offset printing works well for printing books with long print-runs – the longer the print-run, the lower the unit cost. Offset printing is more difficult in the case of short print-runs, however, because the set-up costs involved in preparing the plates, etc., have to be incurred regardless of whether one is printing 500 or 5,000 books. So for short print-runs of 500 copies or fewer, it is often uneconomic to use offset printing – the unit cost would simply be too high to justify the printing given the price at which the publisher believes the book should be sold.

Most digital printers are toner-based printing devices in which toner particles adhere to a photoconductive drum in patterns that are determined by laser beams or light-emitting diodes; the toner is then transferred to paper and fused in place, usually by a hot roller. To be useful for book printing, the devices have to be of sufficiently high resolution to approximate the quality of offset printing, they have to be sufficiently fast to enable a book to be printed in a relatively short time period, and the cost per page has to be sufficiently low to make the printing economic. By the early 1990s, with the appearance of Xerox's DocuTech printer and similar machines from other manufacturers, the quality, speed and cost per page of digital printing devices were beginning to reach levels at which they could compete with offset printing on short print-runs. The quality was not as high and the reproduction of halftones remained distinctly inferior, but with improvements in technology the quality was getting better and better. By the end of the decade, the reproduction quality for straight text was, to the untrained eye, indistinguishable from offset printing, although there was still a discernible difference in the quality of halftones.

As the technology improved, a number of players emerged in the mid to late 1990s offering a range of digital printing services to publishers. Of particular significance in this context were two services: *print on demand* (POD) and *short-run digital printing* (SRDP). POD is the printing of a document in response to the demand of a particular end user. So, for example, if an individual consumer asks for a book, then the book can be printed to meet the request. Essentially, POD is a fulfilment system which uses digital printing to fulfil a specific order. If the book can be printed in response to the order, then in principle there would be no need to keep stock of the book sitting in the warehouse: the book could be kept simply as a digital file on a server and the file would be called up if and when it was needed to produce a printed copy of the book. Physical stock could be replaced by a 'virtual warehouse'. SRDP is simply the use of digital printers to produce small quantities of books – anything from 10 or 20 copies to 300 or 400 copies. It works within the same distribution model as books printed by traditional means – the publisher orders books to be printed, the books are shipped to the publisher's warehouse where they are held in stock and copies are then distributed through the normal channels in the normal way. The only difference is that the books are printed digitally and the quantities are smaller than they would be if the books were printed by traditional offset.

Print on demand emerged out of the business of producing and supplying manuals and documents for the software industry. In the late 1980s, IBM and Kodak entered into a partnership to develop a print-on-demand system for managing around 30,000 documents that could be combined with software products in a variety of different ways and shipped anywhere in the world with a four- to five-day delivery cycle. The logistic problems of organizing a system of this kind were huge, but by 1994 the system was up and running. The organization that created and ran this system became Danka Services International. It was essentially an outsourcing company that produced documents for other companies, in some cases using print-on-demand methods. In August 1997, Ingram, the book wholesaler based just outside Nashville, Tennessee, began to collaborate with IBM and Danka to see whether they could develop a print-on-demand system for books. Ingram wanted to be able to print books in response to an order – no inventory, true just-in-time printing. The whole idea was to reverse the traditional way of thinking which underpinned the publishing industry. As one of the senior managers involved in setting up the system explained, 'It used to be print book, sell book. We say no, no. Sell book, print book.' The printing technology existed and Danka had already developed much of the operational know-how, but the question was whether the costs could be kept low enough to make it economically viable. To achieve this required two things: the whole fulfilment process had to be made as automated as possible, since every time an individual handles an order or a book, it adds cost; and the business had to be scaled up quickly to achieve a high volume of throughput.

> You had to have volume because you had to price initially in such a way so that you could overcome what were very aggressive pricing strategies by commercial printers in the marketplace and still allow everyone within the supply chain to make enough money to make it an interesting business for them. So we looked at this thing six ways to Sunday and said yes, we can do this, but we're going to lose money in the beginning of this thing big time.

This was the beginning of Lightning Print, subsequently renamed Lightning Source, which was to become one of the key players in the print-on-demand business.

Lightning Source set up its POD systems between October and December 1997 and produced its first saleable book in January 1998. It also began knocking on the doors of publishers and trying to persuade them to put some of their titles into the scheme. It wasn't easy, because publishers were accustomed to working in a particular way and it had to try to get them to think differently. 'Here's the way it went,' recalled a senior manager from Lightning Source:

> A normal process for a publisher was to sit down in a smoke-filled room, figure out how many books a particular title might sell and roll the dice with a commercial printer for anywhere from 3,000 to 300,000 copies, whatever it is. Then it was cross your fingers and wait

and see how many get returned. Our proposition was different. Our proposition was give us the content, let us put it in our library, don't worry about the supply chain, don't worry about the sales. Give us the books, we'll line up the channels, we'll interface with the retail community, we'll produce the book, we'll distribute the book and at the end of the month we'll tell you how many you've sold and send you a cheque. It was kind of like – 'Let me understand this. You want me to take my company assets, put them in your library and you are going to tell me how many I sold? I have no idea. You could be sending these things to China and I wouldn't know.' We said, yes, that's exactly right. So you can imagine it took a little while for the publishers to get there.

The fact that Lightning Source was part of Ingram undoubtedly helped to win over many publishers, since Ingram was the largest wholesaler in the US and was already well known and trusted in the publishing world. Nevertheless, growth was slow. It took two years, until the end of 1999, to get 5,000 titles into the system and by then it was only printing 30,000–40,000 books a month – not enough to get the scale it needed. It expanded its services and began to market itself more aggressively to publishers, offering incentives (such as free conversion) to encourage them to participate. In the course of 2000 it grew rapidly: by the end of 2000 it had 20,000 titles in the library and it was printing 150,000 books a month.

Lightning Source began as a print-on-demand service but it quickly evolved into three distinct business lines. One line is what it calls the 'distribution model': the publisher sets up a title in the Lightning Source library; the bookseller or library supplier orders a book from the wholesaler; the wholesaler sends the order to Lightning Source, who prints the book and sends it to the wholesaler; and the wholesaler then ships the book to the bookseller or library supplier. Lightning Source pays the publisher the list price less the wholesaler's and retailer's discount (say 50 per cent for a full trade discount) and less the cost Lightning Source charges for printing the book (say around $4.80 for a 300-page book with a laminated cover). So if the list price was, say, $30, the publisher would receive $10.20, from which it would pay author's royalties using its normal royalty scales. If the book was being sold at a short discount (say 35 per cent for the combined wholesaler and retailer discount), then $14.70 would be remitted to the publisher. Lightning Source takes the orders, prints the books in response to the orders, puts them into the established distribution channels and sends the publisher a statement at the end of the month telling it how many books it has sold and enclosing a cheque.

Lightning Source also developed a second model in which it operated like a virtual warehouse for the publisher – variously called the 'virtual warehouse' or 'drop ship' model. In this model, the publisher continues to take individual orders for a title but rather than keeping the title in stock, it sends the orders to Lightning Source as though it was an extension of their warehouse – a virtual warehouse. The order is accompanied by a 'ship to' address. Lightning Source prints the book, packs it up and puts the publisher's label on it and ships the book directly to the destination defined by the order – that is, drop ships it. In this case, Lightning Source invoices the publisher for the print cost plus a shipping and handling charge, and the publisher collects the revenue from the customer. To make the virtual warehouse model work, Lightning Source establishes an EDI (Electronic Data Interchange) with the publisher so that everything is automated. 'Humans can't touch the order process – it won't work. The economics will not work.' The interfaces effectively integrate the order management system of the publisher with the order management system of Lightning Source, so that the orders can flow directly from the publisher to Lightning Source and get fulfilled directly to the customer. 'More than 90 per cent of our books go out the door in twenty-four hours. A hundred per cent go out the door in forty-eight hours. That's a hell of a good turnaround time.' This model can also work by establishing an EDI connection with the publisher's distributor. In this case, the distributor would act as the publisher's agent, picking up orders for the publisher's books and forwarding them directly to Lightning Source for fulfilment.

In both the distribution model and the drop ship model, the customer who receives the book need not know anything about the systems which lie behind the fulfilment of the order. It is up to the publisher to decide whether it wishes to announce that a book is available through POD. So far as Lightning Source is concerned, it is providing a supply chain service to publishers and it is for the publisher to decide whether it wishes to make this explicit. 'We are invisible,' explained one Lightning Source manager. 'We are the supply chain service provider and we don't want to be visible.' The name 'Lightning Source' appears discreetly on the copyright page as the printer, but apart from that, there may be no visible sign that the book was fulfilled through POD. The customer may not know whether the book comes from a real warehouse or a virtual warehouse, whether it comes directly from the publisher or from a third party, and in all likelihood will not be able to tell whether it was printed digitally or by traditional offset. So long as the book arrives quickly, the quality is high and the price is reasonable, why should it matter to the customer how the book is printed and supplied?

Lightning Source also found that there was a growing demand from publishers for short-run digital printing and it turned this into a separate line of business. Lightning Source had begun as a POD service but increasingly it found itself responding to orders from publishers for short-run digital reprints – by 2001, POD accounted for around 60 per cent of the books it produced, while SRDP accounted for around 40 per cent. Publishers used Lightning Source to replenish their stock – that is, as an inventory management partner who could supply short and ultra-short print-runs of books which were selling slowly but which they wanted to keep in stock. In this case, Lightning Source operated simply like a printer: it took orders to print a given number of books, it printed them, shipped them to the publisher's warehouse and billed the publisher for the books printed.

In 2001 Lightning Source expanded internationally, opening a UK office in Milton Keynes and establishing an alliance with Bertram's, the second-largest wholesaler in the UK. This enabled Lightning Source to develop closer working relations with UK-based publishers and to provide digital printing facilities which are situated in the UK. Given that digital printing does not have the same economies of scale as offset printing, proximity to market is one area where digital printing can offer a competitive advantage. If a publisher wants to resupply its stock of a particular title by, say, fifty copies in the UK and a hundred copies in the US, these copies can be printed separately in the UK and the US and sent to the publisher's warehouses in each country, thereby eliminating the cost of shipping them across the Atlantic. Similarly, if one copy of a book in a POD system is ordered by a customer in the UK, it is much more cost-effective to fulfil that order from the UK rather than from an operation based in Tennessee. By spanning the US and UK markets, Lightning Source is able to offer UK publishers access to the US market and US publishers access to the UK market. 'We have actually brought 15,000 US books into the UK market,' commented a Lightning Source manager in the UK. 'If you look at the number of new titles per annum being generated in the UK, that's a significant percentage.'

To a large extent, Lightning Source found itself dealing with older backlist titles which were nearing the end of their lives in the normal book cycle. They were slow-moving backlist titles which had run out of stock and perhaps even been put out of print, and which could now be given a new lease of life by being reprinted in small quantities or made available through print on demand. However, since most of these books were produced before most publishers had created digital workflows or had become conscious of the need to preserve PDFs, they had to be digitized before they could be put into the system. Publishers had to locate copies of the books and send them off to Lightning Source, which cut them apart, scanned them, cleaned up the image if necessary, colour-retouched the covers and so on. In the early days, Lightning Source covered the cost of 'title accession' for publishers who committed themselves to a certain volume – this was a way of encouraging publishers to sign up and of achieving rapid growth in market share. But over time it has shifted the set-up costs on to the publishers. Publishers can import the PDF files into templates which are provided by Lightning Source, and which enable the files to be slotted into the Lightning Source system. The more that the setup costs were shifted onto publishers, however, the less attractive Lightning Source became. 'When they started charging us set-up charges they lost their competitive advantage,' commented the production manager at one university press. As more players entered the field, publishers were able to compare prices and shop around for better deals.

Many publishers who joined up with Lightning Source in the late 1990s and 2000 soon found that it began to generate a significant new revenue stream. University presses were among the main beneficiaries, both because they had been energetically targeted by Lightning Source as potential clients and because their lists – given that they contained many slow-moving backlist titles – turned out to be particularly well suited to the kinds of services that were being offered. In 2001–2, the revenues generated through print on demand and short-run digital printing were among the few growth areas for some university presses in what were in other respects very difficult years. 'To put it bluntly, that saved our arses for the last year,' said one university press editor. 'Without print on demand it would have been a much more difficult year.' Publishers with deep backlists stood to gain the most, because they had many titles that had gone out of stock and had either been put out of print or were slowly accruing back orders which could not be filled, since the quantities needed were too small to justify a reprint using traditional offset printing. By putting these titles back into circulation either through print on demand or through a short-run reprint, publishers were able to revive dead titles – in effect, to bring them back from the dead – and turn them back into revenue-generating assets. The revenue generated by each title may be small taken by itself, but if there are a large number of titles the sums soon add up.

Spurred on by Lightning Source's success, many other players have entered the field of digital printing and print on demand. As the printing technology improved in quality and the cost of the equipment fell, new players offering digital printing began to appear and both established offset printers and distributors began to offer digital printing services. A range of new suppliers emerged who were able to offer SRDP services to publishers at very competitive rates; some also offered POD fulfilment services, although this was less common simply because the logistics are much more complicated. Publishers who had their own distribution facilities, and distributors who provided distribution services for a number of publishers, began to look at the feasibility of installing digital printing equipment in their warehouses and either running the equipment themselves or bringing in a third party to run it. The advantage of installing this equipment in the warehouse is that it enables stock to be replenished on-site, thereby eliminating the need to ship it from the digital printer. It also means that the publisher or distributor can retain full control of the fulfilment process without outsourcing it to a third party like Lightning Source. The problem is that one publisher on its own, and especially a relatively small publisher like a university press, is unlikely to have the volume of throughput needed to keep the print engines busy and to make the process economically viable. Digital printers generally lease the printing equipment from manufacturers like Xerox and IBM, who charge every month for a specified number of impressions, so the printers have to try to keep the print engines running around the clock seven days a week in order to keep the price per page down. 'If I'm actually only printing half the impressions I'm paying for, my internal costs per page have just doubled,' explained one digital printer. Hence, the installation of digital printing equipment in warehouses is likely to make most sense in those cases where the warehouse is providing storage and distribution services for a variety of publishers.

This is the idea that lies behind the Chicago Digital Distribution Center (CDDC), which was set up in 2001 with the help of a $1.5 million grant from the Mellon Foundation. The University of Chicago Press has a large warehouse and distribution facility in the Pullman district of Chicago's south side. Since 1991 it has provided storage and distribution services to other not-for-profit publishers, and it currently has more than a dozen university presses as clients. In 2001, the press secured funding from Mellon to establish a short-run digital printing centre and a digital book repository – the 'Biblio-Vault' – which would together comprise the CDDC. The idea was to install a SRDP facility in the Chicago warehouse which could be used to reprint small quantities of books for the presses who were clients of the distribution service. A space was cleared in the warehouse and an outside contractor, Edwards Brothers, was brought in to set up and run the digital printing equipment. Money from the Mellon grant was used to facilitate the digital conversion of up to 2,300 backlist titles from the participating presses. The files were deposited in the BiblioVault so that they could be accessed by the SRDP operator when further reprints were needed.

The digital printing service was understood from the outset as an SRDP service rather than a strict POD system. The management system of CDDC highlights titles which are suitable for SRDP based on their sales history and inventory, and the publishers of the titles decide whether they wish to include them in the programme. If so, the book is scanned and deposited in the BiblioVault. The management system recommends a date when the book should be reprinted and a quantity – often around twenty-five copies but it could be more or fewer. The title can then be handed over to CDDC to manage – it becomes, in other words, a 'managed title'. When the stock runs out, the system automatically triggers an order for a predetermined quantity; the order gets in the queue for printing, gets printed, some get sent to the customer and the rest go to the warehouse bin where the title is stored. The press doesn't have to think about it again – 'these are all low-demand books with low margins, low everything, and once you've made the decision you can forget about it,' explained one manager. 'Set your price at something that seems reasonable and let it go – unless somehow it becomes a bestseller and then we'll let you know.' A bin space is kept open for the title and it is topped up as and when it needs to be. Orders are fulfilled in the normal way – in exactly the same way as if the book had been printed by traditional offset. It is not a true POD fulfilment system or a virtual warehouse: it is a real physical warehouse using a normal fulfilment system. But it uses digital printing technology and a computer-based stock management system to keep books in print (or bring them back into print), while minimizing the quantities of stock held in the warehouse and the amount of management time needed to keep them available.

Given that the Chicago warehouse provides storage and distribution facilities for more than a dozen university presses, and given that the backlists of university presses contain many slow-moving titles (52 per cent of all active in-print ISBNs in the Chicago warehouse sell four copies or fewer a month, or fewer than fifty copies a year), it makes a great deal of sense in principle to provide an on-site SRDP service which can be used to replenish stock in small quantities as and when it is needed. The main difficulty in running a system like this is the need to achieve a sufficiently high level of throughput to make it commercially viable for the digital printer. CDDC found that, for various reasons, it took longer than originally planned to get titles into the system. And, even in those cases where titles were put into the system, the stock had not necessarily fallen to levels where a reprint was necessary – given the pace at which many of these books were selling, a small amount of stock might be sufficient to last for a year or more. So there was 'a gap between the concept, which I feel is totally valid, and where we are at the moment in terms of actual need for books to be printed', explained one of the project managers. As a result, Edwards Brothers had to bring in work from other clients to keep the machinery busy. However, this is to some extent a phasing problem which should diminish with time as more and more titles are loaded into the system and as the existing stock on these titles becomes depleted.

In the original plan, Chicago had bolder ambitions for the BiblioVault. In the first instance, it would serve as the digital warehouse or repository for the PDF files that would be used in the SRDP facility, as well as a repository for jackets and bibliograph-ical metadata. But in the longer run, Chicago envisaged the possibility that the Biblio-Vault would have another function: it would become a searchable database that could be accessed by scholars. The plan was to develop a user interface that would enable scholars to search the database to see if any of the titles covered topics in which they were interested. Eventually this could perhaps be developed in the direction of an e-commerce operation. 'My hope, my goal', said one of the project managers, 'is to create a system of online books that is efficiently, cheaply deliverable to the scholarly market, that we can price at points that are relatively economical compared to what the other vendors are able to do but yield more money back to the publisher.' However, this longer term ambition for the BiblioVault is rather loosely defined and it is not clear at this stage whether it will ever materialize.

Lightning Source and the Chicago Digital Distribution Center are just two examples of what has become a burgeoning business in digital printing and print on demand. Most academic publishers have now begun to use digital printing for short-run reprints, but it is not just academic publishers who find this advantageous. Digital printing, both short-run and POD, is particularly suitable at present for those kinds of publishing where sales are relatively modest and prices are relatively high – 'it is low distribution volumes, slightly higher prices and no colour,' explained a Lightning Source manager. So digital printing is becoming increasingly important in professional and STM publishing where, like academic publishing, many titles sell in low quantities and at high prices. Some journal publishers are using digital printing for titles which have low circulations, to supply print copies for journals which are available online and to supply back issues. Digital printing has an important role to play in certain areas of textbook publishing, especially at the upper levels of the curriculum where sales are modest and the textbooks are produced without colour. Sometimes textbook publishers get an adoption which requires them to supply fifty or a hundred copies of a textbook which is no longer adopted elsewhere: short-run digital printing enables the textbook publisher to keep that business rather than simply turn it away. And, of course, digital printing has helped to make possible the rise of the custom publishing business, as we saw in the previous chapter.

In trade publishing, digital printing is most commonly used to produce prepublication editions which can be used for publicity purposes. It is more difficult to use digital printing for trade books simply because most trade books tend to be high-volume, low-priced publications. 'The difficulty with trade is, if it's a big title it justifies litho and our rates will never be competitive. There's also colour in there, and their price points are low. Their price points tend to be below the £9.99 mark. We'll go down to £7.99, but if you start to get below that, it is really not a good model for them.' However, there are certain niche areas of trade publishing, like poetry, history and specialist interests, where short-run digital printing and print on demand can be used very effectively. Moreover, some trade publishers may find that they can keep their slower moving backlist titles in print, and bring back older titles that have gone out of print, by using digital printing.

The rise of digital printing and print on demand has been particularly marked in the US and the UK, and publishers in other countries have as yet been less inclined to make use of digital printing facilities. Digital printers have emerged in the German-speaking world, for example, but most of their business to date is vanity publishing rather than providing printing and fulfilment services to publishers. Why this should be so is not entirely clear; it may simply be a time lag and a lack of familiarity with available technologies, or it may be explained by other factors. In principle, however, the advantages of digital printing are in no way limited to English-language publishing, and indeed they may be even greater in those linguistic fields where the markets are smaller and less global in reach. As one Lightning Source manager observed,

> it may be that what we've got is an enabling technology which opens up a market, which enables publishers who couldn't otherwise have produced books for the market to produce books at a reasonable price. So the Welsh language is a classic example. There are Welsh language books – some, but not as many as perhaps there could be if they were all aware of the possibilities that print on demand gives them.

Digital printing is undoubtedly here to stay. The dedicated digital printers find that their business is growing rapidly – 'we are finding that we've been doubling in size every two to two-and-a-half years,' said one digital printer, 'and we see that the curve just keeps going up.' Some traditional offset printers have also installed digital equipment on their premises so that they can offer their clients the option of doing short-run digital reprints in those cases where the print-runs are too low to justify a reprint using traditional offset methods. There are three issues that are likely to determine the way in which digital printing is used, and the extent to which it is used, in the coming years – cost, quality and speed. Let me briefly comment on each.

As I mentioned earlier, the economics of digital printing are fundamentally different from the economics of offset printing. Once the file has been made available, there are no significant set-up costs for digital printing, but above a hundred copies there are no significant economies of scale either – the cost per copy is roughly the same for printing a hundred copies or a thousand copies. (The unit costs tend to be higher for printing a single copy or for small quantities of, say, ten or twenty copies, because there are some costs associated with setting up a title and changing from one title to another.) In the case of offset printing, there are significant set-up costs that have to do with plate preparation, etc., but there are also significant economies of scale: the more that are printed, the lower the unit cost. If you chart the costs of printing between one and, say, a thousand copies using digital and offset printing, the lines will cross at a certain point: below that point it will be cheaper to print digitally, and above that point it will be cheaper to print using a traditional offset press. The lines and the point at which they cross will vary depending on the extent and size of the book and depending on the suppliers. Table 15.1 gives the figures for reprinting various quantities between 25 and 600 copies of a standard 6 × 9 inch, 224-page book using a traditional offset and a digital printer in the UK in April 2004, and figures 15.2 and 15.3 chart the costs against the print-runs for each (figure 15.2 is based on total manufacturing costs and figure 15.3 is based on unit costs). The lines in figures 15.2 and 15.3 cross at around 450 copies: below this number, it is cheaper to reprint digitally; above it, it is cheaper to reprint using traditional offset printing.

These are figures for 2004, but in practice the thresholds at which it is more cost-effective to use digital printing or offset printing are constantly changing for several reasons. Developments in digital printing technology have brought down the cost per copy and enabled digital printers to push up the level at which they can compete with offset printers. At the same time, traditional offset printers have responded to the

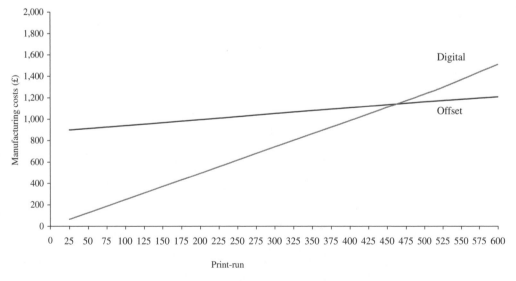

Figure 15.2 Comparison of manufacturing costs for traditional offset and digital printing for various print-runs, 224 pages, 2004

Table 15.1 Comparison of costs for traditional offset and digital printing for various print-runs, 224 pages, 2004 (£ sterling)

	25	75	125	175	225	275	325	375	425	475	525	575	600
Total manufacturing costs													
Offset	899.37	928.38	957.39	986.40	1015.41	1044.42	1073.44	1102.45	1131.46	1160.47	1189.48	1218.49	1233.00
Digital	66.75	194.25	321.25	449.75	578.25	706.75	835.25	963.75	1092.25	1220.75	1349.25	1477.75	1542.00
Unit costs													
Offset	35.97	12.38	7.66	5.64	4.51	3.80	3.30	2.94	2.66	2.44	2.27	2.12	2.06
Digital	2.67	2.59	2.57	2.57	2.57	2.57	2.57	2.57	2.57	2.57	2.57	2.57	2.57

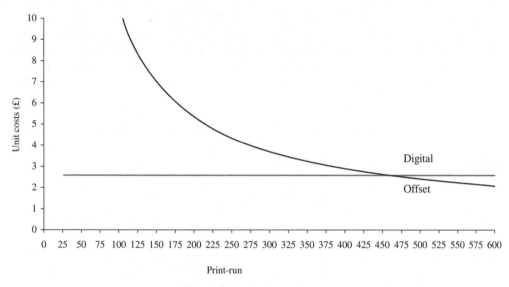

Figure 15.3 Comparison of unit costs for traditional offset and digital printing for various print-runs, 224 pages, 2004

challenge from digital printers by choosing to compete for short print-runs when previously they wouldn't have been interested in this work, and improvements in the technology of offset printing have enabled offset printers to reduce their costs so that their prices are more competitive on shorter print-runs. At any point in time, the switch-over point is the outcome of these two processes which are driven both by technology and by the competitive logic of the printing field. In April 2004, the switch-over point was around 450 copies for a standard 224-page book; a year earlier, in April 2003, figures from the same suppliers generated a switch-over point of around 350 copies, indicating that during this time period the digital printer had effectively raised the level at which it was able to compete effectively with the offset printer. The switch-over point will no doubt continue to change in the coming years with further technological developments and with intensified competition between digital and offset printers.

The second issue that will affect the take-up of digital printing technology is the quality of reproduction. The quality has improved enormously over the last decade – so much so that for straight text it is difficult for the untrained eye to tell the difference between a book printed digitally and a book printed using traditional offset printing. But the quality of halftones in digital printing is still significantly inferior to offset. The quality is reasonably good if the publisher is able to supply the original PDF; if no PDF exists and the book has to be scanned, the quality of the halftones is noticeably worse. Many publishers are therefore reluctant to use digital printing for books which contain a significant number of halftones, or where the quality of the halftones is important. They have to strike a balance between quality, cost and print-run. If they can justify print-runs of sufficient length to give a manageable unit cost, most publishers prefer to use offset for books which contain halftones, although many are prepared to accept the lower quality of digital printing if it enables them to reprint a book – even one containing illustrations – which they would not otherwise be able to keep in print.

The quality problem will undoubtedly be reduced by further improvements in toner-based printers, which are being continuously upgraded. The issue of quality would also be transformed if at some stage toner-based printers were to be replaced by inkjet printers. Inkjet printers use an entirely different method: tiny droplets of ink are squirted onto the paper from a print head containing hundreds or thousands of nozzles. The size of the droplets can be varied, and this allows for variation in shades of grey or colour without resorting to halftone dots. Inkjet printers offer the possibility of improving significantly the quality of digital printing, of producing sharper images in black and white and of adding colour, but high-quality inkjet printers that could be used for book printing are not yet commercially available.

The third issue that is likely to affect the take-up of digital printing is speed. The speed of toner-based printers currently ranges from about 200 pages per minute to about 800 pages per minute, so on a fast machine a book of around 300 pages takes less than 30 seconds to print. By the time the covers have been printed and laminated and the binding added, it takes about two minutes to produce a typical book. With further technological improvements, the time required to produce a book on toner-based printers is likely to be reduced still further. If high-speed inkjet printers were to become commercially viable, this could also reduce the printing time.

Apart from the technological developments, it's also possible that the organization of print-on-demand services will change. Up until now, the main players in the POD business have been linked to wholesalers (as in the case of Lightning Source, for example) or distributors, and there are good reasons for this: setting up the fulfilment systems for true POD and making them work efficiently is a complicated business, and wholesalers and distributors are generally good at this. Moreover, digital printing machines need a high level of throughput in order to be cost-effective, and businesses linked to wholesalers and distributors are well positioned to provide this. The scenario sketched by Epstein and others – namely, that POD would enable publishers to bypass the traditional book supply chain by allowing local bookstores or shops (like Kinko's) to install POD facilities in their premises so that a book could be printed out in a couple of minutes while a customer waits[2] – may have some application in the future, but it bears little resemblance to the current realities of digital printing. However, it is perfectly conceivable that the big retailers – and especially the retail chains like Barnes & Noble and Borders as well as Amazon – might seek to become involved in the POD business. By setting up POD facilities in their own warehouses, they could potentially get the kind of throughput needed to make POD viable while at the same time taking a link or two out of the supply chain. Whether the potential revenue that might be generated in this way would justify the considerable cost and complexity that would be involved in setting up and running a POD system with titles from hundreds or even thousands of publishers is, however, another question.

Reinventing the life cycle of the book

The development of digital printing has created a new set of options for publishers when it comes to the manufacture of books, but it has done much more than that: it has begun

[2] Epstein, *Book Business*, pp. 168 ff.

to transform the basic principles that underlie the book publishing business and the life cycle of the book. The traditional business model of the book publishing business involves publishers taking a decision, an informed guess, about the likely sales of a new title, ordering an appropriate number of books to be printed and then storing those copies in the warehouse until they are sold. If they sell out, a reprint is ordered; if they don't sell, stock is written down and eventually pulped. A substantial amount of a publisher's capital is tied up in stock that sits in the warehouse for an indefinite period of time. It is easy for a publisher to print more stock than it needs, simply because the market for most books is unpredictable and there are strong financial incentives to print more rather than less, since larger print-runs give better margins and better unit costs. But printing more than can be sold in a reasonable time period can have disastrous consequences for the publisher. It may find that it has a warehouse full of unsold and unsaleable stock and when this stock is written off, the loss goes directly to the bottom line.

The traditional business model also defines the normal life cycle for books. In general, a book is kept in print until the rate of sale declines to a level where it no longer makes sense for the publisher to keep it in stock, or until the stock runs out and it is no longer possible to reprint the book in the quantity that would be justified by the rate of sale. At this point, the book is put out of print and its life as an active title is over; the book may continue to sell in the used book market, but it is no longer possible to buy a new copy. The life cycle is made more complicated by decisions concerning hardback and paperback editions – in effect, a title may have more than one life, depending on the editions in which it is issued. A title may be issued in hardback only in the first instance, and even reprinted in hardback if it sells well. After a period of time – say between twelve and twenty-four months – a paperback edition may be released, either by the same publisher or by another publisher to whom the paperback rights have been sold, and the two editions may continue to sell side by side (although typically to different markets). If the hardback then runs out of stock, it is typically put out of print while the paperback is reprinted until it no longer makes sense to do so.

However, the development of digital printing has the potential in some areas of publishing to alter the traditional business model and to transform the normal life cycle of the book. This potential is likely to be greatest in fields such as academic and professional publishing, precisely because these are fields where print-runs are modest and sales tend to be low, but the impact will be felt in other areas of publishing too, especially as titles age and their sales begin to fall off. Already publishers are beginning to move to new models in which initial print-runs are more modest than they would have been in the past and in which new editions and/or reprints are handled increasingly by short-run digital printing. Consider the following:

- *Model 1*   A scholarly book is published in hardback only in the first instance using traditional offset printing. The hardback edition sells out and the publisher brings out a limited edition of 300 copies of a paperback which are printed digitally. If the paperback does well, another short-run digital reprint is done. If it runs out of stock but is selling slowly, it is switched over to a managed title or POD scheme and remains permanently available.
- *Model 2*   A scholarly or upper-level/supplementary text is published in hardback and paperback simultaneously, both printed in modest quantities using traditional

offset. The paperback sells out and the publisher decides whether to reprint it using offset or to reprint digitally, depending on the quantity. If the sales are modest and declining, the publisher orders one last digital reprint of, say, a hundred copies and arranges for the title to switch over automatically to a managed title or POD scheme when the stock is exhausted. From that point on, the title is permanently available.

- *Model 3*   A scholarly or upper-level/supplementary text was published in paperback some years ago and ran out of stock but was selling too slowly to justify a reprint using traditional offset printing. It has remained unavailable for a number of years but back orders have slowly accumulated. The publisher decides to bring it back to life by doing a short-run digital reprint and/or by putting it into a managed title or POD scheme.

- *Model 4*   A scholarly book was published some years ago in hardback only and has ceased to be an active title – it is either languishing on the backlist or is out of print. The publisher thinks there may be a market for a limited paperback run and decides to reissue the book in paperback by doing a short-run digital reprint of 300 copies. If the book does well, another digital reprint is done; if it sells slowly but runs out of stock, it is switched over to a managed title or POD scheme.

- *Model 5*   A scholarly or reference work was published some years ago in hardback only and runs out of stock. The main market for the book is an institutional library market and the case for a paperback edition is not strong, but back orders are slowly accumulating. Using digital printing, the publisher does a small reprint of thirty or forty copies and binds them up as hardback to fulfil the existing back orders and keep the book in print. Both the cost and the price are high – it may cost $20 to print and bind and it may sell for $80 – but the publisher is able to capture a revenue stream that otherwise wouldn't exist and to keep the book alive.

All of these models are now in existence and are being used, often in experimental ways, by academic and professional publishers.

Some publishers are also experimenting with the idea of printing digitally from the outset in the case of new books where the life sales are likely to be low. Rather than using offset printing to do the first print-run, the book is given to a digital printer from the beginning and the life of the title can, if the publisher wishes, be managed by the printer. For example, the printer does the first print-run of, say, 400 hardback, or 200 hardback and 800 paperback (or even fewer). When the stock runs out, the printer will handle the reprint – it will bring out a new paperback edition if it was originally published in hardback only, or it will do a short-run reprint if it was originally published simultaneously. When the sales fall to the point at which the demand is very limited, it would be switched over to a managed title or POD programme. In partnership with the publisher, the digital printer handles the entire life of the title – from the first print-run to the later years of life when stock is automatically replenished in small quantities or when it is no longer stocked at all but is permanently available on demand. As one digital printer explained, 'that book is going to start up in a digital format from day one and it will stay digital until it gets down to the one-off and finally dies, if it ever dies.'

Digital printing is not a panacea for the financial troubles of academic publishers, but it does ease some of their difficulties. It is not a panacea because the basic problem they face – namely, the problem of how to publish scholarly books in a financially viable way given the decline of the institutional market – is not resolved by a technology that enables them to print fewer copies of their books and keep them available longer. They still have to be able to cover all of their overheads and their pre-press costs, and printing and selling fewer books is not going to make it any easier to do this. But digital printing will enable them to manage their resources more effectively. From the publisher's point of view, the real value of digital printing is that it provides them with a new way of thinking about stock management and about how best to invest their resources in stock. It is a way of generating new revenue streams by keeping books available that otherwise would have been put out of print, but it is also a way of *managing cash flow more effectively, saving money and reducing risk*. The problem with the traditional model is that it encourages academic publishers to print more books than they really need in order to achieve an acceptable margin on paper. They print optimistically in order to meet a target gross margin, but the actual sales often fall well short of the original print-run. The figures look good when they finalize the print-run, but cash is tied up in slow-selling stock that will eventually come back to haunt them. As one director of an American university press remarked,

> the best way to go out of business as a scholarly publisher is to overprint and put your capital in your warehouse, and if you run out of capital then you usually won't live to see another day. So there is an enormous cost to this kidding yourself by printing 800 and selling 300. If you are not printing any more than you have orders for, even though you're getting a much lower gross margin, you don't have this incredible aggregate build-up of capital in your warehouse and you will be allowed to probably live longer, all things being equal, than you would if you were doing it the old-fashioned way.

Rather than investing in a substantial print-run at the beginning of a book's life and taking the risk that some of the stock will sit in the warehouse and remain unsold, publishers can reduce the initial print-runs and reduce the risk, knowing that they can reprint digitally at a later date if and when they need to.

If publishers use digital printing and print on demand to print smaller quantities, this will result in higher unit costs and lower margins when the decision to print is taken, but this initial calculation has to be put in a broader context. The figures might look better on paper if larger quantities are printed using traditional offset, but if the costs associated with unsold stock are factored in, the picture looks very different. One digital printer put it like this:

> If publishers are comparing our unit costs to do 500 copies with their costs originally to do 1,000, yes, we are going to be higher. But for years they said they had to get their unit cost to this level, even though five years later half of the books are still sitting in the warehouse. What's their unit cost really if they're not selling the books? It's probably double what they thought it was. Then you throw in the storage costs per year, the cost of tying capital up in stock and so on. More and more publishers are starting to look at that whole picture.

Digital printing provides publishers with a wider range of choices when it comes to deciding how best to invest their resources and a more flexible array of tools for managing their stock. The unit costs may be higher and the margins lower on short print-runs and print on demand, but this has to be weighed against the reduction in risk involved in printing smaller quantities, the fact that less capital is tied up in stock, storage costs are likely to be lower and write-downs are likely to be less. Digital printing enables publishers to respond more flexibly in an overall context of static or declining sales, and enables them to capture revenue streams that would otherwise have been unavailable to them.

The combination of short-run digital printing and print on demand has also transformed the life cycle of the book. In the old model, the life cycle of the book is relatively simple and predictable: a book is generally kept in print for as long as it makes financial sense to reprint it and continue to stock it. The feasibility of a reprint is the outcome of a calculation in which the rate of sale, based on the sales history, is used to determine an optimal stock level, and this is weighed against the unit cost that can be achieved using offset printing. Given the economies of scale built into offset printing, most books reach a point in their lives (and some rather early in their lives) when it is no longer feasible to reprint the book and maintain an acceptable margin – and at this point, the book is put out of print and its active life is over. With digital printing, the life of a book can be stretched out in time – and indeed, stretched out indefinitely, as the book can be made permanently available, if not actually kept in stock, through print on demand. Books that were once dead can be brought back to life and released again either in the same edition or in a new edition. Digital printing – both short-run and print on demand – has become a tool for managing the life cycle of the book. This may not be true for all books. For example, the unit cost on very long books of 500 pages or more may simply be too high to reprint in small quantities (or one at a time) and still achieve an acceptable margin given the price at which the publisher believes the book should be sold. Given the quality issue, heavily illustrated books may also be bypassed for the time being. And undoubtedly there are many books that will not be maintained in life, or recovered from the dead, simply because the rate of sale is likely to be so low that the cost of keeping it available, or bringing it back to life, is likely to exceed the benefits to be gained from doing so. But these qualifications should not obscure the fact that a fundamental change in the life cycle of the book is taking place.

It is one of the great ironies of the digital revolution that only ten years ago, in the mid-1990s, there were many commentators who were predicting the death of the book. The digital revolution will usher in the era of the ebook, they proclaimed, and the printed book will increasingly look like the relic of a bygone age. While it is still too early to say exactly how the online dissemination of content will affect different publishing fields, one can say with some confidence that the prognostications of the early ebook champions were wide of the mark. But this does not mean that the digital revolution has had little impact on the world of book publishing – on the contrary, it has transformed it profoundly. And in so doing, rather than spelling the demise of the printed book, it has given it a new lease of life, allowing it to live well beyond the age at which it would have died in the pre-digital world and, indeed, rendering it potentially immortal.

While the take-up of digital printing in certain sectors of the publishing industry contrasts rather sharply with the much more equivocal performance of ebook vendors, in the longer term it may turn out that digital printing and online content delivery become more closely linked as alternative and complementary ways of delivering content in certain fields of publishing, such as academic, professional and STM publishing. If some of the experiments currently underway in making monographs available online are able to demonstrate that there is an institutional market for delivering scholarly content in this format, then it is possible that academic publishers will be able to diversify to some extent the revenue streams available to them. They may find, for example, that they are able to generate some institutional revenue from the sale of site licences for access to databases of scholarly content, in the manner of Oxford Scholarship Online. At the same time, they may judge that with particular titles, there will be sufficient demand from both institutions and individuals for a print version to justify an offset printing. With other titles, they may judge that the demand will be too modest for an offset printing, but that it will be sufficient to warrant a limited digital printing. In still other cases, or at a later stage in a title's career, they may decide to make the book available in print only through a print-on-demand programme. By mixing the media of content delivery and using the new opportunities opened up by digital technologies in flexible and creative ways, academic publishers may be able to create a more varied range of revenue streams where previously they relied overwhelmingly on one. They may be able thereby to reduce their dependence on the traditional and rather rigid formula of scholarly content delivery – namely, print a fixed number of hardback copies and sell them at a fixed price, a formula that, with the decline of the library market for scholarly monographs, has become harder and harder to sustain. Of course, what remains unclear at this stage is whether the overall revenue generated through these varied revenue streams will be sufficient to cover the publisher's costs and generate enough of a contribution to make academic publishing a more viable and robust activity in financial terms – there simply is not yet sufficient evidence available to provide a cogent answer to this question. But it may well be that, in the longer term, the viability of certain kinds of academic publishing, and the well-being of certain fields of scholarly endeavour, will depend on whether mixed models of this kind can be successfully developed.

Conclusion

Today, at the beginning of the twenty-first century, we live in a rapidly changing information and communication environment. New technologies linked to digitization are transforming the ways in which individuals interact with others and are revolutionizing the industries that have traditionally been concerned with the creation and dissemination of symbolic content. But if we want to understand how the digital revolution is affecting (and is likely to affect) the creative industries, we have to situate these developments within the context of a much more profound analysis of these industries themselves, of how they are organized, how they serve their markets and how they (and their markets) are changing. Technologies do not transform social practices in and by themselves, like some *deus ex machina*; rather, technologies are taken up and used by agents in specific contexts (or not, as the case may be), depending on whether they are seen to be useful or helpful in solving specific problems or capable of providing something of value to them. The terrain of the last few decades is littered with enough examples of misguided speculation about the impact of the digital revolution to make any reasonably sensible person wary of further contributions to the genre.

Focusing on one important but neglected sector of the creative industries, I've tried to show that the digital revolution is part – but only part – of a profound series of changes that are transforming these industries today. To understand these changes, we have to look beyond the digital revolution as such; we have to go back and reconstruct the structure and evolution of the fields within which these industries operate, for only then will we understand the distinctive interplay of economics, technology and culture which defines the logic of each field and the conditions of success or failure within it. Only then will we understand why some sectors of these industries (and some organizations within these sectors) are flourishing while others are experiencing severe difficulties. And only then will we be able to gain a grounded view of the ways in which new technologies are transforming (and are likely to transform) these industries, for only then will we have a firm grasp of the broader context of constraints, opportunities and social practices within which these industries exist and of which they are part.

Two fields, two histories, two very different sets of constraints and opportunities: by reconstructing the logics of the fields of academic and higher education publishing, I've tried to show that these two domains, which to the casual observer might appear to be one and the same, are in fact different worlds which face very different kinds of problems. The key issues with which academic and higher education publishers have to grapple today are the outcome of extended processes of social, economic and technological change which are specific to each field. Exactly how these issues will be addressed in the coming years, and whether the organizations which are active in these fields will find satisfactory ways of dealing with the problems that weigh most heavily on them, are questions to which we cannot provide definitive answers at this stage; certain tendencies can be discerned, but in the rapidly changing information and communication environment of the early twenty-first century, there are too many variables to be able to predict future developments with any degree of confidence. What is clear, however, is that the answers to these questions matter a great deal – and they matter not just to the many individuals whose livelihoods depend directly on a flourishing book publishing industry, but also to the countless others who have come to rely on the availability of books as a medium for the dissemination of ideas and the cultivation of the mind. After more than five hundred years of the culture of print, we have become accustomed to the book and have come in many ways to take it for granted; but this all-too-ordinary cultural object depends on an industry which is undergoing fundamental change and about which we understand very little. Those commentators who, in the late 1990s, were predicting the imminent demise of the book were no doubt wide of the mark – the printed book is likely to prove a much more resilient cultural artefact than these harbingers of a new age were suggesting. But they were right to ask what role books will play in the changing information and communication environment of the twenty-first century, and right to ask how the organizations that have traditionally concerned themselves with the production and distribution of the printed book will be affected by the digital revolution. And these are questions that will continue to demand our attention for some years to come.

Appendix on research methods

The research for this study was carried out over a period of three years, from 2000 to 2003. This was a time of considerable turbulence in the book publishing industry, both because the economic conditions of book publishing were changing in significant ways and because there was a great deal of investment in, and speculation about, the impact of new technologies. The research benefited from being able to study these changes as they were occurring and from the opportunity to interview key players at different points in time. However, given the speed of change, and the speed with which some players have appeared and disappeared from the scene, any study of this kind is bound to be a limited and partial account at best – a snapshot of an industry at the turn of the millennium, as it struggles to deal with a rapidly changing social, economic and technological environment.

The principal aims of the research were to examine how the book publishing industry is changing today, what factors are driving this change and how particular firms are responding to the changing environment of publishing. Among other things, I wanted to explore how the book publishing industry was responding to four key developments:

- the changing nature of the markets for books;
- the growing concentration of resources in large corporations and retail chains;
- the growing internationalization of the book trade;
- the impact of new information and communication technologies.

In order to delimit the scope of the study, I restricted the focus in three ways. First, I focused on two sectors or fields of publishing: the field of academic (or scholarly) publishing, and the field of higher education (or college textbook) publishing. By restricting the focus to academic and higher education publishing, I was able to keep the project manageable and to study in depth two sectors which are often neglected in general accounts of the publishing industry. I was also able to explore in detail those sectors of the book publishing industry which are of particular importance for teaching and research in higher education.

The second restriction is that I limited the study to English language publishing, and specifically to publishers whose principal headquarters were located in either Britain or the United States. The fact that English has become the de facto international language of business, science and higher education undoubtedly confers significant advantages on publishers operating in English, and it would be extremely interesting to look comparatively at the problems faced by publishers working in languages other than English. But it was not the intention of the present study to carry out a multi-language comparative study of this kind.

The third restriction is that the study was limited to the time period from roughly 1980 to the present. While I wanted to situate current developments within a broader historical context, my principal aim was to try to understand how the fields of academic and higher education publishing have changed since 1980, and how they are changing today.

The research design was based on a case-study approach and the use of semi-structured interviews with key personnel. I selected six publishing firms based in the UK and ten based in the US and I carried out intensive case studies of each. In order to select the firms, I conceptualized each of the two sectors – academic publishing and higher education publishing – as structured fields in which the position of firms was determined by the different kinds and quantities of resources available to them. I wanted to ensure that I had a selection of firms that were drawn from different positions within the field and that were active in different geographical markets (in the US, the UK and/or internationally). So in the case of higher education publishing, I included two of the large corporations which were key players internationally. I also selected several medium-sized and small commercial presses who were active in the field of higher education publishing either in the US, the UK or both. In the case of academic publishing, I wanted to study a range of university presses and commercial firms. The university presses included large, middle-sized and small university presses; they included presses in both the US and the UK; and, in the case of the US, they included presses that were linked to state universities as well as presses linked to private colleges and universities, and they included presses located in different parts of the country. I also wanted to make sure that at least some of the presses in both fields were actively experimenting with new technologies.

I was able to gain full access to each of the sixteen firms I chose to study. In most cases I was given unfettered access to staff at every level of the organization, from chief executive officers, chief financial officers and managing directors to editorial directors, editors, production managers, marketing managers, rights managers and anyone else I wished to see. My access to staff was often facilitated by a particular individual who took a special interest in the project and put me in touch with other key people in the organization. Often this individual was a senior manager or managing director, but this wasn't always the case: sometimes it was a senior editor who had been at the press for many years and was widely respected and trusted. Wherever possible I tried to ensure that I retained control over which individuals were selected for interview, and for the most part this was unproblematic. Occasionally I was conscious of an inclination on the part of senior executives to 'manage' my interview schedule, but in these cases I was usually able to set up other interviews on my own. Staff were enormously helpful and cooperative; many had spent their entire working lives in the publishing business and they spoke with remarkable openness and candour about a world which they knew well. Most were happy to be interviewed on more than one occasion; in some cases, I interviewed key individuals on three or four occasions over a period of two or three years. Where firms were active in both the US and the UK, I tried to interview staff on both sides of the Atlantic, although this was not possible in every case.

The interviews were semi-structured and followed a format carefully worked out in advance, but interviewees were encouraged to pursue particular points or lines of thinking that emerged in the course of the interview. The interviews ranged from one to three hours in duration, but most were around two hours long. In the vast majority of cases the interviews were carried out in the offices or at the desks of the interviewees, although in some cases – for instance, when I interviewed someone at a trade fair or someone who happened to be in London or New York on business – they were conducted in a relatively secluded public setting, such as a quiet corner of a hotel lobby. Before the interviews began, I assured interviewees that their anonymity would be protected and that anything they said that was confidential would remain so. All of the interviewing was done by the author, which ensured a high level of consistency in the interviewing process. Most firms were also willing to share financial data, confidential memoranda and policy documents of various kinds. In many cases I was given a tour of the premises and I often had a chance to talk informally with senior managers, sometimes over lunch or dinner. The unfettered access to key personnel gave me an unparalleled opportunity to explore the internal structures and practices of these organizations in depth, to see how they were changing and to gain a well-grounded understanding of the problems and challenges they face.

In addition to the intensive study of sixteen publishing firms, I carried out case studies of a number of new technology firms that are active in the publishing industry and of a number of specific initiatives in the area of electronic publishing. In order to gain a rounded picture of the changes taking place in the industry, I also interviewed key individuals who worked for organizations situated at different points in the book supply chain, such as printers, booksellers and librarians, in both Britain and the US. I also found it very helpful to interview a number of individuals who had worked in the industry for a long time and were very well informed about the changes that had taken place within it, even though they did not work for one of the firms chosen for the case studies.

Since I was focusing on current developments in the publishing industry and in some cases was studying initiatives that were unfolding as I studied them, I tried to reinterview certain people a year or so after the initial interview. This was particularly important for the new technology firms and the experiments in electronic publishing, some of which were being put to the test of the market during the time period of this study. But it was also extremely helpful to reinterview some senior managers in publishing firms, especially since 2001 and 2002 turned out to be very difficult years for many academic publishers.

In total, I carried out more than 230 interviews in Britain and the United States, amounting to more than 450 hours of interview material. All the interviews except two were tape recorded and most were transcribed. (The two exceptions were an interview with a central buyer from one of the large retail chains and an interview with a junior member of staff in the IT department of one of the university presses; in both cases they specifically requested that I did not record the interview but they were happy for me to take notes during our conversation.) The interviews were analysed with a view to highlighting general trends and documenting the ways in which particular firms responded to economic and technological change. The views of individuals were interpreted in relation to their position in the firm and the position of the firm within the field, and in relation to the individual's own personal experience and career trajectory. On the basis of interviews carried out with particular individuals in specific firms, I sought to elucidate the general processes and dynamics that have shaped the evolution of each field. I wanted to identify the key problems faced by publishing organizations within these fields and to show how these problems are linked to broader processes of change. I also wanted to show, through a detailed analysis of specific initiatives and developments, how the digital revolution was actually affecting the strategies and practices of firms.

When I completed a draft text based on the research, I sent it to twelve senior figures in the fields of academic and higher education publishing and invited them to comment on it. They all read it and provided me with detailed feedback – in one case amounting to more than a dozen pages of commentary. This was extremely valuable as a check on my own understanding of the worlds I was seeking to describe; it also gave me the opportunity to test my accounts of the logics of the fields against the experiences and intuitions of key players within them. I sought thereby to produce an account which reconstructed the general dynamic of change within particular fields of publishing while at the same time taking stock of, and helping to shed light on, the varied experiences of particular firms.

Bibliography

ARL Statistics 1999–2000, compiled and ed. Martha Kyrillidou and Mark Young. Washington, DC: Association of Research Libraries, 2001. Available at www.arl.org/stats/arlstat.

Armstrong, C. J. and Lonsdale, Ray, *The Publishing of Electronic Scholarly Monographs and Textbooks*, 1998. Available at www.ukoln.ac.uk/dlis/models/studies/elec-pub/elec-pub.htm.

Bagdikian, Ben H., *The Media Monopoly*, 5th edn. Boston: Beacon Press, 1997.

Bergstrom, Theodore C., 'Free Labor for Costly Journals?' University of California at Santa Barbara, 2000.

Birkets, Sven, *The Gutenberg Elegies: The Fate of Reading in an Electronic Age*. London: Faber & Faber, 1994.

Black, Michael, *Cambridge University Press: 1584–1984*. Cambridge: Cambridge University Press, 1984.

Book Industry Trends 2000. New York: Book Industry Study Group, 2000.

Book Publishing in Britain. London: Bookseller Publications, 1999.

Book Retailing in Britain. London: Bookseller Publications, 1999.

Book Sales Yearbook 2001: An Analysis of Retail Book Sales in the UK during 2000. London: Bookseller Publications, 2001.

Book Selling in Britain. London: Bookseller Publications, 1995.

Bourdieu, Pierre, *The Logic of Practice*, tr. Richard Nice. Cambridge: Polity, 1990.

Bourdieu, Pierre, *Language and Symbolic Power*, ed. John B. Thompson. Cambridge: Polity, 1991.

Bourdieu, Pierre, *The Field of Cultural Production: Essays on Art and Literature*, ed. Randal Johnson. Cambridge: Polity, 1993.

Bourdieu, Pierre, 'Some Properties of Fields', in Bourdieu, *Sociology in Question*, tr. Richard Nice, pp. 72–7. London: Sage, 1993.

Bourdieu, Pierre, *The Rules of Art: Genesis and Structure of the Literary Field*, tr. Susan Emanuel. Cambridge: Polity, 1996.

Bourdieu, Pierre, 'Une révolution conservatrice dans l'édition', *Actes de la recherche en sciences sociales*, 126–7 (Mar. 1999).

Bower, Joseph L. and Christensen, Clayton M., 'Disruptive Technologies: Catching the Wave', *Harvard Business Review* (Jan.–Feb. 1995), pp. 43–53. Available at www.hbsp.harvard.edu/products/articles/hbronpoint.html.

Callender, Claire and Kemp, Martin, 'Changing Student Finances: Income, Expenditure and the Take-Up of Student Loans among Full- and Part-Time Higher Education Students in 1998/9', Research Report RR213, Department for Education and Skills, London, Crown Copyright, 2000.

Chartier, Roger, *The Order of Books: Readers, Authors and Libraries in Europe between the Fourteenth and Eighteenth Centuries*. Cambridge: Polity, 1993.

Competition Commission, *Reed Elsevier plc and Harcourt General, Inc.: A Report on the Proposed Merger*. London: Competition Commission, 2001.

Coser, Lewis A., Kadushin, Charles and Powell, Walter W., *Books: The Culture and Commerce of Publishing*. New York: Basic Books, 1982.

'Course Packs Come of Age', *College Store Executive* (Mar. 1996), pp. 11–12.

Courtney, Dana, 'The Paper–Cloth Conundrum', *Against the Grain*, 14/2 (Apr. 2002), pp. 28–33.

Cox, John, 'The Great Journals Crisis: A Complex Present, but a Collegial Future', *Logos*, 9/1 (1998), pp. 29–33.

Creaser, Claire, *Sconul Library Statistics: Trend Analysis to 1999–2000*. Loughborough: Library and Information Statistics Unit, Loughborough University, 2001.

Crystal, David, *English as a Global Language*. Cambridge: Cambridge University Press, 1997.

Curwen, Peter J., *The UK Publishing Industry*. Oxford: Pergamon, 1981.

Curwen, Peter J., *The World Book Industry*. London: Euromonitor, 1986.

Custom Publishing on College Campuses: Marketing Research Report and Analysis. Stamford, Conn.: O'Donnell & Associates, 1995.

Darnton, Robert, *The Business of Enlightenment: A Publishing History of the Encyclopedia, 1775–1800*. Cambridge, Mass.: Harvard University Press, 1979.

Darnton, Robert, 'A Historian of Books, Lost and Found in Cyberspace', *Chronicle of Higher Education*, 12 Mar. 1999. Available at www.Theaha.org/prizes/gutenberg/rdarnton.cfm.

Darnton, Robert, 'The New Age of the Book', *New York Review of Books*, 18 Mar. 1999.

de Bellaigue, Eric, *British Book Publishing as a Business since the 1960s: Selected Essays*. London: British Library, 2004.

Economic Analysis of Scientific Research Publishing. London: Wellcome Trust, 2003. Available at www.wellcome.ac.uk/en/1/awtpubrepeas.html.

Eisenstein, Elizabeth L., *The Printing Press as an Agent of Change: Communications and Cultural Transformations in Early-Modern Europe*, vols 1 and 2. Cambridge: Cambridge University Press, 1979.

Ekman, Richard and Quandt, Richard E. (eds), *Technology and Scholarly Communication*. Berkeley: University of California Press, 1999.

Epstein, Jason, *Book Business: Publishing Past, Present, and Future*. New York: W. W. Norton, 2001.

Feather, John, *A History of British Publishing*. London: Routledge, 1988.

Febvre, Lucien and Martin, Henri-Jean, *The Coming of the Book: The Impact of Printing 1450–1800*, tr. David Gerard. London: Verso, 1976.

Fishwick, Francis and FitzSimons, Sharon, *Report into the Effects of the Abandonment of the Net Book Agreement*. London: Book Trust, 1998.

The Future of Scholarly Publishing. New York: Modern Language Association, 2002. Available at www.mla.org/resources/documents/issues_scholarly_pub.

Gasson, Christopher, *Who Owns Whom in British Book Publishing*. London: Bookseller Publications, 2002.

Giddens, Anthony, *The Consequences of Modernity*. Cambridge: Polity, 1990.

Graham, Thomas W., 'Scholarly Communication', *Serials*, 13/1 (Mar. 2000), pp. 3–11.

Greco, Albert N., *The Book Publishing Industry*. Needham Heights, Mass.: Allyn & Bacon, 1997.

Greco, Albert N., O'Connor, Walter F., Smith, Sharon P. and Wharton, Robert M., *The Price of University Press Books, 1989–2000*. New York: Association of American University Presses, 2003.

Guthrie, Kevin M., 'JSTOR: The Development of a Cost-Driven, Value-Based Pricing Model', in Richard Ekman and Richard E. Quandt (eds), *Technology and Scholarly Communication*. Berkeley: University of California Press, 1999.

Habermas, Jürgen, *The Structural Transformation of the Public Sphere: An Inquiry into a Category of Bourgeois Society*, tr. Thomas Burger with Frederick Lawrence. Cambridge: Polity, 1989.

Hall, Max, *Harvard University Press: A History*. Cambridge, Mass.: Harvard University Press, 1986.

Hawes, Gene R., *To Advance Knowledge: A Handbook on American University Press Publishing*. New York: American University Press Services, 1967.

Herman, Edward S. and McChesney, Robert W., *The Global Media: The New Missionaries of Corporate Capitalism*. London: Cassell, 1997.

Horowitz, Irving Louis, *Communicating Ideas: The Politics of Scholarly Publishing*, 2nd edn. New Brunswick, N.J.: Transaction, 1991.

Horvath, Stephen, 'The Rise of the Book Chain Superstore', *Logos*, 7/1 (1996), pp. 39–45.

Johns, Adrian, *The Nature of the Book: Print and Knowledge in the Making*. Chicago: University of Chicago Press, 1998.

Kasdorf, William E. (ed.), *The Columbia Guide to Digital Publishing*. New York: Columbia University Press, 2003.

Kay, John, *Foundations of Corporate Success: How Business Strategies Add Value*. Oxford: Oxford University Press, 1993.

Kay, John, 'The Foundations of National Competitive Advantage', Economic and Social Research Council, London, 1994.

Lane, Michael and Booth, Jeremy, *Books and Publishers: Commerce against Culture in Postwar Britain*. Lexington, Mass.: D. C. Heath, 1980.

Levin, Martin P., 'The Positive Role of Large Corporations in US Book Publishing', *Logos*, 7/1 (1996), pp. 127–37.

Lewin, Tamar, 'When Books Break the Bank: College Students Venture beyond the Campus Store', *New York Times*, 16 Sept. 2003.

Lewin, Tamar, 'Students Find $100 Textbooks Cost $50, Purchased Overseas', *New York Times*, 21 Oct. 2003.

Luhmann, Niklas, *Trust and Power*. Chichester: Wiley, 1979.

Luhmann, Niklas, 'Familiarity, Confidence, Trust: Problems and Alternatives', in Diego Gambetta (ed.), *Trust: Making and Breaking Cooperative Relations*. Oxford: Blackwell, 1988.

MacLeod, Donald, 'E is for Error', *Education Guardian*, 8 June 2004, pp. 18–19.

McChesney, Robert W., *Rich Media, Poor Democracy: Communication Politics in Dubious Times*. New York: New Press, 1999.

McWilliams, Gary, 'Questia's Aim: The Big Database on Campus', *Wall Street Journal*, 13 Apr. 2000.

Menand, Louis, 'College: The End of the Golden Age', *New York Review of Books*, 18 Oct. 2001.

Nielsen, Jakob, 'How Users Read on the Web', 1997. Available at www.useit.com/alertbox/9710a.html.

Okerson, Ann, 'Wanted: A Model for E-Reserves', *Library Journal*, 126/14 (Sept. 2001), pp. 56–9.

Pettigrew, Andrew and Whipp, Richard, *Managing Change for Competitive Success*. Oxford: Blackwell, 1991.

Porter, Michael E., *Competitive Advantage*. New York: Free Press, 1985.

Power, Michael, *The Audit Society: Rituals of Verification*. Oxford: Oxford University Press, 1997.

Publishing in the Knowledge Economy: Competitiveness Analysis of the UK Publishing Media Sector. London: Department of Trade and Industry and UK Publishing Media, 2002. Available at www.uk-publishing.info/competitive.asp.

Rickett, Joel, 'Internet Sales Flatten Out', *The Bookseller*, 11 May 2001.

Schiffrin, André, *The Business of Books: How International Conglomerates Took Over Publishing and Changed the Way We Read*. London: Verso, 2000.

Scholarly Communication: The Report of the National Enquiry. Baltimore: Johns Hopkins University Press, 1979.

Schonfeld, Roger C., *JSTOR: A History*. Princeton: Princeton University Press, 2003.

Sconul Annual Statistics 1991–1992. London: Sconul, 1993.

Sconul Annual Library Statistics 1999–2000. London: Sconul, 2001.

Smith, Anthony, *The Age of Behemoths: The Globalization of Mass Media Firms*. New York: Priority Press, 1991.

Smyth, Marney, 'The Community *is* the Content', *Publishing Research Quarterly* (Winter 2001), pp. 3–14.

Sowden, Peter, *University Library Spending on Books, Journals and Electronic Resources*, 2002 Update. London: Publishers Association, 2002.

Spector, Robert, *Amazon.com: Get Big Fast*. London: Random House, 2000.

Student Hardship Survey. London: National Union of Students, 2000.

Student Information Sources and Book Buying Behaviour 2001–2002. London: Book Marketing Ltd, 2001.

Student Information Sources and Book Buying Behaviour 2003. London: Book Marketing Ltd, 2003.

Student Market Today. London: Book Marketing Ltd, 2000.

Student Watch, *Student Buying Habits: Textbooks and Course Materials II*, vol. 6. Oberlin, Ohio: College Stores Research and Educational Foundation, 2000.

Subtext, *Perspective on Book Publishing: 2003–2004: Numbers, Issues and Trends*. Darien, Conn.: Open Book, 2004.

Sutcliffe, Peter, *The Oxford University Press: An Informal History*. Oxford: Oxford University Press, 1978.

Tebbel, John, *Between Covers: The Rise and Transformation of American Book Publishing*. New York: Oxford University Press, 1987.

Thompson, John B., *The Media and Modernity: A Social Theory of the Media*. Cambridge: Polity, 1995.

The UK Book Industry: Unlocking the Supply Chain's Hidden Prize. London: Booksellers Association/KPMG, 1998.

Vista 1995, *The Organizational Impact of Publishing in New Media*. Northwood: Vista Computing Services, 1995.

Vista 1996, *Profiting from Tomorrow's Customers*. Northwood: Vista Computing Services, 1996.

Vista 1997, *From N to X: The Impact of Online Networks on the Publishing Value Chain*. Northwood: Vista Computing Services, 1997.

Vista 1998, *Supporting Creativity: Bringing Technology to Front Office Operations*. Northwood: Vista Computing Services, 1998.

Vista 1999, *Information in Action: Putting Knowledge to Work in the Publishing Industry*. Northwood: Vista Computing Services, 1999.

Wasoff, Lois S., 'Back to the Future ... Are E-Reserves the New Course Packs?', *Professional/Scholarly Publishing Bulletin*, 4/1 (Spring 2003), pp. 1–3.

Waters, Lindsay, 'Rescue Tenure from the Tyranny of the Monograph', *Chronicle of Higher Education*, 20 Apr. 2001, pp. B7–10.

Waters, Lindsay, *Enemies of Promise: Publishing, Perishing, and the Eclipse of Scholarship*. Chicago: Prickly Paradigm Press, 2004.

Watkinson, Anthony, *Electronic Solutions to the Problems of Monograph Publishing*. London: Resource, the Council for Museums, Archives and Libraries, 2001. Available at www.publishers.org.uk/paweb/paweb.nsf/pubframe!Open.

Whiteside, Thomas, *The Blockbuster Complex: Conglomerates, Show Business, and Book Publishing*. Middletown, Conn.: Wesleyan University Press, 1980.

Index